QAUM, MULK, SULTANAT

SOUTH ASIA IN MOTION

EDITOR
  Thomas Blom Hansen

EDITORIAL BOARD
  Sanjib Baruah
  Anne Blackburn
  Satish Deshpande
  Faisal Devji
  Christophe Jaffrelot
  Naveeda Khan
  Stacey Leigh Pigg
  Mrinalini Sinha
  Ravi Vasudevan

QAUM, MULK, SULTANAT

Citizenship and National Belonging in Pakistan

ALI USMAN QASMI

STANFORD UNIVERSITY PRESS
STANFORD, CALIFORNIA

Stanford University Press
Stanford, California

© 2024 by Ali Usman Qasmi. All rights reserved.

No part of this book may be reproduced or transmitted in any form or by any means, electronic or mechanical, including photocopying and recording, or in any information storage or retrieval system, without the prior written permission of Stanford University Press.

Printed in the United States of America on acid-free, archival-quality paper

Library of Congress Cataloging-in-Publication Data
Names: Qasmi, Ali Usman, author.
Title: Qaum, mulk, sultanat : citizenship and national belonging in Pakistan / Ali Usman Qasmi.
Other titles: Citizenship and national belonging in Pakistan | South Asia in motion.
Description: Stanford, California : Stanford University Press, [2024] | Series: South Asia in motion | Includes bibliographical references and index.
Identifiers: LCCN 2023018093 (print) | LCCN 2023018094 (ebook) | ISBN 9781503637283 (cloth) | ISBN 9781503637788 (paperback) | ISBN 9781503637795 (epub)
Subjects: LCSH: Nationalism—Pakistan—History—20th century. | Citizenship—Pakistan—History—20th century. | Pakistan—Politics and government—1947-1971. | Pakistan—Politics and government—1971-1988.
Classification: LCC DS384 .Q265 2024 (print) | LCC DS384 (ebook) | DDC 320.54095491—dc23/eng/20230419
LC record available at https://lccn.loc.gov/2023018093
LC ebook record available at https://lccn.loc.gov/2023018094

Cover design: Jason Anscomb
Cover art: Official instructions about national flag.
Source: File number 138/CF/64, National Documentation Wing, Cabinet Division, Islamabad.

CONTENTS

Acknowledgments   vii

INTRODUCTION   1

1   Noah's Ark?   48
The Making of Pakistan as a Homeland for Muslim Nationals

2   Quilting Islam   109
Pakistan as an Islamic Republic

3   Making the State National   173
Symbols, Flag, and Anthem

4   Over the Moon   232
Ulema, State, and Authority in Pakistan

5   Scripting the National Time and Space   284
Archive, Calendar, Roads, and Museums

POSTSCRIPT
A New Beginning   340
My Fellow Countrymen

Notes   357
Bibliography   405
Index   423

ACKNOWLEDGMENTS

With great relief I present this book, the culmination of years of research and hard work. The journey has been both challenging and rewarding. I want to take this opportunity to acknowledge the intellectual debt I have accumulated and express my deep appreciation for the countless individuals who have supported and inspired me along the way and made this journey possible.

I started working on this project about a decade ago. The inspiration came from a workshop led by Sarah Ansari in London and her project in collaboration with William Gould on citizenship in South Asia. Professors Francis Robinson and Ansari mentored my work and made it possible for me to visit London for archival research as an alumnus of the Newton International Fellowship program. Much of the work on this book was carried out in Pakistan as I extensively probed various archives and public libraries in Lahore, Karachi, and Islamabad. The research was made possible due to generous support from LUMS University's Faculty Initiative Fund (FIF) and research awards from Department of Humanities and Social Sciences' Proposals and Grants Committee. I am grateful to Dr. Ali Khan, dean of humanities and social sciences, for providing additional funds for the successful completion of this project.

My intellectual home for the past twelve years has been the Department of Humanities and Social Sciences, where I have been blessed to work with some of the brightest minds in Pakistani academia, especially Ali Raza, Nida Kirmani, Anushay Malik, Hasan Javed, Tania Saeed, Sameen Mohsin, Zahid Hasan, Umair Javed, Nauman Faizi, Gwendolyn Kirk, Laila Bushra, Khalid Mir, Asif Iftikhar, Ghazal Asif, Ameem Lutfi, Ilyas Chattha, Ateeb Gul, and Mohammad Waseem. I couldn't have asked for better colleagues, critics, and friends. A special shout-out to the department's administrative staff, including Naseer-ud-Din, Sophiya

Anjum, Muhammad Ikhlaq, Haroon Asghar, Ummul Buneen, Hinna Zahid, Muhammad Imran, Fahid Ahmad, and Adeel Ahmed, who made my journey a smooth one.

I was also lucky enough to work with some of the best library staff in the country, especially the late Waris Arslan, who went above and beyond during the pandemic to serve the LUMS community. A big thank you also goes to my students, especially the batch of '21 (you know who you are!), and research assistants Arafat Safdar, Zahra Paracha, Hasnain Akram, Ayesha Lari, Osama Ahmed, Saman Tariq, and Fatima Afzal, who helped collect material for this project.

My research journey took me to various archives and libraries in Pakistan, where I was fortunate to receive the support of (late) Qamar Zaman and Muhammad Saeed Khurram (National Documentation Center), Mazhar Saeed (National Archives of Pakistan), Kaneez Fatima (Freedom Movement Archives, Karachi University), Hamid Ali (Punjab University Library), Shamim Jafri (Punjab Archives), Muhammad Naeem (Government College University Lahore Library), Ejaz Husain (Punjab Secretariat Library), Aurangzeb Malik (Punjab Textbook Board Library). Shahid Hanif did a brilliant job helping me find relevant material on the *ru'at-i-hilal* controversies in Pakistan. Yasir *bhai* assisted in navigating bureaucratic red tape to help me get access to archival material on multiple occasions.

I also had the opportunity to visit Dhaka for research, thanks to the kindness of Iftekhar Iqbal. I am grateful to the faculty members of the Urdu Department of Dhaka University for inviting me. Layli Uddin and Sadia Mahmood facilitated my work by sharing with me their knowledge of Dhaka's research repositories.

During the pandemic, I wrote the bulk of the manuscript, with the remaining chapters written and revised during my stay at the Stanford Humanities Center (SHC). I am grateful to the SHC's director Roland Greene, fellowship program manager Kelda Jamison, and my fellow resident scholars Sharika Thiranagama, BuYun Chen, Anubha Anushree, Radhika Koul, and David Kazanjian for providing me with a wonderful intellectual space. My yearlong stay in Palo Alto was made even better by my wonderful hosts Karen Wigen, Martin Lewis, and the unforgettable

Midnight for a purr-fect experience. Thank you, Priya Satia, Anne Bigelow, Ali Mehdi, Fatima Naqvi, Madihah Akhter, Shandana Waheed, Maira Hayat, and Saad Gulzar for adding flavor to my academic journey with your warm hospitality and impromptu dinner invites. Cheers to unforgettable memories and new friends.

I want to thank my friends in Pakistan and around the world, especially Ammar Ali Jan, Tabby Spencer, Ilyas Chattha, Sadia Bajwa, Nitin Varma, Faizan Abbas Naqvi, Sehar Sarah Sikandar Shah, Ali Raza, Zakra Lakdawala, and Nida Kirmani for their cheerful camaraderie throughout this period. Professor Jamal Elias, thank you for bringing me to the University of Pennsylvania's Department of Religion for an intellectually rewarding experience. Rachael Hickson, your unwavering support made my stay in Philadelphia a breeze. Jamal, Mehrin Masud-Elias, and Megan Robb were warm and welcoming hosts who made me feel at home.

Thank you, Margrit Pernau, for hosting me at the Max Planck Institute for Human Development in Berlin over successive summers to work on this project. Kama Maclean's trust in my abilities as a historian has been a major confidence booster. I am indebted to Ali Raj, who not only translated the lyrics of Hafiz Jallandhari's alternative national anthem but also carefully read sections of chapter 3 and pointed out finer details that I had missed in my analysis.

Special shout-outs to two Kamrans—Kamran Asdar Ali and Tahir Kamran for their unwavering support and encouragement over the years. I wish Ahmad Saeed *sahab* was alive to see this book in its final form. I am forever grateful for the lessons I learned from him.

My family in Pakistan—Abbu, Ammi, my brothers, *bhabis*, nieces, nephews —are the reason for all that is good in my life. I cannot thank them enough for their warmth and love.

I am also thankful to the Stanford University Press team for their professionalism in handling the manuscript and expediting its publication. I am particularly grateful to Thomas Blom Hansen, the series editor, for believing in my project. Thanks to my editors, especially Katherine Faydash, Mariam Rahmani, and Maryam Hasan who critically read and reviewed different versions of the manuscript, making invaluable recommendations to make it more readable.

Some sections of chapters 3 and 5 were published in *Modern Asian Studies* (vol. 53, no. 4), *Nations and Nationalism* (vol. 23, no. 3), *and Finding Jinnah: Contemporary Art from Pakistan* (Karachi: Furqaan Ahmed Collection, 2021). I am grateful to the National Documentation Center, Cabinet Division, especially Farid Ahmad, for allowing me to reproduce images from one of the files in their archival repository. Thanks, Umar, for helping me get the permission in a "smoothless" manner!

I presented parts of this work at the universities of Michigan, Yale, University of Texas at Austin and LUMS, and received valuable feedback, especially from Azfar Moin, Sumit Guha, Maryam S. Khan, Farina Mir, Barbara Metcalf, William Glover, Matthew Hull, Rohit De, and Karuna Mantena. Needless to say, I am solely responsible for any errors or omissions in this book.

I must mention my furry muses, Mitthan and Chumchum, who made it possible for me to work on the manuscript during the pandemic. Their meowing kept me going!

This book is for you, Nousheen. Your love and support have been the wind beneath my wings. I could never do enough to express my gratitude for everything you have done for me. Thank you for being my rock.

QAUM, MULK, SULTANAT

INTRODUCTION

THE *PAKISTAN TIMES* REPORTED on 28 September 1947 that "Mr J. K. Mehra, Station Director, Radio Pakistan, Lahore, embraced Islam . . . at the hands of Maulana Ghulam Murshid of Lahore. Mr. Mehra's Muslim name is Ahmad Selman."[1] This news was published as Hindus and Sikhs from what had become an overwhelmingly Muslim-majority province of West Punjab were forced to flee their homes and move to India. In a similar trend in East Punjab, Muslims were forced to migrate to Pakistan to escape violence. Amid this bloodshed, it was not uncommon for communities or individuals to insist on staying in their ancestral land. One survival strategy was conversion. Mehra/Selman was among the millions on both sides of the border who had to change religions to conform to the normative ideal of citizenship according to the nation-states in which they wished to remain. Mehra/Selman's decision—and most importantly, its public announcement—signaled his intent to live by the ideals of a "Muslim homeland" where faith-based identity was privileged above all others.

Fast-forward to 2016, when another popular story circulated in Indian and Pakistani newspapers. Salma Agha, a veteran actress and singer, applied for an Overseas Citizen of India card to permanently settle in

Mumbai.² In her application to the Ministry of Interior, Ms. Agha emphasized her "Indian roots" by referring to her maternal grandfather, Jugal Kishore Mehra, who was married to her maternal grandmother, Anwari Begum, a star singer in the 1930s and 1940s. It is noteworthy that Agha referred to her grandfather as "Jugal Kishore Mehra" and not as "Ahmad Selman," indicating her tacit understanding of shifts in Indian citizenship laws that privilege Hindu religious ancestry. Even though her mother was a stepdaughter of Mehra, Salma Agha was granted the citizen card on the pretext that she was a British citizen and that her grandparents were of Indian origin.³ But what is most remarkable is that, against Mehra's prior plea for acceptance as a Muslim to stay in Lahore, decades later his Muslim step-granddaughter reasserted his Hindu roots to stay in Mumbai.

Thousands of others, if not millions, chose to switch religion without publicly announcing it. Many low-caste Hindus and Sikhs, landless peasants, and small landowners chose to remain in West Punjab by adopting the official religion of the newly formed state or landowner. In several cases, during the 1950s, Christian missions worked hard to convert low-caste Hindus and Sikhs.⁴ There were also possibly thousands of cases of Muslims stranded in East Punjab, just as there were Hindu and Sikh women and children in West Punjab. Most had been abducted during Partition, giving rise to massive retrieval projects undertaken by the governments of both India and Pakistan.⁵ If Muslim, such individuals were considered "stranded Pakistanis," and if Sikh or Hindu, they were identified as captive Indians.

Consider the case of Charagh Din, also known as Jagjit Singh, of the Bhatinda district of Kotha Guru, who was living in Mian Chunnu's Khanewal district.⁶ Separated from his parents at age sixteen during the Partition violence of 1947, Charagh Din was saved by Zaildar Thakar Singh Sodi, who then raised him as his son and renamed him Jagjit Singh. He lived with his adopted family for eight years, learned Gurmukhi, and memorized parts of the Guru Granth Sahib—the Sikh sacred scripture. In 1955, Charagh Din/Jagjit Singh was reunited with his family in Pakistan, and he later became known as Baba Guru Pakistani.

I cannot fully capture the trials and tribulations of such individuals as Baba Guru Pakistani or J. K. Mehra. Yet I attempt to understand their stories by challenging how the citizen has been legally defined. What kind of legal fiction helps make sense of the countless children and women who could not be retrieved and continued to live with their abductors? What did it mean for Ahmad Selman to be a Pakistani citizen, or for someone like Salma Agha, who lived in Pakistan and later the United Kingdom, to be an Indian citizen? My purpose in raising these questions is to highlight the absurdity of law—especially its refraction through a predetermined ascription of a legal identity based on religion—to settle the citizenship question or the notion of national belonging.

These stories demonstrate how individuals and communities navigated, and continue to navigate, the legal entailments of the state and balance it with their desire for immersion in an intimate social or cultural community. Beyond the membership of the political community—understood as citizenship in the academic literature—the postcolonial state extends or aspires to extend its power to cultivate a majoritarian sociocultural community of the nation. But it's never a one-way process by which the individuals and communities are at the receiving end. They strove to situate themselves in milieus and networks that sustained affective bonds and carried intimate cultural values for economic sustenance and political ascendancy.[7]

In the early 1950s, as new postcolonial states consolidated legal structures and institutions and cultivated a majoritarian national identity, individuals and communities actively engaged in the process. The force of the moment as a foundational one affording the opportunity to build new identities, forge alliances, and seek economic and political opportunities was not lost upon them. Many of these attempts were colored by the overarching influence of a statist ideology and its cultural entrapments. These responses and aspirations took several forms. Take the example of a letter to the editor published in *Nawa-i-Waqt*, an influential Urdu daily, in the early 1950s. A migrant from East Punjab who had settled in a village called Khotiyan—the name means "jennets"—was annoyed at this impropriety.[8] He suggested changing it to "Islamabad" to reflect the Islamic spirit of the new country. This was years before Pakistan developed a new capital and named it Islamabad.

Let me add to these examples of supralegal forms of citizenship and belonging a memory from my childhood. Growing up in Lahore during the 1990s, I remember reading a special issue on Independence Day published by a popular children's magazine, *Aankh Micholi*. The magazine offered a gift in the special issue: a board game about the Pakistan movement.[9] Its instruction manual included a historical essay written by the magazine's editor, Tahir Masud.[10] Starting with the statement by the founder of Pakistan, Muhammad Ali Jinnah, that Pakistan was founded on the day the first person embraced Islam in the subcontinent, Masud gave an overview of Muslim history in the region, recounting various wars, rulers, betrayals, and achievements.

The narrative helped explain which specific historical episodes, events, and personalities contributed to Pakistan's creation and which obstructed its progress. If players landed on, say, the Muslim military's success in the Battles of Panipat, they were rewarded with points or progress in the game. Landing on the "invention" of Din-i-Ilahi—a rather heterodox amalgamation of various religious value systems under Mughal emperor Akbar—would take players back. The implication was that certain historical events and personalities facilitated the emergence of Pakistan, and others obstructed its development. The board game cultivated Pakistani statist ideology by having citizens play out history along a predetermined national temporal grid. The player fought battles for Pakistan, celebrated its heroes and leaders, and identified villains who had hampered the creation of the Muslim homeland. To be Pakistani was not simply to be a legal resident of the country; it also required a sense of belonging and affiliation mediated through history, culture, and literature.

This book is about the mediating practices through which the postcolonial state sought to cultivate a sense of Pakistani national identity and its constitutive elements. At the same time, the book details strategies whereby individuals and communities have contested the power of the state and its nation-making project so that it has remained abortive, always in the process of becoming. I focus on both the legal framing of citizenship and performative acts of state making through such spectacles as the celebration of Eid as a national festival, the commemorative chronology of the national calendar, the renaming of roads and cities, discussions of the national anthem, and so on. In all cases, a particular understanding of Muslim nationalism and the historical narrative of the Islamic nation undergirded the process of state formation, national identity, and citizen making. The narrative itself was subject to change or contested by varying claims to the past. While my focus throughout the book will be on the formation of a normative order of citizenship and on nationhood as both legal membership and majoritarian ethos, I approach citizenship and nationhood as an aspirational project of the postcolonial state: this project aims to hegemonize everyday life, and yet it is haunted by the specter of ambivalent affiliations and fluid identities of the likes of Mehra and Baba Guru.

DOES CITIZENSHIP MATTER?

On the face of it, citizenship is a matter of designating who is a legal member of a political community. It is a documented existence, that is, a corporatized identity that allows the member to benefit from his or her legibility to the state in the form of a passport, identity card, ration card, or any other documentation. But there is a long and continuous history of groups, individuals, and communities who have struggled to get recognition, who demand equality as citizens, and who blur the distinction between citizen and noncitizen. A somewhat abstract and seemingly banal distinction in citizenship has profound consequences for a state's projected self-image and for its majoritarian ethos. In the case of Pakistan and India, it is vital to understand a violent history of state formation that included mass exodus and murder. Equally important are the prehistories of ideas of nationhood and statehood—such as the ideological predispositions of the Indian National Congress and of the All-India Muslim League—that the postcolonial state embodied through legislation and policy. Nevertheless, after these nations' citizenship laws were codified in the 1950s, the "citizenship question" was far from over. This question resonates across the region, shaping ideological posturing, political mobilization, and policy outcomes to this day.

The massive mobilization in India against proposed changes to citizenship law provides a recent example. According to the new amendment to the Citizenship Act of 2003, which builds on previous changes since the 1980s, illegal migrants who were non-Muslim minorities from neighboring Muslim countries—specifically, Pakistan, Bangladesh, and Afghanistan—would not be considered unlawful migrants, and hence were eligible for grant of citizenship.[11] The 2003 amendment also provided a procedure for setting up and maintaining the National Register of Citizens (NRC) in response to controversies such as that in Assam, where illegal Bangladeshi migrants were seen as a potential threat to the region's demographics. During the 1980s, sporadic outbursts of communal violence led to a popular demand that noncitizens be weeded out. As a result, in 1986, the citizenship act was amended to grant citizenship to Bangladeshis who had entered Assam between 1 January 1966 and 24 March 1971. The cutoff date conflicted with the original date set in the constitution. In a thinly veiled jibe that religiously coded the issue, the Indian Supreme Court took up the case of illegal Bangladeshi migrants in the name of internal security threats and supervised the maintenance of NRC. The process started in 2015; by the time it ended in 2019, almost four million people had been excluded.[12] The outcome was not unexpected. In a largely undocumented economy and illiterate society, people did not have the required proof to establish that they had lived and earned their livelihood from there for decades; that is, they could not even establish their corporatized identity as a citizen.

Although the policy was an exercise initially meant for Assam and its particular historical context, the BJP government—whose manifest Hindutva ideology aims to transform India into a Hindu majoritarian state—promised to extend it to other parts of the country. Such an extension would have put the onus on citizens to provide documentary proof in order to be included in the NRC. It is little surprise, then, that the NRC got conflated with the newly proposed constitutional amendment, which excluded Muslims from the category of "illegal migrants," thus aggravating Indian Muslims' fears of further marginalization or even of an outright stripping of their citizenship rights. These fears were not unfounded, given the increase in systematic mob violence against Muslims and astonishingly brutal statements issued by influential Hindutva ideologues. Subramanyam Swami, for instance, flatly refused to acknowledge Muslims as equal citizens and called for their disenfranchisement if they refused to recognize their Hindu ancestry.¹³ Fears of India's citizenship criteria moving from civic nationalism to ethnic nationalism—a process that had been underway for some time—became too real, posing an imminent existential threat to Indian Muslims.¹⁴ In response, they came out to protest against proposed changes to the citizenship laws in large numbers.

Similarly, an announcement made by the Pakistani prime minister in September 2018 expressing his desire to grant citizenship to Afghan and Bangladeshi refugees in Pakistan caused an uproar, especially in the provinces of Sindh and Baluchistan, where nationalist groups feared that this would turn them into ethnic minorities in their own provinces.¹⁵ The number of illegal migrants, workers, and refugees in Pakistan is estimated at five million. Most of them are Afghans displaced from their homes as a result of the 1980s Soviet invasion. Most have since lived in designated campsites, although those with financial resources have managed to obtain forged identity documents for business and travel. The clear majority, now the third generation, continues to languish in camp life, barred from better employment for lack of proper documentation.¹⁶

Given that most Afghan refugees are ethnic Pashtuns, if they were to become Pakistani citizens, it would greatly disturb the ethnic composition of Baluchistan. Roughly half the documented population of Baluchistan is Pashtun. Pakistan's largest province in terms of land but smallest in terms of population, Baluchistan is the most underdeveloped area of the country. As it is, its people are marginalized and exploited, and there is a growing sense of "red Indianization," including fears of a non-Baluch majority. Baluch nationalists are anxious that the situation will only worsen when the proposed expansion of the port city of Gawadar is completed and Gawadar becomes "another Dubai," attracting professionals, corporations, and more workers.¹⁷

Sindh, in contrast, has a distinct history of dealing with migrants. Around the time of the establishment of Pakistan in 1947, migrants from North India settled in Karachi in large numbers. Scions of North India's Muslim intelligentsia—many claimed an elitist ashraf culture as well as landholdings and professional class associations—these Urdu-speaking migrants took over the city, then the capital of Pakistan. Ethnic Sindhis lost control of the province's only major urban center, thus stunting the growth of the community's professional middle class. Over the decades, a new Mohajir (migrant) identity emerged in response to a democratized polity of the 1970s, when Sindhi chief ministers used their electoral advantage to introduce pro-Sindhi measures. Such measures included compulsory Sindhi-language learning in schools and quota systems in jobs and college admissions that enabled the social mobility of rural residents of Sindh. Possessing domicile in rural Sindh became a vital tool of empowerment. Accepting Afghans and Bangladeshis as Pakistani citizens would dilute a Sindhi majority.

Equally paranoid are Mohajirs living in Karachi. Since the 1980s, hyperracialized tensions between Mohajirs and Pashtuns in the city have often resulted in violence. Karachi's increasing Pashtun population weakened Mohajir control over city politics.[18] Formal recognition of Afghans as nationals, Mohajir political groups fear, would further consolidate Pashtun control of the city, especially in electoral politics.

If the possible recognition of Afghan refugees and Bangladeshi workers as citizens causes political turmoil, then the non.recognition of Pakistan's "own" causes a distinct set of problems. As Ammar Jan, Pakistan's leading Marxist academic and activist, satirically points out, Pakistan is perhaps the only country in the world where the majority seceded from a minority—the reference is to the 1971 debacle with East Pakistan, when 54 percent of the population fought a war of liberation to become Bangladesh. Writing in reference to demands put forward by the people of Gilgit-Baltistan (GB) and Federally Administered Tribal Areas (FATAs) for inclusion into the Pakistani federation as full citizens with equal rights, Jan quips that the paranoid Pakistani state looks at these calls for integration, rather than separation, as subversive and unpatriotic.[19] Shaheen Sardar Ali and Javaid Rehman's work gives an excellent account of how minority groups in Pakistan—whether ethnic, linguistic, or religious—enjoy only limited citizenship rights.[20] There exists, in other words, a model of unequal citizenship rather than a careful federal scheme for accommodating ethnic and linguistic differences. Such an arrangement is sharply brought into focus in the cases of GB and the FATAs.

Gilgit-Baltistan, formerly nominally part of the princely state of Jammu and Kashmir, joined Pakistan after an armed struggle in 1947–1948. Although it owed only symbolic allegiance to the ruler of Kashmir, the Pakistani state decided to keep the region's legal status ambiguous until settling the Kashmir dispute. This arrangement has continued to this day, with disastrous consequences for the people of GB. Reduced to an administrative unit without citizenship rights, the region held the vague geographical appellation "Northern Areas" and was administered by a federal secretary in Islamabad. Only in 2009 was some semblance of political autonomy granted to the region, and it was formally renamed Gilgit-Baltistan. However, full citizenship rights for residents of GB remain a far-fetched idea.[21] One possible explanation for this is that granting provincial status to GB would not only bear on pro-Pakistani sentiment on both sides of Kashmir but also create an anomaly of an overwhelmingly Shia-majority province in an otherwise Sunni-dominated Pakistan.

In the case of the FATAs, Pakistan has acted as a successor state of British India, replicating the policy of dealing with the region as a special zone under its own punitive law. Drafted during the colonial period, the so-called Frontier Crimes Regulation (FCR) was a set of rules designed to deal with the empire's restive frontier. In their fetishized Orientalist understanding of Pashtun society, the Raj and its successor postcolonial state recognized the tribal areas for their "peculiar" traits of chauvinism. The colonial-era law endorses such forms of tribal justice as Jirga and punitive punishments like the burning of the homes of an entire clan to atone for the crimes of an individual.[22] Only in 2018 was the formal constitutional procedure for the integration of the FATAs into the province of Khyber Pakhtunkhwa completed.[23] But full-scale integration and equal application of Pakistani law to all residents in the FATAs remains a dream. Different models of citizenship rights continue in provincially administered areas and Azad Kashmir—to say nothing of the vast lists of grievances levied by communities who feel they are effectively treated as unequal or lesser citizens despite being ostensibly recognized as full citizens.[24] Even those Pakistanis who do not encounter the violence of marginalization per se nevertheless face the citizenship question—that is, issues of inequality—in their daily life. To apply for an identity card or passport, citizens who want to register themselves as Muslims must sign off on excluding Ahmadis by designating them non-Muslims in a declaration.

In contrast to this, the recent issuance of identity documents for *khwaja siras*—an umbrella term for the "third gender" in Pakistan—offers an instance of acceptance and negotiation. In a series of judgments issued in the 2010s, the Pakistani Supreme Court reaffirmed the rights of *khwaja sira* communities by officially recognizing the category of third gender on national identity cards. The judgment opened new spaces of state intervention in regulating bodies and sexualities. Commenting on these developments, Faris A. Khan argues that many among the *khwaja siras*, nonnormatively gendered communities as he conceptualizes them, practiced and desired a form of "translucent citizenship—a mode of belonging which involves not only demands for equal rights from the state but also the right to remain hazy to broader publics." While recognizing the potential benefits of access to state resources, the *khwaja sira* communities were also wary of the potentialities of the state's policing of their bodies and sexualities—hence the need for translucent citizenship whereby the community achieves "empowerment through political participation, state recognition and cultural acceptance, while seeking to sustain the many freedoms encapsulated within indigenous patterns of identification and organization, through modes of resistance to fully being 'seen' by the state and society."[25]

WHO IS A CITIZEN? WHAT IS A NATIONAL? THE BIOGRAPHY OF A CONCEPT

The idea of citizenship undergoes various semantic and ideological changes when we shift the focus of the inquiry from the European origins of the concept to its non-European histories. In the South Asian context, for instance, the biography of citizenship reads differently when the interlocutory power of a European concept is read against its own history.

T. H. Marshall's theorization of citizenship has provided an accepted model for the history of citizenship, whereby the concept is understood as originating in England to mean equal membership in society. This transformative idea arose from civil rights discourse in the eighteenth century and was extended to political rights in the nineteenth century, followed by economic rights in the twentieth.[26] Reading Marshall alongside Weber, one can trace the religious roots of modern democratic polity and problematize a supposedly neat division of secular and sacred power. As Turner explains, society for Weber was premised along the division of secular rule of the state and the spiritual rule of the church, corresponding with two distinct forms of citizenship: spiritual citizenship within the community of believers, known as the body of Christ, and worldly citizenship within the political community. As an eschatological religion with a focus on the afterlife, Christianity considered the current world and its worldly powers—the City of Man—insignificant and a prelude to preparation in the City of God. In the postmillenarian environment, the church adopted a this-worldly approach of good citizenship in the City of God, affecting worldly urban politics to attain rights.[27] Thus, contrary to the popular view that the rise of urban citizenship was at the expense—or due to the corrosion—of religious authority and confessional ties, Weber argued that the Christian notion of a faith-based community that transcended differences of blood undermined traditional links in the city and allowed for an associational pattern of urban groupings to emerge.[28]

In Turner's reading of Weber, this marks the triumph of *Gesellschaft* over *Gemeinschaft*, moving from closed, personal relationships to open, impersonal relationships and corresponding to the success of markets over villages.[29] To borrow from Tonnies, who initially thought of this differentiation, the community comes prior to an established political order with cohesive traditional ties, as opposed to the fragmented societal and associational ties that follow as rationalized and individualized structures.[30] Durkheim similarly understood movement from community to society as a function of modernity whereby an individual identification with the collective, contractual relations, and cooperation between groups are established.

Although Durkheim did not romanticize the idea of community as prepolitical and was instead inclined to regard social organization as individuated and differentiated, he nevertheless considered community a prerequisite to strong societal bonds, which in turn effective citizenship requires.[31] In sum, the historical and sociological account of citizenship in the European context describes it as a process involving social differentiation between religious and secular spheres, and the corrosion of traditionally held belief structures; modernity is thus defined as autonomous liberal subjecthood, democratic politics, and economic growth.[32] This forms the basis for coming together as a community and contractually attaining rights, provisions of justice, representation in political life, and protection against social inequality.

It is necessary to emphasize the simultaneity—rather than a sequential unfolding—of these developments and their mutual reinforcement with the rise of the nation-state, the conceptual framework of modernity, and capitalist modes of production. The Marshallian approach assumes a neatly discernible, layered history of citizenship that helps stabilize the forces of discontent and protest. It makes the history of citizenship an idealized temporal grid of an onward triumphalist march and its supposed universality. Such a framework forecloses the possibility of analyzing the constituent elements of citizenship as it emerged as a political concept in the European world, thus effectively reducing much of the current scholarship to an analysis of sociological categories and possibilities for individual citizens' autonomy within a liberal framework. The scholarship of Will Kymlicka, for instance, is primarily concerned with increasing citizens' individual and community freedoms and rights within existing liberal frameworks of citizenship, especially as a way of addressing issues of migrants, the question of assimilation, and debates about multiculturalism in increasingly intolerant European and North American politics and praxis.[33] The study of citizenship in its European iteration, therefore, becomes a description of its various categories (e.g., active and passive rights) or its conceptual basis (e.g., civic virtue, equality, civil society, public sphere) or its models (e.g., civic, republican, ethno-national, communitarian, Marxist).[34] These approaches are bereft of the radical potential that exists within the history of citizenship, especially when that history is read as part of a global history of colonial rule that is based on difference where the distinction between the national citizen and the colonial subject was adamantly maintained.

Engin Isin adopts a similar set of practices that espouses a "bundle of rights" approach but explores the concept's non-European origins. While Isin locates the polis and its genealogy in a vastly imagined European intellectual history from the ancient Greeks to the European Union, his work allows for space "after Orientalism" to study the possibility of a distinct history of citizenship or conception of political membership in non-European societies.[35] Such an intertwining of the Global North and the colonized South helps expose the dubious universalization of the citizen as "male, propertied, white, heterosexual, able-bodied, generally Christian figure" rather than simply trying to retrieve non-European conceptions and practices of citizenship. Isin's project opens up possibilities for understanding how non-European and colonized subjects constituted themselves as "political subjects not in terms of the dominant figure of the citizen and its orientalizing perspective but as a challenge to them."[36]

I take Isin's intervention as a point of departure for tracing the shift from the abstract universalization of citizenship via its European history to a global intellectual project whereby the contestation of rights and the formation of political subjectivities permeated circuits of power that connected the Global North with the colonized South from the nineteenth century onward. In their earliest iterations, these trends can be seen in colonial debates and anxieties about the possibility of recognizing some form of legally sanctioned subjecthood for colonial subjects, whether in the form of cosmopolitan imperial citizenship or according to a much narrower premise. These debates extended well into the twentieth century, coinciding with similar debates about equal citizenship in Europe. The British official and author Lionel Curtis, for instance, favored imperial citizenship based on the idea of loyalty to the sovereign in a commonwealth that brought nations together in a single political framework under the banner of the empire.[37] In contrast, the Scottish novelist and diplomat John Buchan envisioned a cosmopolitan version of citizenship inclusive of national identities and democratic ideals.

However, even such paternalistic notions of inclusion were not extended to Britain's colonies in Asia and Africa in the nineteenth century. The inevitability of legal subjectivity in an increasingly connected world—linked by the exchange of goods and labor—forced the empire to accord its subjects documentary recognition. As Radhika Mongia's work shows, the invention of the passport in the early twentieth century and its extension to the colonies was a technology to surveil and manage bodies that regulated racialized mobility, organizing a massive flow of indentured labor, sailors, agricultural workers, and others across continents. It was within the framework of these racialized categories of surveillance and this global outreach connecting the metropolitan with the colonized—in other words, at the nexus of colonialism and racism—that, according to Mongia, "a notion of the nation as a territorially and demographically circumscribed entity" took shape.[38] In a related study, Radhika Singha traces the genealogy of the passport as shaped by an imperative to keep India's borders porous in order to maintain British interests in Indian labor, including on plantations and in oil works and mines in the Bay of Bengal and in the harbors of Malaya, Burma, and Ceylon.[39] In line with Mongia's argument, Singha sees the emergence of the passport as an act of claiming territorial coherence for what was otherwise a fragmented sovereign power and historically unstable entity: the modern state. Such a project gelled with the compulsion to identify and establish colonial difference, whether for internal administrative purposes, such as granting travel documents to pilgrims or to Indians studying abroad, or in response to external problems, such as regulating maritime traffic and managing the cross-continental migration of indentured laborers and workers. This, in turn, defined the debate and politics around introducing the passport in British India. The granting of a passport, restricted as it was, did not endow any legal obligations or political subjecthood to a person. It made the person a protected British subject only for the purposes of law and classification. The anxiety around underscoring and distinguishing concepts and categories like race, nationhood, and subjecthood was thus central to the development of regimented zones of legal classification with corresponding rights; that anxiety forms a vital feature of the global history of citizenship.

In short, in an increasingly interconnected world, the distinction between citizen and colonial subject was key to the endowment of rights and racialized control of bodies. The domestic differentiation between citizen and national, then, served as an additional marker for making political subjects legible. This categorization was both formal and informal, as in the German case of distinguishing *Staatsangehorigkeit* from *Volksangehoritkeit*, that is, membership in the state from membership in the *Volk*.[40] These terms map onto the conceptual registers of membership in a political community based on formal legal status, and thus the idea of the abstract citizen, and an intimate sense of belonging to a community defined by a majoritarian ethnic, linguistic, or religious ethos.

As Brubaker's work on the conceptual differences between French and German citizenship models shows, the history of French state formation and its consolidation—along with a rhetoric of civic equality as championed by the bourgeoisie revolution of 1789—led to the institutionalization of ideas of political rights in France and to a relatively stable union of nation and state. The French citizen, earlier on than the German one, existed within the institutional and territorial framework of the state.

The German mode, however, was distinct. Legal membership in the Prussian state, for instance, could be dissolved and replaced only by a German national-state after 1871. Brubaker writes: "The initial distinctness of nation and state—ethnic nationality and political citizenship—in Germany gave to the later nationalization of citizenship a specifically ethnocultural dimension that was muted, if not entirely absent in France."[41] Brubaker describes French and German citizenship as based on, respectively, the jus soli (right of soil) and jus sanguinis (right of blood). In both cases, it is only the history of state formation that has differently connected the national type and its majoritarian ethos, though admittedly with distinct outcomes. What does not change is that, in both cases, citizenship is at its core defined as membership in the modern political community, whereby legal recognition by the state serves as a formal basis for a rights-based interaction between the individual and the state.

Citizenship is thus markedly different from nationality, which historically has been a matter of transforming the subject's affective bond with the sovereign into an allegiance to the nation-state, hence reifying the majoritarian ethos.[42] Citizenship, in its pretense of abstraction, universality, and equality, becomes an attempt to override affective bonds of allegiance to the sovereign and intimate connections with the local, as well as identification with the nation via majoritarian values. In Oommen's formulation, citizenship becomes a tool whereby nonmajority groups variously defined along the lines of race, religion, language, or ethnicity can be provided protection, a sense of belonging, and the opportunity for participation.[43] But reducing individuals to legal members of a community is a process of disavowing the political in general and upholding the rights-bearing individual as a normative model and de-ethnicized entity. Such a liberal conception of citizenship is based on an erasure of identities and suprastate bonds, which is prerequisite for equal membership in the political community.

Brubaker's and Oommen's analyses bring us to the heart of Hannah Arendt's formulation about the right to have rights. For Arendt, the universality of rights-bearing subjects was premised on the particularity of an organized community. The experience of statelessness and deprivation of citizenship rights experienced as a German Jew had convinced Arendt of the need to particularize what was otherwise, in its universal form, abstract. But this quest for a place in the world and "a right to belong to some kind of an organized community" as prerequisite to the endowment of rights exposes the fault lines and palpable, unresolved tension between the allure of citizenship as equal membership in a modern political community and an enchantment with the nation as a supralegal, premodern fiction of affiliation and belonging to a homeland—that is, the citizen-national chasm.[44]

I posit that membership in and belonging to a political community are two different things, a distinction that Habermas tacitly recognizes as "the tension between the universalism of an egalitarian legal community and the particularism of a community united by historical destiny ... built into the very concept of the national state."[45] The equivalents would be the juridical identity of the individual as a citizen and the affective belonging to the nation as a majority. As Mamdani has argued, the political modernity of the nation-state is premised on community or society imagined as a nation and then conflated with the state to produce the nation-state, with a permanent national majority and minority. This is not to imply the fixing of boundaries, however, as the definition of the national self keeps on changing to create new minorities and to set the limits for who belongs and who doesn't. This makes national belonging a social endeavor and a legal project, a dynamic that, according to Mamdani, creates a vicious relationship between nation and state, wherein the state exists to serve and aggrandize the nation.[46]

The conjoining of nation and state can occur in civic nationalism, as in the United States, or, at its worst, in exclusionary forms like Nazism, apartheid, Zionism, and Hindutva that put a premium on the purity of the nation.[47] But even in its civic form, the presupposition of the normative value system does not fade; it can only pretend to be more inclusive and pluralistic. As current events involving controversies of free speech show, such as European bans on the public display of religious symbols and a related disapproval over conspicuously Islamic architectural styles in major European cities, the non-European citizen must adapt and convert to the archetype of the ideal European national, a performative act. In that sense, "national" is not, as international legal jargon would have it, equivalent to "citizen." The national is the person who retains or represents the imaginary of prepolitical notions of organic ties of blood and soil. The nation-state, by its very nature and definition, embodies the national as a guarantor of the sovereign nation. In this fashion, sovereignty has been nationalized. This transformation has led to what Nandita Sharma describes as the emergence of national natives, that is, the postcolonial afterlife of colonial forms of state power, violence, and exclusion.[48] The essentialist autochthony in this discourse betrays the promises and possibilities of the anticolonial struggle for sovereignty.

To sum up, there is a problematic triangulation of state, nation, and citizen. To borrow from Arendt, rights are based on sameness, assembling various communities as a nation, and also on difference, to ensure equality between said communities. In the name of sovereignty and nationhood, the postcolonial state seeks to flatten that difference to create a homogenized citizenry, and yet it holds on to the affective power of the national symbol, the archetype, imagining a glorious past to animate the disenchanted present. Managing affective, prepolitical, organic community bonds and their symbols and metaphors is at the heart of state-making projects. The flattening of difference refuses to recognize minority types and whatever does not fit into the imagined national type, dealing with them through eradication or, at best, liberal assimilation, with a corresponding set of differential rights, layered forms of citizenship, and special constitutional categories. When the Mozambican revolutionary Samora Machel says that the tribe must die for the nation to live, Mamdani interprets it as a message that "every potential source of competing identity had to be cleansed in order to homogenize the nation."[49] In other words, this flattening is part of national homogenization, going against the Arendtian idea of establishing artificial equality to constitute the "basic condition of both action and speech" wherein individuals can realize their humanity through public action and speech.[50] This is why in separatist struggles and ethnic movements, the emphasis is often on equality *and* recognition of difference.

There is, therefore, an inherent tension in the processes of state formation, identity articulation, and demands for citizenship rights that is often masked by or necessitates sociological formulations of different modes of citizenship in the name of multiculturalism or the accommodation of diversity. A study of these processes would open interstitial spaces for analyzing the constitutive elements of the nation-state, its claims to sovereign power, and the attempts to cohere a national type that is territorially bound and legally subjected. An understanding of the normative order thus constituted—and of various forms of political mobilization, alternative historical models, concepts of community boundaries, and the quest for sovereign self—offers a rich understanding of ideas about the state, sovereignty, nation, and citizen as part of a global intellectual history of ideas.

THE APORIAS OF BELONGING IN A POSTCOLONIAL NATION-STATE

Understanding the postcolonial context of citizenship rights and nationhood requires understanding the history of the transition from colonial subjecthood to postcolonial citizenship and how ideas of nationhood were imagined. Given the overlap between the European and non-European in the global history of citizenship, it is problematic to conceive of a sequential ordering of political developments that result in legally endowed rights, that is, of a veritable transference from West to East. It is by historicizing the simultaneity of modernity, capital, and right-based politics as the organizing principles of the colonial state and its attempts at organizing itself as a hegemonic entity that we should study the conceptualization of political subjectivities and shaping of their different modular forms as part of a global intellectual history.

In colonial India, for instance, it was the principle of national self-determination that defined the quest for political subjecthood. The articulation of the nation served as the fulcrum for petitioning legal and constitutional rights on behalf of the Indian subject. The nation, national self-determination, and freedom coalesced into a political movement for Indian independence, setting up an independent state in which citizens were to have equal rights. The demand for freedom was as much about finding a rhetorical language of freedom—enabling the soul of India to find utterance, as Nehru famously put it—as it was about, and couched in, finding a precise constitutional language for creating the Indian Republic and the rights-bearing Indian citizen.

Much of academic literature has focused on the rhetorical imagination of Indian nationhood in literature and history and the expressions of the Indian nation in vernaculars and politics. The work of both Partha Chatterjee and Sudipta Kaviraj provides an essential theoretical framework for understanding the development of Indian nationalism in its various phases, inspirations, modalities, creative expressions, and political articulations.[51] It is not just the history of Indian nationhood as a "felt community," but also that of political groups and communities campaigning for constitutional rights, that helps us understand postcolonial developments.[52] Niraja Gopal Jayal's foundational work on citizenship helps trace the history of the constitutional language through which nationalist groups contested the colonial government in a century of disagreements, as she calls it.[53] Her work is a veritable biography of citizenship in the Indian context that covers different shades of thought as various Indian leaders, political groups, and communities—whether as leaders of the Indian National Congress, Dalit campaigners for caste groups, or Muslim nationalists—sought to establish the political subject as a legal entity.

In the earliest phase of Indian nationalism, a handful of Indian elites—subject-citizens, as Jayal calls them—campaigned to cultivate a legal relationship of subjecthood between the Crown and the Indians based on the Queen's declaration of 1858, promising equal and just treatment, as well as commonality of loyal subordination to the Crown.[54] For the prehistory of citizenship in colonial India, Jayal differentiates between imperial and colonial modes of citizenship. With race and class as primary markers of differentiation, the British Empire recognized the status of its Indian subjects as members of the British Empire—that is, as imperial citizens—on par with other subjects of the Crown. Such identities were assigned in cases of indentured labor or to serve other imperial interests in different colonies. The colonial subjects in another part of the empire had to be differentiated from the native population while the Crown entertained their claims to equal or fair treatment.

The colonial citizenship focused on subjects within India and was thus a site of claims for civil liberties and political rights.[55] Although race stood as the primary marker of differentiation, the legal categorization of colonial subjects was further stratified: it distinguished along the lines of non-European, natural-born subjects in the British colony; protected persons in the principalities (British-protected persons); and a third category, including colonial administrators, Eurasians, and poor Europeans.[56] The British administration thus expressed a deep sense of anxiety, distinguishing between natural-born subjects of India and "white subalterns" to maintain racial superiority as the fulcrum of British colonial authority.[57] So while imperial citizenship was deeply hierarchical and racialized, colonial citizenship had no pretense of inclusiveness. This rule of difference signified a political lack and failure to actualize the universalist bourgeoisie project of rights and liberty, and it was addressed, managed, and governed through the spectral violence of legal coercion.[58]

The colonial public sphere was narrowly confined to mostly British-trained lawyers and landlords. In their earlier debates, as Jayal's work shows, these putative citizens of the empire highlighted the paternalistic character of the Crown's new charter and urged the colonial state to honor it. They expressed their disappointment to the benevolent Crown in an empire that did not hold itself up to its own liberal standards. The occasional imperial *darbar* served as the site for the performative praxis of loyal subordination by elitist subjects in return for the Crown's benevolent affirmation of fair treatment and just rule. For the bulk of the Indian liberal elite, a common political citizenship "within the framework of British rule and, even when it aspired to Swaraj, within the empire" continued to be a viable political project well into the twentieth century.[59] But with the entrance of new nationalist leadership in an era of mass-based politics, the language of the nationalist movement changed. However, it was not uncommon for the Indian National Congress to continue drafting constitutional reforms and political rights that it then submitted to the British government.

For instance, in 1918 the Bombay session of the Indian National Congress issued the Declaration of Rights, guaranteeing equality before the law and equal political liberties. The Nehru Report of 1928, which, according to Jayal, "prefigured the Indian Constitution of 1950 in several important ways," not only defined a jus soli criterion for Indian citizenship but also delineated fundamental rights. These included, in addition to political liberties, equality before the law and freedom of expression and of faith, as well as social and economic rights.[60] Many other draft constitutions prepared in the 1940s came up with similar provisions and helped set the tone for discussions on constitutional rights in the postcolonial period.

Although nationalists continued to fault the empire for its unequal treatment of subjects, its denial of political rights, and the limiting of franchise to property owners, their proposed solution was no longer to seek recognition within imperial citizenship, home rule, or commonwealth status, but to demand independence. In other words, from the early twentieth century onward, the demand was not for equal treatment as colonial subjects but for national freedom and the setting up of an independent state as an expression of sovereign power that guaranteed equality, liberty, and universal rights.

The formal language of constitutional law in which these issues were taken up from 1947 was shaped by the prehistory and ideological content of debates on citizenship and by the historical contingencies of political thought that informed them. In addition to the political genealogy of imperial and colonial citizenship, Joya Chatterjee talks about the "original blueprints" of Indian and Pakistani citizenship, which she locates in the Constituent Assembly debates before independence. After elections in 1945–1946, the assembly started functioning in December 1946—although notably the Muslim League, which had gained overwhelming support from Muslim constituencies, chose to boycott the sessions. One of the earliest tasks taken up by the assembly as part of the constitution-making process was to define "the people of India."[61] A proposed definition was to recognize as a citizen anyone born in the union or naturalized according to existing law.[62] But months before a formal transfer of power, as violence erupted and the refugee crisis started simmering, the citizenship debate could no longer ignore the question of those stranded outside of the Indian union as a result of the creation of Pakistan. The matter was deferred, to be taken up only after independence, when the refugee crisis reached such a point that any future outcome of the legal question of citizenship depended on it.

In Uditi Sen's categorization, the "citizen refugee" was the locus of debate as to who was an Indian or Pakistani citizen.[63] However, this question did not necessarily answer who belonged to India or Pakistan. The works of Haimanti Roy and Vazira Zamindar provide a detailed analysis of such aporias of belonging. According to Roy, the divided identities of nationals versus citizens were discursively produced through the categories of refugees, evacuees, and displaced persons, among others.[64] The distinction of national and citizen became a defining feature of the new legal regime of control and surveillance, each category requiring a different criterion of documentary evidence and of affect to establish the notion of belonging. Roy's work is an extensively researched history of the statist imposition of a documentary regime. From as early as 1948, the Indian and Pakistani postcolonial states started defining the legal identities of citizens through travel permits or by granting passports specific to travel between them. Zamindar's work focuses on affective modes of belonging, especially that of the Indian Muslim minority, as people navigated their way through a nation richly imagined as male and Hindu. The division of families across borders and a longing for the lost homeland—along with a strong sense of alienation, anxiety, and displacement in the newly adopted abode—are prominent tropes through which Zamindar offers a rich description of *mohajir*, or migrants, and their dilemmas of belonging.[65]

Despite claims to an obvious choice of jus soli citizenship, there were competing "citizenship discourses," as Ornit Shani describes them, which defined both the legal criteria for membership and the affective notions of belonging. On the basis of an approach to citizenship as a primary mechanism for making claims to the state and state membership in order to develop a shared community or sense of social solidarity, Shani delineates the content of such claims and solidarities in the democratic workings of the Indian nation-state. She identifies four notions of citizenship: liberal, republican, ethno-nationalist, and the nonstatist, which are often in competition with one other as delimiting processes. In addition to universal inclusion in the liberal model and to the predominance of the common good and civic virtue envisaged by republicanism, there is some overlap and tension between the ethno-nationalist model—which emphasizes notions of blood, soil, and majoritarian ethos—and the privileging of the individual as a member of the moral community in the nonstatist model developed along Gandhian lines.

As Shani's analysis of the Gandhian model shows, the abhorrence of the state in Gandhian thought contrasts with the independence of "the self and self-regulated stateless national life."[66] The locus of moral action lies within the individual, who is situated in an idealized community of Ramrajya—a utopia of sorts—"by which he [Gandhi] means a 'reign of ideal justice' of 'self-imposed law of moral restraint.'"[67] Though seeking a nonstatist view of individual action in a moral community, the Gandhian notion was thus couched in a religious idiom and had to be represented in a language transcending the ethno-nationalist conception of citizenship.[68] Village councils, or *panchayats*, were premised on an idealized notion of a self-reliant village community in which everyone cooperated regardless of identity politics, caste distinctions, or Hindu-Muslim affiliation. However, the use of such terms as *bhoodan*, the moral duty of good Hindus—in addition to references to a Hindu cosmological order that was tied up with a moral universe that these councils aspired to achieve—had an alienating effect, failing to counter the impact of the ethno-national narrative.[69] Still, despite their inherent tensions, the polyvalence of views could be held together because of the democratic process of debate and frequently forced repositioning of the state's idea of citizenship. This is why ongoing changes to the citizenship law in India and resulting controversies have caused alarm bells to go off, as there is now an unprecedented challenge to the precarious balance among competing types of citizenship discourses.

The blurring of boundaries that allowed for the dominance of a normative ethno-national model was also built into the country's supposedly liberal constitutional doctrine. Ananya Vajpeyi's work, though meant in adoration of the "founding fathers" of Indian nationhood and its constitutions, directs us to the almost-exclusive reliance on Hindu and Buddhist religious philosophy, imagery, and aesthetics that inspired prominent Indian thinkers. In her analysis of the political thought of individual ideologues of Indian nationhood, she reads Gandhi's politics through the Gita, interprets Tagore's philosophical musings through a longish fifth-century classical poem about longing by Kalidasa, explains Nehru's state-building agenda by its affiliation with Ashokan era edicts and monuments, and locates Ambedkar's radical manifestos for the Dalits in Buddhist canonical literature.[70] It is not surprising, then, that to form a "righteous republic," the new republic's major symbols drew inspiration either from Ashoka as an idealized form of Indian state—centralized, strong, and expansive—or from various shades of classical Hindu and Buddhist religious traditions.

The strength of Indian scholarship and other interest in the academic study of the Indian constitutional democracy and secularism has caused that model to dominate discussions of citizenship in postcolonial nation-states. Until the 1990s, the predominant trend in scholarly literature on Pakistan was to focus heavily on studying the causes for the Muslim League's demand for a separate homeland or on an exploration of debates on the Islamic versus Muslim state for the post-1947 period. In the past few years, there have proliferated new academic works from a growing, critical mass of Pakistani scholars, which has enabled a shift from state-centric views of history to an exploration of subaltern groups, ethnic and linguistic marginalization, women's movements, religious minorities, agrarian revolts, and workers' solidarities.[71]

What I am interested in can broadly be viewed as an intellectual history of Pakistan as a case study in the ideational basis of nationhood, that is, Muslim *qaumiyyat*. Pakistan's transition to citizenship can be studied to delineate state development processes, identity formation, and politics of belonging. The excess of literature on Indian nationalism as theorized by the likes of Nehru and Gandhi, or its critiques by Ambedkar, is in contrast to a paucity of analytical work on Muslim *qaumiyyat*, especially its multiple variants in the state of Pakistan. The idea of *qaumiyyat* and its attendant history and articulation in political thought were central to the project of carving the Pakistani nation-state. A rigorous analysis of the history of this idea and its politics in the post-1947 period is a much-needed corrective to scholarly literature on both the political theory of citizenship and the politics of national belonging in the postcolonial world.

The study of citizenship in the Pakistani context has attracted the attention of a few scholars. Among the latest contributions are Nosheen Ali's work on Gilgit-Baltistan. Given the peculiar history of the region's independence from the princely state of Jammu and Kashmir in 1947–1948, the Pakistani state continues to keep the constitutional status of the area ambiguous. Ali describes the emotional language employed by the GB integrationist movement, in which the claim-making discourse around a push for equal citizenship is expressed through the reigning metaphor of a jilted lover whose desire for communion has not been reciprocated. In Ali's estimation, "love is a compelling constellation through which we may chart how the dynamic of citizenship operates on the ground."[72] Her innovative analytical lens significantly complicates, and thus adds to, our current, more simplistic understanding of citizenship as a legal abstraction.

Coming from a legal, bundle-of-rights approach, Ayesha Siddiqi has developed new theoretical insights by looking closely at disaster management in the wake of the devastating floods that hit Sindh in 2010–2011. Her extensive fieldwork in flood-hit areas shows the breadth of the state's influence. In their claim making, citizens continue to look to the state for the provision of rights. Siddiqi's work speaks about rural Sindh, which is a region that is considered remote and inaccessible, and is largely ignored for developmental purposes. The choice of her fieldwork adds to the importance of her theoretical and empirical contributions. Her central claim is that a "relationship between the state of Pakistan and its citizens does exist," and that the traditional structure of patronage—though still intact—accounts for only one part of that relationship. Her conclusion that the relationship between the citizen and the state is "based on [the] rights and entitlements of citizenship" proves to be the most significant aspect of her research.[73] It leads Siddiqi to claim that the sensationalist specter around Islamists acting as viable alternatives to the state or as service providers because of state failure is overestimated.

While Ali's and Siddiqi's scholarship takes a regional approach to making broader theoretical claims, my analysis is more akin to recent contributions by Sarah Ansari and William Gould. Ansari and Gould provide an overview of general trends in citizenship-making processes through focused case studies. Taking the violence and displacement of the foundational moment of Partition, Ansari and Gould describe the approaches by the Indian and Pakistani states to cultivate notions of belonging through texts and performances and to lay down the basis for active civic and political life. Citizens themselves, emphasize Ansari and Gould, played a significant role in charting the acquisition of rights through their claims, critique, and political praxes, whether through organized, concerted efforts or everyday interactions with the state.[74]

Aside from these exceptional new works, postcolonial studies of citizenship, nation, and the state have focused on India and largely celebrated its continued tradition of a secular democracy unified around a single constitution, as well as the intellectual traditions of those who drafted it. This literature has left Pakistan out of the equation, given its subsequent history: the systematic breakdown of the democratic process and the presence of endemic ethnic and religious violence. An additional assumption is that the plan for a homogenized Islamic identity was, for a Muslim-majority state, a foregone conclusion that did not require debate or much imagination. My work rebuts such myopic views. By offering a rich analysis of the ideological content and political disputes that emerged from Pakistan's postcolonial state-making process, this book contributes significantly to the intellectual history of political thought in the Global South.

QAUM, MULK, SULTANAT: THE CURIOUS CASE OF PAKISTAN

Qaum, mulk, sultanat: these three words, which comprise a stanza in the national anthem of Pakistan, written by Hafiz Jallandhari in Persianized Urdu, are at the heart of my contribution to the study of citizenship, nationality, and statehood in Pakistan.[75] The national anthem is the heralding of the nation, its moment of arrival in state form, built on the glory of the past with an aspirational march toward the future. *Qaum*, *mulk*, and *sultanat* can be translated as "nation," "country," and "state," respectively. As I have previously argued in a jointly written essay, an etymological survey of these terms reveals that they have embodied various meanings and histories that do not necessarily cohere with those meanings emphasized in the anthem.⁷⁶

The term *qaum* has variously been understood as referring to any kind of collectivity, especially those defined along kinship lines. During the election campaign in 1945–1946, Muslim League propaganda denounced *qaum* as antithetical to the universalist conception of a singular, faith-cemented community of Muslims.⁷⁷ Despite the nationalization of the term in the anthem, it retains its vernacular usage, referring to kin groups and other claims to ethnic nationhood.

Mulk defines a literary imaginary, an amorphously bounded land. It is distinct from a modern iteration of the word to mean "state" and from related vernacular terms like *watan* for "homeland." As Mana Kia's recent intervention shows, such transformations in meanings are based on the presumption of an empty space on which political subjectivities are built—a modern phenomenon tied with the specificity of the nation-state's territoriality. Such a conception of space as homogeneous and national overlooks various other modes of embeddedness through which individuals and communities ascribe different meanings of homeland to link people and spaces across regions and polities.⁷⁸ Manan Ahmad has adopted a similar approach by looking at Hindustani regional histories written in Persian in the premodern period, which Ahmad considers the connective idiom that enables intimacy with the land. Ahmad argues that such a conceptualization—which is not to be reduced to a prehistory of the nation or the nation-state—was lost in the positivist histories of India commissioned by the officials of the East India Company.⁷⁹ By the mid-twentieth century, a new term coined for geostrategic purposes became frequent: *South Asia*.⁸⁰

Sultanat is a term that is still widely used to denote an empire in the premodern sense. Its usage in the anthem to refer to the state is presumably due as much to metrical limitations as it is for wont of a better replacement.

In this manner, the conceptual equivalence of terms for modern political thought, concepts, institutions, and their histories, shows how such terms draw upon various legal registers, cultural metaphors, and preexisting categories to cultivate and create modern sensibilities, political subjectivities, and collective identities. Words, as Bakhtin and Voloshinov describe them, are "the most sensitive index of social changes, and ... of changes still in the process of growth, still without definitive shape and not as yet accommodated into already regularized and fully defined ideological systems. . . . [They have] the capacity to register all the transitory, delicate, momentary phases of social change."[81] A genealogical approach, therefore, can help trace the process of transition and translation as words transform to coincide with political processes and institutional change. In the postcolonial context, Muslim nationhood, variously defined and understood throughout the modern period, was at the heart of the movement for a separate state and of later nation-making and state-formation projects. Foregrounding the significance of *qaum* as a social and cultural metaphor before that term became a national type or was collapsed with the legal entity of the citizen offers an intriguing point of entry.

In using the term *metaphor*, I draw upon the cognitive theorists George Lakoff and Mark Johnsen and the literary theorists Paul Ricoeur and Shamsur Rehman Faruqi. All these theorists agree on the need to move beyond the Aristotelian notion of metaphor as a replacement for a word and function of persuasive rhetoric. For Lakoff and Johnsen, human thought processes and conceptual systems are metaphorical.[82] They shift the locus of metaphorical action from words to concepts and from similarity to cross-domain correlations in experiences. Metaphors as conceptual systems are not only historically contingent but also significantly shaped by our bodies' common nature and everyday functionality.[83] Ricoeur is similarly focused on reading the metaphor as a discursive phenomenon rather than simply as a calculated error meant to displace the meaning of a word. "To affect just one word," writes Ricoeur, "the metaphor has to disturb a whole network by means of an aberrant attribution."[84] Moreover, the disturbance produced by metaphor presupposes a logical order, conceptual hierarchy, and classification scheme operating within the constituted order that is temporarily displaced. What if this constituted order, speculates Ricoeur, were begotten by a similar process of displacement? The question "suggests the idea that order itself proceeds from the metaphorical constitution of semantic fields."[85]

The shared poetic idiom and connected histories and geographies discussed by Manan Ahmad and Mana Kia can similarly be understood as constitutive of a discursive order that delineates metaphors for a premodern notion of *qaum* in Hindustan. Such metaphors continued well into colonial modernity given the preponderance of Persian as a classical language, a tradition inherited by Urdu as an embodiment of Indic-Muslim religious, political, and cultural thought, and especially by North Indian languages. To a considerable extent, as emerging scholarship on vernaculars shows, many aspects of metaphysical thought in the *qissa* tradition, for instance, were located in the cosmopolitan Indo-Persian epic traditions and tales circulating via land-based trade routes of the Indian Ocean, which encompasses a vast region.[86] As Sudipta Kaviraj has argued, it was the modernity and its twin political projects of nationalism and state formation as new modes of space making that drove a wedge between the individual and community sense of belonging to the land through the legal-strategic ordering of space and its transformation into sovereign territory of the nation-state.[87] Emphasizing the role of lyricism and poetics in creating an affective surplus, Kaviraj shows how late nineteenth-century nationalist writers invoked premodern religious and literary traditions whose initial vocalizations were specific to their regional contexts in order to conjure an image of the nation that claimed a more significant historical tradition and thus spirited people into action for its glory and safeguarding.[88] The connectivity of nation through land and language, however, was limited by the inherently majoritarian model of the nation in which the Muslim was the "other." Poetry, as Ali Khan Mahmudabad's work has shown, was equally influential in making a powerful claim to the land on behalf of all and in setting a "normative horizon" that was broadly construed.[89] But even if we accept the premise that modern forms of imagining the nation were different—regardless of whether they resulted in a fragmented polity or held the potential for inclusivity—it is the nation as the metaphor for a collectivity, group, or community sutured into a folk (i.e., the people) that requires further scrutiny. It is essential not only to emphasize the richness of language around *qaum*, *mulk*, and *sultanat* but also to historically locate such terms and analyze the processes whereby—to use a term from literary theory coined by Jauss—a concretization of meanings takes place.[90] In applying the term to political processes, my emphasis is on ascertaining modernity's impacts on imposing—or the attempts made by nation-states to impose—an overarching hegemonic authority and consistency in thought.

The best way to understand the layered, overlapping, and sedimented literary and political repertoires is through Umberto Eco's concept of the encyclopedia as a "multidimensional space of semiosis . . . a complex system of shared knowledge that governs the production and interpretation of signs inside communicative contexts."[91] Eco calls these repertoires an encyclopedia because of the heterogeneous nature of this knowledge system. The encyclopedia in this theorization becomes a register within which meanings in a social habitus and cultural unit are recorded, generated, regulated, renewed, and suppressed—or alternately, glossed over. Eco offers "house" as an example, with its correlated meanings of a physically delimited space for dwelling or inhabitation. But metaphorically, the sky is a house for birds, which does not fall within the same semantic values. What connects the uses is the idea of shelter: man takes refuge inside the house, and the bird flies into the open sky, yet both are connected through a shared narrative and cultural frame. In this metaphoric transference, shelter, and open space are condensed as sky despite the mutual exclusion of their ordinary meanings. In this manner, metaphors subvert semantic orders attached to words or terms by dictionaries and establish semantic contamination.[92] Metaphors, therefore, are central to Eco's description of the encyclopedia, in which, unlike the dictionary, words lack fixed meaning and are capable of generating new meanings through subversion, conversion, correlation, deletion, and replication.

Eco describes this understanding of the semiotic system encapsulated in an encyclopedia as resembling the working of the rhizome as theorized by Deleuze and Guattari. In this conceptualization, each point is connected with another point; connections are drawn as lines that can be broken off at any point and later reconnected following other lines. The rhizome has neither an outside nor an inside and can be broken down into its constituent units and modified. For Eco, the most crucial feature of the rhizome is that "only local descriptions of the rhizome are possible . . . [;] every perspective (every point of view on the rhizome) is always obtained from an internal point."[93] This conceptualization emphasizes the interconnectedness and virtual infinity of multiple interpretations in a given culture. It serves as the encyclopedic repository of truth, where *truth* is defined as the discourses about a term posited in any given moment.⁹⁴ Thus, it envisages an open-ended system of knowledge and communicative action, though one that is situated locally. The massive accumulation of knowledge in a cultural system requires selective modes of amnesia and remembrance to offset what Eco describes as a "vertigo of knowledge."⁹⁵ However, that which remains in abeyance remains retrievable for future modes of action.

Within this system of signification and interpretants, Shamsur Rehman Faruqi's description of the cultural content of classical poetry's metaphors—and their histories, subsequent developments, attributions, and ascriptions—can be understood. A leading novelist, critic, and literary theorist, Faruqi adds to literary theories on metaphor by tracing its conceptual genesis and discursive shifts encyclopedically. According to Faruqi, the thematic focus of classical Urdu poetry derived from Arabic and Persian is limited to a few subjects. Through the concept of *mazmun afrini*, poets strive to create new meanings, extending them beyond given metaphorical limits or the surface meanings of a word, sentence, or couplet. Faruqi takes up *giriya-i-ishq* (wailing for the beloved) as an example: this phrase has been used as a metaphor for the weeping eye (*chashm-i-girya*) in an expansive and exaggerated interwoven web of meanings involving rivers, clouds, rain, greenery (*haryali*), jungle, desolation (*virani*), floods, and more. Despite its usage for hundreds of years in Persian and Urdu poetry, the metaphor hasn't lost its freshness, as each poet uses it differently.⁹⁶ In the same fashion, Faruqi traces religious ideals that seep into poetics through the metaphorical imaginary and contends that they serve as a shared poetic idiom across regions. He cites the Sufi poet Rumi's famous *har lehza ba shakal-i-aan but-i-ayyar bar-amad* as a classic example of yearning for the One and being one with the Divine. He then traces this concept in the work of poets who followed Rumi hundreds of years later in North India and the Deccan. Divided across time and space, these poets had what Faruqi calls "mutual comprehensibility" when it came to a shared metaphoric understanding of being one with the Divine.⁹⁷ The same *mazmun* was replicated in classical Urdu poetry innumerable times, and even by Hindu poets like Swami Ram Tirath (d. 1906), whose ghazal carries the unmistakable influence of Sufi influences as Vedantic in his depictions of Ram and of being one with Ram.⁹⁸ Through this broader encyclopedic canvas, Faruqi charts a historical account of how shared comprehensibility across the poetic realm develops ideas across cultural and religious traditions and imbibes them. The corresponding impact is that metaphors either fade into oblivion or transform into a new meaning, or wholly new metaphors are coined to reflect changing sociopolitical contexts.

LOCATING THE MUSLIM *QAUM* IN COLONIAL MODERNITY

Such an elaborate knowledge of the semiotic systems through which cultural units develop, derive, forget, ascribe, or resuscitate meanings to concepts, words, and actions help us understand the metaphors of *qaum*, *mulk*, and *sultanat* over the *longue durée*. My project is not to write a detailed history of the Muslim *qaum* but to reflect on the processes and transitions of postcolonial state and nation formation, analyzing this metamorphosis through a close reading of texts and performances.

To explain historical processes of change, an exploration of the Muslim *qaum*, the colonial context, and the labeling of minority, community, and nationhood in that context is essential. At the outset, it must be said that the existing secondary literature on this topic is almost exclusively focused on North Indian Muslim *ashraf* classes—which also extend into Punjab—and their writings and interactions in Urdu.⁹⁹ There is an astonishing dearth of literature on the histories of Muslim imaginaries of community, kin, and vernacular literature for other areas in the late nineteenth century. The Bengal is an exception that has been covered extensively in the works of Rafiuddin Ahmad, Sufia Ahmed, and Neilesh Bose.¹⁰⁰ Two factors explain the reductive meaning of the Muslim *qaum* thus imagined, suggesting why *qaum* remains a necessary topic of scholarly analysis. First is the nature of the colonial conception of community as religiously bounded and held together by a single set of laws. In colonial India, the individual Muslim subjectivity—with political interests tied to its recognition as Muslim in identities that were shot through with differences of locality, language, ritual practice, belief, and caste—was subsumed within the collective of "the Muslim community."¹⁰¹ Second is the predominance of Urdu in the intellectual milieu of North India, where it became the language of articulation for Muslim interests, sensibilities, and aesthetics. The sphere of Urdu itself, argues Akbar Zaidi, had discursive boundaries that extended to the Deccan, so that the Muslim *qaum* did not constitute a singular entity; instead, it was more of an aspirational project, an attempt by reformist groups and political leaders to create a unified community.[102] This further adds to the importance of retrieving other notions of *qaum* in multiple linguistic registers in colonial India and their prehistories, as they will invariably enrich our understanding of the debate. The current deficiency in the historical literature is responsible for the misconception that the politics of, say, Sindhi or Pashtun nationalism was born only after 1947.

It was the idea of a homogenized Muslim identity articulated via tropes of the past that lay at the heart of Muslim separatism during the twentieth century, and thus it is important to take stock of that intellectual genealogy. As Ayesha Jalal rightly points out, the dismissal of Muslim nationalism as communalism—both in the anticolonial politics of the Indian National Congress in the early twentieth century and in later historiographical accounts of that movement—is the result of misapplying a Eurocentric view of the nation to India. At the same time, Jalal is careful to point out internal inconsistencies in the concept of the Muslim *qaum*. She historicizes the articulation of the Muslim *qaum* as a balancing act between the individual quest for autonomy and the need for delimiting communitarian boundaries for rich pickings in a colonial framework that operated on enumeration along ethnic, religious, and caste lines.[103] She talks about the complexities of layered belongings arising out of the "Muslim's identification with a non-territorial community of Islam and the sense of belonging to a territorially located community," which meant that "space is both infinite and finite at the same time."[104] Faisal Devji, in contrast, theorizes Muslim ontology in colonial India as an unresolved dialectics between the citizen as a universal subject juridically produced, transcending particularity to become a legal ideal and the universality of Muslimhood itself in an ontic-ontological sense.[105]

In tracing the precolonial history of the Muslim *qaum*, Faisal Devji locates "the *moral* city as a site of ethical-political discourse ... created in legal (*shariat*) culture as a public-discursive realm (*am*, *suhbat*, or *jalwat*) which was deemed the arena of Islam *par excellence*." The colonial structures of governmentality and the materiality of colonial power reshaped the notion of *qaum*. Ghalib, a nineteenth-century doyen of classical Urdu poetry, captures the anxiety of this spatial-political and religious change in the following couplet:

> *Iman mujhe rokey hai jo khinche hai mujhe kufr*
> *Ka'aba mere piche hai Kalisa mere agay*

> Faith restrains me while I am tugged at by heresy
> behind me stands the mosque, the church in front of me.[106]

The loss of the moral city theorized by Devji implied a decline in the Muslim elite's social privilege and the ethical-moral code of the self, threatening the self's link with the spatiality of the moral city. The conversion of Hindustan into India, an empty uniform object, severed traditional ties to the place and ideas about place, which had to be reimagined in *ashraf* geography.[107] With the constitutive public of the Muslim elite rendered obsolete by the new colonial order, "the Shurafa were able to build the *qawm* as a new sort of private sphere from the wreckage of the moral city . . . abstracting from it [i.e., the moral city] areas such as the mosque and the (Islamic) school (the courts and market being surrendered to the amoral public sphere of colonialism), and joining them in a new Muslim privacy with the traditionally private areas of the Sufi shrine and the domestic realm."[108] Writing about Syed Ahmad Khan's work on the monuments of Delhi, Devji points to a cartographic perspectival view wherein monuments are fetishized as monumental representatives of the community or as the historical materiality of the *qaum*. As symbols of the religious past and belonging, they are not only poetically meaningful but also reverential, symbols of the Muslim past through which a history of the *qaum* was idealized.[109] Such a sacralization of space, he says, led to the possibility of the offensive politics of designating sacrilege in the nineteenth century onward, forbidding the playing of music in front of mosques or the entering of mosque premises with shoes.

Temporally, the new Muslim self was no longer filiative, dealing with disparate genealogical temporal orders. The new affiliative history interrupted this temporality, thus creating a new ontological space for the *ashraf* in which the present became an entity rather than a passage from past to future. It was a future that was already known either as the present or as a kind of past recoverable by history.[110] The futurity of the historical output of the late nineteenth and early twentieth centuries sought to recover an idealized past of Muslim political supremacy and cultural glory. Much of this creative and literary output was chauvinistically male and approached the *qaum* as a feminine figure embodying male honor.

Another common trope, identified by Zaidi, is that of *zillat*, or utter humiliation, through which much of the debate on *qaum* takes place in print literature, public debates, and religious polemics, especially during the late nineteenth century.[111] The historical fiction of Abdul Halim Sharar (1860–1926); the didactic, reformist literature of Nazir Ahmad (1836–1912); the nostalgic poetry of Muhammad Iqbal (1877–1938) about the Muslim empire; and the many works on the history of Hindustan by Maulwi Zakaullah (1832–1910) are representative popular and intellectual articulations of the Muslim *qaum*.[112] What connects these works is what Koselleck describes as a temporalization of the past, that is, a critical-historical distance from events, texts, and practices, and a recognition of that distanciation.[113] Coupling this concept with Anderson's idea of the awareness of embeddedness in secular, serial time enables the writing of the nation's biography. But unlike persons, who have a beginning and an end, nations do not have identifiable births or deaths. In Anderson's words, "the nation's biography cannot be written evangelically, 'down time' . . . the only alternative is to fashion it 'up time' . . . wherever the lamp of archaeology casts its fitful gleam."[114]

THIS STUDY'S SCOPE

Like other studies on India and Pakistan, in this book I am interested in tracing the history and politics of transition from subjects to citizens. My analysis, however, treats this process as both continuous and interruptive of the prehistories and debates that preceded the Partition of British India. By foregrounding the category of Muslim *qaum* as it developed during the colonial period, I show that citizen making marks a transformation in the metaphor of the nation from a richly imagined historical entity grounded in the cultural unit of Hindustan to the abstraction of a legal entity. In this process, the postcolonial state selectively draws upon the repertoire of the *qaum* to create notions of belonging. But the postcolonial state has a problematic relationship with its own ideological and cultural content. There is deeper anxiety at work: the postcolonial state—a spectacular state, as it is called—cannot disregard the content of the *qaum*.[115] Its "surplus of affect," as Arjun Appadurai calls it, acts as a supplement to the ideological lack in the concept of citizenship.[116] The juridical identity of the citizen is a prerequisite to the granting of rights, but without the notion of belonging it is insufficient; furthermore, citizenship and belonging are not equivalent. Belonging here is essentially national, defined along prepolitical imaginings of soil and blood. Hence the problematic trinity of state, nation, and citizen that heralds a crisis of cohesive weakness of the idea of republicanism, which, according to Habermas, "must learn to stand on its own feet."[117]

Even before its creation in 1947, there were contentious debates about whether Pakistan was just meant to be a Muslim homeland that safeguarded the political and economic interests and cultural identity of the Muslim *qaum* or was meant as an Islamic state wherein Muslims could practice their religion and reestablish an idealized pious republic.[118] These competing views about the *qaum* and the rationale for setting up a new state had a bearing on how the new state was to be run. Even if the version of the Muslim homeland as a politico-economic and religio-cultural refuge was potentially more tolerant of diversity than the Islamic republic version that eventually prevailed, both insisted on the centrality of Muslimness to designating equal or discriminatory citizenship for nationals. The very nature of the demand for a new state based on essentialized differences between Hindus and Muslims—the two-nation theory, as it was called—made nationality reducible to religious identity. Muslimness had to be emphasized to justify Pakistan. If Muslimness was not part of the state or society, or both, there remained little rationale for the state; otherwise, the same could have been ensured under a united India. Yet a large part of the Muslim *qaum* remained outside of Pakistan, as many members of this *qaum* were to stay back in India.[119] As I show in chapter 1, successive Pakistani regimes made passionate appeals to that Muslim *qaum* to stay put in India and adopt it as their homeland. Such a policy has the effect of creating a veritable "Pakistani diaspora" living in India—that is, a permanent threat, foreign element, and outsider, and a source of anxiety for the Indian Hindu right wing, which buys into the logic of Pakistani nationhood and takes it to its logical conclusion. For the Pakistani state, this logic has to remain operational to justify the separate state, hence the need for further emphasis on the religious content of the Muslim *qaum*, which leads to the further marginalization or forced assimilation of those who do not belong.

This is not so much a dismissal of Pakistani nationhood as it is a critique of any form of nationhood in political modernity that serves as the basis for nation-states. Mamdani has skillfully argued that all such models replicate the settler-native, colonial-subject, and majority-minority discursive practices. Yet he remains optimistic about effacing the categories that make citizens permanently nonnationals or unequal nationals. The decolonization of the political, says Mamdani, requires an intricate engagement with history.[120] What I take from Mamdani's work is his idea of historicization as a praxis of undoing, and thus I foreground an analysis of the constituent elements of the *qaum* and its shifting boundaries and changing valuational emphasis, as well as the contingencies of their making. I chronicle the nation-state's abortive, aspirational march toward coherence that always falls apart at the seams and perhaps even at the core. Through such historicization, it is probably possible to efface the citizen-nation difference. The premise of equality enshrined in the citizenship ideal can be retrieved from its radical history and from the nation's symbolic repertoires of anticolonial resistance and its vibrant autochthonous discourses around liberty, freedom, and sovereignty.

For this process of retrieval and historicization, one must look at the so-called foundational moments of the postcolonial period in which these discussions took place. In the case of India, the centrality and enduring democratic legacy of the Indian constitution have led scholars to focus on the assembly debates that resulted in the promulgation of the constitution within three years of independence, in January 1950. As recent work by Madhav Khosla on the foundational moment of constitution making shows, the primary concern of Indian lawmakers was to organize a centralized political entity built on the codification of the law. The constitution served a modernizing and a pedagogical function insofar as it sought to cultivate political subjectivity at the individual level, unmediated by the community.[121] More fundamentally, to paraphrase Shruti Kapila's recent theorization, the constitution and constituent assembly debates grappled with the question of equality and the peaceful coexistence of fraternal groups.[122] According to her, this was a question that had occupied the attention of prominent Indian thinkers since their encounter with the liberal notion of individual liberty and equality in the nineteenth century amid the innumerability of caste, linguistic, and ethnic divides and the uncanny intimacy of familiarity with the figure of the Muslim friend, neighbor, or brother.

In contrast, in the case of Pakistan, there is no single foundational moment that gave rise to a constitutional patriotism of the sort described by scholars of Indian constitutional history. Like most other postcolonial states, there was, among ambitions of decoloniality, a sense of reckoning with ideas of political and social equality that had to be effected into practice.[123] But what was different was the inability of Pakistan's political leadership to answer questions that ultimately delayed the constitution-making process by several years and even decades.[124] Unlike in India, where lawmakers deferred the question of social equality to achieve a consensus on political equality for citizens of the republic, political equality alone was a contentious issue in Pakistan.[125] This was due to an imperative of a substantial non-Muslim minority at home, which forced a reckoning with the intellectual poverty of the two-nation theory: it was inadequate for ensuring the equality of Muslims and non-Muslims as citizens.

This is not to suggest that the question of fraternal coexistence had not been a concern for Muslim political thinkers. Devji explores this debate through Iqbal's writings. Like Gandhi, Iqbal was opposed to the Western notion of territorial nationalism and the way it eschewed the ethical, reducing the individual to an atomistic existence understood in liberal terms of representation in the pursuit of selfish interests. Both Gandhi and Iqbal sought to recenter religion in the public sphere not as part of a political strategy of maximal gain under the liberal registers of representations and self-interests but as a critique of a Western political theory they saw as devoid of ethics and spirituality. For Iqbal, Islam was "an ethical ideal plus a certain kind of polity"; he was wary of any form of territorial nationalism that required eradicating the particular or reassigning it to the private realm as a prerequisite for a concordance with the general. In Devji's reading, Iqbal insists on foregrounding particularity, deferring its moment of universality, which is embodied in the state, given that the language of citizenship invisibilizes social relations and allows for the articulation of only interest-based politics.[126] Iqbal's project was concerned with social relations between Hindus and Muslims beyond the procedural language of liberalism and of representational politics of interest.

These social relations were viewed as a threat by both imperialists and nationalists, as they vitiated the logic of liberal politics and the agenda of singular nationhood, respectively. But for Iqbal, and for Gandhi as well, such relations were "not only inevitable but also valuable because they prevented the complete dominance of liberal principles, which both men saw as posing a far greater threat to humanity than these prejudices."[127] What emerges in Iqbal's poetic and philosophical work is the transformation of Hindus and Muslims into metaphysical categories "relating to one another in metaphors of translation instead of representation."[128] Here, Devji draws on Iqbal's work to cite references from his poetry, invoking the classical Persian-Urdu idiom of enchantment with idol worship as an act of concretized devotion whereby "Islam becomes the secret of Hinduism and Hinduism of Islam, without ever being made equivalent to or a substitute for the other, both having been robbed of all sociological particularity and rendered into metaphysical categories."[129] Instead of reading everyday relations between Hindus and Muslims through liberal categories, assigning them to the realm of prejudice and stereotype creates the possibility of rendering Islam and Hinduism as realms of thought, beyond sociological facts. As Devji concludes, "it is at this point, then, that it becomes possible for such groups to enter into relationships not reduced to those of a liberal order of representation, making each available to the other metaphysically in a translation that retains all the fire of faith, conviction, and idealism"[130]—hence making possible mundane, quotidian conversations about commerce, sexuality, or friendship across languages of intimacy.

For Jinnah, the basis for equality must be sought in the language of the law. Jinnah saw in the postcolonial moment "the first real instantiation of the social contract described by Hobbes, Locke or Rousseau."[131] In this moment that Jinnah saw as of world-historical significance, there was an urgency for exploring a new social contract to build a state that recognized difference but accepted the validity of political equality. Jinnah arrived at a solution in his famous speech delivered at the inaugural session of the Constituent Assembly of Pakistan on 11 August 1947:

> I cannot emphasise it too much. We should begin to work in that spirit and in course of time all these angularities of the majority and minority communities—the Hindu community and the Muslim community— . . . will vanish . . . . You are free; you are free to go to your temples, you are free to go to your mosques or to any other places of worship in this State of Pakistan. You may belong to any religion or caste or creed—that has nothing to do with the business of the State (Hear, hear). . . . We are starting with this fundamental principle that we are all citizens and equal citizens of one State. . . . Now, I think we should keep that in front of us as our ideal and you will find that in course of time Hindus would cease to be Hindus and Muslims would cease to be Muslims, not in the religious sense, because that is the personal faith of each individual, but in the political sense as citizens of the State.[132]

No one knew better than Jinnah himself, a great proponent of the two-nation theory, that his statements nullified the Muslim-Hindu difference that served as the very basis for the newly established state. For Jinnah, the theory had become redundant at the precise moment of its fruition. But in saying so, Jinnah was not claiming freedom from religion but rather freedom to practice religion in a manner that allowed communities their public religious identities while ensuring their political equality as citizens. Equality formed the central plank of Jinnah's vision for organizing the new political community in the newly established state of Pakistan. That alone, he realized, could eradicate distinctions like majority and minority, believer and nonbeliever, Muslim and Hindu, citizen and national. But his reformulation of the identity basis of Pakistani nationhood could not, so to speak, square the circle. It projected a futurity of equality that contradicted a conflictual past of essentialized differences between Hindus and Muslims, which had served as the rationale for establishing a new state. Hence, the postcolonial state had to persist with a differential mode of citizenship and remain haunted by the specter of its inconsistencies. Constitution making was delayed in Pakistan, as there were considerable controversies around what it meant to be politically equal, especially given a new majority-minority distinction along ethnic lines. The question of representation based on political equality was challenged both on religious and ethnic bases. As I show in this book, it took considerable debate, struggle, and acrimony to address this question.

As one of the most important events in Pakistan's history, the liberal potential of Jinnah's speech has never been lost on those aspiring for equality in the new state. No matter which term dissidents use—*secularism*, *pluralism*, or *egalitarianism*—the emphasis has always been on equality as the basis for being Pakistani and as a marker for acceptance of difference. That such a premise is retrievable—whether from Jinnah's prosaic constitutional theory or Iqbal's metaphysical language of poetry—shows how the historicization of the nation-state can yield rich dividends in striving toward equality, effacing the citizen-nation divide and undermining the settler-colonial forms of power exercised by the postcolonial state. But this endeavor must start by exploring the citizen-nation divide and the nature of the assemblage called the postcolonial state. This is what I set out to do in this book. I describe what happened to the nation and show how the citizen was discursively created and mediated through historical, cultural, and religious practices of power and pedagogy. In other words, like Sadia Toor, I am interested in showing how nation understood as a political and moral community is invested with an emotive force to "inspire the kind of passion and loyalty that is required for the idea of the nation to 'work.'"[133]

For this purpose, I trace the making of the label "citizen" and its inscription through state violence and legislative power over citizenship, and also in attempts to create a sense of belonging and affect through such spectacular acts as festivals. In the creation and re-creation of the state through everyday practices, as well as in its subversion—a veritable daily plebiscite as Ernest Renan calls it—the postcolonial state, I argue, draws on the metaphor of *qaum* to incite a transformative aspiration toward majoritarian nationhood, but it empties the metaphor of its richness, plurality, and fluidity of meaning.[134] In this fashion, to borrow from Srirupa Roy's work, the state is nationalized, and the nation is institutionalized.[135]

Roy's work is a crucial reminder that it is important not only to analyze the history of the nation-state but also to explore the discursive basis for and practices of the state, which help create the myth of statehood and help the state establish a relationship with its citizens as nationals. By highlighting the modalities, rationalities, and techniques of nation-state formation, Roy shows that "the reproduction of the nation-state rests not on the existence of individuals who identify with the nation but rather on their ability to identify the state as the nation's authoritative representative."[136] To Roy's formulations I add that what emerges from such transformation are hackneyed notions of both the state and the nation that are drummed into the collective psyche of the citizenry through acts and performances—the "sights and sounds of the nation-state," as Timothy Mitchell calls it.[137] Such acts and performances help the citizen recognize the state and its preferred representation of nationhood.[138] This insistence on establishing a preferred representation of the *qaum*, I argue, building on the works of Thomas Blom Hansen and Srirupa Roy, is because the idea of national sovereignty from the colonial period then becomes incompatible with the dictates of a postcolonial state.[139] The sovereign nation of the anticolonial period is rhetorical and unbounded; it revels in lyrical expression and acts of symbolic redemption. The inherent logic of the state is to regulate the *qaum* through law to enforce homogeneity or to administer a form of diversity that conforms to a preferred national type. This inevitably results in the metaphor of the nation becoming a catechism for the ideal citizen that is analogous to the state's idealized national type. In this manner, the postcolonial state engulfs the decolonial moment's emancipatory potential by hollowing the nation of its mystique and of possibilities for alternative futures, and yet the state relies on it to distinguish between rights-holding citizens and nationals who belong to its self-defined majoritarian ethos.

Although this book may appear state-centric, such a focus helps undermine the hegemonic aspirations of state power by undermining its constituent elements and by analyzing their historicity, and the everyday forms of resistance against the state, offering alternative forms of imaginings. I echo Gyan Pandey's statement that modern historiographies of the nation and state have elevated the nation-state to the end of history, and I set out to decenter the nation-state.[140] In a historical appraisal of the postcolonial nation-state and its apparatuses of power lies the potential of the nation-state's unraveling. This book thus aims to cover two primary areas: first, to analyze the foundational moments of the postcolonial state, considering it a violent act through which the state inscribes the legality of its power on bodies made legible as refugees, migrants, citizens, and so on; second, to historicize the state's conjuring of a preferred notion of *qaum* and enforced through various commemorative acts, archival practices, remembrances of the past, histories, and pedagogies.

In writing about the inscription of state power through various acts and performances, I am reminded of Thomas Blom Hansen's and Finn Stepputat's formulation of the incompleteness of the national-state project, which projects itself as "stable and natural, [but] never completely manages to achieve the status of a 'master signifier' that can stabilize a social order and a set of identities."[141] As to the latter part of this project, I build on Gayatri Spivak's idea of nationalism as a form of negotiation with the private to control the public sphere to show how the postcolonial state's forays into the inner recesses of the *qaum* to carve out a preferred assortment of the national remains a failed project.[142] The postcolonial state may establish itself as a recognized entity through spectral acts of violence, commemorative rituals, and performances, but intimacy continues to be defined through multiple forms of the *qaum* as metaphors for affective belonging to a land, locale, or community.

In summary, this book is about the formation of a national citizenry in the postcolonial state of Pakistan on the basis of an analysis of extensive archival data, close readings of various texts and performances, and explorations of the *qaum* as metaphor. In the first chapter, I trace the history of citizenship making from a largely unexplored archive of the legal debate on what constitutes a Pakistani citizen. I show that despite claims to the contrary, "being Pakistani" was conflated with Muslimness to ensure that the doors were shut for non-Muslim minorities' return to their neighborhoods for emotional and material reasons. Exploring the bureaucratic archive helps us understand the delimiting of barriers between the national and the citizen and the inadequacy of the legal registers of jus soli and jus sanguinis in capturing the lived experiences of marginalized individuals and communities—that is, elucidating the praxis of the law.

In chapter 2, my focus is on state-led activities meant to establish state legibility in order to demarcate the ideal citizenry according to a majoritarian definition. One of the projects through which the Pakistani state achieves this purpose is by managing the debate on the idea of an Islamic state. In my analysis, I go beyond the established practice of focusing on the Objectives Resolution of March 1949, which is thought to have sealed the country's fate as an Islamic state. Instead, I look at archives of cabinet discussions and Constituent Assembly debates—along with an overview of public opinion as expressed in newspapers—to portray a broader picture that represents the range of ideological spectrum on this issue. Theoretically, I approach this debate through the question of naming Pakistan as "Islamic Republic" as performative, symbolic, and communicative. In this theoretically dense debate, I use the works of Laclau and Žižek and employ Gadamer's hermeneutic method to analyze the deliberations of the board of ulema—an archival source that, to the best of my knowledge, has not been utilized before in academic inquiry. I thus provide a broad spectrum of views and contestations whereby the Pakistani state instrumentalized Islam for state-making purposes, using it to divide citizen-believers from nonbeliever minorities.

In chapter 3, my focus lies on the postcolonial state's project of setting up a normative culture for the new citizenry based on the symbolic repertoire of the *qaum*. For this purpose, I have foregrounded themes that historians have generally ignored, such as the debate on the language and lyrics of the national anthem, the choice of symbols to be embossed on office stationery, and the designing of funerary architecture for the founding figures of the new republic. I take the public debates, official correspondence, and anecdotal evidence about such apparently mundane or trivial issues as a delineation of the postcolonial state's political theology. I extend the scope of Schmitt's concept of political theology to consider both the aura cultivated in the idea of the state through such paraphernalia as flags and anthems and the precision expected of the devotee-citizen in interactions with such symbols. I argue that in the case of postcolonial states, the scripting of such protocols, given their newness and the identifiability of their foundational moments, is itself a public act that is both pedagogical and affective. This act seeks to educate citizens about their new faith and to inculcate sentiments of reverence for the state's founding fathers and their sacrifices, as well as for the state's sacred objects (e.g., the "citadel of faith," in the case of Pakistan).

Chapter 4 focuses on the controversy around moon sighting, an issue that continues to be at the heart of popular discussions today. The original question was how to define a procedure for sighting the moon as required by the Islamic lunar calendar, so that Muslim religious festivals like Eid could be properly celebrated, with public holidays for such occasions planned well in advance. In the premodern and even the colonial period, the sighting of the moon and celebration of Eid remained a local event, while for the postcolonial state, managing national time and representing it as rational and scientific—that is, as unambiguous—became crucial. The state approach necessitated quantifying time as calculable and precise in order to enforce, observe, and routinize sacred, secular, and everyday activities. A corollary of this approach, I argue, was to subsume the lunar calendar into the precision of national time, thus leading to a conflict between state authority—which insisted on the possibility of a precise calculation of lunar rotations—and ulema, who contested the state, offering alternative definitions of what constituted acceptable ways of "seeing" the moon. In a first-ever detailed analysis of Pakistani moon controversies, I analyze contestations between the ulema and the postcolonial state on themes of scientific rationality, sovereign power, and religious authority. The chapter looks at these debates as an interactive process whereby the postcolonial state aimed to nationalize religion for state-making purposes by overriding the ulema's claim to act as custodians of religious authority. I analyze the coercive enforcement of the policy of "one nation, one Eid" as a pedagogical tool for fostering national unity among citizens.

As I argue in the chapters that follow, to be Pakistani in the postcolonial moment was not simply a matter of being a legal resident of the country; it also implied a sense of belonging and affiliation mediated through history, culture, and literature. Writing the nation through history was thus central to the project of postcolonial state formation. In chapter 5, I discuss the politics of nationalist historiography as a process of deletion and creative remembrance that aims to develop a master narrative that might then serve as a template for various commemorative acts. A significant contribution of this study is to provide a detailed account of the postcolonial state's idea of a national telos that seeks to set the normative standard for historical imagination. The purpose of the chapter is not to discuss the ideologization of history but to elaborate how history conquers memory through performative acts such as the state's holding commemorative parades, establishing museums that provide a visual narrative about the nation's preferred foundation moment, regulating temporal cycles through the announcement of national holidays, and writing the urban text by naming and renaming roads and cities.

My argument envisages state formation as an abortive project that is always seeking coherence and domination. Accordingly, this book provides an overview of relevant debates and their prehistories, continuities, and afterlives. I do not offer a cutoff date, after which a final settlement on the nature of state power and of the idealized national citizenry was achieved. I do refer to some foundational moments, including the so-called zero hour of 1947, when the new state was created. The bulk of my argument concerns the period between 1947 and 1956. In 1956, Pakistan adopted its first constitution. Although it lasted for only two years and failed to achieve consensus on important issues such as joint electorates and the nature of the federal structure, much debate and committee work over the course of a decade—including constitutional theorizing, debates on the nature of Islamic state, and accounts of the history of nationhood—went into the making of that constitution. Another watershed moment was 1971, when the secession of East Pakistan changed the religious and ethnic demography of the remaining Pakistan. The kind of severe ideological introspection that the traumatic events of 1971 called for did not take place in the public arena. We find a hardening of views on issues related to Islam and its role in state affairs. Treating these various moments, I go back and forth in time, picking out a diverse range of issues and drawing on multiple sources to assemble critical arguments about the process of postcolonial state formation and nation-making.

Last, a few words about the archival material I consulted in this study. Over the years, I visited numerous libraries and archives across various continents to work on this project. But the bulk of my work is based on materials I collected from archives and libraries in Dhaka, Karachi, Islamabad, and Lahore. In particular, I made frequent trips to the National Archives of Pakistan and the National Documentation Center in Islamabad. I was able to consult rich collections of documents from the Ministries of Home, Education, and Information, in addition to records from the Cabinet Division and the Prime Minister's Office. As a result of issues of access and a lack of professional curating, I was not always able to find complete files. In many cases, the scanned material I received was not correctly numbered. In the case of the Zafar Ahmad Ansari Collection of records from the ulema board, held at the University of Karachi, it was difficult to discern any chronological order in documents that are part of the collection. Even the box numbers were hardly legible. Very few papers carried the name of the author. Significantly, in one of the boxes that had no date or name, I found a draft Islamic constitution. In some ways, then, my reading of the archive is influenced by how I approached it—that is, as an assemblage of information—and by my understanding of its curating.

In this book, I have not limited myself to official sources. To understand public thinking about issues of state, nation, and citizenship, I have combed through multiple newspapers in English and Urdu, covering the period from 1947 to 1956. These include *Imroz, Pakistan Times, Nawa-i-Waqt, Dawn, Civil and Military Gazette, Morning News, Pasban,* and the *Pakistan Observer*. Additionally, I have relied on such diverse sources as autobiographical accounts, fatwas, textbooks, newspaper advertisements and cartoons, conference proceedings, archival catalogs, and museum bulletins. My purpose is to show the limitations of the state's pedagogical imposition; in seeking alternative explanations and responses, I supplement my reading of the archive with that of additional, popular sources. This book thus draws on a rich archive of diverse sources meticulously collected over the course of a decade from various public libraries, national archives, and research centers. I use these materials to theorize and critically analyze complex ideas of citizenship and national belonging in the making of a postcolonial Muslim state in Pakistan.

ONE

NOAH'S ARK?
The Making of Pakistan as Homeland for Muslim Nationals

THE EVENTS OF 1947 mark the foundational moment of state-making violence that inaugurated the postcolonial states of India and Pakistan. Following the announcement of the Radcliffe Award in August 1947, which divided the Punjab along religious lines and demarcated the boundaries between India and Pakistan, Muslims living in many parts of East Punjab came to know that they were on the wrong side of the border. The Radcliffe Award handed over many of the Punjab's Muslim-majority areas to India.[1] In the aftermath of the Direct-Action Day agitation in Bengal in 1946 and violence in the Rawalpindi division of Punjab that had broken out in March 1947, the civil administration in both provinces was already on the verge of collapse. The announcement of the award triggered fresh rounds of violence aimed at pushing out Muslims from East Punjab and Hindus and Sikhs from West Punjab. East and West Bengal witnessed a similar trend. The violence, however, was on a slightly lower scale in Bengal. But this meant that the minority population on both sides of Bengal remained a constant target of harassment; there were sporadic incidents of violence throughout the 1950s, which ultimately led to a consistent drop in their numbers. In West Punjab, however, the matter was "resolved" to the effect that almost the entire non-Muslim population, with the exception of a few pockets of Sikhs in holy sites like Nankana, was forced to leave. Muslims of East Punjab met a similar fate.

Much of the violence on both sides was systematic. Because Muslims coming from East Punjab roughly matched the numbers of non-Muslims leaving from West Punjab, the Pakistani government was willing to allow for a complete transfer of population in Punjab.[2] The violence and displacement were not limited to Punjab and Bengal. Sindhi Hindus were forced to leave for India. Many Muslims from North India—and minority provinces in general—opted for the Muslim-majority state of Pakistan.

In the case of North Indian Muslims, migratory patterns were different insofar as they carried at least the semblance of voluntary movement. While forced migration ended in the case of Punjab within a year—both sides were by then largely "cleansed" of their minority populations—in many parts of North India, the back-and-forth of Muslim families continued for many decades. As late as the 1980s, Muslims from North India continued to migrate to Pakistan and were able to get the necessary legal documents for citizenship. The distinct migration patterns of North Indian Muslims gave rise to that population's peculiar sense of intergenerational trauma caused by the splitting up of families, the loss of social prestige, the sense of alienation in a new country, and the displacement of culturally rooted communities.

Beyond a descriptive account, we need to understand the theoretical implications of this violent foundational moment. In describing the 1947 moment as an in-betweenness, or "an ambiguity that prevailed in the initial years of independence, decision making, and agenda setting," Ted Svensson's work provides critical insight.[3] Svensson invokes Žižek's concept of the political as "the moment of openness, of undecidability, when the very structuring principle of society, the fundamental form of the social pact, is called into question."[4] The violence of Partition, and the resulting chaos of millions of refugees on both sides of the border, was one such moment. It delimited the distinction between society's inside and outside and its internal and external boundaries.[5]

In other words, it is only in retrospect that 1947 can be isolated as an "event." Here, I am drawing on Aditya Nigam's conceptualization of event as "an occurrence that institutes a break in the logic of the situation that existed till then and secondly, that this occurrence itself is produced by the coming together of different logics into a kind of unity that then governs, for some time the actions of different players."[6] Such a conceptualization helps understand the process whereby the event of 1947 is reduced to a definable moment in time without a medley of voices and chaos, a veritable zero hour and tabula rasa on which the national biography of the state is scripted. This interstitial space of political openness becomes a point of entry for analyzing the constitutive processes of state making as a praxis of power that coheres the ambiguity of the moment into temporal linearity and directs its telos into a developmental march toward progress, the securing of boundaries, and nation making. It was only after postcolonial states had enforced such an order that they were able to "obscure the contingency of their origin and the voids at their cores."[7] These processes included the production of performative affects of sovereign power and lawmaking and the imagination of a symbolic political order.

As I argue in this chapter, it is on the body of the refugee variously encoded in provisions of law and situated in a moral language of history and affect as a *mohajir* or *sharnarthi* that the statist project operates. As the state seeks to cohere unity out of ambiguity, this body of the refugee served as the site for state action. The present chapter shows that the transformation of the migrant, refugee, *mohajir*, and *sharnarthi* into a citizen, and later or simultaneously into a national, is a central part of the state-making process. Not only in South Asian politics but also in the rest of the postcolonial world, state-founding processes are grounded in inaugural moments of spectacular violence, to which this chapter speaks.

THE MAKING OF THE REFUGEE

The initial impetus of the postcolonial state was to create and recognize the entity of the refugee to regulate his or her movement. The movement of displaced Hindu, Muslim, and Sikh communities stretched across the newly constituted dominions of India and Pakistan. Such movement was not an act of voluntary relocation: almost all communities and families were forced to leave their homes and seek refuge wherever they could be safe. As such, they did not *intend*—a word that acquired considerable legal importance in subsequent discussions about citizenship—to permanently leave their homes. People arrived at Lahore's Walton Camp or Delhi's Kingsway Camp without any legal authorization or paperwork.

From September 1947 onward, both India and Pakistan came up with what Haimanti Roy calls a "document regime" to manage movement across the border and the making of Uditi Sen's "Citizen Refugee."[8] Even with such documentary requirements as visas, emergency permits, India-Pakistan specific passports, and migration certificates, the postcolonial states of India and Pakistan—each in its own way, according to its specific political structures and ideological frameworks—were able to manage the movement of bodies in only a limited sense. The Indian Constitution drafted in 1950 specified citizens' rights, and yet there was no law of citizenship as such until 1955. In the case of Pakistan, the country did not adopt its first constitution until 1956, although it formed a citizenship law in 1951 and amended that law in 1952. But how did India and Pakistan deal with the refugee or migrant without a legally defined criterion for citizens?

First, in July 1948, India had introduced a permit system and the Influx from Pakistan (Control) Ordinance, which made entry from Pakistan into India without a permit a criminal offense. Pakistan responded in October 1948 by adopting its own permit system and the Pakistan (Control of Entry) Ordinance. Zamindar marks this as the beginning of a strict border control regime in South Asia, a move that was not inevitable—and indeed not envisaged by Partition.[9] This regime aggravated the humanitarian crisis that was then emerging due to post-Partition violence and displacement: divided families were further deprived of possibilities of reunion and linkage because of new requirements and bureaucracy introduced by the ordinance, and this was made only further complicated in subsequent years.[10]

Second, the category of "evacuee property" and the ambiguities of the legal application of that category became a point of contention that hindered the movement of minorities across the border. The Joint Defense Council of India and Pakistan, in its meeting held in Lahore on 29 August 1947, had decided to set up the Custodian of Refugees' Property. Once many property owners had fled, leaving behind their houses, shops, bungalows, and agricultural land, the task of the custodian was to manage the properties until refugees could return to reclaim them. As part of the agreement, both governments had agreed not to give legal ownership rights to those occupying the properties.[11] In September 1947, both Punjabs passed the East and West Punjab Evacuee Property (Preservation) Ordinances, and these were later extended to Delhi. The laws' open-endedness and application were highly discriminatory. Many Muslims complained that their property had been declared as evacuated even though they had only temporarily traveled to Pakistan on permits. It came down to long-drawn legal battles about the term *migration* itself.

Most damaging was a later addition to the law whereby "intending evacuees" who had never set foot inside the Pakistani territory could similarly be deprived of their property.[12] Even though, as per the Karachi Agreement of 1949, both states had allowed the exchange and sale of urban property, very few could avail of this concession, as the permit system posed a significant hindrance to traveling to India or Pakistan. In Pakistan's case, only those Hindus and Sikhs who were affluent and well connected managed to dispose of their property.[13] After the Citizenship Law of 1951, Hindus and Sikhs effectively and legally lost their right to return and claim their properties in Pakistan.[14] A sustained anti-Hindu and anti-Sikh rhetoric at home and visible attempts to shape the new state along Islamic lines also discouraged non-Muslim residents from returning to their ancestral lands.

Other than through bureaucratic, legal, and procedural controls, the state created the entity of the refugee through moral language of sacrifice and victimhood. The Pakistani state preferred the term *hijrat* for migration, as it connoted religious sanction and referenced the sacrifices made by the nascent Muslim community during the lifetime of the Prophet Muhammad, who had to leave Mecca to escape persecution. In India, the term *sharnarthi* quickly assumed the character of a persecuted and debilitated Hindu or Sikh refugee, as opposed to a Muslim migrant. Both countries, however, were confronted with the specter of statelessness of a massive number of people who had arrived without any intentional desire to become citizens of the country they were in and without any legal claim thereto. Indeed, this legal claim was only retrospectively conceived of and applied to those who had already migrated. In doing so, the law was drafted and implemented in such a manner that allowed for Muslim migrants to come to Pakistan while disallowing the same right to Hindus and Sikhs who had been forcibly evicted. But such a provision was not officially written into the law, implying that Hindus and Sikhs from East Punjab could still return to West Punjab and claim citizenship as long as they were not citizens of another state—that is, of India, in almost all cases—or living in the larger British Empire as Commonwealth subjects, and they could also fulfill several other different criteria.

To the best of my knowledge, given limited access to archival records, only one Punjabi Hindu family was officially allowed to return to Pakistan to claim citizenship. I did not "encounter" this case in the official archive but found it on a YouTube channel while looking for stories and interviews documenting the lives of Punjabi refugees. Ravinder Kumar's father, Jagat Singh Chibbar, was a *zaildar* in Karyala, Chakwal district. In 1947, following his paternal uncle's assassination during communal violence, the family migrated to India and stayed in refugee camps for a few months. During this period, Chibbar contacted Col. Nur Khan, military attaché in the Pakistani High Commission in Delhi; he was also from Chibbar's native village and a close friend. Khan helped Chibbar and his family return to their ancestral village and claim their property.[15] They are now celebrated as Punjab's only Hindu family who stayed back in Pakistan.

There must have been numerous other undocumented cases of Hindus and Sikhs reentering the country through unofficial channels. For instance, in 1950, an intelligence report from Punjab police's Special Branch mentioned that "the number of Hindus visiting West Punjab to remove buried treasures or other valuable property" was gradually increasing.[16] The "voluntary" conversion to Islam was a more popular route to survival for higher caste groups or propertied classes, as thousands of conversions took place at the time of Partition violence in 1947. The example of Mehra at the beginning of the book is just one prominent example of the politics of religious conversion resulting from the violent compulsions of Partition. There were other reported instances in the secret intelligence reports of the special branch till the early 1950s referring to Hindus and Sikhs returning to Punjab claiming to have converted to Islam.

However, an overwhelming majority of Sikhs and Hindus did not see a point in returning to a place from which they had to leave amid fear and violence, or to live in perpetual fear of reprisal attacks from the majority community. Still, some were not allowed to return or to make legal claims to citizenship because of citizenship laws were implemented so as to effect a majoritarian, Islam-based nationality. Notably, the Pakistani state was far more sensitive about relaxing the law in Punjab than in any other part of the country. As I show later, a select few Sindhi Hindus were able to exercise this right to return but only with the intervention of the minister for interior himself, and not without drawing a backlash from the ministerial staff and bureaucracy. In contrast, in East Bengal, the provincial government continued to manage a sizable Hindu population, which often had to be allowed to cross the border in case of violent rioting. They were then also allowed reentry because of the specific nature of the citizenship by birthright that they enjoyed.

In the case of India, however, such a blockade on Muslims' reentry into India was not legally enforced. But as Vazira Zamindar's work shows, Muslims who had spent time in Pakistan and wanted to return for whatever reason faced considerable social and legal obstacles. Even still, in the case of West Pakistan, the inverse movement was a possibility for Muslims but a near impossibility for Hindus and Sikhs. Such hurdles remained in place despite the Liaqat-Nehru Pact, signed into effect in 1950 by the prime ministers of Pakistan and India, which promised to protect religious minorities on both sides of the border. Under the pact, if minorities from violence-ridden areas wanted to leave, their respective governments provided them protection and did not hinder their movement.[17] However, such a provision clashed with the documentary regime for interdominion travel enacted by the Indian government and matched by its Pakistani counterpart. In that sense, the two postcolonial states effectively endorsed the outcome of genocidal violence that they had not even orchestrated by legally sanctifying its effects and ensuring the impossibility of its reversal.

FROM REFUGEE TO CITIZEN

While drafting the law that would define the legal basis for membership in the Pakistani state, policy makers were confronted with spectral violence that had necessitated the law in the first place. In other words, the law that eventually emerged after prolonged discussions was contingent on the violent context of the new state's originary moment. A direct corollary of these events was the vast body of refugees who had to be admitted as citizens in a manner that conformed with the emerging ideational basis of the state, which required an ideal Muslim citizenry. At the same time, a major consideration for policy makers was to prevent the unfettered migration of North Indian Muslims to and from Pakistan while ensuring that any attempt to plug any legal lacunas did not result in the statelessness of thousands of people who had already arrived. Therefore, the focus of the law was to be on the body of the refugee who had, in mass numbers, entered West and East Pakistan.

Only a few provisions of the law were relevant for those already residing in Pakistan. But what constituted Pakistan was itself a question that the Ministry of Interior and Law had to address. Until today, the boundaries of Pakistan have continued to evolve through such processes as the accession of princely states, the "purchase" of Gawadar, and the exchange of villages with India on the Punjab-Bengal border. In the following sections, I describe these processes and explain their impact on citizenship law. The law primarily had to perform the task of legitimizing a legal void within which refugees operated and rationalizing their movement as a one-off event to attempt to foreclose the possibility of any future influx or outflow. In that manner, the law was to come into force retrospectively, and yet it was also oriented toward the future.

The retrospective renaming, recognition, and transition of the refugee as and into the citizen can be explained through Derrida's reading of Walter Benjamin's critique of violence. According to Derrida, it is through the future anteriority, or return of the law, that the violence accompanying the founding of the state is retrospectively legitimated.[18] The refugee or the migrant, in that sense, does not exist before the law, as the law has yet to come. As Derrida puts it, "A 'successful' revolution, the 'successful foundation of a state' (in somewhat the same sense that one speaks of a 'felicitous performative speech act') will produce *après coup* [afterwardness] what it was destined in advance to produce, namely, proper interpretative models to read in return, to give sense, necessity and above all legitimacy to the violence that has produced, among others, the interpretative model in question, that is, the discourse of its self-legitimation."[19]

The Citizenship Law of 1951 and the discussion that led to it provide the interpretative model through which the state legitimized its violent exclusion of Sikhs and Hindus while creating a legal fiction to justify the inclusion of, and lend legitimacy to, Muslim migrants. The committee drafting the law also had to carefully scrutinize the citizenship laws of Britain and India to discern their possible impacts on Pakistan. Even still, after the bill was passed, it went through numerous revisions, and it continues to evolve in response to challenges posed by various political developments. The breakup of Pakistan in 1971 is one such instance. More important, it was through the interpretative models set by bureaucrats and policy makers—models that were distant from the lived social realities of those bearing the consequences of those decisions—that the state aspired to ascribe coherence to the praxis of granting citizenship and, in turn, to conjure the figure of an ideal citizen.

THE CITIZENSHIP LAW OF 1951: DEBATING THE DRAFT

In this section, I focus on the new archival data from the National Archives of Pakistan dealing with citizenship laws. There have been numerous works on Indian citizenship laws, but Pakistan's bureaucratic practice and legal archive have not been studied because of a broad lack of access to these sources. The result is that academic studies about citizenship are siloed. The three concerned parties—India, Pakistan, and the United Kingdom—deliberated their citizenship laws, each jealously protective of its discussions about whom to consider a potential citizen. I provide a vital, missing link in the jigsaw puzzle of UK, Indian, and Pakistani citizenship to provide a complete picture of how internal debates were carried out in these three contexts: in each country, citizenship depended on the other two's definitions and criteria. Each had to bear in mind that the law they were drafting was not only applicable to residents in their respective states but also effected the status of those living as subjects of another state or an empire.

The initial imperative for a consistent policy on citizenship in Pakistan emerged from a situation wherein millions of Muslim refugees were bound to be permanent residents of—and take up profession in military and government service in—a country in which they neither were born nor had been resident. Amid the acrimony of post-Partition bilateral relations, both countries harbored deep suspicion of each other as enemy states. This anxiety and fear of the unenumerated, unrecognized, and uncataloged mass of bodies were reflected in the West Punjab government's proposal to require public servants to take an oath of allegiance to the new state. Various government ministries, and especially the Ministry of Interior, opposed the idea. The reason for their opposition was that the Constituent Assembly had already set up the Committee on Fundamental Rights to define the qualifications of Pakistani citizenship and the rights and obligations expected of citizens.[20] But because there was considerable delay in the constitution-making process, the Ministries of Law and Interior prioritized the drafting of a citizenship law. In their estimate, the drafting of fundamental rights alone would take at least another eighteen months, to say little of the drafting of the constitution.[21] The United Kingdom had amended its nationality act in 1948, and the Indian constitution was promulgated in 1950, further adding to the anxiety of the Pakistani state. The Interior Ministry's Home Division pointed out in a note that after the change in the British Nationality Act of 1948, and in the absence of any Pakistani legislation on this issue, "technically, persons residing in Pakistan, unless they are definitely aliens, continue to be potential citizens of Pakistan. The absence of a Citizenship Law of Pakistan is, in Pakistan, resulting in every child born after the commencement of the 1948 Act having no nationality at all. Once a Pakistan Citizenship Law is passed such children under the terms of this Act will automatically become British subjects and citizens of Pakistan."[22]

The British were also anxious to quickly define a criterion for identifying "potential Pakistani citizens" and a procedure to register them. Ian Sanjay Patel's detailed overview of British nationality laws in the postimperialist era and Sarah Ansari's analysis of the law's implementation in South Asia and its diaspora help us understand the motives behind British nationality law as well as the anxieties that surrounded its implementation. In Patel's estimation, the British Nationality Act of 1948 was remarkably liberal in accepting the non-English, former subjects of the empire as equal in citizenship rights. As Patel describes it:

The 1948 Act converted the status of all those who had previously been British subjects into the new status of "citizen of the United Kingdom and Colonies," often referred to by politicians simply as "British citizenship." British citizens after 1948—"citizens of the United Kingdom and Colonies"— acquired their status principally through birth either in Britain itself or in a British colony. A person born in Britain and a person born in a British colony had an identical citizenship, and the same right to move to and live in Britain, including political rights such as the right to vote, and the right to hold public office or work in the public sector.[23]

The law was passed despite the acknowledgment that Commonwealth countries had their own laws, whereby they were moving toward alienage, defining nonnationals by law. Britain, in contrast, "was waiving its sovereign prerogative to consider peoples in independent Commonwealth states as aliens."[24] Patel calls this law "explosive" and an "astonishing piece of legislation," as it gave "gave identical citizenship and entry rights into Britain both to white Anglo-Saxons born in England and those born in one of forty-seven territories designated as 'colonies' around the world." The passage of such a law is perplexing. In Patel's view, for the UK Labour government, the law was simply an exercise in constitutional practice, an attempt to regularize the Commonwealth and avoid imperial dissonance.[25] Accordingly, James Ede, the Labor government's home secretary, had to ease paranoia around hordes of non-White former colonial subjects rushing to the United Kingdom by explaining that the change from British *subject* to *citizen* was an adjustment to a new, postcolonial context, a concessionary arrangement: "former subjects" in the present-day Dominions of India and Pakistan would no longer be called subjects because of its historical connotations implying subjected races. The new term of a British citizen for non-Whites retained the older meaning of a person who owed allegiance to the king. He clarified that the term *citizen* as a replacement for *former British subject* did not imply "a person *belonging* to Great Britain."[26] Through such an explanatory note, the British government tried to retain the edifice of the Commonwealth in the aftermath of decolonization while adopting restrictive immigration controls meant to ensure the entry of White Britons to the country and to prevent the entry of others.

Officials working in the Commonwealth Office and in British embassies and consulates abroad were concerned that the ambiguity in the law's wording might incentivize former colonial subjects to claim British citizenship. They scrambled to put together administrative and bureaucratic procedures to ensure that potential Pakistani or Indian citizens who had undefined nationality but were recognized as Commonwealth subjects did not apply for British nationality. There were many reasons for such anxiety on the part of the United Kingdom. Many subjects domiciled in what then constituted India and Pakistan resided in nation-states they were not permanently residents of and in which they had not acquired legally protected status. More important, many such domicile holders—an estimated four million—were spread throughout the British Empire, from Kenya to Singapore, from Burma to Guyana.[27] They had probably settled for life without becoming nationals of those countries and without any expressed desire to return to their so-called homeland. Diasporic Indians and Pakistanis posed a significant challenge to all three parties, as they were neither fully Indian nor fully Pakistani, yet not recognized by their host countries. The diasporic subjects were blissfully unaware of the legal abyss that defined—or ill defined—their citizenship status. Britain was concerned that if they were excluded from the citizenship criteria set by India and Pakistan, the United Kingdom would have to accept their claims to Commonwealth subjecthood as a route to potential British citizenship.

In the case of India, Nehru had initially been an enthusiastic supporter of Indians living abroad. But in the post-1947 context, while recognizing in principle their right to Indian citizenship, Nehru was more eager to urge the Indian diaspora to stay put in its current setting.[28] For Pakistan, the major anxiety stemmed from the fact that anyone who was domiciled in areas that had come to constitute Pakistan would potentially become "diaspora Pakistanis." This would have included many Hindus and Sikhs, who, unlike resident Punjabis or Bengalis of the March–August 1947 period, had not faced violent displacement to the point of no return. To allow unfettered access to those Hindus and Sikhs by recognizing them as citizens would have gone against the unwritten codes of exclusion that privileged Muslim-only claims to citizenship. But the Interior Ministry was also reluctant to dole out unrestricted citizenship certificates to the

Indian Muslim diaspora dispersed throughout Britain's global colonial possessions.

Britain insisted that India and Pakistan recognize all those domiciled in their respective areas as potential citizens by registering them at their consulates, and that they do so urgently. Because India and Pakistan had little diplomatic presence abroad during their early years of independence, many Commonwealth subjects had to register themselves at the nearest British consulate, which Pakistan and India mandated for these purposes. British consulates pushed for unregistered potential Indians and Pakistanis to register for whichever country they could.[29] The fact that those registering themselves had little clue of what registration entailed in terms of lived social realities, economic challenges, and political problems was not of any concern to British consulates. Here, in such informal practices, lies the roots of the Windrush scandal that surfaced in the United Kingdom in 2018, bringing to light the fact that thousands of immigrants, mainly from the Caribbean, were threatened with deportation, even though they had been entitled to enter the country as Commonwealth citizens between 1948 and 1971. Also, as new archival evidence suggests, postcolonial states like India collaborated with the British government to keep "undesirable citizens" at bay by adopting a strict passport policy that actively discriminated against underprivileged caste groups and classes.[30]

In its deliberations on the citizenship bill from December 1949 onward, the Pakistani government aimed not to take responsibility for those who were initially domiciled—or whose grandparents were domiciled—in what was by then Pakistan but had settled in other parts of the world, whether Hindus or Muslims. It had other problems to address, including the continued trickling in of Muslim refugees from India and people who had arrived, left, or were coming and going without the required paperwork. In a meeting held on 21 December 1949, the cabinet took up the question of citizenship criteria for the bulk of the population by considering whether "birth within the country or parentage or a minimum period of residence, or a combination of one or more of these" should be set as the standard.[31] A major limitation was that the existing laws—such as the Naturalization Act (1926), the Registration of Foreigners Act (1939), and Rules for Domicile Registration—given the changed circumstances and a post-1947 upheaval, had become wholly inadequate, unable to address how to asses who was a permanent resident in any given area. In January 1950, the Ministry of Foreign Affairs and Commonwealth Relations advised the Ministry of Interior to carefully consider the repercussions of allowing a person's grandfather's residency to serve as grounds for citizenship because "as stated the concession is very wide: it would allow e.g. an Italian whose grand-father spent a weekend at Bombay in 1870 to obtain a domicile certificate after one year's residence in Pakistan!"[32] The outward insistence on jus soli, or a territorial basis for citizenship, was nevertheless important. In practice, the law's implementation was colored by consideration of a jus sanguinis approach to membership in the "Muslim nation-state."

If domicile or residency in areas of Pakistan and India was to be a qualifying criterion, it necessitated the importance of defining the territorial limits of both Pakistan and India, as well as of British India. As to the last, the law adopted the territorial limits of British India defined at the time of promulgation of the Government of India Act of 1935. Defining Pakistani territory was trickier. Because of Partition's unfinished business with regard to Kashmir and those princely states such as Junagadh and Manavadar that had been acceded to Pakistan but were militarily occupied by India, a policy had to be devised that accepted the de facto position of Indian control but did not compromise on Pakistan's legal claims to these territories. On 1 February 1950, the Foreign Office suggested that people from Junagadh and Manavadar entering Pakistan should renounce their Indian citizenship within six months or automatically lose Pakistani citizenship. Even though the Ministry of Foreign Affairs was of the view that "ultimately, it is inevitable that we shall lose these States," they opposed "any admission of this at this stage."[33]

Other than the disputed territories, the Constitution Act defined Pakistan as comprising of the governors' provinces, the chief commissioner's province, the capital of the federation, any acceding states, and any areas added with the federation's consent. In a note prepared by the Ministry of Law, the last provision referred to tribal areas that were de facto part of Pakistan but not legally so. "To conceal this fact," Edward Snelson, joint secretary at the Ministry of Law, wrote, "I have adopted the device of saying that references to Pakistan shall be deemed to include references to the tribal areas. This avoids public admission of the legal fact that the tribal areas are not part of the Federation."[34] Instead of *India*, the term used in the law was *Indo-Pakistan subcontinent*, as territorially defined by the Government of India Act of 1935. As for the choice of words that could designate subjects of a dominion as members of the Commonwealth, there was considerable unease with continuing to use "British subjects" for "psychological reasons."[35] Eventually, "Pakistani British subjects" became prevalent, until Pakistan became a republic in 1956.

Another problematic category to address was that of seasonal migrants from Afghanistan. The Powindah of Suleman Khel lived on both sides of the border in Afghanistan and Pakistan. As A. B. Shah, secretary in the Ministry of States and Frontier Regions, mentioned in his note on 2 August 1950, the Powindah comprised several migratory tribes, including the Ahmedzai Ghilzai, Sulemankhel Ghilzai, Kharoti, and others. Their homes, lands, and places of birth were rooted in Afghanistan, but they annually migrated to Pakistan for the winter.[36] Stopping them from entering the country, or even subjecting them to a documentary regime, was impractical given their strong tribal connections in the region and the porous nature of the border. Doing so might also have caused a serious diplomatic confrontation with neighboring Afghanistan, which had adopted a hostile stance toward Pakistan and staked claims over its sizable Pashtun area.

In response to the Ministry of Interior's request for notes about the Powindah population, its historical background, and colonial practices of dealing with them, the Ministry of State and Frontier Regions addressed several themes and issues, including, importantly, the question of whether to extend dual nationality to Powindah people or to push them to give up their Afghan nationality. The ministry believed that the Powindah could not be asked to renounce their Afghan nationality, as it would have strategic consequences and because their claims were sanctioned by international law itself. "Even if the Afghan Law were to permit the renouncement of Afghan nationality by the Powindahs," the ministry said, "they would not be prepared to renounce it, for they have by force of habit to go to Afghanistan every year to live there in the summer months. Many of them cannot stand our summers."[37] They could not be asked to denounce Pakistani citizenship either, as that would require them to acquire passports and visas before their winter migration from Afghanistan to Pakistan.

The Powindah, therefore, posed a persistent challenge to the rationale of a legal regime that aimed to mark bodies legible as citizens and to endow those citizens with legally sanctioned rights in order to regulate their movement. In its essence, Powindah migration was not a permanent one from one nation-state to another but part of a seasonal cycle of life, interconnected economies, and sociality of exchange transacted in languages of belonging that arose from kin, tribe, and ethnicity. The language of the law could not recognize such ambiguities, as these circuits of exchange and movement operated outside of the law. The committee deliberating on the issue thus decided to maintain the status quo and not interfere in the migratory patterns of Powindah. In the case of children born during the tribes' sojourn in Pakistan, the committee observed that they could take Pakistani nationality and become dual nationals if Afghan law did not make it compulsory to renounce other nationalities.[38] In making these decisions, officials largely followed the precedent set by the British government during the colonial period and their dealings with border tribes.

The issue was again taken up in 1960, when tensions increased between the governments of Pakistan and Afghanistan. By then, the official language described the presence of Powindah as an *influx* rather than a *movement*.[39] Despite a tense, brief military standoff between Pakistan and Afghanistan, there was no change in the status of Powindah, who soon returned to their routines.

THE PROVISIONS OF PAKISTAN'S CITIZENSHIP LAW

Because of the various challenges, ambiguities, and questions highlighted in the previous section, the process of drafting Pakistan's Citizenship Law was drawn out over two or more years of internal debate and deliberation. Composing the law required addressing several issues of identification of multiple legal categories of residence, setting the criteria for inclusion, and imagining scenarios in which its provisions might fail or be exploited to illegal purpose.

As part of this exercise, the law department created a list of possible scenarios that might occur due to the citizenship bill's adoption and possible responses to and explanations for such concerns or queries—a sort FAQ. On the question of Arabs, Afghans, and Iranians who had been living in "Pakistan" for an extended time but did not have passports of their countries of origin, for instance, the bill explained that these groups were not covered under the proposed law, as citizenship by residence was not allowed in the draft under discussion. There was, however, a provision whereby anyone could apply for a certificate of naturalization by fulfilling a set of requirements. Another question asked about the status of eligible persons for both Indian and Pakistani citizenship. The answer was that they were required to migrate to Pakistan, obtain a domicile certificate, and take an oath of allegiance. The note similarly raised the question of those who were born in India or in states acceding to India before Partition but were currently residing abroad and wished to become Pakistani nationals.[40] In the following pages, I describe the major provisions of the Citizenship Law and how it evolved through bureaucratic framing and interpretation of rules in response to various exceptional cases.

Section 3 of the final draft of the Citizenship Act of 1951 stipulated that every person be deemed a citizen of Pakistan "who or any of whose parents or grandparents was born in the territory now included in Pakistan and who after the fourteenth day of August, 1947, has not been permanently resident in any country outside Pakistan."[41] This reaffirmed the status of those who had ordinarily been resident in "Pakistan" and were also born there while successfully excluding those—almost all of whom were either Hindu or Sikh—who had migrated and were permanently resident in another country.

Clause (b) recognized the claims of those who were born—or those whose parents or grandparents were born—in British India but no longer resided there. To press their claims for citizenship, they had to be domiciled in territories included in Pakistan. The compulsion of domicile worried the British officials. They feared that many potential Pakistanis in far-off areas of the globe would not be carrying a domicile, nor would it be possible for them to go back and get it. For instance, the British Consulate General at Tetuan reported the case of one Mr. Gormukhdas Kessawadas Hingorani, born in Hyderabad, Sindh, in 1924. He had previously held a passport and, in 1955, when applying for a new passport, had been treated as a British subject without citizenship. The consulate nevertheless decided not to renew his passport until his citizenship status had been ascertained. His previous passport was issued from Karachi in 1944, "so there may well be grounds for supposing that he was at one time domiciled in the territories now included in Pakistan."[42] Most of the people of the "Indian race" in Tetuan were Hindus born in Sindh. Therefore, the British consulate was eager to seek the opinion of the Commonwealth Office on whether Hingorani and other Hindus from Sindh were to be considered Pakistani citizens under section 3(b) of the Pakistan Citizenship Act 1951.

Section 3(c) covered naturalized British subjects who had renounced any foreign nationality that they may have acquired before the commencement of the Citizenship Act.

Section 3(d) provided legal cover to all refugees from any territory in the Indo-Pakistan subcontinent who had migrated to the territories then included in Pakistan "with the intention of residing permanently in those territories." The key phrase in the provision was "the intention of residing permanently"—it reverberated in policy debates throughout the 1950s. Theoretically, once the law had come into force, no further conferral of citizenship to migrants was possible. There was no religious qualification set in the law to claim citizenship, although clause (a) did serve the purpose of keeping out non-Muslims who had left the area, excluding them from Pakistan. During the drafting stage and its deliberation, the word *persons* was used instead of *Muslims*, showing no outward, explicit preference on a religious basis. There were numerous slippages in internal correspondence in which Pakistani citizenship was equated with Muslim nationality.[43] Additionally, for the grant of emergency certificates, which were meant to allow entry to the families of Pakistanis stranded in India, the application form asked information relating to religion.[44] It was because emergency certificates were also being used to bring people who were not yet Pakistanis, such as Muslims of Hyderabad Deccan who wanted to leave after India's occupation of the princely state.

Routes to Pakistani citizenship included citizenship by birth (section 4), descent (section 5), migration (section 6), naturalization (section 9), and marriage (section 10). Section 13 allowed for the acquisition of citizens via the incorporation of new territory to the state of Pakistan. To further facilitate the process of assimilation of Commonwealth subjects, section 20 allowed citizens of Commonwealth countries to acquire Pakistani citizenship if they intended to settle permanently in the country and fulfilled several other conditions.

Each section through which citizenship could be claimed, acquired, or granted came with a set of rules and conditions. The law and its regulations detailed such terms as *domicile, residence, registration*, and so on. Often such terms led to legal claims settled by the courts; alternately, officials had to read the rules—liberally, literally, or strictly, depending on the nature of the case—to make provisions for an applicant.

The following sections focus on how government officials addressed many such disputes and claims. This serves two purposes: first, I show the ambiguities contained in the idea of who belonged to Pakistan and describe how the state pretended to foreclose such ambiguity through a legally enforced uniformity; second, I show that by enforcing this uniformity, the state tried to cohere national unity where one did not exist and to which it could retrospectively look back to claim as a foundational or originary moment.

The mediating power of official documents affects everyday social life and its praxis, which in turn affects everyday social life and shapes bureaucratic practices. With their legal specificity and cutoff dates, the citizenship law gave the illusion of the foreclosure and settling of the citizenship question, but in practice it led to more questions than it answered. Even in the seemingly more straightforward cases of Muslims migrating from Punjab, Bengal, and Uttar Pradesh, the idea that such migrants were there to stay, or that they had relocated to areas constituting Pakistan with the intention of permanently residing there, was presumptuous. Many still had businesses and families in India and were averse to the idea of making a permanent choice between the two countries. The citizenship law's cutoff date was meant to imply that the time to think about a preference and choose between India and Pakistan was over. But for many Muslims who had migrated from North India, an alternative future to their current predicaments was still a possibility.

Vazira Zamindar's work provides case studies of Muslim families that relocated from Pakistan to India. Such cases posed a challenge not only for India, which had to accept Muslims who had at some point held a form of legal documentation that associated them with Pakistan, but also for Pakistan itself. India's refusal to accept returning Muslims could have resulted in statelessness for such individuals and families. In the case of Bengal, sporadic communal violence during the 1950s pushed scores of Hindu migrants to West Bengal. The government response had to be flexible enough to accept them back as citizens of Pakistan despite deep-rooted anxieties wherein returning Hindus were viewed with suspicions of disloyalty.

In other cases as well, the narrow framing of the law failed to provide a solution or had to be constantly improvised through bureaucratic practice. For instance, the law was silent on cases of illegitimate children or of unknown parentage. The relevant ministries had to interpret the existing law to address this gap. As M. A. Samad, joint secretary, wrote in his note:

> Under Pakistan law an illegitimate child has no legal father and, therefore, that child acquires no nationality by descent, but only by birth. Consequently the nationality it acquires is that of the country where it is born. The illegitimate children, whose putative fathers are citizens of Pakistan and mothers are United Kingdom citizens, would acquire British nationality if they were born in the United Kingdom. Such children could acquire Pakistan nationality, otherwise than by obtaining a certificate of naturalization, by registration under the proviso to section 9, or more appropriately under sub-section (2) of section 11 of the Pakistan Citizenship Act, 1951.[45]

Other than exchanges about the Citizenship Law already discussed, there were numerous other files in which individual cases with more significant policy impacts were taken up for consideration by the Ministry of Interior. The matter was internally discussed, or referred to the Foreign Office and the Ministry of Law for comments, before deciding. In this way, a citizenship case file is not simply a record summarizing the details of the case. As Matthew Hull describes it, a Pakistani government file is an artifact with signs of its history, which is "continuously and deliberately inscribed upon the artifact itself, a peculiarity that gives it an event-like quality."[46]

The files are divided into two parts: Noting (marked with an *N* in parentheses) and Correspondence (marked with a *C*). Notings are internal exchanges, scribbled notes, comments on drafts, correspondence, and policy issues. As Hull aptly puts it, "A file is both the occasion and the means of a particular form of dialogue."⁴⁷ In addition to the formal bureaucratic language of rationality, there is room in noting sections for social commentary and discussion of the political implications of the decisions made. Notings and correspondence complement each other, although it's difficult to trace the process whereby a response received from a ministry is then commented upon in the note, which, in turn, impacts the position taken by the other ministry. In many such cases, there is considerable exchange among bureaucrats outside of the file and its impersonal language of the law. This is where their social backgrounds, associational linkages, and memories of camaraderie as "batch-mates" among bureaucrats come into play.

In that sense, Pakistan's archives match Stoller's descriptions of the unsureness of colonial taxonomies and the anxieties they generated. The colonial bureaucratic praxis produced classification rules in a piecemeal manner, writes Stoller, but its "grids of intelligibility were fashioned from uncertain knowledge."⁴⁸ To read along the grain of the archive as a subject instead of as a source, and to view archives as "itineraries of their own," helps trace the rule-making process, its disconnect with lived experience, and the anxiety it generated among those responsible for drafting and implementing a coherent policy amid the inherent limitations of insufficiently imagined classificatory schemes. In that manner, section officers' scribbles in the margins become, in Stoller's terms, contrapuntal intrusions emanating from outside the corridors of governance, though centrally located within the sequestered space of the file.⁴⁹ Cumulatively, these processes add to the file as "a chronicle of its own production, a sedimentation of its own history."⁵⁰ My task is to tease out constituent elements of such sedimentation to attempt what can be only a fragmented history about the processes that shaped the idea of the citizen, that is, through bureaucratic practice, interpretation of the law, and a praxis of power.

MANAGING HINDUS: THE LAW'S RELIGIOUS NEUTRALITY AND THE PRACTICE OF COMMUNALIST EXCLUSION

Even though the Citizenship Law itself was jus soli, its implementation ensured that non-Muslims were actively discouraged, and indeed prevented, from exploiting specific provisions of the law to their benefit. From section officers to midcareer bureaucrats and federal secretaries, there was a shared but vaguely defined sense of Pakistan's ideological basis as Islamic and a Muslim homeland, an idea that they were willing to amend only in exceptional circumstances. It is not possible to pin down this permeating influence of ideology to a specific event or piece of legislation. It is also important to highlight that bureaucratic practice was shaped by what were thought to be pragmatic considerations for implementing or not implementing the law. Pakistan could not have afforded a return of Hindus and Sikhs, because refugees, locals, and provincial governments had already taken hold of their property. Thus, the policy decision was less of an ideological position and more of a pragmatic solution. The "pragmatism" of the policy is further clarified by the aversion to the continuous trickling of Muslim migrants from North India that bureaucrats showed and their recommended stern policy actions to block such migrants.

In my analysis of policy decisions reached with regard to applications by returning Hindus (mainly in the case of Sindh), and of the proposed general effort to regulate the continuous traffic of Muslim migrants from North India, I highlight the differences between the two cases, especially when it came to defining terms like *citizen*, *national*, and *homeland*. This helps delineate the ideological content of so-called pragmatic decision-making in cases dealing with Hindu and Muslim migrants. If Hindus were to be kept out because Pakistan was a Muslim homeland and their property could no longer be returned to them, the restriction on excessive Muslim migrants was also rationalized in pragmatic as well ideological terms: an attempt to secure the Muslim homeland and make it economically viable and prosperous. In that sense, there were ideological reasons for being pragmatic and pragmatic reasons for being ideological—either of which could be adopted for deciding cases of Hindu and Muslim applicants. As I show, the decision-making also depended on the predilections of the section officer or bureaucrat writing the note on the file: he could choose the position he wanted to take on a particular case. Furthermore, these officers acquired a disproportionate role in making policy and implementing it. This was because of the unrepresentative character of Pakistan's political setup during the 1950s and frequent changes of government. Amid such uncertainty and lack of democratic transparency, bureaucrats dominated decision-making processes on key policy issues.

The non-Muslim members of the Constituent Assembly saw through the facade of religious neutrality in the law and discerned the ideological and pragmatic reasons with which government officials implemented it. They therefore tried to undermine its unwritten codes of exclusion through various means. For instance, when the Citizenship Bill was presented to the Constituent Assembly in April 1951, Kamini Kumar Dutta proposed an amendment to allow the status of permanent residence for those who had not sold or rented out their property in Pakistan but were presently living in a foreign state. Commenting on the proposed amendment, the Ministry of Interior's Hameeduddin Ahmed—whom we will encounter several times as a hawkish proponent of active discrimination against Hindu applicants—described it as a "very mischievous amendment and if carried would mean the negation of the fact of migration by Hindus into India." He added in his note that

> the [e]ffect of this amendment will be that every Sikh and Hindu who has migrated from Pakistan without letting out his house on rent will be deemed to be a citizen of Pakistan. Not only this but persons having any share in a family house, which will be a common practice in a joint Hindu family, will be assured of this right. Thus Hindus with a single member of their family left in Pakistan, will have the right of Pakistani citizenship inspite [sic] of their being permanent residents in India. This strange test of permanent residence is against all common sense and equity.[51]

Hence, the amendment was thrown out.

The best that non-Muslim members of Pakistan's Constituent Assembly could do was push for a more liberal visa regime and minimal restrictions on cross-border movements. Nevertheless, especially after the promulgation of the citizenship law, the state was further eager to regulate the movement of non-Muslims. Accordingly, a passport scheme was introduced with a more detailed outline for visa requirements and those eligible to apply. As reported by the *Pakistan Times* on 18 August 1952, "A passport duly visaed for Pakistan by an authorised official of the Government of Pakistan will, under an Ordinance as from a date to be notified, be the only document recognised by the Government of Pakistan for the entry of Indians into this country." The permit system that had previously regulated entry into Pakistan was discontinued, and different categories of visas were specified for Indian travelers. Category A was for Indian nationals living within ten miles of the East Bengal border who typically earned their livelihood by working in Pakistan. This included: "(a) Cultivators who have to make frequent journeys in order to cultivate or supervise the cultivation of their own lands and their labourers and hired servants; (b) Artisans, such as blacksmiths, woodcutters, carpenters, petty shopkeepers and petty traders; and (c) Persons the only markets for whose agricultural produce lie in Pakistan territory within 10 miles of the East Bengal border."[52] Other categories included those deriving income from immovable properties, pensions, or other sources of income, or those with relatives in Pakistan. In addition, there were specific visa categories for Indian diplomats, seamen, and passengers in transit.

The changes introduced through the above-mentioned ordinance were later presented in the assembly in November 1952 as the Pakistan (Control of Entry) Bill. The minister who tabled the bill emphasized the importance of introducing passports and visa regimes to control movement between India and Pakistan. Dhirendra Nath Dutta opposed the bill. According to him, the bill did not consider the ground realities of thousands of people who everyday crossed borders. Even though the bill had a provision to provide Category A visas for people earning their livelihood in the border zone, Dutta pointed out that most of them were illiterate cultivators who would not be able to get passports and visas. He said that there was only one passport office in East Bengal and only a few photographers in the district towns who could help the poor applicants fulfill the documentary requirement of three copies of an identificatory photograph for the visa form.[53] He suggested scrapping the passport system between Assam and East and West Bengal, as in that between the two Irelands.

Other non-Muslim members pointed out the logistical problems of getting a no-objection certificate from the Criminal Investigation Department (CID). Seth Sukhdev gave an account of the hardships faced by Sindhi Hindus in obtaining the necessary documents for their travel. In most cases, he said, the applications of Hindus were forwarded for clearance to the CID, where they would lie for months gathering dust. Parsis and Christians, he said, did not receive such treatment. He talked about a particular officer who was in charge of issuing identification documents and told Hindus to their face that the instructions were to send their cases to the CID. The same person, Sukhdev said, had been put in charge of the post of scrutinizing passport applications. "You know, Sir, in Hitler's times there were certain officers who were called Jew baiters," said Sukhdev. "He is a Hindu-baiter. He is trained in that line."[54]

As Bengali members of the assembly pointed out, the primary motive for the bill was the Bengali-language riots that had taken place in February 1952. The government suspected the influence of foreign elements who had allegedly traveled to Dhaka in the form of *jathas* to incite violence. As Nur Ahmed—an assembly member from East Bengal—alleged, young Hindu groups were motivated to undo the partition of Bengal and were sent to East Pakistan in an organized fashion.[55] Raj Kumar Chakraverty countered this approach and urged the government to look inward to find elements of discontent and the reasons for their anger. "Food and clothing," he said, "is the main problem and if the Government can solve that problem they need not worry about the undesirable whom they fear as coming from outside."[56] He also pointed out the absurdity of policing a border as long, convoluted, and porous as the East Bengal–India border.

Although non-Muslim critics of the bill spoke about the hardships faced by the non-Muslim minority and how passport and visa requirements further compounded their difficulties, Mian Iftikharuddin, a left-leaning Muslim member from Punjab, saw the bill as a necessary step toward effectively checking the inflow of Muslim migrants from India. Pakistan, he said, could not possibly accommodate thirty million Muslims living in India, so it was necessary to put in place adequate measures that reduced the number of Muslim influx by specifying some documentary requirements for entry.[57] A long-term solution, according to Iftikharuddin, was to implement the Pakistan Resolution of March 1940 to its fullest extent, guaranteeing minority protection and the granting of equal rights. Without such safeguards, he feared, there would be a thinning out of the Hindu population coming from Pakistan to India and a continuous pouring in of Muslim migrants from India into Pakistan.

Other than as a mechanism for the surveillance and management of bodies across the border, the visa regime was explicitly designed to ensure the impossibility of Hindus returning to Pakistan to claim citizenship. By migrating from Pakistan, Hindus and Sikhs were—to use the term frequently used in the ministerial documents—"hit by section 7" of the Citizenship Law. The relevant section deprived individuals of citizenship if they had migrated to India from what now constituted Pakistani territory after March 1947. In any case, most Hindu and Sikh migrants would have acquired Indian citizenship, as the constitution of the new Indian Republic came into force in 1950. As such, they were already barred from receiving Pakistani citizenship, albeit in extraordinarily rare cases, as discussed later. Even if Hindus and Sikhs had not become Indian citizens and wanted to acquire Pakistani citizenship, they needed to travel under a permit for permanent return or resettlement.[58] The embassies and relevant ministries were reluctant to grant these documents to non-Muslim applicants. The provision did not apply to Muslims migrating from North India, as they had never left the territory that had come to constitute Pakistan. In other words, Muslim migrants were not "hit by section 7" and could still be registered as citizens upon their arrival in Pakistan.

The introduction of passport and visa regimes was only partially successful in addressing the Pakistani state's anxiety about its Hindu citizens, especially in East Bengal. The major anxiety was the cross-border connections—regardless of religion—that communities continued to maintain, especially those who had acquired citizenship as a birthright. Hindus born in East Bengal who had not left the area in the aftermath of Partition violence were one such category.

DIFFERENTIATING CITIZENS FROM NATIONALS: PAKISTAN AS MUSLIM HOMELAND

If the idea of the citizen was built on the refugee's body, it was through an explication of the category of Hindu citizen as "other" that the law cultivated new sensibilities about national belonging to, and affiliation in, a Muslim homeland. The citizen as an opaque category was amenable to the homogenization of identities based on the rational language of the law. At the same time, the enchantment of the national as the rationale for the sovereign state overshadowed the purported universality of citizenship. To explain this dialectic, I take a look at Hindu applicants who requested a return to Pakistan and applied for its citizenship. Through a close reading of these cases, I trace the processes whereby bureaucratic praxis conjures the idea of Pakistan as a homeland for Muslim nationals. In some cases, I find slippages in language that imply a nonbelonging of Hindu citizens; in other cases, the references to Pakistan as a Muslim homeland are more explicit.

The clearest explication of Pakistan as a homeland for Muslim nationals is to be found in the probing file "Question whether the migrant Hindus should be accepted as citizens of Pakistan in case they make applications to the Central Government for registration as citizens of Pakistan." The debate was triggered by an application submitted by Mr. Saha, an East Bengali Hindu who, upon migrating to India in 1950, had lost his Pakistani citizenship. Commenting on this question in April 1956, the Ministry of Interior's citizenship section wrote a detailed note. "Our policy in respect of non-Muslims, particularly Hindus," it specified, "is that we do not grant them the citizenship of Pakistan, except of course, in cases in which they claim it as matter of right." Such a policy, the document goes on, had been adopted because of the following considerations:

(i) Pakistan is a home land for Muslims only. By granting Pakistan citizenship to Hindus liberally, we would be throwing an implied invitation to them, which would not be in accord with the idea under which we demanded a separate state and established Pakistan.

(ii) The Government of India have also adopted similar policy towards Muslims, Pakistanis in particular. They refuse Indian nationality to Muslims even in those cases in which it is admissible to them as a matter of right. If necessary, a few instances can be cited in which Indian Muslims have been deprived of their Indian status on the ground that they have, for some time, served under the Government of Pakistan or lived in Pakistan for a few days before the introduction of passport system.

(iii) Apart from these consideration, we are particularly averse to the grant of Pakistan citizenship to those Hindus who have lost their Pakistani status under Section 7 of the Pakistan Citizenship Act, 1951; for their return to Pakistan would dislodge innumerable Muslim refugees who have since been permanently rehabilitated.[59]

This is one of the earliest, detailed, and clearest explications of the statist doctrine on citizenship. This principle had been in practice for years, even though the law continued to feign religious neutrality in matters of citizenship. This note illustrates the citizen-national binary whereby citizenship for Hindus was reduced to birthright only. At the same time, for Muslims, citizenship extends beyond the realm of law, articulated in a rhetorical, affective language that uses the metaphor of homeland as a more expansive and intimate category of belonging defined for Hindus as India and for Muslims as Pakistan. This notion of national belonging conjoined with nationalism exclusive to the majority group is akin to what a liberal Israeli politician, Tzipi Livni, said about Arabs in the occupied state: "I would like to see the State of Israel be a home for Arab Israelis, but it cannot be their national home."[60] Analogously, Hindus could be Pakistani citizens, but Pakistan could be a national homeland only for Muslims.

Within the ministry, others argued a different stance. M. W. Abbasi, in a note dated 24 August 1956, adopted a more humane position. Abbasi referred to sporadic communal violence. Several Hindu families had been frequently shifting places, and there was, since Pakistan had been declared an Islamic Republic under the constitution of 1956, a general sense of insecurity among the non-Muslim minority. To alleviate their concerns and prevent an international crisis involving India, Abbasi called for a revision in policy that would grant citizenship to returning Hindus. "What is required in the present atmosphere of the Province," he wrote, "is a persistent campaign for restoration of confidence among the Hindu minority and for proving to them that the Islamic Republic of Pakistan is anxious to give them a better treatment than the secular State of India is meting out to its Muslim minority." In case that the reverse migration of Hindus increased to an unmanageable scale, he recommended halting and revising the policy once again. But this fear was, in his estimation, far-fetched, an unlikely contingency.[61]

Hameeduddin Ahmed, serving in the relatively junior rank of deputy secretary, took a hardline stance and played a far more critical role in determining policy. In a note from April 1956, Ahmed gave detailed reasoning for why the policy should not be lax for non-Muslims. To begin with, according to Ahmed, citizenship was a matter of loyalty, and regardless of the reasons for migration, "the fact remains that a person leaving the country has subordinated his loyalty to it to other considerations e.g. economic betterment or a more congenial or apparently safe atmosphere." Once renounced, therefore, citizenship could be restored in only exceptional circumstances, such as involuntary migration or if the person in question was a minor at the time of migration.[62] Furthermore, and more important, Ahmed feared that the number of Hindus wanting to return to East Pakistan was probably lower than those Hindus and Sikhs who were likely to return, if possible, to West Pakistan. Any relaxation in East Pakistan had to be applicable in West Pakistan, and there could not be two citizenship laws for the two wings of the country. The return of an "appreciable number of Hindus would constitute a serious economic and security risk." It would also be unpopular because of "the Government decision to stop the influx of Muslim refugees from India on economic and other considerations."[63] Ahmed did not believe that such a readmittance policy would boost the confidence of minorities. If anything, he said, it would send a signal to Hindus to rush out, knowing that they would be admitted back whenever they liked.

Adopting a more conspiratorial tone, Hameeduddin Ahmed described the Hindu migration from East Pakistan as "perhaps engineered and inspired by India and her agents" rather than the result of Pakistan becoming an Islamic republic.[64] It was, therefore, an issue of national security meant to ward off Indian attempts at politically and economically destabilizing Pakistan. Although there was a similar hardening of views on the part of the Indian government with regard to Muslims wishing to return to India, the numbers of Muslims leaving Pakistan were far greater than those of Hindus allowed to return to Bengal or Sindh. In fact, this same allegation of "one-way traffic" of both Hindus and Muslims leaving Pakistan to enter India had been used as an excuse by the Indian government to introduce the permit system in the first place and was followed by other bureaucratic procedures.[65]

Although in the end citizenship was granted to Mr. Saha, the broader principle of not giving citizenship to non-Muslims other than as a matter of right under section 3 was firmly established. The decision clearly stated that the exception was made for Mr. Saha because of the minister of interior's intervention on an individual basis and without setting precedent.[66] There were only a few other exceptional cases in which Hindus returning to Sindh were granted citizenship.

One such case was that of Kundanmal, who migrated in March 1948 from Sindh to India, putting him under section 7 of the Citizenship Act. This was the main provision whereby anyone who had left areas that constituted Pakistan after March 1947 was automatically denied any claim to Pakistani citizenship. The omission was deliberate, preventing any claims of mitigating circumstances that Hindus and Sikhs could have used to return to their homes. Kundanmal's application was, therefore, initially rejected.

He reapplied to the Ministry of Interior. The note in the file summarizing the case facts observed that

> the Minister took a policy decision that since thousands of Muslims and Hindus had migrated in the years immediately following the independence due to some fears in their mind, the applications of those who wanted to come back and become citizens of Pakistan, should not be rejected on the ground that they had migrated from Pakistan but that each case should be examined and decided on merits subject to the overriding consideration of security. As nothing adverse against Mr. Kundanmal was found on the records of the D.I.B., it was decided to grant him Pakistani Citizenship and a certificate was accordingly issued.[67]

Kundanmal's motives were primarily economic, as he owned sixty acres of land in the Sanghar district and a residential house in Shahpur Chakar. He had left in 1948 but returned in 1955. Such was the importance of this matter that the prime minister himself wished to see the papers on his case and to make formal inquiries. Altaf Gauhar, then deputy secretary in the prime minister's office, sent a letter to the Ministry of Interior to share the record with the Prime Minister's Office.

This case, which demonstrates a strong personal interest in the granting of citizenship to a returning Hindu, was taken during the ministerial tenure of Mir Ghulam Ali Khan Talpur. A later file mentions him for changing the policy regarding Hindus. Before his term commenced in June 1957, the file noted, "migration from Pakistan was considered to be the greatest disqualification and no migrant Hindu was re-admitted to the citizenship of Pakistan."[68] Talpur—a Sindh-based politician who was better acquainted with the situation in the region and with the role the Hindu population played in the economy and society of Sindh—changed this practice, and several migrant Hindus were readmitted, as long as nothing incriminating was found against them. But so much was the control of bureaucratic power, the distrust of Hindus, and the firmly entrenched idea of Pakistan as a Muslim homeland that the officials of the Interior Ministry adopted a policy of "go slow" on such cases, jealously guarding their authority in such matters. At one point, then prime minister Feroz Khan Noon asked the Ministry of Interior to send all cases of granting citizenship certificates directly to his office. The deputy secretary responded that the Ministry finalized almost fifty certificates every day. Only those cases that involved some aspect of policy—not more than seven to eight per week—were sent to the deputy secretary. For instance, if there were a case of a Hindu who had migrated after Partition, the case would be referred to the deputy secretary, and later to the secretary and even to the prime minister. "It is not known," wrote an official at the rank of the deputy secretary in a somewhat tongue-in-cheek tone to respond to the prime minister's directive, "whether the intention of the Prime Minister is to devote so much of his time to such routine cases which even a Deputy Secretary in the Ministry does not see." He then added a handwritten note to the sentence: "Perhaps the intention is in respect of Hindus of doubtful loyalty."[69] The prime minister's principal secretary clarified that the prime minister's interest was only in cases of non-Muslims, "particularly of Hindus who have migrated to Pakistan after partition."[70] The ministry again clarified that there were practically no cases of Hindus migrating to Pakistan after Partition.

With the imposition of martial law in the country in 1958, bureaucrats no longer had to work with leaders who had a more profound, political understanding of the situation and took a personal interest in cases affecting migrants. During the military rule, the policy was to strictly adhere to the granting of citizenship only to those who could claim it as a right. For all other categories, only those applications were to be processed that were put forth by dependents of Pakistani nationals, including those with emergency certificates entering from the Khokhrapar border, highly qualified persons, persons bringing in capital, and persons of Pakistani origin who were permanently resident abroad.[71] For the rest, a "go slow" policy was to be observed.

The exception to the rule was confined mainly to high-profile cases, in which applicants were affluent and politically connected. There were nevertheless also other cases of widows, divorced women, or individuals made vulnerable by unforeseeable circumstances and seeking a favorable review of their applications to return to Pakistan as a citizen. One example is the case of a Hindu widow named Lal Bai Velji Harijan. Born and raised in Karachi, Harijan moved to present-day India at the age of twenty, after her wedding in 1945. After her husband died, she came to Pakistan intending to settle there and applied for citizenship. There was nothing to indicate that Harijan posed a security threat, so the ministry proposed a sympathetic consideration. The problem was that she had left much before the outbreak of communal disturbances and the creation of Pakistan and thus did not qualify for citizenship as a right under section 3. If she had been a Muslim widow, the question of policy relaxation would not have become a matter of review, as the ministry was then accommodating numerous Muslim migrants under different sections of the Citizenship Act.

The exceptional circumstances of Harijan's case warranted a review of the law. Qamaruddin Butt, in his note written in November 1958, a month after the imposition of martial law, called for a lenient response, as the applicant "would not probably have thought of coming back had her husband not died leaving the widow without a breadearner. The only comfort now she can find is among her relatives who might support her in her dark days."[72] But Hameeduddin Ahmed, typical of his hawkish stance on accepting non-Muslims back to Pakistan as citizens of the country, wanted to know if India was extending similar consideration to "Muslim widows from Pakistan for settling in India with their relatives on the demise of their husbands in Pakistan."[73] On the question of whether Harijan was hit by section 7, Assistant Secretary Butt responded that, since the widow went to India in 1945, her case was not covered under section 7, as that was applicable only if the individual in question had migrated to India after 1 March 1947. "Her case is therefore of a commonwealth citizen," he wrote, "and there are ingredients in this case to be considered sympathetically."[74]

As to the policy on Muslim widows wishing to return to India, Butt did not have any information to share. The same query was put to the Foreign Office, which in a note dated 1 January 1959 stated that India would bluntly say no to Muslim widows of Pakistani nationality. While the Indian High Commission, it alleged, on occasions might favorably consider cases of Hindus wishing to repatriate on the basis of individual merits of the case, it was doubtful they would extend similar consideration to Muslim widows whose husbands had migrated to Pakistan before their demise. Although there were several reported instances in which Muslims wishing to return to India had had their wishes granted by the Indian government, the Foreign Office insisted that "the Indian Mission seldom entertain requests of Indian Muslim for repatriation and re-settlement in India, who once came to Pakistan." It therefore advised against taking up this matter with the Indian government, as "the Govt. of India will not be willing to take the burden of Muslim widows for obvious reasons."[75]

This is not to say that no Hindu applicant requesting a return on humanitarian grounds was denied permission for resettlement. I have found at least one case of a Hindu widow, Dadan Bai, who was granted a citizenship certificate, albeit under the ministerial policy adopted by Talpur.[76] But as earlier stated, the ministry rarely took such a humanitarian reading of the law into consideration.

From a legal perspective, a more significant issue for the Foreign Office was the use of a generic term such as *Muslim widow*. Another important consideration was whether these widows were Indian or Pakistani.[77] The question of Pakistani widows or divorced women had been receiving the attention of the Interior Ministry ever since the Citizenship Law was promulgated. There were numerous cases—especially in families from the minority provinces of North India—where one part of the family stayed back in India and the rest moved to Pakistan. In cases involving divorce, the legal process was seldom followed, making it difficult to ascertain the claims of a woman wishing to be reunited with her family who had moved to Pakistan. In case of separation or her husband's disappearance, verifying an applicant's claims was even more challenging. As per the Citizenship Act, married women could be registered independently of their husbands regardless of their citizenship status. Similarly, a Pakistani woman could retain her citizenship after marrying an Indian citizen, provided that she did not take up any other nationality.

While India and Pakistan were in principle committed to reuniting families, in practice, this was not always the case. There were, for example, cases in which a woman who had acquired Indian or Pakistani citizenship was seeking a reversal of her citizenship status to be reunited with her family. Such applications were seldom accepted. According to the ministerial record, only two such cases were accepted. In these cases, husbands were "invalid and were not in a position to undertake the journey from India to Pakistan." In one particular case that led to a discussion about the registration of women as Pakistani citizens, the female applicant "alleged bad treatment of the husband."[78] For the ministry, it was difficult to investigate such claims and bend the rules to accommodate the applicant. In many circumstances, husbands objected to registering their wives as Pakistani citizens without the consent of their wives' male custodians.

Although the file generally speaks in terms of *women* or *widows*, through its use of such terms as *talaq* and *khula*, it is clear that the reference is to Muslim women only and not to "Pakistani women" or widows at large, as the Foreign Office insisted. This accounts for the lenient tone taken by the Interior Ministry when making policy recommendations for Muslim women, as opposed to their recommendation made in the case of Hindu widows. In a note dated 28 January 1957, Hameeduddin Ahmed recommended examining each case of alleged separation on its own merit. He suggested that legal proof was not strictly essential, given that in most cases it was difficult to obtain. It was irrelevant, he said, to ask women to prove their financial status when the same question was not asked to thousands of men crossing the border into Pakistan.[79] In a summary put up for approval, the recommendation was to consider on the basis of individual merit "all requests for citizenship by women who have separated from their husbands or whose husbands are infirm or incapacitated by illness or other disabilities from migrating to this country." The note recommended reasonable proof of separation without insistence on proof of legal separation, as it could not always be established until legally sanctioned through divorce or *khula*. It also recommended that if the husband in question could not migrate to Pakistan because of infirmity or old age, this inability should not affect the applicant's request for citizenship.[80] Ahmed's approach was far more lenient in response to Muslim widows and distressed women than the stance he took to similar appeals for compassion by Hindu applicants.

This brief survey of the Citizenship Law's legal provisions and their interpretation and implementation in cases of Hindu applicants shows that even though the scripting of the law was liberal—meant to accommodate all subjects, regardless of their religion or locality—putting the law into practice yielded different results. With their marginal notes, internal memos, and informal conversations and connections, these bureaucratic files framed the ideological discursive field within which the law operated.

THE LIMITS OF A MUSLIM HOMELAND

The idea of Pakistan as a Muslim homeland established in the internal correspondence of Ministry of Interior officials was implemented by decisions on the applications submitted under various sections of the Citizenship Law. But even with an official policy that was pro-Muslim migrants, there were limits to the state's accommodation of Muslims. This pragmatism overshadowed the ideological plane but was nevertheless couched in ideological language that justified a pragmatic implementation of the law.

Even after the cutoff date of the day of promulgation of the Citizenship Law in April 1951, Muslim migrants from India continued to come to Pakistan. Within a year of the Citizenship Act, several hundred thousand new migrants had entered Pakistani territory, in addition to those who were already in the country before the law came into force. They had not gotten themselves registered. It was thus considered necessary to waive the registration requirement, as it was impossible to register such a vast number of claimants. Accordingly, an amendment was proposed in the Constituent Assembly on 7 April 1952. The interior minister, Mushtaq Ahmad Gurmani, called for rationalizing the law to accommodate eight million refugees already in Pakistan whose required registration would be impractical.[81] Sardar Shaukat Hayat Khan spoke against the decision to keep extending the date for conferral of Pakistani citizenship to "those pouring in from India," because without necessary checks in place, "so many will come into the boat that it is sure to go down under the burden."[82] If the government wanted to keep accommodating migrants,

Khan said, it should ask the Indian government to provide "extra territory in proportion to the number of Indian citizen who are being pushed across the border."[83] So while Shaukat Hayat projected Pakistan as a Muslim homeland—a veritable Noah's ark that would save all who boarded—the fear was that the ark could not accommodate *all* Muslims. Gurmani concurred with this view. In his rejoinder to Khan, Gurmani reaffirmed the idea of land belonging to God, and thus as open to all those persecuted for their beliefs and way of life. He reinterpreted Shaukat Hayat Khan's call for more territory as the need to "increase the capacity of the boat" through effective economic development.[84] This offers the best example of a pragmatic policy decision that was justified on an ideological basis rather than the other way around.

Neither one-off relaxation of the rules nor blanket conferral of citizenship resolved, or even fully addressed, the issue of Muslim migrants from India who continued to enter Pakistan in the thousands via the Khokhrapar border along Sindh-Rajasthan. Given the scale of this migration, and the fact that most migrants intended to permanently reside in the country, Pakistan could not repatriate them. Stopping migrants at the border also could have led to a critical situation, as Karachi's existing, sizable migrant community would have protested the decision. To further complicate matters, the migrants had already risked, if not lost, their claims to Indian citizenship by journeying to Pakistan. As G. A. Ahmed argued in a detailed note dated 24 January 1952, the migrants had become "our permanent liability." He proposed an amendment to section 6(1) of the Citizenship Act "to abrogate the date line by when migration to this country may entitle a person to the citizenship of Pakistan."[85] Although the one-off amnesty was meant to provide legal cover for thousands, if not millions, of Muslim migrants already residing in the country without any possibility of going back, it certainly did not deter the continuous stream of migration via Khokhrapar. The limits of the Muslim homeland had been exhausted.

The crisis came to a head when one Mr. Yad Elahi, who had entered Pakistan via the Khokhrapar border, applied for a passport to visit his family in India. The application led to a sustained and detailed discussion in the Ministries of Interior, Law, and Foreign Affairs about the legality of all those who had entered Pakistan via Khokhrapar, and continued to do so, even though the statutory time limit for such migration had long expired.

The Ministry of Foreign Affairs and Commonwealth Relations was, according to a note dated 25 March 1955, of the opinion that Pakistan was already issuing emergency certificates to Indians to visit their families in Pakistan and allowing them unfettered access via Khokhrapar (the ministry does not disclose that these certificates were primarily given to Indian Muslims). The Foreign Office thus had no objection to supplying them with travel documents as well, even though "such persons are not citizens of Pakistan in the legal sense but when we allow them to come to this country for permanently settling here, there should probably be no objection to provide them travel facilities as to our own citizens in order to avoid statelessness from them."[86] The Ministry of Interior was careful to distinguish between those who arriving in the country on a valid passport, visa, or emergency certificate and those illegally crossing the border. Accepting the Foreign Office's proposal, the Ministry of Interior wrote in its comments that it " would mean our placing a premium on the entry of Indian Muslims via Khokhrapar. This would be a direct incentive to enter through Khokhrapar instead of passports. This, we would certainly oppose as we want to discourage the illegal influx of Indian Muslims via Khokhrapar."[87] Its recommendation was not to issue passports to persons entering Pakistan through Khokhrapar after 13 April 1951, unless they registered themselves as citizens.

The Foreign Office stuck to its view that granting citizenship to migrants from Khokhrapar was inevitable. Instead of registering them individually, the office suggested the automatic conferral of citizenship on all those who had entered Khokhrapar after April 1951, whether illegally or on the strength of emergency certificates.[88] By keeping the Khokhrapar crossing open, the Foreign Office insisted, the Pakistani state had "in effect threw a general invitation to refugees from India to come and settle down in Pakistan." Refusing citizenship to even a few hundred would "creat[e] a class of stateless persons who came to this country on our implied invitation and whom we are now refusing to absorb. They owe loyalty to none and yet be our responsibility. They would in the long run create a disgruntled element of our population many of whom would perhaps become fifth columnists."[89] Moreover, the Foreign Office reminded the Ministry of Interior, the established position in official circles was that a passport was not, in any case, conclusive proof of nationality.

The Citizenship Section of the Ministry of Interior dismissed what it called "sentimental considerations." The question of millions of unregistered migrants, claimed officer M. R. Ali in one note, posed a serious security threat to Pakistan: "the fact remains that entry through Khokhrapar is illegal and we cannot encourage it in any way, especially when we know that Indians agents and spies find their way into Pakistan through this route."[90] That general distrust extended to any potential migrant from India—all of whom were Muslims, in this case—signaled an attempt at closure: political stability was enabling the Pakistani state to set definite limits to the idea of citizenship and its legal criteria. An initial massive influx of migrants had considerably subsided, allowing state control over its borders for a regulated and documented movement of citizens, aliens, and refugees. The Ministry of Interior was clear that those arriving from India via Khokhrapar after April 1951 would continue to be stateless unless they registered themselves and formally initiated the proper procedure for becoming Pakistani citizens.[91] It opposed the idea of another extension of blanket amnesty, whereby anyone could be accorded citizenship simply by ending up in Pakistan.

The Ministry of Foreign Affairs insisted on taking a historical overview of the situation, accounting for bilateral agreements to which Pakistan was signatory. The ministry referred to the Prime Ministers' Conference and to the Liaqat-Nehru Pact of 1950, whereby any Indian allowed to migrate to Pakistan had to be accepted as a Pakistani citizen, even if the individual had not arrived with proper documents. In the past, the Foreign Office added, several recommendations were given to the cabinet to control the influx of refugees via Khokhrapar—including sealing the border and resorting to aerial firing—but the government had been averse to such suggestions for political considerations.[92] Now that people had arrived, the open border at Khokhrapar in combination with the provisions of this bilateral pact meant that "citizenship of Pakistan cannot be refused to Muslims who entered Pakistan for permanent settlement through Khokhrapar without travel documents. They will have to be given Pakistan citizenship sooner or later."[93] Notably, the ministry took a generous view here in the case of millions of Muslim migrants. However, during the same period, Hindu applicants requesting reentry on emergency or humanitarian grounds—and especially those from Sindh—were mostly rejected.

In a terse response in a note dated 9 June 1956, the Ministry of Interior criticized the Foreign Office, to whom the legal position had many times been explained and "yet they harp on the same string that citizenship of Pakistan cannot be refused to Muslims who entered Pakistan, for permanent settlement, via Khokhrapar without any travel documents."[94] It further added that the Liaqat-Nehru agreement was meant to facilitate the free movement of people, especially minorities, from one country to another and was "designed to eliminate the possibility of their movement being hindered in the country which they were leaving."[95] But things had since changed. Since October 1952, the passport system had been in place, requiring a passport and visa to enter either of the two countries. This statutory requirement was mandatory. If it had not been implemented at Khokhrapar, it did not follow that the government was bound to exempt such crossings from the other statutory requirements of citizenship law.

The Ministry of Interior took a stern position on the idea of an automatic conferral of citizenship on all illegal entrants via Khokhrapar, as it would be "fraught with dangerous possibilities and security risks." Already, the ministry observed, the massive influx through Khokhrapar "has resulted in a large number of *bad characters*, even the culprits on bail, finding their way into Pakistan and that a good number of them have not yet come to the notice of the authorities concerned simply for want of the records in respect of them."[96] As was the case with any other application for citizenship, proper screening of applicants was a prerequisite, ensuring that none of the persons permitted posed a security risk to Pakistan. In a related note, the Ministry of Interior's Political Section referred to a cabinet meeting held in August 1951, at which specific standard operating procedures were adopted that took note of the particulars of the refugees entering Pakistan via Khokhrapar. A standardized form was prepared, which included information about an entrant's name, parents, Indian address, age, occupation, and date of entry, as well as their fingerprints.[97]

Screening applicants—even the state's capacity to do so was somewhat limited in practice—was an essential part of the citizenship process. Even those who had entered Pakistan on emergency certificates could not be considered bona fide citizens of Pakistan or granted passports without proper checks. Neither was Pakistan bound by any law or bilateral agreement to accept them as citizens.

Per the opinion of the Ministry of Law, persons entering via Khokhrapar without valid documents could be prosecuted under the Pakistan (Control of Entry) Ordinance of 1948, or the Pakistan (Control of Entry) Ordinance of 1952 that updated it. Such persons could be prosecuted for committing an offense under section 4 of the said act and sent back to India under section 7. They did not meet the provisions of section 3(d) of the Pakistan Citizenship Act, as their migration to Pakistan was not a migration in the legal sense.[98] If they had entered Pakistan even on a temporary permit, the Ministry of Law said, it could have been regarded as a legal migration with entitlement to Pakistani citizenship.

Edward Snelson, the secretary of law, called for a more cautious and humane approach in a note from 13 February 1956. Regardless of illegal entry, such a person had come to Pakistan to make it his or her permanent home. By this act, that person had already lost Indian citizenship. If then externed from Pakistan as a noncitizen, "then he faces the dreadful situation of becoming a stateless person whom every country will reject. It is a serious question whether this situation should be inflicted on anyone without very grievous reasons."[99] But the Ministry of Interior insisted that a blanket endorsement of citizenship claims would invalidate the procedures in place for the formal granting of citizenship based on residence permits, visas, and emergency certificates.

But the ministry overlooked the problems faced by Muslim migrants in acquiring this documentation. Mere suspicion that someone was intending migration from North India could trigger draconian clauses that governed evacuee property, resulting in a loss of land or home. Also, the Pakistani High Commission and Pakistani consulates in India lacked the capacity to deal with the enormous demand for such documents. In the end, the ministry relented, mentioning in the note, "We have hitherto been and will always be liberal in the matter of conferment of Pakistan citizenship on Indian Muslims; *for Pakistan is a home land for Muslims only.*"¹⁰⁰ Even though the ministry was eager to put in place effective checks to ensure that unfettered access to the Muslim homeland by Indian Muslims was curtailed, its pragmatic reasons for doing so were different from the reasoning applied to Hindu applicants. For "illegal" Muslim migrants from North India, the policy was ideologically construed to ensure that Pakistan remained a Muslim homeland on far more accommodating terms.

In official correspondence dated 18 February 1956, the Ministry of Interior summed up its debate with other departments. The ministry was not opposed to the idea of granting citizenship to entrants via Khokhrapar but insisted only that such a conferral was not automatic; since April 1951, every new claimant had to first register. At the current moment, it noted, "all such persons are therefore stateless because they have lost their Indian status on account of their migration to Pakistan and do not have the status of a citizen of Pakistan till it is conferred upon them."¹⁰¹ In an oblique response to the Foreign Office's arguments in the relevant notings, the Ministry of Interior said that under the provisions of the Control of Entry Act, entrants from Khokhrapar were committing an offense. The fact that the government was neither using force against such entrants nor prosecuting them did not amount to endorsing their illegal action or to an open invitation that would result in a further inpour of refugees from India.

By the mid-1950s, the Pakistani state had amassed enough power and achieved enough stability to ensure that the Muslim homeland was closed off to further claimants and entrants via various border crossings. The rationale for maintaining Pakistan as a Muslim homeland while simultaneously sealing it off to new entrants from India required a carefully drafted policy addressing the inherent contradiction of such a position.

This question was finally addressed in the late 1950s in response to a query about the possibility of granting domicile to migrants while their citizenship cases were pending. Such an exception was requested to make educated and highly skilled young men eligible for superior government service, allowing them to compete with those Pakistanis who had acquired citizenship by right.¹⁰² In the comprehensive policy review that followed, the Ministry of Interior shared background information about the Citizenship Law and its subsequent changes, highlighting important considerations in the law's implementation. In particular, the notes exchanged talked about the relaxation in policy for Sindhi Hindus adopted by Minister of Interior Talpur, reiterating that such actions marked a departure from the treatment of Pakistan as a Muslim homeland that recognized Hindu citizenship only in the case of birthright.[103] To offset the policy adopted by Talpur, which encouraged the granting of citizenship to affluent Hindus returning from India, the ministry adopted a "go slow" policy. It thus prioritized very few cases, namely those of minors dependent on Pakistani nationals, women married to Pakistanis, elderly parents of widows dependent on Pakistani nationals, and highly qualified or technical persons. All other certificates were withheld, resulting in the number of certificates issued falling from four hundred to thirty and an accumulation of over five thousand applications.[104] Persons whose applications were put on hold included new migrants via Khokhrapar who had entered Pakistan with or without documents; persons who were alone, without any relatives in India or Pakistan; married women whose husbands were in India; Indian men who arrived in Pakistan after 1955 and married Pakistani women; and educated boys and girls whose parents were in India but who themselves were residing in Pakistan with close relatives.[105]

The ministry observed that all those who had already acquired citizenship or had been residents for more than three years seemed to have severed all their connections with India and looked to Pakistan as their homeland. In a remarkable departure from its previous position—stated only two years prior—the Ministry of Interior recommended granting citizenship to all those who had come to Pakistan via Khokhrapar, as they had become "our permanent and legal liability and cannot be pushed back to India. There is, therefore, no point in keeping them stateless. In fact the grant of Pakistan citizenship in their cases will be a sort of regularization of their national status."[106] In addition, it suggested granting citizenship to the following people: dependents of Pakistani nationals (e.g., widowed sisters, aunts), women married to Pakistani citizens, old and invalid persons who lacked financial support in India and came to Pakistan to live with their close relations, divorced and widowed women coming to Pakistan to live with their close relations, persons with high qualifications, minors dependent on brothers, uncles, and parents permanently resident in Pakistan and "persons of Indo-Pakistan origin (particularly Muslims) residing abroad" as many of them "though residing in foreign countries for years together, took upon Pakistan as their home-land."[107] Because most "diaspora Pakistanis" were well established either in business or in service abroad, they were not seen as a burden on Pakistan's finances and economy. But the ministry was careful in setting the prerequisites for capital and educational credentials for persons in other categories to qualify for citizenship; in one particular case, the ministry noted, "a person who smuggled stolen Indian films was deemed to have brought capital."[108] Last, the ministry emphasized that the term *highly qualified person* applied to those with degrees in engineering and technology and not those who had graduated in arts.[109]

Such a dramatic reversal proposed by the Ministry of Interior shows the complex interplay of pragmatism and ideology in policy making. When the ministry opposed the blanket conferral of citizenship and insisted on following guidelines and filing paperwork, there were still thousands of potentially stateless Muslim migrants. The numbers may have remained more or less the same; that is, there was nothing ideological that called for a change in position other than the fact that the relevant bureaucrats recognized the conferral of citizenship as the only pragmatic solution.

On the basis of these notes and this background, A. R. M. Fazlur Rehman, deputy secretary to the government of Pakistan, prepared a detailed note addressed to the chief secretaries of East and West Pakistan and the administrator of Karachi on 14 June 1960. It gave a comprehensive summary of the Citizenship Law, its history, and how its various provisions had changed over time. While regulating the "national status" of currently stateless persons residing in Pakistan, the note gave a comprehensive plan of action to plug the gaping hole in Pakistan's citizenship policies and the rationale for doing so. Rehman wrote that Pakistan's citizenship laws were reasonably generous in awarding citizenship, especially to those in Pakistan or those who had migrated to Pakistan before the commencement of the act:

> This is an unusual provision which very generously accepts any one and every one as a citizen of the country provided he has years of its coming into being. The Act provided a further facility to those persons who though still in India had their hearts in Pakistan and who on hearing of a separate citizenship for Pakistan from that of India being ushered in by the Act may wish to migrate to the former country. . . . The Government which enacted this legislation in 1951 rightly thought that those who were ideologically attracted towards Pakistan reached right at its inception, either voluntarily or by being compelled by the actions of the Indians to leave India because of their support to Pakistan. Considerable numbers followed during the subsequent years because of communal riots which were an aftermath of the partition of the sub-continent.[110]

The situation had, however, changed. All those who intended to migrate to Pakistan had already done so. Even those held back by India's laws on evacuee property no longer had an excuse, as the laws had been repealed. All financial considerations as well as any "ideological incentive for migration" had entirely disappeared: there was no longer any justification for migrating to Pakistan. By 1956, strict enforcement of the Citizenship Law was to come into play "without any demur on moral or other considerations."[111] The martial-law regime was simply going to enact what had been originally envisaged in 1951, at the time of the implementation of Citizenship Law.

Forced to confront the inherent contradictions that lied in the logic of Pakistan as a Muslim homeland that was to remain open to all Muslims from India, Rehman had to make the uncomfortable admission that Indian Muslims had to reconcile themselves to being Indian citizens. "They are finding their feet again in the political and other spheres of their country's activities," he wrote. "Any continuance of their exodus to Pakistan will militate against the Indian Muslims' interest. It will continue to make the loyalty of Muslims to India suspect in the mind of the Hindus who would regard it as a proof of the allegation that the Indian Muslims' hearts lie in Pakistan." Rehman thus exhibits a new kind of ideological rationalization of pragmatic decision-making, whereby it was deemed in the interests of Indian Muslims not to migrate to Pakistan. An economically prosperous Pakistan was also seen to be in the benefit of Indian Muslims, as "in Pakistan's strength lies the guarantee for their receiving good treatment at the hands of their Government and of other communities living in India. Both these considerations demand that the exodus to Pakistan should cease."[112] For sustained growth of the Pakistani economy and to secure any gains that had been made, Rehman considered it essential to keep a check on population growth. The government was already investing in family-planning schemes. Any further influx in the population would jeopardize Pakistan's economy and had to be checked. As to the question of divided families or a humanitarian crisis, the note said, there were already bilateral arrangements between India and Pakistan that could address such issues.

Rehman also addressed the issue of statelessness in cases where individuals arrived on a visa, registered themselves for citizenship, and then refused to go back to India, pleading that they had already lost their Indian citizenship. To ensure that the government of Pakistan was not burdened with such persons, he asked provincial governments and the Karachi administration to "tighten up their vigilance over Indians coming into Pakistan on short visits and to ensure that all such Indians leave the country during the period of validity of their passports."[113] Anyone exceeding the duration of legal stay was to be prosecuted and returned to India.

Once citizenship was to be considered only in cases of divided families and based on qualifications of capital and professional expertise, Rehman urged Pakistani foreign missions to be vigilant in ensuring that those applying for visas had families in Pakistan and were thus covered under the bilateral agreement between the governments of India and Pakistan on divided families and their dependents, or they were highly qualified or had sufficient capital that they wished to transfer to Pakistan.[114] The last provision was specifically important for the sizable Muslim population of Indian-Pakistani origin residing in Africa. If there was any other reason for which an applicant sought Pakistani citizenship, that reason had to be diligently scrutinized.

Such a strict implementation of the policy, Rehman predicted, would lead to Indian propaganda against the Pakistani state and "its allegedly restrictive policy against Indian Muslims."[115] It needed to be pointed out that this restrictive policy did not apply to persons of Indo-Pak origin living outside India. They were to be covered under section 8 of the Citizenship Act instead of section 20. To counter Indian propaganda, the humanitarian aspects of the Citizenship Law and the liberal view it had taken over many decades were to be emphasized. Rather than aiming at restriction in movement or assisting the migration of a particular group, the then-current policy was mainly inspired by economic reasons, Rehman insisted. It was also to be publicized that "after 13 years of Independence it can be presumed that people in India have made their final choice of the country in which they would stay. They are under no ideological compulsion to migrate to Pakistan or to become its citizens."[116] Through such counterpropaganda, Rehman wanted to project Pakistan's humanitarian credentials, which had accommodated Muslim migrants for India for over thirteen years as a Muslim homeland; at the same time, he wanted to signal to Indian Muslims that they were no longer welcome and should stay back for their own good. This refusal was on economic grounds and to save Indian Muslims from charges of disloyalty as citizens of India. In Rehman's estimate and that of the martial-law regime that endorsed it, the strategy intelligently managed to retain the tag of "Muslim homeland" while effectively closing off Pakistan to Indian Muslims. Yet the policy faltered: it effectively projected both India and Pakistan as Muslims homelands where Muslims could continue to live without reason to migrate to any other country.

Drafted in 1960, this policy set the norm. On some occasions, such as communal disturbances in India, there were demands to relax the policy to accommodate Muslims. But a full-on policy review was out of the question; from the Pakistani government's perspective, the situation had considerably stabilized.

Following the outbreak of communal violence in West Bengal, National Assembly member Abul Quasem in 1962 tabled a bill to amend section 6 of the Citizenship Act "with the object of dispensing with the requirements of domicile certificate for the grant of Pakistan citizenship to persons who have migrated Pakistan for fear of communal disturbances or persecution from any part of India or any territory occupied by her at any time after 1st March, 1947."

The Ministry of Interior—in its comments meant for internal circulation only—opposed the amendment, as it would "open a door to any number and sort of persons to migrate from India, creating economic and security problems for Pakistan."¹¹⁷ The ministry also feared the amendment would open the gate for persons from Goa—recently annexed by India—to come to Pakistan to escape persecution, and for Kashmiris, which would deprive them of their right to vote in a plebiscite when and if one was held.¹¹⁸ As an alternative, the ministry advised the rehabilitation of Muslims displaced in East Bengal without creating an open public policy on the issue.

The ministry's response reiterated the need to consolidate Pakistan's economic gains and keep Indian Muslims secure in their own country to thwart attempts by the Indian government to liquidate its Muslim population.¹¹⁹ Even a rich country like Canada, the official note of the ministry read, had to cap the number of immigrants entering its territory while seeking to increase its population. Therefore, granting citizenship to applicants from India was to be selective, restricted to the following categories:

(a) *bona fide* dependents from amongst close relations of citizens of Pakistan;
(b) technically/highly qualified persons;
(c) persons who wish to transfer substantial capital (at least worth Rs. 2 lacs) to Pakistan; and
(d) persons seeking Pakistan citizenship for very special reasons not covered by either of the two aforesaid categories.¹²⁰

The Standing Committee of the Assembly on Home Affairs, State, and Frontier Regions met on 15 October 1962 to discuss the bill's provisions and, after deliberations, voted unanimously to drop the bill. Still, under section 20 of the Citizenship Act, it was possible for persons of Commonwealth states, including India, to register for Pakistani citizenship. The list covered persons of Indian-Pakistani origin in other parts of the world who qualified as British-protected persons. Successive governments chose not to exclude India from the list of countries whose citizens could use this provision. Thus, a loophole was maintained in the legal framework at hand to make room for Indian Muslims or, more generally, for any person who could not otherwise be accommodated under the Citizenship Law's other provisions. The cases of Dadan Bai and Kundanmal mentioned above are examples of persons who were granted citizenship under section 20 of the law. While Kundanmal fulfilled the financial criteria of holding sixty acres of agricultural land in Sanghar, Dadan Bai—by the ministry's admission—did not hold property and was accommodated purely on a humanitarian basis.

THE PAKISTANI DIASPORA

Other than Muslim migrants from North India, the second major chunk of Muslim migrants, or potential Pakistani citizens, were Muslims of British Indian origin who had lived for some time outside of the Indian territories as defined by the Government of India Act of 1935. One such person was Fazaldin, born in Amritsar in 1889, who went to Manila, Philippines, in 1910 and died there in 1958. The same year, his brother had approached the ministry to determine his deceased brother's Pakistani citizenship status in order to execute his power of attorney. For the ministry, the vital question was "of intention rather than of the duration of the stay."[121] As long as it could be argued that Fazaldin continued to look to Pakistan as his home—even if he had lived almost his entire life in the Philippines, without once setting foot in the territory that constituted Pakistan—he could be considered a Pakistani citizen. In the end, the Ministry of Interior refused to accept Fazaldin as a Pakistani citizen because he did not fulfill the criteria of residence or domicile.

Questions of permanent residence, intention, and ideas of homeland were not merely legal abstractions. They posed severe existential threats to the future of communities settled across the former British Empire. In the 1950s, for instance, the Pakistani embassy in Rangoon sought an opinion from the Foreign Office about the status of Muslims and Hindus in Arakan. Resident in Burma for many decades, most of these Hindus and Muslims had originally migrated from East Bengal during the colonial period. In its summary note, the Ministry of Interior identified two categories of persons:

(i) Those who are originally born in the territories now included in India, and subsequently shifted to Burma; and

(ii) those who were originally born in territories now constituting Pakistan, (in fact East Pakistan) and subsequently shifted to Burma.[122]

The persons mentioned in the first category were not Pakistani, except in cases where they had registered themselves under section 8 of the Citizenship Act, which allowed for registration "as a citizen of Pakistan any person who, or whose father or whose father's father, who born in the Indo-Pakistan subcontinent and who is ordinarily resident in a country outside Pakistan at the commencement of this Act." This provision did not explain the status of those whose families had migrated to Pakistan. Persons in the second category were Pakistanis if they had not acquired Burmese nationality. Irrespective of whether they were Muslims or non-Muslims, the note said, if they "look upon Pakistan as their homeland, their Pakistani status remains intact under section 3(a)."[123] Contrary to the position taken in several other cases and departmental exchanges, a note prepared by A. R. M. Fazlur Rehman and dated 3 September 1959, reaffirmed the religious neutrality of Pakistani citizenship laws: "The Citizenship law of Pakistan as well as the Constitution of Pakistan do not provide for any discrimination or reservation among Muslims and non-Muslims in so far as their national status is concerned. If Hindus of East Pakistan origin resident in Burma have not, so far, acquired the nationality of that country either by long residence or by formal registration and look upon Pakistan as their homeland, they shall be deemed to be citizens of Pakistan, by right, under section 3(a) of the P.C. Act [Pakistan Citizenship Act], 1951."[124] Such an approach ensured that the policy did not simply extend to the Muslims of Arakan but also to all those of East Bengali origin resident in Burma. As I have stated earlier, policy decisions were made depending on context, choosing either an ideological reason for pragmatic decision-making or a pragmatic basis for ideological decision-making, as seemed fit. In a case like this, the officer's personal worldview led to a rather liberal reading of the law, even though his individual act was unable to make a larger impact on the framework that had by then been settled with distinction along the lines of Hindu citizens and Muslim nationals.

Most of these persons had lived in Burma for several decades without returning to East Bengal, and had married local women and raised families with them, and yet were still not legal residents of Burma. Their situation raised questions about the nature of law, belonging, and loyalty. Section 8, under which such persons could register themselves as Pakistani citizens, used the term *ordinarily resident* in an area outside Pakistan. Officials from various ministries grappled with semantics to figure out the precise meanings of *residing, living*, or *dwelling* in an area. As Abdullah Akhund, undersecretary in the Ministry of Interior, wrote in his note dated 18 May 1957:

> The words "residence" and "place of abode" are flexible and must be construed according to the object and intent of the particular legislation where they may be found. Primarily, they mean the dwelling and home where a man is supposed usually to live and sleep; they may also include a man's business abode, the place where he is to be found daily. . . . A residence is different from a domicile. Residence indicates permanency of occupation, as distinct from lodging or boarding, or temporary occupation, but does not include so much as "domicile," which requires as intention continued with residence. A person may be permanently residence in one country while having his domicile in another.[125]

The note sums up the problem of blandness of legal language. For wont of a better legal term, the note uses the category of domicile registration to explain the affective notion of national belonging to the homeland. As the note shows, terms like *living, dwelling*, and *residing* could be understood only as legally defined categories without capturing the ideological excess that the terms embodied.

In response to the query sent by the Pakistani embassy in Burma about persons of Pakistani origin, Akhund, commenting on behalf of the Ministry of Interior, described their living there as an aim to earn their livelihood. Even though they were "ordinarily residing" outside of Pakistan, the domiciled status of East Bengalis remained unaffected, especially when they had not acquired Burmese nationality and had registered themselves with the Burmese Foreigners Registration Department as Pakistanis. The same rule applied to persons who were married to local women and had been living in Burman for twenty or thirty years but had not acquired Burmese nationality.[126] At the same time, Pakistani officials did consider the possibility of unfavorable circumstances in Burma whereby non-Burmese Bengalis could be pushed out and asked to go back to their places of origin. In their assessment of "Pakistanis in Burma," the Ministry of Interior in its memorandum sent to the Ministry of Foreign Affairs in June 1958, observed that chances were remote of *"Pakistanis residing in Burma* coming back to East Pakistan en-masse, yet there is a likelihood that in the event of some unfavorable economic or political development in future, they may rush to Pakistan either of their own accord or under pressure of the Burmese authorities."[127] To prevent this outcome, the Pakistani embassy in Burma was asked to tactfully convey to the persons of East Pakistan origin residing in Burma that they should withhold applying for Pakistani citizenship certificates. They should be persuaded, the note said, to reside there, as citizens of Burma. Even if they could not acquire Burmese citizenship but continued to reside there and did not apply for Pakistani citizenship certificates either, they were to "remain citizens of Pakistan under the provisions of Section 3 of the Pakistan Citizenship Act 1951 . . . provided, of course, they continue to look upon Pakistan as their permanent home and do no acquire the citizenship or domicile of Burma or any other country."[128] Such a generous view about "Pakistanis in Burma" was based on the assessment that most of these persons were comfortably settled in their family life in Burma and had little intention of returning to their "homeland." But the Muslims of Arakan remained a liability. Even when they had acquired Burmese citizenship, there was a lingering, underlying fear that the question of their national belonging might jeopardize their future juridical stature as Burmese citizens.

As did residing abroad, residing inside the country often resulted in contested claims to citizenship. In the case of Sir Mohammed Currimbhoy Ebrahim, son of late Sir Currimbhoy Ebrahim, the claim was that he resided in Pakistan before the commencement of the Citizenship Act. Government officials contested such a view. In their reading of sections 3(b) and 3(d), the "claim for citizenship is conditional to intention of migration which can be proved by a certificate of domicile." Sir Ebrahim's father, it was said, had no intention of living in Pakistan. The "intent" to migrate for residing permanently in an area was a vague legal term that required interpretation.

In many cases, officials in the Ministries of Interior, Law, and Foreign Office interpreted the relevant provisions, generally calling for evaluating cases on their individual merits. But in some cases, the matter was taken to court. In *Roochomal Daryanomal v. Province of West Pakistan* (1959), Justice Constantine looked at the facts of the case in which the appellant, Roochomal Daryanomal, of the Sanghar district, had in 1948 gone to India on a temporary permit. After the permit's expiration, he visited the Pakistani High Commission in Delhi, which issued him a temporary permit and asked him to get his permanent permit from authorities in Pakistan. Daryanomal applied for a permanent permit in April 1949. His case remained pending for years. Five years later, in December 1953, he was told that he would be forcibly deported from Pakistan. He subsequently applied to the government of Sindh for citizenship. Looking at the facts of the case, Justice Constantine observed that the lower courts had misunderstood the word *migration*, and it fell on him "to consider whether on the evidence the appellant migrated to India with the intention of permanently residing there."[129] Because the appellant, like many Sindhi Hindus, had left the region because of safety concerns amid rampant communal violence, he did not intend to live there permanently. He overstayed his temporary permit by only two months and applied for a permit to return to Pakistan soon afterward. Justice Constantine was therefore convinced that the appellant was entitled, prima facie, to Pakistani citizenship under section 3(a).

Although the interpretation of migration with the intention of permanently residing in Pakistan could provide a defined legal basis for citizenship, the possession of a valid legal document like a passport did not in all cases carry the same weight. In the case of Currimbhoy, both father and son had been issued passports, but that did not suffice to prove an intention to permanently reside in Pakistan. The passport was merely a document issued to facilitate the applicant's travel to India and the United Kingdom.[130] This passport was different from the passport specific to travel only between India and Pakistan, yet it was considered insufficient as a legal document to claim citizenship. As a note from S. H. Firoz at the Ministry of Foreign Affairs explains, Pakistan could, as a member of the Commonwealth, issue passports to the citizens of any other country of the Commonwealth. In those Commonwealth countries where Pakistan did not have diplomatic representation, the External Affairs Department of that country could similarly issue a passport to a Pakistani citizen: "The issue of a Pakistani passport to any such person, therefore, does not necessarily mean that he is a Citizen of Pakistan."[131] A passport had been issued to Currimbhoy because he was a British subject and a citizen of a Commonwealth member state.

That possession of a passport did not equate to citizenship had become an essential part of Pakistani citizenship policy. Many persons of subcontinental origin in different parts of the world who thus qualified as former subjects of the British Empire and then Commonwealth subjects were registered by British consulates as Pakistani British subjects. In an earlier note dating to November 1951, S. H. Firoz from the Passport Office of the Ministry of Foreign Affairs had observed that passports were being issued to help these persons in emergency cases. But he cautioned against the practice, pointing out that some people from Hyderabad Deccan were given Pakistani passports even though they were foreigners.[132] In Firoz's view, British nationality laws were kept simple with the purpose of registering as many people as possible so that "in view of the international crisis, which crops up every now and then, desire to enroll as many British subjects as possible, so that if conscription is notified, they could raise a very large army immediately." But such a conspiratorial view was at variance with the actual position taken by the Commonwealth Office, which was, in fact, eager to rid itself of the liability of accommodating "potential" Indians and Pakistanis as British citizens.

NEW CITIZENS: THE CASE OF GAWADAR

In September 1958, the port city of Gawadar in Baluchistan became a territory of Pakistan after the government of Pakistan paid an amount equivalent to 1.5 million pounds to the Sultanate of Muscat.[133] The Baluch had served as traders, courtiers, and mercenaries in various trade circuits and different littoral states on the Indian Ocean, and even in far-off areas like Zanzibar.[134] Such connectivity had led to Omani influence on Gawadar's politics. Since the state of Qalat was outside the political domain of colonial India, Oman's informal control of Gawadar continued, and the territory did not automatically pass to Pakistan after the lapse of British suzerainty in India. In the 1950s, the Pakistani government entered into negotiations with the Sultanate of Oman to acquire control of Gawadar;

such control was formally agreed on in 1958, with compensation paid to the sultan.

Unlike other territories that had become part of Pakistan in 1947 and were covered under the Citizenship Law—whether provincial units of colonial India or princely states—the addition of a new territory meant the addition of new citizens. The law did have a provision to cover such an event. Under section 13 of the Citizenship Act, "if any territory becomes a part of Pakistan the [President] may, by order, specify the persons who shall be citizens of Pakistan by reason of their connection with that territory: and those person shall be citizens of Pakistan from such date and upon conditions, if any, as may be specified in the order."

On 28 November 1958, R. A. Mahamadi from the home division put up a summary stating that now that Gawadar had become part of Pakistan, the first step was to apply the Naturalization Act of 1926 and Pakistan Citizenship Act of 1951 to the area.[135] Qudratullah Shahab, a career bureaucrat and famous Urdu writer, had become a close adviser to General Ayub Khan after the latter had imposed martial law. Shahab's primary concern concerning Gawadar was that it was "reeking with Hindu businessmen who are nationals of India. Automatic conferment of Pakistani nationality on them will not change their loyalties. On the contrary, it will give them a good cover to retain their domination on the local business. They will enjoy all the legal immunities of Pakistani nationality while, in practice, they will always remain a strong fifth column both in business and otherwise."[136] Shahab's use of the term *national* is not in the legal sense of citizenship, as the Hindus of Gawadar did not have any such legal identification. It is instead used in an affective sense, whereby a Hindu was naturally an Indian; in this way, Hinduness was conjoined with Indianness. Shahab thus advised caution before issuing an "omnibus order of naturalization." He wanted Hindus to be flushed out before they could be given a chance to claim Pakistani citizenship.

Upon inquiry, it was found that 263 Hindus resided in Gawadar at the time it was ceded to Pakistan; 127 had since left, and the remaining 136 were contemplating migrating. Following Shahab's advice, the government decided "to hold the issue of the proposed notification in abeyance until such time the remaining Hindus also quit Gwadur for good." In this fashion, the note advised, Pakistan would not have to confer citizenship in a discriminatory manner by preferring Muslims and excluding Hindus. Such a step was likely to invite criticism from the Indian press. The best course of action was to wait a couple of weeks, "until we get rid of the undesirable elements without an effort of our own."[137]

The policy was reminiscent of the approach taken by the Indian government after its forceful annexation of the princely state of Junagadh, which had acceded to Pakistan. Following the occupation by India, many Muslim residents had fled to escape violence. Some Muslims of Junagadh had been living in Ceylon and Burma for decades to run their businesses. In their absence, their property was declared evacuee property. They had to make several pleas to the local administration and to ministerial officers in Delhi to emphasize their attachment to the land and their loyalty to the Indian nation-state.[138] The Muslims of Hyderabad Deccan faced a similar experience after its forceful annexation by the Indian military in September 1948.[139]

In the case of Hindus in Gawadar holding Indian passports (if there were any), the Ministry of Law mentioned in a note that once the citizenship order came into force, Indians or Indian Hindus would automatically lose their right to Pakistani citizenship by the operation of section 14(1) of the Citizenship Act. There was some legal confusion as to the deadline for renouncing other nationalities, but in the case of dual citizenship, the loss of Pakistani citizenship would happen automatically.

The potential of the selective conferment of citizenship to the residents of Gawadar on the basis of religious affiliation caused alarm among the Hindu community. The Indian parliament took up the issue, and the Indian High Commission in Pakistan sought permission to visit the area to look after Hindu residents' interests. The Ministry of States and Frontier Regions was strongly opposed to giving such permission. Hameeduddin Ahmed, contrary to the position taken by Shahab and his earlier anti-Hindu stance, took a bureaucratic view of the situation, given that it concerned the law. He considered all inhabitants of Gawadar, both Muslim and Hindu, Pakistani citizens after the territory's cessation—a textualist reading of the law. Yet at the same time, Ahmed expressed deep anxiety over what bonds of loyalty and commercial and political connections such

Hindus might want to sustain with India. According to him, there was a danger "that the Indian Officer sent from here will re-establish and espionage and smuggling base through the assistance of these Hindus. The likelihood of such an eventuality is not remote particularly because of the very strong position of Indian currency in the Persian Gulf."[140] This was yet another example of a disjuncture between Hindus' Pakistani citizenship and national belonging to Pakistan, which was imagined to be tied with India. Even though other non-Pakistani citizens, such as Ismailis with British passports, lived in Gawadar, the government's anxiety was only about Hindus and the possible impact their decision to stay there as citizens might have for Pakistan.

I would like to end this discussion of citizenship law by referring to a proposed amendment to the Constitution of 1956 that would have made citizenship part of a person's inalienable, fundamental rights. This amendment was proposed by several opposition leaders—not only Hindus but also Bengali Muslims—who were distrustful of the law and dissatisfied with its lack of protection. Abul Mansur Ahmad's amendment proposed adding the definition of a citizen to the section of the act that dealt with fundamental rights. His definition of the citizen was simple: confirming the citizenship of those who were already citizens "in the strength of the Constitution" to safeguard those who might acquire citizenship status after the promulgation of the Constitution.[141] Speaking from experience, Zahiruddin—who had been subjected to an externing order despite his Pakistani citizenship—supported the amendment. The fiery opposition leader and later founder of Bangladesh Sheikh Mujib-ur-Rehman also supported the amendment. His stated concern was that in the absence of a constitutionally guaranteed safeguard, anyone could tell him that "O Mr. Mujibur Rahman you are not a citizen of Pakistan and, therefore, you get out of Pakistan."[142] I. I. Chundrigar from the treasury bench referred to clause 222 of the Constitution Bill, which defined a Pakistani citizen as "a person who is a citizen of Pakistan according to the law relating to citizenship."[143] But the law of citizenship that it referred to—that is, the Citizenship Act 1951, was easily amendable, because it was not part of a constitutional provision. Despite the opposition's apprehensions and its demand for more effective safeguards, the motion was negatived.

The significance of this discussion lies in the insistence of key leaders to foreground the centrality of being a Pakistani citizen as the fountainhead of all rights based on equality and in an expressed eagerness to protect those rights and enforce them without discrimination along religious, ethnic, or linguistic lines. A failure to achieve consensus on this point was one reason for the country's trajectory of democratic breakdown that was to follow, a point I take up in more detail in the next chapter.

"There is good reason to write the political history of a community of citizens around the moments when it has been open or closed," writes Étienne Balibar.[144] Such moments include when legal definitions and debates about citizenship—and the related questions of who does and does not belong, and who is excluded from what and how—are debated and decided. Using the foundational moment of 1947 as a point of entry, I have investigated the extensive legal regime whereby the state formulated inclusionary and—for Balibar, equally important—exclusionary criteria of membership as "indicators of essential instability of citizenship."[145] Inclusion itself, says Balibar, can be a violent process. As we have seen in the case of India and Pakistan, the everyday violence of bureaucratic practices, securitized borders, and allegations of divided loyalties forced individuals and families to choose one side over the other. That is, to be included as a member of one nation-state only to be definitively excluded from that of the other.

The imperative for such a decision was driven by the state's anxiety and need to enforce closure and stabilize a legal process that was inherently vague, relying on violence for its coherence and enforcement. The postcolonial state set cutoffs and retrospectively created criteria to make its legal authority legible and to ascribe legitimacy to migratory movements that had already taken place or continued to take place outside the praxis of state and law. Even after the imposition of the Citizenship Law and its relatively organized control over border movements through permits, visas, and passports, it was mainly through bureaucratic note writing, musings on policy, and departmental squabbles over the interpretation of specific provisions that "the Pakistani citizen" continued to be constituted as a legal entity. The process lacked consistency and was primarily reactive, responding to individual requests that destabilized a set definitional or interpretative consensus over law and praxis.

There is thus neither a consistent timeline that might be followed from the enunciation of the Citizenship Act of April 1951 nor a cutoff after which formal closure took place. In principle, Pakistan as Noah's ark was packed to capacity by the late 1950s, and Muslims were asked to stay put in India. The intensity of migratory traffic declined as individuals, families, and communities on both sides of the border were forced to reconcile themselves to their local settings. Despite all bureaucratized controls and securitized borders, the two postcolonial states continued to wrestle with the problem of unregulated migrants. Even for Punjab, where an almost-complete exchange of population along religious lines had taken place, to think of a true closure would be erroneous. As Ilyas Chattha's recent work shows, Pakistan's eastern border at Punjab continued to be porous, as borderland communities found profitable smuggling ventures despite the artificial barriers imposed between such interconnected economies. The same could be said for migration patterns on the Sindh-Rajasthan-Gujarat border. The inpouring of Muslim refugees from North India to Pakistan via Khokhrapar continued well into the 1980s. It was no longer a deluge, but it undoubtedly was a consistent trickle. Through established family connections or intermarriages, newly arrived immigrants were able to acquire such documents as a passport and an identity card.

Other than institutional corruption and social connections that allowed the bypassing Pakistan's citizenship laws, the definition of Pakistani citizenship has continued to face legal challenges arising from further incidents of violence and displacement. The breakup of the country in 1971 necessitated an amendment in the act to allow for "stranded Pakistanis" to return home. At Partition in 1947, Urdu-speaking Biharis had migrated to East Pakistan. The establishment of Bangladesh, which emphasized ethnic and linguistic identity of Bengalis, resulted in the targeting of Urdu-speaking Biharis, who became "Pakistanis" living in Bangladesh. In one catastrophic moment of foundational violence, Biharis were rendered stateless. The state of which they were nationals had ceased to exist in their area. The newly established Bangladeshi government put Biharis in internment camps and insisted that the Pakistani government take them back. For three years, the government of Pakistan did not have diplomatic relations with Bangladesh. Later, when it did, the country's ethnic politics were so fragile that the state was reluctant to take the Bihari population back. Upon their return, Biharis inevitably preferred to stay in the urban cities of Sindh, where other Urdu-speaking migrants from North India were also living.

Through an amendment to its citizenship laws, the Pakistani state carried out the extraordinary feat of canceling the citizenship of its majority population, that is, the erstwhile East Pakistanis.[146] Those "West Pakistanis" who were stranded in refugee camps in Bangladesh became stateless because the Bangladeshi government did not recognize them as citizens and Pakistan refused to repatriate them all. The issue of Bihari statelessness as a humanitarian catastrophe continued for several decades, until the early 2000s, when the Bangladeshi Supreme Court granted them citizenship rights.

The massive influx of Afghan refugees has, since the 1980s, posed another challenge to Pakistan's legal citizenship regime. Even though a third generation of Afghan refugees today lives in Pakistan, those of Afghan descent are technically confined to camps and not allowed to open bank accounts, acquire identity documents other than those for refugees, or find work. The predominant middle-class Pakistani view of Afghan refugees is one of disdain, accusing them of bringing heroin and "Kalashnikov culture" into the country. During the height of the Taliban insurgency and in the waves of terrorist attacks in Pakistan that have hit the country since 2004, hysterical calls for the forceful eviction of Afghan refugees have been made, accusing them of subversive activities.

Bangladeshis and Rohingyas living in Karachi in large numbers pose another challenge as illegal refugees who lack documentation. As discussed earlier, the Pakistani prime minister initially floated the idea of granting citizenship to Afghans, Bengalis, and Rohingyas. The proposal received a massive rejection from Pakistan's embittered ethnic groups, who feel marginalized and fear changes in local demographics.

In short, no single legal answer exists to the question of who is a Pakistani. The definition of Pakistani has continued to evolve and is subject to political developments. The social and ideological factors that determine the question of being Pakistani—whereby a certain correspondence is achieved between the nation and the state, and the decline of the citizen as a universal category of equality and the rise of a privileging of the nation defined by the state along religious lines—further this debate. It is a contestation that takes place in a discursive milieu shaped by competing ideas of Islam, state, *qaum*, law, and belonging. In addition to exclusionary legal criteria, the debate involves setting the limits of what Balibar calls "internal exclusion," whereby legally entitled communities are excluded from being included in the larger national community.[147] By understanding the identity base of what constitutes the normative Pakistani national identity and how that identity was debated and continues to evolve, we can understand the nature of inclusionary violence against those who are Pakistani citizens, yet are not equated to having Pakistani national identity or seen as representing its majoritarian ethos.

In the introduction, I referred to Baba Guru Pakistani's return to Pakistan as a confounding example that I cannot wrap my head around. The reason Baba Guru and hundreds of other children like him were brought back to Pakistan was not because they were Pakistani citizens but because they were Muslims.[148] Yet even that ascription of Muslim identity was solely based on the idea that they were born to Muslim parents, even though, for all practical purposes, such children had been raised to become practicing Sikhs. One could say that because their families back home had become Pakistani citizens, they demanded that the state recover and repatriate their children stranded in India. But many of the children were abducted as infants, without any memory of their parents or knowledge of their whereabouts, and raised—often lovingly—by foster parents who were Sikhs or Hindus.[149] Their biological parents were not known. No official record of their whereabouts or complaints about their disappearance or abduction had been registered. On their return, these children were raised in shelter homes and orphanages. In their case, it was clear that they had not intended to migrate, nor were their parents alive or present to press for their return. What obligated the state of Pakistan state to retrieve them was simply that they were known in the village neighborhood as born Muslims.

Furthermore, from the perspective of the two states, abduction was less of a legal infringement and more of a moral outrage, as women embodied national honor and children held the key to the nation-state's future. This is why the state did not prosecute the abductors; it simply forced them to give up the abductees in their possession. The same rule applied to foster parents. What is also important to deduct is that no matter how tightly the law was scripted, it could not enforce the closure that the postcolonial state had aspired to, nor could it cover all the bases. Eventually, through a call to a supralegal basis in the name of the nation, the two postcolonial states conducted a massive, joint operation of the recovery and repatriation of abducted women and children. As the comprehensive lists prepared by the two states show, they were not looking for Indian and Pakistani citizens; they were tracing Hindu and Sikh women and children in Pakistan and Muslim women and children in India. There is much more to the notion of belonging, and to national imagination, that supersedes the law. It is thus important to historicize transitions from the concepts of citizen to that of the nation or *qaum*, and from the legal to the metaphorical, exploring their mutually dependent yet problematic relationships. The remainder of this book focuses on this history and its politics.

TWO

QUILTING ISLAM
Pakistan as an Islamic Republic

IN HIS LECTURES FOCUSING on democracy, sovereignty, and citizenship in the age of populism, Partha Chatterjee refers to the formation of the state in its colonial and postcolonial iterations. Instead of giving a historical overview of the development of state structures, which he and theorists like Sudipta Kaviraj have covered in their previous works, Chatterjee focuses on the discursive basis of the nation-state. In nationalist histories he locates the historical possibility of state formation and the state's extensive sovereign jurisdiction over much of India during the British Raj and its attendant structures of administrative, bureaucratic, and legal apparatuses. Concomitant to this is Chatterjee's idea of the people-nation, "discursively formed through a much more fragmented, disparate, and contentious field of history writing" from the late nineteenth century onward, touching on such diverse themes as caste, social reform, and regional histories.[1] Drawing a distinction between the centralized regime of power inherited by the postcolonial nation-state and the discursive practices that constitute the people-nation, Chatterjee's theorization borrows from Gramsci's idea of the integral state, in which, in Chatterjee's terms, "the ruling bourgeoisie exercises hegemony by using the powers of the state to carry out a guiding or disciplining function over civil society without collapsing the distinction between the two domains."[2] This approach helps emphasize the pedagogical role of the postcolonial state as deploying dispersed, governmental techniques of power.

What results from this formulation of postcolonial state and its forms of power is a lack of both the essentialization of ideological state apparatuses and of the idea of a center as a fixed locus, allowing for a conceptual borrowing from Ernesto Laclau's concept of discourse as a "purely differential ensemble."[3] For Laclau, identities do not preexist the relational complex but are constituted by it. In a Saussurean sense, language has no positive terms, and there are only differential relations to something else: "whatever centrality an element acquires, it has to be explained by the play of difference as such."[4] The only possibility for conceptually grasping such a totality of differentials is to differentiate the totality from something other than itself—something that is not another difference or a neutral element, but "an excluded one[,] something that the totality expels from itself in order to constitute itself."[5] All other differences are equivalent to one another in their common rejection of the excluded entity. In such a manner, all identities, argues Laclau, are "constructed within this tension between the differential and the equivalential logics."[6] Given the insurmountable logic of difference and tensions of equivalence, a hegemonic identity is what Laclau calls an impossible object—that is, an emptiness, a failed totality, a horizon and not a ground. Through what Laclau calls the process of condensation, a privileged signifier has to perform the function of signification, which is then defined as a synecdoche, a figural representation of totality as a class, nation, people, or in our case, the Muslim.

I draw on this theoretical framework to explain the condensation of popular identity in Pakistan around the signifier of Islam, which, in its abortive attempt to achieve fullness or closure, produces the excluded figure, first that of "the Hindu" and later of Ahmadis: the former to foreclose the discourse on citizenship and contours of the new state, and the latter to delimit the boundaries of people-nation.[7] This also explains the catachrestic nature of Islam as an empty signifier (or also as a floating signifier, as I show later) in Pakistan, where it can be invoked for a range of acts, objects, and issues, and yet remain an elusive, undefined, and ambiguous entity. This catachrestical nature serves as a precondition for Islam's functioning as the name given to a totalizing project that is both impossible and necessary.

FRAMING THE REPUBLIC AND ITS CONSTITUTION

In many works on the history of Pakistan, the focus has been on tracing the ideological indoctrination of the state education system, the Islamization of laws, and various other projects that the state undertook to superimpose an Islam-based identity with an overriding power to curtail any assertion of regional, ethnic, or linguistic identities. In this chapter, I extend this debate, supplementing the works of scholars such as G. W. Choudhary, M. Rafique Afzal, and Kausar Parveen.[8] I do so by exploring the debate on the naming of the republic to enter into an interrelated set of debates on and contestations of what it meant to be Islamic in the immediate aftermath of Pakistan's independence, given the political developments and constitutional debates that followed.

In this chapter, I primarily draw on the debates of the Constituent Assembly of Pakistan, which are a copious source of information about the early years of Pakistan's history and politics. Given the voluminous nature of the record, which runs into the thousands of pages—not counting similar records for the provincial units of Punjab, Sindh, North West Frontier Province (NWFP), and Bengal—I focus on a selected reading of these documents. These debates covered a wide variety of issues, such as state ideology and the ideas of a multiethnic federation, and thus offer a robust critique of governmental policies and engagement with prevalent discourse on democracy and secularism.

Like the Indian Constituent Assembly, the Pakistani variant comprised mainly the landed elite and high-caste men. Unlike India, no direct elections were held in Pakistan to replace the pre-1947 assembly. The first Constituent Assembly comprised members elected during the 1945–1946 elections.[9] Because many of its non-Muslim members—especially those from West Pakistan—had migrated to India, the assembly was reduced to sixty-nine members. Some new members were added to accommodate Baluchistan, the princely states and tribal areas that had become part of the new state. The Muslim League enjoyed an overwhelming majority, with fifty-nine members, followed by the Congress Party, with predominantly Hindu members elected from East Bengal.

Despite its narrow basis for electoral legitimacy and its elitist composition, the first Constituent Assembly had a diverse ethnic and religious membership. Most important, several Hindu members elected from East Bengal had stayed back in Pakistan—unlike in Punjab, where not a single Hindu or Sikh member remained. Hindu assembly members were vocal critics of attempts to give an overtly Islamic bent to the constitution and state institutions. From West Pakistan, only erstwhile "communists" like Mian Iftikharuddin offered a spirited defense of the non-Muslim minority in attempts to establish a centralized state structure. When elections were held in Bengal in 1954, the ruling Muslim League was routed and replaced by an overwhelming majority of members drawn from the United Front, an agglomerate of several Bengali political parties such as the Awami Muslim League, the Krishak Praja Party, and the Ganatantri Dal, that was led by popular leaders like A. K. Fazlul Haq, Husain Shahid Suhrawardy, and Maulana Bhashani. They espoused a collective, twenty-one-point agenda seeking constitutional autonomy and other demands, such as the adoption of Bengali as a national language, the nationalization of the jute trade, the building of a memorial to honor the martyrs of the Bengali-language movement, the release of political prisoners, and the repeal of repressive public safety acts.[10] Although the coalition fell apart quickly after the elections, the entry of fiery Awami League leaders like Sheikh Mujib-ur-Rehman ensured a more powerful encounter and exchange between the government and the opposition.

When Governor-General Ghulam Muhammad dissolved the first Constituent Assembly in 1954—an act that was initially dubbed unconstitutional by the Sindh High Court, only to be overturned by the Federal Court in the name of doctrine of necessity[11]—a new assembly was constituted on the basis of proportional representation from the provincial assemblies, which had gone through popular elections after 1950. The first-ever national-level elections with adult franchise took place in 1970, twenty-three years after the country's independence and after two periods of marital law, several prime ministers, and the abrogation of two constitutions.

The Constitutional Convention, as ordered by the Federal Court in a 1954 verdict, was convened in May 1955. It had eighty members: forty from East Pakistan, with the remaining seats allotted to provincial units from West Pakistan, princely states, tribal areas, Karachi, and Baluchistan. Although the Muslim League had an absolute majority in the first Constituent Assembly, its numbers in the new assembly had considerably declined—primarily because of the party's defeat in the 1954 East Bengal provincial elections.

Even though the assembly was indirectly elected, Choudhury describes it as "more representative in character," as the provincial assemblies that had served as an electoral college for the new assembly had been elected on the basis of adult franchise.[12] Some old stalwarts like Khawaja Nazim-ud-Din and Sardar Abdul Rab Nishtar, and academics like Dr. Ishtiaq Hussain Qureshi and Mehmud Husain, were missing. But the presence of leaders like Husain Shahid Suhrawardy, A. K. Fazlul Haq, Mian Iftikharuddin, and Sheikh Mujib-ur-Rehman gave the assembly considerable strength. It made it vocal in opposition to various measures proposed by the government.

With twenty-five members, the Muslim League remained the single-largest party in the new assembly, followed by the United Front and Awami League, with sixteen and twelve members, respectively. Despite such odds, the government could push through such controversial acts as the reconstituting of multiple federating units of West Pakistan as One Unit in 1955. Instead of going into the details of the changing ministries, the dissolution of the assembly, court cases, and other such events that occurred during the 1950s, I focus here on the content of assembly debates on a range of issues—and especially on records from 1956, when the Constitution Bill was finally debated for approval. This is not to suggest that such ministerial changes were incidental to overall political developments. Following Prathama Banerjee's theoretical interventions, I do not posit a distinction between "the political" as the philosophical content of political theory and the routinization of "politics" in the form of assemblies, ministries, and elections.[13] The irreducibility of the two helps me read the Constituent Assembly debates as a political act of opposition and subversion, and most important, enables me to theorize ideas of state, sovereignty, democracy, federation, and equality in Pakistan's postcolonial moment.

Of the constitutional debates, the Objectives Resolution of March 1949 has received considerable attention.[14] The resolution was meant to serve as a blueprint for the country's future constitution and for its destiny as an Islamic state. While presenting the resolution, Pakistani prime minister Liaqat Ali Khan described it as the fulfillment of the Pakistan independence movement, as it was envisaged to set up a state where Muslims could live their lives per their religious beliefs. This state was also meant as a veritable laboratory of Islam that could provide solutions for the modern world, which was plagued by excesses of materialism and the destruction those excesses have caused.[15] By doing so, Khan surmised, the Pakistani state was fulfilling the Islamic injunction to follow its religious commandments in all aspects of life. In particular, Khan's focus was on the disjunction between the separate realms of public and private, of religion and state. From his lengthy speech, it is clear that by projecting religion back onto the state, he was claiming to undo the Machiavellian notion of statecraft and bringing a much-needed ethical imperative to statecraft. Such a view of pious politics was in his vision of Islam not only as a complete code of life but also as a divine truism whose validity had become apparent because of the wanton destruction and violence the world had seen in the recent past. In other words, his conception rendered Islam an ethical critique of Western liberalism and of its procedural language of interests.

In its inaugural session of 12 August 1947, the Constituent Assembly also created committees to draft reports on fundamental rights of citizens, matters relating to minorities, franchise, and other issues related to the making of a new federal structure. These committees' interim reports were released in 1950 and their final reports in subsequent years. Therefore, to understand the process of constitution making in Pakistan, it is important to take note of the following chronology: the passage of the Objectives Resolution in March 1949; the publication of interim reports of the Basic Principles Committee (BPC) and Committees on Minorities and Fundamental Rights in 1950; the release of BPC's final report in 1952; the introduction of so-called Muhammad Ali formula in October 1953, which helped achieve agreement on the representative structure of the federal legislature; and the adoption of the BPC by the assembly in September 1954, after extensive debate.

The assembly was close to adopting the Constitution Bill when Governor-General Ghulam Muhammad, reacting to the clipping of his viceregal powers, dissolved the Constituent Assembly in October 1954. After a long, drawn-out constitutional battle, the eventual exit of the governor-general, and the convening of a new constitutional convention based on proportionate representation from the provincial assemblies, the Constitutional Bill was finally presented for approval on 8 January 1956. After lengthy discussions, it was eventually adopted on 29 February 1956, even though vocal opposition members staged a walkout and did not vote for its approval.[16]

MULLAHS' ISLAMIC STATE AND MODERNISTS' ISLAMIC PRINCIPLES

What is more important than a chronological account of the various ministerial changes in Pakistan during the 1950s is analysis of the contestation of an ongoing ideological debate of what constitutes an Islamic state in the modern period and the measures required to bring it into existence. The Objectives Resolution had laid down the basis for setting an Islamic state on what it referred to as Islamic principles of democracy and egalitarian values. Such a pronouncement was in line with the worldview of Muslim modernists who dominated the Muslim League, including Prime Minister Liaqat Ali Khan. Islamic modernists like him believed in the vitality of scriptural teachings and their relevance, and in the possibility of successfully adopting them in contemporary settings through a creative process of textual reinterpretation. It would be erroneous to assume that the Objectives Resolution was simply political gimmickry. Leading members of the Muslim League widely shared their ideas about Islam as a democratic and rational force. This is clear from the writings and speeches of Muslim League leaders during the Constituent Assembly debates, some of which I refer to later in this chapter.

What justifies the term *modernists*, and what differentiates the proponents of these ideas from the ulema whom they pejoratively dismissed as "mullahs," is the methodology by which each group approached the "reservoir of data" from a vast corpus of Islamic texts—as Nelly Lahoud explains—to "pick and choose aspects relevant to contemporary concerns."[17]

While one group's level of exposure to Western education, knowledge of English, and class background also distinguishes it from the other, the central characteristics of the modernist are his methodology toward Islam and deductive tapping of the Islamic reservoir. For the ulema, *modernist* is a shorthand for a "brown sahib," "a product of the British colonial rule and its English education system, who is contemptuous of the teachings of Islam, incompatible as they are with the Western lifestyle he has adopted."[18] The modernists drew on the centuries-old trope of the mullah as regressive and puritan to describe the ulema as lacking in Islam's "true spirit," which, in their estimate, was rational, modern, progressive, and egalitarian.

I want to expand on this distinction—and especially on the methodological differences at hand—by focusing on the Board of Ta'limat-i-Islamiyyah (Board for Islamic Teachings) created by the government following the Objectives Resolution. Comprising prominent scholars who were mostly migrants from India, the government appointed the board to advise on drafting an Islamic constitution. Even though not all the board's suggestions for an Islamic Pakistan were accepted, the government made several concessions to accommodate the ulema, as there was a growing public perception fueled by official rhetoric about the religious nature of Pakistan's state and polity.

I draw on the board's archives, as preserved in the Zafar Ahmad Ansari collection, which, to the best of my knowledge, has not yet been explored in detail. Focusing on the ulema's musings about the Islamic state and the incommunicability of their idiom with the modernist language of the state, I analyze the overall project of Islam as a tool for state formation in Pakistan and the inevitable question of religious authority that comes with that project.

The board was not the first institution created by a Pakistani government to advise on matters relating to the setting up of an Islamic state. A year before its establishment, the government of West Punjab had established the Islamic Reconstruction Department (IRD). With a name that took inspiration from Iqbal's monograph *Reconstruction of Religious Thought in Islam*, a philosophical revisioning of the Islamic scholastic tradition, the department was headed by Muhammad Asad, a Jewish convert to Islam and renowned scholar. *Imroz*, a left-leaning Urdu newspaper in Lahore, was skeptical of the government plan. Although the paper supported the creation of an Islamic academy, it wanted to know the details of the IRD's structure. *Imroz* alleged that the British also used to support such initiatives, but with the intention of furthering their own vested interest in creating a class of loyal Muslims and suppressing their passion for freedom. If the academy was closely tied to the government, warned the newspaper, the government might try to use the IRD for its own purposes and, in the name of Islam, impose dictates that had nothing to do with Islam.[19] The paper thus called on the government to make the academy completely autonomous. *Imroz* then took a similar, critical stance against the Board of Ta'limat-i-Islamiyyah, especially after the board's report became public.

Writing in another paper, the Indian Constituent Assembly member Raghib Ahsan described the creation of the IRD as a step toward fulfilling the dreams of great Muslim scholars such as Shah Wali Ullah, Iqbal, and Jamal-ud-Din Afghani, an attempt to rewrite the history of Islam, which had, since the Battle of Karbala, fallen prey to Arab imperialism and Byzantine heathenism.[20] While appreciating the scholarly credentials of Muhammad Asad, Ahsan pointed out that Asad was essentially a European with little knowledge of the realities and problems of Muslim life in Pakistan and India. Ahsan accused Asad of holding views that were opposed to general Islamic principles, as unanimously accepted by all schools of Islamic thought. He recommended the creation of a *majlis*, or a council of eminent Muslim scholars, such as Shabbir Ahmad Usmani, Sulaiman Nadavi, Mir Ibrahim Sialkoti, Maulana Azad Subhani, Abdul Majid Daryabadi, Dr. Hamidullah, and Manazir Ahsan Gilani. Although there was no reason for the Pakistani government to listen to Ahsan's proposal, let alone to act on it, the final membership of the Board of Ta'limat-i-Islamiyyah did indeed include some of these names, as well as other ulema who were closely related to or associated with them, sharing their worldview on Islamic thought. Asad's IRD, however, ceased to function because of a lack of support from the successive Punjab government.

Commissioned in 1949 by the Constituent Assembly of Pakistan, the Board of Ta'limat-i-Islamiyyah was initially comprised of Sayyid Suleman Nadawi, Mufti Muhammad Shafi, Syed Jafar Husain Mujtahid, and Dr.

Hamidullah. The scholars were paid a generous monthly salary of one thousand rupees, with additional travel expenses covered. Zafar Ahmad Ansari served as the *mu'tamad*, or secretary, of the board. His duties included translating documents and maintaining correspondence with the government, legislators, and ulema. His collection of papers serves as an excellent source of information about the workings of the board and its insights and disagreements with the government.

To understand the nature of the ulema's insights into the Islamic state, one needs to understand their methodology of arriving at the idea of an Islamic state. Following Gadamer's theoretical framework, we can describe the ulema's discussions, draft constitutions, and critiques of government proposals as a hermeneutic reading of classical texts of jurisprudence, using them as an answer to the question of what an Islamic state is in the modern period, and how it might be constituted and modeled for the rest of the world. We can then attempt to understand the ulema's interpretation of the normative political order of Islam as part of a discursive tradition that has also undergone the transformative impact of colonialism and modernity.

It is, of course, impossible to arrive at a singular notion of the state or Islamic political thought; their histories span centuries, cover multiple empires, and are witness to various contestations, schisms, and violent confrontations. But what is important is to ascertain the historical horizon in which the ulema situated their ideas about state and political thought. Without access to the source material used by the ulema in their deliberations and the references to classical works they made in their reports, we can arrive at their normative model only through existing academic literature on the topic, checking it against the ulema's declaratory statements.

As Emad El-Din Shahin sums up, the classical constitutional theory of government in Sunni Islam was primarily focused on six principles: the establishment of authority as a religious and rational necessity; the election of the head of state by the influential elite serving as electors; the combining of religious and political authority in the leader; the status of the leader as a successor to the Prophet; the extension of his power over all Muslim territories; and the obligation to obey him as long he performs his duty under Islam.[21] To follow up with Patricia Crone's astute observation, we can conclude that the purpose of an Islamic state was first and foremost to establish and maintain a moral order.[22] Such a conceptualization differed from the modern Western state, which sought violent hegemony for internal order organized against the external defense. At least in its Sunni iteration, the idea of an Islamic state emphasized the importance of holding on to a central authority in obedience, despite its possible excesses, failures, and oppression.

But this does not mean that classical scholars did not recognize the distinction between a regressed state authority and the idealized state, in which the community was guided by its allegiance to the Prophet and later by the Rightly Guided Caliphs—only to be followed by a monarchical government that lacked legitimacy. Whether imam or king, that leader was nevertheless to head the Muslim community, as without him, "there was no saving vehicle in which to travel along with the legal highways revealed by God. . . . All the social and political arrangements of the Muslims would cease to be distinguishable . . . from those of infidels. The abode of Islam would merge with that of unbelief."[23] In the absence of a righteous imam, the ulema provided an effective check, or erected an idealized mode of practice, for dealing with the worldly power of the King in practice, administering Islamic law for the maintenance of a Muslim community. While Islamic teachings, and the order sustaining them, pervaded and covered the entire public realm, that does not mean that there was a lack of understanding of the distinction between *din* and *dunya*, or power of the government and that of the ulema.[24]

Brilliantly summing up the Islamic structure of power, its normative ideal, and changes to it over the centuries, Crone describes the domains of religion, state, and society as three circles that were concentric during the Prophet's time.[25] In subsequent periods, the circles gradually come apart, and the ulema yearn for that idealized past. We find this ambitious vision in the deliberations of the Board of Ta'limat-i-Islamiyyah and its recommendations. The board did not seek to restore medieval forms of political authority or to rectify the yawning gap that existed between the three circles after the decline of Muslim political power, the increasing secularization of public life, and an increased reliance on human-made law. Instead, their goal was the reactualization of the perceived golden age of the Prophet's time and his successors, with the goal of combining the ruler's political authority and moral righteousness for a harmonious social existence based on Shariat. The pursuit of this goal required undoing the impact of the colonial interruption to this history, which the ulema identified as a significant factor for the Muslim community's moral decline.

In doing so, the ulema, in their own way, shared the modernist vision of Pakistan as a project that could serve as a model for the rest of the world to emulate. To realize this ideal, they drew on classical texts—but not as subjective readers who see the text as an external object to which to apply a rational mode of interpretive techniques. To borrow from Gadamer, the process of "encounter with the tradition that takes place within historical consciousness" involves a tension between the text and the present. "The hermeneutic task consists in not covering up this tension by attempting a naïve assimilation of the two," writes Gadamer, "but in consciously bringing it out."[26] In this way, the horizons are distinct, but they cannot be formed without each other. In transposing themselves to the horizon from which the traditionary text speaks, the ulema were cognizant of the historical otherness of their present, and of the horizon of the past they emanated from being in the world. With their horizon superimposed on a continuing tradition, there emerges the possibility of a recombining with what it has foregrounded "to become one with itself again in the unity of the historical horizon that it thus acquires"—a process that Gadamer describes as historically effected consciousness.[27] The historical gap between past and present is thus overcome. Gadamer describes this temporal distance as a productive condition for enabling understanding that "overcomes the alienation of meaning that the text has undergone."[28] This requires, according to Gadamer, rising above what one is conscious of and regaining "the concepts of a historical past in such a way that they also include our own."[29] The ulema's writings, comments, critiques, and discussions about the Islamic state were thus not merely attempts to reconstitute medieval forms of political authority; instead, we must read them in an interpretive manner as a productive engagement with the past and the present aimed to arrive at a new horizon of Islamic political thought.

The ulema's deliberations in April 1950 that led to their first report, which was submitted to the BPC in June, can be analyzed by two main points.

First, the ulema were convinced that Pakistan was an ideological, not a national, state. In their understanding of the Objectives Resolution, Pakistan was to be an Islamic state where "the Divine Order, as contained in the Holy Quran and Sunna, reigns supreme and the entire Government business in its various spheres is conducted with a view to executing the will of Allah as laid down in Shariat." It naturally followed that only those who believe in the state's fundamental basis and "conform to the minimum standard of conduct necessary to ensure sincere execution of the code promulgated under that particular ideology" should have power in it.[30] In this regard, they cited the example of the Soviet Union, where a person disagreeing with the Soviet ideology of communism could not be expected to occupy a key post. Although the modernists shared the idea of Pakistan as an ideological state, the ulema added the proviso for the head of that ideological state to be the best exemplar of that ideology; thus, making space for themselves to serve in positions of political and moral authority.

Second, the ulema also shared the euphoric spirit of the time, imagining new possibilities in the exigencies of the postcolonial moment. Instead of drafting a constitution modeled on the British parliamentary tradition or copying the Indian variant, the ulema urged the government to take an alternative course: borrowing from Islamic traditions rather than emulating the Western democratic model. Here, again, the ulema shared the broader goal of making Pakistan a laboratory of Islam, but they worked with a different formula to develop a parallel model of the new Islamic state.

In outlining the proposed Islamic state, the ulema focused on the figure of the head of state. The precise form of government and the nature of the distribution of power were, at best, issues of secondary importance. In the draft proposal for an Islamic constitution for Pakistan, the ulema started with the office of the head of state and the method for his election. The head of state was to be a Muslim man of sound mental and physical health over the age of puberty, and with mental maturity, erudition and learning, a virtuous character, wisdom, sagacity, and composure. The ulema explained "erudition and learning" as having sufficient knowledge of Shariat, the limits prescribed by Allah, and an understanding of Islamic laws based on the Quran and hadith. The minimum age was set at forty, as this was when the Prophet Muhammad achieved prophethood; it was thus regarded as the ideal age of combined physical and mental maturity.[31]

There were several instances in which the ulema read the classical juristic tradition to make amends and arrive at the new horizon of a historically constituted interpretation. To begin with, they were reluctant to set a limit on the tenure of the head of state. Although it was not a religious commandment per se, and they admitted a reasonable limit could be prescribed, "to keep semblance with the precedents and practices of early Islam." The board nevertheless recommended a procedure that allowed for lifetime tenure, with removal only theoretically possible. According to this provision, the constitution was not to limit the terms of the head of state. After each terminal election, the legislature could in its inaugural session decide to remove the head of state by majority vote.[32] The head of state could also step down himself as a matter of convention or unwritten law. To set conditions for removing the head of state, the ulema borrowed from classical texts. Requirements for doing so included apostasy, captivity by an enemy country, physical disability such as blindness, treason, and open indulgence in "dissoluteness and profligacy against Islam and disregard of the provisions of Shariat."[33] To ascertain the head of state's character around his election or removal, it was deemed necessary to have the Federal Committee of Experts on Shariat, who would serve as ex officio members of the Upper House.

The ulema's concept of the Islamic state and the rationale for establishing it remained tied to the idea of setting a moral order based on Shariat. Because it was incumbent on Muslims to act as the vicegerents of Allah and work for the glory of Islam, wrote the ulema, it was the duty of the head of state to work to implement the Islamic way of life in its fullness and to follow the code of *amr bi'l ma'ruf wa nahi an'al munkir* (commanding right and forbidding wrong), to make provisions for the carriage of justice, and to preserve human dignity and spread Islamic learning.[34] Maintaining domestic peace and protection from external threats was mentioned later in the ulema's note.

The centrality of the dictum of *amr bi'l ma'ruf* was in line with classical Islamic thought, which the ulema wanted to be enforced as the cornerstone of an Islamic polity. As Patricia Crone argues, this principle was a collective duty performed by the ruler through the institution of *muhtasib* (censor and market inspector).[35] *Muhtasib* served the task of roaming the streets to ensure that people adhered to Islamic norms, such as abstaining from public consumption during Ramadan and drunkenness, and observing Friday prayers. What people did in their private affairs was left untouched. There is voluminous literature, commentary, and discussion on the role of individuals in enforcing the virtues and eradication of evil.[36] The establishment of an Islamic state could be described as necessary to maintaining the normative moral order so as to ensure a preservation of the Islamic way of life. The responsibility for that moral order did also devolve to individual men. Given that ulema identified the modern age as infested with obscenities—indeed, they demanded provisions in the law for eradicating such obscenities—it is no wonder that they reaffirmed that the Islamic state was predicated on the principle of *amr bi'l ma'ruf*.

To perform the multifarious tasks required by an Islamic state, Muslims were to elect "the wisest and most God-fearing person from amongst themselves as their head to discharge these duties and responsibilities on their behalf and in consultation with pious and sagacious members of the Millat enjoying their confidence."[37] A single advisory council was to help the ruler perform his extensive legislative, executive, judicial, and propagative powers, duties, and functions. Thus, the board envisaged a presidential form of government for Pakistan, in which the advisory council served ministerial functions. This power structure is further clarified in the mitigated role of the legislature as proposed by the ulema. According to the board, such Islamic injunctions had been expressly mentioned in the Quran and Sunnah or were determined by consensus by those well versed in these teachings. Only for matters explicitly covered in Quran and Sunnah could the head of state pass laws, and only after consulting the representatives of the *millat* (Muslim nation) that constituted the legislative council.[38] Here, too, the proposed constitution gave bulk of the power to the head of the state and his advisory board, both of whom were to be selected primarily for their knowledge of religious teachings, to serve their roles effectively. While the draft does discuss committee procedures for giving assent to legislative bills and even the possibility of a bicameral legislature, these are seemingly issues of secondary importance. The primary purpose of the ulema was to emphasize the extensive powers of a virtuous head of state who was elected for life and exercised his authority with the help of learned scholars.

Another note with the same title but a different date further elaborates the ideas in the document. Here the board justified the centrality of power under the president, the limited role of the legislature, and the extensive reliance on the advisory board for the execution of powers. To this purpose, the board highlighted the difference between an Islamic and a democratic state. Unlike a democratic state, which is geared toward implementing the people's will, wrote the ulema, the purpose of the Islamic state is to execute Allah's commandments. The scope of legislation was thus limited. Nevertheless, in case of a disagreement, the matter should be referred to "men of wisdom and character who have deep insight into, and a comprehensive knowledge of Islam in its various aspects and are conversant with the necessary requirements of the age."[39] Another possible area of legislation was to address current issues for which the Shariat might lack explicit guidance. Here, too, "maximum conformity with the nature and spirit of Islam" was to be ensured. The board clearly said that the legislature could not hold any additional powers. Even though there was no explicit prohibition against the delegation of such powers as approving the budget and ratifying treaties to the legislature, the ulema disliked it because they thought it imitated either British parliamentary traditions or the provisions of the Indian constitution. They invited the members of different committees set up by the Constituent Assembly to realize the importance to "exonerate ourselves from the charges of servile imitation betraying the mental bankruptcy of the Millat."[40] To this purpose, the board recommended what it considered an acceptable reading of Islamic tradition: to delegate additional supervisory roles to the legislature.

This larger representative body was to be called the *majlis ahl al-hal wa'l 'aqd*, thus transforming the learned and noble elite of traditionary political theory into elected assembly members with specified qualifying criteria. The ulema proposed various translations for this body, such as the General House, the House of Representatives, and the House of the People.[41] In translating the term, the ulema were not looking for a literal transposition but attempting a conceptual equivalence. This act is indicative of their cognition of the historical distance that they sought to creatively overcome.

Given the requirement that this house be representative and popularly elected, the ulema were further confronted with the possibility of having to accommodate women and non-Muslims in this institution. The board was more sympathetic to the representation of non-Muslims than of women. Even though the juristic tradition did not allow for the inclusion of non-Muslims in a consultative body of an Islamic state, "given the exigencies of time and other factors," the ulema allowed for their inclusion provided that it did not affect in any manner the implementation of Islamic injunctions.[42] Non-Muslim members were allowed to represent their community interests and give opinions about the country's general well-being.

As to women, the ulema adopted an uncompromising, hard stance against their role in public affairs. In the ulema's understanding, the "innate capabilities, natural tendencies and special characteristics of women-folk" made women perfect for their prescribed role in establishing an Islamic social order:

> The pivot of the activities of women is her home and her real function is to manage the domestic affairs efficiently, bring up children with such physical, menatl [mental] and spiritual training that they should fear none but Allah and obey none but Allah and come forward equipped with best moral virtues, as promoters of human welfare and prosperity. They are responsible for creating such atmosphere within the four walls of the house as can help men perform their social functions prescribed by Islam, with happiness and traqquillity [tranquility] of mind. No burden of any other social duty has been placed on the shoulders of women so that their main functions may not be hampered and the collective progress of man kind may not thereby be allowed eventually to suffer.[43]

Yet the board was mindful of requirements of the modern age, and reluctantly allowed for the inclusion of women, provided they were at least fifty years of age and observant of purdah as defined by Shariat. The "anti-women" posturing of the ulema, especially after the report's contents became public, led to criticism. *Imroz*, published a cartoon depicting a furious, bearded man—the caricature of a mullah—carrying a sword and chasing women with a menacing look.

The ulema's proposed outline of the Islamic state and the provisions of that state and the Basic Principles Committee report for the overall federal structure received a backlash at the deliberations held in Nathiagali in June 1950 to discuss constitutional committee reports. The opposition parties from East Pakistan rejected the first BPC report because it did not recognize the numerical majority of the Bengali population in distributing seats. The ulema objected to the report because it lacked Islamic content. At the same time, the committees working on, and reviewing proposals for, various aspects of the constitution either rejected or asked for an explanation for most of the ulema's recommended provisions for an Islamic constitution. For instance, the committee asked for the rationale behind having the head of the state lead congregational prayers and the relevance of that clause to constitution making. For the ulema, the explanation was straightforward. They responded that one could not expect a capitalist whose beliefs and practices were in stark contrast to the communist ideology to run a communist state.[44] Eventually, when the BPC agreed on the requirement that the head of the state be Muslim, the treasury benches used the same explanation—ideological character of the state—to justify the provision. But with their language of liberal constitutionalism, the treasury benches differed from the ulema in their interpretation of the symbolism of an Islamic head of state and of the nomenclature of the "Islamic republic."

For the ulema, the symbolism extended to include the performance of some religious obligations, such as leading Friday prayers and Eid prayers, and collecting zakat. Another explanation provided by the ulema, which was then later used to justify the provision in assembly debates, was to refer to European countries in which the head of the state also had a religious affiliation, such as the United Kingdom, Norway, Denmark, Sweden, Spain, and Belgium. The ulema also pointed out that, given the legitimate desire of Pakistanis to have a Muslim ruler, it was natural that the head of the state would always be Muslim. The ulema wrote that, unlike countries that ostensibly allowed anyone to be elected as head of state but in which that never happened in practice, Islam does not adopt such a hypocritical approach.[45] Tied with this religious affiliation was the provision that the head of the state be a man, since a woman could not perform some of the duties highlighted by the ulema, such as leading prayers.

Thus, it was not only the BPC members who objected to the ulema—the ulema also had reservations against the BPC and what they saw as its inability to think beyond the frames of Western constitutional theory. The ulema's critique was sharpest on the interim report released in 1950 that dealt with the fundamental rights of citizens and matters related to minorities. The interim report called for equal rights and opportunities for citizens of all religious backgrounds, regardless of caste, creed, and gender. In a strongly worded note, the ulema wrote:

> The report throughout betrays a deplorable lack of Islamic ideology and Islamic vision and shows that the Constitution of Bharat, the Government of India Act, and a few outdated constitutional principles borrowed from the Western countries is all that seems to have provided the ideological basis in the framing of this report. If the contents of the report are to be incorporated in the very constitution of about which our leaders have vociferously been declaring that Pakistan is going to demonstrate before the world an altogether new order of life for this age and to make a unique experiment based on the principles of Islam, then this report is enough to repudiate and belie all such claims. Leaving aside the question of providing for the positive requirements of Islam in this behalf even negatively speaking it cannot be said that the contents of the report are not opposed to the Islamic principles.[46]

The ulema also targeted specific aspects of the report, such as the possible conscription of non-Muslims in the military. In other instances, they indirectly objected to its provisions on gender equality by proposing new provisions. For example, the note recommends declaring family as the natural unit of society and arranging to "ensure that women are not driven on account of economic necessity or by any other method of exploitation, engage themselves in a ny [any] such labour or outdoor occupation as may cause hindrance to the discharge of their sacred and important household duties or in occupations which according to the Islamic shariat, are derogatory to feminine dignity."[47]

The note suggested adding the right to minimum wage, calculated at no less than one-fortieth of the remuneration of the highest-paid employee in state service. Among other duties to be performed by government servants, the ulema also expected them to observe Shariat.

In official notes addressed to the BPC, and other government members, as well as in their public dealings, the ulema became increasingly vocal in their disavowal of the constitution-making process. Their primary criticism concerned the ignorance of assembly members in understanding the principles of Islamic state—such as its existence to serve and uphold a moral Muslim community; the reliance on the strong figurehead of a Muslim man holding extensive executive power in a consultative manner; the domesticated role of women and the limited scope of religious activities for non-Muslims. Overall, the ulema also bemoaned the lack of intellectual courage or creative outlook among the political leaders to think beyond Western models of constitutional democracy.

These points were effectively summed up in *Fundamental Principles of an Islamic State*, formulated by a public gathering of prominent Muslim scholars in January 1951.[48] The conference unanimously rejected the BPC and the report on fundamental rights for its incongruity with Islamic teachings. Other than the points of disagreement summarily highlighted already, a major point of contention was the ulema's insistence on using state power to curb vulgarity, growing atheistic tendencies in society, and social vice, broadly defined.

The board wanted the state to command right and forbid wrong—*amr bi'l ma'ruf wa nahi an'al munkir*. They clearly spelled this out in their proposed amendments to the second BPC report. In their comments, the board suggested adding sections on eradicating drinking, gambling, and prostitution within three years of the constitution's enforcement; the elimination of interest; and the prohibition of obscenity.[49] Apart from provisions for Islamic teachings in educational institutions, the ulema wanted government servants to receive education on the basic tenets of Islam. This overall structure of political organization and societal behavior was part of the ulema's vision for the Islamic state "to plan, organize and co-ordinate the work of Amr-bil-Maruf and Nihi anil Munkar (promotion of virtues and suppression of vices)."[50] As functionaries of an ideological state, the ulema wanted public office holders to take an oath vowing to uphold injunctions from the Quran and Sunnah in their public and private lives.

Tied to this ideologically driven Islamic state was the requirement for learned Muslim scholars to oversee the implementation of Islamic ideology and to ensure its conformity with the Quran and Sunnah. Therefore, the board suggested that reputed experts of Islamic law who possessed the qualities of justice and piety (*adal* and *taqwa*) be appointed to—with one scholar assigned to each—the Supreme Court, the High Court, and district courts for at least ten years. They were to serve as experts advising on cases from an Islamic point of view.[51] The ulema were not appointed as aides to the judges, but their demand for a committee of Muslim scholars who oversaw legislation and ensured its conformity with Islam was accepted in all constitutions adopted by the Pakistani state. The induction of ulema as judges was then carried out during the tenure of General Zia-ul-Haq, whose government created a federal Shariat court. This federal court, however, is not the highest court of Pakistan; appeals against its decisions are heard by the Shariat Appellate Bench of the Supreme Court.

Although many of the ulema's demands and directives—including differentiating the believer citizen's rights from the nonbeliever's, forming state policy to spread Islamic teachings and obscenity, and setting up of a council of learned scholars of Islam to oversee legislation and, to lesser extent, the judicial process—were gradually incorporated into Pakistan's successive constitutions, their most persistent demand for a limited public role for women was never accommodated. After the second BPC report in 1952, the ulema warned against "the fruits of dragging women into fields of such activities" and demanded that women be relegated to their roles as mothers who nurture the nation.[52] At most, the ulema agreed, a separate chamber might be created for female representatives, with three to eleven members elected by female voters alone. With members' minimum age reduced to forty, and with the requirement that any member not be "engaged in an occupation which militates against the dictates and injunctions of Islam," the chamber would "initiate and consider proposals relating to health, education and general welfare of women and children, i.e. female hospitals, maternity homes, nursing-homes, child education, female education, first aid training, industrial homes, relief measures for orphans and widows, and protection of women's rights."[53] The ulema's uncompromising opposition to women's representation was matched in intensity only by their persistence in demanding that Ahmadis be declared non-Muslims and thus represented by the same mechanism as other non-Muslim minorities.

The officially released version of the second BPC report in December 1952 did not consider many of the ulema's proposals, although its content was, to the discomfort of non-Muslim members of the assembly, excessively peppered with Islamic content. A brief pamphlet, *Should We Be Ashamed of an Islamic Constitution? An Illuminating Comparison between the Proposed Islamic Provisions and the Existing Constitutions of the World*, is included in the Zafar Ahmad Ansari collection.[54] The pamphlet sums up many of the arguments given by members of the board and justifications for the creation of an Islamic state given in the Constituent Assembly. It also draws comparisons with other states in the world, describing their provisions for an official religion, invocation of God in oaths, and so on. Similarly, there are pamphlets in the collection published in the mid-1950s, at the height of arguments about an Islamic constitution, that discuss the rights of non-Muslims, the concept of fundamental rights in Islam, and other related topics.

In January 1953, the board met to discuss the provisions of the second BPC report. The BPC had agreed to the proposal of a Muslim head of state and a panel of Muslim scholars to ensure the conformity of any future laws passed to Islamic teachings. The ulema were not satisfied. They demanded a time frame to bring all laws in accordance with Islam. They repeated their earlier demands for building government employees' Islamic character and even for making that good character a criterion for appointments and promotions.[55] Merely propagating Islamic teachings was not enough; the ulema demanded the criminalization of the "propagation of atheism and infidelity and the insulting or ridiculing of the Holy Quran or the Sunnah."[56] They also demanded the codification of Islamic law, a process that would require translating the juridical ambiguity of Shariat into Western-style procedural law. Despite the loss of meaning inherent to such a process, in codification the ulema saw a pragmatic way of seeking the implementation of Islamic law.[57] In reviewing such discussions among ulema and their frustrations in dealing with a government that conversed in the liberal language of constitutional law, we can conclude that the ulema saw in the law's codification a chance for their enhanced role in, and closer scrutiny of, state affairs.

At this point, I want to bring to the discussion a draft constitution prepared by the board, as it uses a language different from that of liberal constitutionalism and rights theory. As Patricia Crone reminds us, the absence of a Western-style theory of rights and duties is not to deny the existence of rights in classical Islamic political thought but to emphasize that the medieval Muslim scholar viewed human society and its relationship primarily through the lens of duties. According to Crone, individuals did not have rights and duties in themselves; they had rights and duties conferred to them by God.[58] It follows that when jurists talked of human rights, they did not mean that in the modern sense of the phrase, as encoded in a bill of rights, enforced by the sovereign state, or guaranteed by courts, but rather in terms of individuals' claims on each other. They did not view them as rights vested in them by virtue of their human nature.

In the absence of a precise language of rights in the modern legal sense as discussed by Crone, and given the ambiguity of lawmaking through the inherent indeterminacy of applying human reasoning to Shariat as argued by Wael Hallaq, we have to search for the traditionary language available to the ulema, through which they scripted a legal document for the new Islamic state.[59] As I have shown, the ulema primarily wrote general statements about the rationale for an Islamic state and proposals for setting it up in a certain fashion. It is important, then, to look at the draft constitution in order to analyze the language gap between classical Muslim political thought and modern Western constitutional democracy and the incongruity of meanings, and incommunicability, that resulted.

The constitutional draft does not carry a date; nor does it mention name(s) of the author(s). The file cover describes the draft as compiled by "a few ulema." It has several edits and versions, and was likely drafted before the first BPC report to serve as a model constitution prepared by the ulema. I have not seen the ulema members of the board refer to this document in any of their concept notes or critiques of the BPC. What makes the draft unique is that the ulema do not seek to translate Islamic political theory into a modern idiom. By "translate," I refer to the conceptual equivalence for Islamic terms, institutions, or practices. The draft refers to the head of the state as *amir-i-am* elected by *majlis ahl al-hal wa'l* '*aqd* for life, and inaugurated into office (*masnad nashini*) by the Sheikh-ul-Islam (chief Islamic scholar).[60] In addition, the Sheikh-ul-Islam was to supervise *majlis peshwan-i-mazahib*, *majlis ehtasab* (which oversaw *akhlaq* and measures for eradication of vulgarity), *auqaf*, *ifta*, zakat, the committee of ulema and *fuqaha*, the Council of Non-Muslim Leaders, and *nizam-i-hifazat wa taqwiyyat-i-din*.[61] In line with Crone's understanding of medieval Islamic political thought, the draft constitution referred to "rights" for both Muslims and non-Muslims, such as the right to life, freedom, property, and so on. In its understanding of natural resources and their utilization, the draft constitution had a different understanding from modern nation-states: it called for the public ownership of rivers, canals, timber, and other natural resources that do not require human efforts for production and growth.[62] Everyone had the right to use these resources for their individual needs.

The constitution granted citizenship to all Muslims who wanted to become part of the state. For non-Muslims, the draft constitution uses the term *zimmi* but remains generous in recognizing their fundamental rights and equality before the law. What is remarkable is the document's adherence to classical jurisprudence that recognizes non-Muslims' rights to propagate their religion—albeit only to other non-Muslims—and also to criticize Islam.[63] In lieu of military service, non-Muslims were to pay an additional tax, although the ulema did not use the term *jizya*. Additionally, non-Muslims were given cultural autonomy, with the right to have an assembly of their own to deal with their cultural and religious affairs and present their grievances to the government.

The *amir* held the executive power appointed by a select group of men. The *amir* was expected to be popularly known for his piety and knowledge of Islamic teachings. Continuing with the classical Islamic tradition of not seeking a position of authority, a major disqualification for being an *amir* was to aspire to become *amir*. In aid to the *amir*, the *majlis-i-shura* implemented and interpreted Shariat on the principles of *qiyas*, *ijtihad*, and *istehsan*.[64] The *majlis* had limited legislative powers. It could not legislate on matters where clear Islamic injunctions existed. However, it did have a right to decide on cases or issues where more than one interpretation existed, applying *qiyas* and *ijtihad*. Also, the *majlis* could infer subsidiary laws (*furu'i ahkam*) from main commandments (*usuli ahkam*). The *majlis* could legislate on matters for which no clear injunctions were available as long as it conformed to Islam's collective system and spirits. There was to be no party system.

A distinctive feature of the document is that it lacks legal precision. In a poetic idiom, its equivalent of directives of state policy talks about establishing a system of justice where "an ordinary worker, a poor peasant and a voiceless beggar (*faqir-i-bay nawa*) would have the right to challenge even the ruler of the country.[65] The poetic excess of the ulema's *dastur* sharply contrasts with the prosaic precision of the constitutional law of the modern state. This is not to suggest that the language of Islamic political thought cannot be precise or to hint at its inherent irrationality or emotional excess. Indeed, subsequent developments in Pakistan's legislative and constitutional history show the successful use of legal language to accommodate the ulema's demands for an Islamic state, especially for the purposes of defining who is a Muslim or criminalizing blasphemous content.

As I argued earlier in the chapter, the major difference with Western constitutional democracy was methodological. Both Islamists like Maulana Maududi and modernists like Khalifa Abdul Hakim sought to overcome the mediating discursivity of Islamic tradition. They did so by forced erasure, summary dismissal, or feigned amnesia, and for varying purposes, establishing an Islamic state that helps institute an Islamic society by using the coercive tools of the modern state apparatus or one that uses diffusive egalitarian elements of Islamic principles to influence social and moral outlooks. This similarity in methodological inference by distilling meanings from the past without the mediating role of the tradition reifies Islamic practices in different ways. In saying so, I am not projecting tradition as a "permanent precondition" but merely describing the difference in method whereby "we produce it ourselves inasmuch we understand, participate in the evolution of tradition, and hence further determine it ourselves."[66] The difference between the ulema's interpretation and that of the modernists is the incongruity of their language. For instance, the ulema's hermeneutic reading of the tradition about *shura* as a consultative process headed by an all-powerful male ruler elected for life does not correspond with the modernist interpretation or search for a conceptual equivalence in the democratic principles of elections, legislation, and responsible executive authority. Yet given the very nature of hermeneutic reading as interpretation, the ulema are as much involved in the process of trying to create a democratic state as the modernists are striving for an Islamic one. The ensuing gap is that of a common language. In this regard, the modernists had more in line with the members of the opposition—both Hindu and Muslim—who opposed the idea of an Islamic republic than with the ulema hired by the government to advise on an Islamic constitution. To explore this further, we should focus on the incongruity of language in the politics surrounding Islam and on the historical developments that shaped such politics in 1950s Pakistan.

WHAT'S IN A NAME? PAKISTAN AS AN ISLAMIC REPUBLIC

The first Constituent Assembly decided on 2 November 1953 to designate Pakistan an Islamic republic.[67] The contention was not limited to the naming of the republic alone but also to the choice of words for its various institutions. The BPC had set up a committee for nomenclature that comprised Dr. Abdul Haq, Dr. Mahmud Husain, and Dr. Ishtiaq Husain Qureshi; they would decide on "Muslim terminology" for the constitution and on a complete English translation. The committee considered terms like *amir* (for "head of state"), *shura* (parliament), *awan-i-wilayat* (the house of units), *awan-i-jamhur* (the house of the people), *wali* (the house of a unit), *mir-i-adal* (chief justice of Pakistan), *suba* (province), and *riyasat* (state). In working on a suitable nomenclature, the BPC consulted the Board of Ta'limat-i-Islamiyyah and, in a meeting held on 17 November 1952, recommended that the board come up with terminology that did not contain any difficult words or have "undemocratic associations."[68] This led to an interesting exercise. The ulema and nomenclature committee members drew up lists of English terms with their proposed Urdu translations in "Pakistani Urdu," "Indian Urdu," modern Persian, and, in some cases, Arabic. Even when it came to linguistic references and not conceptual equivalences, it was difficult to agree on codified language and to ignore the historical antecedents shaping meaning and usage.

For "The Islamic Republic," the board recommended Jamhuriyyat-i-Islamiyyah-i-Pakistan, roughly an Urdu translation of the same term.

Non-Muslim objections to this name, the ulema noted, were not valid and should not stop them from naming the country as an Islamic republic.[69] The report used an "ideological states" argument, emphasizing the peculiar ideological content in appellations such as "Soviet Socialist Republic." A similar suggestion was given by Raghib Ahsan, who proposed the name Jamhuria-i-Shora'iya-i-Islamiya-i-Pakistan to link Pakistan's name with *shura*, which in the Quran serves as the basis of Islamic democracy, just like "the name of the Union of Socialist Soviet Republic of Russia—the USSR—links Russia with the spirit of Marxism."[70]

This rhetoric about Pakistan's ideological mission and Islam as a moderate middle ground builds on preexisting ideas about the so-called spirit of Islam. This concept reverberates in scholarly literature produced by Pakistani ideologues throughout the Cold War. Such views about Islam became an official policy line that was popularized by government-sponsored institutes such as the Institute of Islamic Culture, including the writings of its director, Khalifa Abdul Hakim, who "seemed more indebted to the Hegelian march of history than to a study of the Muslim past."[71] Scholars like Syed Suleman Nadawi, a member of the Board of Ta'limat-i-Islamiyyah, shared this worldview. From his deathbed, Nadawi issued a statement reminding the leaders and the ulema of the urgency of the historical moment, and of building Pakistan as a democratic Islamic state and beacon light for the entire Islamic world, which faced challenges posed by the capitalist West and the communist East. Though frustrated in his efforts to bridge the gap between his understanding of a democratic state and modernists' understandings of an Islamic state, Nadawi nevertheless firmly believed that Pakistan had the potential to use Islam to mediate between these ideological camps "for the scientific synthesis of the matter and the spirit, the Here and the Hereafter, Laissez Faire and regimentation of life."[72]

In this understanding, Islam serves to offset the excesses of both material consumption and spiritual asceticism, critiquing the West's secular modernity and its Christian religiosity. What enables the emergence of Islam as a closed system is not only the sociological language of structures that shapes aspects of modern life. Faisal Devji refers to Cantwell Smith's sampling of twenty-five thousand Arabic books from before the nineteenth century. Smith noted that of the twenty-five thousand titles, only eighty-four titles used the term *Islam*, out of which only fifteen could be said to have used it as a proper noun. He argued that the frequency of using Islam as a proper noun increased by many times in the nineteenth century, especially in titles that were translated from European languages or written by non-Muslim authors or responses to their works.[73] From Smith's findings, Devji concludes that Islam became a proper name in the nineteenth century, with a corresponding impact on its juristic methods and theological reasoning. One example of this shift, according to Devji, was the emphasis placed on *Islam* and *Muslims* to replace terms like *Mohammadenism* and *Mohammaden* at the turn of the twentieth century.[74] While, for example, earlier leaders and organizations in late nineteenth-century colonial India had styled themselves as the Mohammedan Anglo-Oriental College or the Mohammedan Educational Conference, they had shifted to the term *Muslim* by the turn of the century. Hence, the major political entity set up in 1906 to serve Muslim interests was named All-India Muslim League.

The separation of religion from the name of its founder was, in the opinion of famous jurist and historian Syed Ameer Ali, a unique feature. In his magnum opus, *The Spirit of Islam*, Ali wrote: "The religion of Jesus bears the name of Christianity, derived from his designation of Christ; that of Moses and of Buddha are known by the respective names of their teachers. The religion of Muhammad alone has a distinctive appellation. It is Islam."[75]

Thus, Islam as a proper noun was central to stylizing Western-educated elite as Muslims who believed in Islam as a complete code of life. In discussions about the future constitutional framework of the Pakistani state, there was little disagreement on the all-encompassing nature of Islamic teachings; there was, however, a lot of discussion about the appellation *Islamic* for the new republic.

Much of the discussion that followed in 1953 coincided with the fallout from the anti-Ahmadi movement of March 1953, which had led to widespread violence in Punjab and the imposition of martial law in Lahore. The discussions on proposals to name the country "the Islamic Republic of Pakistan" and on requirements that the head of the state be Muslim took place against the backdrop of what opposition members described as the natural outcome of the excessive use of religious rhetoric in political affairs. Later, in 1956, as the final round of debates—albeit by a newly formulated Constituent Assembly—took place, assembly members were keen to refer to the findings of the Munir-Kiyani report, a judicial inquiry into the violence of the 1953 movement in which the authors had talked about the impossibility of setting up an Islamic state. Given the existence of a voluminous debate at various levels, including during committee deliberations and discussions of the committee reports submitted to the assembly, I focus on discussions from January to February 1956, when the larger debate was summarized and brought to a conclusion.[76] On many occasions, the speakers referred back to earlier claims, alluded to Pakistan's political history, and drew on prior arguments and counterarguments presented in this prolonged and checkered constitution-making process.

The thrust of the opposition's criticism of the term *Islamic Republic* was twofold: non-Muslim members emphasized the aporia of the term and that it made them uncomfortable; for Muslim members, the term was unjustified, as it did not do justice to what they described as the egalitarian spirit of Islam.

Among other non-Muslim assembly members, Rasa Raj Mandal, S. K. Sen, and Peter Paul Gomez objected to the nomenclature of the new republic. According to Mandal, his objection was not inspired by any religious bias but by a regard for the principle of equality enshrined in the idea of a republic that should treat all citizens equally, regardless of their caste or creed. The name *Islamic Republic*, Mandel argued, might frighten people, as if the new republic were only for Muslims.[77] Peter Paul Gomez expressed similar reservations about the implied exclusion of non-Muslims from the state, ignoring sizable non-Muslim communities of Hindus, Buddhists, and Christians living in Pakistan.[78] Gomez criticized as discriminatory other aspects of the proposed constitution, such as enabling Muslims to live their lives according to the Quran and Sunnah. He argued that the constitutional draft did not extend such policy statements to cover other religious communities in Pakistan and simply presumed them irreligious.[79] On a similar note, S. K. Sen appreciated the establishment of the Islamic Research Institute as proposed by the constitution but stated that there should also be research institutes to study the Gita and Vedas.[80]

Other than the inherently discriminatory nature of the term and the potential fear that it would cause among the non-Muslim population, members like Bhupendra Kumar Dutta laid out the contradictory nature of the term: "As it is, if it is Islamic, it is not a Republic. If you call it 'Islamic,' you assign the near about a crore of non-Muslims in the State a subordinate position to the limit of obliteration. The position they are faced with is that either they remain here as serfs or *zimmis* or clear out. In the latter course, the name becomes consistent."[81]

Furthermore, as S. K. Sen argued, the nomenclature was unnecessary: other Muslim-majority states like Turkey and Indonesia did not use it, nor were there Buddhist, Christian, or Jewish republics; furthermore, because the popular imagination of Pakistan was that of a Muslim state, no additional adjective was required to emphasize the point.[82]

Some Muslim members were also critical of the move. In their opinion, it was an attempt by the government to instrumentalize the name of Islam for political gains. Sheikh Mujib-ur-Rehman referred to what he saw as an inherent contradiction between the ideals of an Islamic state and wealth inequality in Pakistan:

> I challenge my honourable friends to quote a single injunction in Islam whereby a man may be permitted to hold ten or fifteen lakh acres of land and simultaneously another Mussalman may die of starvation on the streets of Karachi and Dacca. Can they show such an injunction in Islam? . . . How long will they bluff the people of Pakistan in the name of Islam? You are insulting Islam before the whole world. You are discrediting Islam. Can they prove that Islam means some people working in mills for Rs. 30 per month and other people going round the world squandering people's money? Islam means equal distribution of wealth.[83]

Sheikh Mujib warned against the consequences for Indian Muslims of adopting a religious appellation for Pakistan. "Have you ever imagined what would be their fate if you declare Pakistan 'Islamic Republic of Pakistan'?" he rhetorically asked. "If you declare today that Pakistan is an Islamic Republic and name it as an 'Islamic Republic of Pakistan,' the fanatic Hindus such as R. S. S. and Mahasabhaista might agitate tomorrow for declaring India a 'Hindu Republic of India.'"[84]

Dispelling the propaganda that the Awami League was opposed to the Islamic constitution, Mujib-ur-Rehman said that he and his party were opposed to a reactionary constitution that was trying to fool the Pakistani people in the name of Islam. In contrast, his political party stood for a democratic constitution with the fundamental principles of Islam—including equality, fair play, and the equal distribution of wealth—enshrined in it.[85] With such a disregard for equitable redistribution of wealth and dismissal of the demands of East Pakistan for autonomy, Ataur Rahman Khan described the constitution—and especially its Islamic content—as an eyewash meant to appease "the Mullah"; it hence resembled "a liquor shop over which a signboard of Islamic Sharab Khana [Islamic Liquor Store] is placed."[86]

To bring conformity between Awami League's avowed position of communion between Islamic principles and social justice, Abul Mansur Ahmad proposed an amendment to the first clause of the constitution bill, whereby "Pakistan shall be an Islamic Socialist Federal Republic and shall be called Federal Republic of Pakistan.[87] The emphasis on Islamic socialism, according to Abul Mansur Ahmad, ensured distance from communism while upholding the cherished goal of ending inequality, exploitation, capitalism, and feudalism in Pakistan. Such an emphasis, he claimed, was the kind of ideological character that the country needed, from which rulers had shied away because of a lack of moral courage on their part.

From the treasury benches, Mian Abdul Bari and Pir Ali Mohammad Rashdi cited examples from other countries to justify the appellation and referral to Islam as the state religion. Bari emphasized the religious nature of the Pakistani project, as compared to that of Afghanistan, Egypt, and Turkey, "because all these empires have been built up not on Islamic basis but on national basis." Pakistan, he said, was "the first State which was established in the name of Islam, Islam and nothing but Islam."[88] This was reflective of the new state's faith in the universality of Islam, and Pakistan's version of a universal Islam was compared to the narrower bases of identification adopted by other counties. Rashdi referred to, for example, the Hashemite Kingdom of Jordan, which was named after a dynasty, and mockingly exclaimed, "If I had called this country as the Rashdi Kingdom of Pakistan, my friends would probably have committed suicide."[89] He gave the examples of England, where the Queen carried the title "Defender of the Anglican Faith," and Greece, where the role of the Orthodox Church was officially recognized. To further support the claim that the Pakistani constitution was genuinely reflective of Islamic teachings, Rashdi referred to statements by the Grand Mufti of Palestine, Naquib al-Ashraf, and the custodian of the *dargah* of Ghaus-i-Azam Abdul Qadir Jilani, both of whom had lauded the Pakistani constitution's Islamic provisions.[90]

Drawing a comparison to India and responding to objections by non-Muslim members who were uncomfortable about living in a country named as an Islamic state, Bari stated that Muslims never objected to the term *Hindustan*, which means "the abode of Hindus"—and lived there, and even ruled it, for centuries. Even when India had reverted to call itself *Bharat*—a name from a bygone era when Muslims did not exist in the country—it still prided itself as a secular state.[91] An essential part of Bari's speech was to justify naming Pakistan an Islamic republic as akin to John Austin's illocutionary speech act, in that it was performative, symbolic, and communicative. Responding to Mujib-ur-Rehman's argument that the misdoings or lack of character of an Islamic state would give a bad name to Islam, Bari argued that he and Mujib should change their names to Danga Ram and Manghu Ram because they are bad Muslims and neglectful of their religious duties: "The name has the greatest importance in the world. Name makes a thing what it is, it sets the whole outlook of it. The whole outlook of it is governed from the day a child is born. The first thing is to give it a name. Everybody knows that it was the power of naming on account of which human beings have been given the sovereignty over this universe."[92]

Mushtaq Ahmed Gurmani and Mumtaz Daultana gave similar arguments in response to Hussain Shaheed Suhrawardy and his objection to the republic's name. The appellation was unwarranted, said Husain Shaheed Suhrawardy, the main opposition leader in the Constituent Assembly, because the Constitution failed to live up to the name it had chosen for itself: "When you will provide every person in this country with food, clothing, shelter, employment, medical aid, education, then call yourself Islamic State." To this, Gurmani responded, "why bear Islamic names; why do you not change names unless and until you become true Muslims."⁹³ Suhrawardy was unfazed. For him, the state was not Islamic and only pretended to be so; it would be called, he stated, "in the world at large as the *Munafiq* Republic of Pakistan."⁹⁴ On the distinction between Muslims or Islam or the rationale for adopting an Islamic name when the overwhelming majority of citizens were Muslims, Daultana said that "Pakistan" itself was as much an Islamic name as "Hussain Shaheed" was a Muslim name: "I think it is more Islamic than Muslim," Daultana mockingly remarked. "Consider, Hazrat Husain, and then not just ordinary Husain but Shaheed Husain [martyred Husain], could there be anything more Islamic? (*Laughter*)."⁹⁵

In a way, Suharawardy and his critics are engaged in a debate on descriptivist and an antidescriptivist approach to naming. To understand the debate in terms of Saul Kripke's thought, even if Suhrawardy's outward appearance or praxis as a Muslim were to be removed, the "rigid designator" of Husain—and that too a *Shahid* (martyred Husain)—would remain, and the same would have been true if he were named Dinga Ram.⁹⁶ By avoiding a fixed correlation between the signifier and the signified, or "emancipating the signifier from any ethralment [sic] to the signified,"⁹⁷ the Muslim League leaders wanted to keep *Islamic state* as a term amenable to change and filled with content that tallied with their version of Islamic modernist values.

Thus, the country's naming was rationalized by the government as an aspirational act, a form of action and striving. The late nineteenth-century Muslim scholar Ameer Ali had conceived the term *Islam* as a proper name, which "made the religion into an ethical as much as political phenomenon of a distinctly modern sort."⁹⁸ In this aspirational modern Muslim subjectivity from the colonial period and in its concretization in the political project to acquire a sovereign state, Islam served as the singular element in what Laclau would call an "equivalential chain."⁹⁹ In that manner, the particularity of a demand—say, Islamic state in our context—becomes the signifier of a wider universality: it embraced, through equivalential links, contents such as economic concerns of "salariat classes," desire for a *truly* Islamic state, protection of cultural rights, the importance of Urdu language, and concerns about the future of Islam and Muslims in majoritarian Hindu India—all of which condensed during the decisive phase of the Pakistan movement in the 1940s.[100] To paraphrase Laclau's reference to Althusser, all the antagonisms in the debates about Muslim political subjectivity and its idealized solution in any future federal polity or separate sovereign entity were condensed in a ruptural unity around Islam.[101] It was in the emptiness of the terms being articulated that they could be transmitted into demands and "become the *names* of a universality that transcended their actual particular contents."[102]

However, as Laclau reminds us, "the empty character of the signifiers that give unity or coherence to a popular camp is not the result of any ideological or political underdevelopment; it simply expresses the fact that any populist unification takes place on a radically heterogeneous social terrain."[103] As in any other hegemonic formation, particularity is not entirely eliminated and continues to be contested. Given this heterogeneity of the links in an equivalential chain, a coherent articulation is contingent on transference: from the conceptual order of the logic of difference to that of a nominal one. Thus, the name becomes the ground of *the thing*, an assemblage of heterogenous elements kept equivalentially together by name, and hence the radical contingency of naming.[104] The retroactive effect of naming is that that name becomes the signifier of what is heterogenous and excessive, and becomes available for the articulation of demands that remain unfulfilled.

But to play such a role, theorizes Laclau, the name has to be an empty signifier. By that, Laclau does not mean a signifier without a signified, as such a notion is self-defeating and would constitute only noise. Instead, as Laclau explains, an empty signifier is a place within the system of signification that is constitutively irrepresentable, in the sense that it remains empty, yet it is an emptiness that can be signified, as it deals with a void within signification. Laclau uses Paul De Man's analysis of the Pascalian zero as the absence of a number, but when given a name, that naming transforms "zero" into a "one."[105] Naming *the thing* "Islamic" to make the equivalential chain meaningfully coherent thus seeks to condense the polyvalence of voices, demands, and aspirations. At the same time, it is possible that the signifier operates as a floating signifier rather than an empty one. Laclau's idea of the popular formation of the equivalential chain, and its crystallization in a unified entity through the production of empty signifiers, was based on the givenness and fixity of an antagonistic frontier. As he develops the model fully, he explains that frontiers are unstable and constantly in a process of flux. He subsequently introduces the concept of floating signifier, whose meaning is suspended. Whereas the empty signifier presupposes a stable frontier against which an equivalent chain is coalesced, the floating signifier emanates from the displacement or blurring of such a frontier. There is still a considerable overlap between the two categories, as there is neither a possibility of permanent dichotomous, immobile frontier nor a pure floating with any partial fixation.[106] To sum up using Laclau's words: "The emergence of the 'people' depends on the three variables I have isolated: equivalential relations hegemonically represented through empty signifiers; displacements of the internal frontiers through the production of floating signifiers; and a constitutive heterogeneity which makes dialectical retrievals impossible and gives its true centrality to political."[107]

To simplify it further, as Chatterjee explains, "the heterogeneous elements that have to be stitched together into chains of equivalence could change over time."[108] This structural transformation in the signification process is necessary to make adjustments for the applicability of the theory for a postcolonial context where the populist movements are not directed at an external, hostile frontier but against an a priori, homogeneous notion of *the people* postulated from a center of power.[109] Also, this theoretical tweak enables a better understanding of the changing patterns and multiplicity of demands for Islamic state in the Pakistani context as it figures prominently for a range of political purposes and demands for socioeconomic justice, whether articulated as Bhutto's Islamic socialism or Imran Khan's Riyasat-i-Madina. As the preceding discussion has shown, such populist articulations are linked with the history and praxis of naming through equivalential relations of contiguity, whereby the contingent moment of naming acquires a central and constitutive role.[110]

EXCLUDING THE INTERNAL AS THE OTHER

I argued at the beginning of this chapter that the coalescing of an imagined, hegemonic totality was predicated on the exclusion of an internal. In this section, I discern the processes whereby the Pakistani state sought to achieve this ideological consistency through the exclusion of Ahmadis as the internal other.

As the debate on naming shows, Hindus and Christians felt that the Islamic state excluded them from the universality of equal citizenship rights. During the debate, opposition members also pointed out the inherent exclusion that was constitutive of such a naming practice, especially when it came to ascertaining the religious status of the head of the state. When the Basic Principles Committee and the draft constitution that resulted proposed that the head of state must be a Muslim, several assembly members pointed out the need to define "Muslim," a demand that was at the center of the anti-Ahmadi movement in 1953. The ulema at the forefront of the campaign had justified their demands on the basis of the BPC report. Because the consensual opinion of Islamic scholars was that Ahmadis were non-Muslims, the ulema demanded a legal and constitutional sanction for their juristic opinion. The Munir-Kiyani report commenting on the ulema's demands turned the question on its head. Instead of commenting on the unanimity of ulema's opinion about the status of Ahmadis, the judges asked the ulema to define a Muslim. The lack of consensus by ulema on which beliefs or practices defined a Muslim then gave the judges maneuvering space, and they ultimately described the disagreements over the definition as irreconcilable.

Other than a couple of religious scholars—including, most notably, Maulana Maududi, the head of the Jamat-i-Islami—there was no opposition to the Munir-Kiyani report. Despite its criticism of the idea of an Islamic state, the report was popular with the ruling elite as well as the opposition for its espousal of broad-based democratic principles of state making and its condemnation of clerics' authority to dictate religious commandments. But while the government actively sought to replace the clerical authority with its own legitimacy to instrumentalize Islam for nation-building purposes, the opposition was critical of such attempts, citing the Munir-Kiyani report, and especially the Ahmadi issue therein, so as to embarrass the government.

The government was mindful of possible fallout from such anti-Ahmadi agitation. Further, the ulema exploited the proposed clause in the constitution that the head of the state be Muslim, thus necessitating the definition of a Muslim or ensuring that Ahmadis as non-Muslims were not allowed to take that position. In a document from the Prime Minister's Office that can probably be dated August 1952 and was undersigned by the president of the Muslim League, it was proposed that the "Government should not declare Qadianis to be a non-Muslim minority, or demand resignation from a minister on the grounds of his religious views." The document pointed out that when a party member had presented a resolution to declare Qadianis non-Muslims at a Muslim League session, Jinnah did not permit it: "The Muslim League will, therefore, be discarding a fundamental part of its creed, and would be going against its entire history and the policy consistently followed by the Quaid-i-Azam, if it were to weaken in its opposition to sectarianism and to accept demand for declaring a certain group claiming to be Muslims a non-Muslim minority."[111] Publicly, however, the government did not show similar resolve in its ideological commitment to what it understood as Jinnah's vision. The government kept deferring the matter until the finalization of the constitution draft, rather than taking a definite position. When the movement became violent, the government used excessive force to suppress the movement, and continued to shy away from committing to ensuring the religious and political status of Ahmadis.

This purposeful lack of clarity on a public level was warranted by a possible backlash from even those ulema who were supportive of the government and directly employed by it. The members of the Board of Ta'limat-i-Islamiyyah were clear in their denunciation of the Ahmadis as non-Muslims. In their comments on the proposed draft of the second BPC in 1952—just as anti-Ahmadi rhetoric was brewing in Punjab—the board suggested adding a new column for "seats reserved for Qadianis" in the section dealing with the representation of Muslims in the assembly. They even provided a definition of Qadiani as a person "who professes to believe in Mirza Ghulam Ahmad of Qadian as his religious leader."[112] In a separate but related note, the ulema added an explanation to describe Qadiani as "a person who professes to believe in the late Mirza Ghulam Ahmad of Qadian, as an apostle, prophet, the promised Messiah, the promised Mahdi or Mujaddid."[113] Per the criteria for electoral representation that the ulema suggested, "for filling up the one seat of Qadianis in Punjab, the

Qadianis of other areas in Pakistan will also be entitled to vote and eligible for membership."[114] To my knowledge, this was the first occasion after 1947 in which the ulema made a concerted effort to legally and constitutionally enforce a fatwa against the Ahmadis. They chose a language that excluded Ahmadis, without necessarily providing definite criteria for membership in the Muslim community or engaging with the controversy on the finality of prophethood. They simply dismissed the legitimacy of following of Mirza Ghulam Ahmad as a prophet or even as a revivalist of Islam.

From the ulema's point of view, the exclusion of Ahmadis was a non-negotiable issue. "With all the emphasis at our command," the ulema implored constitution makers to

> not be un-aware of how delicate and tense the situation has become in areas where a considerable number of Qadianis are living along with Muslims. They should not be have [sic] like our erstwhile rulers who did not care to take cognizance of the hindu-Muslim problem until the four corners of un-divided India had become blook-stained [sic] on account of the Hindu-Muslim disturbances. For our constitution makers, belonging to this country as they do, it would be a tragic blunder that they should refuse to realize the existence of a Qadiani-Muslim problem which needs an urgent solution until such time as they find that it has grown into a wild fire.[115]

The ulema accused Ahmadis of posing themselves as, and mixing with, Muslims, and at the same time, declared all non-Ahmadis Kafirs. As suggested by the ulema, the remedy was to declare Ahmadis a "minority altogether separate from the muslims [sic] as had been proposed by the late Allama Iqbal twenty years back."[116]

Because of such harsh views on the rights of women and minority groups, the government was too embarrassed to make the findings of the ulema's report public. As Sris Chandra Chattopudhyaya said in the assembly, the government was spending about five thousand rupees a month on the board—a substantial sum in the early 1950s—but did not share the report or the ulema's findings with even the members of the Constituent Assembly: "Are they afraid of showing us to what are those Islamic principles which the Board has enunciated. If they are good we will accept them but why do you not show them to us. Now these are supposed to be great Maulanas because each of them gets a salary of Rs. 1,000. They are respectable Maulanas. Why are you shy of showing that report to us."[117] Referring to the demand for the removal of Sir Zafarullah Khan from the post of foreign minister, not because of his performance but because of his Ahmadi faith, Chattopudhyaya warned against a policy of making distinctions between believer and nonbeliever citizens, and of thus according separate electorates for Muslims and non-Muslims. Such a policy, he warned, would lead to similar demands for the exclusion of other sects from the electoral rolls. The Muslim and non-Muslim distinction, argued critics of the provision for separate electorates and Islamic provisions of the constitution, was cannibalistic: it hurt the Muslims more. As Zahiruddin pointed out during debates on finalizing the Constitution in 1956, because the ulema were clear about the non-Muslim status of Ahmadis, given the latter's denial of the doctrine of *khatam-i-nabuwwat*, the Constitution must mention that "a Qadiani cannot be elevated to the exalted office of the President. I am therefore saying that by placing the word 'Muslim' you have created difficulties. You have not only created a difficulty between the Hindus and Muslims, but here and now you have sown the seeds of disruption for the Muslims arid in the Muslim polity itself."[118]

Zahiruddin said that this had created a situation in which a person could exploit the provision to challenge the religious credentials of the person elected to the highest office in the state; doing so was a great disservice to Islam and Muslims, as it would open the floodgates of accusations of heresy and lead to a repetition of the carnage in Punjab.

In wrapping up the debate on the Constitution Bill, Suhrawardy re-emphasized the anomalies arising from the need to define "Muslim" in order to choose a head of state; it would be impossible to define. "Who is a Muslim after all?" asked Suhrawardy. "Can anybody define it what is Muslim? Have we not recently—only recently—had large bloody riots on this question as to who is Muslim?"[119] The government response was to cite examples from other constitutions, in which the head of the state was required to be a Christian or a defender of faith and church. For Daultana, the office of the president held a symbolic value. Just as the flag and its crescent and star held symbolic value, the president's being Muslim, according to Daultana, had a symbolic value.[120] Suhrawardy pointed out that all such examples were from kingdoms in which hereditary rulers were anointed to the throne, and thus the practice was unsuitable for a republic with an elected president. "Over here what do we have?" asked Suhrawardy. "You say that the Head of your State, merely because in this country only Muslims happen to predominate, shall be a Sunni Muslim or a Shia Muslim or a Qadiani Muslim or what?"[121] His referral to Ahmadis as Muslims went unchallenged, as the government was, once again, reluctant to publicly address the issue.

According to Suhrawardy, ascertaining religious identity, as required per the provision for separate electorates, was also going to cause havoc: "If you are going to have separate electorate you shall have to decide in which category you are going to place Qadianis. If you place them in Muslim category you are going to have riots."[122] Eventually, the matter of joint or separate electorates was deferred to the provincial assemblies in order to get the Constitution through without further delay.

But such a step only postponed the crisis rather than addressing it. For the opposition, and especially its non-Muslim members, the focus on the definition was not just a gimmick meant to embarrass the government on the Ahmadi issue; rather, they meant to take to its logical conclusion the possible implications of using faith—that is, a set of beliefs internal to an individual—as a minimum criterion for voting and holding office or citizenship rights, rather than relying on more external features of identification in the form of documentation. A cultic, conspiratorial view of the minority and its "activities" further fueled suspicions of what *they* held in *their* hearts, which was impossible to discern. As S. H. Koreshi, a reader from Karachi, wrote in a letter to the editor, the lack of a definition in the Constitution would provide a loophole for saboteurs. During the Second World War, he said, there were rumors about Hitler and Mussolini's converting to Islam. He cautioned against the ready acceptance of neo-Muslims into the electoral rolls. It is only after a minimum of five years of a proclaimed acceptance of Islam, he suggested, that a person should be entered on the electoral rolls.[123] This sums up the difficulty, or impossibility, of exorcizing the internal other to constitute it as an external one.

The question of defining or identifying who was a Muslim resurfaced in the 1960s as General Ayub Khan's martial-law regime solicited opinions for a new constitution. In a letter to the president by Muhammad Hasan Cheema, an advocate from Gujrat, it was suggested that a definition of a Muslim in the constitution should be provided for to deprive the "mullah"—"Pakistan's most dangerous enemy"—from using the powerful tool of *takfir* or issuing of decrees declaring people as non-Muslims.[124] In 1961, Qudrat Ullah Shahab, a close aide to the regime, wrote to I. H. Qureshi, then director of the Institute of Islamic Research, and asked for his opinion. Qureshi responded with a brief historical background about the evolution of "a catholic definition" of a Muslim in Sunni "orthodoxy." Citing Abul Hasan al-Ashari (d. 330 AH), Qureshi defined a Muslim who recites and professes *kalima*. Various minority Muslim sects, he said, also shared this definition. Qureshi further noted:

> This is to say that if a person or group of persons state that they are Muslims—recite the Kalima of Shahadah—and there is no reason to believe that they are deliberately lying, then they are legally Muslims and no Fatwas of Kufr can confiscate this right from such people, i.e. legally cast them outside Islam. This[,] however, does not imply that a particular belief or a set of beliefs and/or practices may not be criticized as being un-Islamic, varying degrees, by a person or a set of persons. The decision whether a certain person, as head of State, is also effectively a Muslim—i.e. whether, Islamically speaking, he has the confidence of the Community as a whole—must, in the final analysis, rest upon the good sense of the Community as a whole exercised at the time of election.[125]

Qureshi's proposed definition was in line with the colonial precedence for identifying a person as Muslim for the purposes of law on the basis of the outward profession of Muslim faith. At the same time, Qureshi provided judgmental social scrutiny to ascertain the Islamicness of an individual by his or her actions and practices. By giving this responsibility to society at large, Qureshi was perhaps trying to salvage more space for individual freedom in belief and action, arguing against the state's authority to define Muslimness.

In a note dated 21 November 1961, Shahab disagreed with Qureshi's solution. He read this as opening the gate for others to decide on and judge someone's inner convictions. By allowing people to ascertain views about someone's faith depending on "whether he recites it with his whole or half heart, and whether he becomes a good, bad or indifferent Muslim are matters entirely between the man and God and nobody else has any jurisdiction in it."[126] Shahab thus dismissed both legal and social means of ascertaining an individual's faith. He suggested recognizing anyone reciting *kalima* and professing his belief in it as a Muslim and making it punishable to declare any such person as *kafir*.[127] In the margins of this note, Manzur Qadir, the principal architect of the 1962 Constitution, shared his proposed legal definition of a Muslim: "The word 'Muslim' means a person who declares his faith as Islam and professes belief in the Kalima, 'there is no god except Allah, and Mohammad is his messenger.'"[128] Ayub Khan wrote in the margins approving this definition. However, the 1962 Constitution—like the previous constitution—did not provide any definition for *Muslim*, although both contained the provision that the head of the state must be a Muslim. Thus, the Munir-Kiyani report's sharp-witted comment on the impossibility of defining a Muslim gained further credence.

When the anti-Ahmadi pogrom started in 1974, and the so-called Ahmadi question came up for discussion in Parliament, the ulema leading the movement were fully aware of the challenge posed by the Munir-Kiyani report. One of their primary concerns during parliamentary debates, and in the discussions that preceded them, was to arrive at a definition of a Muslim so contrived that it targeted specific aspects of the Ahmadi faith and then to incorporate that into the constitution.[129] But even the second amendment to the 1973 constitution, which resulted in the declaration of Ahmadis as non-Muslims, did not provide the definition of a Muslim; it only defined a non-Muslim, and then in a manner designed to outlaw the religious beliefs of Ahmadis.

Nevertheless, a later change to the constitution during General Zia-ul-Haq's martial-law regime also defined *Muslim*. The current law and practice, as when acquiring a national identity card or passport, is that an affirmation of the Oneness of Allah or of Prophethood of Prophet Muhammad alone is not enough to qualify as a Muslim; the applicant must sign a disavowal of Ahmadi beliefs and the figure of Mirza Ghulam Ahmad to be eligible as a Muslim. This is how, to rephrase Laclau again, the common rejection of the excluded identity provided internal consistency to an equivalential ensemble of an Islam-based name of *the thing*.

DEBATING THE FEDERATION

The debates in the 1950s about the appellation of the new republic and provisions relating to franchise and representation were not limited to the constitution's "Islamic features"; they were also directly related to the federation's overall structure and ideas of citizenship and national belonging. In critiquing these provisions, opposition members articulated an alternative vision for the Pakistani federation and for citizens' rights that could accommodate Pakistan's non-Muslim minority and ensure equality of all citizens. In showing these issues' interconnections and analyzing their critiques in the assembly, I attempt to provide the political theory of an alternative federal structure, which we can retrieve from the debates of the Constituent Assembly. For that, I draw on Chantal Mouffe's idea of the political community as a discursive surface where ideas about "us" are inscribed along with the correlative idea of a common good.[130] If politics is about competing interpretations of shared principles in order to define what constitutes the common good, then we can apply Mouffe's definition in the Pakistani context: proponents of an Islamic constitution proposed equality of citizenship rights based on the "Islamic" principles of tolerance and the fair treatment of non-Muslims; opposition members pushed for a rights-based approach, envisaging universal equality as the defining feature of Pakistani citizenship. In that sense, applying Mouffe's reading of Wittgenstein's conception of practices and languages, both groups agreed on the language they used—a precondition for procedural consistency for normative concerns to help achieve agreement.[131] The government that proposed an Islam-centric constitution was as wary of the role of the Board of Ta'limat-i-Islamiyyah, and of the incommunicable gap with *their language*, as were the opposition members critiquing the government and positing an inclusive democratic structure.

Mouffe emphasizes the need to distinguish between public and private, religious and secular, and church and state, rather than collapsing them under the same rubric or in an equation in which each requires the other. This is why she is opposed to the Rawlsian and Habermasian versions of deliberative democracy that prioritize right over good, vacating divisive issues like religion to allow for rational consensus on moral, universalizable concerns. In what she calls the model of agnostic pluralism and democracy, there is room to acknowledge religious forms of identification as legitimate motives for political action. This is not to justify "the use of religion in state affairs" but to devise a nuanced theoretical approach and avoid a summary dismissal of the voluminous Pakistani debate on the broader theme of the Islamic state and Muslim citizenry. A non-reductive approach to Pakistan's constitutional history will help uncover the discursive formations of the political community in Pakistan, its constitutive and interconnected elements in other aspects of state structure, and the "grammar of conduct" shaping its ethical-moral principles.[132]

In the Pakistani context, religious interjections overwhelmingly derived their legitimacy from, and were constitutionally delimited by, the signifier of Islam. But for the period under discussion—from 1947 to 1956—their articulation was not hegemonic. Hence, it is possible to retrieve from within the same democratic debate dissenting views of what could have been, and thus the potentiality of what the proponents of these ideas thought inhered in the Pakistan project. Such an approach takes the debate on Pakistan's constitutional history beyond the lament of an unfulfilled promise, as I discuss in the introduction in reference to Jinnah's speech on 11 August 1947. My purpose is to show how Pakistani assembly members posited a different idea of the common good, and of equality and rights, for an alternative imagining of and ideational basis for the republic.

To begin with, on the more substantive issues of belief-based divisions—especially the issue of separate electorates—Suhrawardy opposed the move, in the name of establishing a unified national identity where "the Hindus and Muslims shall co-operate with each other jointly in the service of the nation and in working out the problems of the country." According to him, it would give Hindus confidence about their status as equal citizens "because we want to keep the Hindus in Pakistan and this, for us, Sir, is a very[,] very important problem."[133] To justify the ideological justifications for his proposed vision of Pakistani nationhood, he pointed out the strategic implications of the Islam-centric view, which would, in his opinion, lead to a mass exodus of Hindus, with repercussions for Muslims living in India.

To shape this alternative basis for national inclusion and equal citizenship, opposition members had to anchor their arguments as much in strategic pragmatics as in legal rationality and ideology. Basanta Kumar Das's speech was an excellent example of this approach. He referred to the two volumes of world constitutions that Jinnah had distributed to all members of the Constituent Assembly to serve as a guide and aide in the constitution-making process.[134] Jinnah had asked the volume editor to write a preface for each constitution included in the volumes. In the section dealing with the Turkish constitution, the editor paid glowing tribute to Turkish republican values. Das sees this as an attempt on the part of Jinnah to nudge the direction of discussions on constitution making and offer his vision for Pakistan as modern and democratic.[135] In Jinnah's explanation of the ideology of Pakistan, the demand for a separate homeland was based on the theory of the exclusivity of Muslim nationhood "with a view to separate the Muslims from the Hindus giving them a separate homeland for their own development being freed from Hindu domination." But since there was nowhere in India—not even in Muslim-majority regions—where Hindus and Muslims did not coexist, Jinnah demanded an exchange of population to secure homogeneity in the Muslim homeland.[136] But such an end was impossible to achieve, said Das, so "the Pakistan that was created could not be the country where the Muslims were the only exclusive people and, therefore, Pakistan could not become a country exclusively for the Muslim nation. People professing other different faiths living in Pakistan remained to be as good citizens of Pakistan."[137] According to Das, Jinnah was farsighted enough to understand that any further emphasis on the two-nation theory would be detrimental to Pakistan's development. To avoid a continuing specter of communal violence in the aftermath of Partition, Jinnah, in his role as governor-general and president of the Constituent Assembly of Pakistan, set the tone of constitution making and state making by reminding assembly members that the state was inherited not only by Muslims but also by followers of other faiths. Although in subsequent statements, Das admits, Jinnah sometimes referred to the teachings of Quran and Sunnah, that was meant to highlight the lines of conduct Muslims should follow; otherwise, "he always emphasised that he wanted a Pakistan State of a Pakistani Nation."[138]

Das suggested viewing Pakistan in territorial rather than religious terms. In emphasizing the territorial basis of Pakistani statehood, religious belonging would become irrelevant. As another member, Gomez, said, even though non-Muslims were going to lose elections in a Muslim-majority country because of the joint electorates—the same justification that Sardar Nishtar had given for introducing the provision for separate electorates in 1953—he still demanded them. This was because "the non-Muslims want that they be integrated into the nation as one entity. They do not want to remain politically separate, but they want to be one with the Muslims, not in the religious sense, but in the political sense."[139] Statements by Das and Gomez sum up the debate about demand for equality by providing an ideological basis for it within the larger intellectual milieu of the "nation's past."

The idea of territorial nationalism that Gomez proposed and that Das seconded was different from the scheme adopted by the Pakistani state in 1955, known as the One Unit Scheme. According to the plan, the constituent, provincial units of West Pakistan were amalgamated to form a single administrative unit. This move was opposed not only by legislators from East Bengal, who saw it as an attempt to create a false sense of parity in population numbers between the two wings, but also by numerous groups and leaders from West Pakistan, and especially Sindh, who saw it as an attempt by the Punjabi-dominated military and bureaucracy to exploit resources of smaller provinces and use the consolidated unity of the region to gain a bargaining advantage over the eastern wing. Conceptually, One Unit was predicated on the organic unity of the regions of West Pakistan, which were interconnected geographically and functioned as a single economic market. But such a "natural" affinity in the region still required a justification for overriding the multiple ethnic and linguistic formations of what was to become the One Unit of West Pakistan.

Mumtaz Khan Daultana, the former chief minister of Punjab, delivered a speech in the assembly to provide historical justification for the merger. He argued the historical unity of the region since time immemorial. Daultana stated that the region had always been monotheistic in spirit long before it embraced Islam: "From the very earliest time, our history has been one: Mohenjodaro, Harappa, Taxila, the great Empire of the Emperor Kaniska, throughout the ages we have faced the world as one unity. Sir, we have always fought together the same enemies; we have faced the same problems; we have made identical adjustments; we have answered the same challenges with the same responses, from time immemorial."¹⁴⁰ To allay fears of Punjabi domination, Daultana convinced assembly members that Punjab was a single geographical entity. Unlike Sindhi or Pashtun identity, each rooted in ethnicity and language, so would continue to exist even after the dissolution of those provinces, the same did not hold for Punjabi identity, which would cease to exist once One Unit was constituted.¹⁴¹ Therefore, he claimed, it was an act of sacrifice on the part of Punjab rather than a matter of gains to be made.

In Daultana's conceptualization, the state preceded the nation, yet the nation remained Islamic as in the projected state narrative, and Islam served to override claims to ethnic nationhood. Critics of the Islamic state were as much opposed to this form of territorial nationalism—with much passion and energy, in fact—as they were to reducing the national identity to the triumvirate of Islam, Muslim, and Urdu. The thrust of the opposition's critique was to gain recognition for ethnic and linguistic identities while insisting on the erasure of differential rights. Thus, while non-Muslim minority members resented the separate electorate, as it would have created discriminations along the lines of Buddhist Pakistanis, Hindu Pakistanis, and Christian Pakistanis, they did not agree to subsume their identities into an ahistorical entity of West Pakistani. The absurdity of the identity can be seen from the promotional programs and slogans proposed by Pir Ali Muhammad Rashdi to popularize One Unit, including "Unite the Indus Valley" and "Consolidate the platform of the poor."¹⁴²

In opposing West Pakistan, the One Unit scheme, and the Islamic state, minority members were not demanding that the "particular" be kept strictly private. In many of their speeches, members of the assembly pointed to the overwhelming majority of Muslims in the country; even with the sizable Hindu community of East Bengal still intact, Muslims accounted for about 85 percent of the population. As many argued in the assembly, this numerical superiority was bound to have an impact on the working of the state and to ensure that only a Muslim would become the head of the state. Their approach was to keep the particularity of religious and ethnic identification intact while equally participating in deliberations on the common good, thereby setting ethical-moral normative standards that accommodated polyvalent voices and interests.

It is essential to consider how interconnected the decade-long debates on religion, identity, and citizenship were. As a proposed territorial unit, One Unit carried an in-built religious element. Islam kept the disparate ethnic elements together even though the logic of One Unit was that geographical conditions and economic contiguity provided an essential basis for union. A centralized state structure was thus directly linked with an Islam-based identity. Each depended on the other for sustenance and support. To oppose the religious component of this ideological paradigm, the opposition resorted to Jinnah's model of equality. The opposition challenged the unitary form of government in the shape of One Unit by repeatedly referencing the Lahore Resolution of March 1940, popularly known as the "Pakistan Resolution," when the Muslim League publicly demanded separate sovereign states for Muslim-majority areas of British India.

Without a unitary form of government—whether in the form of One Unit or the proposed distribution of powers in the federal, provincial, and concurrent lists of the 1956 constitution—the state could not have used a coercive apparatus to shape a homogenous citizenry that overrode the particularities of ethnicity and language. Without an Islamic anchor, the state could not have justified a claim to national homogeneity. Abul Mansur Ahmad from Bengal recognized the symbiotic relationship between the statist impetus toward centralization and (or for) de-ethnicization. He became a vocal proponent of the Lahore Resolution, using it as an effective strategy to counter the centralized power structure and a unitary form of government. Even after the dismemberment of Pakistan in 1971, Ahmad continued to plead the importance of the Lahore Resolution. He described the emergence of Bangladesh as an endorsement of the original scheme rather than a deviation from it.[143] In the discussion on the distribution of powers between center and the provinces, Abul Mansur Ahmad referred to the peculiarity of Pakistan's geography, which was divided by distance as well as by language, traditions, culture, and even diet and calendars. Because of these peculiarities of differences, argued Ahmad, the Lahore Resolution was drafted in the way it was. This was also why the coalition of Bengali political parties contested the elections of 1954 by focusing on full provincial autonomy in accordance with the Lahore Resolution.[144] In invoking the resolution, even fiery leaders like Sheikh Mujib-ur-Rehman and Suhrawardy interpreted it not as a demand for two states but as one for autonomous states.¹⁴⁵ Such a stance was in accordance with Mujib-ur-Rehman's proposed amendment to use the terms *state government* and *state legislature* instead of *provincial government* or *provincial legislature*. He argued that the Indian and American constitutions used the same terms.¹⁴⁶ As another member, Zahiruddin, explained, the word *province* came from the British administrative system and corresponded to the Mughal term *suba*, both of which connoted unitary forms of government. To dispel the impression of a unitary form of government, he suggested using the term *states* for federating units and requested that the House consider his amendment on its constitutional merit rather than "reading any hidden meaning" in it.¹⁴⁷ But it was difficult to overlook the underlying tones of assertions of sovereignty in using the term *states*. The government had to provide an explanation of the term as used in the foundational text of the Pakistan movement. Also, it had to assert that the provincial units did not have a sovereign, prior existence and that they had voluntarily exercised in 1947 to join the Dominion of Pakistan. Even though the Lahore Resolution continues to resonate in Pakistan today and is often alluded to in public discourse about maximizing provincial autonomy, its crucial impact on the question of sovereignty, or lack thereof, of provincial units has largely been overlooked.

Mushtaq Ahmad Gurmani, a senior leader of the Muslim League and minister in the government, gave an account of the constitutional history of British India, the emergence of various administrative units, and the question of provincial sovereignty. He argued that the presidencies in Calcutta, Madras, and Bombay were initially independently administered before a unified, central government was gradually established to control the entire Indian territory. A gradual devolution of power started with nominal Indian representation in local, provincial, and imperial councils, then gave way to the constitutional reforms of 1919 and to the Government of India Act of 1935, the bedrock of much of the federal structure inherited by India and Pakistan in 1947. Gurmani conceded that the Lahore Resolution envisaged two Muslim states, one in the Northwest and the other in the Northeast. But such an outcome, he said, was contingent on the inclusion of the undivided provinces of Punjab, Bengal, and Assam, which would have meant an absolute, but not substantial, majority of Muslims (62 percent in West Pakistan and 52 percent in East Pakistan).[148] Only after Congress insisted on a division of provinces, claimed Gurmani, did the Muslim League give up the plan to establish two independent sovereign Muslim states, agreeing to establish "one national Muslim State." Accordingly, at the Muslim League Legislators' Convention held in Delhi in 1946, Suhrawardy himself presented a resolution modifying the earlier "two-state solution" of the Lahore Resolution. Gurmani concluded, "It will thus be seen that the resolution of the Muslim League which formed the basis of Pakistan as it emerged was not the Lahore resolution of 1940 but the resolution of the Muslim League legislators Convention passed in Delhi in 1946."[149] If that had not been the case, two Muslim states with their own federations would have been established.

But in giving this narrative to the history of the two-state demand, Gurmani deliberately omitted other important events between the Lahore Resolution of 1940 and the Delhi convention of 1946. In his seminal work on the history of the Lahore Resolution and its evolving meaning throughout the 1940s, Muhammad Aslam Malik refers to the annual meeting held at Madras from 12 to 15 April 1941, in which the amended resolution stated the following: "the establishment of complete independent states formed by demarcating geographically contiguous units into regions which shall be so constituted with such territorial adjustment as may be necessary, that the areas in which the *Musalmans* are numerically in majority as in the North-Western and North-Eastern zones of India, shall be grouped together *and* constitute independent states as Muslim free National Homelands in which the constituent States shall be autonomous and sovereign."[150]

It was eventually in the Delhi convention that the Muslim League legislators amended the resolution to provide for the creation of one state. The first half of the resolution pointed out the features of "Hindu Dharma and Philosophy" and the impossibility of a single nationhood in India. The latter half gave the details of the proposed Pakistan scheme: "whereas the Muslims are convinced that with a view to save Muslim India from the domination of the Hindus and in order to afford them full scope to develop themselves according to their genius, it is necessary to constitute a sovereign independent State comprising Bengal and Assam in the North-East zone and the Punjab, North-West Frontier Province, Sind and Baluchistan in the North-West zone."[151] Even the initial draft for the Delhi convention, Malik notes, used the word *states*. When Abul Hashim from Bengal pointed out that the original resolution had used the word *states*, Jinnah gave the evasive reply that it was a typographical error. No one else raised any objections.[152] But this is not where the importance of the Delhi convention lies. In Malik's interpretation, the Delhi convention did not amend the Lahore Resolution per se; it only fulfilled one of the conditions it laid out. The resolution had envisaged sovereign provinces coming together to form a federation. In the Lahore Resolution, an agency was to be created and entrusted with the task of forming a federal government in each of two separate federations. The Madras amendment had eliminated the necessity of such an agency. This created a lacuna, as a federal government could be established only with the consent and approval of provincial units: "The legislators convention, therefore, embodied the 'consent' of the representatives of their respective provinces, the only acknowledged democratic way of ascertaining the will of the people."[153] For Malik, it was no less significant than had been *foedus* between the sovereign provinces of American federalists at the Philadelphia convention.[154]

This reading of the Lahore Resolution and its subsequent amendment during the Delhi Convention of 1946 contradicts Gurmani's position on the question of sovereignty of provincial units that joined the federation. Gurmani had insisted that at the time of Partition, the Crown transferred power to the two constituent assemblies of India and Pakistan and not to any provinces: "It was transferred to the area as a whole and on the basis that the areas constituting Pakistan would have one single Sovereign State."[155] This transfer, Gurmani admitted, was a departure from the earlier practice of devolving powers to the provinces, as part of the gradual constitutional development of India during the British period. But with this final act, a central authority emerged as the sovereign entity, with the provinces subordinated to it. Such an outcome, from Gurmani's perspective, was in line with a popular demand of the Pakistan movement, "the demand for a Centre . . . which will have the strength to preserve the sovereignty and the solidarity and integrity of the Nation."[156] Gurmani cited the example of Congress, which agreed to cede territory to a Muslim state rather than accept a weak center, as offered by the Cabinet Mission Plan. This, for Gurmani, best explained the importance of a strong center in the project of nation making and state formation.

Both Zahiruddin and Sheikh Mujib-ur-Rehman contested the constitutional and legal position taken by Gurmani. They insisted on a legal position and constitutional history in which the provinces as sovereign entities voluntarily came together to form a federation. Zahiruddin moved the following amendment for the second paragraph of the preamble of the proposed constitution:

> AND WHEREAS the autonomous and sovereign Provinces of Muslim India in the famous Lahore Resolution of 1940 agreed to form sovereign independent States in which the constituent units shall be autonomous and sovereign;
>
> AND WHEREAS on the 14th August, 1947, Pakistan was created on the basis of the said resolution;
>
> AND WHEREAS the autonomous Provinces of Western Zone have voluntarily integrated into one sovereign autonomous State of West Pakistan;
>
> AND WHEREAS the people of autonomous and sovereign States of East Pakistan and West Pakistan have voluntarily agreed to federate into one sovereign independent State for their common weal, progress and defence.[157]

The amendment was rejected, as was his demand that the Lahore Resolution be added as a preamble to the constitution.

Through this proposed amendment and reading of the Lahore Resolution, Bengali legislatures were keen to emphasize that the nation, however defined, preceded the state and was the embodiment of sovereign power before voluntarily acceding to the new federation. Such an approach enabled claims for maximum autonomy for the provinces, the contingent nature of the relationship between center and province, and the indivisibility of the historical roots of ethnic nationhood as existing before any later amalgamation in an Islam-based national project. In other words, the centrality of sovereign nations trumped the ideas of both a unitary state and an Islamic basis for differential citizenship.

In this way, a contextualized reading of assembly debates allows for a new political theory of federation, citizenship, and equality. It was not posited as a simplistic binary of secular and sacred but was offered in the form of a critique and liberal reading of the foundational texts in Pakistan's constitutional history. It thus retains the possibility of a reclamation for an alternative imagining in which a radical notion of equality serves as the basis for Pakistani citizenship, national belonging, and people's sovereignty.

INSTITUTING THE ISLAMIC STATE

The partial ideational foreclosure of issues of language, the electorate, differential citizenship rights, and the role of Islam in state affairs could take place only gradually, and that too with the formal onset of martial law in 1958. The language of Islam in Pakistan shifted from a "decolonial" moment in the 1950s that sought an alternative ethical mode of the political to the assumption of a liberal-Kemalist authoritarian idealism in the 1960s. In a paternalistic pedagogical mode, Kemalism proffered the blueprint of "modern Islam" for nation-making purposes. It was the failure of this project in the aftermath of the breakup of Pakistan in 1971, as well as the vacating of political space for dissent and critical debate that had been available in the 1950s that set the tone for a sacralized language of the law. This is where I find Sadia Saeed's theorization of desecularization to be a better description of what scholars in academic works on Pakistan generally refer to as the "Islamization" process. The term *desecularization* allows for "a better understanding of the ways in which people engage in sacralizing their worlds within the structural confines of the modern nation-state form."[158] Desecularization, in its historical specificity, as elaborated by Saeed, "does not entail an erosion of the secular disciplinary and symbolic powers of the nation-state."[159] Contrary to Saeed's assessment of the process of desecularization as generative and one that might strengthen the nation-state, I show here that Ayub Khan's vision was premised on a similar presumption of the productive use of Islam for strengthening the nation-state, leading to unthought-of consequences—namely, enhancing the scope of the ulema as nonrepresentative determinants of religiopolitical discourse in Pakistan and weakening of the state structure.

There has been an extensive discussion of the Kemalist project of Ayub Khan's Islamic modernist policy, but there remains little understanding of the major transformations that shaped the policy. During consultations for the new constitution, Ayub Khan outlined his vision for utilizing Islamic ideology to counter "the offensive of Communism and Hinduism."[160] At the same time, he was skeptical of sacralizing the constitution's language. His young adviser, Zulfiqar Ali Bhutto, understood the dilemma perfectly and suggested a deft solution. To unite the nation into an indivisible entity through the force of Islam, Bhutto recommended state actions outside the Constitution through political, economic, and social measures. "It is not uncompatible therefore," wrote Bhutto, "for a preamble to make minimum reference to ideology and at the same time for the State to advance the cause of Islam for the good of its people."[161]

Accordingly, Ayub Khan's policies entailed changing the content of the ideological field but trying to create distance from even a descriptivist attachment to the rigid designation of Pakistan as an "Islamic state." In the new constitution that General Ayub Khan promulgated in 1962, *Islamic* was dropped from the state's nomenclature. However, the first task of the newly convened, indirectly elected national assembly was to propose an amendment to change the name back to Islamic Republic of Pakistan. Ayub Khan nevertheless understood the importance of referring to the title or designation of *Islam* or *Islamic* in public discourse.

In a major policy huddle in 1964 to discuss the "religious problems of Pakistan," it was recommended that reference to Pakistan as an Islamic state be minimized. Instead of the prevalent state-sanctioned historical narrative that "Pakistan was fought for and won in the name of Islam," the new policy was to describe the "Pakistan movement [as] a re-action to the narrow-mindedness and tyranny of the Hindus."[162] The note thus suggested avoiding expressions like "Pakistan was won in the name of Islam" in public speeches and statements, as well as in textbooks. The Governors' Conference held in Karachi 14–16 January 1964 maintained that the expression "Islamic State" was not even meaningful, as "the Holy Prophet never called his state an Islamic State."[163] The conference attendees did, however, recognize the difficulty of a complete reversal on the slogan of "Islamic state," as it had become widespread.

Ayub Khan's regime drew battle lines with what he conceived of as an egalitarian concept of Islam and the "mullahs' exploitation" of religion. As the Governors' Conference concluded, the mullah asserted authority over religion because of the educated classes' lack of information about Islam's teachings. The conference attendees saw as their primary target the Jamat-i-Islami, for the group's ability to permeate the middle class with effective propaganda techniques, articulating a religious language that resonated with them. For a counterstrategy, the government was to churn out its religious literature following the model of Jamat's literature, which was "popular because they were cheap, easily available and well turned out."[164] The government was also going to set up large-scale publications of Islamic literature, such as a collection of authentic hadith and the book of Sirat (Prophet's biography). A Quranic society on the model of international Bible societies was also proposed.

While the conference attendees were skeptical of frequent referrals to Islam in the public sphere, they simultaneously sought an increased Islamization of national life. It was a question not of dissociating Islam from public life but of how to establish the state's management of Islam in public life. Thus, while the conference left it to society "to decide what is Islam and what is not Islam,"[165] it at the same time proposed using the power of union councils to control prayer leaders by bringing them into salaried positions, in order to make them dependent and disciplined, and also giving them talking points for Friday sermons in place of their usual "out-of-date sermons in Arabic and Persian."[166] To further ensure the prevalence and popularity of the state-backed idea of Islam, the government was to set up model mosques and seminaries for religious education.

Such a modernized overhaul of the madrassah, mosque, and shrine network was one of the top items on General Ayub Khan's list when he imposed martial law in 1958. The purpose was the same: to establish the state's authority on Islam by setting up model mosques, training prayer leaders in modern education, and sanitizing shrines as exemplars of Islam's "spiritual essence." This activity's departure from the goals of the 1950s is indicated in a document prepared by the Ministry of Interior, which recognizes Islam as a force "which should not be ignored because of the harm it could do if allowed to remain unchecked, as well for the good which can come out of it if it is suitably channelized."¹⁶⁷ Delving into a historical account of religious institutions, the note claims that the temporal authority of the Caliph and other Muslim rulers during the premodern period also extended to religion. The Mughals, for instance, used land grants as a tool to control religious institutions and figures.¹⁶⁸ Even during the British period, princely states such as the Hyderabad Deccan continued to exercise control over religious affairs. This is why, the note claimed, during his stay in Hyderabad Deccan, Maulana Maududi was confined to a role of religious thinker and writer; he became a politico-religious figure of importance in Pakistan because of the "lack of these inhibitive institutions which prevented exploitation of religion for selfish and political ends."¹⁶⁹ The note expressed similar concerns about minority groups like Ahmadis and Shias. As to Hindus, the note referred to the activities of the Ramakrishna Mission in East Pakistan, describing it as "the nucleus of subversive activity engineered by the Indian Mission in Pakistan and anti-Muslim organizations in India."¹⁷⁰ The Ministry of Interior observed that all these groups needed to be controlled.

There had been little government action during the 1950s to exercise authority over Islam. The successive governments had primarily been setting a particular narrative about Islam in the modern world rather than enforcing that narrative. As the note pointed out, in the wake of the 1953 anti-Ahmadi movement, there was a proposal that the state wrest control from mosques and religious endowments. In principle, the cabinet agreed to this and referred it to the Ministry of Education for implementation, but there was no follow-up after the initial discussion.¹⁷¹ Meanwhile, the mullah took control of the religious discourse that opened up after 1947. The ministry observed that both Deobandis and Barelvis were consolidating themselves by creating a federation of their religious institutions across Pakistan.

Amid these developments, the martial-law regime made concerted attempts to establish state authority over Islam in the name of using it "as a force for moral and spiritual uplift of the people," and by freeing it "of the hold of reactionary groups monopolising to themselves the task of interpreting religion and making of it a fetish and a conglomeration of rituals."¹⁷² To this purpose, there was a proposal to set up a department of religious affairs to ensure the registration of religious institutions, the supervision of financial assets and resources of sacred sites, the licensing of preachers, and research on sociopolitical problems from an Islamic perspective, as well as to encourage organizing preaching missions outside Pakistan. In addition, prayer leaders were to undergo training programs and refresher courses. Much of the reformist agenda was to be implemented through a coordinated effort of the newly established Auqaf department, the National Reconstruction Bureau, and the Basic Democracy system at the union council level, along with relevant ministerial support.

Despite such measures, the martial-law regime remained skeptical of the impact of policies on national integration. In particular, the regime was paranoid about the reception of ideology in East Pakistan. Therefore, the Bureau of National Reconstruction—a department set up by Ayub Khan with extensive powers to plan policies and enforce decisions—prepared a document outlining its short-term plan for East Pakistan. This revealing document sums up the Pakistani state's ideological approach for state formation and national integration. There were two main points of the plan: depoliticization and the patronizing of madrassahs to create a pliant citizenry. The plan was to move the campus of Dacca University away from the city. "So long as the student community remains concentrated in Dacca City," the bureau observed, "it will continue to influence the thinking and sections of the Government in power, with the result that Government's decision will not be dictated by considerations of national welfare but by the desire to please the student community."[173] Another pretext for setting up the new campus on the periphery was to provide students with a more peaceful environment to concentrate on their studies and not be distracted by activities that the state authorities considered unacademic, seditious, and distracting.

The bureau members believed that subversive elements in the student community mainly came from English schools and universities. The report observed: "Those who have studied in the Madrassas are much less disposed to falling prey to subversive influences. It is necessary that this section should receive attention and encouragement." The government was to encourage the building of madrassahs in the region: "these Madrassas would be a source of real strength to Government."[174] Ulema living in Karachi and other parts of West Pakistan were to be encouraged to go to East Pakistan to help improve the quality of madrassah education there. Accordingly, the government was to finance the building of madrassahs in East Pakistan and to encourage the printing of Bengali books in Arabic script.

In its comments on the Bureau of National Reconstruction's draft, the Education Department observed that the cause of subversion was not English education but the fact that "all ambitious and forward looking people send their children to such schools and universities. The vivacious men and women students from amongst them who take to subversive activities do so due to frustration when opportunities for suitable jobs or other careers do not exist or are not promised to them."[175]

On other occasions, government departments in East Pakistan consistently had to clarify their stance on various new proposals and initiatives on national integration launched by the martial-law regime. As to the curriculum changes proposed in 1967, for example, the East Pakistan Textbook Board felt that it was being unfairly targeted for not implementing proposed changes in its curriculum and textbooks. In a response submitted to the central government, the board dispelled the impression that the textbooks did not conform to the ideology of Islam and Pakistan. The board said that a committee had recently scrutinized its books. It found them to be free from such defects, as the board followed the recommendations of the Curricula Committee set up by the Commission on National Education.[176] However, the Government of East Pakistan had reservations about using the same textbooks in both wings. The government's position was that it would not be feasible to have primers in both Urdu and Bengali for such subjects as social studies, geography, arithmetic, and languages, as "the geographical and living conditions in the two wings of Pakistan are appreciably different and, hence, books prepared centrally on the subjects mentioned above will not suit the educational requirements of both the wings equally."[177] Plans for a single textbook—along with the efforts to introduce Ayub Khan's life story in school and college curriculum—were eventually dropped as the country's political situation deteriorated, resulting in the ushering in of a second martial-law regime led by General Yahya Khan.

The decade-long, centralized, authoritarian efforts to instrumentalize Islam for state-making and nation-building purposes came to a symbolic end with the resignation of the martial-law regime's chief adviser on Islamic matters, Dr. Fazlur Rahman. The publication of Rahman's scholarly work, *Islam*, caused a stir in religious circles. His nuanced, philosophical reading of scripture was misinterpreted as implying that he was referring to the Quran as the Prophet's words or creation. Given that the regime was already on the brink because of the mass movement of trade unionists and students, it was unable to counter the ulema's propaganda against Rahman. As a result, the regime decided in September 1968 to dissociate itself from Rahman's book. "It would serve no useful purpose if government took upon itself the responsibility to expound and defend the views of Dr. Fazalur Rahman," the cabinet decided. "He should defend himself and government should only provide him the necessary assistance and the backing. The relevant portion of his book which was being mis-interpreted should be translated in Urdu and Bengali and widely publicised."[178] But even with Rahman's resignation, agitation did not subside: ulema and religious parties opposed Ayub Khan's larger plan of what he thought was a modernist Islam vis-à-vis his categorization of "mullahs' Islam."

Ayub Khan's vision of state formation and nation building through claims to religious authority for an egalitarian interpretation of Islam fell flat during his stay in power. His strategy was to sacralize society by institutionalizing a "reformed" Islam while jealously guarding the secular language of the law. The strategy backfired. By the end of Khan's regime, the ulema had emerged as a far more potent influence than they were in the 1950s. Despite numerous strategies of the regime to discipline the ulema by bringing them under regimented bureaucratization, they became the mediating force through which statist policies of social Islamization were negotiated, disputed, and implemented.

Post-1971, the secular language of the law was also diluted. There were two reasons for this: first, brushing more closely with the workings of modern representative structures as members of the assembly, the ulema had developed a familiarity with the language of constitutional law; second, and more importantly, the independence of Bangladesh meant a loss not only of territory but also of the vocal, majority population opposed to the triumvirate of Islam, Urdu, and Muslim. In the first-ever countrywide general elections based on adult franchise, in 1970, the share of the ulema's seats was eighteen in an assembly of three hundred. This was an impressive achievement, given that the ulema had not been elected to a national or provincial assembly in such numbers.[179] Other right-wing religio-political parties had secured seats in West Pakistan, where the bulk of the seats—that is, 81 out of 138—were won by the left-leaning Pakistan People's Party. In an assembly of a united Pakistan, the ulema's influence would not have been significant, but in what remained of Pakistan after 1971, the ulema emerged as a vital part of the opposition. Through their ability to mobilize the masses, they could bring to the forefront an Islamist agenda that populist governments could not ignore. Unlike in the 1950s, when the Bengali opposition checked the government's push for a sacralized polity, in the new Pakistan that emerged after 1971, there was no disagreement on, or fierce opposition to, the agenda of Islamization.

It is beyond the scope of my work to closely analyze the Islamization in post-1971 Pakistan that has affected law, society, and state institutions—a process that Jamal Malik refers to as the colonization of Islam in Pakistan.[180] What is nevertheless relevant here is that following these developments, Pakistan was no longer "Islamic" in the sense of espousing a "Muslim" ideology of national distinctness and vague adherence to modernist principles. The post-1971 Pakistani state freely legislated on matters of belief and practice to ensure purity of faith and the protection of Islam. In the post-1971 period, the Pakistani state accommodated most of the demands that the Board of Taʻlimat-i-Islamiyyah recommended, with the following two exceptions: the exclusion of women from public life and the setting up of an authority for commanding the good (*amr biʼl maʻruf*). The social sanction of women remains at the forefront of debate and dispute in everyday conversation in Pakistan and in religio-political and cultural discourse. The state has not been able to accede to the ulema's demands against women due to the active political opposition organized by women's groups: from the All Pakistan Women Association (APWA), which dates to the 1950s, to the Women Action Forum (WAF) and Sindhiyani Tehrik in the 1980s, to the current wave of young radical feminists, and specifically, Aurat March, a group active since 2017.[181]

To give one example, in the deliberations on the 1973 constitutional draft, the ulema again proposed that the head of the state invariably be a Muslim male. Objecting to this provision, Begum Nasim Jahan reminded the ulema of the recent history of the Pakistan-India War and the Arab-Israel War. The women in charge—Indira Gandhi and Golda Meir, respectively—had inflicted humiliating defeats on Muslim armies. Jahan stated: "They say our 93,000 prisoners of war have gone to India. Whose prisoners of war they are? Are not they POWs of a woman[?] Are you not ashamed that they are a woman's prisoners[?] Has not a woman defeated you most shamelessly? And what happened to our Arab brothers? Did not a woman defeat the Muslim world? This is because you are keeping your women in chains. You don't want them to come out."[182]

As to the enforcement of moral code, the closest ulema came to achieving their agenda was the Hasba Bill, proposed by the ulema-led government of the province Khyber Pakhtunkhwa in 2003. The Pakistani Supreme Court blocked implementation of the bill in 2006. In line with the initial plan proposed by the ulema in the 1950s, the Hasba Bill proposed setting up the institution of *mohtasib* to implement the Islamic way of life in line with the commandment of *amr bi'l mar'uf*.[183] The bill's scope was not limited to eradicating only obscenity or vulgarity but whatever counts as injustice or an abuse of power in society or government offices, vaguely defined.

Meanwhile, on a range of other issues, from the "Islamic" validity of polio drops and the COVID-19 vaccine to implementing Quranic translation pedagogy in schools and scrutinizing textbook content, the ulema undisputedly established themselves as the bearers of religious authority in Pakistan. But even with a sacralized state structure, institutions, and law, the state has continued to resist the demand for a *hasba*-style code of moral policing as a means of enhancing its authority in the name of setting up an Islamic state. Its reluctance is perhaps less due to possible international backlash as it is a realization of the state's inability to claim the religious authority to exercise this arbitrary power.

Since 1971, Pakistan's broad political spectrum has had consensus on Pakistan as an Islamic state. This was not possible during the brief moment in the 1950s when Bengali intelligentsia and political opposition offered a spirited defense and alternative conceptualization of nationhood, citizenship, and sovereignty. Ironically, in Pakistan, there is nostalgia for the 1960s as a period of "openness," but not for the 1950s, when in fact there were more sustained and deeper engagements with the ideas of state, nation, and citizenship. The dismemberment of Pakistan in 1971 was, then, a loss not merely of territory but also of the radical inheritance of these debates and the possibility for envisaging other trajectories for Pakistan.

The instrumental use of Islam to legitimize policies and polities has been a recurrent feature in Pakistan from the very beginning. A humorous, satiric take on everything's being Islamic in the new state was also recurrent, especially in English newspapers. Ashabuddin Ahmed from Comilla College expressed his irritation at political leaders' excessive invocation of Islam in their statements: "Now, Sir, Insha Allah, Masha Allah, Islamic life, Islamic death, Islamic dress, Islamic culture, Islamic society, Islamic State, Islamic education, Islamic Commerce—things very good in themselves—have been repeated ad nauseam without any practical implementation. They have become as irritating to us as sagoo and barely to a patient. We like to hear something new and refreshing."[184]

To understand this "overdose" of Islam in Pakistan's history and politics, it is crucial to explore the theoretical basis whereby Islam in Pakistan was quilted for a retrospective naming of *the thing*, through which could be created the ideological self-experience on an existential, everyday level.

In his work on ideology, Žižek builds on Mouffe's and Laclau's idea of proto-ideological floating signifiers "structured into a unified field through the intervention of a certain 'nodal point' (the Lacanian *point de capiton*) which 'quilts' them, stops their sliding and fixes their meaning."[185] The very fact of these floating signifiers being nonbound and nontied elements in an ideological space necessitates that they are articulated in a chain with other elements and thus generate meanings through their attachments, as part of a structured network of equivalences. The meaning of these signifiers, in other words, depends on the chain they are part of, "but this enchainment is possible only on condition that a certain signifier—the

Lacanian 'One'—'quilts' the whole field and, by embodying it, effectuates its identity."[186] Quilting halts their meaning and delimits it to a structured network of meaning in an ideological field. To modify Žižek's example, an Islamic state is not ideologically predetermined. It can be a liberal Islamic state, as proposed by Liaqat Ali Khan in the Objectives Resolution; a socialist Islamic state, like that of Abul Mansur Ahmad; or the variant proposed by the Board of Ta'limat-i-Islamiyyah. The quilting process gives the term fixity through which free-floating ideological elements are delimited and conferred meaning.

The *point de capiton* serves as a nodal point for the quilting process, that is, as the word that unifies the given field and constitutes its identity; "the word to which 'things' themselves refer to recognize themselves in their unity."[187] Thus, the nodal point retroactively confers meaning to *the thing* once it has been sewn into it, providing us the unity of our historical experience mediated through a process of symbolization. To quote Žižek's famous example of Marlboro's America, the effect of quilting takes place only after Americans start to identify themselves in the image of Marlboro's advertised self-experience of being American. What is at stake in the ideological struggle, argues Žižek, is ascertaining which of the nodal points will totalize and fix the meanings of the free-floating elements.

In the Pakistani context, one needs to look at the quilting processes and the changing nodal points that have had a corresponding impact on the ideological field, retrospectively conferring meaning on what it meant to be an Islamic state: Liaqat Ali Khan's laboratory of Islam, Ayub Khan's Kemalist modernism, Bhutto's Islamic socialism, Zia's Islamic Shariat, Musharraf's enlightened moderation, and Imran Khan's welfare state of Riyasat-i-Madina. The "Islamic state" has generated meaning in the context of equivalential chains in the ideological field in which it has existed. The fact that the state remains Islamic is the effect of the signifier as the "rigid designator," to use Kripke's concept. The retrospective effect of naming itself supports the identity of the object even after its properties have changed. It is that surplus in the object that remains the same, lacking positive reality or consistency "because it is just an objectification of a void, of a discontinuity opened in reality by the emergence of the signifier."[188]

Thus, the real has no necessary mode of symbolization and is merely a historical constellation that can be symbolized in various ways—hence the importance of nodal points. For this chapter, my focus was on the quilting of Islam in the 1950s and on the changes in Islam's nodal points made during the 1960s, which resulted in a differentiated set of meanings. As I have shown, the ideological field continued to retain the descriptivist title of "Islamic state" but with a distinct set of social correlates, public enunciations, and political articulations.

THREE

MAKING THE STATE NATIONAL
Symbols, Flag, and Anthem

THE POSTCOLONIAL STATE'S juridical categories that identified migrants as citizens and determined those included or excluded from that category had put the people, to use Judith Butler's words, in "quite a state."[1] The Pakistani state's praxis had tried to establish a correspondence between state and nation. Such a communion, according to Butler, assumes a national identity through a concerted consensus on the nation, as well as a correspondence between state and nation.[2] But the process of achieving such concordance, which enables the state to derive its legitimacy from the nation, is a contested process. As we have seen, the Pakistani state theoretically worked on a jus soli basis for citizenship but practically pursued an ideological policy that privileged religious belonging. But even that policy was inherently contradictory and unsustainable beyond a certain degree, so the state had to scrap it for a more pragmatic praxis.

Different kinds of state practices emerged during the post-1947 period in Pakistan. As we saw in chapter 1, there was an active process of nonrecognition, whereby non-Muslims were purposefully kept out of state boundaries and not allowed to return. Chapter 2 addressed a process of recognition, whereby groups were produced as minorities, in contrast to majoritarian praxes of religion, ethnicity, or language. Finally, this chapter addresses how the contested nature of the nation-state's majoritarian basis increasingly involved articulating the notion of *qaum* as a metaphor that embodied a North Indian–centric, Urdu-based cultural and literary landscape. *Qaum* became the master trope delimiting Pakistan's legal, cultural, and political boundaries. I follow Srirupa Roy's dictum that discourses about nation-states are constitutive of nation-states, in order to locate the materiality of discursive processes in various state policies that dictate the symbolic repertoire of the nation, and in citizens' everyday interactions, both among themselves and with the newly emerging power constellation of a postcolonial state structure.

THE SYMBOLIC NATION AND ITS IDEOLOGY

Commenting on the role of ideology, Clifford Geertz described ideology as an anchor and a signpost that directs decisions on a range of sociopolitical issues. What enables or strengthens the hold of ideologies, according to Geertz, is the breakdown of traditional societies, a point "at which a political system begins to free itself from the immediate governance of received tradition, from the direct and detailed guidance of religious or philosophical canons on the one hand and from the unreflective precepts of conventional moralism on the other."[3] He described the high, figurative nature of ideology an essential attribute of its function to "render otherwise incomprehensible social situations meaningful."[4] Geertz described the ideological ferment in much of the postcolonial world as symptomatic of the transformative political changes of overthrowing ruling elites and rationalizing administrative structures and of such social phenomena as mass literacy. The breakdown of "tradition" thus leads to a search for an alternative framework for "formulat[ing], think[ing] about, and react[ing] to political problems."[5] These factors accounted for the popularity of such ideological frames as Marxism and nationalism in the postcolonial moment.

What Geertz has overlooked is the role of ideology in the postcolonial project of state formation and nation making, as it undermines or seeks to erase tradition to replace it with a narrative structure that conforms to an idealized form of rationality and modernity, and thereby enables a conjoining of the nation and state. Thus, to use Geertz's formulation, while ideology does function to make autonomous politics possible, it does so by hollowing out the social and traditional of their excesses, making them amenable to control, appropriation, and manipulation. Ideology is therefore both a cause and an effect: it causes tradition to slither away, with the effect that an alternative formulation can become rationally acceptable. Yet the cause of the effect is never fully able to achieve its end and results in an ambivalence—the double time of the nation, as Homi Bhabha puts it. The state's operationalization of rationalized modernity on the patches of tradition's cultural signification is a project that is filiative and affiliative at the same time. To quote Bhabha, it is "in the disjunctive time of the nation's modernity . . . that questions of nation as narration come to be posed."[6] The very positing of the question of how to narrativize the nation reveals the irreconcilability of the disjunction of the archaic nation and its homogenized modernity. These disjunctures are best explained in policies and debates on such issues as the adoption of national symbols, rituals for state ceremonies, and so on.

First, let us consider the example of the national flag, the first item of symbolic order to be decided by the Pakistani state. What was adopted as the national flag of the newly established state of Pakistan was essentially the flag of the Muslim League, the political party that led the demand for a Muslim-majority state. The flag comprises a white crescent and star against a dark-green backdrop. The precise history of the Muslim League flag—including the date of its creation or the name of its designer—is not documented. Nevertheless, its symbolism is clear: green is the color of the dome of Prophet Muhammad's tomb in Medina, and has been since Ottoman rule, and the crescent has been associated with Islam throughout its history, perhaps given the importance of the lunar calendar. Indeed, such popular symbols are often incorporated, in one way or the other, into the flags of other Muslim nations and organizations.

By the first quarter of the twentieth century, the crescent on a green cloth had become associated with the Muslim League in an almost metonymic fashion, and for Jinnah, the founder of the Pakistani state, it carried sentimental value. In 1938, at a flag-hoisting ceremony in Bombay, the premier of Punjab, Sir Sikandar Hayat Khan, did not attach any historical or symbolic significance to the Muslim League's flag. He described it as any other flag, just as every regiment in the military had a flag of its own with distinct color scheme. Jinnah quickly refuted this idea, calling the flag distinctive because it was new and deep rooted at the same time.[7] In describing the flag as bequeathed to Muslims by the Prophet himself and, in its modern incarnation, as a symbol of Muslim political consciousness, Jinnah established a link between the flag as a modern symbol of the state and the notion of an *'alam*, with the latter's metaphorically laden meanings in Islamic history of upholding valor and serving as the bearer of truth.[8] While the postcolonial state inherited this emotional attachment with the flag as *'alam*, and such a connection helped the state claim authenticity through the past, it was also a source of anxiety: the historical richness and complexity that the idea of *'alam* carried could be invoked for multiple political projects. Hence, as previously outlined in the theoretical framework of this book, stabilizing the symbolic meaning of the national flag was an important task for the Pakistani state.

It is not surprising, then, that one of the first businesses of the newly convened Constituent Assembly of Pakistan was to finalize the new state's flag.[9] The Pakistani prime minister, Liaqat Ali Khan, submitted the flag's design to the assembly for approval. He described it as the flag of the Pakistani nation, representing freedom, liberty, and equality.[10] The Hindu members of the assembly were quick to point out that the flag of the Muslim League, with slight changes, had been adopted as the country's national flag. As Dhirendra Nath Datta from East Bengal pointed out in a speech, the flag should have been designed in consultation with all communities to help "creat[e] enthusiasm over the flag."[11] In responding to the objection that the flag carried Islamic symbols, Liaqat Ali Khan said that the moon and stars were everyone's property. Kiran Sankar Roy from East Bengal reminded him that the sun, too, was a shared property. Khan could only respond rather humorously to say that "the sun's heat is scorching and moon's light is soothing."[12] It is interesting to note that when East Bengal gained independence, becoming Bangladesh, it chose the sun as its dominant symbol, signifying a new dawn, while preserving a green background, to represent the Bengali landscape.

The press reported Congress members' criticisms of the flag as their refusal to respect it for its "Islamic content." In an editorial dated 13 August 1947, *Pakistan Times* described the flag as fulfilling the primary function of a symbol of Pakistani state authority. It was not a religious flag, because, the editorial claimed, "Islam enjoins no particular flag for Muslims. . . . It was a flag of a party and represented the urge of a large section of the Indian peoples for freedom in the same way as the Congress flag did."[13] The *Times* suggested that all accept the modified flag and become loyal citizens of the new state, just like Muslims in India had accepted the modified Congress flag in India. Some citizens raised objections to the change in the flag's original design. In a letter, Ayesha Rashid from Calcutta wrote that the official Muslim League flag did not have a star and was closer to the "original Islamic flag." Among the proposed new designs, there was one with five stars, representing the five provinces, and a stripe of white, red, or another color. "Such a flag," she wrote, "will be grotesque and antagonistic to the underlying motif of all Islamic art—simplicity."[14] She suggested a flag with a crescent against a green background and a white stripe in the edge to represent minorities.

The flag's design and symbolism claimed inspiration from Islamic civilization and history. But the richness of the past was a problem in itself and had to be managed through narrativization in rationalized, bureaucratic language. The Pakistani Ministry of Information published a brief booklet that gives precise geometrical calculations for the flag, lists rules for flying or unfolding the flag, and provides a brief description of its history.[15] The flag's symbolism was taken for granted during the colonial period. But when in 1948 the UN Secretariat wrote to the Pakistani government requesting information on the symbolism of Pakistani flag, the ministry compiled a booklet on the flag to provide an official commentary on its symbolic content. Additionally, the postcolonial state was eager to popularize its understanding of what the flag stood for to offset any counterhistorical representations. In an article published in *Imroz* on 24 August 1948, for instance, Abdul Ghafur Qureshi from Karachi explained the historical significance of the flag by referring to Iqbal's couplet:

> *Taighun ke sa'ye mai hum pal kar jawan huway hain*
> *Khanjar hilal ka hai qaumi nishan hamara*

> Brought up in the shadow of the sword, we reached maturity;
> The scimitar of the crescent moon is the emblem of our community.[16]

Qureshi said that in a letter Iqbal wrote to Ghazi Abdul Rahman in May 1916, he gave a brief history of the crescent. He reported Iqbal's saying that Muslims did not use the crescent during the Prophet's period or his companions; they probably used it for the first time after the victory of Constantinople, and some said its use started during the Crusades. In his estimation, its usage must have been accidental: if Christians used the cross, Muslims must have adopted the crescent as a mark of distinction.

Muhammad Asad, influential Muslim thinker and the author of *Road to Mecca*, helped draft the official explanation of the flag. At the time, he was working with the government to help prepare a vision for a modern Islamic state. Asad mentioned in his note that the Prophet had used different banners at different times. It was the Fatimids who adopted the color green. When Sultan Salim proclaimed himself caliph after the Abbasids, he chose green, which gradually became "the most widely accepted colour through-out the Muslim world." As for the crescent, Asad ascribed it to "an old tribal sign, which in its earliest form may have been a horseshoe. From the 16th century onward, the combination of crescent and star was the symbol of the Ottoman Empire," and eventually, it became the "symbol of Islamic power and gradually of Islam itself."[17]

Asad's matter-of-fact opinion about the flag was a multilayered yet demystified account that did not provide the symbolic affect required for the flag to serve as a sacred symbol of the state. Such an account was furnished by G. Rasheed, undersecretary to the cabinet. In a note dated 17 February 1949, Rasheed theorized the significance of the crescent and star as reflective of Islam's ideas of creation, the active and the receptive, which, according to him, could be described in Sufi language as *jalal* (glory—which he translated as fury) and *jamal* (beauty); the crescent and star represented a balance of these two forces of creation. To his credit, he did admit to making this statement without the backing of any authentic sources and called his interpretation a "pure guess."[18] The note described white as a symbol of peace, justice, and equality that also represented minorities, an affirmation of the government's resolve "to act up to this symbolic declaration."[19] The addition of white to the traditional Muslim League flag was thus an act of expediency to indicate a commitment to minority rights. Similarly, quoting the comments of Liaqat Ali Khan from the flag debate in the Constituent Assembly, the undersecretary to the cabinet wrote that the flag had been designed in Delhi by a few leaders. It was the same flag used by the Muslim League, "except for the prominent white stripe which was included as representative of the minorities and of the fair attitude promised to them."[20]

Eventually, on 8 July 1949, the cabinet approved the following statement to explain the significance of the color and symbols used in the Pakistani flag:

1. The white and dark green field represents the peace and prosperity.
2. The crescent of the flag represents progress. (The crescent has for centuries past been used as their emblem by many Islamic countries, and this is one of the incidental reasons for adopting it for Pakistan).
3. The Pakistan flag, therefore, represents that the State stands for peace, prosperity, progress and enlightenment.[21]

In this manner, the resulting statist narrative flattened the complexity of varying interpretations and overlapping civilizational traditions. The official statement ascribed preferred meanings to various colors, motifs, and symbols used in the flag to arrive at an explanation that suited the purposes of the nation-state.

WHICH COLOR IS MY FLAG? FIFTY SHADES OF GREEN

Although a sanitized historical account was required to explain and justify the flag's green color for nation-making purposes, consistency in color was an equally important prerequisite for the standardization and homogenization required of a state-formation project. The resolution passed by the Constituent Assembly of Pakistan had recommended simply dark green for the Pakistani flag, without any further specifications. But as the Ministry of Defense took up the practical question of making an *ur*-flag for the nation, it consulted experts and vendors from the chemical industry. The question of standardization was of great importance. As the Prime Minister's Office mentioned: "We cannot afford to be haphazard about this . . . a British Colour Council registered number is the only way of perpetuating the original 'Pakistan green.'"[22] To do so, the color was to be determined by the flag presented to Jinnah at the time of Pakistan's creation. Part of the cloth was removed and sent to the British Colour Council for exact determination. The council informed the Ministry of Defense that the color of the cloth was "Tartan green" and its code was BCC 26.[23] But apparently, the council had erred in its assessment of the color, so to arrive at an authentic "Pakistan green," the home division also conducted tests in collaboration with the local chemical industry. However, the Ministry of Defense insisted on Tartan green as the closest to the color in the sample. They attributed the slight variation to fading from wear and tear. Jinnah's flag had faded and could not serve as the standard anymore.

The next question was to establish a suitable material for the flag. In a detailed note by Deputy Secretary J. G. Kharas, from 27 December 1951, the Ministry of Interior recommended woolen bunting, as this was the standard material for flags throughout the world was "considered to be the only suitable material for the purpose as it is loosely woven and allows the flag to fly freely and prevents whipping and destruction of the trailing edge."[24]

A last issue was that of dyes: the formula sent by the Ministry of Defense was suitable only for wool fabrics, but the Home Ministry also required formulas for spray printing, cloth printing, and paper printing.[25]

While standardizing the historical narrative and color were adequately addressed from a statist perspective, the flag's symbolism continues to be a problem. The crescent drawn in the flag depicts a declining moon. This issue was brought before the cabinet on various occasions, as early as 1948, with continued debates into the 1970s. Even today, many astrologers point to the waning position of the moon on the Pakistani flag as a reason for the country's decline and decay. For instance, *'Aina-i-Qismat*, a well-known Urdu astrology magazine and publisher of astrological almanacs, published the photo of the Pakistani flag on its cover page, pointing to a distinction between *hilali chand* (crescent) and *wabali chand* (cursed moon).[26]

Because of the potentially harmful effects of the "wrong crescent" depicted on the Pakistani flag, the Ministry of Interior suggested sending the matter to the Constituent Assembly to modify the position of the crescent on the flag to make sure it always appeared as a waxing moon. But because the design had been in circulation as a popular symbol of Muslim political organization since the early 1920s, and had been formalized as a state symbol by the Constituent Assembly in August 1947, it was considered imprudent to change the flag's design. However, for other state symbols such as currency notes, official seals, and postage stamps, the government decided to change the shape of the crescent.[27] So while the crescent appears in a waning position on the national flag, it is in a waxing position on all other state symbols and official documents. As pointed out at a later cabinet meeting, the rationale was this: "if the Flag is seen from right to left with the white portion of the Flag nearest the mast being on the right hand size, the position of the Crescent should be correct as it would then be in the waxing position."[28] This explanation satisfied the existing position of the waning moon on the flag, giving the appearance of a waxing moon from a standing position. Because the Constituent Assembly's resolution applied to the flag alone, a change in the position of the crescent and star when used as an official emblem was justified.

Not everyone was on board with this decision. The Embassy of Pakistan in Washington, DC, sent a letter to Foreign Minister Sir Zafarullah Khan on 2 February 1949 commenting on the cabinet's revised position on the crescent and star. The embassy appealed to the cabinet to reconsider its decision, so that the emblem would correspond with the national flag as Jinnah and the Constituent Assembly had originally approved it: "Neither the Quaid-i-Azam nor the Constituent Assembly considered that this would be inappropriate or that waxing or waning had anything to do with the matter." The memorandum gave examples of Turkish and Egyptian flags where the crescent faces east. Also from an artistic perspective, the memorandum stated, it was better to depict the crescent facing northeast than northwest, as it "gives a far better balanced and pleasing effect."[29] The cabinet rejected the proposal.

The debate resurfaced in post-1971 Pakistan. It can be conjectured that Zulfiqar Ali Bhutto's government believed in the superstition associated with a waning moon and held it responsible for Pakistan's humiliating military defeat, moving the government to take up the question of changing the crescent's shape. Hamid Jalal, a minister in Bhutto's cabinet, brainstormed with vexillologists to find ways of changing the crescent from a waxing to a waning position without having the rules amended by the national assembly. His solution was "to amend Rule 18 and allow the Pakistan Flag, when displayed on a wall, to have the white stripe to the right of the person facing the Flag." The amendment was to replace the provision that the white stripe be on the left when facing the flag, thus putting the crescent in the wrong position.[30] According to Jalal, the flag resolution specified only how the flag was to be drawn, not how it was displayed. He cited Dr. Whitney Smith of the Flag Research Centre: "A national flag must be shown (to a person facing it) with its mast on the left. To me it seems possible that the mast-on-the-left portrayal of national flags has something to do with the writing of most European scripts from left to right. The Saudi Arabian flag is shown, in publications like the United Nations flag chart, as flying from the hoist to the left of the person facing it."[31]

No final decision was taken on this matter; the cabinet deferred it.

Although the flag's symbolism and its excess were brought under control through rationalized bureaucratic language, the flag also had to be invested with a sacral aura, so that it could act as a modern-day totem, to use Durkheim's analogy. Hence the flag comes with a strict list of rules that limit its usage and dictate the protocol to be observed in its presence. Reading the rules for the Pakistan flag brings life to an inanimate object that is to be picked up, handled, hoisted, and folded in a ritualized manner. Among other instructions, the booklet of flag rules stipulates that, in case the flag is hoisted alongside the flags of other countries, "the place of honour shall be reserved for the Pakistan Flag." In case of more than two flags, "the Pakistan Flag shall be placed in the centre if the number of flags is odd." In case of an even number of flags, the Pakistani flag "shall be flown the first to the right of the centre."[32]

The flag as the omnipresent bearer of state sovereignty does not allow for partnership with other flags within its realm. A recent example of such violation of sovereign authority was the hoisting of an Indian flag in Okara by a local man. In January 2016, the tailor Umar Daraz stitched an Indian flag and hoisted it atop his rooftop in adulation of his favorite cricketer, Virat Kohli, of India. It became a scandal, and the young man was immediately arrested on charges "reserved for crimes considered contravening Pakistan's sovereignty and carrying a sentence of up to 10 years in prison."[33]

The act of hoisting another country's flag does not violate any explicit provision of the penal code. It was by stretching the legal interpretation of sedition and of endangering public peace and order that Daraz could be charged with committing a heinous crime. Only the postcolonial state had the right to authorize the use of another country's flag during, say, an international event or a sports tournament, a ritualization through which national space could be prepared to receive such a foreign object. Anyone bypassing this ritualist performance was guilty of transgression.

In the 1950s, when Pakistan was still a Dominion under the British Crown, a recurrent issue for the state was how to accommodate the Union Jack, especially on such special occasions as the Queen's birthday. As mentioned earlier, the usual practice of displaying flags at official ceremonies did not cause any concern, although their display also required legal etiquette. But hoisting the flag of another country—in this case, that of the former colonizer—on a state building carried considerable political risk and required an imagination that the available legal fiction failed to provide. During negotiations over the transfer of power, the British government insisted on maintaining the sanctity of the Union Jack, which, according to it, represented the entire Commonwealth. Despite its pro-Western policy, the Pakistani government was reluctant to grant equal status to the Union Jack, even on special occasions. Through Pakistan's emissary in the United Kingdom, the British government reminded Pakistan of the agreement among Nehru, Jinnah, and Mountbatten to fly the Union Jack on specified days.[34] Pakistan refused to accept the stance on the ground that the Pakistani flag was as much "the King's flag in Pakistan as the Union Jack."[35] Because the sight of the Union Jack was a reminder of criminal colonial rule, the government risked losing popular support by allowing it on government buildings. By the late 1950s, the British government gave up on the policy and stopped reminding Pakistan of its pre-Partition contractual obligations.

As the most visible representation of the new state, the flag figured prominently in public discourse on patriotism and discussions about how to cultivate respect for the country's national symbols. Numerous citizens regularly wrote letters to the editor to report acts of disrespect toward the flag, express their dismay, and call for educating the masses, in order to make them realize the flag's importance and the need to honor it. A frequent complaint was about the cinema. Because Pakistan did not officially adopt an anthem until 1954 (as further discussed later), the government introduced the policy of showing the Pakistani flag on cinema screens as a pedagogical tool meant to familiarize citizens with Pakistani national symbols. The public response was divided. S. R. Osmani, from Dacca, was opposed to displaying the flag in a cinema hall, as it was not a "holy place," and such constant display could trivialize the significance of the flag.[36] Shawkat Ali Khan disagreed. He said that the Union Jack was also displayed in cinema houses before Partition, and people used to give homage to it.[37] Others debated whether the flag should be displayed at the start of the film or after the show. Atia Zahooruddin, from Narayanganj, wrote that displaying the national flag before the film's beginning was not a good idea, as cinemagoers do not arrive on time. Once they arrive, they hurry to occupy their seats, so they might miss the display. She wrote that "if the people can sit in the hall for three hours just to see the film it will not be difficult for them to wait for a few seconds [after the film ended] in honour of the National Flag, which is a symbol of our independence, which has taken sacrifices from millions of people."[38]

Later, once the anthem was approved, a new concern among citizens was the disrespect shown to the anthem and the flag. Some citizens debated playing the anthem before or after the film. D. Andrews, from Dacca, proposed a middle ground. He recommended playing the anthem "immediately after interval and before the main picture is screened. . . . If the front-row 'patrons' would only be kind enough to stand to attention, the view of the screen would be obstructed and people in the near will have no alternative but to stand up also."[39]

From a statist perspective, it was necessary to familiarize people with the most important national symbol through the broadest circulation possible, but such a practice also raised concerns about citizens' casual approaches to national symbols after they become too familiar with them. The *Pakistan Observer* published a full-length article on this theme as early as August 1949. Titled "Our National Flag: Appeal to Maintain Its Sanctity and Prestige," it called for a calculated use of the flag on the select occasion specified by the state to ensure the sanctity of the national flag as "the sacred symbol of a country's freedom." The article recognized the importance of the official manual for flag use for its potential to discipline the citizens. "Not all, however, can unfurl the Crescent and the Star as and when they please," the article reads. "Such indiscriminate handling of the Flag will reflect not only on our good sense but will also belittle the ideals for which the Pakistan Flag stands—Peace, Prosperity, Progress and Enlightenment."[40] Despite the government's clear regulations about flag use, the public seldom followed them, nor were people drawing the flag according to specifications. As a correspondent from a later date, Zakia Mustafa, of Dacca, wrote in March 1958, flag rules were not properly followed during Republic Day celebrations. For example, at the office of the inspector of schools, the "flag was tied to a piece of Bamboo stick and disgracefully tied with the 'Inspector of School' board."[41]

Unrestricted use of the flag was allowed on only four days of the year: the birthday of the Holy Prophet, Pakistan Day (14 August), Jinnah's birthday, and the King's or Queen's birthday. The *Pakistan Observer* insisted that it was every patriotic citizen's duty to fly the flag on these designated days only "to give vent to his enthusiasm."[42] To preserve the dignity and prestige of the flag, the article recommended that it was important to refrain from indiscriminate flying of the flag. Regulating the passions of citizens and disciplining their bodies was part of the postcolonial state's pedagogy for nation making.

It was neither possible nor desirable to enforce the prescribed mannerism for use of the national flag. On the contrary, a popular attachment to the flag helped cultivate a sense of patriotic belonging. At the same time, the ritualized practices associated with the flag helped create an aura about it, making it a sacred relic and an object of devotion. The story of the flag's symbolism exemplified a similar dilemma. A popular narrative grounded in radical histories associated with *alam* and its emotive, lyrical language gives the flag a different meaning, especially among the masses. The official version, too, draws on Islamic civilization but for a more sanitized reading of the past. It ensures that the flag becomes a popular symbol of Muslim nationhood, but that its meanings are stable and amenable to control. The internal correspondence about the story of the flag was not meant for public consumption, nor was there any certainty that the statist version of the flag would prevail. Yet from a statist perspective, it was important to provide such a narrative: it helped set a vision for the new state, connecting its imagined past with an idealized future.

SYMBOLS OF THE NATION

To extend Durkheim's formulation, currency notes and stamps are semiotic objects of desire to which sentiments attach themselves.[43] In that sense, official seals, currency notes, and postal stamps conjoin state and nation in their ideational and material forms. They can be in circulation and daily use without losing prestige while still reinforcing the symbolism of sovereign power. But as Geisler reminds us, the attachment to symbols is not spontaneous, as Durkheim claims. Geisler describes the process as a mass media system that has "developed their own differentiated modes of articulation or 'genres' (flags, anthems, currency, monuments, etc.) . . . [and] establish and maintain a power structure."[44] This framework helps explain daily, multiple exposures to and interactions with, symbols such as waving the flag during a cricket match, seeing the "national landscape" and crescent on currency notes, listening to a national song on the radio, etc. Through such "recursive communication," argues Geisler, national symbols "stabilize our sense of collective identity."[45] Because of such objects' ability to tell a story about the nation, states are careful to design and plan their symbolism, as much as they are careful to, in the case of currency, establish security features to prevent counterfeit.

Using the symbolic communicative powers of currency is not limited to the modern nation-state. The strategy has been practiced for centuries, with numerous academic works explaining the symbolic coding of various signs, scripts, and images used by kings, empires, or local chiefdoms to establish sovereign authority and claim legitimacy. In the modern period, currency notes and postage stamps have become important bearers of national sovereignty as portraits of the nation.[46] In their performative role, they serve a much more critical function in the modern era of interstate, international relations than in the premodern period. This aspect is clearly brought forth in disputes of territory or around commemorative practices associated with an uncomfortable past or contested history. For instance, in the case of Palestine, the designing of a new currency under the British Mandate after World War I was a highly political act to achieve the recognition of Jewish sovereign claims over the region. To use the title of Yair Wallach's paper, the British were creating a country through currency and stamps.[47] By adding Hebrew to Arabic and English on new currency notes and stamps—not to mention, other designs and symbols—the British policy normalized the Zionist presence in and claims to Palestinian land.

A similar study of symbols and language in Pakistani currency, stamps, and state seals helps us understand the national story that circulated via these objects.[48] Issuing Pakistani banknotes and stamps was a significant marker of Pakistan's sovereignty, given that Indian banknotes continued as legal tender up to 1948. Until the end of September 1948, Indian notes circulated, but with two inscriptions on the front proclaiming Pakistan's name.[49]

On 1 March 1949, the government issued two currency notes worth one and two rupees depicting historical places located in Pakistan. These included the Naulakha Pavilion of Lahore Fort, with denominations in Bengali, Urdu, and English. Two-rupee notes showed part of the wall encircling the tomb of Jehangir. Five- and ten-rupee notes issued on 1 September 1951 depicted a waxing crescent and star.[50] Currency notes of different values carried images of Jinnah—note that none has an image of Iqbal—or of Jehangir's tomb (thousand-rupee note), and Islamia College Peshawar. Initially, the proposal to add Jinnah's photograph to the currency note was dropped because it was thought that the representation of living persons would not be acceptable to the Pakistani public.[51] To represent East Pakistan, scenic pictures with boats were typically used. The new generation of notes introduced in 1974 removed East Pakistan's landscapes and Bengali numerals. For the first and perhaps last time, the new one-rupee note of 1974 carried the monetary denomination of the currency note in all four regional languages.[52]

It was difficult for successive governments to choose flora and fauna reflective of "Pakistani character," as there was disagreement on the utility of such symbols. A more troubling issue was that of standardizing the emblem itself. In 1954, the government chose the tiger and narcissus as symbols and emblems of Pakistan. When these symbols were initially approved in November 1950, S. M. Ikram wrote a note to explain their significance: "The Bengal Tiger is so famous and its association with East Bengal are so great that it may well claim the place of honour among Pakistani animals. It has also associations with our literature where it is the embodiment of courage, valour and strength. The Jasmine too is a flower of great popularity in Pakistan. The two taken together will stand for bravery softened with culture. These symbols are distinctive, do not smack of idolatry[,] have not been borrowed from other countries[,] represent both East and West Pakistan and will look elegant on a panel."[53] But when it came down to designing the symbols in a standardized manner, government officials encountered problems: there were various varieties of narcissus and multiple images of the Bengal tiger to choose from. To resolve this, bureaucrats worked with artists to take specimens of narcissuses and the Bengal tiger from *National Geographic*, the *Washington Post*, and the *Times Herald*, as well as *Chamber's Encyclopedia Britannica*, *Wild Beasts of India*, *Sirat-un-Nabi*, and *Tehzib-ul-Akhlaq*.[54] In the case of the narcissus, the ministry pointed out that the variety grown in Pakistan was "that of the white lily Nargis with a single bunch of about 20 to 50 flowers," whereas the specimen photograph shared earlier was "that of the popy [sic] or the cosmus [sic] types."[55] The officers in charge sought help from the British Council's representative in Pakistan in May 1956 to supply books "about the significance of various flowers" and improve the existing floral designs. They were also anxious about the ideas associated with such symbols. For instance, the ministry referred to the "bad association in Greek mythology" with narcissus, signifying sightlessness.[56]

In a review process starting in June 1961, it was proposed that the narcissus be replaced with jasmine. The summary presented before the cabinet justified the decision by the abundant growth of jasmine in East and West Pakistan, its soothing fragrance, and wider popularity among the people. Besides, the summary claimed, jasmine carried historical significance, figuring prominently in folklore and in Mughal paintings and murals.[57] A search to find a match for the jasmine variety depicted in Mughal miniatures was begun. Salahuddin Ahmad from the Ministry of Agriculture wrote in a note that the variety found in Mughal-era works was *Grandi-*

florum Linn (*chameli*). But if historical validation was not important, his suggestion was to opt for another variety: *Jasminum sambac* (*motia*).[58] In a note dated 3 September 1964, the section officer Faiz Mohammad differed from this opinion. He said that although *motia* had a fragrant smell, it did not remain evergreen, shedding its leaves in autumn.[59]

Eventually, given the complexity of identifying a standard archetype for Pakistani narcissus or jasmine, the idea was shelved altogether. The spoken rationale for abandoning the task, however, was that in choosing such a symbol, Pakistan was being guided by Western convention. In the presence of a coat of arms, then used on state documents and stationery, such symbols did not serve a purpose. "In view of this," Faiz Mohammad wrote on 24 April 1965, "as well as in consideration of the fact that a majority of the Islamic countries of the Middle East has not adopted any floral symbol, other than the Coat of Arms," the committee decided to drop the search for a floral symbol.[60] As Muizuddin Ahmad's summary for the cabinet in June 1965 argued, symbols and emblems were relics from "the days of the Crusades where secret emissaries of the Knights needed marks of identification."[61]

The government had approved the official crest in the early 1950s. In September 1953, Mushtaq Ahmad Gurmani presented a proposed design before the Constituent Assembly: "In designing the proposed Crest of Pakistan, an attempt has been made to embody, in a pictorial form, the national ideals and the characteristics and factors which inspire them." The crescent (in waxing position) symbolized progress, the five-rayed star represented light and knowledge, and the green field represented prosperity. "The ear of wheat and the jute stalk on either side of the crescent and star on a base of cotton pods," explained Gurmani, "represent the bounties of nature with which Pakistan is endowed."[62] A Quranic verse—*hasbuna llahu wa-ni'mal-wakil* ("Allah is sufficient for us, and He is an excellent trustee;" 3:173)—was inscribed on the bottom of the crest.[63]

A new crest was introduced in 1954 with slight but significant modifications. The new design comprises a shield with four quarters surrounded by a wreath of jasmine resting on a scroll. A waxing crescent is depicted at the top of the crest. The four quarters of the shield show wheat, cotton, jute, and tea, major crops of East and West Pakistan. On the scroll is inscribed Jinnah's famous motto, "faith, unity and discipline."⁶⁴ The syntax and their Urdu translation has been an issue of dispute. As Aqeel Abbas Jafri's research shows, the initially proposed order was "unity, faith and discipline," translated into Urdu as *ittihad, iqan aur nazm*. Over the years, however, as the Pakistani state inched toward a greater public role for Islam in public affairs, the order was changed to its present form, with "faith" translated as *iman* to connote religious significance rather than firmness or determination.

Other provincial governments have followed a similar pattern of using the crescent in a waxing position and adding an agricultural landscape to highlight regional specificity. For instance, the official crests of Baluchistan and Punjab depict rivers and camels. The common denominator in the case of all provincial government and official departments is the waxing crescent and star. The waxing crescent and star have thus become a metonym for the Muslim state, which is encountered on a daily basis and widely circulated through a range of objects. Increasingly, major Pakistani institutions have chosen to inscribe a Quranic inscription on their insignia. For instance, the logo of Radio Pakistan, designed by Abdur Rahman Chughtai, symbolizes an eagle in flight with its wings spread out enclosing a crescent and star—a depiction based on Iqbal's poetry, in which the *shahin* (falcon) shows a fiercely independent character.⁶⁵

(AD)DRESSING THE NATION: JINNAH'S WARDROBE

Dress, or choice of fabric, figured prominently during anticolonial resistance. In the case of India, Gandhi was the chief proponent of using dress as a strategy. Susan Bean describes Gandhi as a semiotician who used "his appearance to communicate his most important message in a form comprehensible to all Indians."⁶⁶ By choosing to wear hand-spun, coarse cloth, Gandhi challenged the foundations of colonial modernity undergirded by its industrial prowess and protested the mechanization of life. Gandhi also used *khadi* as a commodity and political strategy of the Swadeshi movement to argue for India's economic autonomy and political independence.⁶⁷ To cite Lisa Trivedi, Gandhi "used *khadi* to construct a common visual vocabulary through which a population separated by language, religion, caste, class, and region communicated their political dissent and their visions of community."⁶⁸ With such a connection in the making of Indian nationhood, it was natural that *khadi* was incorporated into the body politic of the Indian Republic after independence.

In the case of the Muslim League, although there was a flag associated with the movement, dress did not formally enter the discussions. In 1944, Sami Ahmad, a Muslim League supporter from Ramna Bagh, Patna, wrote to Jinnah about the importance of national dress. Jinnah responded that the question was irrelevant under the present circumstances: "There is no such a thing as one dress even for the Mussalmans. Dress has its importance no doubt, but I think you are attaching too much important to it. If we can have one dress for all Mussalmans, then I think it will stand out as a national symbol."⁶⁹ But this does not mean that Jinnah did not himself signal preferred political and social behaviors through dress. His being well dressed was often contrasted with Gandhi's abnegation of self and his fakir-like simplicity. Once the Pakistan movement started in the 1940s, Jinnah often donned *sherwanis* to indicate a connection with a North India idea of gentrified Muslim nobility. Such a practice helped establish a claim in favor of the *sherwani* as a national dress. The catalog of items at a national museum that lists Jinnah's possessions, published by the government of Pakistan, explicitly mentions his *sherwanis*: "It is generally believed that Quaid-i-Azam started wearing Pakistani dress only after being elected President of All-India Muslim League in 1934 but a China silk Sherwani in this collection tailored by Hoar and Co. Bombay in 1925 (S. No. 13) belies this point of view."⁷⁰

The discussion of the importance of dress as an identity marker for community formation had been the focus of attention among Muslim groups and individuals since the late nineteenth century. The Turkish cap popularized during that period was a symbolic act of allegiance to the Ottoman caliphate. In later periods, Muslim clerics frowned on "Westernized" Aligarh graduates who opted for European dress. None of the debates or disputes, however, centered on a particular piece of clothing, as they did in the case of *khadi* as debated by the Indian National Congress. As works on Muslim figural representation in India show, *shalwar-qamiz*, *sherwani*, and the *fez* nevertheless acquired enduring significance as "Muslim attire."

This colonial context shaped the debate on choosing a national dress for the Pakistani state at the official and public levels. India's choice for Nehru cap and waistcoat, kurta and pajama, and Gandhian-style dhoti in the post-1947 period did not go unnoticed. In its news commentary, the daily *Imroz* gave a brief historical overview of the Muslim contribution to dress in India. Claiming that before the arrival of Muslims, Hindus simply wrapped themselves with a piece of cloth, newspaper writers identified turbans, *achkans*, and *angrakha* as Muslim attire that had evolved as a result of Muslim rule in India.[71]

Because of the association of the *sherwani* and *shalwar* with a broadly defined Muslim political authority and civilization, general newspaper readers often complained about the head of an Islamic state's donning of Western attire. N. Javid, from Dacca, wrote that since Pakistan had become an Islamic republic, the president should wear national dress: *sherwani*, *shalwar*, and a Jinnah cap.[72] A cartoon in *Pakistan Times* from the mid-1950s depicts a distressed woman turning her face away from her husband wearing a *sherwani*. "But believe me, honey, I am not going to grow a beard when Pakistan becomes an Islamic Republic," assures the husband.

At the official level, the postcolonial state exercised its disciplinary powers to fashion the body of the nation by prescribing the ideal dress for formal occasions. In the file dealing with formal dress for officers, the note prepared by the Ministry of Interior stated that there was no recognized national dress in Pakistan. It thus sets out to create one, claiming that, "in spite of this diversity of mode of dress . . . it seems that a combination of Sherwani with the various types of Shalwars and Payjamas has in actual fact become more or less our accepted national dress."[73] The dress had to be suitable to Pakistan's extreme climate, in addition to being "dignified, sober, practical and easily procurable as well as inexpensive." After the final decision had been made, the ministry was to provide a list of reputable tailors and outfitters who could stitch such clothing following approved guidelines for style, cut, and fabric. Schedule II of the note gave precise descriptions of the measurements, color, and design for each item of suiting prescribed as formal dress. In the final decision, as communicated to provincial governments and other departments through a notification issued by the Ministry of the Interior's Home Division on 18 February 1950, formal dress during winter (from 1 November to 31 March) was to be as follows:

DAY WEAR.

Black *sherwani* with 7 buttons (the length of the *sherwani* not to be below the knees).

Black Jinnah cap.

Black shoes and socks.

Striped trousers (as worn with European morning coat) or white shalwar or any other type of pyjama.

EVENING WEAR.

Black *sherwani* with 7 buttons (the length of the *sherwani* not to be below the knees).

Black shoes and socks.

Black evening dress trousers or white shalwar or any other type of pyjama.[74]

The cabinet made the decision in a hurry, in light of an impending visit of the Iranian emperor to Pakistan. Yet there remained some outstanding issues, as indicated in a note sent by the Interior Ministry in July 1950. The note raised such questions as to which dress was to be worn during summer and the detailed specifications for such garments. Another outstanding question was whether police officers were to wear a uniform or formal attire, and whether such dress would be adorned with medals.

The precise description of dress is a homogenization that constitutes yet another instance of a loss of excess: the *sherwani*'s historical significance as the attire of the Muslim nobility, and the multiple meanings that held, were reduced to a singular purpose for official statehood and subjected to bureaucratic rules. The *sherwani* had to be tailored to attend to the need for homogenization required for nation making, made to serve as a symbol of the state.

The quest for a national dress did not end there. Subsequent Pakistani governments continued to play with the idea of national dress and to project a preferred kind of subjectivity—whether "modern," as reflected by a fine-cut suit, or "traditional," in the form of *sherwani*—depending on political orientation. For both trends, successive governments turned to the same source for inspiration: Jinnah's wardrobe.

The official photographs of Jinnah hung on the walls in government offices across Pakistan and embassies abroad depicts him wearing a suit and Jinnah cap, gazing benignly at the viewer. But this was not always the official version of Jinnah's image. Like debates about "Jinnah's Pakistan," his official image has also evolved to correspond with the idea of an Islamic, or liberal, Pakistan. In 1948, soon after Pakistani independence, worried that there was no official photograph of Jinnah and several competing, unofficial versions in circulation, the Ministry of Interior, Information, and Broadcasting issued a press note inviting photographers to submit a portrait of Jinnah for official use. On 17 September 1952, the government eventually selected Arthur Sequeira's photograph of Jinnah as the officially recognized image of Jinnah.[75] The photograph of Jinnah in his suit and an eponymous cap was taken in the studio of I. Sequeira & Sons in Karachi and used for Jinnah's passport. It has become the iconic, official image of Jinnah, used on banknotes since 1957.

However, the matter did not end there. Sequeira demanded a fee that was higher than the market rate. One of the government's options was to introduce special legislation, in line with other countries of the world, "relating to the photographs of national heroes which do not have a copyright." But the government was cautioned against such a course of action, mainly because Sequeira belonged to a minority community.[76] Eventually, in a cabinet meeting on 14 October 1953, it was decided that the portrait submitted by Messrs. Zaidi also be accepted as an official photograph of Jinnah. Sequeira's photograph was then accepted as an official photograph under the same terms.

At the same time, the government decided to limit the usage of Jinnah iconography to purely official purposes. The Pakistan Names and Emblems (Prevention of Unauthorized Use Act) of 1957 was modeled on similar Indian legislation for Gandhi: "no person shall, except with the previous permission in writing of, and in accordance with the conditions, if any, imposed by the Central Government or any officer authorized by it in this behalf, use or continue to use a name or emblem in any trade-mark or design or in the title of any patent or for the purposes of any trade, business, calling or profession, or for any other purpose whatsoever."[77] The schedule attached to the law listed "the name, title or semblance" of Jinnah—along with the Pakistani flag and official seals—as items covered under its purview.

The two photographs continued to enjoy official status and were displayed in all official buildings, parliament, embassies, and other such places. During General Zia-ul-Haq's period, the question of replacing Jinnah's official portrait again came up. In a letter sent by the Directorate of Films and Publications on 14 April 1981, the president's secretariat asked the cabinet division to share a copy of the file dealing with Jinnah's official portrait.[78] The official file ends at this point.

What prompted Zia's interest in revisiting Jinnah's portrait, a relatively unimportant issue that the cabinet had already settled in the 1950s? Instead of Jinnah's image in Western clothing, Zia likely opted for a photograph in which Jinnah was wearing a *sherwani*. Perhaps *sherwani* could be considered "Pakistani dress" in a manner that a suit could not, and Zia's purpose was to minimize the notion of imitation of the west—or "Westoxification," as Iranian thinker Jalal Al-e-Ahmad famously described it—associated with wearing an English suit. This was part of a larger project of seeking the Islamization of the Pakistani state and Pakistani society. Zia wore a *sherwani*—in contrast to his predecessors in the military who, as martial-law administrators, preferred to wear suits. Zia's choice of clothing was in line with a specific political project for which he sought an appropriation of Jinnah's portrait. Eventually, his martial-law regime promoted a new official portrait, in which Jinnah wore a *sherwani*. Although my evidence is primarily circumstantial, the fact that there is documented interest regarding Jinnah's portrait in the official correspondence from Zia's regime, or autobiographical accounts from the period, indicates that there was an intentional shift toward portraying Jinnah in a *sherwani*.[79] For Zia, the interest in Jinnah's portrait was to resignify that image with a different set of meanings that would bring it in line with his own projected image of Jinnah as the founder of an Islamic state. By the mid-1990s, when new currency notes were issued, the Sequeira photograph was modified to show Jinnah wearing a *sherwani* with a cap.

HAGIOGRAPHY OF THE NATION: NARRATING THE NATION THROUGH JINNAH AND IQBAL

Jinnah and Iqbal served as the two major national icons through which the postcolonial state narrated the story of the nation. In this story, Iqbal was the visionary who conceived of Pakistan, and Jinnah the legendary leader who executed that idea. As father figures of the new state, Jinnah and Iqbal appear on more than notes, coins, and stamps; the state has instituted their memory through a range of discursive practices that enable and justify a certain kind of polity and ideational basis for Pakistan and Muslim nationhood. It is not only the iconography of Jinnah and Iqbal, but also their biography and musealization, that is central to the shaping of Pakistan's national character and its historical narrative.

In the case of Iqbal, given his stature as a towering intellectual, political leader, and poet, there was widespread appreciation for his work. The process of an ideological curating of Iqbal's life, ideas, and works through commemorative practices started soon after his death, nine years before the creation of Pakistan. A centralized Iqbal Day committee was constituted, organizing the first Iqbal Day in April 1939; the committee was presided over by Justice S. A. Rehman, who later became chief justice of Pakistan.[80] At the end of his life, Iqbal had written letters to Jinnah to convince the latter to work toward a centralized Muslim authority or separate state within India. This close collaboration between Jinnah and Iqbal justified the Muslim League to project Iqbal as the ideological founder of the idea of Pakistan; the Muslim League organized special services to mark the anniversary of his death during the 1940s. Jinnah regularly paid homage to Iqbal on such occasions and recognized his services as a Muslim poet-philosopher who laid down the vision for a Muslim state.

Work on Iqbal's mausoleum had also started soon after his death in 1938. The burial site was nestled between the Lahore Fort and the Badshahi Mosque, iconic symbols of Muslim political and spiritual power in India. Given the grandeur of the surrounding structures, Iqbal's mausoleum had to have a simple aura that blended in with the immediate built environment. One design was rejected because it had a "Catholic ethos." Another design by an architect from Hyderabad Deccan, Zain Yar Jang, was more suitable but "too delicate." The architect was called to Lahore, where Chaudhry Muhammad Husain took him to the poet's grave and said: "Look, Nawab Sahib! On one side is the mosque, which represents the religious glory of the Muslims, on the other is the fort, which represents their worldly power. The tomb between them will look nice if it effuses simplicity with strength."[81]

Eventually, the committee for Iqbal's mausoleum, which comprised Muslim notables from Lahore, chose a mixture of Afghan and Moorish architecture. Writing to S. A. Rehman in January 1940, the influential poet and friend of Iqbal, M. D. Taseer, expressed his concern about the architectural style: it was from the late Mughal period and carried Hindu influences. "Oh God, this is so insulting," he wrote. "In any case, the intent of doing good is there. Whether it is friendly foolishness or foolish friendliness. But if this building gets constructed, it would be difficult to find anything more stupid existing on a permanent basis. This building is supposed to be the pilgrimage site of the world of Islam. What would the seeing eyes say about it."[82]

The funding for the mausoleum was to come from Iqbal's admirers, friends, and followers. The construction was delayed because imports of Jaipuri red stone were interrupted after Partition. The same went for marble, which came from Makrana in Rajputana. The delay caused anguish among citizens and the literati, who viewed Iqbal as the central ideological figure for the newly established state. In a letter to the editor, Shah Abdul Aleem from Lahore lamented that even after two years of Pakistan's creation, Iqbal's *mazar* had not been completed. He said that foreign tourists, and especially Iranians, would like to visit it. He urged speeding up the construction, arranging for the mausoleum's maintenance, and appointing a guard to prevent stray animals from loitering at the site and young men from playing cards.[83] Finally, after construction was completed in 1949–1950, the site was declared a protected monument.[84] The total cost incurred was more than one lakh rupees. King Zahir Shah of Afghanistan contributed the sarcophagus, made of lapis lazuli.[85]

In its initial decades, the mausoleum was not a national site with material signs of sovereign power. At the time of Iqbal's birth centenary, during Zulfiqar Ali Bhutto's regime, the government decided to post military guards, from the army, air force, and navy, at the mausoleum on a rotating basis.[86] In addition, gun salutes were to be offered to Iqbal on his birthday, and a grand ceremony of the changing of the guard was to take place to mark Independence Day. Such statist appropriation of the space ensured that Iqbal was no longer only a poet but instead a national poet; his final resting place was no longer merely a shrine for celebratory remembrance but a site to perform state power through the regimented rituals of gun salutes and parades.

A similar transformation occurred at Iqbal's birthplace in Sialkot and at his last residence in Lahore. The Department of Archaeology and Museums acquired the Sialkot residence in May 1971, although it was still occupied and used by Iqbal's extended family. The Sialkot municipality had taken the initiative. By declaring Iqbal's place of birth a national asset, there was the possibility that the government would forcibly acquire the site; thus, after some initial reluctance, Iqbal's family agreed to sell the property.[87] The owners also donated a few items of old furniture, books, and photographs that were then in the Iqbal Manzil, some of which had been in use since the days of Iqbal. The government acquired additional material from Iqbal's son in Lahore, including Iqbal's personal belongings, which were to be displayed in a museum as artifacts of national treasure.

According to the official bulletin of the Department of Archaeology and Museums, the government of Pakistan purchased the house in 1971 at a total cost of 125,000 rupees and "placed it under the control of the Department of Archaeology to be maintained as a historic house."[88] At the time of purchase, the house was in bad shape and needed immediate repairs and a renovation. Although the report claims that the original style was kept intact, the layout was in fact considerably modified to add a library, reading room, visitor's reception, and other structures typical of a museum. One of Iqbal's descendants, Khalid Nazir Sufi, has written a nostalgic account of the building where he was born and spent a significant part of his life. Sufi's account, while reverential of the achievements of the great poet, is also an intimate account of a residence that meant something to its residents: "For others, probably, it is just a house where great poet and thinker of the East was born," but for Sufi, "it is like a friend, the cradle of [his own] childhood."[89] This intimacy was excised by converting it into a museum; several structural changes had to be made to the building. A national museum was thus built by flattening a personal site, erasing the intimate to make the space familiar yet impersonal.

In addition to regulating the mausoleum as a national site through spectacular state power, the Pakistani state nationalized the poet by sponsoring specific readings and interpretations of Iqbal's works. The work of Iqbal, a poet, philosopher, and political thinker, lent itself to a range of ideological causes, from Islamic socialism to anti-Ahmadi legislation. When a virulent anti-Ahmadi movement raged in Punjab in 1952–1953, the government and religio-political groups spearheading the campaign fell back on Iqbal as an ideological anchor. The government sponsored a set of writings titled *Iqbal and Mullahs* to highlight Iqbal's disdain for religious obscurantist forces.[90] The religio-political groups reprinted Iqbal's writings against Ahmadis to justify their demands for the political and religious exclusion of Ahmadis as non-Muslims.

The creation of state-sponsored research institutes to study the life and works of Iqbal was, therefore, an attempt to regulate scholarly literature on Iqbal's thought and poetry. The Iqbal Academy funded by the federal government and a Bazm-i-Iqbal supported by the Punjab government was instituted soon after independence. The purpose of both institutions was to promote research on Iqbal and to translate his works to introduce him to the world, and especially the Muslim world, as a global thinker. Although the rationale was to promote Iqbal on the world stage, even within Pakistan itself, there was little agreement on Iqbal's national status. The government of East Bengal was interested in granting a similar status to Qazi Nazrul Islam, a famous Bengali poet.

The Iqbal Academy set up by the central government was tasked "to perpetuate the memory of the late Allama Iqbal." An initial grant of one lakh rupees for 1948–1949 was allocated for this purpose. Sir Abdul Qadir and Maulvi Abdul Haq served on the Foundation Committee set up by the Constituent Assembly.[91] In the case of Punjab, the Bazm was set up in 1950 with an initial grant of two hundred thousand rupees.[92] The Bazm planned to publish scholarly works in Persian, Arabic, Turkish, and various European languages, focusing on, among other topics, on Iqbal's ideas about *millat*, Shariat, and philosophy.

Examples of such projects include Abdul Wahab Azzam's translation of *Asrar-o-Rumuz* and its free distribution using academy funds. Similarly, the academy subsidized the publication of Dr. Abbas Mahmud's Arabic translation of Iqbal's major philosophical treatise *Reconstruction of Religious Thought in Islam*, with a supplementary grant of 2,500 rupees. Later 450 copies of the book were purchased for free distribution in the Arab world.[93] Similar subsidies were offered to scholars translating Iqbal's works into Turkish and Persian.

The Iqbal Academy was particularly concerned with making Iqbal's work available in regional languages, especially in Bangla. In 1961, the Iqbal Academy established its branch offices in Lahore, Peshawar, and Dacca. A plan was sketched to introduce Iqbal in Bangla. This included translating selected poems into Bangla and publishing translated books on Iqbal's politics and philosophy, especially those that focused on the demands for a Muslim state in South Asia.[94] The academy contacted the East Pakistan Textbook Board to convince its members to include chapters about various aspects of Iqbal's life, poetry, and philosophy.[95] Such chapters were subsequently added to textbooks. Selected portions of his poetry were also published in many of Pakistan's languages.

To date, the poetry and prose of Iqbal have been translated into at least twenty-six languages, and about two thousand works have been published on Iqbal in twenty-two languages worldwide.[96] Most of this work has been sponsored by the Iqbal Academy and Bazm-i-Iqbal. In addition, these research institutes have been responsible for collecting documents related to Iqbal and setting up an archive for his life and works. Bazm-i-Iqbal set up a committee of leading scholars and close associates of Iqbal to sponsor an authoritative biography of Iqbal.[97] Among other material, the academy was also interested in acquiring such memorabilia as handwritten letters of Iqbal and first editions of his books.[98] The academy sponsored conferences and other events to celebrate Iqbal's life and work internationally. For instance, in April 1968, the academy spent 4,200 rupees on the unveiling ceremony of a memorial plaque installed in Munich. The Bavarian minister of education and culture, Dr. L. Huber, performed the ceremony.[99] A similar memorial had earlier been erected in Heidelberg, in September 1966.

Besides sponsoring research on Iqbal, the Pakistani state also promoted Iqbal as a national icon by setting up numerous educational institutions and hospitals in his name, naming roads after him, and issuing commemorative stamps. For instance, in 1977, the People's Open University was renamed Allama Iqbal Open University as part of the Iqbal centenary celebrations.[100] In the late 1970s, Iqbal's birthday became a national holiday, a practice that continued until the early 2010s.

The "birth" of a national poet was a gradual process that required state patronage. The actual birth of the poet, and debate over its accurate date, was also part of the process. This process was crucial to Pakistan's claim over Iqbal as the national poet of the Muslim state he had purportedly helped to establish.

Despite all its investments in Iqbal, the Pakistani state was oblivious to the approaching centenary of Iqbal's birth in 1973. This date was contested by scholars from India and Pakistan and debated down to the last possible document. The Indian government had taken the lead in celebrating the Iqbal centenary in 1973, while Pakistan was taken off guard. The controversy about the centenary started because of a letter sent out by All India Radio at the beginning of 1973, which declared 22 February 1873 as Iqbal's date of birth for centenary celebrations. Ghalib Academy in Delhi and Iqbal Academy Hyderabad Deccan celebrated the centenary, but Aligarh University's Urdu department was more cautious in its approach.[101] Professor Aal-i-Ahmad Suroor of Aligarh University sent invitation letters for a seminar on Iqbal but was careful not to mention that the seminar was being held as part of centenary celebrations.[102]

To make matters worse, the Indian government had obtained a copy of Iqbal's doctoral dissertation from Munich on the pretext that he was an "Indian national," and it planned to celebrate his birth centenary in 1973.[103] The Pakistani government saw this move as an attempt by Indira Gandhi's government to appease Muslim voters before upcoming provincial assembly elections in Uttar Pradesh.[104]

The resulting embarrassment for Pakistan led to frantic efforts at the government level to convene a committee of specialists in 1973 to determine the exact date and, more importantly, the year, of Iqbal's birth. The committee comprised notable scholars and several close aides and relatives of Iqbal, including Dr. Muhammad Ajmal, Dr. Javed Iqbal (Iqbal's son), Justice S. A. Rehman, Sayyid Nazir Niyazi, Sheikh Ejaz Ahmed (Iqbal's nephew), Professor Hamid Ahmad Khan, Ghulam Rasul Mihr, Sayyid Abdul Wahid, Dr. Wahid Qureshi, Mehmud Ahmad Khan, and Professor Muhammad Usman.[105] The Ministry of Education wrote to Professor Usman requesting an early decision about Iqbal's date of birth, as it was "a matter of national interest"; the ministry had been "receiving letters from our Foreign Embassys [sic] stating the various Associations in England and Europe intend to celebrate Iqbal Centenary in 1973."[106] But it was difficult for the committee to speed up its proceedings. It had been tasked with probing multiple sources, such as autobiographical accounts, Iqbal's official documents, and records of birth and death registered at the Sialkot municipality. In addition, the committee also had to conduct interviews with Iqbal's family and the elders of Kashmiri neighborhood in Sialkot.

All these sources were telling a different story. The most challenging task for the committee was to reconcile several of Iqbal's signed documents with contradictory dates of his birth. In his dissertation submitted to the Ludwig Maximilian University of Munich, Iqbal gave his date of birth according to the Islamic calendar. He wrote 3 Zil-Qaʿda 1294 as his birth and roughly converted it into the Georgian calendar as December 1876. In 1931, when Iqbal applied for his passport, he mentioned only his year of his birth, cited again as 1876. At the time of his death, *Inqilab* cited December 1876 as his date of birth. But soon after, the newspaper clarified that Iqbal was born on 22 February 1873.[107]

The fact that Iqbal had given a precise hijri date—an uncommon thing to do in an era when the Georgian calendar was the marker of measuring exact time—was a strong argument to choose it as the definite date for Iqbal's birth. But he had erred in converting the hijri date. Also, in his official documents for Lincoln's Inn and Cambridge, Iqbal had used another hijri date and combined it with the Georgian calendar, Muharram 1876. Durrani was inclined to accept this date as valid, as it carried the additional advantage of coinciding with Jinnah's year of birth. Thus 1876 would have been a blessed year for Indian Muslims: the birth year of both Jinnah and Iqbal.[108]

More embarrassing and difficult to account for were several of Pakistan's official documents and objects such as stamps that cited February 1873 as the date of Iqbal's birth. The committee constituted by Bazm-i-

Iqbal to write an official biography of Iqbal had also agreed on 24 February 1873 as Iqbal's date of birth. On 21 April 1958, on the twentieth anniversary of Iqbal's death, the Pakistani government issued three sets of postal stamps with Iqbal's verses printed on them; they mentioned Iqbal's date of birth as 1873.[109] An urgent task for the committee was to change the date on Iqbal's grave. The committee sent a letter to the Archaeology Department to make immediate arrangements.[110]

Official municipality records told a different story. The birth and death registers of Sialkot municipality showed Iqbal's date of birth as 29 December 1873.[111] Khalid Nazir Sufi's research was most rigorous, as he was not just a scholar. He had the added advantage of being part of Iqbal's larger family. According to him, Iqbal was born on neither 22 February 1873 nor 9 November 1877, but on 29 December 1873. On the basis of oral testimonies collected from his family, Sufi established that Iqbal's elder sister, Ta'ley Bibi, was three years his senior. His younger sister, Karima Bibi, was three years his junior. According to the municipality record, two brothers were born between the two sisters. One died; the other survived. The first girl was born on 6 September 1870, followed by two sons on 22 February 1873 and 29 December 1873, respectively, and a daughter on 14 November 1876. The entry for the name of *mohalla*, occupation, and the person reporting it vary slightly. They refer to either Mohallah Churigaran, *qaum* Kashmiri, or Musalman *khayat*.[112] According to Sufi, Iqbal's mother gave the child born in February 1873 to his *dewrani* (husband's sister-in-law), who did not have a son. The child died in infancy, but Allah liked this gesture so much that another son was born to them after about ten months in December 1873. This child, according to Sufi, was Iqbal.[113] Thus, personal family history collected by Sufi corresponds with documented municipality records of births and deaths. The problem, however, was that for the girl born in 1876, the father's name in the papers is Sheikh Muhammad Rafi rather than Sheikh Muhammad Rafiq. Sufi calls it a typing error, as the names sound very similar.

Other family members of Iqbal—and especially his nephew, Sheikh Ijaz Ahmad, who was nominated by Iqbal as a custodian for his children—contested Sufi's findings. According to Ahmad, there was not only one Sheikh Muhammad Rafiq, alias "Nathu," in Sialkot. Professor Muhammad Usman had found between twenty-five and thirty different persons named Nathu in different *mohallas* of Sialkot, as reported in birth and death registration records. So it was difficult to accept that entries claimed as births taking place to Nathu referred to Iqbal's father, especially when the *mohalla* and occupation given were different.[114]

Eventually, the committee declared in February 1974 that the date mentioned by Iqbal on his PhD dissertation—3 Zil-Qa'da 1294—which, in the Georgian calendar, is 9 November 1877, should be accepted as the correct date of Iqbal's birth. But there was no consensus around this: some of Iqbal's closest aides, such as Ghulam Rasul Mihr and Sayyid Nazir Niyazi, as well as such leading scholars as Professor Hameed Ahmad Khan and Dr. Waheed Qureshi, were inclined to accept 1873 as the year of Iqbal's birth. There were nevertheless strong reasons to take 9 November 1877 as the accurate date, as its exact hijri equivalent had been mentioned by Iqbal himself. Also, the date aligned with the widely held view in Iqbal's family that he was born on a Friday. The major problem with the officially accepted new date was that it did not have a matching entry in the birth register of Sialkot. On the contrary, as pointed out by Wahid Qureshi, Iqbal's mother died on 9 November 1914, making 9 November a date, and unfortunate coincidence, that he could not have overlooked.[115] That his mother died on the date he was born should have figured in Iqbal's writings, especially the poem he wrote in his mother's memory. Qureshi also pointed to Iqbal's preference for hijri dates over the Georgian calendar. In most of his historical poems, with few exceptions, observed Qureshi, Iqbal used the Islamic calendar. This made the case for accepting the precise hijri date Iqbal gave in his official documents even stronger.

Because of such missing leads and loose ends, the draft submitted for approval before the committee stated that "until some fresh material becomes available, the date of birth given on Allama's Ph.D. dissertation should be accepted as definite." But when the communiqué was officially released, this quoted portion was expunged.[116] Accordingly, the Pakistani government announced centenary celebrations to be held in 1977. By this calculation, Iqbal died at the age of sixty-one. As Faqir Sayyid Wahid-ud-Din wrote in article, to die between the ages of sixty-one and sixty-three was, according to prophetic tradition, the sign of a true devotee of Prophet

Muhammad, as his demise had taken place at the age of sixty-three.[117] This became another reason to sanctify the new date as Iqbal's year of birth.

Following Pakistani lead, Turkey and Iran also accepted this date and issued stamps to commemorate Iqbal's centennial birth celebrations.[118] According to Jagan Nath Azad, even in India, serious Urdu scholars accepted 1977 as the birth centenary of Iqbal.[119] The All-India Iqbal Birth Centenary Committee was formed in Delhi with Durga Prasad Dhar as its chairman and Inder Kumar Gujral, the future prime minister of India, as vice-chairman.

During his lifetime, Iqbal never bothered to correct anyone or provide an accurate description of his biographical details. When Munshi Muhammad Din Fauq inquired with Iqbal about his date of birth for a book on prominent Kashmiris, Iqbal responded to his query in a letter in 1922: "As far as my biographical details are concerned, what is in there to describe[?]"[120] Nawab Zulfiqar Ali Khan, in his book *A Voice from the East*, published in 1922, cited 1876 as Iqbal's year of birth. Other reference works published during Iqbal's lifetime, such as *Who Is Who in India* and the *Indian Encyclopedia*, gave different years.

For a project aimed at nationalizing the poet, such imprecision cannot be taken lightly. Although knowing the exact date had no bearing on interpretations of or the reception of Iqbal's work, it was a statist project that sought to reclaim Iqbal as the national poet of Pakistan. The government of Pakistan was keen to take official responsibility for monopolizing research on his work and celebrating his life through centennial commemorations, the naming of airports, educational institutions, and the issuing of stamps.

A NARRATIVE FOR JINNAH

Unlike Iqbal, who died even before the demand for Pakistan was formally presented, and whose poetry could also be claimed by the Indian government as part of its nationalist project, Jinnah's stature as the undisputable founder of the Muslim state could not be denied. After the late 1930s, his unswerving championing of Muslim political rights and claims to sovereign nationhood had catapulted him to the pedestal of the greatest leader—or *Qaid-i-Azam*—of the Muslim community in India.

But this does not mean that Jinnah's life and ideas did not carry elements that required a sanitized biographical account to serve nation-building purposes. A prime example is Jinnah's faith. Born an Ismaili Khoja, Jinnah later converted to the Isna Ashari form of Shia Islam. As the founder of one of the largest Muslim states with an overwhelmingly Sunni population, Jinnah's Shia credentials became increasingly incongruent with the outlook of an Islamic state that was becoming more obscurantist and exclusionary. For instance, Jinnah's funeral rites were performed twice: once in his home, where Shia rituals were performed; and once publicly, when the funeral pyre was carried under an *alam*—a visible symbol of Shia religious practice—but the funeral prayer was led by a noted Sunni Deobandi scholar, Allama Shabbir Ahmad Usmani. In another instance, while deciding a court case on Jinnah's property and the question of applying Shia personal law, the Sindh High Court ruled that Jinnah was *just* a Muslim, so neither Shia nor Sunni personal law could be applied as such.[121]

Narrativizing Jinnah's life was part of a statist project to seek legitimacy for the ideological basis of the new state of Pakistan. Jinnah's vision of the new state was frequently invoked for various political agendas, whether to establish an Islamic state as enshrined in the Objectives Resolution passed by the Constituent Assembly in 1949 or to argue for a presidential form of government in the country. As I explain in chapter 5, an extensive project was launched in the early 1960s to scientifically preserve Jinnah's documents and rigorously catalog them to make them available for researchers. Since then, multiple volumes of Jinnah's letters, speeches, and statements have been officially published. The complete record of Muhammad Ali Jinnah's papers, Fatima Jinnah's papers, and the Muslim League papers are available in the reading room of the National Archives of Pakistan. Any Pakistani citizen can access them, simply picking them off the shelf, without putting in a request for archival material. The process of archival research can otherwise be frustratingly long in Pakistani archives. For most other area of research, the documentation does not exist, is difficult to access, or simply lies dumped in sacks without proper cataloging. In this manner, the Pakistani state facilitates research on Jinnah and the Muslim League, preserving officially released documents and making them available to researchers and the general public.

Soon after independence and well into the 1950s, material about Jinnah and the Muslim League was unavailable to even official historians such as Ishtiaq Husain Qureshi, who held cabinet positions as influential intellectual figures in the political setup. Much of Jinnah's archive lay with his sister, Fatima Jinnah. She had increasingly been isolated and estranged from successive Muslim League leaders and governments that came into power after her brother's demise in 1948.

The lack of crucial documentation on Jinnah became a national crisis when the government of Pakistan hired an internationally renowned biographer, Hector Bolitho, to write a lucid account of Jinnah's life for an international audience. Known for his biographical accounts of the British royalty, Bolitho had little knowledge of Pakistan's history and politics. Hired at an exorbitantly high rate of fifty thousand Pakistan rupees, in addition to a lavish hotel stay and use of first-class international travel facilities, Bolitho soon hit a dead end after he arrived in Pakistan.[122] The government had appointed him without consulting Fatima Jinnah, so the latter gave the cold shoulder to his request for cooperation. Frustrated, Bolitho sought a revision in the terms of the agreement. Under the contractual arrangement, the government of Pakistan was supposed to provide archival sources for Jinnah's biography. Because the government of Pakistan was unable to fulfill its side of the bargain, Bolitho threatened legal action if the hefty amount promised to him, along with damages for the time he had already spent, were not paid. That a British author was paid a hefty fee, yet no official biography was being published, became a public scandal. This question was raised in the assembly and covered in the national press—so much so that the government's Press and Information Department had to issue a clarification about Bolitho's hiring and Fatima Jinnah's refusal to cooperate with him. A press note dated 18 January 1952 justified hiring Bolitho to introduce Jinnah to the international world. Bolitho was the right person for the job, the note claimed, as he was a well-published and respected author and biographer.[123] At the same time, the note said, the government was putting in efforts to collect all possible material relating to the life and works of Jinnah.

Even with whatever material Bolitho was provided to write a biography of Jinnah, veto power lay with the government of Pakistan, which had the authority "to decide on the correctness of material proposed to be used and hence whether it may or may not be included in the biography."[124] This led to several instances where Bolitho had a falling out with Majeed Malik of the Press Information Department, who had been appointed to scrutinize drafts submitted by Bolitho. Any attempt by Bolitho to humanize Jinnah was deleted by Malik. "I am sorry you wish me to delete the story about Jinnah 'sneaking a free ride on the footboard of a gharry,'" wrote Bolitho in his correspondence with Malik. "I like it because it removes the hint of piggishness and makes him more human. I remember when writing the story of King George VI as a boy, I related the incident of his letting off fireworks in lavatories at school, and of his being punished for it. No body objected to such a human story. I would like to induce you to allow me to leave this story of the gharry-ride in."[125] But wary of an adverse public reaction, Malik and his superiors in the cabinet cautioned against any such attempts to humanize Jinnah. They feared that their critics would "pluck this story out of its context and exploit it against us when the book is published."[126]

On another occasion, fed up with delays and interference from the ministry, Bolitho warned that "the book will be 'dull' without such lively episodes which only add to Jinnah's bigness—since little eccentricities are part of the stature of a really great man."[127] He reminded the official of the Press and Information Department that the book was primarily meant for an American and English audience, few of whom knew of Jinnah or were interested in his greatness as a political leader. "If the little human touches . . . are removed," wrote Bolitho, "Jinnah will emerge as dull and unwarm, and uninteresting."[128] Eventually, Bolitho's apprehensions proved correct. The final version that appeared was not received with much acclaim; it lacked proper documentation of Jinnah's life and was unable to present a lively picture of his personality.

The editorial board of Dacca's *Morning News* and its readers were brutal in their criticism of the biography. M. S. Ashraf from Karachi described the book as that of a "miserable, lonesome and snobbish midget, more devoted to his monocle than to other serious things of life. This was the work of an 'artist' as the Government called Mr. Bolitho."[129] Responding to many critical letters, articles, and editorials, Bolitho issued a statement to *Morning News* to explain his position. He acknowledged the support received from Majid Malik, but none from the prime minister of that period, Khawaja Nazim-ud-Din. He found more help in Bombay in one week, he said, than from the entire official machinery in Pakistan in six months.[130] According to Bolitho, he was repeatedly forced to explain his position, as he was "weary of being described as a 'foreign hireling' and of my task being described as a 'blasphemous project.'" He wrote that if he had known that the government had not consulted Fatima Jinnah about this project, he would never have sailed for Pakistan. Responding to the charge that hiring him had been a waste of public money, he argued that the government did not cover his expenses during the two and a half years in which he was writing his book. To rebut the claim that the book gave a negative view of Jinnah, Bolitho referred to reviews by Pakistan-friendly academics, such as Ian Stephens, who were appreciative of his effort.

Other than managing the archive for a desirable understanding of Jinnah's life and politics, the Pakistani state has pursued similar objectives through the musealization of his residence and personal items of daily use, and by building a mausoleum. Acquiring Jinnah's possessions was akin to the process of creating an archive of his personal papers through which his life could be studied. Such a museum-as-archive was to be built on Jinnah's private and official residences in Karachi to provide a visual narrative of his life and politics. A committee was set up under M. A. H. Ispahani and Raja Sahib Mehmudabad—both Jinnah's close associates—with Dr. F. A. Khan, director of archaeology, as its member, to acquire Jinnah's personal items from his residence. The process was started in 1970, three years after Fatima Jinnah's death. The court case to decide the division of Muhammad Ali Jinnah and Fatima Jinnah's estate among their siblings was then still pending before the Sindh High Court.

The deputy commissioner of Karachi unsealed the rooms where Jinnah's articles were housed, finding the room dusty and filled with a foul odor.[131] A special grant of fifty thousand rupees was sanctioned to clean and chemically preserve the relics after they had been identified and sorted by Ispahani and Raja Sahib Mehmudabad. Meanwhile, Shirin Bai, the sole legatee of Muhammad Ali Jinnah and Fatima Jinnah, had been granted a succession certificate by the Sindh High Court. To deal with her as a legal heir was, therefore, incumbent. Bai agreed to cooperate with the commission and hand over relics on the condition that her right to private ownership was safeguarded. Because the relics ran into thousands of pieces, their sorting could take months, and it was to be carried out elsewhere. She also demanded immediate possession of Fatima Jinnah's house and its articles.[132] The commission found the terms agreeable.

The commission's idea was to acquire as much material as possible to furnish at least five rooms in the house converted into a museum. The commission also eyed the furniture from Jinnah's Delhi residence, especially those items that were used on important formal occasions. Shirin Bai agreed to hand it over if the government provided her with a replacement. Accordingly, a dining and sofa set of Bai's choice was arranged for her at the cost of 7,875 rupees.[133] The commission was excited about Jinnah's wardrobe and its overall significance in portraying Jinnah's elegance. The commission's report gleefully noted the recovery of such dressing items as suits, *sherwanis*, ties, collars, *kurtas*, *churidar pajamas*, *shalwars*, caps, and gowns. Among the "Pakistani dresses," each of which showed "the high taste of that great leader," the commission was excited to find the chocolate-colored *sherwani* that Jinnah reportedly wore to important historical occasions.[134] The commission was also excited to find among twenty-five pairs of Jinnah's footwear, the shoes he wore to the oath-taking ceremony as the governor-general of Pakistan.

If the nation-state is, to use Srirupa Roy's words, an object of desire and enchantment, it is because of its power to animate artifacts and establish an affective relationship with them as symbolic embodiments of the nation by investing in their aura through ritualized repetitive performances. Curated in a museum, what was otherwise simply a pair of shoes or a formal dress was exoticized into a national asset. Along with other similar objects, it became part of a visual narrative about the struggle for the Muslim homeland where elegantly dressed Jinnah is shown negotiating with the British and outcharming the seductive appeal of Gandhi's "wicked simplicity."

A MAUSOLEUM FOR THE STATE

While Jinnah's personal items and private and official papers helped represent Pakistan's history through musealization or archival documentation, his mausoleum served the statist project of offering a routinized, sober display of the state's power and grandeur. As Jinnah was the undisputed founder of the new state whose burial site was to be visited by foreign dignitaries on official visits, choosing an appropriate burial site and constructing an elegant mausoleum were important considerations.

Hashim Raza, who was serving as the commissioner of Karachi, recorded the discussion among top leadership about the burial site in his memoirs. Most of Karachi's graveyards, he recalled, were in Lyari. But burying Jinnah there was out of the question, given the lack of proper roads to Lyari and because its drains turned into a river after heavy rains.[135] Eventually, with "heavenly help," Raza chose the current site in Karachi's Jacob Lines: it was a central location accessible to ordinary citizens and situated on an elevated, level ground.[136]

For almost a decade, no further developments took place; the design of Jinnah's mausoleum could not be finalized. Because the mausoleum was going to be the first Pakistani monument of national significance, it had to reflect the aspirations of a modernist Muslim state. In their reverence and love for Jinnah, Pakistanis expected a veritable Taj Mahal to be built in his memory. As Islam Salmani from Karachi wrote, a modern-day Taj—nay, a mausoleum superior to the Taj—should pay homage to Jinnah.[137] Unlike Shah Jahan's Taj, which reflected only an individual's aesthetics, he wrote, Jinnah's memorial should reflect the entire nation's culture and taste. He recommended building a vast garden full of fruits and flowers, better than the Shalimar Gardens of Lahore, with trees planted "in the way like that of the Hanging Gardens of Bombay just near to which the Quaid lived for a long time at Malabar Hill."[138] Salmani was not the only individual with an opinion about the required aesthetic grandeur of Jinnah's mausoleum. There were many other citizens as well, especially experts, and those many deliberations and objections delayed the designing and construction of the mausoleum.

To speed up the process, the Pakistani government allocated sixty-one acres of land in 1957 for the burial site. In the same year, the Central Committee of the Quaid-i-Azam Memorial announced an international competition to select a design. Fifty-seven architects from seventeen countries took part in the competition. A jury was set up to choose the best design; in February 1958, it announced its decision in favor of the London-based firm, Raglan Squire and Partners.[139] The proposed design was a modernist structure without any element of traditional Islamic-Mughal features. The designs submitted by A. Vasfi Egeli and Nawab Zain Yar Jang were also in the competition. Eventually, Yahya C. Merchant's design was approved because of Fatima Jinnah's insistence and severe criticism of Raglan Squire's proposed design in the national press.

Merchant's design, according to the architect, "reflects the founder of Pakistan's grand character, personality and unflinching determination."[140] The domed white-marble structure is simple and elegant, combining the traditional Mughal architectural styles with a modern outlook. But for Merchant's critics, the proposed structure was not Islamic enough. Abdullah Chughtai, for instance, proposed surmounting the dome with a golden pinnacle, adding cupolas to the building's four corners, and inscribing Quranic verses on the interior and exterior of the tomb in calligraphy.[141] Chughtai also objected to the mausoleum's three arches, contending that they were based on the idea and tradition of the Christian Trinity (*taslis*), and he sought their removal, or their accommodation in an Islamic style. Writing under the pseudonym "Fikri," another author criticized Chughtai's approach to the mausoleum design. He commented that Chughtai was reading too much into simple architectural styles. If Chughtai's reading of the arches was valid, he wrote, "one is also justified in taking these arches to mean Unity, Faith and Discipline, the three golden principles given to the Nation by the late Quaid-i-Azam."[142]

Despite the simplicity of the proposed design, there were numerous technical and operational issues to be sorted out. Merchant submitted his design in 1959, and construction work started the following year. Difficulties included procuring enough marble and finding engineers and laborers who had experience using marble in modern-day construction. The major marble structures built during the previous few centuries, noted the official publication on Jinnah's mausoleum, had been constructed in areas outside of Pakistan; hence, local artisans lacked the required experience.

Eventually, supervision was given to former chief engineer of British India, Mohammed Solaiman. He had supervised the repairs of the Taj Mahal in 1944 and the construction of the Viceregal Palace, which later became the Rashtrapati Bhawan, or Presidential Palace, in India, along with the Central Secretariat Buildings in New Delhi. He was assisted by Khushi Mohammed Choudhry, who supervised the construction of Bahawalpur's Jama Masjid. Several marble dressers and artisans were identified who had migrated from Makrana and Jodhpur after 1947. The marble came from a site near Mardan. It was tested at a laboratory in Munich for its strength and quality.[143]

To infuse a patriotic spirit into the project, the government appealed to citizens' love for and devotion to Jinnah to raise donations. The government set up the Qaid-e-Azam Memorial Fund for this purpose. The fund also received contributions from central and provincial governments. In addition to the mausoleum, other memorials were also proposed. These included Jamia Masjid in Karachi, Dar-ul-Ulum in Multan, and the National Institute of Technology in East Pakistan.[144]

The mausoleum construction was finally completed in January 1971—more than two decades after Jinnah's death (1948), thirteen years after the design was approved (1958), and almost a decade after construction officially started (1960).

In March 1972, on Bhutto's instructions, arrangements were made for posting army, navy, and air force personnel at the mausoleum for the changing of the guard. In addition to performing this ritualized practice during official visits by foreign dignitaries, the presence of uniformed guards also served the function of disciplining citizens' bodies, claiming to give a solemn and graceful look to the mausoleum and "educating the visitors in giving due sanctity to the Mazar and to ensure that the Mazar is not used as a picnic spot. They also ensure that the visitors enter the main Mazar for Fateha [prayers for the departed soul] only and do not touch the grills."[145]

As in Iqbal's mausoleum, the state intervened to establish Jinnah's mausoleum as an apolitical space, doing so in the name of championing the space's sanctity. Jinnah's mausoleum is protected under the law—the Quaid-i-Azam's Mazar (Protection and Maintenance) Ordinance of

1971—with specific legal provisions detailing permissible and impermissible activities inside the mausoleum and adjoining area. In the case of both Jinnah and Iqbal, their status is not sacred-reverential but state-reverential: visitors are expected to behave like patriotic and disciplined citizens paying homage to the founders, and not like Sufi devotees seeking blessings or performing rituals that fall outside the purview of secular law or its logic of state praxis. This aspect of the mausoleum arose when, in November 2020, the retired captain Safdar—spouse of opposition leader Maryam Nawaz Sharif—raised pro-democracy slogans inside the mausoleum. The incident sparked a huge controversy, as the incumbent Sindh government refused to take action against Safdar for his act of "sacrilege" that violated the sanctum sanctorum of the nation-state. A top military commander in Karachi swept into action, ordered the abduction of the chief of Sindh police in the wee hours of the day, and forced him to sign arrest warrants for Safdar. When the case details surfaced publicly, the Sindh police reacted sharply, as officers refused to work under such stressful conditions. Eventually, the military was forced to issue a statement admitting the wrongdoing of senior officers who "overzealously" took matters into their hands and ordered a departmental inquiry against them.[146] Safdar's use of shrine space to articulate a political ideology is certainly not an unprecedented event. Still, the fact that it raised such a reaction is a reminder of the sharp distinction between the sacred reverence of a Sufi shrine and the state reverence of a national hero's funerary monument. In the case of a Sufi shrine, the voices of concern on the display of "un-Islamic practices" are couched in the language of religious reform, but the reaction against the sacrilege of a mausoleum as a national site was voiced in the language of law. It serves to manifest the state as a secular entity while embodying the aura of the sacred—the emergence of a veritable political theology, as Carl Schmitt called it.

THE SOUND OF THE NATION: A NATIONAL ANTHEM FOR PAKISTAN

To borrow Carl Schmitt's famous formulation, the concept of political theology implied a translation of theological notions about God into secularized theological concepts about the modern state. In particular, Schmitt cites the example of God's omnipotence replaced by the state as the lawgiver whose power to decide the rule of exception was analogous to that of a miracle in religious metaphysics.[147] One could extend the scope of Schmitt's metaphor to find similarities in the aura cultivated in the idea of the state through such paraphernalia as national symbols—such as the flag and the national anthem—and in the precision expected of the devotee or citizen in interacting with such objects. In postcolonial states, given the newness of the state and presumption of a zero hour, or foundational moment, the scripting of such protocols is itself a public, performative act. It is both pedagogical and affective insofar as it seeks to educate citizens about their new faith and to inculcate in them sentiments of reverence for its founding fathers, their sacrifices, and the sacred objects associated with that faith.

With this understanding, the anthem can be likened to a daily chant prescribed for the devotee or citizen to reaffirm resolve in the new faith and renew expression of devotion to its cause and any sacrifice that might entail. In such aspects, the anthem as an official declaration differs from nationalist songs. Nationalist songs help mobilize resistance and cultivate political sensibilities, but they lack formal ritualism and regularity. For instance, in the case of South Asia, various nationalist songs captured the imagination of the people and helped mobilize the anticolonial movement on a mass scale. "Bande Matram" is one example that, despite Muslim criticism of the song as religiously offensive, was widely sung in public rallies. Post-1947, the Indian government opted for Tagore's "Jana Gana Mana" as its national anthem, in order to express the republican spirit. Other than the communal tinge associated with "Bande Matram," its warlike sloganeering did not suit the sobriety required of a national anthem. Even "Jana Gana Mana"—written in heavily Sanskritized Bengali—needed to be sanitized to serve the statist purpose. For this reason, the officially prescribed pronunciation for the anthem is Hindi, as it would sound differently if recited in a Bengali accent.[148] It is this remedial approach to accents, and the anxieties undergirding an elusive search for homogeneity and consistency, that serves as an opening point for looking into the language of state performativity.

Just as a green flag with crescent and star enjoyed widespread popularity in the early twentieth century, several *milli* songs also widely circulated among the Muslim community. I do not use *nationalist songs* here, as the content of these songs did not necessarily correspond to the Eurocentric idea of a nation defined by ethnicity or language. Some examples include songs based on Iqbal's poems or on poetry that eulogized Muhammad Ali Jinnah.[149] While there were numerous songs and poetry about the Muslim *qaum* popular during the colonial period, not one was considered suitable to become the national anthem after the creation of Pakistan.

While the Constituent Assembly was able to agree on the flag's design in its inaugural session, it took the government seven long years to decide on an anthem. There were several reasons for that. As Majid Lahori, a famous Urdu columnist from the period, satirically wrote, the government was caught in a chicken-or-egg dilemma in creating the anthem and had failed to decide whether it should first adopt a tune or lyrics.[150] The other major issue was the anthem's language. The debate about national language continued to rage in Pakistan until the mid-1950s, as East Bengalis—the majority population—demanded that Bengali hold official status equal to that of Urdu. The third challenge was to create a tune that was easily played by military bands and orchestras at official ceremonies throughout the world.

To popularize the process for choosing the national anthem and to generate wider interest, the Ministry of Interior, Information, and Broadcasting in June 1948 announced two prizes of five thousand rupees each for the best tune and lyrics for the national anthem.[151] This generous award was donated by Ahmad A. R. Gani, of Klerksdorp, South Africa. A committee was set up in December 1948 with Sardar Abdur Rab Nishtar as chairman and Z. A. Bukhari, Hafiz Jallandhari, and S. M. Ikram, among others, as members. Jasimuddin, a folklore poet of Bengal, was also on the committee. Bukhari had worked at All India Radio for years. Jallandhari was famous for his poetic brilliance, especially for the work *Shahnama-i-Islam* (Epic of Islam). Ikram was a bureaucrat and man of letters who excelled in a knowledge of classical poetry and Indo-Muslim history.

A key member of the committee, Zulfiqar Ali Bukhari, was opposed to the idea of a national anthem altogether. Muslims, he said, never had a national anthem, as it is "tantamount to artificial respiration administered to those who have no other inspiration to keep them alive." Bukhari pointed out various problems, including those of language and music. He lamented the woeful inability of Urdu poetry's vocabulary, which, with the exception of Hali and Iqbal, had not been "able to use a language for any living or serious purpose. Their vocabulary has remained severely restricted to the expression of carnal love and beauty."[152] While Urdu's poetic diction was, in Bukhari's estimation, one impediment, other major challenges of "Eastern" music included the single-line melody and the compulsion to play instruments in unison. Unlike Western music, "Pakistani music" does not have vertical harmony. Furthermore, it also does not have scales, he argued, the way Western music does: "Music must be sung and National Anthems must be sung to the accompaniment of musical instruments. I can hardly imagine the nationals of Pakistan rising at the role of tabla or the attack of a bow on the strings of a sarangi or violin. Therefore as far as the nationals of Pakistan are concerned a musical National Anthem as such seems out of question."[153]

But because a national anthem had become a prerequisite for statehood in the twentieth century, Bukhari nevertheless suggested adopting Surah Fatiha, the first chapter of the Quran, as Pakistan's national anthem. The Fatiha was known to most Muslims both in Pakistan and abroad, and it could be recited in a musical manner; it was thus perfectly capable of instilling reverence in the hearts of nationals. The Fatiha would be acceptable to followers of all religions, Bukhari claimed; Gandhi, too, used to recite it in his public prayers. Another added advantage was that the adoption of Fatiha would ensure that it was recited only on solemn occasions and not in cinema halls or cocktail parties.[154]

Bukhari was not the only person to recommend adopting a part of scripture as the national anthem. A. M. Mumtazuddin Khan, from Karachi, wrote to Fatima Jinnah on 2 October 1954 suggesting that the national anthem for Pakistan ought to be from the Quran, as the Islamic Republic's constitution was also going to be based on the Quran. He claimed to have "discovered" an Urdu translation of a famous Surah whose name is not disclosed in the text. He had also composed a tune for it. He wrote: "The most important feature of the Anthem is that when it is being recited every Musalman of the world is bound, by orders of God, to not only pay the necessary respect to it, but also to repeat himself the last verses of the

Anthem. This, I think, will play a great part in uniting the Muslim world, which is the main object of Islamic Republic of Pakistan."[155]

Bukhari's suggestion was overlooked, and the committee went ahead in its deliberations. Later, Bukhari himself wrote an anthem and presented it before the committee for approval.

The committee was clear that it intended to adopt an anthem that was "in consonance with the ideology of the state" and also "have a universal appeal ad might emphasize abiding values like equality, fraternity and human dignity." The committee wanted the tune of the anthem be such that it was "capable of being written or reduced to notation."[156] Tunes composed by Ahmed Chagla and Sajjad Sarwar Niazi of Radio Pakistan were played by the band at *HMPS Dilawar* on 4 June 1953.[157] But these were not the only artists who had submitted entries for the national anthem. Artists and individuals motivated to be part of a project of national importance reached out to Fatima Jinnah as well with their contributions and ideas. Even before the officially appointed committee had started its deliberations, Rex A. Manuel, bandmaster of the First Punjab Regiment, wrote to Fatima Jinnah on 1 September 1947 to submit his tune for the national anthem. "The modern style of music this Anthem is written in, in preference to the old and hackneyed modes prevalent, manifest the modern trend in Pakistan," he wrote. "It further renders the Anthem to be universally played, understood and appreciated."[158]

Of all the entries received, the selection committee was most enthusiastic about that submitted by Chagla. Abdus Sattar Pirzada, chairman of the National Anthem Committee, claimed the tune was based on melodies that had developed in the Indo-Pakistan region during the Muslim period and could suitably be played by international orchestras.[159]

The committee's work—and its delay in deciding an issue of national importance—was routinely criticized in the press. The left-leaning Urdu newspaper *Imroz* criticized the secrecy surrounding the working of the anthem committee. It wrote about random news in circulation about a composer whose composition had been selected. The paper lamented the lack of transparency in a process of vital national importance.[160] In another article in the same newspaper a few months later, Rafiq Ghaznawi wrote a column titled "Qaumi taranay ki zarurat aur ahmiyyat." The article gave a brief history of the origins of the idea of a national anthem and an overview of different anthems. He then built on this historical background to argue that a country's national anthem should reflect the people's character, culture, aspirations, and beliefs. The article then discussed the tune for the Pakistani anthem composed by Chagla, which it described as an awful noise, a grand funeral in which people, wearing black with heads down, followed it and beat their chests. According to Ghaznavi, it reminded one of an old tune from the Christian priests of a grand church that was full of irregular noises. While recognizing the poetic brilliance of Hakim Ahmad Shuja, Hafiz Jallandhari, and Jigar Muradabadi, whose poetic contributions were all being considered as the anthem was finalized, he said that this task of writing the anthem was not simply for a poet, but the job of someone who had spent a lifetime in the arts and crafts.[161] Decades later, Jallandhari spoke about the tune of the anthem in similar terms. In an interview he recorded for the Luftullah Khan collection, Jallandhari reminisced on mimicking the tune, making it sound like a lament in order to convince committee members that it was unsuitable as a national anthem.[162]

Despite such criticisms, Chagla's composition was finalized, and poets were invited to submit entries for the anthem's lyrics. The composition was played on the radio and, in the absence of a complete anthem, on formal occasions. Of more than two hundred submissions received, the committee shortlisted the anthems written by Hafiz Jallandhari and Hakim Ahmed Shuja in a March 1951 meeting. Both anthems were in Urdu. Eventually, Jallandhari was the clear winner, given his superior skills as a poet. The committee further recommended that in addition to the anthem, two songs, one by Iqbal and one by Nazrul Islam, be selected as national songs.[163] Nazrul Islam's song "Chal Chal Chal," as amended by Jasimuddin, was to be one of the national songs. In the case of Iqbal, instead of adopting one of his poems, the committee recommended inviting prominent poets to write *tazmin* of Iqbal's verse (*sabaq parh phir shujat ka*), making a six-line stanza.[164]

In addition to being an excellent poet and lyricist, Jallandhari had the advantage of knowing Chagla, so that he could work with his tune to adjust his lyrics accordingly. During World War II, Jallandhari had served as the director general of "peace publicity" and was responsible for getting songs recorded in various languages. Jallandhari also had prior experience writing another national anthem, that for Azad Kashmir. According to Jallandhari, Chagla's tune was elegiac (*matami*), but Jallandhari's lyrics gave it a militaristic touch (*rijzyiya andaz*).[165] Jallandhari expressed his frustration with other members of the committee, who insisted that he change his lyrics to be more in tune with the composition. The committee also pressurized Jallandhari to incorporate a stanza from Z. A. Bukhari's submission in his draft. This was being demanded to placate Bukhari who carried considerable influence in official circles. Jallandhari flatly refused and responded mockingly, criticizing Bukhari's lyrics for being rhythmless. If Bukhari could prove that even a single verse of his was in sync with the tune, Jallandhari claimed, the latter would forever quit being a poet.[166]

In this back-and-forth correspondence between the poet and the bureaucrat, Hashim Raza wrote another letter to Jallandhari in July 1954 asking him to explain the use of particular words. The word *parcham*, Raza pointed out, lexicographically meant "a piece of cloth tied to a flag," while it had been used to connote a flag in the national anthem.[167] Jallandhari, in his response, pointed out that the dictionary meaning of other Persian and Arabic words, such as *'alam*, was also similar to the one pointed out by Hashim Raza in his letter: "It is to be understood that the flag, though merely a piece of cloth, is a symbol of national identity and sovereignty. The Pakistan's flag manifests grandeur, high ideals and dignity of the State of Pakistan. These words are to be understood metaphorically."[168]

Because of this prolonged discussion, the national anthem was not officially adopted until 1954, three years after the committee had selected Jallandhari's composition. The lack of a national anthem had become a source of embarrassment for the Pakistani state and the public at large. The noted progressive poet and fiction writer Ahmed Nadeem Qasmi recalled an incident in which a delegation of Pakistani authors visited China in the early 1950s. After other countries' anthems were played, the Chinese stood up out of respect for the Pakistani anthem, which they expected to hear. Because there was still no official anthem, there was an awkward moment of silence before one of the delegates, Maulana Akhtar Ali Khan, stepped forward and started reciting his father Maulana Zafar Ali Khan's poem, "Wo shama ujala jis nay kia chalis baras tak gharon mai."[169] Aqeel Abbas Jafri talks about similar incidents in which, in the absence of an official anthem, individuals and groups recited poems and songs to represent Pakistan on various official occasions.[170] He gives the example of a national song recited by Pakistani scouts at international forums.

The national anthem was played for the first time on Radio Pakistan on 13 August 1954. It was then replayed every evening for a few weeks to familiarize people with its lyrics.[171] Given its highly Persianized language, popularizing the anthem required a major pedagogical exercise. Students, children, and the general masses had to be taught to read the lyrics and recite them in sync with the official tune. The Education Department of Punjab took measures to introduce the anthem in schools and colleges. One such official, Younas Kamal Lodhi, visited Government College Lahore, Lahore College for Women, Junior Model School, Pak Boys Scout Group, and PAF Officers Mess to impart a daily one-hour training.[172]

Once the anthem had been officially released, a flurry of criticism followed. To make this public discussion of the anthem understandable, I provide here the original text of the anthem, along with its official English translation:

> *Pak sar-zamin shad-bad*
> *Kishwar-i-hasin shad-bad*
> *Tu nishan-i-azam-i-alishan*
> *Arz-i-Pakistan*
> *Markaz-i-Yaqin shad-bad*
> *Pak sar-zamin ka nizam*
> *Quwwat-i-ukhuwwat-i-awam*
> *Qaum, mulk, sultanat*
> *Painda tabinda-bad*
> *Shad-bad manzil-i-murad*
> *Parcham-i-sitara-o-hilal*
> *Rahbar-i-taraqqi-o-kamal*
> *Tarjuman-i-mazi, shan-i-hal*
> *Jan-i-Istiqbal*
> *Saya-i-Khuda-i-Zuljalal*

> Blessed be the sacred land
> Happy be the beauteous realm
> Thou symbol of high resolve
> Land of Pakistan
> Blissful be the citadel of faith
> The order of our sacred State
> The might of the brotherhood of man
> May the nation, the country and the State
> Shine in glory everlasting
> Thou blissful goal of ambition
> Our flag of the crescent and the star
> Guide to progress and excellence
> Symbol of the past, glory of the present
> Soul of the future
> Shadow of God Omnipotent[173]

Critics—most of them ordinary citizens—were appalled at their alienation from lyrics that were incomprehensible to the large majority. Both English and Urdu newspapers from West and East Pakistan joined hands to criticize the anthem. They expressed their disappointment with the unintelligible text of the anthem and its uninspiring tune. In its editorial on 24 August 1954, Dacca-based *Pakistan Observer* wondered what the verses of the newly released national anthem meant: "Since it has been characterised as a national anthem its purpose is, of course, understood, but not the words until one has managed to procure by borrowing or buying Arabic and Persian lexicons and delved deep into them for the significance of the words composing the anthem."[174] It recommended that the selection committee members look into the works of Nazrul Islam for a suitable composition. Arshad Kakwi, professor of Urdu at Victoria College, Comilla, objected to the Persianate language of the anthem, which was incomprehensible to 80 percent of the population and "uninspiring, cold, static and dull." Kakwi suggested presenting this anthem to Iran; it had all the right qualities for serving as the Iranian national anthem.[175] For Aziz Ahmad Bilyameeni, of Dacca, the major failure of the anthem was not its language but its inability to inspire people.[176] Another Dacca-based English daily,

Morning News, wrote in an editorial that half the cabinet members, the majority of members of the Constituent Assembly, and 80 percent of the population of Pakistan were unable to understand the national anthem. According to the newspaper *Baba-i-Urdu*, Maulvi Abdul Haq also disapproved of it. He was reported as criticizing the anthem for lumping together Arabic and Persian words, which did not stir the emotions and sentiments of the people of Pakistan. Abdul Majid Salik—another notable poet and journalist—observed that the anthem sounded as if it were not to be sung but simply set to the music. Its tune was Western rather than Eastern. He was disappointed that the anthem was written not in Urdu but an alien language. Ehtashamul Haq Thanvi and Abdul Hamid Badayuni, talking to *Morning News*, also disapproved of the anthem.

Majid Lahori wrote a satirical piece saying that the only purpose the anthem could serve "was to set as a piece for matric students to be 'rewritten in simple Urdu.'" *Zamindar* reported that the anthem was pedantic, and one had to be at least Munshi Fazil to understand it. "Some MA students and their professors may, however, sing it at their convocations." *Zamindar* narrated the story of a journalist who gave the anthem to his son to read; the son came back to ask his father who "Kishwar Husain" was—a play on the term *kishwar-i-hasin*, or "beautiful land."[177]

Some critics felt that Hafiz Jallandhari could have done better had he not been forced to follow the tune. M. A. Khaliq, from Karachi, felt that Jallandhari faced the compulsion of sticking to "the rigid frames of the bars of music," thus coining such terms as *istiqbal*, which he otherwise wouldn't have used. The dictionary definition of an anthem, Khaliq said, was that it be adopted by the people. *Morning News* echoed similar sentiments in an editorial. The result of Jallandhari's confinement to a set tune was an "uninspiring, grotesque caricature of a national anthem which eighty per cent of the people of Pakistan will not even understand."[178] In another editorial, the newspaper said that the anthem lacked rhythm and beauty. It was a queer mixture of Urdu and Persian oddly grafted on to a tune that had already been selected, putting the cart before the horse.[179] The editorial stated that the anthem should have been chosen by the representatives in the Constituent Assembly.

The newspapers persisted in criticism even after a year of the anthem's promulgation. Writing under the pseudonym of Diogenes, an author gave an account of an Independence Day reception in August 1955: as the military band played the anthem, none among the elites recognized it. According to the author, the tune of the anthem was "neither stirring like the martial 'Marseillaise' nor loyally appealing like 'God Save the Queen.'" As for the lyrics, Diogenes was of the opinion that "in this land of 'mushairas' or poetical 'soirees' any 'shaher' or even a poetaster, aided and abetted by a composer of orchestral music can easily replace the Persian text with an Urdu one, and the simpler the language, the better from every point of view." Now that after seven years, the country had produced "a mouse of a National Anthem, let us try and make a lion of it by changing its text and making it popular by playing and singing it everywhere."[180]

Adding to the rising choir of criticism of the anthem were demands from East Bengalis to have an anthem or set of national songs in Bengali. Various national songs had been produced in East Bengal. For instance, the ad for one such song, "Zamin Firdos Pakistan ki hogi," sung by Abbasuddin Ahmed, was available on record as early as October 1947.[181] A Bengali national song, "Pakistan Zindabad," by Nazir Ahmed, was already popular in East Bengal and sung in schools there in the 1950s.[182] A. Rashid, from Chittagong, demanded another anthem for East Pakistan. The current version, he said, was incomprehensible and might serve as the proverbial last nail in Pakistan's coffin, as it would fail to serve the purpose of national cohesion. He asked how India could adopt Tagore's anthem when Bengali was not even spoken in most parts of India.[183] As the government finally announced the launch of new national songs in Bengali, *Morning News* reminded its readers that the newspaper had, upon the anthem's launch, pointed out its unintelligibility to a large section of the Pakistani population, but the anthem was still accepted because "Hafiz Jullundhari's claim . . . was backed by a fellow-Jullundhari"—a jibe at then prime minister Chaudhary Muhammad Ali, who was also a migrant from Jallandhar.[184] Given that Bengalis were unable to recite the Persianized anthem, a Bengali national song was to be launched. The editorial anticipated the announcement for a Bengali national anthem in addition to the Persianized one and criticized such an outcome. The newspaper argued that this would further fester regional divides and the demand for two separate economies, which had already become a rallying cry. This theory of two national anthems, however, failed to materialize. One could compare this situation with similar demands by marginalized Hispanic groups in the United States for the national anthem to be in Spanish alongside English. While such a demand strikes at white superiority as the basis of American state, it can also be read as an aspirational value for equality through and as inclusion in the state, and in its official narrative and national paraphernalia.[185]

From Jallandhari's point of view, the most serious challenge was directed at him by his fellow poets. In a detailed essay published in *Nawa'i-Waqt* on 30 August 1954, he responded to his critics, especially Abdul Majid Salik and Sufi Tabbassum. Jallandhari's rejoinder is a remarkable piece of writing: he discusses his poetic brilliance, flays his opponents for their jealous behavior, and explains the anthem verse by verse to show that the language he had used was from everyday life.

Jallandhari's main line of defense was that his creative canvas had been constrained: he was forced to conform to Chagla's tune, which he had opposed. Within the confines of that tune, Jallandhari had to find words that could reflect, and be worthy of, an Islamic society and state and Islamic values. "It is true," he wrote, "that I haven't said in this anthem to 'Go, grab a sword and invade, bring the entire world under subjugation.'"[186] The ideational basis of the state, Jallandhari contended, was not to conquer the world but to reestablish the Islamic way of life and promote Islamic values and brotherhood. He claimed that his lyrics matched these lofty values and were understandable to anyone who listened to the speeches of Muslim leaders and read the newspaper, and furthermore, familiar to the people of Afghanistan, Iran, Iraq, and the rest of the Muslim world. This clearly shows that Jallandhari's intended audience for the anthem was literate and transnational.

Before responding to the literary merits of the criticism against him, Jallandhari responded to the personal slander. He said that while he was not jealous of anyone's success and did not criticize others' poetic craft, others were envious of his accomplishments. He had been ridiculed for writing *filmi* songs and at the same time taunted for his religiosity as he had written a twelve-thousand-verse epic on Islamic history. He said that a newspaper claimed that Hafiz Jallandhari wrote the anthem dead drunk, and dancing girls (*randiyan*) were singing it.[187] The reason his anthem had been selected out of hundreds of submissions, Jallandhari wrote, was not because of any conspiracy or act of personal favor but because the committee thought it was the best entry.

As for the literary criticism, Jallandhari justified using Persian words for every line by either citing references from contemporary sources or simply adopting a mocking tone in addressing his opponents. To begin with, it was not as if the Urdu world had not heard of words like *kishwar* (country), *markaz* (center), *yaqin* (faith), and *sar-zameen* (land). *Shad-bad* (blessed) was as Persian as *zinda-bad*. Why use *alishan* ("high" or "grand"), he wrote, and why not Hindi or Punjabi words such as *wadda*, *wadera*, *uccha*, and *lamma*? He went on with a similar satirical tone to taunt his opponents, who critiqued him for using words like *sultanat* because it implied emperorship. Iqbal might have used the term *sultani-i-jamhur* (the government of the people), wrote Jallandhari, but such an understanding of the term was unacceptable when applied to the anthem.[188] A longer excerpt from the essay helps sum up the mix of satire and knowledge of linguistics and poetics that Jallandhari used to justify his position:

> And what is this *manzil* [goal], we don't have any *manzil*, we haven't oriented ourselves to any direction, so how come there is a *manzil*! Furthermore, what is this *parcham* [flag]? Well, we do write unfurling the flag [*parcham kushai*] and flying the flag [*parcham lehrana*] in Urdu, [but] this flag of crescent and star [*parcham-i-sitara-o-hilal*] is Persian. And then this *tarjuman-i-mazi*—what is a *tarjuman*? Tarjuman-ul-Quran [monthly magazine published by Jamat-i-Islami] makes sense, this is our everyday speech, [but] what is this *tajuman-i-mazi*. From which language is the word *shan* [pride]? What is *hal* [present]? We have never heard in Urdu *mazi* [past], *hal* [present] or *mustaqbil* [future]. No sire, this isn't our language.[189]

As to the Arabic roots of the word *zuljalal*, Jallandhari wrote, Pakistanis are used to referring to their kings as "the shadow of God," so why couldn't they apply it to the Pakistani flag? Jallandhari's argument is an apt description of Schmitt's formulation of the state replacing God as the omnipotent sovereign. At the end, Jallandhari quotes from the highly Persianized poetry of his critics Salik and Sufi Tabassum, adding a tongue-in-cheek remark that such verses do not have a single word of Persian or Arabic. As to Maulvi Abdul Haq, known as "the grand old man of Urdu" (*Baba-i-Urdu*), who criticized Jallandhari for writing an anthem in Persian, the latter quips that the title *Baba-i-Urdu* is itself Persian.[190] Jallandhari finishes the essay by challenging colleagues and senior poets who were busy criticizing him to try writing an anthem of their own.

In response to Jallandhari's criticism, Salik wrote a letter on 1 September 1954 clarifying his position. He had not criticized Hafiz; he had simply stated that Hafiz was forced to adjust to the tune. Salik reiterated his position that the anthem was full of Persian and Arabic words that people could not understand and that could not move them. The anthem, he said, would be only played, not sung. He added that he himself wrote Persianized poetry—such as that cited by Jallandhari—because he did not write for the common person. In contrast, an anthem was meant for the masses and should be in a language they could understand.[191]

The most significant objections to the national anthem were of its language and perceptions of it as an uninspiring tune. Little criticism was made of its content: the idea of land as an abstract space. None of the regions of Pakistan is named. This is in sharp contrast with the Indian anthem, which refers even to Sindh, although no part of that region is now in the Indian Republic. The thrust of the Pakistani anthem was futuristic, meant to serve as an inaugural moment of state formation that promised a prosperous future with an earnest prayer to God to protect the homeland. The anthem does not engage with the past, other than referring to the state as the embodiment of the past's glory. It rhythmically overrides the complexities of the past and its many contradictions by keeping it undefined while acknowledging the country's glorious heritage to build the foundations of the new state, heralding an era of progress, and establishing a bastion of faith.

Given his poetic brilliance, it was not difficult for Hafiz Jallandhari to write an anthem in a more straightforward language with a more intimate description of Pakistan's history and its landscape. In fact, when Prime

Minister Liaqat Ali Khan first approached him as early as December 1947 to write an anthem, Jallandhari came up with a much simpler draft that the committee rejected. This original version is as follows:

> *Aay meray Abad Watan Azad Pakistan*
>   *Zinda-bad Pakistan*
>   *Zinda-bad Pakistan*
> *Teray Samandar, Teray Darya*
>   *Kohisar wa Maidan*
>   *Izzat, Shaukat, Shan*
> *Khuda-i-Pak ka hai Ihsan*
> *Tu hai Pak Amanat*
>   *Jis par Zindigiyan Qurban*
> *Tujh pay Nichawar Mal, Jan, Aulad, Pakistan*
>   *Zinda-bad Pakistan*[192]

> O my flourishing homeland, my free Pakistan
>   Long live Pakistan (2)
> Your seas, your rivers
>   Hills and plains
>   Honour, grandeur, glory
> Blessing of Holy God
> You are a sacred trust
>   For which we will lay our lives (2)
> All our wealth, lives, progeny are for you
>   Long live Pakistan (2)[193]

For the national anthem to function as a daily chant, its language had to be liturgical, though not explicitly scriptural or derived from scripture as proposed by Zulfiqar Ali Bukhari. Like India's national anthem, the lyrics did not have to be communicative or accessible. The nation's grandeur required genealogical linking with a civilizational core—Persianate, in the case of Pakistan, in its initial decades—and its expression in a classical language that was lyrical enough to be memorized without being understood. In that sense, it served a similar purpose to a religious prayer recited in Arabic or Latin, which few can understand unless translated into vernacular language. The same holds for Pakistan's national anthem: its highly ornate, Persianized Urdu must be simplified and explained to its listeners. Yet the anthem carries a functional value recognized by everyone. A major reason for the anthem's legibility is the elaborate ritual practice prescribed by the state to enforce the sanctity of the anthem. Like flag rules, there are officially prescribed procedures for playing the anthem: "Rules for Playing the National Anthem of Pakistan" details the occasions on which the anthem is to be played, and the mannerisms that are to be observed while it is played. A separate "Regulations for Defence Services Regarding Playing of the National Anthem of Pakistan" specifies the role of military and pipe bands.[194] For instance, both bands are to play when the toast "Pakistan" is proposed. The anthem's rhythmic repetition on public occasions and its regular observance in educational institutions ensure that the "sights and sounds" of the anthem are drummed into the lives of Pakistani citizens.

A few years ago, a controversy about Pakistan's national anthem surfaced in the electronic media. From an interview of the India-based Urdu poet, Jagan Nath Azad, published a month after his death in 2004, a journalist claimed that Azad wrote the first national anthem of Pakistan. According to the report, Azad was approached by none other than Muhammad Ali Jinnah himself to write an anthem for Pakistan. The fact that a Hindu writer was tasked with drafting the Muslim state's national anthem made for a flashy headline in the *Hindu*: "A Hindu Wrote Pakistan's First National Anthem."[195]

The Pakistani liberal intelligentsia celebrated this discovery as another validation of Jinnah's pluralistic and "secular" vision for Pakistan. It is true that Azad's anthem was regularly played on national radio until the 1950s, but as Aqeel Abbas Jafri has conclusively shown in his research, it was a *tarana* (national song), not a *qaumi tarana*, or official state song or anthem.[196] In the copious official documentation of the public debates around the anthem that exists from the 1950s, there is no reference to an existing national anthem that Jallandhari's replaced. But the fact that such a controversy exists, and that there are many among the intelligentsia who are eager to believe in the fiction of an alternative anthem, is indicative of aspirations to influence the state narrative and to have the state recognize an ideological framework of liberal nationalism.

This chapter has given an account of what can be described as "identity constituted by historical sedimentation," referring to Homi Bhabha's commentary on Julia Kristeva's theory of nationalism. I read this phrase as an accumulation of meanings ascribed to different objects, whether forms of dress, artistic symbols, or poetic metaphors. I interpret Bhabha's description of "the loss of identity in the signifying process of cultural identification" as the exorcising of excess to stabilize meaning by overwriting its metaphorical depth and layered genealogical complexity.[197] These twin pedagogical and performative processes create a new meaning of abstract simplicity to give a definite narrative shape, flattening difference, as required by the homogenized conjoining of the nation with the state. While the nation was built on the surplus meaning attached to these symbols, and on their use in multiple ways to assert a sovereign existence and to articulate distinct nationhood, the very basis of this nationhood expressed through symbols has to be regulated by the state to ensure their preservation and sustenance. In other words, the state existed, or was required, to protect the nation. In statist logic, the nation, through its use of symbols in its excessive, emotion-laden language, cannot sustain the sovereign expression of nationhood unless its meaning is stabilized as part of the state-making project. Such a statist project is aspirational and continues to strive for a foreclosure of the meaning of the nation and its constitutive historical and cultural elements.

But it is the failure to achieve such closure that marks the anxiety of the nation-state and its imperative for violence to achieve homogeneity. Despite the legally sanctioned rules about using the flag, for instance, the Pakistani flag is approximated in all sorts of ways. It is seldom drawn following precise calculations and seldom hoisted on private, or even official, buildings in the prescribed manner.[198] Jinnah's mausoleum is one of the major picnic spots for the residents of Karachi. As an investigative TV report showed, the mausoleum is the most popular dating spot for young couples.[199] The anthem has been remixed and rendered in different styles by artists and corporations. The crescent and star figure on all sorts of advertisements, signboards, and other designs and objects. Regardless of what the state thinks of as "Pakistani dress," popular attire is, in varying forms and shapes, *shalwar qamiz*. People continue to draw on what the state has tried to appropriate as symbols of nationhood with regulated meanings, instead using them as objects in everyday life. It is by tracing the history of this appropriation and its limitations that the enduring significance of these symbols and their usage as contestation—that is, as a form of banal nationalism, or resistance against it—can be understood.

FOUR

OVER THE MOON
Ulema, State, and Authority in Pakistan

ON 17 MARCH 1961, Maulana Ehtasham-ul-Haq Thanawi, a prominent religious scholar based in the country's capital—Karachi—announced that that year the crescent had not been sighted anywhere in Pakistan; therefore, the festival of Eid would take place on 19 March, the last day of Ramadan. Thanawi's statement contradicted the declaration made by Pakistan's meteorological department, which had announced Eid for the following day, 18 March. This led to mass confusion. Given Thanawi's status as the leading religious scholar in the city, most people followed his statement, ignored the official declaration, and chose to fast on 18 March. Even in Pakistan's brief existence, from 1947 to 1961, it was not the first time that Eid was celebrated on two different days. But it was the "moon controversy" of March 1961 that sparked a public debate that continues to reverberate today.

The debate centers on such questions as the idea of sovereign power, the role of scientific rationality, the authority of the ulema, and the public role religion should play in the context of a Muslim-majority state. In General Ayub Khan's Kemalist vision for Pakistan, Islam could serve as a modernizing force for state formation and nation building. Khan insisted that the moon and its movements could be calculated years in advance, to the last fraction of a second. It was a "simple" matter of relying on scientific calculations to prepare a lunar calendar listing all major religious occasions for years to come, enforcing it across the country, as is done in places like Egypt. The twin principles of authoritarianism and scientism thus lay at the heart of a statist discourse about Islam as part of the nationalizing project. From Ayub Khan's perspective, it was essential to establish the state's control over the interpretation of Islam, which in turn required diluting the influence of the ulema as guides in matters of belief and practice.

For the ulema in the postcolonial context of a majoritarian Muslim state such as Pakistan, enchantment with state power and its ability to alter how society operated offered an opportunity to assert their role in determining normative Islamic beliefs and practices. But to claim leadership, guiding the Muslim state in the quest to establish an ideal Islamic society, required a revisionist approach to Islamic discursive tradition; this tradition had originally emerged in a context in which a constellation of power apparatus such as the modern state had not existed.

In this chapter, I study the disputative engagement between the postcolonial state and the ulema by focusing on the issue of the sighting of the new moon. I look at these debates as an interactive process that has been shaped by the imperatives of state formation and by epistemological crisis. The cumulative impact of these processes is that, in practice, the ulema have adopted a revisionist approach toward classical juristic texts to make "tradition" adaptive to contemporary changes.

For the sake of clarity, I discern three, nonhierarchical levels of debate: at the public level, a question of a conflictual binary between science and religion, that is, an understanding of the zeitgeist as an onward march of reason, questioning whether Islamic beliefs and practices are egalitarian and rational enough to cope with that spirit; at the state level, the question of establishing sovereign power to interpret Islam and the challenge posed by the ulema, who claim religious credentials for interpretating of Islamic law; and last, a debate within the larger Islamic tradition as ulema grapple with the impact of modernity to reengage with classical texts of *fiqh* and law, addressing questions concerning everyday belief and practice.

The contingency of state power, as well as an enchantment with it, shapes the ulema's engagement with their own tradition, which they then bring to bear on shaping the state itself. The ulema's two-way engagement with state power, while requiring a revision of tradition, also enhanced the scope of their authority and the public role of religion. In the case of religious festivals that require a moon sighting, I draw on fatwas from the colonial period—from the early nineteenth century to well into the twentieth century—covering major Sunni denominations, to show that the Eid celebration was traditionally a local event restricted to a community of believers in a neighborhood, village, or city. With the acquisition of state power in 1947, new meanings were attributed to the festival. Both the ulema and the Pakistani state contributed to such meaning making. In the context of a nation-state eager to project the concept of "one nation, one Eid," but with boundaries as far apart as 1,200 miles between its eastern and western wings, the ulema had to adopt an expansive approach to reread locale, community, neighborhood, and city as conceptually equivalent to the territorialized unit of the nation-state.

At the same time, they affirmed a literalist reading of the term *sight* to sublimate scientific rationality to authentication by the ulema and their scholarly credentials. I offer a reading of the semantics of this debate and the process whereby ulema brought about this change in meaning while ensuring that the process remain within the larger discursive tradition of Islam. The moon-sighting controversies thus provide an exciting perspective for understanding the process whereby ulema adapt in the face of what MacIntyre calls an "epistemological crisis" while still maintaining the status of, to use a term coined by Muhammad Qasim Zaman, "custodians of change."[1]

DEBATES ON THE MOON AND ASTRONOMY IN THE CLASSICAL PERIOD

The moon figures prominently in different forms and ways in Islamic art, treatises on astrology, poetry, and texts on *fiqh*. The new moon, or *hilal*, regulates the cycle of the Islamic calendar, in turn affecting religious observance and practice. Of particular significance is *hilal-i-Eid* (also *ghurra-i-shawwal*), which marks the beginning of the month of Shawwal that immediately follows Ramadan, and thus the celebration of Eid. The moon as a celestial body is central to medieval texts on astrological calculations and various manuals that advise daily routines and schedules of specific colors, costumes, and food. The lunar eclipse is another common theme, with debates on which religious practices should be observed to protect oneself from its impact. The centrality of the moon is not unique to Islamic civilization; there are similar imaginings to be found in all societies across time and space. What is noteworthy, however, is the extensive literature, including canonical texts, poetry, and horoscopes, that has accumulated over centuries and continues to regulate quotidian life among Muslims.

The moon, or more specifically, *hilal*, has been a popular metaphor in classical Persian and Urdu poetry. Its appearance on the horizon is indicative of a regulatory regime specific to a month. In Ramadan, it signals a month of repentance and abstinence. *Ghurra-i-Shawwal*, in contrast, marks the end of the disciplinary bodily regime of Ramadan, thus spurring joyous celebrations. This is captured in a couplet attributed to the Mughal emperor Jehangir, in which the *hilal* is likened to the key to a tavern that had been lost for a month. Another popular invocation of *hilal-i-Eid* emphasizes the rarity of its occurrence, the eagerness with which it is awaited, and the difficulty with which it can be sighted; these features combine to liken the sighting of a new moon to seeing the beloved: each is an eagerly awaited, delightful sight that requires a great deal of effort.

Hilal-i-Muharram triggers an entirely different set of emotions and festivities. Marking the first year of the Islamic calendar, Muharram has become synonymous with the martyrdom of Husain, Prophet Muhammad's grandson, along with his family, in the Battle of Karbala. In an essay on the observance of Muharram in colonial Lucknow, Mushirul Hasan summarizes the sudden change in mood and atmosphere marked by sighting the Muharram crescent. As soon as the moon was sighted, the city became enamored of a festivity of a different kind: *majalis* (gatherings) to commemorate the martyrdom of Husain, reciting of *nauhas*, and self-flagellation. Muharram practice includes abstaining from meat, tobacco, and pan (betel leaf); wearing black clothes; and giving up perfumes.[2] With the sighting of the moon, the rhythm of life changes.

The scriptural rubric of observance of religious practices based on the lunar calendar has generated multiple life forms of its own. In this chapter, however, I limit myself to debates on the calendar itself and, more specifically, discussions of the act of moon sighting.

As David King's extensive research on astronomical works published during the premodern period shows, calculations of time and the calendar had such a substantial impact on daily Muslim observance that a scholarly tradition dedicated to such issues came into existence as early as the second century *hijri* (eighth century AD). This tradition focused exclusively on astrology, astronomy, geography, and mathematics to calculate lunar cycles, tabulating this information for astronomical and astrological purposes. Information about such aspects as the longitudes of the sun and the moon at sunset, the altitude of the moon above the horizon, and the apparent velocity of the moon, was recorded in astronomical handbooks (*zij*) and treatises on astronomical timekeeping (*miqat*).[3] Dale has identified more than two hundred *zij* compiled by scholars between the eighth and the nineteenth centuries. Additional material about the movements of celestial bodies was often supplemented in the form of an annual *taqvim* (almanac) that "extracted from the latest zij the relevant astronomical and astrological data."[4] These various genres about celestial bodies contributed to a repository of knowledge that was required to determine the length of the day, to schedule daily prayers, to set the timing of *sahar* and *iftar* during Ramadan, and to orient mosques toward the Ka'ba. In short, during the premodern period, mathematical calculations for determining the new moon were not exceptional.

For jurists, the question was of the validity of claims made on the basis of mathematical calculations: should it be supplement to, or could they replace, the actual sighting of the moon? Per a well-known hadith attributed to the Prophet, Muslims are enjoined "to start fasting when they see the moon and end it when they see the moon." The question was how to determine the role of mathematically calculated tables prepared by Muslim scholars in *seeing* the moon. As Dallal points out, jurists had a problem believing the accuracy of mathematical calculations. Those same calculations could be used in the service of astrology for activities deemed impermissible from a religious point of view. A lack of precision was a problem for jurists, and not the idea of relying on specialized knowledge of mathematicians, geographers, and astrologers. These debates, as summarized by Dallal, span centuries. Rather than bifurcating the religious and rational sciences, scholars drew on one another's works, *répliques*, and countercritiques to evaluate the merits of particular methods in ascertaining the direction of the Ka'ba according to the requirements of Shariat.

For example, the late seventeenth-century scholar al-Arabi Ibn Abd al-Salam al-Fasi refers to the distinction between the qibla's *jih* (direction) and its *samt* (azimuth).[5] His text responds to a group of scholars who believed that a general direction toward the qibla sufficed, without ascertaining exact mathematical coordinates. Al-Fasi makes a distinction between *jih* and *samt* to emphasize the importance of precise mathematical calculations and the use of knowledge of geometry. With a mastery of specialized knowledge, Fasi claims, it is the astronomer, and not the jurist, who has the authority to exercise *ijtihad* in matters of the direction of the qibla.[6] Unlike the *ijtihad* of jurists on issues of their own expertise, which can have multiple outcomes and thus be subject to revision, the astronomer's *ijtihad* about the qibla is definite and reaches a high level of certainty. Widespread and constitutive of the Islamic culture of inquiry as they were, such discussions, Dallal reminds us, took place in the broader epistemological space at the intersect of science, religion, and philosophy.[7]

During the late eighteenth and early nineteenth centuries, the emergence of modern state authority—both as a concept and as an apparatus of power—affected the Islamic intellectual tradition. These new constellations of power coincided with the epistemological crisis following colonial modernity, which invariably shaped the practice of Islamic juristic and scientific thought. The nature of the technology involved and its corresponding impact on social practice serves as an additional area of inquiry. The question was not simply about technology but also about the sociality of technology and its epistemic basis. If scientific observance itself is a socially embodied practice—"a highly contrived and disciplined form of experience that requires training of the body and mind, material props, techniques of description and visualization, networks of communication and transmission, canons of evidence, and specialized form of reasoning"[8]—then the observatory methods of the premodern period inevitably yielded ritualistic practices that were different from the current usage of astronomical calculations.

This is where Heidegger's distinction between old and modern technology becomes important. Heidegger describes modern technology as a form of revealing that does not unfold into a bringing-forth, in the sense of poiesis—the creative act of bringing into being what did not exist before. This revealing, however, is a challenge that enables mastery and control.[9] Technology sets upon nature, in the sense of challenging it. Heidegger gives the example of a hydroelectric plant on the Rhine that reduces the river to "a water power supplier." There is, thus, the same river with two titles: "'The Rhine' as dammed up into the power works, and 'The Rhine' as uttered out of the art work" in Holderlin's poetry.[10] In a Cartesian perspective in which the world was no longer to be read as a divine text but rather to be seen as situated in a mathematically regular spatial-temporal order, the moon becomes a celestial body calculable by technological precision—thus subjecting it to technological conquest; it becomes a mere unit of calculation, exorcised of its mythical aura, which is at the heart of ritualistic observance, and of longing and poetic metaphors.[11]

CHANGING TIMES: THE AGE OF COLONIAL MODERNITY

Given the long history of the ulema's engagement with scientific calculations of, and tools for measuring, time, distance, and direction, eighteenth-century ulema were eager to learn and adapt to new technological tools. As Daniel Stolz's work shows, mechanical timepieces had become popular in Ottoman Cairo long before European influence. But the fact that the mechanical clock enabled the precise timing of the daily prayers did not lead to a decline in the ulema's authority; it supplemented that authority. A new genre of manuals came into existence instructing users on how to adjust the watch hand's movement to the cyclical phenomena of the rise and fall of the sun, and thus to the call to prayer.[12] Through their mastery of the science of *miqat*, the ulema became the mediators through which these objects became popular in everyday use. Based on the Ottoman-era sunset hour (*gurubi sa'at*) method of timekeeping, the day begins at sunset. Given that mechanical clocks keep equal hours, they had to be adjusted daily to keep midday aligned with the changes in sunset that occur throughout the year.[13] Thus, "the mechanical clock on the *gurubi sa'at* system would show a different time for apparent noon in February, and quite another in July."[14]

In Istanbul, the institution of timekeeping, often attached to a mosque, was vital: it helped maintain concordance between accurate clock time and prayer times.

In the late nineteenth century, the trend changed. Following Mehmed Ali Pasha's centralization policies, a new generation of Egyptian bureaucracy emerged, along with specialists trained in European universities. By the mid-1870s, the residents of Cairo were familiar with a new sound—cannon fire—as a signal for timekeeping.[15] The shift from the call to prayer to a cannon firing at noon, instead of sunset, was accompanied by, and indicative of, several other changes. The most important were centralized state control and a shift in social relations whereby technocrats replaced ulema.

Eventually, by the beginning of the twentieth century, British surveyors synchronized time signals in Egyptian cities with the Greenwich Mean Time, thus plugging Cairo into the larger global circuit of standardized time. Cairo's signal was regulated within a telegraphic network rather than a sun-triggered citadel cannon or a muezzin's call to prayer.[16] By the 1920s, the Ministry of Religious Endowments made it compulsory for mosques in Cairo to call the *adhan* in strict compliance with the almanac published by the Survey Department.

By the first quarter of the twentieth century, debates about a mathematically computed calendar were also starting to emerge. Ebrahim Moosa has translated a tract penned in 1939 by Ahmad Shakir (1892–1958), in which Shakir—an Egypt-based scholar—stresses the need to adopt a lunar calendar based on scientific calculation. This required an argument against the established practice of collecting evidence for the new moon at the local level, allowing for valid moon sightings that took place outside of the local sphere.[17] Therefore, the critical term in Shakir's tract is *ikhtilaf-i-matali'*, a difference of horizon. This phrase was at the center of classical juristic disputes. The majority of jurists maintained that the difference of horizons was not to be taken into consideration in deciding on the moon for Ramadan or Eid. Such a view was based not on the denial of differences in horizons but on disagreements about whether such a difference should have a bearing on the religious practice. Therefore, a new crescent sighted anywhere was binding for another region, provided that the news had reached the people living there in accordance with Shariat requirements for the transmission of evidence. One could argue that the ulema did not take into account the consequentiality of *ikhtilaf-i-matali'* because an individual's capacity for daily travel in the premodern period was limited to a certain distance that could not have been long enough to result in a change of the horizon. Determining the minimum distance at which the horizon would alter also varied among different scholarly authorities. For instance, some Shafi'i jurists proposed a distance of eighty-nine kilometers, as it was the threshold for shortening prayers (*masafat al-qasr*) during travel.[18]

According to those scholars who believed in the applicability of the notion of *ikhtilaf-i-matali'*, Shakir summarizes, every locality must have its own calendar based on when the moon was sighted. But with new technologies that considerably reduced distances and brought regions closer together, the fact that a difference in horizon from one region to another affected each could no longer be denied. Believing that those "who reject the consideration of difference in horizon and favor the validity of one sighting as compelling for all regions of the earth grasp the true reality" and that "the first day of every lunar month is the same [lunar] day all over the globe," Shakir anchors a single, global point of reference as the point of conjunction where the moon wanes behind the earth. That place, in his opinion, could only be Mecca, the center of Islam.[19]

To establish that the moon sighted anywhere in the world—or in Mecca, as suggested by Shakir—should be become *hujjat*, or binding, for Muslims elsewhere to start Ramadan or celebrate Eid, was simultaneously both enabled and prevented by new technologies: technology enabled precision in calculating the sighting of the new moon, but it also nullified the popularly accepted view among the ulema on the invalidity of *ikhtilaf-i-matali'*. The new moon sighted with the help of technology or predicted with precision in any part of the world, and the news thereof transmitted to believers in any region at lightning speed, was to become binding on believers, regardless of differences between horizons. As a result, despite traditional views and established historical practices, the ulema had to reconsider their opinion about the inconsequentiality of *ikhtilaf-i-matali'*. Similarly, unlike in premodern times when news about the new moon was shared locally at a personal level, with new technology it could be relayed from one region to another via telegraph. In which case, even with the same horizon, people could be separated by a large distance and unable to receive the news about the new moon through a direct encounter. Much of the debate among the ulema and nontraditional scholars was, then, about the mode of news transmission and the prescribed role of technology in seeing or predicting the sighting of new moon.

In the case of Egypt, the debate was led by reformists and modernists who, out of a desire to create unity, uniformity, and discipline, preferred a fixed calendar, rather than a continuation of the traditional method that allowed for local variance. Throughout his long career, the famous scholar Rashid Rida (1865–1935) was asked this question on multiple occasions. His responses, as summarized by Stolz and Ogle, indicate a gradual shift in his stance. In his early responses, Rida favored the local practice of *ru'at* (sighting), as it was more egalitarian and did not require dependence on scientific equipment. In these texts Rida held the view that the scripture prioritized, or mandated, sighting over calculation.[20] However, later in his career, as the Ottoman Empire disintegrated, the Caliphate was abolished, and European Mandates were established over Egypt, the Levant, and Iraq, Rida relented for the sake of achieving greater unity in the Muslim world.[21] A consistency in global ritual practice and a regulated lunar calendar meant to achieve political unity among Muslims has since become a popular theme, and the subject of various proposals among proponents of "Muslim unity" across the globe. Yet as I highlight later in this chapter, its iteration in the case of Pakistan is specific to a project that nationalizes Islam rather than forges an internationalist connection of Muslim solidarity at a global level.

THE SOUTH ASIAN CONTEXT

As we can conclude from the preceding sections, due to a longer history of centralized management of religion, the Egyptian state was able to subordinate various aspects of Islamic religious practice, including the adoption of a standardized lunar calendar. The gradual standardization of time and its enforcement served as a disciplinary technology of homogenization. It strengthened the Egyptian state and was also used by the state to further its influence, especially by regulating religious practices.

Such a normative, institutional Muslim political authority was not in existence in South Asia until the emergence of Pakistan in 1947. Before British rule, and even at the height of Mughal rule, state power was fragmented or, at best, limited to core areas closer to the central seat of authority. Hence, *Fatawa Alamgiri*, the bulky compendium of collated juristic opinions on a range of religious issues and practices compiled under the direct patronage of Mughal emperor Aurangzeb Alamgir, does not approach the question of *ru'at* in terms of exercising state authority in regulating the lunar calendar. Rather than concerning itself with procedural arrangements for uniformity in observing Eid, the text was concerned with the criteria for evaluating witnesses who claimed to have seen the crescent. In the *Fatawa*, such factors as clarity of the sky, reputation of the witness (a discussion of which leads to further subdivisions and discussions), and so on, were listed as prerequisites for a valid moon sighting.[22] Although the role of the *qazi* in evaluating witnesses was discussed, as was the ruler's discretionary power in acting on witness accounts when there were doubts, the collated opinions did not translate into a regularization of *ru'at* as an organized statist praxis.

The same goes for the colonial period. The ulema were not concerned with coordinating their efforts toward a centralized system of moon sightings. To them, the more urgent task was to respond to queries about the use of the telegraph and telephone as modes of transmitting the news about the moon sighting. They reinterpreted *Fatawa Alamgiri* and *Durr-i-Mukhtar*, along with hadith and other classical works of jurisprudence within or outside Hanafi tradition, to grapple with such questions.

This debate had several parallels with general questions about the use of technology. As Altaf Mian's work about Mufti Shafi's fatwa on loudspeakers shows, the ulema's primary anxiety was how to adhere to authentic living or being as prescribed by Shariat—a path put in danger by technology.[23] In the case of the loudspeaker, the fatwa focused on the nature of sound itself, assessing whether amplification through electrical transmission kept it a human sound. If the worshipper following the imam were acting on a sound other than the imam, the ritual observance would be null and void. A similar concern would later be raised about the vision provided by a high-powered telescope, asking whether that qualified as seeing the moon with the naked eye.

The ulema's anxiety concerning telegraphs and telephones as modes of news transmission stemmed from a dictum in which information about the moon sighting was not treated like any other news. It was an anxiety that was shared by ulema across the Muslim world, regardless of whether under a centralized political authority. As Vanessa Ogle's brilliant study shows, there was a similar moon controversy in Egypt in 1910: there, ulema could not agree on the veracity of news received via telegraph. The debate generated a flurry of pamphleteering, such as Jamal al-Din al-Qasimi's *Guiding Mankind on Acting upon the Telegraphic Message*, disseminated in 1911.[24] Qasimi was among those who were acceptive of telegraphy. He argued that the telegram itself was not the source of the news, only its communicator; that is, the telegram was a medium, not the testimony. His contemporary Muhammad Bakhit, a judge in Alexandria who was involved in the 1910 moon controversy, shared Qasimi's views, writing a book to explain his position. Bakhit pointed out that there was no difference between a mailman and a telegraph operator; both were "mediums in the sending of the message from its sender, and neither one of the two was a sender."[25] Still, the ulema had considerable reservations about the electronic transmission of news, which was only symptomatic of the alienating aspect of technology, which made an authentic way of being seemingly impossible.

At least in the South Asian context, the critique of, or skepticism about, electronic transmission was not about whether the news had been accurately relayed but about the need to distinguish news from testimony: the Shariat had separate requirements for evaluating each. The reports of the new moon for Ramadan and Shawwal were not judged as news or information (*khabar*) but as testimony (*shahadat*). Therefore, they were subject to the same degree of scrutiny as court testimony. Just as courts rejected testimony via telephone, some ulema argued, the same held true in Shariat in matters of *ru'at*. As the ulema argued, it was essential to judge the witness's character. In a query sent to Mufti Kifayat Ullah, for example, the questioner asks about evaluating the testimony of villagers of Jaganpur in Faizabad district. The ordinary Muslims residing there, the questioner wrote, did sport beards, and yet indulged in such vanities as watching dances, listening to *qawwalis*, and participating in *tazia* processions. At the same time, they offered their prayers and listened to gatherings in which ulema imparted moral-ethical training; their good and bad habits were there for all to see.[26] In response, the mufti left it to the discretion of the qazi to decide and evaluate the quality of testimonies received from the villagers.

However, the bulk of queries addressed to Mufti Kifayat Ullah and others during the colonial period remained focused on the validity of testimonies received via electronic devices. In the various fatawa collections from the period that I have come across, none discusses the impending crisis arising of a lack of Muslim political authority—or it is certainly not the major concern. For instance, in most queries sent to the prolific Sunni Hanafi scholar Ahmad Raza Khan Barelwi, who was active during the late nineteenth and early twentieth centuries, and in Barelwi's detailed treatises on the issue of *ru'at-i-hilal*, there were several questions about acting on reports of moon sightings in other parts of India, whether received via newspaper or telegraph, or even sometimes in person. Like other scholars, Barelwi focused on specifying the standards set by Shariat in ascertaining the account of a witness.

This is not to deny that classical jurisprudence and its interpreters in the colonial period outrightly dismissed the ruler's power on this matter. But the absence of central authority does not appear to have triggered a crisis that endangered the practice of the faith. In this regard, the lack of ulema's responses is different from their active engagement in questions concerning Friday or Eid prayers in areas that did not have a Muslim ruler. Congregational prayers were central to Muslim practice and had historically served as a legitimizing tool for the ruler as the guardian of faith, so their continuation in a context where Muslims did not have political power caused numerous debates among the ulema. But we do not find similar debates about the announcements of moon sighting as dependent on centralized Muslim political authority. Nor was much importance given to the idea of a mathematically calculated lunar calendar that might bring about uniformity among Muslims in celebrating Eid. In most fatwa collections from early twentieth-century colonial India, questioners were eager to confirm the religious validity of methods that they could use to avoid confusion about the moon sighting.

Those who argued for adopting new techniques were also arguing for a uniform practice to achieve Muslim unity. For example, Anjuman-i-Numaniyya, a Lahore-based organization that aimed to reform Muslim society through education and a better understanding of Islam, wrote to the famous Deobandi scholar and Sufi, Maulana Ashraf Ali Thanawi, to ask about the possibility of regulating the Islamic calendar for Ramadan and Eid through a coordinated ensemble of telegraph messages received from different parts of India. If news about the new crescent were received via telegram through numerous locations, they asked, would it reach the level of *matwatir* (continuous transmission); that is, would it be equivalent to the status of certitude required for testimony? Thanawi agreed that numerous reports of moon sightings from different parts of India would reach the level of *matwatir*, but a similar degree of multiplicity would be required for it to be actionable for those who receive it via telegram in one particular area.[27] Thanawi, offering his personal opinion, advised against setting up a permanent setup for this purpose, as it would incur a lot of expenditure that could be spent for more useful purposes. In addition, he predicted, it might cause disunity among Muslims, as they could disagree with this arrangement.

During much of the colonial period, the question of a centralized authority regulating the cycle of Ramadan and the announcement of Eid did not become a major site of contention. In Lahore, for instance, the usual practice was for people to rely on announcements made locally, via the mosque or newspaper, or by telegram. In 1930, on one occasion, the daily *Inqilab*, advised its readers to "contact Karnal Shop in Anarkali for accurate news about ru'at-i-hilal. On the occasion of Eid, the owner of this firm gets news about Eid via telegram [*paigham-i-barqi*] from all the big cities."[28] The proprietor of Karnal Shop published an ad in the same newspaper urging people to come to the shop to get reports about moon sightings, as he had arranged for telegrams to be received from Karachi, Calcutta, Peshawar, Delhi, Agra, Jaipur, Bahawalpur, Saharanpur, and Karnal.[29] For the proprietor of the Karnal Shop, a shoe store, the incentive was to attract people to do their Eid shopping there.

Central mosques, however, remained focused on collecting testimonies from witnesses and making an announcement accordingly. The mosque and its prayer leader's roles in evaluating the witness, and the inadmissibility of telegraphic or telephonic testimony, gave an influential position to the ulema—a power they were reluctant to give up once the postcolonial state had set up a centralized authority.

MAKING EID A PLANNED NATIONAL FESTIVAL

In August 1948, hardly a week before the first anniversary of Pakistani independence, preparations were being made to celebrate another festive occasion, Eid. Lahore's grand central mosque, the Badshahi Masjid, was then run by Anjuman Islamiyyah, which published an appeal in the newspaper asking worshippers to observe discipline when coming to the mosque to offer Eid prayers. A decision about the moon sighting, the report said, would be made on the evening of 29 Ramadan after *maghrib* prayers, when members of the executive committee would meet to evaluate testimonies.[30]

Despite appeals for keeping prayer lines straight and orderly, what happened during Eid prayers was beyond anyone's imagination. As soon as the prayers finished and worshippers from the central courtyard rushed toward the exit gate to put on their shoes, those behind caused a rush, resulting in a stampede. Close to a dozen worshippers died. In assessing the tragedy, *Inqilab* observed that it had been caused by the city's substantially increased Muslim population after all its non-Muslim inhabitants had been expelled during the Partition riots. The congregational prayer was the largest that had ever taken place, with little added in terms of facilities. There were few tents in the courtyard, making the ceremony unbearable for worshippers in the hot and humid weather of Lahore, causing them to try to exit as soon as prayers had finished.[31]

The introspective calls for remedial action in the future emphasized the need for disciplinary control as a core feature of the Islamic belief system. For a newly established Pakistani state still scrambling to set up effective administrative management and to assert sovereign political power, pursuing a nationalizing project for disciplining citizens' bodies through Eid became part of the state-formation process. As early as 1949, an op-ed published in the *Pakistan Times* called on the government to "make 'Id a planned national festival." The article lamented the lack of national festivals in the country. Traditional festivals such as *basant* and *besakhi*, the author wrote, had become redundant since Pakistan's non-Muslims had left. Local fairs had a parochial flavor, lacking a national character and broader appeal. Projecting Pakistan as heir to the Mughal empire, the article discussed the pageantry of life during Mughal rule, as evident in the observance of a range of festivals celebrating "the New Year, the spring, the rains, the flowers and whatever else came in handy." The author bemoaned the lack of joy in people's routines and the sorrows that had entered their lives. This could be addressed by developing Eid as a national festival and expression of national culture. "We too can organise flag-marches, plays, flower shows, sports, symposiums, and social parties on this day on a national scale," the author wrote, in addition to "competitions for town decoration, for clean streets, for window-displays . . . and also teach people how to get in and get out of the mosque without crushing a certain number to death."[32]

What is evident here is an idea of Eid as a disciplining tool that constitutes an orderly citizen, and a related definition of Eid an embodiment of various local practices of joyous celebrations assembled under the banner of the nation. If it were to be celebrated on a national level, Eid required homogeneity and standardization, especially in regulating the lunar calendar, as the festival could not have regional variations.

In line with this vision, a committee was constituted as early as 1949, under the chairmanship of then interior minister Khawaja Shahab-ud-Din. In addition to announcing the moon, it was also tasked with regulating hotels during Ramadan to ensure that they observed the sanctity of the month by not openly selling food and drink.[33]

The idea of Eid as a national festival did not get approval from the ulema. In the first instance, the ulema found the very idea of Eid as a "festival" lacking concordance with Islamic teachings. The board of ulema set up by the government of Pakistan to advise on the drafting of an Islamic constitution for the country dismissed the idea outright. The board was clear that the Prophet of Islam, and the Companions who followed him, did not attach any significance to uniformity in observing Ramadan. They admitted that this could have been because of a lack of efficient communication tools. But if the issue had carried any religious importance, they opined, arrangements could at least have been made for Madina and its neighboring satellite towns. On the contrary, the note submitted to the government on this issue states, "on occasions when the idea of this sort of uniformity came up in any form it was discouraged by the most accredited authorities."[34]

Although the government had only just shown the intention of implementing a principle of uniformity to the celebration of Eid, the ulema applied such a principle to all forms of Islamic worship to show that such an attempt at enforced uniformity was not only uncalled for but also would jeopardize the spirit of Islamic observance. For instance, in the case of *salat*, or daily prayers, the difference between time zones would result in a call to prayer for *maghrib* prayers in Karachi being broadcast to the rest of the country when it was already time for *'isha* prayers.[35] The same holds for daily timings of *sahar* and *iftar* in Ramadan, which differ for every city depending on the particular position of the sun at a given hour. The board did, however, keep the option open of celebrating the Eid on the same day by stating that it was possible only if it could be ascertained that the lunar horizon for the entire country—including East Pakistan, which was 1,200 miles away from Pakistan's far west—was the same. The prerequisites for collecting evidence and transmitting news about the moon sighting were to be prepared by the ulema.[36] In this manner, the ulema dismissed the government's attempts at creating a centralized authority for moon sightings while ensuring that any such endeavor in the future remained indebted to their role in carrying out the necessary textual reinterpretation required for such an undertaking.

STATE VERSUS ULEMA: THE GOVERNMENTALITY OF EID

Disapproval from the board of ulema did not end the state's attempts to develop a centralized structure for regulating the Islamic calendar. Even before the imposition of martial law, which expedited discussions on this issue, there were several bureaucratic exchanges about bringing about uniformity in practice. The calls for such a policy were made in the name of scientific rationality and the need to foster national unity. As S. M. Ayub observed in a note dated 2 August 1958, "the so-called atomic clock[s] . . .

are so perfect that they can detect irregularities in the speed of the earth itself! That means in 'time' itself, in a way!"[37]

Anwar Ali, notorious for his role as a noncommissioned officer working in the special branch during the British period, who then became a prominent figure in the civilian and military governments after 1947, described the model adopted by several Arab countries with admiration. Emphasizing the role of the state in making decisions about religion, he noted that in United Arab Republic "the government selects convenient and pliable ulemas who make the pronouncement whether the moon is sighted or not on the advice of the Meteorological Department."[38] The Pakistani officials reporting on procedures for declaration of Eid in the Arab world were impressed with how these states relegated ulema to a position of submission. The embassy of Pakistan in Cairo, while commenting on the practice of moon sighting in the United Arab Republic and Saudi Arabia, reported with envy the high-handedness of these states. They reported that in those countries the ulema cooperated with the state, and the state's decision in these matters was accepted without a murmur. They also observed: "Government do pay considerable attention to Sheikh ul Azhar and other prominent Ulema but they have been made to understand that no interference in the administration will be tolerated. I wish we could take the same strong line with our ulema specially reverend Ihtishamul Haq."[39] The twin principles of authoritarianism and scientism as aides in the process of nation building and state-formation were thus at the heart of debates about *ru'at* after 1947.

One of the best examples of the ulema's response to official discourse is Mufti Muhammad Shafi's treatise on this issue. Widely known for his erudition as a scion of a family of Deobandi scholars who had played a crucial role in supporting the Muslim League and its demand for Pakistan, Shafi's opinions carried considerable weight. In his slim volume on the topic of *ru'at-i-hilal*, written during the height of the moon controversy in the 1960s, Shafi undertook what MacIntyre would describe as the task of a tradition-constitutive inquiry constituted by tradition itself. Shafi's text is an example of grounding tradition in its broader historical text to enact a further stage in its development.[40] Applying MacIntyre's theorization of epistemological crisis as the "dissolution of historically founded certitudes," I draw on Shafi's text to trace the history of the crisis within the tradition as well as "the invention or discovery of new concepts and the framing of some new type or types of theory." Doing so helps to, from his perspective, address the epistemological crisis, explaining the reasons for tradition's incapacity to respond to the crisis before ulema intervention—whether his or others'—while simultaneously establishing "some fundamental continuity of the new conceptual and theoretical structures" with the beliefs and principles that had defined the tradition and its method of rational inquiry up to that point.[41] Rather than pitching his argument strictly in terms of a contest between ulema and state, Shafi adopted an approach aimed at translating the classical edicts for adoption within the framework of a modern state. This translation project is significant insofar it is indicative of Shafi's departure from the classical position and of the incongruities that come with transposing conceptual categories from classical jurisprudence onto the "institutionalized languages of modernity."[42] I later expand on Shafi's rereading of the tradition by focusing on four aspects of the debate on *ru'at*: the nature of religious observance, the necessity of recording testimonies, the idea of nation-space as a new category, and the question of authority.

Shafi wrote *Ru'at-i-Hilal* after the moon controversy of 1961. In continuation of his earlier stance on technology, Shafi described scientific tools as Allah's bounty, which were to be used with an expression of gratitude while also ensuring that no religious commandment was violated in using them.[43] Ali Mian describes such an approach as a concept of technology that aids in the attempt at authentic living insofar as it helps one get closer with the dictates of Shariat. Written against the backdrop of the government's attempt to streamline the lunar calendar to ensure consistency in the practice of Eid, Shafi started by making a clear statement about the nature of Eid: Eid is not a festival (*tehwar*), he wrote; it is a form of prayer or worship (*ibadat*).[44] As *ibadat*, it must be observed in a manner prescribed by Shariat. Muslims must follow these rules without questioning their rationale, just as the number of *rak'at* to be observed in *salat* are fixed, per Allah's commandment, which must be obeyed.

Rather than dismissing the productive role of technology or scientific calculation in enabling believers to live their lives in accordance with the

Shariat, Shafi adopted circuitous reasoning that helped subordinate technological usage to the authority of the ulema. Shafi argued that the moon remains on the horizon at all times; it is simply because of the sun-moon conjunction that it ceases to be visible. There is, hence, no such thing as a new moon. According to Shafi, what science can predict—though that, too, by limited accuracy—is when the moon will again become visible. But it cannot speak with certainty about chances of seeing that new moon with the naked eye, which was the main condition set by Shariat, based on Prophet Muhammad's hadith.[45] As to this condition of seeing the moon with the naked eye, Shafi argued that Islam was meant to be a universal religion for peoples of all times, ages, and places. If it had been compulsory for believers to use scientific equipment to search for the moon—for scientific methods and techniques were widely practiced in that era—it would have caused a lot of trouble for people living in jungles and villages. Only affluent citizens (*sarmaya-dar shehri*) would have been able to fulfill the requirement, given their access to such facilities.[46] He further elucidated the point by referring to the obligation to pray in the direction of the qibla. In his reading of Quranic verse 2:144, the scripture did not specify the Ka'ba, or *bait Allah* (house of Allah), but rather *masjid al-haram*, which carries a much wider geographical expanse. Also, instead of *ila*, the word used is *shatar*, which indicates the direction toward *bait Allah* rather than *bait Allah* itself.

As discussed earlier, such calculations with scientific tools were not alien to Muslim scholars. But Shafi argued that making a more precise requirement would have added to the difficulties of those in far-off areas, without access to such tools and knowledge systems. In Shafi's estimation, the Shariat adopted a lunar rather than a solar calendar for the sake of universality, ease, and access; the latter required precise calculations using astronomical tools.[47]

Shafi saw the demand for a scientific basis for estimating the appearance of the moon rather than using the traditional method of *ru'at* as a problem arising "from the basis that Eid should be declared as a festival or national function or national day."[48] Historically, he stated, no such precedent was to be found, nor was any instruction given by the Prophet or any attempt made by Muslims from the earliest period of Islamic history to observe Eid on a single day—not even in Medina and the adjoining areas of Syria.⁴⁹ For more than a thousand years, when Muslims ran a vast empire, there was never an arrangement in place to celebrate Eid on the same day. This was because, according to Shafi, Eid was more than just a matter of celebrating a national festival: it was about making sure that one set of religious practices—fasting—had come to an end and the next religious observance, Eid, might begin. This required reaching a degree of certainty, which was not the same as knowing that the moon existed somewhere on the horizon. The moon also had to be seen with the naked eye. Just as *salat* that cannot be simultaneously observed throughout the country due to vast gaps in day and night, the same held for Eid, which was another religious commandment of Allah to be followed in accordance with the criteria set for it.

There was thus no virtue in insisting on the observance of one Eid for the entire country, as there was no precedence for it. Every region celebrated Eid by making its own arrangements and without causing disagreements. For the sake of a vague idea of unity, Shafi wrote, the government was opening the door to many quibbles and difficulties.⁵⁰ If the idea was to simply make things convenient for people traveling to other cities to celebrate Eid with their families, then the government could easily do so by increasing the number of holidays for Eid. This question came up only for Eid al-Fitr, as it was announced at the final hour, unlike Eid al-Adha, which invariably took place on the tenth day of the month of Zil-Hajj, according to the Islamic lunar calendar.⁵¹ In any case, Shafi wrote, an Islamic state like Pakistan should celebrate the most joyous occasion for Muslims in a befitting manner, granting more public holidays.

Yet Shafi opened up the possibility of bringing about uniformity in practice, suggesting that ulema and scientific experts be incorporated into *ru'at* committees to be set up across Pakistan. His only condition was that East and West Pakistan should have the same horizon. His acknowledgment of the existence of *ikhtilaf-i-matali'* as casting a significant impact on the lunar calendar was itself a departure from what was a near-consensus position in Hanafi doctrine. To make this doctrinal shift possible, Shafi argued that the possibility of news about *ru'at* traveling from east to west in a matter of hours did not previously exist. That is why, in his humble opinion, jurists like Imam Abu Hanifa did not consider it beyond a hypothetical question that would not have any actual consequences in matters of religious observance. But once it had become a possibility, the difference in horizons was to be recognized, especially in those areas that were at such a distance from each other that "as a result of accepting *ru'at* from one area for another area, the number of days in the month are reduced to 28 or increase to 31."[52]

Through a reconceptualization of ideas of territory and horizon, Shafi and others who have since followed him make room for national space and standardized time, which in turn helps transform Eid from a religious observance into a national festival. For them, the central question was to define the territorial unit and the geographical expanse over which the rubric of the lunar calendar was applicable. For this purpose, the ulema had to work with several categories used in the classical tradition.

Classical Islamic literature on history, philosophy, geography, and jurisprudence uses different terms to describe land, home, and territory. As Antrim's work shows, the "discourse of place" in classical literature is an expression of "articulating desire, claiming authority, and establishing belonging."[53] Arab geographers reworked the Ptolemaic system to derive classificatory categories for such geographical schemata as climes (*iqlim*) "to refer to regional entities of different size, shape, and provenance."[54] In addition to terms denoting notions of belonging or climatic zones, the idea of a broad *mamlakat al-Islam* also existed as "an identifiable region, like the climes and other territorial divisions . . . singled out on the basis of a particular coherence or meaning." The appellations for land, space, and territory in the works of classical geographers were, in other words, climatic, regional, and political, making the inhabitable world legible. They did so by sometimes through "the description of frontiers or dividing lines determined by mathematical calculations or political realities past and present." On other occasions, the process of geographical demarcation "involved the close association of land and people according to theories of climatic determinism, divine design, or the ethnographic impulse current in the world of *adab*."[55] From the perspective of Shariat, however, other dimensions of space conceptualized on a distinct basis—but at times overlapping with the above categories—were more important. The term *dar*, for instance, is used in Islamic legal texts as territory "with reference to this-worldly geography, and to various forms of political, social, and religious boundaries." In Sarah Albrecht's reading and theorization of classical legal texts, the term *dar*—in its various iterations as the abode of Islam, infidelity, peace or war—best captures "questions related to religious authority, identity, and the interpretation of Islamic norms."[56] Such a variegated approach to territory is less about the fragmented nature of authority in the classical period and more a reflection of a quest for a term to encapsulate the modern idea of a nation-state as a territorialized unit subject to a singular sovereign authority. As Hallaq points out, the terminology of *dawlat* used in classical texts refers to dynastic rule rather than offering a conceptual equivalent to the modern state.[57] The problem is confounded when modern states project themselves as inheritors of the Islamic classical tradition, seamlessly morphing modern notions of citizenry and nation-state onto premodern empires, realms, and communities. When moving from space as territory to space as horizon, yet another dimension is added to the problem.

In the current context, the question of "one state, one Eid" required envisioning the nation-state as a singular territorial unit under not only a sovereign authority but also a single horizon. According to a fatwa dating to 1954 and issued by such leading scholars as Yusuf Banori, Mufti Muhammad Shafi, Maulana Zafar Ahmad Usmani, and Maulana Ahmad Ali Lahori, a new moon sighted in any part of Pakistan was binding on Muslims all over the country, because the *wilayat* was under the authority of the same ruler.[58] However, two regions with the same *matali'* but different *wilayat*—for example, Pakistan and India, or Pakistan and Afghanistan—would not be bound to follow the same *ru'at* until and unless sanctioned by their respective *wilayat*. Such a ruling created the absurd situation in which a reported sighting from an adjacent area with the same *matali'* but a different *wilayat* (e.g., Afghanistan) was dismissed but that from a different *matali'* under the same *wilayat* (e.g., East Pakistan) was accepted. Until at least 1971, the ulema were agreeable to rereading ideas about organized space as a territorial unit, nation-state, or Islamic government, without necessarily engaging with the more vexed question of different horizons that made it impossible for uniformity of practice under such a state.

Mufti Shafi, for instance, was concerned with recognizing the state's authority in deciding Eid by appending that authority with the sanction given by ulema. He arrived at this conclusion by emphasizing that reports about the *hilal* sighting were to be evaluated on a specific standard set by Shariat. Involved ulema were required to be members of the committees that the state was to set up down to the district level. In his prescribed procedures for collecting evidence, Shafi emphasized the status of the committee members as vice-regents of the head of state. Any decision reached by the committee was not to be read out from the radio like any ordinary news item. The announcement had to be carefully worded, as specified by the committee, with added emphasis that it was made on behalf of the head of state; the areas of the country to which the announcement applied were also to be clarified.[59] Shafi insisted on including ulema in the committee because of the necessity to differentiate between *khabar* (report) and *shahadat* (testimony). Any information about the *hilal* was not like any other report; it required the scrutiny applied to legal testimony. Just as a court would not accept testimonies via telephone, wrote Shafi, testimonies about the new moon could not be accepted unless the witness came to the qazi in person to record his testimony.[60] But the same rule did not apply to announcing the decision: the new moon could be announced via radio, which, according to Shafi, was in the modern era a better way of making a declaration than firing a cannon, as done in the premodern period.

In his ruling, Shafi then gave an account of the requirements set by classical jurists for a *ru'at* witness.[61] The witness must be an adult Muslim of sane mind and sight. The testimony of non-Muslims is unacceptable, and that of a minor is not trustworthy. The most important condition is that the witness should be known for his good character and virtuous behavior.[62] A long list of prerequisites and conditional behaviors is provided, in case the witness does not have any of the prescribed features. The prescribed features themselves are subject to revision, depending on the evening's clarity of horizon and such factors as whether the witness is a slave or a female. The overwhelming number of people reporting the moon also alters the requirements of *shahadat*, or witnessing.

The critical point is that Shafi insisted on ulema's presence in the committee. They alone can apply these numerous conditions and ensure that the announcement made via radio was definite and trustworthy. Supervising the work of the committee placed a heavy responsibility on the shoulders of ulema, Shafi wrote, as they would be held responsible for any misreporting that results in people missing obligatory fasts or other religious observances.[63] Shafi's text is silent on the question of the dichotomy between scientific calculations about the moon's visibility at a given hour and given place and the actual sighting reported by a trustworthy witness.[64]

Here, a ruling by the modern-day scholar Mushtaq Ahmad serves as an excellent supplement. Ahmed points out that the reason for classical jurists' reluctance toward scientific calculation of the lunar calendar was inexact nature of science in their age—a distrust passed on to present-day scholars. Because scientific calculations about the moon and its various stages have reached a status of certitude in the contemporary period, any testimony about sighting the moon that stands in stark contrast with scientific reports about the impossibility of *ru'at* at that moment should be rejected. According to such an approach, scientific tools and calculations can be used to set the time and area where the new moon shall become visible, but *ru'at* would be finally settled on the basis of an actual moon sighting.

Although Shafi maintained that Eid was not to be falsely equated with any other kind of national festival, he did nevertheless create the possibility for Eid to be transformed from a religious observance to a festival celebrated at a national level under the authority of the state, and with the religio-moral sanction of the ulema. He achieved this by revisioning the idea of the state, space, and sovereign power. Shafi's treatise and its politics therefore serve as an essential reference point against which to read similar texts, polemics, and political disputations that seek to either dismiss the ulema's authority or assert their influence over the state. In either case, the respective claims and their rational justifications do not necessarily confine themselves to a close reading of juristic texts; they extend to cover general questions about scientism and the authoritarian management of religious affairs.

MODERNIST REBUTTAL

Shafi's critics were opposed to the idea of ulema determining the lunar calendar under state patronage. The scholars with a modernist approach to Islamic texts argued for a praxis that bypassed the ulema's claims to authority in determining matters of belief and practice. Such a counterpoise was not only an epistemological challenge; it also required state power to follow a policy of "curbing the Mullah," as practiced in 1960s. These policies were not limited to the question of *ru'at* but extended to the larger gamut of contestations broadly construed along the heuristic binaries of science-scripture, rationality-orthodoxy, and modernity-obscurantism. The polemics and policies touched on such issues as the regulation of madrassah education, the use of mosques to promote a preferred version or interpretation of Islam, and the state's management of shrines. In this encounter, religious scholars and leaders—often dubbed "mullah" and "maulwi" in official discourse, playing on a popular understanding of the term in which mullahs have become synonymous with retrogressive, opaque thinking—were looked at with suspicion, disdain, and scorn.

At the discursive level, the state's sponsorship of modernist Islam—as in the case of *ru'at-i-hilal*—was primarily carried out through officially supported centers for research. Maulana Jafar Shah Phulwarwi's *Ru'at-i-Hilal* was published by the Institute of Islamic Culture in 1967. Trained as a scholar of classical Islam, Phulwarwi was known for his modernist approach, as is clear from his work supporting such contentious issues as family planning, the registration of marriage and divorce, and limits on polygamy. In moon sighting, as in much of his other work, Phulwarwi emphasized the spirit of the commandment and its implementation in the contemporary period. The commandment for physically sighting the moon, argued Phulwarwi, was to be followed in spirit only; seeing the moon with the naked eye was not necessary. Phulwarwi drew a comparison to the injunction on believers to train their children in horseback riding to prepare them for jihad. If someone were to learn to operate a tank, he stated, that would be a viable interpretation of the same commandment, not an outright rejection thereof.

According to Phulwarwi, scientifically calculating lunar movements was definitive and, historically, found acceptable by several scholars during the classical period. He interpreted some ulema's rejection of innovation as the continuation of a pattern wherein ulema expressed reservations against other technologies before later relenting to accommodate them, such as using loudspeakers in mosques or of the printing press for the Quran. Phulwarwi was convinced that, inevitably, the scientific method would prevail, as it was in perfect accordance with Islam's vision of the cosmos as an ordered entity predictable in its rhythmic consistency.[65] In response to the issue of *shahadat*, or testimony, requiring different criteria for evaluation, Phulwarwi contested the term itself, insisting on expanding its meanings. *Shahadat*, according to his redefinition, was not restricted to giving testimony in person; it encompassed accurately getting to know something. Measuring body temperature and blood pressure using medical tools, for example, was also a means of recording *shahadat*.[66] Phulwarwi read the authority of qazis as described by classical texts, deeming them arbiters of final decisions in matters of *ru'at* to the extent that "if someone has completed thirty days of fasting, even then he cannot break the fast on the thirty-first day to celebrate Eid without the [consent of] Imam. This is the kind of national unity and discipline (*qaumi nazam-o-zabt*) that for the jurists mentioned above is no less important, nay even more important, than fasting and Eid."[67]

He extended the authority of the qazi or imam to the modern state and urged people to repose as much trust in the state as they did in the local butcher who claimed to be selling them halal chicken or lamb.[68]

Other than scholarly engagement, a more popular rebuttal of the so-called mullah's obscurantism has been through humor. The moon controversy has inspired countless cartoons, satirical pieces, and poetry. In his autobiographical account, Syed Hashim Raza shared an interesting anecdote about the first *hilal* committee, which he gathered in Karachi in the early 1950s. According to him, there was a clash between two leading clerics of the city, Maulana Ehtasham-ul-Haq Thanawi and Maulana Abdul Hamid Badayuni: each wanted to arrange for the moon sighting from the mosque where he led prayers. Raza decided that the session would be held on the rooftop of the Karachi Municipal Corporation Building. The following year, Raza arranged for an aircraft to enable committee members to look for the moon at an even higher altitude. The aircraft flew at an altitude of eight thousand feet for half an hour, and yet members returned to the ground without reaching a unanimous verdict. Four said they had seen the moon, and two said that they hadn't.[69] In response, Syed Muhammad Jafri wrote a humorous poem:

> This year, appearance of Ramzan's moon was happier,
> When the Orient Airways chartered its carrier,
> On boarding it, the Maulvi became much merrier.
> To the moon and stars, he scanned like a cavalier,
> Among the dwellers of the sky, there was a commotion,
> What a look it was! What a vision!
>
> When the Maulvi beheld Ramazan's moon,
> At once he came under trance-like swoon,
> Reddish was the chicken soup, whitish bread as moon,
> In milky-way he lay the edibles, what a boon!
> Some beheld the moon, others only heard,
> Some saw that moon which the real moon had blurred.[70]

THE OFFICIAL MOON FOR A NATIONAL EID UNDER THE STATE'S UNIFORM CALENDAR

I now turn to the official correspondence in which the practical problems of developing a framework for moon sighting were worked out to serve the purposes of a scientifically calculated, predetermined annual calendar required for unity in the celebration of national festivals.

In the period of martial law under Ayub Khan, the existing provincial committees that helped announce Eid at the district and division levels were abolished, replaced by a central mechanism. On 25 March 1959, the Bureau of National Reconstruction, the leading organization through which Ayub Khan's Kemalist vision of a modern Pakistani state was implemented, sent an official memorandum to the Ministry of Interior. The bureau noted the practice of celebrating Muslim festivals at different dates throughout the country, and even in the same city, with concern. This was causing confusion, giving a bad name to the country, and undermining the unity of the people.[71] The internal correspondence referred to various examples from Muslim states to emphasize that a central authority was required to make decisions about Eid that would be binding for the entire country. In his note, Hameeduddin Ahmed gave the example of the Hyderabad Deccan, where the nizam had set up an observatory that gave forecasts about the date of the appearance of the moon according to astronomical calculations. Their predictions were hardly inaccurate. As an additional safeguard, the Ecclesiastical Department collected information about the moon's appearance on the evening of the expected date of moon sighting from designated officers in each district. Reports received from any districts were accepted as the basis for officially declaring Eid throughout the realm, through special broadcasts, local announcements, and the firing of canons.[72] The concluding part of Ahmed's note summed up the rationale for centralized control, explaining its basis in a peculiar idea of state power; evaluated the challenge posed by the ulema, and explained the nature of Eid as a particular set of practices or celebration:

> The Eids have been observed throughout Muslim history as a State function and right from the start of Islam the presence of the Head of the State or his representative has been a recognised condition for the performance of the prayers on such occasions. On this basis there is full justification for Government to take a hand in such matters and not to leave it to individuals Maulvis to declare Id on different dates at different places as an exhibition of their authority and power . . . Islam recognises no priesthood or prior rights to persons over others in regard to religious matter. The function has been relegated to the State throughout the centuries.[73]

In official discourse, there was less concern about the actual visibility of the moon and more about its presence in both parts of the country on the same day. In a note sent to the ministry in July 1959, the director of meteorology claimed that although in the previous decade, it had never been the case that the moon was not visible in both wings of Pakistan on the same day, there was still a remote possibility that it could be visible in West Pakistan while invisible in East Pakistan. There was, however, certainty that the moon would always be visible in West Pakistan if visible in East Pakistan and, in general, in both wings on the same day. But if, on some rare occasion, this was not the case, "we should not feel shy in accepting the differences and celebrating the festival on two different days in the two wings," as it would be in keeping with Quranic injunctions, just as the timings of various prayers in a day. He wrote: "This inherently implies the observance of the same religious function at different times at different places on the terrestrial sphere depending upon their respective longitudes and latitudes, i.e., the geographic locations."[74]

On the actual sighting of the moon, the director's position was again similar to that of the ulema. In cases when the moon was to be visible only for a short duration or not at all, given a lack of visibility, he recommended deciding the issue on the "basis of authentic evidence about actual observations" whose testimony should be evaluated based on a set standard.[75]

The government's interest in the lunar calendar generated a great deal of public response and some unsolicited recommendations. Self-taught astrologers contributed to the debate by writing newspaper articles or sending their proposals directly to the ministry. One interesting example is penned by "Lookman," from Lalukhet (the contributor's real name was Syed Raza Luqman). Lookman added the affix *muhajir* to his name to indicate that he was a refugee from Amroha, specifically, the famous quarter of Mohalla Danishmandan. He was a master astrologer who wrote a detailed treatise titled *Hamari Haqiqi Fitri Taqwim or "Part I of Our Original Creational Calendar = 1339 (leap year) H.F. Era*. Luqman's major breakthrough was that the Islamic calendar was solar. He called the lunar calendar man-made and a blot on Islam.[76] An officer who read the statement commented that "the Hijri Era is based on Lunar system" and that the "critic seems to be lunatic."[77]

"A Plea for the Reform of the Calendar" was written by Mohsin Ali, a consultant at National Planning Board. His article had first appeared in June 1958, four months before the coup that brought Ayub Khan into power, and was later made part of the file on moon sighting. Ali gave a detailed historical outline of calendars adopted by various civilizations, making snarky comments about the impact of the moon on "the physiological life of half the human race (the better half!), and, as a consequence, even if to a lesser degree, of the other half also."[78] To him, this, among other reasons, determined the continued significance of the lunar calendar. The major takeaway from Ali's article was that rather than depending on the visibility of the new moon, regulating the calendar by calculations of the formation of the new moon should be enough. He referred to a formula worked out by Fatimid caliphs in the fourth century AH—a perpetual calendar, as he called it—that continues to be used in Egypt and among Ismaili communities in Africa, Yemen, Syria, and the Indian subcontinent.[79] The response to this article and the ongoing debate about reforming the calendar in English-language news media expressed support for statist discourse on centralization and scientism. In one letter to the editor published on 27 May 1959 in *Dawn*, the author talked about the mathematical precision of stellar movements and "in the age of Sputniks, wireless telephones, telegraphy and television," the possibility of calculating exact movement on the moon. To ensure the sanctity of "sacred days," the author requested that the "revolutionary government" of Ayub Khan announce holidays in the official gazette.[80]

On the basis of internal deliberations and responses from a narrow section of public opinion, the government proposed a new scheme to regulate the calendar. In a letter addressed to the provincial governments of East and West Pakistan on 10 October 1959, the Ministry of the Interior ordered the abolition of local *ru'at-i-hilal* committees. The reason given was that it had become possible to calculate the moon's "forecast astronomically to the last second." Calendrical precision was to help government offices, private firms, and banks plan ahead. Such an approach, the letter stated, was scientific and in line with the prescriptions for observance of such occasions "by a progressive and rational religion such as Islam."[81] Yet at the same time, the ministry was careful not to rule out the requirement of seeing the moon with the naked eye. The letter emphasized that while "the visibility of the moon within certain limits of its age and time of remaining above the horizon during twilight can be forecast with certainty . . . in certain conditions of inadequacy of age or of remaining above the horizon for insufficient time during twilight that the element of doubt comes in."[82] On such occasions, the Department of Meteorology—through its thirty observatories across East and West Pakistan—was to assist in the sighting of the moon, bound to be a much better arrangement than lay observers looking for the moon on their own.[83]

I have already noted the ulema's opposition to the proposed scheme and the reasons for it. The provincial government of East Pakistan also opposed the arrangement suggested by the central government. The reasons for East Pakistan's objections were not religious but practical and political. Soon after independence, there was a growing sense of disenchantment in the eastern wing with the Pakistani state. Bengalis viewed the central government as dominated by a section of West Pakistani elite—that is, mostly Punjabi bureaucrats and military men. Over the years, this sense of alienation grew. Political parties in East Pakistan and a large section of its intelligentsia viewed West Pakistan as a colonizing force that had a parasitic relationship with the resources of East Pakistan. Surprisingly, such strong feelings were not reflected in several policy issues in which the government of East Pakistan took a stance in stark contrast to the preferred direction indicated by the central government.

In a letter written on 19 November 1959, the government of East Pakistan pointed out the practical hurdles of observing religious festivals on the same day for a country set apart by a huge distance. The government's main objection was that the moon might not appear in either of the two parts of the country in any given year, and if that happened, there would be no religious sanction for enforcing the observance of Eid. It therefore advised against fixing a particular day to observe Eid. Despite the drawbacks of a calendar that required an actual moon sighting, it was not such a serious shortcoming that required government intervention.[84] In both the central government's explanation and the response from the government of East Pakistan, there was no reference made to the juristic concept of *matali'*. Although the term *horizon* had been used in the sense of "atmosphere" or in relation to the sky's clarity, it was not used in reference to debates about the sameness or difference of *matali'* between East and West Pakistan.

The response from leading ulema and religious institutions was strongly adversarial. Majlis Ulema Shia sent a letter to the Ministry of Interior informing of the existence of a parallel Shia *ru'at-i-hilal* committee comprising leading mujtahids and representatives. In no uncertain terms, the letter stated that "in future the findings of this committee only shall be acceptable to the Shias in general."[85] The Sunni ulema were largely critical of relying on science to determine the Islamic calendar. In a letter written by Maulana Ahmad Ali of *Anjuman Khuddam-ud-Din*, the author recognized the authority of the Muslim government to announce Eid through its appointed qazi or magistrate. If the government wanted to achieve unity through the celebration of Eid, Ali stated, it needed to appoint a judge from the superior court who would announce the decision "without referring to science" and by listening to the testimonies about *ru'at*. According to Ali, even if one had the capacity to go beyond the skies and split the clouds open to see the moon, it was ultimately on the basis of testimony scrutinized by a qazi that the final decision must be made. He wrote that there was no harm in having different dates of Eid observance as long as that did not create confusion (*intishar*).[86]

But Wafaq-ul-Madaris Multan, the umbrella organization for Deobandi madrassahs across Pakistan, was more critical of unanimity in celebrating Eid. Wafaq-ul-Madaris described it as unnecessary from a religious point of view. It endorsed the government's authority to empower a qazi or magistrate to decide on moon sightings testimonies and relay the news using its resources, as long as the basis of *ru'at* itself was observing the moon with the naked eye.[87]

Abdul Hamid Badayuni, an important Barelwi scholar, sought an audience with the President to discuss this issue in detail. His concern, and that of other Barelwi ulema who had submitted a joint statement, was not only about Eid but also about the duration of *iddat* and the celebration of such occasions as *ghyarween sharif* and *barhween sharif*, which also depended on calculating the lunar calendar.[88] Like other ulema, Barelwi scholars dismissed reliance on "some modern instruments" and emphasized the importance of *ru'at* with the naked eye, in accordance with the Islamic principles of *shahadat*.

Zafar Ahmad Usmani wrote a strongly worded letter to the president. Given that Usmani was the scion of a Deobandi family of scholars that had been supportive of the idea of Pakistan since the early 1940s and carried influence among madrassahs across India, Pakistan, and Afghanistan, his criticism had to be taken more seriously. Usmani described the practice of reliance on astronomical calculations as the practice of *rawafiz*, a strong word used to denounce various Shia groups. He wrote that no mathematical calculation could make it possible for Muslims worldwide to observe Eid on the same day as a single community of believers (Ummat), an idea that has a Quranic sanction. If it was not possible to do so for a Quranic commandment about the singularity of Ummat, why bother for an issue that did not even carry such divine sanction?[89] Like others, Usmani focused on the question of *shahadat*. He repeated the ulema's line of argument that the use of telephone or radio was unacceptable in a court of law; even a verdict announced using such instruments would not carry legal weight.

In the end, the government relented and reached out to another Deobandi scholar, Maulana Ehtasham-ul-Haq Thanawi, for appeasement. Following his meeting with the president, a statement was issued on 6 January 1960 in Thanawi's name to allay apprehensions about the proposed scheme. It quoted Thanawi:

> The President told me that the calendar, and the findings of the Meteorological Department would have a bearing only on such Government holidays, which were necessary to be determined before hand. They will have no effect on the practices followed under the shariat to determine the beginning of "Ramazan" and other matters by the appearance of the moon.
>
> In short, the Government is interested only in bringing about uniformity in Government holidays, which was possible by following the calendar. They have no intention of up-setting the practices followed according to the shariat.[90]

Nevertheless, a controversy did take place in 1961, and Thanawi was the one to lead it.

A new flurry of bureaucratic activity and religious debate followed the controversy. In a meeting on 8 April 1961—a few weeks after the "moon debacle" of March 1961—the cabinet recognized the importance of tradition, which "warrants that certain festivals be governed by the sighting of the moon." Although this condition was unchangeable, the cabinet members argued, the actual act of moon observation was to be kept in pace with advances in human knowledge and science. Since it was possible to exactly calculate the moon sighting, all "religious festivals will be observed on the days to be announced in advanced," in line with the practice of several other Muslim countries.[91] In internal correspondence, the government agenda was clear: to centralize the procedure for moon sighting to dilute the strength of religious scholars and their claims to a specialized knowledge of Islam.

By June 1961, the new policy had been finalized. Anwar Ali, secretary to the government of Pakistan, wrote a letter to the chief secretaries of East and West Pakistan on 16 June 1961 explaining the new policy for the "fixation of dates of national festivals." According to this policy, the Meteorological Department provided carefully calculated dates on which the new moon was expected to be visible on the horizon, determining the months of Ramadan, Shawwal, and Zil-Hajj. The official list of holidays issued by the Ministry of the Interior at the beginning of every year was to be drawn up in accordance with these dates. Based on these calculations, district magistrates in East and West Pakistan were directed to "arrange within their respective jurisdictions for an alert to be maintained on the first day on which the moon is expected to show itself." Following any information, which they were then to evaluate on their own, the magistrates were required to send a telegram to the Home Department in a specifically worded format.[92] On the receipt—or lack thereof—of reports about the sighting of the moon, the Home Department was to convene a meeting of secretaries and leading ulema of Rawalpindi, announcing the decision through a special radio broadcast. Because two days of holiday for Eid were specified in the annual list of gazetted holidays, it was possible to ensure that, even if there were deviance from the date initially calculated by the Meteorological Department, there would still be an additional holiday on which Eid could be celebrated throughout Pakistan on the same day.[93]

In November 1961, close to the trial of the new system, the Ministry of Interior prepared a working paper to summarize the procedure to be adopted for the collection of information about the new moon. The paper details the bulletins to be prepared by the Meteorological Department, the meetings to be convened at the local level by district magistrates, and instructions for relaying local evidence to the ministry in Rawalpindi via telegram after due verification. The central committee, which included a leading scholar of Rawalpindi, considered all the reports collected from across Pakistan. In response to this note, the director general of the radio expressed his concerns about the possibility of a clash between predetermined dates issued at the beginning of the year and the actual official announcement about the observance of the religious festival a day or two before the event. If Radio Pakistan announced predetermined dates, he said, it would contradict the announcement made by the committee.[94] The ministry, in its response, recommended that the radio announcement be based on the dates fixed by the committee, even if that contradicted the predetermined dates for Ramadan, Shawwal, and Zil-Hajj. For other months, Radio Pakistan was allowed to follow the predetermined calendar. The ministry was not sure about reactions from the Shia community in case of conflicts between the predetermined dates and announcements made by the committee.[95] Shias could, it was observed, follow their own inclinations if they had problems with the official announcement made by Radio Pakistan.[96]

The Shia dissent came up the very next year. The Meteorology Department had estimated that Ashura would fall on 13 June 1962. However, due to bad weather conditions, sighting the moon was not possible. It was reported that the "common people and the ulema, not having seen the new moon with their naked eyes," had decided to observe Ashura on 14 June. Accordingly, the cabinet decided to announce a holiday for Ashura that day. In the future, and even for Ashura, the note stated, the procedure laid down for other religious celebrations would be followed, with the amendment that a Shia scholar would be made part of the process.[97] Despite all arrangements and subsequent amendments to address any issues or disagreements, the system remained far from practical and failed to achieve its purpose of bringing about uniformity in the Islamic lunar calendar.

Following the brief war with India in September 1965 and the growing economic disparities between the two wings of the country, opposition from political parties and religious groups intensified. In their attacks to undermine the government, among the targets were Khan's pet projects, organizations, and individuals who could be identified with his Kemalist vision. This explains the ulema's protest against Dr. Fazlur Rahman, who was forced to resign from the Council of Islamic Ideology, an institution set up to reconceptualize Islam along modernist lines. Ayub Khan's regime did not simply recognize ulema as a political threat; it saw them as a potent force capable of undermining its religious vision. The arrangements made for moon sightings and the bid to enforce uniformity in observing Eid as a national festival were visible symbols of Khan's authoritarian ambitions. Therefore, opposition to the committee's announcements about the moon and observance of Eid was taken up as an act of subversion to undermine Khan's control. In January 1967, Maulana Mawdudi, Ghulam Ghaus Hazarwi, and Ehtasham-ul-Haq refused to accept the decision announced by the committee about the celebration of Eid. Late in the night, they announced that the moon had not been sighted, implying that fasting should be observed on the following day.[98] This was even though the committee had been reconstituted to increase the ulema's membership. The government had also taken action to prevent counterclaims about moon sightings or nonsightings, invoking laws against the use of loudspeakers that could be used by "local maulvis" for their "mischief." But at the end of the day, as the home minister wrote in a note to the president, the "Government cannot force people to observe the Eid or for that matter any function, if they do not want to do so. All the Government can and must do is to prevent mischief-makers from intimidating and misleading people."[99]

The government eventually gave up on the idea of forcing people to observe Eid on a single day. After Ayub Khan had been ousted from power and replaced by another military dictator, General Yahya Khan, the cabinet decided to abolish the central *ru'at-i-hilal* committee in a meeting on 8 October 1969. In cabinet discussions and the preceding ministerial correspondence, officials expressed concern about the inconsistency between having a fixed calendar and making official announcements for a particular event. Other than the admission that the government should not get itself involved in controversies about the moon sighting, the meeting also highlighted such difficulties as delays in communicating information by deputy commissioners all the way to Rawalpindi, the difference in longitudes between the two wings, and disagreements among the ulema on the entire exercise. It was also noted that it was not possible to forecast the moon's visibility with great accuracy: "The decision to observe or not to observe the festivals on any particular day should, therefore, be left to the people."[100] The government was only to facilitate the process of relaying information about the moon sighting without getting directly involved or forcing people to observe a festival on a specific date.

The correspondence between various officials and the minutes prepared for the minister pointed out that the government's previous policy in deciding on the moon sighting had caused considerable turmoil and controversy, at times resulting in a countrywide law-and-order problem that compelled the government to resort to the preventive detention of dissident ulema. As a result, "the public, specially the Ulema, have developed a grouse that the Government in the shape of the Central Ruat-i-Hilal Committee has been interfering in their personal and religious affairs."[101]

As a result, the central *ru'at-i-hilal* committees were disbanded and replaced by provincial committees mainly comprising nonofficial members and ulema, which continued to receive information about the moon sighting from district-level committees.[102] In the official press release about the new arrangement, the reference to provincial committees was missing. A section officer in the Ministry of Interior observed that the press note had received considerable public appreciation. He inquired whether the government should clarify its stance on the convening of a provincial committee. The interior secretary thought that the provincial committee would face the same issue as the central committee. After getting verbal approval from the president, the secretary dropped the idea of a provincial committee.[103] Under the revised procedure, deputy commissioners throughout the country were to convene a meeting of "influential persons and eminent Ulema" in their respective regional headquarters on the twenty-ninth day of the lunar month to collect and sift detailed information about the appearance or nonappearance of the moon. Any definite news about the sighting or nonsighting of the moon was to be passed onto divisional commissioners via telephone or telegraphs and released to the public.[104] The official letter sent to the provincial governments of East and West Pakistan communicating the change of procedure stated that "the decision to observe or not to observe a festival, on the basis of this information, will, however, rest with the people."[105] This arrangement worked well for Eid, where two public holidays were reserved; either of the two holidays could be used for celebration. But the communiqué was silent on occasions where only one public holiday was reserved. Because religious observances like Muharram and Milad took place on the tenth and twelfth day of the lunar calendar, respectively, it was still possible to relay information about the sighting of the moon at the start of the month. The ministry simply requested that the provincial governments keep it informed about the dates of the sighting of the moon for these two occasions.

ONE HORIZON, MULTIPLE PERSPECTIVES

Although the government gave up on enforcing uniformity in observance of Eid in 1969, it returned with the idea in 1973–1974, albeit with two major differences. Following a protracted war of liberation, East Pakistan became Bangladesh in December 1971. The dismemberment of Pakistan meant that the remaining part of the country was a more cohesive geographical unit. It put an end to longitudinal disparities, although regional differences remained a persistent problem, playing into religious debates. The other major difference was in the composition of the proposed central committee for *ru'at-i-hilal*. With a stark break from the legacy of Ayub Khan's modernizing authoritarianism, Zulfiqar Ali Bhutto—who became prime minister after the first nationwide elections in Pakistan based on adult franchise—drummed up rhetoric that addressed the demand for an "Islamic system" and redistributive justice; thus, the slogan "Islamic socialism." As part of his populist strategy, Bhutto undertook a massive nationalization program and appeased the more conservative part of his constituency, especially in Punjab, by acquiescing to such demands as declaring Ahmadis non-Muslims. Continuing a similar trend of appeasing conservative forces, the Bhutto government set up a central *ru'at-i-hilal* committee that, in a clear departure from the precedent set during the 1960s, gave credence to the ulema and their views about *ru'at*.

Unlike previous attempts to constitute centralized mechanisms through executive decrees, the new committee was set up through an act of parliament. The resolution to set up a new *ru'at* committee was presented in the assembly on 22 December 1973. It aimed at "putting an end to the controversy that usually arises on the sighting of Eid moon." The committee, convened by the federal minister for Haj and Auqaf, comprised nine members with reputable ulema of all schools of thought represented in it.[106] Maulana Kausar Niazi, the minister for religious affairs, gave the rationale for setting up the committee by repeating the arguments made by notable ulema in their criticism of previous committees. Niazi concurred with the ulema's views that Eid was not a festival; it was the culminating point of a month-long religious obligation of fasting. The sighting of the new moon, he noted, marks the beginning of one religious obligation and starts the other.[107] In a reverential tone, he referred to the ulema's viewpoint and agreed with the religious necessity of sighting the moon with the naked eye. The moon's existence alone somewhere on the horizon was not enough, said Niazi; it must be seen as well, as the moon remains in existence throughout the month. Without directly naming Shafi, Niazi reused the latter's argument about the nonavailability of scientific tools to people living in jungles and far-off areas.[108]

Niazi's argument for a new central committee was about neither the need for a uniform lunar calendar nor the superiority of science in recording the movements of the moon. He framed his argument strictly in terms of enabling the Muslims of Pakistan to observe a religious obligation, rather than an attempt on the part of the Pakistani state to meddle in their personal beliefs and practice or to force them to observe Eid on a particular day. He said that the government was willing to let ulema from a broad section of religious backgrounds join the committee and frame rules whereby testimony was to be collected and relayed via radio, television, and newspapers.[109] The new arrangement, he insisted, was different from previous attempts in which the committee was nonrepresentative, comprising the secretary of information, secretary of the interior, and the prayer leader of a local mosque in Rawalpindi.[110] Because of the nonrepresentative character of the committee, opined Niazi, its decisions lacked credibility among the people and led to various disagreements.

The ulema—especially those who were also members of the parliament—were not convinced of the committee's neutrality or its autonomy. Niazi reiterated his position about the committee's change in character and the reasons for which the government was constituting it.[111] In response to a suggestion about punishing those who disobey the committee's announcement, Niazi stated that the committee's purpose was to create unanimity by involving scholars from different persuasions and thus saving people from falling into chaos and disagreement. The government could not force people to celebrate Eid on a given day, but it could help create a situation in which no one would be available, or willing, to lead

Eid prayers on a different day.[112] With minor amendments to the original draft, the assembly passed the resolution, and the first committee was constituted, with nine scholars from different religious groups.

Over the years, the basic structure of the committee has remained unchanged, although its membership has continued to increase. The current membership stands at twenty-six. Every year committee members vote to elect a chair. In addition to a central committee, various provincial, district, and zonal committees have also been set up. However, the decision-making power remains with the central committee. In the beginning, the committee was assisted by the Department of Meteorology, but it is now provided technical assistance by the Pakistan Navy, Pakistan Air Force, Pakistan Space and Upper Atmosphere Research Commission (SUPARCO), provincial Auqaf departments, district coordination officers, and the Ministry of Information and Broadcasting.[113] The committee initially decided on *ru'at* for Ramadan and Eid, but it now decides the entire Islamic calendar.

Despite the importance of the committee and the controversy it generates every year during the month of Ramadan, there is little scholarly literature on this issue. In 2016, Abid Husain, a journalist working for the Karachi *Herald*, wrote a fascinating account of the inner workings of the committee. After a long photography session in which many people who were neither committee members nor helping with the actual task of searching for the moon took selfies with ulema, the committee offered *maghrib* prayers and sat for a while, receiving phone calls. It deliberated on data presented by various government departments. Afterward, Mufti Munib-ur-Rehman—the long-running chairman of the committee who was later removed—read out a live statement on camera, as eagerly awaited by millions of Pakistanis.[114]

Every year, Munib-ur-Rehman, in his trademark style of slowly reading a carefully drafted statement, gradually moves toward the climax, when he announces whether the moon has been sighted. Accordingly, Eid would take place the next day or the following day. The announcement has a considerable impact on people's activities planned for the evening. If the moon has not been sighted, then there is an additional day of fasting, which means that people will have time to prepare for Eid and go to a barber's shop to get a haircut. If Eid is announced for the next day, it causes a rush to the market for some last-minute shopping. In the context of a booming consumerist middle-class Pakistani society, the announcement of the sighting of the Shawwal moon can, therefore, have a massive impact on sales, as an unexpected, early Eid might cause a decline in consumerist spending.

However, this sense of anticipation and excitement about the new moon also causes anxiety and frustration. In 2019, Fawad Husain Chaudhary—a minister in the government of former prime minister Imran Khan—demanded that the committee be disbanded. As minister of science and technology, Chaudhary launched an app for spotting the moon. In introducing this technology, Chaudhary described the task of sighting the moon as simply taking out a mobile phone, downloading an app that gives the moon's direction, looking to the sky in the direction indicated, and finding the moon "right there."[115]

Chaudhary's language of scientific triumphalism discards any serious engagement with the concepts of horizons or visions that had marked decades of debate on this issue—and for this reason elicited a positive response from an urbanized Pakistani middle class that shares a similar worldview about scientific rationality and about Islam as a rational religion. The ulema, and especially Mufti Munib-ur-Rehman, were incensed. In a series of articles, Rehman tried to explain the position of the ulema in this matter. Rehman was critical of media anchors and columnists who poked fun at the committee and criticized its financial burden on the Exchequer. They often demand spending this money for more useful purposes. If disbanding the committee helps the cause of launching a spaceship or landing on the moon, Mufti Rehman stated, then they should please go ahead and do so. In responses reported in the media and published in newspaper articles, Mufti Rehman gave details about the remuneration paid to committee members. The amount paid to committee members is indeed a paltry sum, but the office carries respect and prestige. The most important of these privileges is that the head of the committee gets to make the most important, most anticipated statement about the moon, which millions of viewers watch on their TV screens.

Another common criticism was that there were several other practices—most importantly, the five daily prayers—that depended on calculations requiring precise information about the sun's movements. But rather than keeping track of these movements, worshippers simply checked the time on their wristwatch and offer prayers. The same principle should be applicable in the case of the lunar calendar as well, where actual sighting of the moon with the naked eye should not be a prerequisite. A scientifically calculated calendar with precise details about its movements throughout the year should guide the preparation of a calendar with dates for major Islamic events given in advance. Mufti Rehman offered two responses: first, he said that the timings of daily prayers were also calculated by the ulema. He referred to the centuries-old techniques that had been part of madrassah education, whereby such tables were usually compiled and continued to inform the practice in the contemporary period. To say that this was a problem of ulema's rigidity in embracing new technologies was thus ignorant of facts. Second, according to Rehman, the Prophetic command for seeing the moon with the naked eye was so clear and unambiguous that no metaphoric meanings can be ascribed to it.[116] Referring to scholars like Javed Ahmad Ghamidi, who think that the essence of this commandment was to have definite knowledge about the new moon, which can be achieved with certainty using modern scientific tools, Rehman responded that such a revisionist approach was not acceptable in cases where the actual meanings of the terms used were clear and unambiguous, with consensual interpretations by ulema for centuries.

ULEMA VERSUS ULEMA

If the earlier attempt under General Ayub Khan was meant to achieve national unity through an authoritative implementation of a modernist view of Islam, the post-1971 model anchored the idea of Pakistani nationhood in a version of Islam in which ulema set the contours of religious discourse and used their political influence and effective mass mobilization to get it sanctioned by the state. Over a period of time—especially during General Zia-ul-Haq's martial-law period—the Islamization of state institutions was mainly overseen by the ulema, or they were key contributors in the process. But this attempt to achieve national cohesion through Islam had also not been successful. The issue of *ru'at-i-hilal* itself is the mechanism whereby such fault lines often get highlighted and, hence, the reason for the anxiety felt by a large section of Pakistanis over the question of moon sighting and Eid.

The ascendency of ulema in the process of setting the agenda of Islam in Pakistani politics has caused more groups, individuals, and institutions to stake a claim to the process based on their claims to religious authority, doctrinal differences with others, and more importantly, regional political aspirations and identity politics. This is best reflected in the ongoing controversies about the moon between the central *ru'at-i-hilal* committee led by Mufti Munib-ur-Rehman and the informal committee convened by Mufti Poppalzai in Peshawar. Since the early 2000s, Mufti Poppalzai is the popular face of dissent on national television, and thus the source of disunity and a major reason Pakistanis cannot celebrate Eid on the same day. This has given rise to various jokes about the moon in Peshawar happening earlier than in any other part of the country.[117] In his actions, Poppalzai is not alone. There are reasons for his seemingly chaotic methods. The choices he, and many others like him, make in his juristic interpretation are affected by his location and historical relationship with the state.

Khyber Pakhtunkhawa—formerly, North-West Frontier Province—was essentially a border zone developed during the colonial period to protect the borders of British India from the imagined threat of tsarist expansion, a paranoia inherited by the postcolonial state of Pakistan at the height of the Cold War. Politically, the province was restive; it was the only Muslim-majority province where the Muslim League had lost elections in 1946. The Khudai Khidmatgar, or Red Shirts, led by Bacha Khan, was a mass political movement that challenged the Muslim League and, later, the central government of Pakistan. To offset its influence, the central government supported various rival groups, especially ulema, and their influence in a largely conservative Pashtun society. Faced with decades of state oppression and exclusion from mainstream politics, Awami National Party (ANP)—the direct inheritor of Bacha Khan's politics, led by his son, Wali Khan—finally emerged as a political party that became an active player in Pakistani politics after 1971. The region's dynamics changed dramatically after the Soviet invasion of Afghanistan and the subsequent jihad. Given its pro-Soviet credentials and a general aversion to religious rhetoric, ANP lost considerable political mileage vis-à-vis ulema and their religio-political organizations. Still, ANP retained considerable political support in the province and managed to form coalition governments on various occasions. Over the years, it remained Pashtun nationalist in orientation but became a part of mainstream, federal politics. Still, it retains a strong nationalist agenda for regional autonomy. As coalition partners in the province between 2008 and 2013, senior ministers belonging to ANP went to Masjid Qasim Jan, met with Mufti Poppalzai, and accepted his decision about the observance of Eid. This caused an embarrassing situation for the central committee since Mufti Poppalzai's decision had been endorsed by the provincial government, which had announced the celebration of Eid the following day. As a result, Mufti Rehman was forced to announce Eid.

Maulana Abdul Haq, of Akora Khattak, is another example of a scholar caught in a whirlpool of contrasting interests and affinities, including the burden of tradition, identity politics, and a beneficial relationship to the state. As custodian of one of the major seminaries associated with Afghan Jihad, Haqqani had largely supported the Pakistani state's drive toward Islamization and its instrumentalization for state-making purposes, especially in Pashtun areas, to dilute the impact of nationalist or pro-Afghanistan forces. In numerous responses to questions of *ru'at*, Haqqani had been reluctant to dismiss the role of the central committee altogether or to undermine the religious credentials of the ulema represented in it. Yet he made it clear that if the same procedure could be replicated at the local level under the guidance of reputed ulema. Because the questioner had asked explicitly about the binding authority of decisions by local ulema for government servants, Haqqani made it clear that regardless of whether the person was privately employed or a government servant, the dictate of Shariat applied to everyone.[118]

Mufti Muhammad Farid—also based at Madrassah Haqqaniyya in Akora Khattak—was more explicit in his dismissal of the role of central committee or validity of its decision for government servants. In 1978, soon after General Zia-ul-Haq's martial law, a *khatib* based at a military mosque asked Farid about celebrating Eid in accordance with the dictates of Shariat as duly confirmed by local, reputed ulema, though not announced by the central committee. Mufti Farid stated that everyone—whether civilian or military—was bound to accept the decision of local ulema if based on the requirements of Shariat.[119] No validation from the central committee was required. At the same time, Mufti Haqqani believed in the idea of unity, or organization (*ijtimayyat*), as a cardinal feature of Islam and hence advised the questioner from the border area of Pishin to keep trust in the ability of the committee to announce Ramadan or Eid. But in the same breath, he added that this task could be performed by a local scholar as well, and authority did not lie exclusively with the central committee.[120] He reasoned that the committee did not accept rulings from local ulema and instead relied on scientific calculations to reject evidence presented by ulema—a practice that, in his estimation, clashed with Shariat. Haqqani wrote that if the committee were to stick to its rules and not connect with the local ulema, then people should better listen to their local ulema.[121]

Dr. Muhammad Mushtaq Ahmed's more recent commentary on *ru'at-i-hilal* explained this attitude based on the history of political organization in Pashtun areas. In areas like Swat and Dir, which had Muslim princely states, a centralized authority existed to ensure the regulation of religious affairs. Therefore, the people of these areas, according to Ahmed, were trained to accept central authority and few disagreements about Eid were reported. In contrast, writes Ahmed, in areas like Peshawar, Mardan, and Charsada, the loss of Muslim political authority entailed the destruction of the institutions necessary to maintaining religious order. In these circumstances, the ulema advised believers to take guidance in religious affairs and day-to-day obligations from scholars or men of good repute. This tradition has existed firmly since then.[122] Given their historically constituted role in their respective communities, local ulema wielded considerable power. Denying them a role in the *ru'at* committee undermined the credibility of the entire structure. In the original procedure for the central committee laid down by Mufti Shafi, Zafar Ahmad Usmani, and Yusuf Banori, zonal and local committees were also given the authority to decide for the entire country in case of moon sighting.[123] However, such a proposal was unfeasible, as it would have led to fragmentation of the decision-making process and enabled every union council to decide for itself.

Nevertheless, Ahmed's argument has limited validity; other parts of Pakistan also experienced a dissolution of Muslim political authority during the late eighteenth and early nineteenth century. Yet the demand for local committees, or recognition of their importance in the overall process, does not lead to questioning the central committee's decision in areas like Punjab and Sindh. This is both because of more effective control of state power in these areas and a general lack of interest among the local population to yield to ulema's advice, at least on this particular issue. The "Pashtun exception," therefore, is not only a question of a lack of Muslim political power or of gaining recognition from the state to play a role in the process of moon sighting; it is primarily a reflection of regional assertion for autonomy. In that sense, the situation is akin to opposition to the imposition of standardized time during the British period, which might be understood as an anticolonial act. What started as an initiative to connect colonial India with global circuits of capital hegemonized by imperial powers led to active resistance in the early part of the twentieth century as "local matters became a valve for communicating disapproval of imperial rule" and for creating the possibilities of "carving out autonomous time spaces that did not stand in any meaningful relationship to the prime meridian at Greenwich."[124] Preserving "local time," in other words, can be read as part of preserving the local itself and its autonomy.

This aspect of opposing standardization of time as an act of resistance is even more pronounced in the Pakistani state's troubled relationship with tribal areas. Formerly clustered as Federally Administered Tribal Areas, these seven tribal units have been made part of the Khyber Pakhtunkhwa provincial government. As tribal areas, they previously were not subject to Pakistan's criminal and civil laws. This was in continuation with the colonial policy of "difference," whereby tribal areas were not to be subjected to the same set of laws meant for what the colonial administration described as "settled areas." In effect, neither the British government nor its postcolonial successor maintained effective sovereign power over the region. Because of their geographical proximity with Afghanistan, historical ties between tribes on both sides of the border, and lack of effectiveness of power exercised by the state, the tribal areas constituted a peculiar political and a religious category. The political ambiguity of the region and its impact on religious praxis is summed up in a response given by Mufti Muhammad Farid to a question asked by Maulana Fazal Ullah in 1989.

Writing from Mohmand Agency, Fazal Ullah asked about its peculiar locale, which was "situated in a region where there was neither Pakistani government nor Afghan, instead, it is a completely independent area [*azad ilaqa*]." Some residents followed Saudi announcements for fasting and Eid, while others didn't. Mufti Farid responded that because the difference of *matali'* was not a problem, people living in the east could rely on the *ru'at* of people living in the west.[125] His response was in accordance with the prevalent practice of the local ulema deciding the matter on their own or coordinating their calendars with Afghanistan, which, in turn, relied on announcements made by Saudi Arabia. In an era of modern nation-states that were jealously protective of their frontiers and eager to exercise sovereign power over their subjects, tribal areas present an interesting case study of an indeterminate zone. This ambiguity about sovereign claims over the region made it possible for Mufti Farid to evade the question of *wilayat* and the notion of centralized authority, and instead enjoin believers to follow their local ulema in deciding religious issues and practices.

In this way, in the settled areas of Khyber Pakhtunkhwa and in the tribal areas, the distrust of the central *ru'at-i-hilal* committee is expressed differently. In the case of the tribal areas, it could be described as a matter of indifference: the region is neither under complete control of the Pakistani state nor socially linked with the sizable consumerist market of Eid as other parts of the region. In the case of the settled areas of Khyber Pakhtunkhwa, aspirations for local recognition and identity politics play an important factor because a large part of the Pashtun population has established a more significant stake in Pakistan's bureaucracy, military, and—more importantly—economy.

The question of recognition is also played out based on doctrinal positions. The Ahl-i-Hadith, who constitute a small fraction of Pakistan's predominantly Sunni population, are given token representation in many religious institutions set up by the state. In various fatawa relating to the issue of *ru'at*, the Ahl-i-Hadith ulema have dismissed the requirement of a centralized arrangement. During the 1960s, one of the fatawa written by Muhammad Ismail stated that because Dhaka had a different *matali'*, it was incorrect to declare Eid in East Pakistan by a new moon sighted in West Pakistan. The fatwa ruled that celebrating Eid on two different days would not hurt the unity of the Ummat.[126] In the same fatwa, Ismail warned against the trend of overemphasizing the difference between *shahadat* and *khabar*, as much of hadith transmission was based on *khabar*. He recognized the difference but argued that there was no difference when it came to accrediting or confirming something. Thus, a single woman could not give *shahadat* for the moon, but she could provide *khabar* about it.[127] Similarly, an important Ahl-i-Hadith journal, *al-A'itasam*, consistently criticized the idea of insisting on one Eid or Ramadan cycle.[128] Instead, it recommended strengthening local committees at the city and district levels.

Ulema who have historically been close to the Pakistani state and have continued to benefit from its support and patronage have consistently maintained strict obedience to a centralized authority. Mufti Taqi Usmani—who inherits the religious and political legacies of Shabbir Ahmad Usmani, Zafar Ahmad Usmani, and Mufti Muhammad Shafi—considers it obligatory to follow the command of the central authority. A questioner once asked him about Oman, where Maliki *fiqh* is followed. The questioner's concern was about the compulsion of Hanafis to obey Maliki *fiqh*, especially when respected local ulema expressed doubts about the state-controlled process of managing a lunar calendar and there was disaffection among people about their decisions. In his response, Mufti Usmani clearly stated that the central decision had to be followed. In case of any concerns, the best solution, he said, was for the local ulema to convey grievances or misapprehensions to the central committee. In situations when official committees were not operating—whether in Pakistan or abroad—Usmani emphasized that advice should be taken from reputed local ulema, rather than following what "ordinary people" had decided. It was a strictly religious issue, he stated. Because ordinary people were not well versed in ascertaining the criteria set for *shahadat*, one should always approach respected ulema for guidance.[129] It can be inferred that by maintaining such a doctrinal position, Usmani justified the state's authority and the ulema's endorsement, in addition to justifying an exclusive role for the ulema when there was no centralized system to enforce Islamic Shariat.

The moon controversy is not specific to the recent tussle between Mufti Munib, Fawad Chaudhary, and Mufti Poppalzai. It has a much longer history, not only in Pakistan but also in the broader world of Muslim scholarship and social-cultural practices. This history is part of a conversation about presumed binaries of, and conflictual relationships along the lines of, science and religion, modernity and tradition, belief and superstition, and faith and reason in matters involving Islamic beliefs and practices. What gave this debate a peculiar dimension in colonial South Asia and, afterward, Pakistan, was the added question of state authority. Similar debates in the wider Middle East, for instance, did not assume a similar character, given the strict state management of religion. As I have shown, such a mode of authoritarian statecraft is a desirable model both for those who aspire to a liberal-secular democracy in which religion has no role to play in state policy, and for those who see Islam as a progressive force for nation building, provided it can be exorcised of the influence of the ulema, who are seen as exercising a retrogressive influence.

The debate about the moon required the ulema to engage with such questions as the ideas of space, locality, vision, transmission, and authority. The cumulative impact of these debates marked various transmutations, internal contradictions, and breaks from the past that have resulted in a polyvalence of doctrinal positions that derive their strength from the same tradition but speak to different audiences. In a process that Jamal Malik calls the colonialization of Islam in Pakistan, it is important to highlight the role of each the state and the ulema in this process.

By exploring the moon controversy, I have addressed broader questions related to epistemic crises in Islamic discourses and their impact on the religious authority of the ulema. Furthermore, I explained how this contestation influences state praxis, offering critical insights into establishing a cohesive temporality and scalar homogeneity as crucial prerequisites for postcolonial citizenship. The state's insistence on reducing the debate about *ru'at* to the simplicity of the process of locating the moon, thereby overriding the complexity of the issue and its prehistory, is as important as the erasure of the ambiguities of jurisdictional disagreements on the part of the ulema for an attempted homogenization of a doctrinal position where one has not historically existed. Rather than approaching the contentious issue of *ru'at* as a conflictual binary between state and ulema, science and tradition, and reasoning and scripture, I have tried to show that the intertwined context in which these themes came up and became a source of epistemological crisis. It was negotiated at multiple levels under the impact of various ideological aspirations, doctrinal positions, and projects for nationalizing of Islam. In other words, the direction of reform, revision, or the contestation of authority has not taken place in isolation and without influencing, or getting influenced by, a range of disputative positions.

In the end, the newly constitutive tradition itself remains fragmented and open to further development, with an uneasy relationship to the history of its own making. The ulema are thus as much custodians of change and bearers of charismatic authority as they use that charisma and custodianship to alter that very tradition—under a range of influences, contingencies, and contemporary developments—which bestows this charisma and custodianship in the first place.

I have demonstrated this dynamic through the issue of *ru'at-i-hilal*, where ulema drew on tradition to alter their doctrinal position about the undesirability of homogeneity in Eid. It required them to revise the idea of space as *wilayat* and the concept of *matali'* to seek the clarity and authority required for Eid as a nation-making festival. While for the Pakistani state, the operational ideology is of "one nation, one Eid," the ulema have approached the disputation about Eid as an attempt to achieve concordance between *wilayat* and state, *matali'* and space, *ru'at* and seeing, and *hilal* and calendar to arrive at the nationalized space and homogenized time required for one nation, one Eid.

Such an interactive, interdependent relationship has enabled nationalization as the colonization of Islam in Pakistan. This synthesis is not just limited to the regulation of the calendar but increasingly lies at the heart of Pakistan's ideational fabric. In other words, Pakistan's national idea depends much more on the moon on the horizon than previously thought. The moon sighting is one of the major ways the *wilayat* of Pakistan gets sanctified and seeks to achieve homogeneity in time and space for its aspirational project of state-building, drawing on the nation's symbolic repertoire.

Ulema's responses to the regulation of lunar calendar show that the history of global standard time is far from a seamless morphing of "disciplinary power of new scientific practices" to passive recipients.¹³⁰ One must also add that the ulema might have resisted attempts to enforce an empty, homogeneous national time, that does not mean that they remain unfazed by its enchantment of regimented power. They have sutured into coherence an ideational basis for regularizing time and space required for a national Islam that depends on their mediative role. This reminds me of Vilashini Coopan's referral to William Kentridge's 2012 multimedia video installation, *The Refusal of Time*, which was inspired by an anarchist's attempt to time-bomb the Greenwich meridian in the 1880s. This attempt tragically failed, as the planner was working with a faulty clock.¹³¹ The anecdote points to an "abiding sense of the futility both of imperial modernity and of the fight against it." What ulema's resistance to the modernizing rationality of the state has led to is yet another modernizing logic of regimentation, with the difference that organizing a unified national Islamic time and space in Pakistan takes place under the ulema's custodianship.

In this manner, the revisioning of tradition has emptied the unregulated lunar calendar of its temporal enchantment and ambiguity, and vacated the affective spatial excess of the locale as the unit of dwelling and being part of the community. What then results is a regimented routine of proceedings of the *hilal* committee, the predictability of its deliberations on the reports received about the new moon, and the mechanistic outcome that renders alien what was once familiar and intimate.

FIVE

SCRIPTING THE NATIONAL TIME AND SPACE
Archive, Calendar, Roads, and Museums

IN AN ESSAY ON the role of ideology in stabilizing a predictable system of meanings for a socially integrated meaningful action, Paul Ricoeur defines ideology as a "function of the distance that separates the social memory from an inaugural event which must nevertheless be repeated."[1] He gives the examples of "founding acts" of the American Declaration of War, the French Revolution, and the October Revolution, the historical intimacy of the social group who witnessed or organized it, and the urge to perpetuate it beyond the period of evanescence by making it the creed of the entire group. According to Ricoeur, ideology serves these purposes as a doxa—a simplified, schematic code—to give an overview of not only the group and the group's representation of itself for itself, but also of history in general and the world at large. The inherent justificatory role of ideology is operative rather than thematic, and its transformative capacity is achieved when the ideas it conveys become opinions. As Ricoeur puts it, ideology "operates behind our backs, rather than appearing as a theme before our eyes. We think from it rather than about it."[2] In this manner, ideology causes the narrowing of the field for possibilities of interpretation about the founding moment, although it ineluctably retains sedimented, excavatable layers of the event constituting the historical community whose perpetuation a dissimulative ideological praxis seeks to achieve.

We can look at the master narrative of history institutionalized through archives and replicated in a historical discourse in academic works and school textbooks through a similar lens. The ideology of Muslim nationalism as discussed in previous chapters provides a justificatory framework shaping the self-image of Pakistan as an Islamic republic and a range of representations and conversations involving art, leisure, film, food, and other mundane activities. The purpose of this chapter is to talk not about the ideologization of history but about how history conquers memory through such performative acts as commemorative parades, setting up of a museum as a visual narrative about the state's preferred foundation moment, regulation of temporal cycle through announcement of national holidays, and writing of urban text by the naming and renaming of roads and cities.

Memory is individual and fragmented, and as Maurice Halbwachs has argued, it is through a community membership with its religious, cultural, class, and national outlook that people acquire and recall their memories.[3] Modern memory, as Pierra Nora tells us, is archival as it is increasingly dependent on the materiality of the trace. *Lieux de mémoire*, or realms of memory, as he calls it, are indicative of the lack of spontaneity in memory—a memory that is no longer socially embedded or fleeting, gradually making it an experience from within a distant possibility and hence the "need for external props and tangible reminders of that which no longer exists except *qua memory*."[4] Nora describes memory and history as antithetical. In his estimation, memory ties us to the eternal present, is a phenomenon of emotion and magic, and thrives on vague, telescoping reminiscences of specific symbolic details. History, according to Nora, is a reconstruction of what is no longer; it is a representation of the past, an intellectual nonreligious exercise that ferrets out memory's mode of sacred remembrance and turns it into prose.[5] The poetics of social memory is transformed into history's prosaic language of the state.

Such a theorization is important to emphasize the locale of memory as social and individual and that of history as national and statist. It is the historical frame through which the state seeks to regulate the power of the collective held by memory to forge a sense of sharedness and bring fellow citizens together for the imagining of a united, national self. The purpose of this chapter is to study the process of the national construction of identity as a collective self through various performative acts.

ON RECORD: ARCHIVE AS "RAW MATERIAL FOR HISTORY" OF PAKISTAN'S MASTER NARRATIVE

Writing the nation through history is one among the state effects of power to institutionalize authority and replicate ideological power apparatuses. Like the issuance of currency notes, the building of monuments, and the choosing of national symbols, telling a story about the nation's past is part of the same process of building state power through attempted hegemonization of the narrative. The ingredients of this story are like the narrative structure of fiction as specified by Hayden White.[6] The figurative speech of history masks its fictionality with truth claims based on the construction of archive as a repertoire of factual information. This is why, to quote Achille Mbembe, "there is no state without archives—without its archives."[7] Yet at the same time, reminds Mbembe, the archive is a constant source of anxiety as well. The state's power lies in its ability "to consume time, that is, to abolish the archive and anaesthetise the past"—an act of chronophage, as Mbembe calls it, that creates the state.[8] But any act of writing the past through a process of elision and creative remembrance does not exhaust the possibilities of alternative narratives to emerge from the archive. Any master narrative constructed to serve as a template for various commemorative acts and historicizing the nation can only aspire to a hegemonic status but is always subjected to alternative narratives seeking to subvert the dominant discourse about the past. The state can try to abolish the archive and erase its materiality, but it only serves to inscribe the memory of the archive and its contents in the form of double registers of fantasy and phantom. Destruction or prohibition of the archive removes it from sight and provides it with additional content as it allows for a rich possibility of all sorts of imaginations about what could have been. Similarly, the destroyed archive haunts the state in the form of a specter transformed into a demon by the touch of death and "receptacle of all utopian ideals and of all anger, the authority of a future judgement."[9]

There are numerous academic works documenting processes of nationalizing the past or writing the nation through history.[10] They point to the centrality of historical imagination in the stitching of the nation and legitimation of the state. The key themes in these works involve identifying the master narrative, that is, the dominant accounts of the past shaping the historical identity of a community. Krijn Thijs refers to "the hierarchy of masterliness on an intertextual level by locating the power of the master narrative in their characteristically dominant relation to other narratives."[11] In this way, the master narrative shapes numerous other partial stories to have a much wider acclaim, power, and acceptance in the larger society. The master narrative is built on the archive collated by the state and animated with an aura of truth.

In the post-1947 period, the agenda of writing "authentic" history free of biases was not simply an intellectual exercise but closely tied with the larger project of state formation and nation making. The demand for Pakistan, articulated politically, was based on a historical narrative that was built around the centrality of the Muslim *qaum* in India and its distinctness in terms of religious beliefs, cultural traits, and historical traditions. History was, therefore, central to the idea of Pakistan and its importance was not lost on the government and the intelligentsia of the newly created state. As I show later in the chapter, the government generously patronized historians, the public took active part in criticizing their work, and the history conferences during the 1950s were major events attended by Pakistan's top leadership.

One of the reasons for an overwhelming interest in tracing the basis for Pakistani statehood and nation in history was that the "newness" of Pakistan was more pronounced.[12] It was because India's nomenclature and civilization had been known globally for centuries. Pakistan was a new term coined by a Cambridge-based Indian Muslim student, Chaudhry Rehmat Ali, in the 1930s, which went on to become a rallying cry for those espousing an independent homeland in the Muslim-majority areas of northwestern and northeastern India. This difference between India and Pakistan was not lost on the leaders of the new state immediately after 1947 and led to "PR stunts" to project Pakistan as a distinct and new nation-state with a rich civilization and history dating back to antiquity. This task of introducing Pakistan and its rich civilization to the world was performed by historians as well.

The urgency of rewriting history for a nation-making project was tied with the anxiety of accessing records required for the writing of this history. As in other areas where distribution of resources between the two dominion states had adversely affected Pakistan, the library and archival material along with museum artifacts was another issue on which Pakistan felt deprived of its due share. Unlike India, which inherited the major chunk of colonial records and a large number of public libraries and private collections, in Pakistan the only major university was Punjab University and Punjab Archives the only proper archive in West Pakistan. In other words, Lahore was the only city in both wings of Pakistan that had retained some cultural capital from the Mughal and colonial past. As Ishtiaq Husain Qureshi—a Cambridge-trained historian of medieval India and the chief architect of Pakistan's master narrative—pointed out in his presidential address at the annual history conference in 1954, Pakistan was "denied the raw material for history" because of its deficient inheritance of libraries and archives.[13] "It was essential," he said, "that all the raw material of history should now begin to be collected, sorted, catalogued, described and preserved scientifically."[14] Because this job of preservation and collection of documents was technical, he stressed the need for professional archivists to preserve the material scientifically and protect the records against the damaging effects of weather or insects.

Of the various committees set up in 1947 to discuss issues relating to transfer of power and Partition, one was specifically entrusted with the task of dividing cultural assets between the two dominions. This was in addition to sharing and transfer of purely administrative records, which were required by both dominions for efficient workings of their respective governments. This had been warranted in large numbers because of the huge influx of refugees from areas that had become part of the rival dominion. To ascertain the property claims made by these refugees, it was necessary to have relevant information certified from the other dominion in possession of such records. The mutual dependence of dominions on one another to acquire these records and their importance for administration was, therefore, self-explanatory and created much urgency. The same enthusiasm was, however, not shown for the transfer of cultural and intellectual assets. This was largely Pakistan's loss, and the government quickly realized the urgency of the matter as it affected the larger ambition of the rewriting of history to achieve singular nationhood.

Soon after independence, the Educational Conference held in November 1947 passed a resolution for the setting up of a Historical Records and Archives Commission for Pakistan "to suggest ways and means of preserving all manuscripts, records, and documents of historical and cultural interest."[15] The commission, set up in April 1948, was to comprise representatives of provincial and state governments, along with prominent archivists and representatives from Pakistani universities. On the recommendations of this commission, the Directorate of Archives and Libraries started functioning in Karachi in 1951.[16] The more pressing task was to negotiate with the British government to acquire the India Office collection at the British Library, or to claim major chunks of it. To negotiate with the British authorities—a process that continued well into the 1950s—the government sent Qureshi and A. S. Bokhari to London. Professor Storey, a professor of Arabic at Cambridge University, was to assist the Pakistani delegation in an advisory capacity.

According to a detailed note prepared by the Ministry of Interior's education division in 1948, the British government had set up a committee that "collected factual data regarding the nature of the Indian Office contents and the circumstances of their acquisition." Other than the collections of the archives and rare material, it also took stock of the furniture of the building "which is old and valuable, [and] is stated to be a legacy from the East India Company."[17] The major task of the committee, however, was to discuss the possibility of dividing the India Office and its contents between India and Pakistan and settle a framework on the basis of which it could be carried out.

As for the manuscript collection and books, "Orientalist" scholars advised the British government to keep them in England, as the library had become an international institution. For the claim that most of the holdings were purchased out of Indian revenue, the British government argued this could not be applied to the entire library as a considerable amount of material was acquired before 1833, "when it was laid down by Parliament that the surplus profits of the East India Company should be held in trust for his Majesty for the service of the Government of India."[18] It was difficult to establish which of the books were purchased from utilizing Indian funds. The committee suggested perpetuating the library as a separate institution under a specially instituted trust body with representatives from India and Pakistan as well. The master of the rolls, custodian of the public records in United Kingdom, was to be asked about the records kept at the India Office. As for pictures, the British government claimed ownership since the bulk of it comprised portraits of British statesmen, soldiers, and officials who had served in colonial India. "These pictures are like a family portrait gallery illustrating the British connection with India," the report said, "and their value resides as much in their completeness as a collection as in their intrinsic artistic worth."[19]

From as early as 1948, the government of Pakistan decided that it should claim the entire contents of the India Office library and most of the manuscript collections. In an earlier brief prepared for Qureshi and Bokhari pleading Pakistan's case, a subsidiary argument was that Pakistan's capital, Karachi, had a geographical superiority over Delhi and London. As an international naval base and airport, it was a hub of traffic and conveniently accessible to Indian scholars, as it was nearer to the west than Delhi. Karachi as Pakistan's capital was "bound to develop as a cultural centre and it is the moral duty of the mother Dominion, the U.K., and the sister Dominion, India, to help in this development."[20] The brief claimed the entire collection by projecting Pakistan as the cultural inheritors of the Mughal Empire. Because the Mughals had de jure sovereignty over India until 1857, the brief said, all the purchases and acquisitions made by the East India Company—even if it held de facto power—was still technically owned in the name of the Mughals. On the basis of that, Pakistan had "an automatic claim" to everything purchased using Indian revenues to 1857 and a proportional claim to the rest.[21]

Because of the maximalist position taken by India and Pakistan, discussions and disagreements between the two governments stretched over seven years. Despite an attempt to reach a settlement as part of negotiations led by the education ministers of the two countries in 1955, the deadlock remained. Maulana Abul Kalam Azad from the Indian side insisted on the indivisibility of the collection and for keeping it in Delhi while offering additional copies, microfilms, and other facilities for Pakistani researchers. Such an outcome was most undesirable for the Pakistani side led by Colonel Imam Husain. In the end, both countries just agreed to disagree and issued a joint press communiqué to continue discussing the issue. The only point on which both parties agreed was that the India Office library and its contents belonged to the successor dominions of India and Pakistan.

The Ministry of Education, realizing the impossibility of the task arising out of the noncompromising claims of both sides, drew up alternative plans and a basis for negotiated settlement. For this purpose, the Ministry of Education set up a committee in 1955 comprising twenty scholars—all men—from East and West Pakistan. The committee met in Karachi in September 1955 to deliberate on various aspects of the collection and ways for an equitable distribution. The report drafted by the committee lamented the decisions of the Partition Council, as a result of which Pakistan had lost everything of value in regard to the division of libraries and records. This included the Imperial Library Calcutta, along with several other large, well-stocked libraries owned by the British Indian government. In the case of records, the Partition Council allowed one printed copy of the records of interest to Pakistan, if available, and left it for the Pakistani government to arrange to obtain microfilmed copies of the material of special interest. Because the Indian government had already obtained the bulk of books and records, and "already possess[ed] enormous advantage over Pakistan in the provision of cultural facilities," Pakistan was also to get its fair share as "Pakistan is as much a meeting ground of various indigenous cultures as India."[22] Thus, Pakistan's stance was that it was only fair that the entire content of the India Office be given to Pakistan.

As part of this strategy, the committee recommended insisting on acquiring books in sixteen of the ninety-three languages. This included Arabic, Persian, Urdu, Bengali, Sindhi, Pashtu, Baluchi, Punjabi, Turkish, Multani, and Kashmiri. The rationale was Pakistan's interest in promoting cultural ties with "Oriental countries." The scholars from these countries, the committee insisted, could easily visit Karachi for research. As a negotiating tactic, the alternative was that among the "Oriental" books, Pakistan was not to consider books in Avesta, Pahlavi, Hebrew, or Syriac. Pakistan did not object to handing over manuscripts in Sanskrit, Chinese, or Burmese to the Indian government. Punjabi books in Gurumukhi script were also to be given up.[23] This was being done to reduce the number and percentage of books demanded by Pakistan. By excluding these languages and scripts, the percentage share demanded by Pakistan would have been 36 percent. The explanation to be given to the British authorities was that, although Pakistan was interested in all works of art and culture preserved in the India Office, "its main interest lies in the material relating to Muslim and Buddhist cultures since Pakistan is pre-eminently a Muslim country with a large Buddhist population."[24] This was a projection of the two-nation theory onto the archival material, as it was based on a proposed division of "Islamic material" for Pakistan and "Hindu material" for India. Pakistan's claim over the "Buddhist material" was to serve the needs for scripting an ancient history for Pakistan that excluded Hinduism but accommodated Buddhism as part of Pakistan's national history and civilizational traditions.

For administrative records from 1757 to 1858, the committee advised against region-based distribution criteria, as northwestern India became a part of British India at a much later date, and so the content relating to present-day Pakistan would have been much less. It was therefore suggested that India should be convinced to agree to a division of records on a 50–50 basis. The proposal was for Pakistan to keep the original proceedings of the records whose counterparts were available at West Bengal's Calcutta Record Office with a reciprocal offer for India to take the original files for East Bengal.[25] The committee suggested similar alternatives to the division of records, the bulk of which was already in India. If India agreed to the sharing of government proceedings and selections, Pakistan was to reciprocate by giving India proceedings and selections relating to areas within its territorial limits from 1758 to 1947 in exchange for records from Delhi, Bombay, and Calcutta relating to Baluchistan, the North-West

Frontier Province, tribal areas, princely states acceding to Pakistan, and Sindh (including the period when it was part of the Bombay presidency).

The committee realized the limitations of its arguments about Pakistan's claim of Mughal inheritance and insistence on acquiring the entire manuscript collection relating to Islamic history. If the entire collection could not be handed over to Pakistan and there had to be a basis for division, what was nonnegotiable for the committee was that the ratio of this division must not be less than 60–40, or three to one between India and Pakistan. The committee felt that Pakistan would not be able to build up a proper national library and archive if it got less than 33 percent of the contents of the India Office. Such a division, the committee predicted, would have an abysmal outcome for Pakistan, as it would "neither be able to attract foreign scholars interested in the oriental learning nor will it benefit the Pakistani scholars in their research work."[26] The committee insisted on rejecting India's proposal to adopt the criteria set by the Partition Council for other forms of assets and liabilities. As the committee pointed out, the proposition of 82½ and 17½ for India and Pakistan, respectively, was applicable only to the division of the "unallocated debts" between the two countries and did not have any bearing on the physical division of assets.[27] The libraries, records, and manuscripts, the committee said, were items of cultural importance and administrative value, and it was not possible to assess their value in terms of money.

Because of the failure of India and Pakistan to agree on a negotiated settlement and the British insistence on the indivisibility of the archives and the collection, the records remained in London. But successive Pakistan governments continued to negotiate with the British authorities to arrange for acquiring copies of relevant material. Eventually, an agreement was signed in 1975. Under this exchange agreement between the newly constituted National Documentation Centre and the India Office Library, microfilmed copies of records, official publications, private collections, departmental papers, press materials, and maps were to be provided to Pakistan. A Camera Unit was to be set up in the India Office library at the expense of the government of Pakistan.[28] The exchange of material since then has greatly enriched the availability of colonial records relating to the regions of present-day Pakistan.

A similar understanding was agreed on in the Partition Council, whereby Pakistan was to be allowed access to record listings and indices in Delhi for a possible sharing of these records.[29] This arrangement, however, never materialized. In the resolutions passed at the Pakistan History Conference, the government of Pakistan was routinely reminded to "make renewed efforts . . . to implement the decision of the Partition Council in respect of the division of archives of the pre-Partition Government of India at any early date and to secure the share of the Government of Pakistan." The government representatives attending the conference told the historians that they were negotiating the matter with the government of India.[30]

For its part, the Pakistani government held back Indian shares of the material it desperately needed. For instance, in 1958, before the scheduled meeting of the Punjab Partition Committee, the Ministry of Education advised holding back India's share from the Lahore Museum (8,125 coins and 785 library books) until it handed over to Pakistan its due share in the Delhi Museum and other important historical records.[31] A similar decision was taken with regard to records from the Punjab archives, as India was refusing to give copies of records to East Bengal.

Until the formal acquisition of material from the India Office and in the absence of collaboration with the Indian government, the Pakistani government took other measures to set up libraries and archives for the task of history writing as a national project. The bulk of what came to be established as the national archives were the records of Jinnah papers, Muslim League papers and Fatima Jinnah papers. The Ayub Khan regime, under the pretense of cracking down on the corrupt practices of the Muslim League government of the preceding decade, had seized its records from the party headquarters and dumped them in a cellar. When I. H. Qureshi came to know about the deterioration of the Muslim League records lying in the cellars of the Special Branch office, he used his influence over Ayub Khan and convinced him to hand over the documents to Karachi University, where they could be properly preserved and cataloged. A freedom movements archive was then established at Karachi University. A huge preservation project was undertaken to preserve the cache of documents received from the Special Branch office. When these documents were finally brought to Karachi University in 1966, they were in extremely bad shape. They were packed in 123 gunny sacks and 46 steel trunks. The inventory included one hundred thousand documents, including over twenty-five thousand of the Pakistan Muslim League.[32]

Around this time, perhaps after the death of Fatima Jinnah in 1967, the Jinnah papers had also been acquired by the government of Pakistan. The Historical Records and Archives Commission for Pakistan discussed this collection at length. It was initially left with the Ministry of Education, but because it lacked the expertise and facilities for such a collection, the commission recommended setting up an autonomous organization along the lines of the Atomic Energy Commission for proper preservation and maintenance of these records of "vital national importance."[33] The project of safekeeping the Muslim League records and making them available to scholars for research had still not been completed as the process was estimated to take at least three more years. This meant that even by its fifth meeting held in 1970, the commission had not been able to set up a national archive or make available vital records relating to the Muslim League and Muhammad Ali Jinnah. All it could do was to continue to urge the government to redouble its efforts to acquire Pakistan's share from the India Office library or, pending the final outcome of these negotiations, at least pay for the acquisition of copies immediately required by scholars.[34] The Pakistan Historical Society had by that time lost most of its initial energy and political support. Its own stated mission of reprinting Persian classics and works on the freedom movement had not resulted in more than a dozen publications.

A purpose-built building for the archives was finally constructed in Islamabad in the late 1980s. Since then, the National Archives in Islamabad has become the repository of material relating to Muhammad Ali Jinnah's private and public life, the files he had personally seen as Pakistan's first governor-general, Fatima Jinnah's private papers, and All-India Muslim League records. All this material has been copied and made available for open, off-the-shelf access in the main reading room. The underlying idea was to enable and facilitate research in areas conducive to the growth of awareness relating to Muslim nationalism, the role of the Muslim League during the colonial period, and contributions of such figures as Jinnah and Fatima Jinnah. This regimented labyrinth of the "record" aligns with Mbembe's concept of the architectural dimension of the archive's power and status encompassing its physical space, motifs, columns, room arrangement, and other features.[35] The archive shapes the master narrative as much as the master narrative shapes the archive.

This discussion shows how the historicization of archives works to create national narratives by prioritizing and privileging specific stories and peoples.[36] Officially sanitized archives have been collected in such a manner as to curate the past through a specific lens of deterministic evolution of the Muslim community in South Asia and its march toward the acquisition of statehood. In addition, it has influenced the way in which numerous officially sponsored cultural organizations patronize academic works on Iqbal, Islam, Urdu, and art. In this manner, the Pakistani historical narrative shaped largely by such ideologues as Qureshi has been sustained through a research infrastructure that seeks to promote a selective approach to academic research and history writing.

INSTRUMENTS OF HISTORY MAKING: THE ALL PAKISTAN HISTORY CONFERENCE

Despite their official connections and intellectual prowess, scholars-cum-politicians and bureaucrats like Ishtiaq Husain Qureshi and Sheikh Muhammad Ikram were not the only ones involved in the rewriting of the history project. There were a number of other historians involved, including members of the larger public commenting on these issues. For instance, immediately after Pakistan's creation, Abdullah Qureshi wrote an article in *Nawa-i-Waqt* in which he emphasized the need to revise the history curriculum. Qureshi talked about the biases of both Hindu and British historians who, according to him, had purposefully maligned the reputation of Muslim rulers and undermined their achievements. Because the examiners in the universities were mostly Hindus, said Qureshi, Muslims had no option but to abuse their Muslim heroes to score higher marks.[37] Qureshi's opinions were echoed by an editorial published in *Nawa-i-Waqt* in April 1949 criticizing the continuation of old Urdu textbooks that talked about the benefits of British rule and the importance of showing obedience to it.[38]

The impetus for a professional historians' forum—the Pakistan Historical Society—and its annual All Pakistan History Conference came from another eminent historian, S. Moinul Haq. He was supported in this endeavor by Fazlur Rahman, the minister for education.[39] The society was to serve as a "permanent body which was to produce historical literature of national importance, add to country's cultural wealth and intensify patriotic feelings among educated classes."[40] For this purpose, a meeting of historians was convened in September 1950, which eventually set up a historical society registered under Act XXI of 1860. The first All Pakistan History Conference was then held in March 1951 in Karachi, inaugurated by then governor-general Khawaja Nazim-ud-Din. Rahman had also set up a board for "preparing a history of the Subcontinent based on original sources and containing an objective study of the problems of history."[41] The book published by this board was entitled *A Short History of Hind-Pakistan*.

Convened by S. Moinul Haq for the first time in 1951, the annual sessions of the Pakistan History Conference continued to be held for many decades. Although the conference lost its significance in later decades, in the 1950s it was accorded a great deal of importance. The proceedings of the conference were covered on the front pages of the major English dailies, and leading Pakistani politicians delivered keynote addresses at its meetings. The *Civil and Military Gazette*, for instance, covered the proceedings of the conference with a lead headline on the front page: "Call to rewrite history of Islam"[42]—words taken from Fazlur Rahman's speech in which he had highlighted the role of historians in building an Islamic state. In its editorial the next day, the *Civil and Military Gazette* described the conference as attended by "a galaxy of history scholars." It lamented that the history textbooks so far had only fed the Muslim youth a caricatured account of Islam's revolutionary spirit. Echoing Rahman's idea, the editorial advised historians "to bring out the inner urge that provided the dynamism behind the history of Islam."[43] One finds a replication of this theme in subsequent years as well, since all presidential speakers in different history conferences spoke about it. Fatima Jinnah, for instance, while inaugurating the Society of Islamic History and Culture at Karachi University, called for "the study and re-writing of Islamic history and re-assessment of Muslim culture in a correct and rational spirit."[44]

The Pakistan Historical Society, then, promoted the writing of history through the lens of "Islamic ideology." At the first conference held in 1951, for example, there were only two sessions: the first on Islamic history and the second on the history of the subcontinent, along with an exhibition of Islamic art and artifacts. In his keynote address at the first All Pakistan History Conference, Nazim-ud-Din reiterated the problem of historical distortions. The history written and taught at schools and colleges to Muslim students during the colonial period, he said, either ignored Islamic history or presented it in a biased manner, with the result that "their hearts were empty of any feelings of pride in the achievements of their ancestors because they were ignorant of them."[45] The issue of rectifying historical biases and prejudices was repeatedly taken up during the 1950s. In his address, Iskandar Mirza, too, talked about the need "to re-evaluate the history of Muslims in Indo-Pakistan sub-continent and rescue it from inaccuracies and prejudices which have developed around it either through ignorance on our part or by the design of others."[46]

The conference panelists and historians associated with the Pakistan Historical Society did not simply give statements about these issues; they also strategized to overcome deficiencies in the historical literature. To this end, the annual conference passed resolutions to seek funds from the central government. In 1952, Fazlur Rahman, Pakistan's education minister, set up a board of historians "to prepare an authentic History of the Freedom Movement of Muslims in the Indo-Pakistan sub-continent covering the period from the death of Emperor Awrangzeb in 1707 to the establishment of Pakistan in 1947."[47] It was to be chaired by Dr. Mahmud Husain, minister for Kashmir affairs, and its members included I. H. Qureshi, minister for refugees and rehabilitation; Professor A. B. A. Haleem, vice-chancellor of Karachi University, and Sayyid Suleman Nadwi. The committee thus constituted was notified in the official gazette as well. The bias in favor of a North Indian Muslim aristocratic and intellectual elite in the membership of the committee was evident. After Nadwi's untimely death in 1953, the board was reconstituted to include S. M. Ikram; M. B. Ashraf, who, like Ikram, was an officer from Pakistan's civil service; Dr. A. Halim, professor of history at the University of Dhaka, and Dr. Muhammad Nazim.[48] The first volume in the planned series was published in 1957. By the time the second volume appeared in 1960, the project had been wrapped up. Subsequent volumes were published under the auspices of the Pakistan Historical Society from 1970 onward.[49]

Even before the publication of the first volume in this series, another work—produced under official tutelage and commissioned specifically for the purposes of writing an "authentic" history of the subcontinent—was published in 1955. *A Short History of Hind-Pakistan* was produced by the Pakistan History Board, which comprised Mahmud Husain, I. H. Qureshi, A. B. A. Haleem, A. Halim, M. B. Ahmad, and S. Moinul Haq. Contributors included A. Halim, A. H. Dani, Riazul Islam, S. M. Jaffar, S. M. Ikram, S. Moinul Haq, M. H. Siddiqi, and R. E. M. Wheeler, among others. In his foreword to the book, Rahman reemphasized the importance of history—or the rewriting of history—for the nation-building project, especially where society was being raised based on an ideology.[50]

This book was, therefore, the first specimen of a master narrative of history that has since been reproduced, with some revisions, in Pakistan in officially sponsored histories, biographies, and textbooks, and also promoted through the availability of selective information in the archives, libraries, and institutes of cultural and historical research. It focuses on all the issues that have been relevant to the shaping of a Muslim identity in the twentieth century. This involves such questions as the following: What is the history of Islam in India? What have Islam as a religion and Muslims as a civilizational force contributed to Indian society and religion? How do we evaluate the role of Muslim monarchs in the region? Is it possible to "own" the history of the premodern era as a period of glorious achievements for nation-building purposes while adjusting it to the requirements of the modern state?

The first, most noticeable thing about this book is its title, which uses the term *Hind-Pakistan* instead of *South Asia*, *subcontinent*, or *Indian subcontinent*. This reflected a concern on the part of the Pakistani intelligentsia, which, after giving up on the heartland of "high culture" of Muslim civilization in North India in exchange for an independent homeland, still extended civilizational claims to the wider region. In many ways, this book follows the pattern set by historical works written during the colonial period. It starts off with a chapter on the geography of the region and its relevance to the course of historical events that had unfolded since antiquity. This is followed by chapters on the prehistoric period, the Indus Valley Civilization, Aryan invasion, Greeks, Mauryas, Guptas, and so on. There is even a separate chapter on the "Neo-Hinduism" of the South and the dynasties of Cholas, Pallavas, and Chalukyas.

It does not try to skip over the "Hindu part" of the history or hide it under the broad cover of Aryan history. It describes the Vedas, the Mahabharata, and the Gita in general terms without any negative criticism and does not gloss over the cultural achievements of the pre-Muslim period. About the Gupta period, for example, it says: "The Gupta Age marked the culmination of ancient Indian culture. It was a period of great development in art, sciences and literature, as well as in contacts with the outside world."[51] It does, however, refer to the caste system and devotes a chapter to Buddhism and Jainism, described as a revolt against this rigid classification and oppression.

The book's appraisal of Islam and Muslim rulers is almost uncritical. This can be seen from its description of figures like Mehmud of Ghazna and Aurangzeb, and the defense, or even glorification, of some of their actions, which had become contentious since the advent of academic historical research in India. The book describes the Somnath expedition of the eleventh century as "an outstanding military feat in the annals of Islam" whose success "sent a thrill of joy through the Islamic world," with the Caliph responding with delight by conferring the title of sultan on Mehmud.[52] The book could easily have described the event of Somnath without eulogizing it, but it deliberately adds descriptions of appreciation in line with the idea of a distinct Muslim identity or Muslim nationalism as established by the two-nation theory. In his presidential address on the historic occasion of the Lahore Resolution in March 1940, Jinnah said: "It is quite clear that Hindus and Mussalmans (Muslims) derive their inspiration from different sources of history. They have different epics, different heroes, and different episodes. Very often the hero of one is a foe of the other and, likewise, their victories and defeats overlap."[53] Mehmud's invasion and victory is the best example of such a historical conflict between heroes and villains.

Despite official patronage and wide availability of resources, the Pakistan History Board's academic output was unimpressive. The *Morning News*, in its editorial published on 12 January 1956, criticized the performance of the conference, which, despite its existence since 1951, had failed to produce more than translations and reprinting of manuscripts. The newspaper noted that the Asiatic Society and Munshi Nawal Kishor Press could "claim to have done more, in half a decade, for the cause of Islamic history than the History Conference of Pakistan."[54] It acknowledged the difficulties faced by historians, such as lack of access to required material but asked as to the measures that had been taken to address this problem.

The situation changed with the imposition of martial law in 1958 and Ayub Khan's vision to set up a "modern Islamic state." Like any other strict disciplinarian from a military background, Ayub Khan had a vision of authority and power that emanated from the center. Such centralized authority required a singular idea of nationhood as well. To materialize it, he established the National Reconstruction Bureau to initiate major reforms, invite proposals, and set up commissions to probe issues relating to education, curriculum, national language, and script, among other things. Ishtiaq Husain Qureshi shared this vision and was one of the chief collaborators working on different projects relating to the rewriting of history.

Working with the government to use history for nation-building purposes was in perfect concordance with Qureshi's views about history and the tasks performed by historians. It is not merely through geographical proximity, said Qureshi in his presidential address at the annual history conference, that a feeling of oneness is created: it is history that makes nations. If the historical triumphs or failures of one group create opposite feelings in another group, the historical project of molding people into one nation cannot be accomplished. This was evident, he said, from the recent experience of Hindus and Muslims and their mutual contestations regarding the events and interpretations of history. Therefore, it was important "to instil a sense of a common past among a people if it is to be moulded into a well-integrated nation with loyalties seated within the deepest recesses of the heart. This process need not be a falsification of history; it can be its discovery."[55] It is with this vision and motive that Qureshi penned his most important work, *The Muslim Community of the Indo-Pakistan Subcon-*

tinent (610–1947), which was first published in 1962. It was written during his visiting professorship at Columbia University after the dissolution of the Constituent Assembly in 1954 of which he was a member and a cabinet minister.

By the late 1950s, after the imposition of martial law, Qureshi had been approached by the military regime to help draft a new education policy. He returned to Pakistan, where he quickly became involved in various projects. One of the many projects assigned to Qureshi was to follow Ayub Khan's instructions to write a book on the role of the ulema in the Muslim political movement of South Asia.[56] This became the basis for another important work by Qureshi, *Ulema in Politics: A Study Relating to the Political Activities of the Ulema in the South-Asian Subcontinent from 1556 to 1947*. His most important task was to head a committee of historians appointed in January 1965 to write an authoritative account of the history of Pakistan.

Unlike *A History of Hind-Pakistan*, this venture was to receive direct official support and was meant to be a more rigorous academic work for students as well as scholars. Members of the committee included S. M. Sharif, I. H. Qureshi, S. M. Ikram, A. R. Mallick, A. H. Dani, Abdur Rashid, Waheed-uz-Zaman, and Muniruddin Chughtai, among several others. *A Short History of Pakistan* was published by the University of Karachi and comprised four volumes, with I. H. Qureshi serving as its general editor. Each volume was to be written by a different author or group of authors. To ensure internal consistency in the text, the committee drafted a detailed conceptual note.

The name of the cabinet file containing these proposals is revealing and self-explanatory: "Compilation of Books on (i) the need for a strong centre and (ii) the history of Muslims in East Pakistan." This was in line with Ayub Khan's vision of the centralization of authority for cultivating a sense of national unity.

In the committee discussions, the members noted that because the book was going to be brief—just 650 pages—the emphasis would be on the present-day regions of Pakistan. Other parts of the subcontinent were not to warrant detailed coverage. For example, in the case of South India, the committee suggested that attention be paid only to Muslim settlements and dynasties "whose achievements in the field of culture contributed to the mainstream of the Culture and Civilisation of the people of Pakistan."⁵⁷ In the name of making history contemporaneous with regional and world developments, it was suggested that "emphasis should be laid on the contiguous countries to the North West and in case of East Pakistan the role of that part of Pakistan in the South territories as a bridge between India and South East Asia."⁵⁸ Pakistan's proximity to Southeast Asia through its eastern wing was a rationale for Pakistan's membership of the American-led Southeast Asian Treaty Organization (SEATO), which included member states from that region. To serve the strategic purposes of seducing a Buddhist clientele, Qureshi had molded his writings accordingly, for example, for an audience in Thailand. In a lecture series sponsored by SEATO, Qureshi talked about Buddhism's rich legacy in Pakistan. He said: "As a matter of fact, we ourselves have only recently been rediscovering our Buddhist past. We look upon it as a part of our history and we are proud of it. A measure of that pride, perhaps, you can see from the fact that we have a little documentary film to show to our own people and to people in other countries what a glorious past we had in the realm of art contributed by our Buddhist ancestors and forefathers."⁵⁹

Qureshi used the opportunity to talk about oppressive Brahmanical forms of Hinduism which made it difficult for Buddhist culture and religion to survive, and the points of congruence between Islam and Buddhism as a result of which Buddhists either voluntarily converted to Islam or simply enjoyed the benefits of a more peaceful life under tolerant Muslim rulers.

The task of official history writing was, therefore, to serve these strategic interests, and to establish the history of Pakistan as distinct from that of India. Recent historical works, the committee said, "deal with the history of the sub-continent as one unit and treat the history of Pakistan as having branched off from the main stream of historical developments in the area. [The h]istory of Pakistan, thereby, is relegated to a position of secondary importance and is in the process dwarfed."⁶⁰ This marks the beginning of the process whereby the use of the term *Indo-Pakistan subcontinent* or *Hind-Pak* was discouraged.

A precedent for it had been set a couple of years earlier in 1964, when, in response to an advertisement published in *Times* magazine describing Khyber Pass as a gateway between Afghanistan and the "Indian-subcontinent," the Pakistani government deliberated alternatives for a nomenclature that either failed to account for Pakistan's distinct entity or subsumed it as part of any indivisible Indian whole. The note prepared by the Bureau of National Research and Reference listed some options. It referred to *Dawn*'s practice of distinguishing between British India and independent Bharat as one example. This division, the note said, portrays Pakistan as a secessionist state. Although the note was appreciative of the Pakistan Historical Society's coinage of *Hind-Pak* for undivided India, it observed that Hind, like Bharat, lacked popular currency globally. A pro-Pakistani British historian, Ian Stephens, had proposed—"semi-seriously" according to the note—to combine the names of the two capitals Delhi and Karachi and to call the region Delkaria.[61] The Pakistani government was eager to adopt a nomenclature that did not leave any ambiguity about India and Pakistan as two distinct states, carried a historical sanction, and was likely to gain global currency and wide usage.[62]

Failing to arrive at a solution and finding even *Indo-Pak subcontinent* too India-centric, the proposed history project was to ensure disengaging Pakistan altogether from the subcontinent by giving Pakistan a history distinct from that of India or a narrative that was not centered on India. This was why the committee, in its guidelines for authors, made suggestions such as emphasizing the importance of Mehmud Ghaznawi's attempts to "incorporate the Punjab into his kingdom with a definite purpose."[63] Mehmud's empire did not extend far into areas of post-1947 India, but the fact that a major chunk of territory of present-day Pakistan was tied up with a dynasty based in present-day Afghanistan meant that a disconnect with the history and geography of India could be argued for. In a similar vein, the process of the expansion of power or invading armies—whether of Muslims or non-Muslims—was to be explained as a movement from the northwest or northeast to other parts of India. The conquest of India was to be interpreted "as the eastward expansion of West Pakistan and the westward expansion of East Pakistan."[64] For example, the Indus Valley Civilization, Aryan invasion, and the ancient great kingdoms started from the northwest and ultimately made their influence felt in the east as well. Similarly, it was from East Pakistan that the kingdom of Sasanka and the rulers of the Pala and Sena dynasty moved to North India to conquer the upper Gangetic valley.⁶⁵ This showed the thrust of movement from northwest and northeast, that is, from West and East Pakistan rather than India, establishing the importance of a region that comprised Pakistan as the center of historical developments in South Asia rather than tying it (in a subordinated manner) to the history of India or the Indian subcontinent. However, it was not just Islam but non-Muslim invaders who served the purpose of showing the timeless territorial integrity of West and East Pakistan, their congruity of purpose, and distinctness from the landmass of India. In such a historical understanding, the state precedes the nation—a narrative that contradicts the Muslim League's projection of Pakistan as a homeland or sovereign state for a Muslim *qaum* that had always existed from the moment of its arrival in South Asia.

The new narrative proposed by the committee envisaged East and West Pakistan as sharing the same historical timeline and serving as centers of activity that influenced developments taking place in India. Temporally synchronized and geographically significant, militaries from these regions were to be shown as moving toward India in a pincer movement. India, in this way, becomes a site of invasion and conquest where East and West Pakistan intersected, thereby bringing about a national unity of the two regions. This is how the Indian empire of the Muslims was to be explained: a joint effort by East and West Pakistan. To further strengthen the argument for national unity, the need for centralized authority was to be emphasized by describing "the role of a strong Central Government in giving unity to the Muslim nation, maintaining its power and prestige throughout its history."⁶⁶

The deliberations of this editorial board resulted in the publication of *A Short History of Pakistan* in 1967. As the general editor of the book, I. H. Qureshi theorized about the possibility of writing a history of Pakistan. He asked whether it was possible to sufficiently disentangle the history of Pakistan from the history of India. His assessment was that for certain periods of history, it was possible, while for other periods, events had such regional and localized impact that for proper contextualization an understanding of developments taking place within the larger area was required.⁶⁷ This stood in stark contrast with Qureshi's earlier works, already discussed in this chapter, in which his entire focus was on tracing the historical roots of Muslim identity through the developments taking place in the "high culture" zone of Muslim aristocracy in North India. But he seemed to persist in his understanding of Muslims as outsiders in India, as he distinguished between the history of India and Muslims as the arbiters of India's history. Qureshi was himself aware of the controversy generated by such an approach. He further added: "This fact needs recognization [*sic*]. And if it is recognized, no eye brows will be raised on the title of this book, even though sometimes the most significant drama may have been played outside our boundaries. Sometimes movements have taken birth or received their inspiration in Pakistan, though they worked themselves out in India as well. When the novelty of some of the ideas put forward in this book wears off, there will be less reluctance to accept its approach to history in placing the emphasis on Pakistan and Pakistanis."[68] This discontinuation of the established historical tradition of approaching Muslim history within the category of the Indo-Pak subcontinent (*barr-i-saghir Pak wa Hind*) posed a serious intellectual question for Qureshi, as he himself had been a practitioner of this tradition. In line with the guidelines set by the regime of Ayub Khan, he had to emphasize the importance of the present-day regions of Pakistan as the source of many historical developments that took place within the wider region. For those historical events that could not be explained within this framework, Qureshi uses the metaphor of the history of "this land and these people" as a stream "which sometimes flows by itself and sometimes it commingles its waters with other streams." But this stream was never lost, he writes. Because Islam alone could not have given this historical narrative the much-needed antiquity and continuity required by a nation-state, Qureshi talks about the unity of the regions of Pakistan as having "existed, by whatever names they might have been known before the present country of Pakistan came into existence."[69] This is an indirect reference to non-Muslim invaders from the northwest and northeast.

In this manner, the historical origins of Pakistan, the maintenance of its geographical boundaries, the distinctiveness of its cultural milieu, and its influence on the history of "India" (rather than the other way around) serves as the central, connecting theme in all four volumes of this book, which covers the period from the Stone Age to the end of British rule in 1947. This required a major theoretical revisioning of the overall way of writing history, which was deliberated by the committee in its concept note and elaborated by Qureshi in his introduction.

NATIONS AND COMMEMORATIONS: A NATIONAL CALENDAR FOR PAKISTAN

The selectivity of the process whereby certain aspects of the past are emphasized through commemoration or celebration of events while others are ignored or suppressed are both parts of the same process that seeks to give a certain direction to the narrative of the history of the nation and the nation-state. These aspects of national memory and amnesia—a commemorative narrative, as Yael Zerubavel calls it—is common to every project of identity formation, but its peculiarity is more pronounced in a postcolonial state like Pakistan which has certain cutoff dates and ruptures but is simultaneously eager to emphasize certain continuities in its trajectory and antiquity in historical tradition.[70] The arbitrariness of shaping a commemorative master narrative is, therefore, more pronounced in Pakistan's case, as rupture and continuity figure prominently and simultaneously.

Some major aspects of this commemorative narrative were settled during the lifetime of Jinnah and his tenure as the governor-general of Pakistan. On 12 December 1947, the prime minister of Pakistan, Liaqat Ali Khan, suggested that the birthday of the founding figure of Pakistan—Muhammad Ali Jinnah—be celebrated as an official holiday. Because Jinnah was born on 25 December—already a holiday because of Christmas—it was suggested that Jinnah's birthday be celebrated on 26 December. This suggestion was then approved by Jinnah himself.[71] As a result, 26 December was declared as a closed holiday and various ceremonies, such as flag hoisting and parades, were performed on that day. For subsequent years, however, Jinnah's birthday was celebrated on 25 December and no separate holiday was announced for 26 December.

A major decision during Jinnah's lifetime and tenure as governor-general that shaped the commemorative narrative was on the celebrations for Independence Day. Liaqat Ali Khan wrote to Jinnah recommending the celebration of Pakistan's Independence Day on 14 August instead of 15 August.

Jinnah agreed to this suggestion. It was clearly stated in the official correspondence that this was not particular to that year alone; rather, Pakistan's Independence Day was going to be celebrated on 14 August every year.[72] The decision to opt for 14 August was highly arbitrary and did not conform to a strict chronological rationale. The British lapse of paramountcy took place on the midnight of 14–15 August. India and Pakistan had not become independent until the clock struck midnight. But the arbitrary decision to opt for 14 August as Independence Day was meant to establish the distinctness of Pakistan and the "birth of the nation" by its separation from India.

Additionally, the government decided to co-opt the Islamic calendar to give a sacred aura to the founding moment of Pakistan's creation. As per Liaqat Ali Khan's statement, the date of 14 August 1947 was doubly auspicious for Muslims, as "it was a lucky coincidence that it fell on the 26th of the holy month of Ramzan—the day preceding the night—'the night of power and excellent' (*Lailat-ul-Qadr*). It was in the middle of that night the Book was opened to the thirsting soul. According to the Islamic calendar the anniversary should have been held on the 26th Ramzan."[73] Therefore, Khan's government announced celebration of Thanksgiving Day on Ramadan 26, that is, 2 August 1948. For "convenience sake," however, state celebrations to mark the first Independence Day were held on 15 August 1948. But the *hijri* dates remained an important part of the debate on the national calendar and demands were occasionally made by private citizens and religious organizations to introduce it in Pakistan and replace the Georgian calendar. Mufazzal Haider Chaudhury, a lecturer in Bengali at Jagannath College in Dacca, also objected to the continued use of the term *AD* as it stood for *anno Domini*—in the year of the Lord. "Now the question is," he wrote, "whether we can call Jesus Christ our Lord" because only Allah is our Lord.[74] Dr. Sukumar Sen, of Calcutta University, suggested a way out by using the term *AC*—after Christ.

Various public performances and displays of power also served a pedagogical function of cultivating a sense of loyalty and striking awe in the citizens as spectators. The celebrations of some of the national days were carefully planned in advance with minute attention to detail in curating them. For instance, in the case of Milad—the Prophet Muhammad's birthday—both these purposes were ideally served.

The demand raised in the Constituent Assembly of Pakistan in April 1950 to celebrate Milad as a "state function" led to discussion in the cabinet about the term and the performances expected for such an occasion. Being cognizant of the varied practices in Muslim countries, ranging from the holding of a reception by the head of the state and the delivery of speeches to the flying of flags and observance of a holiday, the cabinet approved similar celebrations for Pakistan. A public holiday was to be observed, with flags hoisted on government buildings and such activities as special radio transmissions, local meetings to celebrate the occasion, and feeding of the poor.[75]

A more elaborate pedagogical performative was developed for the first Independence Day—Yom-i-Istiqlal, as it was called. It started with prayers for Pakistan's safety and well-being in mosques and other places of worship. The national flag was to be hoisted on government and nonofficial buildings. For a spectacular show of state power, "a three-mile long column of the Pakistani military was to march from government house on the Mall road to Zamzam (near the office of Lahore Corporation). The Governor would take the salute of honor (*salami*) near Queen's statue."[76] There was to be free distribution of food, lighting up of buildings, and a *jalsa* (public gathering) by the Muslim League outside Mochi Gate. Detailed instructions were issued urging the citizens to observe discipline:

(a) The Pakistani army is your army. This is one of the world's best fighting forces. You should be proud of it. You are invited to come and see the parade [performed] by this army on *Yom-i-Istiqlal*, and while you are witnessing it, follow the instructions of police to maintain discipline and order [*zabt wa nazm*].

(b) People will not be allowed to assemble between the government house and the Queen's statue. People will be allowed to stand in two lanes from Narain Das building till the Zamzam.

(c) At the pedestal [*salami lenay ki jagah*], a few people will be allowed to enter. For this purpose, permits will be issued. For special guests, seats are being arranged.

(d) Children should be kept safely. They must be prevented from crossing the Mall road to the other side. The path for the military parade must remain absolutely clear.[77]

The parade was therefore as much about the expression of the state's sovereign authority as a spectacular performative tool to discipline the bodies of the citizens. The state has replicated these practices and routines for major events like Independence Day, Republic Day, and Defense Day.

A curious anomaly in performative practices as a form of pedagogy for citizenship was the observance of the centenary of the Indian revolt in 1957. Given the anxieties about the political fallout and the rekindling of acrimonious, anticolonial sentiment in the Commonwealth, the British government was eager to prevail upon India and Pakistan to tone down the celebrations. Still, Suhrawardy's government at that time demonstrated considerable enthusiasm in planning an elaborate series of activities to commemorate the centenary in Pakistan.

One of the reasons was the Pakistani government's eagerness to preempt India's attempt to take the initiative and distort the history of the Pakistan movement and discredit Muslims.[78] To prevent that, the cabinet approved a weeklong celebration starting with a public holiday on 11 May 1957—the outbreak of the Meerut rebellion—and "culminating in a grand climax and the last day of the week also be declared a public holiday." Public meetings were to be held throughout the country, starting with a recitation of the Quran and *fateha* for the martyrs of the struggle. "Mammoth public processions" in all important cities were planned "headed by and interspersed with Units of the Pakistan Armed Forces." Special flags commemorating the event were to be designed and sold to the public to raise funds, which would be used to construct parks and hospitals as memorials. One day of the commemorative week—Zafar Day, as it was called—was to focus exclusively on Bahadar Shah Zafar, the last Mughal emperor. The cabinet note proposed that exhibitions be held to highlight the history of the revolt, chairs set up in universities for Mughal history, and foundation stones laid for the construction of town halls and public parks to be "given appropriate names like Zafar Memorial Hall or Bahadur Shah Park."[79]

The government also planned special radio broadcasts featuring songs "in praise of the exploits of the Mujahideen" along with discussions on the writings of poets and writers like Ghalib, Shefta, Mufti Sadruddin

Azurda, Altaf Husain Hali, and Hasan Nizami to highlight various aspects of the struggle. According to the original plan, several books on the history of the revolt were to be published. These included a book in English, Urdu, and Bengali on "Muslim Resistance against the foreign rule leading up to the 1857 struggle," an anthology of revolutionary verses, a short biography of Bahadur Shah Zafar, leading Muslim personalities of 1857 and so on. Important works on this theme, such as Syed Ahmad Khan's *Causes of the Indian Revolt* and Hunter's *The Indian Musalmans*, along with works of Ghalib, Zafar, and other poets were to be reprinted.[80] The government vowed to appoint scholars "to examine original documents of the early British Period available in the sub-continent or in the 'Indian Office'" to produce "authentic records of the history of those days." But hardly any of these elaborate plans were executed. Although a notification was issued on 2 April 1957 to observe the first day of the centenary week, that is, 10 May 1957 as Zafar Day and declare it a closed holiday, none of the numerous scholarly activities came to fruition. Even the armed forces were to be kept away from celebrations on the pretext that it was going to cost a lot of money to the government. There is no mention in the file as to why these elaborate plans were suddenly dropped, especially when the cabinet had given approval and even issued a notification for the declaration of a public holiday. A milder version of the centenary week did take place, as newspapers in East Pakistan, at least, covered Prime Minister Suhrawardy's address to the nation on Zafar Day and wrote an editorial on the commemorative activities. Even with its toned-down version, the centenary week of 1857 and Zafar Day show the importance of commemoration in transforming a historical event to an episode of national biography required for scripting the nation in a preferred narrative structure.

A SUITABLE NAME: ISLAMIC STREETS, MUSLIM CITIES, AND DE-ETHNICIZED PROVINCES

The national temporal template for ordering the rhythm of life is similarly projected on the spatial plane to produce power effects of the state, its sovereign performativity and intrusion into the realm of everyday interactions. Two aspects of these effects and performances are in the naming or renaming of cities, institutions, and roads, and dotting of the urban text with a semiotic order of symbolic power with selective monumental designs, statues, and cultural artifacts.

There is extensive literature on the naming or renaming of street names, often with a focus on the changes in nomenclature following the collapse of an authoritarian regime. The examples of regime change leading to renaming practices include the dismantling of South African apartheid, the destruction of Saddam's Iraq, and the liberation of the former Soviet bloc in Eastern Europe, among many others. Like newly liberated states emerging from authoritarian rule, postcolonial nation-states like Pakistan seek to rewrite the urban space as a political act of resistance to deconstruct the violence of the past, by dishonoring the individuals associated with it and replacing them with those identified as national heroes. What is different, however, is the nature of the urban text itself.

In the case of the Global South, modern cities with their "civil lines" were adorned with symbols of colonial authority and apparatuses of power. For instance, as William Glover's work on the making of modern Lahore shows, the British colonial authorities implemented a rational order of space with the Mall as the main artery dotted with such structures as the High Court, General Post Office, Aitchison College, and the Punjab Legislative Assembly. It was a deliberate attempt to move away from the labyrinth of congested old streets and narrow lanes, which the British viewed as diseased, irrational, and uninhabitable. The old city was built with its own sense of spatial ordering in the form of intricate webs of interconnected *mohallahs* and *katras*, often named after the community or predominant kin group, craftsmen, or artisans living there. The newly built roads and boulevards, however, were named after colonial officers and administrators.

In the case of former Soviet satellite states, many boulevards already existed and were not built under communist rule; only their names were changed to reflect the ideological tilt of the state. In the postcolonial context, the politics of renaming is about not a reclaiming or rectification but an active, ongoing contestation of the past. The recognition of this distinction is significant, as it can help explain the outcome of the politics of renaming in postcolonial states, setting it apart from other similar cases.

In Pakistan, the politics of nomenclature was less about erasing the colonial past and more focused on giving an Islamic orientation to the urban text by renaming places formerly associated with non-Muslim residents and notables. Soon after independence, the Lahore Municipal Corporation started planning "Islamic names" for seventy-six roads.[81] The most bizarre example of this is found in the discussions of the Lahore Municipal Corporation, where, in 1952, one member, Malik Muhammad Akhtar, proposed a change of Lahore's name to Dasht-i-Muhammadi.[82] This was probably to give Lahore an aura of sanctity and also to nullify the mythic association of the city with Ram's son Loh. Akhtar also suggested renaming roads after Muslim scholars, Sufis, and martyrs who, according to him, brought this region out of darkness, fought jihad against the infidels, and made Lahore the abode of martyrs (*ganj-i-shuhada*). Other members made a number of similar suggestions as well. A councilor demanded that the name of Guru Tegh Bahadur street be changed to Aurangzeb Street, as Tegh Bahadur was an enemy of Islam and Aurangzeb.[83] Another councilor's recommendation was that because Muhallah Ram Garh was populated by Muslim *muhajirs*, it should be renamed Mujahid Abad, and Ram Garh Colony should be renamed Mujahid Colony.[84] After the Pak-India war of 1965, Mian Muhammad Sharif, councilor from ward 26, Jamia Ashrafiya, presented a resolution demanding that all roads named after non-Muslims should be renamed after the martyrs of the 1965 war.[85] The resolution was passed and a subcommittee was constituted. The government, however, said that it would not be advisable to change all names at once. In the light of this advice, the committee changed only the names of major roads. Housing schemes, buildings, and parks were to be changed later. A list of sixty major roads was prepared. It included McLeod, Nicholson, Abbott, Club, and Lawrence roads, among many others. Other than the martyrs of the 1965 war, Muslim notables were also to be honored. The list included the names of Hamid Nizami, Malik Barkat Ali, Hafiz Kifayat Husain, Husain Shaheed Suhrawardy, Ata Ullah Shah Bukhari, Gama Pehalwan, Aurangzeb, Sultan Salahuddin Ayyubi, Sheikh Ahmad Sirhindi, Shabbir Ahmad

Usmani, Ashraf Ali Thanawi, Maulvi Abdul Haq, Hazrat Bilal, Amr bin Aas, Imam Malik, Imam Shafi, Imam Abu Hanifa, Imam Bukhari, Imam Hasan, Imam Husain, Imam Muslim, and many others.

Not all members were supportive of a blanket erasure of non-Muslims, especially Hindus, from the urban landscape of Lahore. In an earlier discussion on this issue in 1955, Malik Ghulam Nabi and Sheikh Rafiq Ahmed argued against the changing of names. They called it a cheap publicity stunt and emphasized the need for preserving history. If heroes were to be honored, Rafiq said, schools and parks should be built and named after them. He said that if Indians started doing it, no place with a Muslim name would be left in India.[86] Not all demands for name change were driven by an anti-Hindu agenda or led to a more Islamic name of the area. For example, the proposal was to change Cooper Road to Bijli Ghar Road, Beadon Road to Mina Bazar Road, Circular Road to Gol Sarak, and so on.[87] Montgomery Road was to be renamed Shahra-i-Rumi to mark the occasion of an international conference on Rumi studies attended by scholars from Afghanistan, Iran, and Turkey.[88]

The demands for removing Hindu names or honoring a national hero were regularly raised by citizens in the national press. Abdul Alim Morris from Karachi wrote in a letter to the editor that renaming of roads was long overdue. According to him, Hindu-dominated municipalities were biased in naming major thoroughfares after Hindus. There was a road named 45th Indian National Congress Road in the city. He did not favor changing all the names, just those that caused offense. For him, a tit-for-tat backlash from India was not a concern, as such a process was already underway. Jinnah Memorial Hall in Bombay had been renamed Congress House, he wrote, and Islamic College of Calcutta had become Central College, while Mirzapur Park of Calcutta was renamed Sradhanand Park. As to hurting the feeling of minorities, he asked "a pointed question": "Is every act of ours, however, Islamic, patriotic, reasonable and rational, to be determined by the feelings of the Hindus? Has not the Islamic name of our Republic been adopted in spite of the opposition of the Hindu members of the Constituent Assemblies? And what about the clause in our Constitution that the Head of the State should always be a Muslim? Then why strain a gnat when you can swallow a whole camel?"[89]

In similar words, other citizens from Karachi regretted continuation of "Hindu names" in the city or congratulated the commissioner of the city for such acts as restoring Shivaji Park to Aurangzeb Park.[90] A related concern for fellow citizens was to demand naming of a road to honor a national hero. This was especially true for citizens from East Pakistan who persistently wanted acknowledgment of an iconic status for Nazrul Islam. In May 1951, a proposal was made by the Youth League to change the name of Nawabpur Road to Nazrul Avenue. In a letter to the editor, Begum Husne Ara and Burun Nahar recommended choosing an area of academic and cultural significance to dedicate it to Nazrul.[91] Rafiqur Rahman Bhuyan, from Dacca, lamented that Nazrul, a legendary Bengali poet, was paid a stipend of 150 rupees per month, whereas Maulvi Abdul Haq, a respected Urdu scholar, was paid 500 per month. He suggested weeklong celebrations in May to mark the poet's activities and included demands for naming a hall after him in Dacca University, declaring a holiday (on the date of the Bengali calendar), naming a road and school after him, increasing his stipend, and sending him abroad for medical treatment.[92] The official position was to decline such requests because of Nazrul Islam's lack of association with the ideology of Pakistan. In his note dismissing the proposal to rename Fuller Road to Nazrul Avenue in 1950, D. K. Power, secretary to the government of East Bengal, observed that while Nazrul Islam was the most famous Muslim Bengali writer to date, he did not have any "intimate association" with Pakistan, as he was living in India. He was mentally unbalanced, and before he became imbalanced, "he married a Hindu girl and gave up, at least partially, an Islamic mode of living."[93] Honoring such a person in an Islamic state was going to arouse trouble, wrote Power, especially when many of Pakistan's more illustrious sons had not yet been commemorated. Besides the political objection, Power raised a linguistic concern as well. Nazrul Avenue, he wrote, would be a misnomer, as it did not convey the meaning unless the complete name of the poet was used.

At the government level, no consistent policy was pursued. On the one hand, successive governments were keen to keep good relations with the British Commonwealth, but on the other hand, they also recognized the importance of scripting an ideological agenda by renaming streets, cities, and institutions. In a summary for the cabinet prepared by the Bureau of National Reconstruction in January 1962, the martial-law regime evaluated the rationale of renaming as undoing traces of colonial legacy and because "some of the names do not come off the tongue easily as a large section of our population is not well-versed in English."[94] Deciding on the feasibility of changing the names of streets proposed by the Karachi municipality, the cabinet urged a cautious approach, as there were also several cities named after colonial officers, such as Lyallpur, Montgomery, and Cambellpur. Before taking any final decision, the cabinet warned that extending the policy to include Hindu names—such as Gandhi Gardens in Karachi—would invoke an Indian response of renaming Jinnah Hall in Bombay. Also, the cabinet urged that the approach to Britain not be "coloured by the sentimentalism of a young nation emerging out of a colonial past." It therefore recommended that only those names might be changed which "in some way commemorate the extension or reinforcement of British imperialism," whereas names given "as a mark of recognition to individuals who were responsible for the founding of a new settlement or for the development of a new area or a new place may be retained."[95] Similarly, the cabinet allowed the retention of "non-British names" for the time being. However, this policy could not be sustained for too long as the names of Montgomery, Cambellpur, and Lyallpur were gradually changed to Sahiwal, Attock, and Faisalabad, respectively, and became widely popular. Following the policy of honoring "benevolent colonialists," the names of Jacobabad and Abbottabad have remained unchanged.

A related concern was to rectify the spellings of districts and towns that had been Anglicized during the British period. The initiative was taken by the government of East Pakistan in January 1958. Following the precedent set by India in restoring the correct phonetic order of local names, the government of East Pakistan proposed Dhaka for Dacca, Sillat for Sylhet, Bogura for Bogra, Jashohar for Jessore, Maimansingh for Mymensingh, Komilla for Comilla, and Chittagong as Chatgaon.[96] Various ministries of the central government opposed this proposal. The Ministry of Defense argued that these spellings had been in use in international maps and records for a long period of time. The Ministry of Communication took a similar stance, especially on the names of Dacca and Chittagong, since they were part of the international postal and telecommunication network.⁹⁷ The Ministry of Interior thought the proposed change was unnecessary, as resources would be wasted in changing names in official records, and it would take time to popularize the new spellings. It also pointed out the inconsistencies of the Indian policy that had apparently prompted the demand from the East Pakistan government. While India had changed the spellings of Benaras and Cawnpore, the Ministry of Interior's note highlighted, it retained the spelling of Delhi which should have been "Dehli." Instead of mimicking the Indian action, the note suggested following the Islamic tradition where "our Prophet (peace be on him) did not change the pre-Islamic name of Mecca and Medina or the spellings thereof."⁹⁸ The Department of Railways urged the government of East Pakistan to be mindful of the historical significance of the name of Chittagong, commemorating peace between the king of Arakan and the residents of the place, and to take into consideration the efforts put in to popularize the city as a major international port.⁹⁹ In practical terms, the proposed "original" spellings were hardly an improvement on the given ones or failed to capture the lived reality. As Ziauddin Ahmad, of the Ministry of Education, pointed out, there was hardly a difference in spelling Comilla as Komilla. As regards Sylhet, he said, Sillat did not exactly match the popular Bengali name, Silet. For a more meaningful relationship between the place, its name, and pronunciation, Ahmad recommended Sil-hat, that is, a marketplace for stones.¹⁰⁰ Because of this overwhelming barrage of criticism from various ministries, the proposal was eventually shelved.

While successive governments remained uneasy about the "sentimental" approach of erasing all traces of the colonial past by renaming roads and cities, they agreed on the importance of nomenclature for provincial units in cultivating a sense of national cohesion. The focus of this approach was on the divided provinces of West Punjab and East Bengal. The move was ostensibly planned to respond to the Indian government's naming of East Punjab and West Bengal as Punjab and Bengal in the new constitution. The urge to enforce a severance from India was so entrenched that there were reports of a proposal to change the unit of Pakistani currency from rupee to *hilal* to differentiate it from Indian currency.¹⁰¹

In November 1949, the central government proposed the name East Pakistan for East Bengal—a proposal supported by that provincial government as "the name 'East Pakistan' has already achieved considerable popularity and currency."[102] The problem with this appellation, as pointed out by the Ministry of Law, was that there was not a corresponding Western wing of a single unit of East Pakistan—an "anomaly" that was finally rectified in 1955 with the promulgation of One Unit in West Pakistan by merging all its constituent provincial and administrative units under one government.[103]

For West Punjab, various proposals were floated. The Ministry of Finance proposed renaming the province as Pak Punjab or Iqbalistan.[104] Writing in a letter to the editor, Muhammad Aziz Khan suggested using Pak Bengal for East Bengal.[105] At the official level, the Ministry for Industries agreed with the name Pak Punjab, because Pakistan had inherited five rivers, and the major region was historically known as Punjab. For North-West Frontier Province, the minister suggested the name Sairab to denote the province's water resources and possibilities of future growth and fertility. But because this name lacked any historical precedence, the minister recommended changing it to Khyber.[106] The purpose of all the names was to play down the ethnic content of the provinces rather than rectify the geographical anomaly resulting from Indian appropriation of provincial names. Of all the names, only East Pakistan was legally adopted and constitutionally enforced. West Punjab simply became Punjab. It took a long, drawn-out struggle to get North-West Frontier Province's name changed to Khyber Pakhtunkwa in 2010. The Pakistani state had deep-rooted anxieties about giving ethnic credence to the term Pashtun or Afghan because of neighboring Afghanistan's irredentist claims over Pakistan's large Pashtun-dominated areas.

The East Bengalis were not all happy with the proposed name change. In various letters to the editor, concerned citizens argued that it would be unfair to deprive the people of East Bengal of their historical identity. Professor D. N. Banerjee, professor of political science at Calcutta University, in a letter to the editor argued that such a move would deprive the Hindus of East Bengal a connection with the Hindus of West Bengal—the connection of being Bengalis.[107] Also, he said, it would be a unilateral modification of the terms of the Independence Act, which both dominions had agreed on. Maula Bakhsha, of Dacca, was opposed to the change, as provinces were component parts of the whole and "a unit cannot unduly associate with it the name of the whole of which it is a part only."[108] He further added that the major part of the undivided Bengal—Bangala as he called it—belonged to Pakistan, while Rhur or West Bengal was with India. He, therefore, demanded the province be called Bangla, as even Bengal was Anglicized.

There was limited support for the move to override the ethnic identity at the expense of Muslim nationalism. Hafiz Abdus Samad, from Chittagong, supported the change, as Bengali "always had the sense of a 'Hindu Bengalee,'" and the Muslims of the province, whenever prompted to introduce themselves, referred to their Muslim identity rather than calling themselves Bengalis.[109] Still, the right-wing Urdu press and its readers supportive of Muslim nationalism as the exclusive form of identification for the citizens of the new state were anxious about any traces of ethnic identity in Bengal. In a letter to the editor, Hakim Muhammad Husain was concerned about "brotherly relations" between East Bengalis and Hindu Bengalis, which, as such, was not a bad thing, but it could pose a serious threat in prevailing circumstances. According to him, credible sources confirmed the preference of East Bengalis for Hindus of East and West Bengal over the Muslims of West Pakistan. "In these circumstances," wrote Husain, "it is important that the name Bengal is erased altogether from Pakistan [*Bengal ka naam Pakistan kay safah-i-hasti say mita diya jaye*]. This name should not appear in writing so that eyes can't read it nor in speech so that ears can't hear it."[110] It was with this mindset of Bengali-phobia that the Pakistani state established the One Unit scheme to effectively enforce a unitary form of government. As part of the new policy, East Bengal eventually became East Pakistan in 1955.

A public debate about "suitable names" started again in the late 1950s, when Ayub Khan's regime decided to transfer Pakistan's capital from Karachi to a new location closer to the military headquarters in Rawalpindi in the Pothohar plateau of Punjab. The government announced a competition, inviting proposals from the citizens to recommend a name for the capital city. M. D. Altafur Rahman, from Rangpur, suggested the name Paindabad. Every time someone pronounced it, he wrote, it would bless the capital.[111] Alimuddin Ahmed, from Dacca, proposed Pakbad for the new capital, as it was "short, simple and sonorous."[112] Akhtar Husain from Karachi suggested two names—Urooj and Faizan: Urooj reflected the lofty ideals of Ayub Khan for progress and the geography of Pothohar; Faizan was to be the name of the second capital in East Pakistan, as it was "to establish closer contacts with our brothers living hundreds of miles away and to strengthen the bonds of unity that the second capital is to be built in that province." Also, it would show that the eastern wing would not be neglected and should "receive the fullest benefits of the revolution."[113] In the end, however, the regime decided on Islamabad as the name for the new capital. It was not the first city to be named as such. As already mentioned in the introduction to this book, a resident of Khotiyan had recommended Islamabad as a new name for his village to replace the more embarrassing meaning associated with its appellation. M. Alay Hasan, from Dacca, wrote in the newspaper—a couple of years before the government even started planning the building of a capital city—that the old name of Chittagong port mentioned in maps and books was Islamabad.[114] During the British period, Chittagong was abandoned and the Calcutta port flourished. Once an Islamic republic had been established, he wrote, it was in tune with its ideological basis to restore the original name and call it Islamabad Port.

The sovereign performative power through naming is thus a product that de Certeau would describe as "imaginary totalizations produced by the eye," articulating "constellations that hierarchize and semantically order the surface of the city" aligned with a preferred rationalized historical framework.[115] Through a discussion of the politics of naming in Pakistan, I have understood this framework as constitutive of the erasure of certain names, the privileging of Muslim heroes, and a praxis privileging an idyllic Islamic past and undermining an ethno-linguistic basis of identity. In other words, it is a "semiotic structure of city-text" through which to read the master narrative of history undergirding it and the ideological discursive order stabilizing its meaning.[116]

SCRIPTING THE SPACE: STATUES AND MONUMENTS

The visual objects as an aspect of commemorative narrative of the city-text were of central significance. As bearers of symbolic authority—whether of the colonial state or its successors—these structures adorned the major thoroughfares, crossings, and public buildings, and they communicated a language of power through which to legitimize authority and inscribe a normative politico-moral code among subjects or citizens. In the postcolonial moment, the erasure of colonial symbols of authority carried as much importance as instituting newer modes to serve a connection with the foundational basis of the new state. What was common to acts of erasure and remembrance was their performative, almost ritualistic nature. For instance, in November 1949, a grand ceremony was held to reopen the gate of Lahore Fort—a symbolic, inaugural act of the Pakistani state as a continuation or inheritor of the Mughal state.[117] The fort had remained closed to the public and served as a garrison for almost one hundred years after the British annexation of Punjab in 1849. What gave this act a spectacular mythical aura was the widely held view of the fulfillment of a prophecy that the Lahore Fort would reopen only once Muslim rule was reestablished in the region.[118] To further augment this connection between Pakistan and the revival of preexisting Muslim authority, S. M. Aslam—a reader from Bombay—suggested that Jinnah should visit Bahadur Shah Zafar's grave to pay homage and also because "such a visit from the first Governor-General of Pakistan to the last Emperor of India may perhaps bridge the gap between 1857 and 1947."[119] He also suggested building of a "befitting monument" there. To mark the inaugural moment as a triumphalist reassertion of Muslim rule, the Lahore Improvement Trust had suggested the building of a tower or victory monument outside Shah Alami Gate in Lahore. Writing an essay in a newspaper in 1950, Professor Syed Abdullah Muhammad Shuja-ud-Din recommended copying the Qutub Minar as an appropriate design for a victory tower and the area of Begumpura as an appropriate site, where an enemy of Muslims, Banda Bairagi, was put to death, and where his executioner, Abdul Samad Khan, Nawab Zakariya, and his daughter Sharf-un-Nissa, were also buried.[120] For him, the purpose of the monument was to keep the memory of the victor of Delhi alive so that the future generations could follow his footsteps and "the idea of expanding the boundaries of Pakistan remains fervently alive [*mojzan rahay*] in their hearts."[121]

But except for a few funerary monuments of national importance, successive Pakistani governments were less interested in constructing material symbols of authority in the form of towers, swords, or other artifacts, and more focused on dealing with the legacy of symbolic, visible remnants of the colonial past in the form of statues and crosses. Even for the British on the eve of Partition, the preservation of these symbolic visual artifacts was of key importance. Built from a colonial perspective of instituting colonial authority as a civilizational force or to commemorate the violence of the 1857 war, these public monuments were considered by the British to be important to preserve as a reminder of the empire's "contributions" to the region. Throughout the 1950s, the British Foreign Office anxiously followed the developments in India and Pakistan as both countries actively worked to remove statues and other public symbols remindful of the colonial past. As Paul McGarr's extensive documentation on the removal of British statues of queens, kings, and colonial officers shows, the British interest was seldom promoted by an aesthetic consideration but was to preserve intact the symbolic power of the empire.[122]

There is extensive archival material in the British Library and the National Archives at Kew Gardens dealing with the protection of British-era monuments, especially cemeteries. The Commonwealth Relations Office, along with the British High Commission in India and Pakistan, worked closely with voluntary associations like the groups of former civil servants or local churches to ensure the maintenance, protection or, in some cases, the transportation of the monuments. Writing in 1960, the British High Commission reported 206 cemeteries in Pakistan, most of which were abandoned or closed, with only 35 open.[123] Other than these, there were a number of important tombs of British soldiers and administrators, such as that of John Jacob at Jacobabad and Sandeman at Las Bela, and the Nicolson monument on the Grand Trunk Road, the Vans-Agnew monument at Multan Fort, and the Miani battle monuments near Hyderabad. Following the advice from the British High Commission in Delhi, the Karachi office sought to cultivate better relations with the Archaeology Department, as, by law, it was custodian of the monuments. The policy worked well for monuments, as they were different from cemeteries, which could easily fall into neglect if not regularly maintained, or statues that could be removed from the public square. Nicholson's column, for instance, is a towering structure that has remained unharmed while statues have been removed and the cemeteries poorly kept. The only change was a government decision in 1969 to rename Nicholson's column as Margalla Monument. Instead of a glorification of Nicholson's victory, the following text was to be inscribed on the monument: "John Nicholson, Brigadier-General in the British Army, was shot dead in 1857 by the freedom fighter Kaleh Khan."[124]

Paul Patrick, of the Commonwealth Relations Office, laid down the initial policy regarding removal of statues. In a letter dated 27 October 1948, he recommended getting in touch with the governments of India and Pakistan "if a particular memorial is dealt with contemptuously or offensively." He agreed with the idea of taking over smaller transportable objects, such as paintings and busts, and the handover to local committees and associations if they could pick up the cost of transporting them.[125] As a matter of policy, the Commonwealth Relations Office was of the opinion that no notice should be taken against random actions or demands for removal of a statue "unless a demonstration was held of a nature derogatory to British prestige; or unless the statue was relegated to a contemptuous new site or wantonly demolished."[126]

Most statues of any historical or sentimental value for the British were in India. These included memorials in Kanpur and Lucknow to commemorate the killings of European women and children in 1857, and numerous statues of former viceroys and governors-general in Lytton's Delhi or the former imperial capital of Calcutta. Nehru's policy was that historically significant statues that did not cause offense were to be installed in the museum. The rest could be taken by anyone interested in them. In the case of Pakistan, two British-era statues acquired significant political importance and alarmed the British High Commission and the Commonwealth Relations Office. One of them was Queen Victoria's statue at Charing Cross and the other was the Lawrence statue on the Mall.

The statue of John Lawrence erected in 1887 in front of the Lahore High Court had a long turbulent history and was at the center of a sustained anticolonial resistance movement for its removal. Lawrence was the first chief commissioner of Punjab after the annexation of the region in 1849 and was credited with laying down the administrative structure of imperial rule in Punjab. In this larger-than-life statue, Lawrence was depicted as arrogantly holding a pen and a sword, provocatively putting to "the natives" the question: "Which will you have, pen or sword?" The statue became the focus of nationalist agitation from 1899 onward. The nationalists demanded the removal of the offensive inscription or replacement of the statue. The British refused to budge. Finally, in 1925, Lawrence's pen and sword were broken by some "unknown assailants." The police arrested the beggar who had initially reported the incident. In a poetic rendition of this act, Zafar Ali Khan—the editor of an Urdu daily and a prominent political figure of Punjab—took a jab at the broken sword and pen of Lawrence as a sign of its redundancy in India's changing political climate.[127] Even if the British still had the bayonet, he wrote, the ascetic power of a fakir's club was powerful enough to counter it.

The statue remained in a damaged condition until the end of the British Raj. The *Nawa-i-Waqt*, in an editorial on 11 April 1949, lamented the continued existence of the Lawrence statue with its inscription, which, after agitation, was changed to say: "I have served you with the pen and the sword." But as the editorial pointed out, "Lawrence *bahadur* was holding the pen and showing the sword in a manner that [it is difficult] to believe his 'service' [*khidmat*] and his posturing [*tewar*] [do not] suggest as if General *sahib* is making a threat."[128] Finally, in August 1950, the provincial government removed the statue and put in the Lahore Fort. *Nawa-i-Waqt* celebrated the act as the removal of a relic of a brutal past and appreciated the policy of putting these artifacts in the Lahore Fort, "where many relics of the past stare at each other."[129] In a follow-up editorial, *Nawa-i-Waqt* criticized the government for taking so long over the decision. It took three years of hard work, campaigning, and dozens of reminders, the editorial said, after which the *tunda lat sahib*—a pun to describe the statue's broken arm—was removed to Lahore Fort.[130] Other than statues, what the newspaper found even more oppressive was the Christian cross for medical services in Pakistan. Even in secular Turkey, it said, the Red Crescent was used instead of the cross. Similarly, there were various regiments that had the cross on their flags. A flag's purpose, it said, was to inspire a soldier. A Christian cross would fail to inspire a Muslim soldier for jihad, and so it demanded a replacement of all such symbols and relics.

To avoid the specter of a populist movement demanding the removal of statues, the central government was forced to deliberate on the issue and come up with a policy statement. The issue of statues at public places in Pakistan was not limited to commemoration of colonial rulers but also the celebration of non-Muslim public, political, or philanthropic figures. With regard to colonial relics, successive Pakistani governments had to act carefully so as not to alienate Western allies or hurt their sensibilities. In a comprehensive review of the policy on statues discussed in 1951 before the removal of Queen Victoria's statue, the central government invited comments from provinces and various ministries. In its preparatory note, the Ministry of Home Affairs described colonial-era monuments as an anachronism in a free Pakistan and repugnant to Muslim sensitivities. It therefore proposed the removal of the statues from public places to museums.[131] All provincial units supported the policy without reservations. But a serious concern was shown by the Foreign Office. In a secret telegram sent to the prime minister on 26 February 1951, Ikramullah, of the Foreign Office, cautioned against the policy, as it could have significant political repercussions. "The existing statues are at best relics of a bygone period and may be left standing," he wrote.[132] He also submitted a supplementary note about practices in Iran, Turkey, and Egypt, where "the exhibition of statuary does not offend the susceptibilities of the public."[133] Even if the statues were allowed to stay in public, Ikramullah said, no one was going to worship them. After prolonged discussions and several postponements, in a notification dated 15 June 1951, the government of Pakistan decided to remove the statues to museums "gradually and only after certain amount of publicity had been undertaken in support of this policy, such publicity laying emphasis on installing them in museums rather than their removal from public places."[134] As a result, Queen Victoria's statue was removed from Lahore's Charing Cross.

As the *Pakistan Times* coverage of the event showed, Queen Victoria's statue was removed, put on a cart, and dumped in the basement of the Lahore Museum. According to the paper, about two dozen persons were engaged in removing the statues, starting at nine in the morning. Underneath the statue was a sealed glass jar with a seventeen-page booklet listing the names of donors who had contributed to the construction of the statue. The information in the booklet recorded that total subscriptions of twenty-seven thousand rupees were raised, and the total cost of the statue was twenty-four thousand rupees.[135] By eleven o'clock, the statue had been "de-platformed" and put on a cart for its transportation to the museum amid a large number of spectators.

In an article published in the *Civil and Military Gazette*, the step taken by the government to remove statues was hailed as the right move to save this historical legacy from damage. By placing them in the museum, "the intention is," the author said, "to collect all such precious monuments from every nook and corner of the country to enrich the National Museum and preserve them from possible damage and destruction. The statues are crystallised remembrances of a past, which is cluttered with hope and glory, frustration and despair. They are projections from a period of our national existence out of which the present is a fulfilment in evolution. Sad or sweet, that past is ours and it can never fail to be of invaluable guidance and absorbing interest occasionally to have glimpses into past struggles and fulfilments."[136]

The article then criticized any variant of extreme nationalism that might revel in vandalizing such important works of art and history. It also pointed out the religious sensibilities in the country against sculptural representation of human figures which, according to the author, was another reason to remove statues from public places. It was in deference to this feeling of repugnance, the author said, that not a single statue had been raised in the memory of Quaid-i-Azam, who was worthy of utmost respect and adoration. The author went on to say that even Pakistan's postage stamps and currency carried no human images.[137] The article rebutted the suggestion to hand over these statues to the church since they were not erected because the monarchs belonged to a particular faith, but because of their importance in the history of British India. The author, therefore, described the removal of statues not as an anticolonial, nationalist act but to safeguard and preserve history by putting them in the national museum.

The handout issued by the Press Information Department on 28 July

1951 also emphasized the historical importance of these statues as the reason for their removal from public places. The note stated that the Pakistani government intended "to remove *all* statues, irrespective of nationality, from public places to various museums in the country. These statues are historically and artistically important to Pakistan and there is absolutely no question of Pakistan parting with them. There [*sic*] removal from public places implies nothing in their permanent preservation in national museums as significant historical monuments."[138] The UK high commissioner who sent these news items and handouts to the Commonwealth Relations Office mentioned that the article in the *Civil and Military Gazette* was written in the Ministry of Information and could be read as an official policy of the government. He also confirmed that the removal was not the result of an organized protest against the statue. The British diplomat could do little more than to rely on "native superstition" as a source of comfort for himself and the Commonwealth Relations Office and to write that "the Statue itself is still locally revered and the opinion has been expressed that its removal is a bad omen."[139] Still, the British authorities were satisfied that the statue was kept in a museum with limited public access as opposed to the Lawrence statue, which was lying in the fort. A campaign was therefore launched for the recovery of the Lawrence statue as it became one of the very few artifacts that the British authorities were interested in protecting.

The official policy was that the government could not spare funds for its removal from Pakistan and repair and preservation in the United Kingdom, as it would lead to numerous similar requests. The initiative for protecting the statue was taken by the Old Boys' Association at Foyle College in Northern Ireland, of which Lawrence was a prominent alumnus. The association relied on the network of old Imperial Civil Service officers who still maintained active links with Pakistan and carried the goodwill of many of its civil and military officers. L. G. P. Freer, secretary of the Ministry of Health and local government in Northern Ireland, and himself from Foyle College, wrote to Edward Muir in the Ministry of Works on 12 May 1958 about the possibility of transporting Lawrence's statue, the cost to be borne by his friends from the college who had floated the suggestion. Muir passed on his request to the Commonwealth Office.[140] The fact that

General Nicholson's statue was successfully transferred from Dehradun to Belfast added to the enthusiasm of those behind this initiative.

By the time the UK High Commission got involved in the negotiations on behalf of Foyle College's association, General Ayub Khan had imposed martial law in the country. The High Commission thought it would be expedient to delay the request, as the new regime, "with their respect for things British and their possibly greater appreciation of the historical significance of British statues may perhaps restore those which have been removed."[141] There was never popular demand, wrote the high commissioner, to remove the statues in the first place and the masses were mostly indifferent on the issue. A number of "sensible people," he said, would like to see the statues back. On 19 August 1959, W. S. Ferguson, of the Old Boys' Association at Foyles, was informed by the High Commission that Pakistani authorities seemed keen to retain the statue and display it in a museum in Lahore Fort once renovations were done.[142] Failing to achieve this purpose, the High Commission contacted the new government about the possibility of a handover. A representative from the High Commission visited the statue in Lahore Fort and found it to be "an imposing piece of work because of its size."[143] The statue was in good shape, except for the damage done to its sword and scabbard.

The decisive role in the handover was not played by the High Commission but by Sir Olaf Caroe. As a former Imperial Civil Service officer and author of a popular work on Pashtun history, Caroe commanded considerable respect among Pakistani officers. He personally wrote to General Ayub Khan to request the transfer of the Lawrence statue from Lahore to Northern Ireland. Writing on behalf of Khan, Lt. General K. M. Sheikh told Caroe about the president's decision to remove the statue from Lahore to England provided its original inscription was not restored.[144] On receiving the president's letter, Caroe wrote to E. W. Trotman, secretary of the Imperial Civil Service (Retired) Association, to convey Pakistan's concern. But Caroe thought it was important to restore the pen and sword while agreeing with Pakistan's request for not restoring the inscription.[145] On its arrival in the United Kingdom, Trotman informed Foyle College about the condition of the statue and the repairs it needed which, in his estimate, would cost around £225.¹⁴⁶ Eventually, the statue was reinstalled and unveiled at Foyle College in 1963.

While it was easier, despite the threat of diplomatic pressure, for the cabinet to remove the colonial relics for their painful memories and the possible public backlash, the policy regarding statues of notable non-Muslims from the area presented a different set of challenges. Gandhi's statue in Karachi was one such problem. The government was wary of an unpleasant incident targeting Gandhi's statue which would cause international embarrassment. On the pretext that Pakistan could not provide round-the-clock security to the statue, and a general agreement on the nonpermissibility of representations of human figures in Islam, the government allowed the removal of statues of prominent non-Muslim personalities.¹⁴⁷ Gandhi's statue was taken over by the Indian High Commission and is now installed at its building in Islamabad. Statues of Lala Lajpat Rai and Sir Ganga Ram had been removed from Lahore and were given to the government of East Punjab soon after independence. In a letter to the editor published in *Imroz* in April 1948, Muhammad Din, from Lahore, demanded restoration of the statues. Din was of the opinion that regardless of his political views, Lajpat Rai was a great man of Punjab who started agitating against the foreign government when political awareness was lacking among the people.¹⁴⁸ Din was opposed to a general policy of the removal, as statues largely served commemorative purposes and it was not as if people were worshipping them.

This policy decision taken in 1951 was considered discriminatory by the local Hindu and Parsi communities, especially those living in Karachi. Between June and August 1957, seven statues were removed in Karachi. These included the statues of Hasa Singh, Sobhraj Chetumal, Herchand Rai Vishandass, Eduljee Dinshaw, Nader Shaw Eduljee, King Edward VII, and Lokmanya Bal Gangadhar Tilak, in addition to eight bronze decorative figures and statues of King Edward and Queen Victoria in Frere Hall. The Parsee community protested against the decision and demanded the restoration of these statues. When the matter came up for discussion at the cabinet level in 1957, N. M. Khan, the chief commissioner of Karachi, in a detailed note dated 24 August, advised against the restoration of statues in the city. He agreed to the handing over of Parsee statues to the community only if they were to be installed in areas exclusively inhabited by members of that community. He strongly disapproved of restoring the statues of the British monarch or the bust of Tilak, "as he had very little sympathy with the Muslims."[149]

The symbolic undoing of the Raj or dissociation from its material past was not just limited to the statues. As a Dominion of the Commonwealth—not to forget the extensive institutionalized presence of colonial administrative inheritance—Pakistan's legal and symbolic order was embedded in a subservient, deferential mode toward the Crown. A public avowal of it was politically disastrous and incongruent with the practical realities of Pakistan as a sovereign entity. Yet the Pakistani state had to faithfully follow this legal fiction with theatrical grandeur. When Queen Elizabeth ascended the throne, the government of Pakistan was confronted with the problem of devising an appropriate wording for her title. The United Kingdom had described her as "Elizabeth the Second by the Grace of God of the United Kingdom of Great Britain and Northern Ireland and of all other realms and territories, Queen, Head of the Commonwealth, Defender of the Faith." The cabinet summary noted variances in declarations issued by other members of the Commonwealth. Given the sensitivity of this issue and the projection of Queen Elizabeth as the Grace of God, the cabinet offered the following description: "Elizabeth the Second, Queen, Head of the Commonwealth."[150] This was approved by the cabinet on 18 June 1952, but the decision was deferred as the government continued to engage with the British government about their expectations for Dominions that were part of the Commonwealth. Eventually, the *Gazette of Pakistan* officially notified: "Her Majesty Queen Elizabeth the Second, has now become the Queen of her realms and territories and head of the Commonwealth." As per the notification issued in the *Gazette Extraordinary* on 10 February 1952, a public holiday was to be observed on 15 February 1952 on account of King George's death.

In the meeting held on 13 February 1952, the prime minister told the cabinet of his consultation with Mufti Muhammad Shafi and Abdul Hamid Badayuni on the possibility of attending a memorial service for the late king. Both of them opined against it. Shafi said that if "there were a hall separated from the hall in which the service is held it would be unobjectionable for Ministers to be present in that hall during the ceremony." It was pointed out that memorial services held during the British period were not compulsory for non-Christians.[151] As an alternative to a memorial service, therefore, it was decided to observe a two-minute silence and a fifty-six-gun salute on the day of King George's funeral on 15 February 1952, which had already been marked as a holiday. The government of Pakistan was clueless about the protocol to be observed for the coronation of Queen Elizabeth. It looked at the precedent followed in British India in 1937 and the celebration programs issued in South Africa and New Zealand. It eventually decided to issue a notification for a public holiday.

Another attempt at dissociation from the burden of the colonial past was made by calling for disavowal of military badges and colors of honor earned for battles against Muslims and their own countrymen. In a meeting held on 6 April 1960, the cabinet decided that these honors should not be carried on new colors. The summary for the cabinet drafted by S. Fida Hassan on 24 March 1960 referred to a Divisional Commanders' Conference at which the question was raised "whether honours for battles fought under the pressure of foreign yoke, by the Indian Army Unit, now forming part of the Pakistan Army, against Muslims of Afghanistan, Persia, Turkey, etc. and against their own countrymen in Mysore and during the Mutiny of 1857 and against the Frontier Tribes, etc., should be retained or not." Most commanders agreed that it was a matter of shame and should not be continued. The opposing view was that "history cannot be changed." The honors were granted for "battle efficiency, fighting qualities, discipline and *spirit* [sic] *de corps*, etc., than anything else."[152] The commander in chief of the army, however, was of the opinion that the honors were a matter of shame and must not be carried on the new colors. Despite the army chief's approval and the cabinet's endorsement, the decision was rescinded on the General Headquarters' (GHQ) insistence. In its defense, the GHQ argued that it was anomalous to allow individuals to retain decorations for their acts of gallantry and deny the same privilege to a unit for their collective performance. Besides, such awards, the GHQ argued, were "always in recognition of the performance of acts of gallantry or distinguished service, and should, therefore, have no bearing whether the opposing force was our own countrymen or other Muslim countries."[153]

A NATIONAL MUSEUM FOR PAKISTAN

Foucault described museums and libraries as "heterotopias of indefinitely accumulating time" and reflective of modernity's will "to enclose in one place all times, all epochs, all forms, all tastes, the idea of constituting a place of all times that is itself outside of time and inaccessible to its ravages, the project of organizing in this way a sort of perpetual and indefinite accumulation of time in an immobile place." We can further complement Foucault's reading of the museum as a general archive by alluding to his description of the archive as such which determines that there is no endless accumulation in an amorphous mass nor an inscription in an unbroken linearity, and to ensure that "they are grouped together in distinct figures, composed together in accordance with multiple relations, maintained or blurred in accordance with specific regularities."[154] In that sense, museums function on the basis of an "archeological epistemology" to give the material fragment of the past a place in a coherently knitted visual representation of the national historical narrative. In this manner, museums mediate the past, present, and future by giving a "material form to the authorized versions of the past" and enabling states to use museums "to represent themselves to themselves, as well as to others."[155] But this process of "defining themselves," as I have been arguing, is a contested process, and this contestation is played out in the case of museums as well. Also, museums do not simply serve to legitimate ideology or encompass the national historical narrative; they are institutive of it as well. As Mrinalini Venkateswaran's work shows, the collection of artifacts and its curating are part of the process of forming a metanarrative of the national history. She cites extensive archival evidence to document it as a process "in which historians, archaeologists, art historians, museum curators, and archivists all play a role."[156] In this manner, Venkateswaran brings museums to the center stage of discussion about the nation-making process and a pedagogical tool through which to educate the citizens about the ideas of heritage, antiquity, history, and belonging.

Amid the chaos and violence following partition, the Pakistani government did not lose sight of the importance of the cultural artifacts and their significance in building a national historical narrative of the origins of Pakistan as an ancient land with a young nation. The discussion of museums was among the agenda items of the Partition Council. With regard to the museums, the Partition Council had decided that the museums should be divided on a territorial basis. The original items removed from a museum for temporary display from 1 January 1947 were to be returned. Accordingly, the government of Pakistan forwarded a list of fourteen items to the government of India of exhibits removed from Taxila and Mohenjo-daro. Despite several reminders, no response was received from the government of India.[157] An additional problem was the condition of the Lahore Museum, which had suffered a great deal as a result of Partition. As "A visitor" wrote about the experience of visiting the museum in 1952, the Lahore Museum lacked an expert curator, guidebooks, informative lectures, qualified staff well versed in history, and postcard-size pictures of important collections for sale. The author lamented that there were no worthy successors of such eminent curators as Sita Ram, Gupta, Fabri, and Maulvi Zafar Hasan. Instead of holding informative lectures, as in pre-Partition days, it was being treated simply as a "show-house of curiosities and a centre of recreation during leisure hours."[158] The process of rehabilitation and reorganization of the museum started in 1955. The tussle for administrative control was finally settled when, in 1969, an autonomous board of governors was created under the West Pakistan Government Educational and Training Institution Ordinance 1960.[159] In 1975 the administrative control was transferred to the Information and Cultural Wing of Services, General Administration and Information Department.

At the time of Pakistan's creation in 1947, the country only had sixteen museums. Since then, thirty more museums have been added. This includes the Archeological Museum in Saidu Sharif, to house Buddhist and Iron Age material excavated by an Italian mission, followed by another archeological site museum at Banbhore. Mughal and Sikh galleries were established at Lahore Fort in 1964. In addition to the building of a new Mohenjo-daro museum during the 1960s and renovation of Taxila Museum, several other museums, such as for forestry in Abbottabad, the

Barrage Museum at Guddu Barrage, a natural history museum, science museum, army museum, air force museum, and Folk Art museum were also built.[160] As an Italian mission was carrying out important excavations in the Swat Valley, a museum along the lines of Mohenjo-daro and Taxila was considered necessary. The *wali* (ruler) of Swat provided the land, and the Archeology Department paid the cost of construction.[161] In 1958, a proposal was floated to set up a museum at Umerkot—the birthplace of the Mughal king Akbar.[162] Alongside this, the government was eager to renovate the protected monuments, clear them of jungles and encroachments, and pay for repairs and renovations. These included excavated sites like Mohenjo-daro, Harappa, Taxila, Paharpur, and monuments like Jehangir's Tomb, Nur Jehan's Tomb, the Old Fort, Shalimar Gardens, Thatta Idrakpur Fort, Jaji Gunj Fort, and Khandkar mosque.[163] But the most important intervention of museal curation of a national historical narrative was the construction and planning of the national museums at Karachi and Dhaka.

As early as November 1949, the government of East Pakistan had put forward a request to set up a museum at Dhaka. For a national museum in East Pakistan, the central government was less enthusiastic. In its note dated 26 June 1956, the Ministry of Education gave the opinion that this was a provincial matter for which the central government could only provide technical or financial assistance. The Archaeology Department had already established a museum at Paharpur in East Pakistan, but setting up a "general" museum was not within its domain.[164] Moreover, the ministry was opposed to setting up more than one national museum in the country. The director of archeology, Raoul Curiel, was supportive of the idea. Even though a museum was a provincial subject, he wrote, the central government could still subsidize it. The museum would be national, he said, in the sense that "it will be representative not only of the local culture and civilization of East Bengal but also of all the cultures and civilisations of Pakistan at large."[165] He further argued that the existence of a national museum at Karachi did not preclude another museum in Dhaka. "As a matter of fact," he argued, "the peculiar character of Pakistan, with its two wings situated far apart from each other and belonging each to different and original cultures, necessitates the establishment of a National

Museum in East Pakistan also."[166] Since setting up a national museum was to be a long and expensive project, the director suggested first setting up a museum for history, archaeology, ethnography and art with Dacca University Museum to serve as the main site for the proposed museum and later handed over to the Department of Archaeology. But the ministry insisted that the responsibility lay with the government of East Pakistan to find a suitable site and construct a building for the museum, though it could later approach the central government for technical assistance, such as for provision of specialized equipment.

The Dacca museum that was eventually established was purposefully designed to exclude the Hindu heritage of the region. As Andrew Amstutz's work argues, the Pakistani state preferred to project itself as an ancient state on the strength of major Buddhist sites and the Gandhara civilization but chose to ignore its rich Hindu traditions. The Amstutz thesis is valid, especially in case of East Pakistan, where the Pakistani state showed considerable anxiety about the "Hindu connection" of the region, whether it was in the form of the Bengali language and its script, or the overall impression of the Bengalis not being "proper" Muslims. Therefore, the provincial museum eventually established in Dacca only displayed Islamic artifacts.[167] Meanwhile, the central government remained focused on building a national museum in Karachi and expanding its collections.

Originally inaugurated in 1950, the national museum in Karachi presented the "records of the cultural history of the country."[168] In its reporting of the inauguration, *Nawa-i-Waqt* was particularly excited about the prehistoric section that had the bust of "an extremely ancient inhabitant (*bashinday*) of Pakistan" from four hundred thousand years ago excavated from the Soan Valley.[169] Still, the museum lacked the artifacts required for fulfilling the purposes of a national museum. By focusing on the detailed proposal to set up a National Museum at Burns Garden in Karachi, I follow Tony Bennett's reading of Foucault's governmentality by focusing on distinctive relations of power that are "constituted in and by the exercise of specific forms of knowledge and expertise, and on the ways in which these give rise to specific mechanisms, techniques and technologies for shaping thought, feelings, perceptions and behavior." It is by looking at those mechanisms instead of looking through them to decipher the modes of power that lie behind them, argues Bennett, that we can "identify how particular forms of power are constituted *there*, within those mechanisms, rather than outside or behind them."[170] Such a theoretical formulation for reading museal curation is even more significant in the context of a postcolonial moment where the process is deliberative and draws upon "expert knowledge" to establish power effects of the state as a governmentalist tool of disciplining the gaze of the subjects.

The proposal to set up a national museum and relocate it from Frere Hall was made by the education adviser and joint secretary to the government of Pakistan in March 1958. He pointed out the inadequacy of the Frere Hall's plan, size, orientation, and lighting as expected of a national museum to "present the cultural history of the country in a fit and proper manner."[171] The shift to Burns Gardens would have allowed for more open-air displays, especially of Bengali thatched huts and Buddhist stupas.[172] Most of the garden was to remain an open space accessible to the public. The plan was, therefore, twofold: to assemble collections from East and West Pakistan and to develop a curated space that served the educative purposes of a museum.

To make the museum "truly representative of our great cultural heritage," F. A. Khan, director of archaeology, emphasized the acquisition of artifacts from private collections and new excavations—especially for the Muslim period, where, the director observed, the collection was poor and inadequate.[173] Because the construction of a purpose-built national museum was going to be a slow and gradual process requiring expertise from abroad as well as the purchase of antiquities, Khan requested a nonlapsable budget that could be used over the following five years. For this purpose, he drafted a detailed proposal—"Note on a New National Museum of Pakistan"—and submitted it to the educational adviser on 15 April 1959. The note outlined the features of the new museum, the collection of artifacts for it, and the specificity of displaying the collections.

According to F. A. Khan, many priceless artifacts were dumped in Frere Hall because of not only lack of space or its unsuitability to serve as a museum but also because "the conspicuous and overwhelming Victorian-Gothic architecture is marring whatever little can be displayed."[174] The note proposed a modern architecture for the museum. The local character was to be highlighted through the use of traditional materials and gardens, "which by their planning, their water-basin, the presence of certain trees and flowers, will be consistent with an ancient Muslim tradition of the Sub-continent."[175] Other than details about a spatial layout for exhibition, reserves, offices, workshop spaces, auditorium, canteen, foyers, corridors and so on, the note also highlighted aspects of curating whereby "visitors should be able to visit the different sections in a certain order, and they should have at the same time the possibility of by-passing certain sections in order to reach easily the section of their choice. . . . The circulation should not only be easy, it should also be controlled."[176] This pedagogical aspect of display was central to the plan, and objects were to be "selected and displayed according to a plan, in order to convey an intended meaning."[177] No exhibition, therefore, was to be permanent and would be subject to change with the increase in the collection. Such a regulated aspect of a museum's curating is what makes museums resemble temples of the nation in their architectural layout and the functions they serve.[178] It is a prescribed ritual of seeing through which museums discipline the gaze of the citizen.

The pedagogical function of the proposed national museum was to be further enhanced through guided tours and careful labeling of the artifacts. "Not only has the exhibition of objects in the galleries to convey a 'message,' to increase the culture of the visitors, to enrich them by a spirited and aesthetic display, and this with the help of labels, diagrams, photographs, etc.," wrote Khan, "but also and mainly the museum to organise guided tours, to contact teachers and professors, to attract them to the Museum and to explain to them how the Museum can help them in their mission of imparting knowledge to others. . . . Civilisation, technology, art can thus be made more easily understandable than by mere lessons and lectures."[179] He recommended mobile exhibitions in different parts of the country, including towns and villages, to further enhance the scope of the museum in its ability to educate the nation about its past.

F. A. Khan's proposal did not just aim to train the citizen's gaze, but it also planned what the citizen was to see. For this purpose, Khan devoted considerable energy to detailing the collection at the museum. With its focus on art, archaeology, history, and ethnography, the museum was to have a section on prehistory focusing on the Stone Age, protohistory with a focus on Harappa and Mohenjo-daro and Kot Diji, along with other areas showing the Bronze Age culture of Baluchistan and the Indus Valley, including Bahawalpur. Other than prehistory and protohistory, the third section mentioned in the concept note was devoted to Buddhism, covering Gandhara, Taxila, and important discoveries in East Pakistan in Paharpur and Mainamati. The fourth section was titled "Hindu Cultures," where, Khan said, the national museum was still very poor. He recommended more excavations and acquisitions to build a larger collection for the Gupta and Pala schools, as the Hindu cultures had played an important role in the region "to which we cannot be indifferent."[180] For the fifth section on the Muslim period, Khan wrote that the exhibits were not adequate or impressive enough, as "the National Museum of the Islamic Republic *should* be one of the richest of the world in this field. It should be representative not only of all the Muslim periods in the Sub-continent—so rich in cultural and artistic achievements, but also for all the particular Muslim cultures in the rest of the world."[181] It was even going to cover the Abbasid period, the Ottomans and Safavids up to contemporary Pakistan. The sixth and seventh sections were to have manuscripts and coins and gems, respectively. The eighth section was for an ethnographic collection that, according to Khan, had hitherto been ignored. It emphasized the importance of collecting dresses, jewelry, textiles, and so on, many of which were fast disappearing. The ninth and last section was called "Comparative Section," to give the visitors "an integrated conception of the development of Human Civilisation based on a concrete approach: that of the civilisations and cultures of Pakistan."[182]

The detailed outlay of the proposed national museum helps outline the institutionalized versions of an imagined national past retrieved from monumental structures, relics, and artifacts. It is by collating and curating these fragments of the past that they are ascribed a coherent linearity and stability of meaning out of an accumulated, chaotic, indifferentiable mass of ancient objects distanced from their site, context, and point of action. Therefore, what the citizens see and internalize as they walk through the scripted space of the museum is a planned emphasis on "ancient" Buddhist sites as part of Pakistan's rich heritage, a blurry vision of the Hindu "interlude," and a nostalgic yet gleeful spark of the glories of an imagined Muslim past and its bright, utopic future.

This chapter has shown the constructedness of historical tradition and national identity, and the transitory nature of this process. For this purpose, I have given a detailed account of how the postcolonial state tried to shape collective memory through power effects of commemorative rituals in the form of observance of national holidays, military parades to mark the independence celebrations, gun salutes on Jinnah and Iqbal's birthdays, the lighting up of official buildings on religious occasions, adorning chowks and squares with preferred symbols, renaming road names, removing statues and ordering of material objects to curate the past as a preferred, linear unfolding.

Commemorations are an important part of identity formation in the postcolonial state. To quote de Certeau, "memory is a sort of anti-museum: it is not localizable."[183] But the frequent iteration of statist symbols of authority and an associational linkage with a constructed past aspire to produce a template—a memory frame of sorts—on the members of the political community organized under a state. It is, by its very constitutive methodology, collective and seeks to override the personal and the individual. Yet it also aspires to an intimacy through attachment to symbols and from ritual performances. As Srirupa Roy has argued, rituals of national commemoration perform two different but related functions: first, they project a seamless, linear, and teleological narrative of national time, which has a homogenizing effect insofar as the rituals are performed every year and showcased as uniformly significant to all members of the nation; second, they help give shape to a nationalist communal solidarity across time and space.[184] "It is through repeatedly encountering rather than believing in the official imagination of nationhood," says Roy, "through recognizing the sights and sounds of the state rather than 'buying into' its mythologies, that the nation-state is formed and reproduced."[185] It is the description and the analysis of the sights and sounds of the postcolonial nation-state of Pakistan and its commemorative ritual praxis to tame the past that has been the focus of this chapter.

POSTSCRIPT

A NEW BEGINNING
My Fellow Countrymen

IN THE END, I want to draw attention to the public debate on appropriate forms of address, greetings, and honorifics that occurred immediately after Independence. Throughout this study, I have referred to ways in which Pakistanis—even if only literate ones, a small portion of the entire population—contributed to debates by writing letters to the editor about what it meant to be a citizen of a free country and helped define the religious nature of the Pakistani polity and propose a blueprint for its future trajectory. We can understand these responses, contributions, debates, contestations, concerns, and—often unsolicited—opinions as reflective of the republican spirit of the time, and thus, of a genuine enthusiasm about alternative futures. In this manner, the "editorial space as a critical archive" serves as an important new source for historians to explore the relations between the postcolonial state and its citizenry.[1]

For instance, myriad public responses demanded that "the nation" be rid of its colonial past by establishing equality in social rank and eradicating distinctions, thereby reducing people to their individual and collective identities as Pakistanis. In writing a letter to the editor, Mehmud Mirza, of Lahore, lamented the presence of "foreigner Pakistanis" like Shaukat

"Thanawi," Hafiz "Jallandhari," and Waqar "Ambalvi," who were holding on to their places of origin in India even though they had permanently settled in Pakistan.[2] Taraullah, from the Government Girls School in Habiganj, objected to the use of "your obedient servant" in official correspondence as the legacy of a slavish mentality. "An officer of the Azad Pakistan State," she wrote, "is not a servant of any other individual officer, superior of inferior to him. He is more appropriately a Khadim or servant of his own State and this he must be conscious of in one and every work that he does for his State."[3] She wanted this wording to be replaced by *Khadim-i-Pakistan*, or "Pakistan's most faithful and honest servant," in all state correspondence.

To explain these disparate approaches to what it meant to be Pakistani in the liberating spirit of the early postcolonial moment, I refer to a discussion initiated by the Lahore-based Urdu daily, *Nawa-i-Waqt*, in November 1949 about the eradication of distinctions and inequality based on caste, or *biradari*. The newspaper asked its readers to suggest alternative appellations to family names, which emphasized a pride in one's ancestry, and to the form of address *mister*, a relic of the colonial past.[4] A lively debate followed that lasted about a month and continued to reverberate in various newspapers throughout the 1950s.

Nawa-i-Waqt floated the idea of addressing people as *Sayyid*. Khawaja Ibad Ullah Akhtar suggested the term *akhi* (brother) or *rafiq* (friend). Khaliq Qureshi, of Lyallpur, wrote that even though *Sayyid* was used in the Arab world as equivalent to *mister*, it had a different, rather religious connotation in the subcontinent, referring more specifically to the descendants of Prophet Muhammad.[5] Other suggestions included *pir* (spiritual mentor) as an address of respect, with the additional benefit that it would help get rid of "fake Pirs," who were widespread in Pakistan. Syed Najam-ul-Hasan suggested adding the title *Pak* to individual names, such as Pak Muhammad Ali Jinnah and Pak Liaqat Ali Khan.[6] Haji Firoz-ud-Din from Lahore cited examples from other countries where people were addressed with the same title, whether as *mister*, *monsieur*, *sheikh*, or *sayyidi*. For Pakistan, he recommended the title *bhai sahab*, *bhai ji*, or *bhai jan*. Hayat Niazi from Mianwali had problems with the title "Mian," as, according to him, it reeked of lowly status.[7] He supported titles like *akhi* or *khan*.

It is clear from this summary of the debate that participants were trying to translate the republican ideal of equal citizenship into a brotherhood of men for that equality to be meaningful in their individual and collective lives. But such a view of equality as Islamic brotherhood hit a snag, conflicting with the colonial conceptualization of Muslim identity, especially in Punjab, pandering to their economic and political interests. To safeguard their interests, the colonial state recognized Muslim landowners' status as agriculturalists in Punjab but, at the same time, allowed them religion-based voting and representation.[8] For landowning purposes, Punjabi Muslims were recognized as members of *biradaris* of agriculturalists; for voting purposes, they were Muslims. Thus, there was a duality between *biradari* and *qaum*, even though *qaum* also carried negative connotations, as it was frequently used to refer to *biradari*. As David Gilmartin's work shows, the Muslim League—especially during its campaign for Pakistan in the 1940s—sought to overcome this duality by cultivating a singular identity rooted in the language of an ethical and moral community of Islam. In the postcolonial state, this duality was to be eradicated—or that was the goal of proponents of new appellations. When the debate slipped into a tirade against the Land Alienation Act, which distinguished between agriculturalist and nonagriculturalist classes, a number of people jumped in to argue in favor of keeping these distinctions, claiming the value of kinship as a marker of social identity.

G. A. Jhajat, of Gujrat, critiqued the Land Alienation Act for dividing Muslims along the lines of agriculturalists and nonagriculturalist classes. Not only was this division un-Islamic, he wrote, it was also irrational: a Muslim cultivator could work for hours in the field and yet be a nonagriculturalist, whereas a man who had never tilled a field could still be an agriculturalist.[9] Jhajat asked for the abolition of this division, so that any Muslim could take up whatever profession he wanted. He suggested that just like Sikhs used the title *sardar*, Muslims should address each other as *khan sahab*. Khaliq Qureshi, of Lahore, identified the colonial system of classification as the root cause of problems, advised the abolition of *zat*-based privileges and called for their replacement with equal rights for all Pakistanis.[10] Abdul Ghafur Chughtai of Muzaffargarh wrote that, without changes in the Land Alienation Act, it would not be possible to strike at the roots of kin pride. It was only by altering the act that the distinction of agriculturalist and nonagriculturalist could be eradicated, making it possible for the adoption of a single title.[11] Chughtai argued it was nothing wrong to use the word *mister*, as it was already well known and widely popular, and furthermore, there was nothing inherently wrong with borrowing something good from another culture.

There was a vociferous countercampaign against the flattening of differential ranks, whether for the use of uniform titles or in the abolition of the Land Alienation Act. Ghulam Haider Mashhadi, of Lahore, opposed the use of *biradari* titles in a casteist sense but justified their use for the purposes of recognition. Those calling for the eradication of *biradari*-based distinction, he wrote, would refuse to enter into matrimonial alliances with a *qaum* they perceive as having lowly status. A donkey and horse could be interbred to produce a mule, he said, but that would still be unnatural.[12] Muhammad Amin, of Lyallpur, was concerned that abolishing the distinction between agriculturalist and nonagriculturalist classes would embolden the lowly castes (*kamini zatain*) to become more assertive (*ankhain dikhani shuru kar dain gi*).[13] Syed Muin-ud-Din Hasan of Jehlum wrote that at least true Sayyids—as descendants of the Prophet, Fatima, Ali, Hasan, and Husain, the lords of paradise—should be allowed to carry the title *Sayyid* in Prophet Muhammad's *ummat*.[14] In a similar vein, Nisar Haideri objected to those who failed to recognize the distinguished status of Sayyids, who, per the Quranic verses of *tathir* (Q 33:33), were granted respect by Muslims. If even in Egypt Jogindar Nath Mandal—the Dalit member of Pakistan's Constituent Assembly—was referred to as "al-Sayyid Jogindar Nath Mandal," argued Haideri, then there was not a logical argument for not doing the same in Pakistan. He wrote that the Quran did not eradicate distinctions as such but limited them to purposes of recognition. Moreover, he wrote, the Quran itself had granted titles such as *Khalil Allah* and *Zabih Allah*, and the Prophet conferred titles to his Companions such as *Siddiq*, *Farooq*, and *Zun-Nurain*.[15] In an article titled "Hasb-o-Nasb ka imtiaz zaruri hai," Dr. Jafari Naz Sonipati took a similar stance, alluding to the Quran's references to the Prophet of Islam as *Sayyid al-Anbiya* and *Sayyid al-Mursalin*, and thus justifying a distinction in status even among prophets. Sonipati took a social Darwinist view of things and wrote that there was scientific evidence for the genetic transference of habits, traits, and diseases. Besides, he wrote, the concept of equality needed to be properly understood. In a world where everyone was a king, no one would be left to do menial tasks (*Tu bhe rani mai bhe rani, kaun bharay pani*).[16] As Muslims, everyone was equal, but in terms of habits, temperament, and knowledge, according to Sonipati, there were distinctions that should be maintained. In any case, wrote M. Akbar Khan Shakargarhi, of Lahore, if lowly castes like *mochi*, *mirasi*, *nayi*, and *taili* wanted to win a title, they should develop distinct qualities and achieve something in the battlefield of jihad; then they could earn the titles of *ghazi* (holy warrior) and *shahid* (martyr).[17] Despite *Nawa-i-Waqt*'s strong advocacy for an Islamic brotherhood as a version of republican equality, the debate remained inconclusive—and in fact became more divisive, threatening economic interests tied to the colonial rationality of a social hierarchy of interests and political identities.[18]

The debate coincided with what citizens saw as a foundational moment in the history of the country as it planned and discussed ways of drafting a new constitution and adopted or altered the semiotic order through construction of public monuments and introduction of commemorative practices for replication of preferred symbolic values. The adoption of the constitution in 1956 heralded a similar moment, rekindling the debate, albeit briefly, about appropriate forms of formal address meant to achieve distance from the colonial past and to establish a republican equality of citizenship in a postcolonial state. Writing "A National Nomenclature" in November 1956, Diogenes—a regular feature writer for *Morning News* using a nom de plume—referred to words used for official servants such as *Babu* and *Maluvi* as remnants of the imperial past that continued in Pakistan to distinguish a central service officer from a provincial service officer—a form of derogatory distinction "carried on by our pseudo-imperialists manning their bamboo frame of Pakistan, which succeeded the steel."[19] India, claimed Diogenes, had abolished these particular social and official distinctions, replacing *mister* and *Babu* with *Shri* for Hindus and *Janab* for Muslims. Eventually, in this manner, "The 'Mr.' for an Indian national disappeared from the body politic as well as the body social of Bharat that was India."[20] Diogenes recommends suitable nomenclature in Pakistan such as *janab, sahib, maulvi,* or *maulana* but found that most lacked a female equivalent. *Begum,* he noted, had become popular. D. M. Alam, of Karachi, commented that coining the term *janabi* for women would be difficult, as, if pronounced as "jana-bee," the word meant "one having just completed a vulgar act" in Arabic.[21] Luthful Kabir Siddiqui, from Chittagong, raised the question of a suitable Bengali term for *miss* or *lady.* According to him, *bhadramahila* or *mohashaya* were not proper substitutes. For *miss,* he recommended the use of *khuki* or *kumari.*[22]

The debate was not limited to nomenclature; it included the issue of dressing, an important aspect of national life in the new republic. In fact, the debate on dress—along with that on language—has had a more enduring presence in the biography of the postcolonial nation-state. The main targets of the debate were women and heads of state, who were held responsible for embodying the symbolic value of national dress. F. Z. Kitchlew, of Lahore, lamented the increasing use of European dress by Pakistani women, which, in addition to its "other undesirable features," created the impression that "we have no national dress of our own." Therefore, he recommended setting up a "Committee of prominent ladies and fashion experts . . . [to] consider the question of a national dress of Pakistani women."[23] For the president of the Islamic Republic, N. Javid, from Dacca, recommended Pakistan's national dress: *sherwani, shalwar,* and a Jinnah cap.[24] But there were other citizens who objected to dress distinguished along national or foreign lines. K. B. Sajjad, of Dacca, objected to the suggestions of introducing *sherwani* and pajama as "Islamic dress" and replacing *Mr.* and *Mrs.* with *janab* and *janaba,* respectively: "The peoples of this country have realised the advantages of Western dress and hence has adopted it. This is why the majority of nations of the world have adopted the Western dress, instead of the Sherwani Pyjama. I fear that some people in the near future may demand the introduction of the baggy dress of the Arabian people, calling it 'purely Islamic,' because the users of these dresses live nearest to Mecca."[25]

But B. W. Rahman, of Dacca University, responded that there was a need to distinguish between national and Islamic, a distinction that was lost on K. B. Sajjad: "This is not a question of comfort or convenience; this is a necessity of national prestige and distinction. . . . History gives us evidence that every country got used to a particular kind of dress not because of religion but because of local conditions and national sentiment. There is no reason to neglect the lessons of history. There is no pride or dignity in putting on of peacock's plumage perpetually."[26] In concluding the debate by writing the last letter on this issue for the *Pakistan Observer*, A. Mawaz, of Chittagong, made a case for national dress based on local climatic conditions. "'Western' dress pant, coat and shirt-tail tucked in is not suitable for local climatic conditions," he wrote.

> Due to the high percentage of humidity at high temperatures, the dress should be well ventilated, and the material chosen should have a sufficient absorbent factor. . . . A dhoti, loongi or pyjama and kurta are far more comfortable. The sari is equally good for the summer as well as winter. . . . Similarly for shoes. The "English" shoe (Oxford) with laces, is also not suitable for this land, as it is designed for cold regions, to keep the feet fully enclosed, air-tight and warm. . . . . Open type of shoes are called for, which can be easily taken off under the table, or when the feet are out of sight.

While prescribing a form of national dress, he advised keeping scientific and local considerations in mind.[27] Such a "scientific approach" to dressing, he said, was in line with Islamic teachings and could be seen in Arab dress, in which "the white dress reflects the strong sunlight, and the flowing robe insulates the body from the fierce surrounding temperature."[28] However, Mawaz did not find it expedient to prescribe a single form of national dress; there was not one form equally suitable for the widely divergent climatic conditions of East and West Pakistan.

These brief exchanges show the limitations of Islamic brotherhood as a basis for equality—even among believers, let alone all citizens—without a corresponding emancipatory ideal for the eradication of social distinction and economic interests. In other words, this brief encounter shows how political equality depended on social equality to bear significance and fulfill aspirations of decolonization and freedom. The Islamic brotherhood model alone was unable to serve that role. The proponents of this model demanded the retention of distinguishing markers for the continuation of social and economic privileges. Such a demand is at variance from that of minority groups, which insisted on the recognition of difference. But the minority groups' emphasis on the recognition of difference is meant as a prerequisite for enforcing and sustaining equality—the end goal is missing from the writings of those who insist on the recognition of clan-based economic interests. In other words, minority groups defined along religious, ethnic, or linguistic lines insist that the state recognize them as equal citizens without overriding their identities as Sindhi, Pashtun, Siraiki, Christian, Hindu, or Baluch.

In addition to a culturally specific, religiously loaded, and socially particular idiom of brotherhood among citizen-believers, there is a statist language of equality as the loss of privilege. In his essay "On the Jewish Question," Marx argued that despite claims of the political annulment of distinction based on birth and social rank, and the state's proclamation that "every member of the nation is an *equal* participant in national sovereignty," the state only exists on the presupposition of these distinctions above the particular elements to constitute itself as universality.[29] It does lead to equality in the sense that the dissolution of civil society into individuals under a political state produces a relationship among men based on law instead of privilege.[30] Even this aspect of equality before the law, incomplete as it was for Marx in the absence of a social revolution, held considerable importance for the ongoing democratic struggle and the anxieties of the political elite in the aftermath of decolonization. Hence, both models—religious equality among believers as Muslim citizens and the loss of privilege as equality before the law—failed to live up to the emancipatory potential of the postcolonial moment. Still, both served an important reminder of the enchanting pull of these ideals during the initial years of the postcolonial state.

To better explain, I refer to a document in the national archives about literally rolling out the red carpet for heads of state and officials at airports and train stations. In a letter written to the director general of railways on 15 February 1951, the chief minister of Khairpur State asked the railway department for the loan of a ceremonial red carpet for the upcoming visit of the prime minister. According to the existing practice, reminded the chief minister, a ceremonial red carpet was laid down at stations for royalty, the governor-general, provincial governors, and the commander in chief.[31] Because the prime minister's designation was missing from the list, the Ministry of Interior recommended adding it to the list, given the importance the role in the new state. The Interior Ministry was also of the opinion that among the designated areas for performing this ceremony, the airport must also be included, as most dignitaries preferred to travel by air.[32]

But Hameeduddin Ahmed, whom we encountered in chapter 1 as a hawkish, anti-Hindu bureaucrat, had different ideas. In the current document, he emerges as an upholder of the republican spirit. The contradiction of locating oneself in multiple political registers is indicative of how citizens and civilian officials, as well as political leaders and military officers, were eclectic in the choices they made to arrive at a model of democratic governance in the general spirit of possibilities in the postcolonial moment. Ahmed observed in a note dated 13 March 1951 that such rules were a relic of the days when the country was governed on behalf of a king. In his view, red-carpet protocol "should not now be extended to include the Prime Minister who is a representative of the people. The carpet should therefore be spread only for the Governor General or visiting Royalties or Heads of State. It should not be spread for H.P.M. or the Provincial Governors (who are now representatives of the Governor General and not of the King), or the Commander-in-Chief, whose position is now entirely different to what it was in undivided India as the seniormost [sic] member of the Vicerory's [sic] Executive Countil [sic]."[33]

But Ahmed's view was not accepted.

The question of protocol for rulers of the formerly princely states invoked a similar discussion. As the Nawab of Bahawalpur was scheduled to visit Karachi, the Ministry of Frontier Regions was eager to get the Interior Ministry's approval to implement the earlier precedent of gun salutes for rulers of the princely states (nineteen guns for Kalat, seventeen for Bahawalpur, fifteen for Khairpur, and eleven for Chitral), along with a red-carpet welcome.[34] The Ministry of Interior was of the view that with the approval of the prime minister, only the governor general, visiting heads of state or royalty, and prime ministers were entitled to a red carpet. The second category included, it clarified, only independent foreign states, not states that had acceded to Pakistan. Still, the ministry allowed, as an exception, red carpet for the Nawab of Bahawalpur. But as a rule, Secretary of the Interior G. Ahmed maintained in a note on 21 April 1951 that these rulers "should not be allowed the paraphernalia of royalty in the present set up and general temper of the country."[35]

The Ministry of Frontier Regions, however, took a different view of the situation. For it, the Pakistani government was from the very beginning committed to observing royal protocols for princely rulers that had been observed during the British period. "These Rulers who still enjoy internal sovereignty in their States," the ministry argued, "should not be allowed to get the impression that their accession to Pakistan has detracted from their past position and personal privileges."[36] As for the argument that this royal paraphernalia was not in keeping with the general temperament of the country, the ministry warned against succumbing to the "shortsighted popular clamour against Rulers." The ministry noted: "If we can satisfy the democratic aspirations of the people by suitable progressive administrative reforms without disturbing the constitutional position of the Rulers, we should prefer this policy to that of merger followed in India." It thus advised the continuation of the ceremonial grandeur and ritualistic paraphernalia of a red-carpet welcome, the guard of honor, gun salutes, police escorts, and formal receptions. The ministry was of the opinion that "it will not be a bad bargain if the Government of Pakistan can secure the goodwill of these Rulers by extending to them such small courtesies as spreading a strip of Red Cloth or rare ceremonial occasions."[37]

Contrary to the Ministry of Interior's objection to ceremonial grandeur as a relic of the colonial past, Z. H. Burney, of the Ministry of States and Frontier Regions, justified the practice as a way of giving respect to local rulers. Unlike in the British period, wrote Burney, when governors were above rulers because "the foreign Government wanted to show the superiority of its officers and nationals over even the Rulers," in Pakistan "the Rulers belong to our own nation and, just as we show our respect and regard to His Excellency the Governor-General and Hon'ble the Prime Minister as heads of the Government, the Rulers of States also deserve to be treated with consideration according to their position."[38] They were no longer former autocrats but were part of the new constitutional framework, fully cooperating with the national government to democratize their states.

In response to the Ministry of Interior's insistence that rulers of state come after governors in the revised warrant of precedence and that the ruler of an acceded state was not a sovereign, Burney emphasized that the rulers—despite signing instruments of accession or agreeing to give powers to the federal legislature to frame laws for their states in areas of the acceded subjects—were "still 'sovereign' without any doubt."[39] To resolve this issue, Mushtaq Ahmad Gurmani, minister of interior, had to intervene. Gurmani observed: "These obsolete practices do not fit in with our democratic system. It would be cruel not to help the rulers to forget about these old practices and to adjust themselves to the changed conditions. . . . The Public opinion is definitely opposed to and critical of these feudal and imperialist customs being continued in a democratic state which we claim to be."[40]

In this fashion, the debate about ceremonial red carpet ended on a note reaffirming faith in democratic traditions as a new era was heralded for Pakistan. The promise of Pakistan, and of being Pakistani, was about the arrival of a new age, a postcolonial moment, a republican spirit, a break from the past and an affirmation of democratic values, whether defined as liberal equality or Islamic brotherhood. Even if the Pakistani state has since failed to live up to this promise, these normative ideals have continued to serve as aspiration, offering a standard against which to measure the deviance of statist praxis and ideology.

In this book I have analyzed the political processes shaping the idea of being Pakistani as a citizen and/or Muslim national. As I have shown, the postcolonial state has juggled the universalist pretense of equality that is the premise of citizenship with the majoritarian ethos of the *qaum* and its symbolic repertoire. The overriding triumvirate of Islam, Muslim, and Urdu, with its epistemic and political violence, has aspired to achieve a homogenized Pakistani identity. Given a plurality of ethnic, linguistic, and religious diversity, such a project was always fraught, a false aspiration and an impossible becoming. Several academic works explain how political movements in Pakistan have struggled against statist violence— again, epistemic and political—to resist enforced assimilation. There is also a long history in Pakistan of movements for social equality, including student-led protests in the late 1960s, general strikes organized by workers, and the farmers' movement, to name only a few.[41]

Yet in the aftermath of statist violence and the neoliberal atomization of communities, there has also been some measure of success for the Pakistan state project. With new technologies of governmentality, the state is able to document and surveil its citizens, but also to dole out massive relief packages; invest in infrastructural development, bringing connectivity to far-off areas; and conduct huge social and food security programs.[42] Partha Chatterjee calls these processes the governmentalization of state, whereby governance becomes less a matter of politics and more one of administrative policy. This results in a conceptual demarcation of a civil society connected to the nation-state, which is founded on the logic of popular sovereignty and of a population connected with the government and its agencies for various projects and policies of security and welfare.[43] The former is the domain of civil society, which is an associated form of life limited to a specific section of right-bearing, culturally equipped citizens; the latter refers to political society, which covers a much larger expanse and myriad inhabitants.[44] While political society has been subject to rigorous state intervention, civil society, too, has undergone tremendous transformation—especially since the early 2000s, with the commodification of the symbolic repertoire that serves as the ideational basis of the nation, and with which the modernizing national bourgeoisie identifies itself. As Kaur has argued, it is no longer the historical value of these symbols, but the way they can be packaged to enable a certain kind of consumption, that is the basis of new national identities. It is National Belonging 2.0 in much of the postcolonial world, whereby "twentieth-century nation building is increasingly being replaced by twenty-first-century nation branding."[45] Reflections of this rebranding of the nation can be seen in multiple projects.

Coke Studio is an example of how a new national narrative can be reimagined through cultural production, in this case, musical media consumed by virtual and digital audiences.[46] Najia Mukhtar describes the content producers of Coke Studio as "intentional Muslim actors, producing alternative ideas for, and about, Muslims, with a view to challenging dominant notions in society that tend towards (often violently) suppressing religious difference."[47] The aesthetic mode of this ideational struggle is not limited to establishing the ascendancy of "good Muslim" over "bad Muslim." Its aesthetics require unison amid a multivocality of ethnicities and languages achieved by amplifying the noise of Western or global notations to choreograph local audiation. This "sound of the nation"—the tagline for Coke Studio—thus becomes a celebration of Pakistani authenticity and its cultural traditions in modern packaging that conforms to contemporary standards and is sellable to a global audience.

The Pakistan Super League (PSL) in cricket is another example. With teams named after major cities, players are selected both domestically and internationally. But domestic players do not have to belong to the city they represent, because they will make it into an intranational contest. As in other sports franchises around the world, the branding of PSL is done to ensure a brand selection by the consumer, not consumer identification with a team as a national. In the cases of PSL and Coke Studio, this rebranding is meant for global citizens to recognize the nation and partake of it through consumption of its music, sports, ethnic food, and exploration of its heritage sites and snowy peaks in the "northern areas."

But it would be erroneous to conclude, on the basis of urban consumption patterns, that the cumulative impact of developments in state, society, and the economy has been to create a Pakistani nationalism or de-ethnicization of communities. The rebranded nation does not erase the disputative past of the symbolic repertoire or stabilize their meaning. It keeps them open to contestation, retaining the memories of conflict that are constitutive of them. Nevertheless, a situation has emerged in which, in Akbar Zaidi's assessment, there is a greater incentive for competing groups and ethnicities to look to Islamabad for redress, claiming their share of the pie, rather than restricting themselves to provincial enclaves. What has enabled this outcome is massive urbanization—a silent and "unplanned revolution," for Arif Hasan.[48] The logic of the capital and of statist pedagogy over the decades has successfully instilled a peculiar subjectivity—an urban-mindedness—that puts a premium on religious sensibility. With the continued support of Islam-based movements acting as a policy tool to enhance the statist project, there has been a mushrooming of Sunni madrassahs in areas such as rural Sindh, or even southern Baluchistan, that were previously considered insulated from the preying eyes of the Pakistani state. The extent of the impact of these decades-long policies can be seen in the rapid increase in the electoral popularity of groups like Jamat Ulema-i-Islam in areas like Larkana in Sindh, and also in the ability of

Jamat-i-Islami to successfully organize a huge rally in the port city of Gawadar in Baluchistan.

Despite the successes of Islamization as an instrument of state intrusion, the "nationality question" in Pakistan continues to simmer. In the absence of a legal language or consensual constitutional framework that recognizes nationalities, ethnicities, and language groups, and enables their acceptance within a federal structure based on these differences, ethnic movements continue to derive their strength from a range of cultural activities that address issues of economic exploitation and political marginalization. At the same time, one must consider a new political language that is claimed by marginalized groups, which draws on the Pakistani constitution of 1973 as a fundamental guarantor of rights and equality. A prime example is the Pashtun Tahaffuz Movement (PTM), which seeks the demilitarization of Pashtun areas, the rehabilitation of internally displaced persons (IDPs) who had to relocate from tribal areas due to military operations, and an end to discrimination and racism suffered by Pashtuns in Pakistani cities.

If PTM's ideal citizenship model is based on the idea of the right to life, then Aurat March (Women's March), which is organized by various radical feminist organizations and volunteers, demands the right to bodily autonomy, the eradication of patriarchal violence, and equality for all genders and sexualities.[49] In the Arendtian sense, both movements demand constituting an artificial equality that is the premise of an organized political community and creating legal personhood through and in which individuals can realize their humanity through public action and speech.[50] It is this realization of equality through speech and action, which is essentially a demand for inclusion and recognition, that is the hallmark of new movements that have emerged in Pakistan.

These movements, along with a number of other organizations representing farmers, workers, and professionals, demand a rewriting of the social and the legal matrix that underpins the idea of citizenship in Pakistan. Disillusioned groups and protestors proceed from the assumption that they are Pakistani citizens and have inalienable rights guaranteed by the Pakistani constitution. As to how and why this moment of radical potential has been possible despite years of authoritarian rule and fractured democratic structures is another topic that demands a much deeper analysis of the post-1990s era of Pakistani politics than that to which I have rudimentarily summarized in broad strokes in the preceding paragraphs. But a detailed analysis is warranted, as this unprecedented moment in Pakistan's history offers new possibilities and challenges.[51] Although it is reflective of a real possibility of a "constitutional patriotism" of some sort to become the enabler of a truly federal polity, the challenge is to overcome and defeat the rule of fear, as Ammar Jan calls it, which the overdeveloped institution of the military has established over the past seven decades as the apparatus of governance for the country. The most potent challenge to the military comes from an ongoing protest movement, mostly in Punjab and Khyber Pakhtunkhwa, following Imran Khan's removal from power in April 2022.[52] To borrow another conceptual category from Ammar Jan's political theory, Imran Khan's massive, cross-sectional popularity since his ouster has enabled him to become Pakistan's "moral sovereign," momentarily superseding legal-political structures and institutional bases of the state. How that pans out in the long term in terms of impact on the military's institutional chokehold on Pakistan's fragile democratic system remains to be seen.

In summary, the blossoming of new political and social movements rallied around the constitution heralds a new era in which Pakistan's polity seeks a fundamental alteration in its militaristic approach to address national dissent and demands for social justice and equality without necessarily agreeing on the conceptual and political basis of these ideals. New Pakistani movements have diverse agendas: eradication of the patriarchal roots of discrimination, the demilitarization of society, the abolition of discriminatory religious laws, ecological justice, land rights, accountability, ending dynastic politics, and so on. The future of these movements is anyone's guess. What the present work can help us understand are the historical roots of these questions and the state's attempts at addressing them through violence, undemocratic means, and what it takes to be the overriding force of Islam-based identity. Through a historicization of the citizen-national distinction, my work has explored the radical potential of equality that inheres in foundational political texts, as well as the potential for mobilizing the autochthony of the *qaum* to bring about disintegration of the national native. Such an approach requires that we do not dismiss the question of citizenship as settled or approached in a narrow legal sense but instead bring it to the forefront of political contestation by teasing out a historical narrative that connects with the present moment in the life of the republic, thus enabling alternative futures and multiple political subjectivities.

NOTES

Introduction

1. *Pakistan Times*, 28 September 1947.
2. *Deccan Chronicle*, 30 May 2016.
3. Anwari Begum had married Rafiq Ghaznawi, with whom she had a daughter, Nasreen, who was Salma Agha's mother. Anwari married Mehra following her divorce with Ghaznawi. I am grateful to Professor Ishtiaq Ahmed for sharing this information with me.
4. Ilyas Chattha, "The Impact of the Redistribution of Partition's Evacuee Property on the Patterns of Land Ownership and Power in Pakistani Punjab in the 1950s," in *State and Nation Building in Pakistan*, ed. Roger D. Long, Gurharpal Singh, Yunas Samad, and Ian Talbot (London: Routledge, 2016), 31–52. Chattha is currently working on a full-length book project tracing the history of Christian conversion in Punjab in the aftermath of Partition and the role of various missions in this process.
5. On the abduction of women and children during the Partition and the details of their recovery, see Urvashi Batalia, *The Other Side of Silence: Voices from the Partition of India* (Delhi: Viking Penguin India, 1998); Ritu Menon and Kamla Bhasin, *Borders and Boundaries: Women in India's Partition* (Delhi: Kali for Women, 1998); Pippa Virdee, *From the Ashes of 1947: Reimagining Punjab* (Delhi: Cambridge University Press, 2018).
6. "Baba Guru Pakistani || Charagh Din Jagjit Singh || Kotha Guru, Batninda To Pakistan || Punjab 1947," YouTube video, posted by Desi Infotainer, https://www.youtube.com/watch?v=lKO7799iU9E.
7. Elisabetta Iob's *Refugees and the Politics of the Everyday State in Pakistan: Resettlement in Punjab, 1947–62* (London: Routledge, 2018) gives a lively account of how refugees navigated life in a new country. In particular, she focuses on the importance of patronage networks in interactions with the postcolonial state, providing rich insight into the everyday life of the migrants as they strove to become citizens of the republic and draw economic sustenance from it by building political alliances.
8. I came across this letter in the file of *Nawa-i-Waqt* and took notes as well. Unfortunately, in the "digital heap" of collected archival material, I lost the precise date and year of publication. A village of this name still exists in Chakwal district.
9. *Ankh Micholi*, August 1990. The special issue was called "Dil Dil Pakistan" after a famous patriotic song popularized by a pop sensation—Vital Signs.
10. Tahir Masud, "Manzil Pakistan," *Ankh Micholi*, August 1990, 93–99.
11. Anupama Roy, "The Citizenship (Amendment) Bill, 2016 and the Aporia of Citizenship," *Economic and Political Weekly* 54, no. 49 (14 December 2019): 28–29. The 2003

amendment specified that citizenship by birth will be granted only in cases where at least one parent is of Indian origin and the other one is not an illegal migrant.

12. Niraja Gopal Jayal, "Faith-Based Citizenship: The Dangerous Path India Is Choosing," *India Forum: A Journal-Magazine on Contemporary Issues*, October 31, 2019, 4, https://www.theindiaforum.in/article/faith-criterion-citizenship.

13. Uzma, "Indian Muslims Have Hindu Ancestry: Subramanian Swamy," August 25, 2011, https://archive.siasat.com/news/indian-muslims-have-hindu-ancestry-subramanian-swamy-212976/.

14. Jayal, "Faith-Based Citizenship," 1.

15. "Imran Khan Pledges Citizenship to Afghan and Bangladeshi Refugees," *Al-Jazeera*, September 17, 2018, https://www.aljazeera.com/news/2018/9/17/imran-khan-pledges-citizenship-to-afghan-and-bangladeshi-refugees.

16. Sanaa Alimia's recently published monograph on the Afghan refugees and their role in the making of Pakistan's urban fabric captures the experiences of everyday lives of Afghan refugees in the country: *Refugee Cities: How Afghans Changed Urban Pakistan* (Philadelphia: University of Pennsylvania Press, 2022). For a similar work on Bengali and Rohingyas, mostly living in Karachi, see Nausheen H. Anwar, "Negotiating New Conjunctures of Citizenship: Experiences of 'Illegality' in Burmese-Rohingya and Bangladeshi Migrant Enclaves in Karachi," *Citizenship Studies* 17, nos. 3–4 (2013): 414–28.

17. Hafeez Jamali's PhD dissertation, "A Harbor in the Tempest: Megaprojects, Identity, and the Politics of Place in Gwadar, Pakistan" (University of Texas at Austin, 2014), is a detailed ethnographic study of the fears and anxieties of Baluch residents of a small fishing harbor that is undergoing massive social change as a result of, what the nationalists view as, extractive mega-developments in the area.

18. For a detailed historical overview of the Mohajir national identity and the politics of urban violence in Karachi since the 1980s, see Laurent Gayer's *Karachi: Ordered Disorder and the Struggle for the City* (New York: Oxford University Press, 2014). On criminal networks and political patronage—especially in the Lyari neighborhood of Karachi—see Nida Kirmani, "Mobility and Urban Conflict: A Study of Lyari, Karachi" (Crossroads Asia Working Paper No. 28, University of Bonn, 2015).

19. See Ammar Ali Jan, *Rule by Fear: Eight Theses on Authoritarianism in Pakistan* (Lahore: Folio Books, 2021).

20. Shaheen Sardar Ali and Javaid Rehman, *Indigenous Peoples and Ethnic Minorities of Pakistan: Constitutional and Legal Perspectives* (Surrey, UK: Curzon Press, 2001).

21. "Gilgit-Baltistan Autonomy," *Dawn*, 9 September 2009, https://www.dawn.com/news/843990/gilgitbaltistan-autonomy.

22. For a historical overview of the Frontier Crimes Regulation and its provisions, see Benjamin D. Hopkins, "The Frontier Crimes Regulation and Frontier Governmentality," Journal of Asian Studies 47, no. 2(May 2015): 369–89.

23. "President Signs KP-Fata Merger Bill into Law," *Dawn*, 31 May 2018, https://www.dawn.com/news/1411156.

24. Anam Zakaria's work provides a rare insight into the lives of ordinary people living in Azad Kashmir and their struggle for constitutional rights: *Between the Great Divide: A Journey into Pakistan-Administered Kashmir* (Delhi: HarperCollins India, 2018).

25. Faris A. Khan, "Translucent Citizenship: Khwaja Sira Activism and Alternatives to Dissent in Pakistan," in "Sedition, Sexuality, Gender, and Gender Identity in South Asia," special issue of *South Asia Multidisciplinary Academic Journal* 20 (2019).

26. Will Kymlicka and Wayne Norman, "Return of the Citizen: A Survey of Recent Work on Citizenship Theory," in *Theorizing Citizenship*, ed. Ronald Beiner (Albany: State University of New York Press, 1995), 285.

27. Bryan S. Turner, "Religion and Politics: The Elementary Forms of Citizenship," in *Handbook of Citizenship Studies*, ed. Engin F. Isin and Bryan S. Turner (London: Sage Publications, 2002), 260.

28. Ibid., 261.

29. Bryan S. Turner, "Islam, Civil Society, and Citizenship: Reflections on the Sociology of Citizenship and Islamic Studies," in *Citizenship and the State in the Middle East: Approaches and Applications*, ed. Nils A. Butenschon, Uri Davis, and Manuel Hassassian (Syracuse, NY: Syracuse University Press, 2000), 31.

30. My understanding of Tonnies's differentiation between community and society is borrowed from Gerard Delanty's "Communitarianism and Citizenship," in *Handbook of Citizenship Studies*, ed. Engin F. Isin and Bryan S. Turner (London: Sage Publications, 2002), 159–74.

31. Ibid., 161.

32. Turner, *Religion and Modern Society*, 11.

33. See, e.g., Will Kymlicka, *Multicultural Citizenship: A Liberal Theory of Minority Rights* (Oxford: Oxford University Press, 1996).

34. For instance, see Thomas Janoski, *Citizenship and Civil Society: A Framework of Rights and Obligations in Liberal, Traditional, and Social Democratic Regimes* (Cambridge: Cambridge University Press, 1998).

35. Engin Isin, *Being Political: Genealogies of Citizenship* (Minneapolis: University of Minnesota Press, 2002); Engin Isin, ed. *Citizenship after Orientalism: Transforming Political Theory* (Basingstoke, UK: Palgrave Macmillan, 2015).

36. Engin Isin, introduction to *Citizenship after Orientalism: Transforming Political Theory*, ed. Engin Isin (Basingstoke, UK: Palgrave Macmillan, 2015), 5.

37. Daniel Gorman, *Imperial Citizenship: Empire and the Question of Belonging* (Manchester, UK: Manchester University Press, 2006).

38. Radhika Mongia, *Indian Migration and Empire: A Colonial Genealogy of the Modern State* (Durham, NC: Duke University Press, 2018), 113. As Kalyani Ramnath's monograph shows, the postcolonial subject continued to wrestle with the specter of such policies of racializing bodies and actively sought to overcome them. Ramnath, *Boats in a Storm: Law, Migration, and Decolonization in South and Southeast Asia, 1942–1962* (Stanford, CA: Stanford University Press, 2023).

39. Radhika Singha, "The Great War and a 'Proper' Passport for the Colony: Border-Crossing in British India, c. 1882–1922," *Indian Economic and Social History Review* 50, no. 3 (2013): 289–315.

40. Ulrich K. Preuss, "Citizenship and the German Nation," *Citizenship Studies* 7, no. 1 (2003): 37–56.

41. Rogers Brubaker, *Citizenship and Nationhood in France and Germany* (Cambridge, MA: Harvard University Press, 1996), 52.

42. Saskia Sassen, "Towards Post-National and Denationalized Citizenship," in *Handbook of Citizenship Studies*, ed. Engin. F. Isin and Bryan. S. Turner (London: Sage Publications, 2002), 278–79.

43. T. K. Oommen, *Citizenship, Nationality and Ethnicity: Reconciling Competing Identities* (Cambridge, UK: Polity Press, 1997), 45.

44. Hannah Arendt, *The Origins of Totalitarianism* (New York: Harcourt, Brace & World, 1966), 297.

45. Jürgen Habermas, "The European Nation-State: On the Past and Future of Sovereignty and Citizenship," *Public Culture* 10, no. 2 (1998): 405–6.

46. Mahmood Mamdani, *Neither Settler nor Native: The Making and Unmaking of Permanent Minorities* (Cambridge, MA: Harvard University Press, 2020), 252 and 334. In case of Israel, for instance, the idea of a Jewish homeland is at the heart of the settler-colonial state. So while the settler-colonial state actively disenfranchises non-Jewish Arabs as full citizens, it also vigilantly monitors the boundaries of Jewishness to determine the eligibility of those who can be full citizens. The state adopts an orthodox interpretation of Jewishness (*halacha*) to settle or apply Jewish law in personal matters, but it accepts a more fluid, open-ended definition and claims of ancestry to qualify for full citizenship status of Israel. Ibid., 256.

47. For my argument, I have drawn on an excellent analysis of Arendt's political theory by Seyla Benhabib, especially from her book: *The Rights of Others: Aliens, Residents, and Citizens* (Cambridge: Cambridge University Press, 2004), ch. 2.

48. Nandita Sharma, *Home Rule: National Sovereignty and the Separation of Natives and Migrants* (Durham, NC: Duke University Press, 2020), 14–15.

49. Mamdani, *Neither Settler nor Native*, 14.

50. Quoted in Andrew Schaap, "Enacting the Right to Have Rights: Jacques Rancière's Critique of Hannah Arendt," *European Journal of Political Theory* 10, no. 1 (2011): 26–27.

51. Partha Chatterjee, *Nationalist Thought and the Colonial World: A Derivative Discourse* (London: Zed Books, 1986); *The Nation and Its Fragments: Colonial and Postcolonial Histories* (Princeton, NJ: Princeton University Press, 1993); Sudipta Kaviraj, *The Imaginary Institution of India: Politics and Idea* (New York: Columbia University Press, 2010).

52. I have borrowed this term from Rajat Kanta Ray's *The Felt Community: Commonality and Mentality before the Emergence of Indian Nationalism* (New Delhi: Oxford University Press, 2003).

53. Niraja Gopal Jayal, *Citizenship and Its Discontents: An Indian History* (Cambridge, MA: Harvard University Press, 2013), 23.

54. Ibid., 36–37.

55. Ibid., 28–29.

56. Ibid., 31.

57. See Harald Fischer-Tine, *Low and Licentious Europeans': Race, Class and White Subalternity in Colonial India* (New Delhi: Orient BlackSwan, 2009).

58. Purnima Bose, *Organizing Empire: Individualism, Collective Agency and India* (Durham, NC: Duke University Press, 2003), 8.

59. Jayal, *Citizenship and its Discontents*, 41–42.

60. Ibid., 137–38.

61. Joya Chatterji, "South Asian Histories of Citizenship, 1946–1970," *Historical Journal* 55, no. 4 (December 2012): 1049–71.
62. Ibid., 1052.
63. Uditi Sen, *Citizen Refugee: Forging the Indian Nation after Partition* (Cambridge: Cambridge University Press, 2018).
64. Haimanti Roy, *Partitioned Lives: Migrants, Refugees, Citizens in India and Pakistan, 1947–1965* (New Delhi: Oxford University Press, 2013), 5.
65. Vazira Fazila-Yacoobali Zamindar, *The Long Partition and the Making of Modern South Asia: Refugees, Boundaries, Histories* (New York: Columbia University Press, 2007).
66. Ornit Shani, "Gandhi, Citizenship and the Resilience of Indian Nationhood," *Citizenship Studies* 15, nos. 6–7 (2010): 659–78.
67. Ibid., 662.
68. Ibid., 667.
69. Ibid.
70. Ananya Vajpeyi, *Righteous Republic: The Political Foundations of Modern India* (Cambridge, MA: Harvard University Press, 2012).
71. Some examples are Maria Rashid, *Dying to Serve: Militarism, Affect, and the Politics of Sacrifice in the Pakistan Army* (Stanford, CA: Stanford University Press, 2020); Aasim Sajjad Akhtar, *The Politics of Common Sense: State, Society and Culture in Pakistan* (New Delhi: Cambridge University Press, 2018); Ammara Maqsood, *The New Pakistani Middle Class* (Cambridge, MA: Harvard University Press, 2017); Ayesha Khan, *The Women's Movement in Pakistan: Activism, Islam and Democracy* (London: Bloomsbury, 2019); Taimur Rahman, *The Class Structure of Pakistan* (Karachi: Oxford University Press, 2012); Mubashar Rizvi, *The Ethics of Staying: Social Movements and Land Rights Politics in Pakistan* (Stanford, CA: Stanford University Press, 2019); Anushay Malik, "Public Authority and Local Resistance: Abdur Rehman and the Industrial Workers of Lahore, 1969–1974," *Modern Asian Studies* 52, no. 3 (2018): 815–48.
72. Nosheen Ali, *Delusional States: Feeling Rule and Development in Pakistan's Northern Frontier* (New Delhi: Cambridge University Press, 2019), 3.
73. Ayesha Siddiqi, *In the Wake of Disaster: Islamists, the State and a Social Contract in Pakistan* (New Delhi: Cambridge University Press, 2019), 6.
74. Sarah Ansari and William Gould, *Boundaries of Belonging: Localities, Citizenship and Rights in India and Pakistan* (Cambridge: Cambridge University Press, 2019). Rohit De's work shows how the Indian constitution, and its charter of rights, was taken up on its word by citizen for a range of litigations, which in turn affected the reading of the law and its implementation while showing how citizens cultivated a relationship with the state through exercise of rights. Rohit De, *A People's Constitution: The Everyday Life of Law in the Indian Republic* (Princeton, NJ: Princeton University Press, 2018).
75. Although I had grown up in Pakistan singing the national anthem in school, it was when Capital TV—a news channel launched in 2013—adopted *qaum, mulk, sultanat* as its tagline that I thought about the significance of this stanza and worked toward theorizing it.
76. Ali Usman Qasmi and Megan Eaton Robb, introduction to *Muslims against the Muslim League: Critiques of the Idea of Pakistan*, ed. Ali Usman Qasmi and Megan Eaton Robb (New Delhi: Cambridge University Press, 2017), 10–19.

77. David Gilmartin, "A Magnificent Gift: Muslim Nationalism and the Election Process in Colonial Punjab." *Comparative Studies in Society and History* 40, no. 3 (1998): 415–36.

78. Mana Kia, *Persianate Selves: Memories of Place and Origin before Nationalism* (Stanford, CA: Stanford University Press, 2020), 6.

79. Manan Asif Ahmad, *The Loss of Hindustan: The Invention of India* (Cambridge, MA: Harvard University Press, 2020).

80. For a detailed history, etymology, politics, and policy implications of the new term, see Aminah Mohammad-Arif, "Introduction. Imaginations and Constructions of South Asia: An Enchanting Abstraction?," *South Asia Multidisciplinary Academic Journal* 10 (2014).

81. Pam Morris, ed., *The Bakhtin Reader: Selected Writings of Bakhtin, Mededev and Voloshinov* (London: Arnold, 2003), 53–54.

82. George Lakoff and Mark Johnsen, *Metaphors We Live By* (Chicago: University of Chicago Press, 2003), 6.

83. Ibid., 244–45.

84. Paul Ricouer, *The Rule of Metaphor: The Creation of Meaning in Language* (London: Routledge, 2003), 23.

85. Ibid., 24.

86. An excellent example of this emerging scholarship on the importance of reading the vernaculars for an alternative conceptualizations about language, literary theory, and social history, see Pasha Muhammad Khan's *The Broken Spell: Indian Story Telling and the Romance Genre in Persian and Urdu* (Detroit: Wayne State University Press, 2019). Taimoor Shahid's doctoral research uses the *qissa* of Saif-ul-Muluk—the story of a prince traversing oceans and continents in search for his beloved—and traces it in multiple languages across the wide stretches of the Indian Ocean, embodying various registers of love and intimacy, as well as shades of Sufi and Yogic philosophical thought. Retrieval projects of this sort will benefit immensely from Maryam Wasif Khan's theoretical intervention in which she examines the Orientalist conceptualizations of language, literature, and canonical texts to explain the emergence of "classical Urdu literature" in the colonial period. Maryam Wasif Khan, *Who Is a Muslim? Orientalism and Literary Populisms* (New York: Fordham University Press, 2021).

87. Sudipta Kaviraj, "A Strange Love of the Land: Identity, Poetry and Politics in the (Un)Making of South Asia," *South Asia Multidisciplinary Academic Journal* 10 (2014): https://doi.org/10.4000/samaj.3756.

88. Ibid.

89. Ali Khan Mahmudabad, *The Poetry of Belonging* (New Delhi: Oxford University Press, 2020).

90. Hans Robert Jauss, *Literary Hermeneutics* (Minneapolis: University of Minnesota Press), xxxi.

91. Paolo Desogus, "The Encyclopedia in Umberto Eco's Semiotics," *Semiotica*, no. 192 (2012): 501. For an understanding of Umberto Eco's ideas about encyclopedia and labyrinth, I have relied extensively on Desogus's commentary on Eco's works.

92. Ibid., 514.

93. Umberto Eco, *From the Tree to the Labyrinth: Historical Studies on the Sign and Interpretation* (Cambridge, MA: Harvard University Press, 2014), 54–55.

94. Umberto Eco, *Semiotics and the Philosophy of Language* (Bloomington: Indiana University Press, 1986), 83.

95. Eco, *From the Tree to the Labyrinth*, 93.

96. Shams-ur-Rehman Faruqi, *Sher-i-Shor Angez: Jild Chaharum* (New Delhi: Qaumi Council Bara-i-Farugh-i-Urdu Zaban 2008), 93–95.

97. Ibid., 147–48.

98. Ibid., 149.

99. Akbar Zaidi's book provides a descriptive account of the *qaum* in colonial North India, which can serve as a point of departure for further forays into more intimate languages of *qaum* in vernaculars in other parts of "Muslim India." S. Akbar Zaidi, *Making a Muslim: Reading Publics and Contesting Identities in Nineteenth-Century North India* (New Delhi: Cambridge University Press, 2021).

100. Rafiuddin Ahmad, *The Bengal Muslims 1871–1906: A Quest for Identity* (New Delhi: Oxford University Press, 1981); Sufia Ahmed, *Muslim Community in Bengal, 1884–1912* (Dhaka: University Press Ltd., 1996); Neilesh Bose, *Recasting the Region: Language, Culture, and Islam in Colonial Bengal* (New Delhi: Oxford University Press, 2014).

101. Ayesha Jalal, *Self and Sovereignty: Individual and Community in South Asian Islam since 1950* (London: Routledge, 2000), 41–2.

102. Zaidi, *Making a Muslim*, especially the introduction and ch. 1. In his detailed analysis, Zaidi points out the differences along caste, *baradari* and sectarian lines that had to be addressed or negotiated for the imagining of a unified Muslim community.

103. Jalal, *Self and Sovereignty*, 40–42.

104. Ibid., 10.

105. Faisal Devji, "Muslim Nationalism: Founding Identity in Colonial India" (PhD diss., University of Chicago, 1993), 20.

106. Mirza Ghalib, "iman mujhe roke hai jo khinche hai mujhe kufr," Rekhta, https://www.rekhta.org/couplets/iimaan-mujhe-roke-hai-jo-khiinche-hai-mujhe-kufr-mirza-ghalib-couplets.

107. Devji, "Muslim Nationalism," 45.

108. Ibid., 74.

109. Ibid., 77–78.

110. Ibid., 157–63.

111. See Zaidi, *Making a Muslim*, ch. 2. In Zaidi's words: "*Zillat* was both a location/place and a condition or state-of-being in which people had fallen. *Zillat kā maqām*, a phrase frequently used by Muslim writers in Urdu after 1857, signified a condition of being humiliated as much as it showed that people had fallen to a place where they had been subject to this humiliation" (83).

112. For details about these literary figures and historians, and their creative and intellectual output, see Mushirul Hasan, *A Moral Reckoning: Muslim Intellectuals in Nineteenth-Century Delhi* (New Delhi: Oxford University Press, 2007); Khan, *Who Is a Muslim?*; Christopher Ryan Perkins, "Partitioning History: The Creation of an *Islami Pablik* in Late Colonial India, c. 1880–1920 (Philadelphia: University of Pennsylvania,

2011); Iqbal Singh Sevea, *The Political Philosophy of Muhammad Iqbal: Islam and Nationalism in Late Colonial India* (Cambridge: Cambridge University Press, 2012).

113. Reinhart Koselleck, *Futures Past: On the Semantics of Historical Time* (New York: Columbia University Press, 2004), 10–11.

114. Benedict Anderson, *Imagined Communities: Reflections on the Origin and Spread of Nationalism* (London: Verso, 2006), 205.

115. Laura Adams, *The Spectacular State: Culture and National Identity in Uzbekistan* (Durham, NC: Duke University Press, 2010).

116. Arjun Appadurai, "Full Attachment," *Public Culture* 10, no. 2 (1998): 446.

117. Habermas, "The European Nation-State: One the Past and Future of Sovereignty and Citizenship," *Public Culture* 10, no. 2 (1998): 408.

118. For an overview of disparate approaches towards the idea of Muslim *qaum* leading up to the creation of Pakistan, see Qasmi and Robb, introduction to *Muslims against Muslim League*.

119. As Saadia Toor argues, the creation Pakistan was in the negation of the idea of Muslim nationhood itself as a substantial population of the *qaum* was to remain in India. Saadia Toor, "A National Culture for Pakistan: The Political Economy of a Debate," *Inter-Asia Cultural Studies* 6, no. 3 (2005): 320.

120. Mamdani, *Neither Settler nor Native*, 20.

121. Madhav Khosla, *India's Founding Moment: The Constitution of a Most Surprising Democracy* (Cambridge, MA: Harvard University Press, 2020). Khosla has outlined the basic premise of his book and responded to his critics. Khosla, "The Possibility of Modern India," *Global Intellectual History* 8, no. 1 (2021): 105.

122. Shruti Kapila, *Violent Fraternity: Indian Political Thought in the Global Age* (Princeton, NJ: Princeton University Press, 2021).

123. One finds similar trends in case of Bangladesh and the challenges faced by the members of the Constituent Assembly that became operative soon after the country's independence in 1971. See Dina M. Siddiqi, "Secular Quests, National Others: Revisiting Bangladesh's Constituent Assembly Debates," *Asian Affairs* 49, no. 2 (2018): 238–58. As Siddiqi's article shows, the Bangladeshi Constituent Assembly—besides the remarkable ethno-linguistic congruity of Bangladesh—still struggled to strike a balance between a "core" idea of Bengali nation and Bangladeshi citizens with full legal rights.

124. Maryam S. Khan's ongoing research is a theorization of Pakistan's constitutional history which she dates from the late 1960s to give an account of the making of the 1973 constitution as Pakistan's foundational moment—at least for the new Pakistan that emerged out of the dismemberment of 1971.

125. This is not to suggest that the question of social equality was of any less significance, as it figures prominently in a range of political movements, left-wing mobilizations, and even artistic expressions. Kamran Asdar Ali's *Surkh Salam Communist Politics and Class Activism in Pakistan, 1947–1972* (Karachi: Oxford University Press, 2015) offers a lively account of this period and its movements for social justice. My focus is primarily on the question of political equality as the basis of formulating a shared sense of rights under the umbrella of citizenship. I am grateful to Anubha Anushree for drawing my attention to emphasize further the notion of equality in debates on nationhood in colonial India and the postcolonial nation-states.

126. Faisal Devji, "Illiberal Islam," in *Enchantments of Modernity: Empire, Nation, Globalization*, ed. Saurabh Dube (New Delhi: Routledge, 2009), 248.
127. Ibid., 257.
128. Ibid., 261.
129. Ibid., 255.
130. Ibid., 262.
131. Faisal Devji, "An Impossible Founding," *Global Intellectual History* 8, no. 1 (2021): 6.
132. *Constituent Assembly of Pakistan Debates*, 11 August 1947, vol. 1, no. 2 (Karachi: Government of Pakistan Press), 20.
133. Saadia Toor, "A National Culture for Pakistan: The Political Economy of a Debate," *Inter-Asia Cultural Studies* 6, no. 3 (2005): 319. Also see Saadia Toor, *The State of Islam: Culture and Cold War Politics in Pakistan* (London: Pluto Press, 2011).
134. Lyn Parker, *From Subjects to Citizens: Balinese Villagers in the Indonesian Nation-State* (Copenhagen: NIAS Press, 2003), 206.
135. Srirupa Roy, *Beyond Belief: India and the Politics of Postcolonial Nationalism* (Durham, NC: Duke University Press, 2007), x.
136. Ibid., 14. Emphasis original.
137. Quoted in ibid., 18.
138. Ibid., 18.
139. Thomas Blom Hansen, "Sovereigns beyond the State: On Legality and Authority in Urban India," in *Sovereign Bodies: Citizens, Migrants, and States in the Postcolonial World*, ed. Thomas Blom Hansen and Finn Stepputat (Princeton, NJ: Princeton University Press, 2005), 178; Srirupa Roy, "Instituting Diversity: Official Nationalism in Post-Independence India," *South Asia: Journal of South Asian Studies* 22, no. 1 (1999): 79–99.
140. Gyanendra Pandey, *Routine Violence: Nations, Fragments, Histories* (Stanford, CA: Stanford University Press, 2006), 18–19.
141. Thomas Blom Hansen and Finn Stepputat, introduction to *Sovereign Bodies: Citizens, Migrants, and States in the Postcolonial World*, ed. Thomas Blom Hansen and Finn Stepputat (Princeton, NJ: Princeton University Press, 2005), 3–4.
142. Gayatri Spivak, *Nationalism and the Imagination* (Calcutta: Seagull Books, 2015), 90.

Chapter 1: Noah's Ark?

1. Lucy Chester's *Borders and Conflict in South Asia: The Radcliffe Boundary Commission and the Partition of Punjab* (Manchester, UK: Manchester University Press, 2010) provides an extensive overview of the proceedings of the Boundary Commission headed by Cyril Radcliffe and is based on analytical rigor of a wealth of archival documents.
2. As mentioned in the introduction, although the scale of violence and displacement was large enough to affect communities across the class divide, there was still a considerable population of Dalits, *mazhabi* Sikhs, and other low-caste groups that did not encounter the effect of Partition in the same manner. Many subaltern groups—with considerable religious ambiguity in terms of their affiliation and praxis—continued to live as landless tenants and agricultural workers. It was through a slow process of conversion that these groups became Christians, resulting in a steep rise in Christian population in Punjab.

3. Ted Svensson, *Production of Postcolonial India and Pakistan: Meanings of Partition* (London: Routledge, 2016), 5.

4. Ibid., 26.

5. Ibid., 6.

6. Aditya Nigam, "A Text without Author: Locating Constituent Assembly as Event," *Economic and Political Weekly*, 22–28 May 2004, 2107.

7. Ted Svensson, *Production of Postcolonial India and Pakistan: Meanings of Partition*, 29. Despite Svensson's emphasis on the ambiguity and openness of the process, he limits his analysis by looking for precise moments of closure after which the state was able to take stock of its own past. For instance, in case of Pakistan, Svensson describes the passage of Objectives Resolution in March 1949 calling for the establishment of an Islamic state, as a moment of closure. 27. As we will see in chapter 2, such an assessment fails take into account internal contradictions, counterproposals, and sustained political movements and ideological critiques that continue to inform the public discourse on the issue of an Islamic state in Pakistan. The very purpose of such debates was to challenge the notion of closure on this issue or to treat it as settled.

8. Haimanti Roy, "Paper Rights: The Emergence of Documentary Identities in Post-Colonial India, 1950–67," *South Asia: Journal of South Asian Studies* 39, no. 2 (2016): 329–49; Uditi Sen, *Citizen Refugee: Forging the Indian Nation after Partition* (Cambridge: Cambridge University Press, 2018).

9. Vazira Fazila-Yacoobali Zamindar, *The Long Partition and the Making of Modern South Asia* (New York: Columbia University Press, 2007), 82.

10. Zamindar, in *The Long Partition*, quotes a quatrain from Rais Amrohi who, in a humorous vein, sums up the tragedy of the situation:

> Wife in Hindustan, husband in Sindh
> Both have complaints against fate's partition
> What severe punishment that in order to meet
> Permit they need—how will it be obtained from the gatekeeper. (102)

11. Ibid., 123.

12. Ibid., 125.

13. Ilyas Chattha's work gives a detailed overview of the complications arising out of the evacuee property, their forcible occupation by migrants, the institutionalized forms of corruption and long-drawn legal battles that continued to dominate Pakistan's political landscape till the early 1960s. Some of the court cases continue to this date. Ilyas Chattha, "Competitions for Resources: Partition's Evacuee Property and the Sustenance of Corruption in Pakistan," *Modern Asian Studies* 46, no. 5 (2012): 1182–1211.

14. There were always some exceptions for those with power and influence. As Manav Kapur's ongoing research on evacuee properties shows, there were rare instances in which non-Muslim Punjabis were able to get control of their properties in Pakistan, as late as the 1960s.

15. "Chakwal Ki Landlord Hindu Family—Partition Ke Waqt India Janay Se Inkar Kar Diya Tha," YouTube video, posted by UrduPoint.com, https://www.youtube.com/watch?v=CUjypwQ8xUI.

16. "Hindus, Sikhs and Achhuts," para 271, March 1950, West Punjab Special Branch

Police Abstracts, Roberts Club Archive (Lahore), p. 177. I am grateful to Ilyas Chattha for his help accessing the archive and finding this information.

17. Pallavi Raghavan, *Animosity at Bay: An Alternative History. Of the India-Pakistan Relationship, 1947–1952* (London: Hurst, 2020), 65.

18. Jacques Derrida, "Force of Law: The Mystical Foundations of Authority," in *Deconstruction and the Possibility of Justice*, ed. Drucilla Cornell, Michel Rosenfeld, and David Gray Carlson (New York: Routledge, 1992), 35.

19. Ibid., 36.

20. Muhammad Mukhtar, Ministry of Interior, Home Division, note, 30 July 1948, file no. 46, Ministry of Interior (N), "Proposal for the West Punjab Government to Require All Officers to Take the Oath of Allegiance to the Constitution of Pakistan," *National Archives of Pakistan* (herewith NAP), 4. The question of oath of allegiance had other political implications as well. Maulana Maududi, the head of the Islamist political group Jama'at-i-Islami, had spoken against allegiance or oath for a state not grounded in Islamic principles. It was only after the Objectives Resolution of March 1949, which promised to transform Pakistan into an Islamic state, that Maududi accepted the legitimacy of Pakistani state. See Ali Usman Qasmi, "Differentiating between Pakistan and Napak-istan: Maulana Abul Ala Maududi's Critique of the Muslim League and Muhammad Ali Jinnah," in *Muslims against the Muslim League: Critiques of the Idea of Pakistan*, ed. Ali Usman Qasmi and Megan Eaton Robb (New Delhi: Cambridge University Press, 2017), 135.

21. M. W. Abbasi, Joint Secretary, Ministry of Interior, Home Division, note, 22 March 1949, file no. 46, Ministry of Interior (N), "Proposal for the West Punjab Government to Require All Officers to Take the Oath of Allegiance to the Constitution of Pakistan," NAP, 12.

22. Muhammad Mukhtar, "Summary," Ministry of Interior, Home Division, note, 7 April 1949, file no. 46, Ministry of Interior (N), "Proposal for the West Punjab Government to Require All Officers to Take the Oath of Allegiance to the Constitution of Pakistan," NAP, 16.

23. Ian Sanjay Patel, *We're Here Because You Were There: Immigration and the End of Empire* (London: Verso, 2021), 95 (e-book).

24. Ibid., 98.

25. Ibid., 99.

26. Ibid., 100. Emphasis added.

27. Jayal, *Citizenship and Its Discontents*, 54.

28. Ibid., 54–56.

29. Sarah Ansari, "Subjects or Citizens? India, Pakistan and the 1948 British Nationality Act," *Journal of Imperial and Commonwealth History* 41, no. 2 (2013): 300–305.

30. Kalathmika Natarajan, "The Privilege of the Indian Passport (1947–1967): Caste, Class, and the afterlives of indenture in Indian Diplomacy," *Modern Asian Studies* 57, no. 2 (2022): 321–50.

31. "Meeting of the Cabinet Held on Wednesday, the 21st December, 1949," file no. 46, Ministry of Interior (C), "Proposal for the West Punjab Government to Require All Officers to Take the Oath of Allegiance to the Constitution of Pakistan," NAP, 39.

32. T. B. Creagh Coen to S. N. Bakar, Deputy Secretary to the Government of Pa-

kistan, Ministry of the Interior, Home Division, 10 January 1950, file no. 46, Ministry of Interior (C), "Proposal for the West Punjab Government to Require All Officers to Take the Oath of Allegiance to the Constitution of Pakistan," NAP, 43.

33. T. B. Creagh Coen, "Memorandum by the Ministry of Foreign Affairs and Commonwealth Relations on the Bill to Provide for Pakistan Citizenship," file no. 46, Ministry of Interior (C), "Proposal for the West Punjab Government to Require All Officers to Take the Oath of Allegiance to the Constitution of Pakistan," NAP, 61.

34. Edward Snelson, note, 3 February 1950, file no. 46, Ministry of Interior (N), "Proposal for the West Punjab Government to Require All Officers to Take the Oath of Allegiance to the Constitution of Pakistan," NAP, 65.

35. "Special Committee to Consider the Bill to Define Pakistan Citizenship—Minutes of the Meeting held on 1-4-50," file no. 46, "Proposal for the West Punjab Government to Require All Officers to Take the Oath of Allegiance to the Constitution of Pakistan" (N), NAP, 105. In another meeting held on 25 July 1950, the Law Division was asked to consider the possibility of replacing the phrase *British subject* with *British citizen*. Ibid., 122.

36. A. S. B. Shah, "Note," 2 August 1950, file no. 46, Ministry of Interior (N), "Proposal for the West Punjab Government to Require All Officers to Take the Oath of Allegiance to the Constitution of Pakistan," NAP, 143.

37. Note by Ministry of States and Frontier Regions, 29 July 1950, file no. 46, "Proposal for the West Punjab Government to Require All Officers to Take the Oath of Allegiance to the Constitution of Pakistan" (N), NAP, 141.

38. "Proceedings of the Meeting of the Sub-Committee of Cabinet on Citizenship Bill held on 18th August 1950," file no. 46, "Proposal for the West Punjab Government to Require All Officers to Take the Oath of Allegiance to the Constitution of Pakistan" (N), NAP, 180–2.

39. "Influx of Powindahs in Pakistan," file no. 517/CF/60, Cabinet Division, Government of Pakistan, National Documentation Centre Islamabad (henceforth NDC).

40. File no. 46, Ministry of Interior (N), "Proposal for the West Punjab Government to Require All Officers to Take the Oath of Allegiance to the Constitution of Pakistan," NAP, 101c.

41. For this section, I use the text of the Citizenship Act of 1951, available at Refworld: https://www.refworld.org/pdfid/3ae6b4ffa.pdf.

42. "Pakistan Citizenship Legislation," Dominions Office and Commonwealth Relations Office, DO 35/6392, National Archives, London (NA).

43. For a comparative perspective on how an apparently slight change in wording can be indicative of fundamental shifts in the ideological settings of the law, one can look at the trajectory of the Turkish citizenship law and its various amendments during the 1920s and 1930s. Even though Turkey had become a republic, it continued to accommodate former "Ottoman subjects" from the Balkans and the Arab territories who had moved to the mainland by a certain cutoff date. Article 6 of Law 1312 was, however, applicable to Muslims only. The continuity of an empire-based affiliation was gradually replaced by an emphasis on Turkish ethnicity as a prerequisite for citizenship. By the early 1930s, the term *Turkish* had replaced *Muslim* in reference to immigrants, but it

was later changed to the more neutral *persons*. Soner Cagaptay, "Citizenship Policies in Interwar Turkey," *Nations and Nationalism* 9, no. 4 (2003): 601–19.

44. Serial no. 99, "Question of the National Status of Kashmiri Refugees, etc." (N), Ministry of Interior, NAP, 36–39.

45. M. A. Samad, Joint Secretary, "Note," 9 November 1955, file no. 82, "Law regarding Illegitimate Children," (N), NAP, 2.

46. Matthew S. Hull, *Government of Paper: The Materiality of Bureaucracy in Pakistan* (Oakland: University of California Press, 2012), 116.

47. Ibid., 126.

48. Ann Laura Stoller, *Along the Archival Grain: Epistemic Anxieties and Colonial Common Sense* (Princeton, NJ: Princeton University Press, 2010), 1.

49. Ibid., 2.

50. Hull, *Government of Paper*, 117.

51. Hameeduddin Ahmed, Office on Special Duty, file no. 47, "Pakistan Citizenship Bill, as Amended by the Select Committee in the Light of the Interim Report of the Committee on Fundamental Rights of Citizens of Pakistan etc., and Finally Passed by the Constituent Assembly" (N), Ministry of Interior, NAP, 47–48.

52. *Pakistan Times*, 18 August 1952.

53. *Constituent Assembly (Legislative) of Pakistan Debates*, Monday, 24 November 1952 (Karachi: Government of Pakistan Press), 598.

54. *Constituent Assembly (Legislative) of Pakistan Debates*, Tuesday, 25 November 1952 (Karachi: Government of Pakistan Press), 614.

55. Ibid., 630.

56. Ibid., 635.

57. Ibid., 610.

58. Abdullah Akhund, Undersecretary to the Government of Pakistan, to Home Secretary, Government of East Pakistan, February 1956, serial no. 103, "Clarification of Section 7 vis-à-vis Section 20 of the Pakistan Citizenship Act, 1951" (C), Ministry of Interior, NAP, 6.

59. File no. 91, "Question Whether the Migrant Hindus Should Be Accepted as Citizens of Pakistan in Case They Make Applications to the Central Government for Registration as Citizens of Pakistan—Policy regarding Migrant Hindus of East Pakistan" (N), Ministry of Interior, NAP, 2.

60. Quoted in Mamdani, *Neither Settler nor Native*, 251.

61. M. W. Abbasi, file no. 91, "Question Whether the Migrant Hindus Should Be Accepted as Citizens of Pakistan in Case They Make Applications to the Central Government for Registration as Citizens of Pakistan—Policy regarding Migrant Hindus of East Pakistan" (N), Ministry of Interior, *NAP*, 9.

62. File no. 91, "Question Whether the Migrant Hindus Should Be Accepted as Citizens of Pakistan in Case They Make Applications to the Central Government for Registration as Citizens of Pakistan—Policy regarding Migrant Hindus of East Pakistan" (N), Ministry of Interior, *NAP*, 3.

63. Ibid., 4.

64. Ibid., 4–6.

65. Zamindar, *The Long Partition*, 94.

66. File no. 91, "Question Whether the Migrant Hindus Should Be Accepted as Citizens of Pakistan in Case They Make Applications to the Central Government for Registration as Citizens of Pakistan—Policy regarding Migrant Hindus of East Pakistan" (N), Ministry of Interior, NAP, 7.

67. Serial no. 104, "Refusal of C.C Karachi to Deliver Two Citizenship Certificates Granted by the Central Government" (N), Ministry of Interior, NAP, 13.

68. Serial no. 124, "Policy regarding 'Go Slow' in the Matter Granting Pakistan Citizenship to Indian Nationals and Foreigners" (N), Ministry of Interior, NAP, 7.

69. S. M. Ayub, Deputy Secretary, 15 July 1958, serial no. 115 (untitled file) (N), Ministry of Interior, *NAP*, 2.

70. A. A. Hamid, Principal Secretary, to Prime Minister, 17 July 1958, serial no. 115 (untitled file) (N), Ministry of Interior, NAP, 2.

71. A. R. M. Fazlur Rehman to A. K. Soofi, Secretary to Administrator of Karachi, 29 June 1960, serial no. 124, "Policy regarding 'Go Slow' in the Matter Granting Pakistan Citizenship to Indian Nationals and Foreigners" (C), Ministry of Interior, NAP, 14.

72. Serial no. 122, "Question Whether India Has Been Accepting Muslim Widows from Pakistan for Settling in India with Their Relatives on the Demise of Their Husbands in Pakistan" (N), Ministry of Interior, NAP, 1.

73. Ibid., 2.

74. Ibid.

75. Ibid., 3.

76. Serial no. 104, "Refusal of C.C Karachi to Deliver Two Citizenship Certificates Granted by the Central Government" (C), Ministry of Interior, NAP, 8.

77. A note dated 28 January 1959 read: "The expression 'Muslim Widow' is vague—Pakistanis or Indians? Or what? Min/Interior want to cover with this team [*sic*] all Muslim women in Pakistan who fall widow?," serial no. 122, "Question Whether India Has Been Accepting Muslim Widows from Pakistan for Settling in India with Their Relatives on the Demise of Their Husbands in Pakistan" (N), Ministry of Interior, NAP, 4.

78. Serial no. 94, "General Policy regarding Grant of Citizenship to Women Separated from Their Husbands in India" (N), Ministry of Interior, NAP, 1.

79. Ibid., 4.

80. Ibid.

81. *Constituent Assembly of Pakistan (Legislature) Debates*, 7 April 1952 (Karachi: Government of Pakistan Press), 1157.

82. Ibid., 1160.

83. Ibid., 1161.

84. Ibid., 1163.

85. G. A. Ahmed, "Amendment of the Pakistan Citizenship Act," serial no. 59, "Pakistan Citizenship Rules 1951—Comments by This Ministry" (N), Ministry of Interior, NAP, 50.

86. Serial no. 80, "Issue of Passports to the Citizens of India Who Enter Pakistan through Khokhrapar" (N), Ministry of Interior, NAP, 1.

87. "Reference Preceding Note of the M/FA&CR," serial no. 80, "Issue of Passports

to the Citizens of India Who Enter Pakistan through Khokhrapar" (N), Ministry of Interior, NAP, 6.

88. Serial no. 80, "Issue of Passports to the Citizens of India Who Enter Pakistan through Khokhrapar" (N), Ministry of Interior, NAP, 8.

89. Serial no. 80, "Issue of Passports to the Citizens of India Who Enter Pakistan through Khokhrapar" (N), Ministry of Interior, NAP, 11–12.

90. Ibid., 11.
91. Ibid., 12.
92. Ibid., 15.
93. Ibid.
94. Ibid.
95. Ibid., 16.
96. Ibid.
97. Ibid., 21–22.
98. Ibid., 18–19.
99. Ibid., 20.
100. Ibid., 25. Emphasis added.
101. Serial no. 80, "Issue of Passports to the Citizens of India Who Enter Pakistan through Khokhrapar" (C), Ministry of Interior, NAP, 3.

102. Serial no. 128, "Query from F.P.S.C. Whether Requirement of Domicile Certificates Should Not Be Insisted upon Indian Nationals Applying for Pakistani Nationality," Ministry of Interior, NAP.

103. Serial no. 130, "Policy regarding the Grant of Citizenship and Naturalization Certificate" (N), Ministry of Interior, NAP, 2.

104. Ibid., 3–4.
105. Ibid.
106. Ibid., 5.
107. Ibid.
108. Ibid., 22.
109. Ibid., 49-J.
110. From A. R. M. Fazlur Rahman, Deputy Secretary to the Government of Pakistan, to Chief Secretary to the Government of East Pakistan, Dacca, and Chief Secretary to the Government of West Pakistan, Lahore, 14 June 1960, serial no. 128, "Query from F.P.S.C. Whether Requirement of Domicile Certificates Should Not Be Insisted upon Indian Nationals Applying for Pakistani Nationality" (C), Ministry of Interior, NAP, 6.

111. Ibid., 7.
112. Ibid.
113. Ibid., 8.
114. Ibid.
115. Ibid., 9.
116. Ibid.
117. Serial no. 149, "Amendment in the Pakistan Citizenship Act 1951 with a View to Facilitating Acquisition of Pakistan Citizenship by Indian Muslims—A Bill Introduced by the Hon'able Mr. Abul Quasem" (N), Ministry of Interior, NAP, 4.

118. Ibid., 5.

119. "Note for the Minister of Home and Kashmir Affairs," serial no. 149, "Amendment in the Pakistan Citizenship Act 1951 with a View to Facilitating Acquisition of Pakistan Citizenship by Indian Muslims—A Bill Introduced by the Hon'able Mr. Abul Quasem" (C), Ministry of Interior, NAP, 10.

120. Ibid., 9.

121. Serial no. 132, "Determination of National Status of Late Mr. Fazal Din Who Died in the Philippines" (N), Ministry of Interior, NAP, 1.

122. File no. 87 (untitled) (N), Ministry of Interior, NAP, 28–29. According to the summary provided by the ministry, the issue of Muslims in Burma had first surfaced in 1955.

123. Ibid., 28–29.

124. Ibid., 29.

125. Ibid., 14.

126. Ibid., 16.

127. "Office Memorandum," M. Zia Husain, Assistant Secretary to the Government of Pakistan, to Ministry of Foreign Affairs and Commonwealth Relations, 12 June 1958, file no. 87 (Untitled) (C), Ministry of Interior, NAP, 13. Emphasis added.

128. Ministry of Foreign Affairs and Commonwealth Relations to Chancery, Embassy of Pakistan in Burma, November 1958, file no. 87 (Untitled) (C), Ministry of Interior, NAP, 16.

129. *Roochomal Daryanomal v. Province of West Pakistan* (1959), The All-Pakistan Legal Decisions (PLD).

130. G. A. Khan, Assistant Secretary, 23 September 1953, file no. 71 (Untitled) (N), Ministry of Interior, NAP, 5.

131. S. H. Firoz, Ministry of Foreign Affairs and Commonwealth Relations, 21 October 1953, file no. 71 (N), Ministry of Interior, NAP, 9.

132. S. H. Firoz, Passport Officer, 7 November 1951, serial no. 59, "Pakistan Citizenship Rules 1951—Comments by This Ministry" (N), Ministry of Interior, NAP, 2–4.

133. *Pakistan Observer* (Dacca), 9 September 1958.

134. For details, see Ameem Lutfi, "Conquest without Rule: Baloch Portfolio Mercenaries in the Indian Ocean," (PhD diss., Duke University, 2018).

135. Serial no. 112, "Question regarding Citizenship Rights of the Residents of Gwadur" (N), Ministry of Interior, NAP, 16.

136. Ibid., 18.

137. Ibid., 19.

138. For details, see Rakesh Ankit, "The Accession of Junagadh, 1947–48: Colonial Sovereignty, State Violence and Post-Independence India," *Indian Economic and Social History Review* 53, no. 3 (2016): 371–404.

139. For more details, see Taylor C. Sherman, *Muslim Belonging in Secular India: Negotiating Citizenship in Postcolonial Hyderabad* (Cambridge: Cambridge University Press, 2015).

140. Hameeduddin Ahmed, Joint Secretary, Government of Pakistan, to Ataullah Jan Khan, Joint Secretary, Ministry of States and Frontier Regions, 14 October 1958, serial no. 112, "Question regarding Citizenship Rights of the Residents of Gwadur" (C), Ministry of Interior, NAP, 4.

141. *Constituent Assembly of Pakistan Debates*, Thursday, 2 February 1956, vol. 1, No. 62 (Karachi: Government of Pakistan Press), 2314.
142. Ibid., 2317.
143. Ibid., 2316.
144. Étienne Balibar, *Citizenship* (Malden, MA: Polity Press, 2015), 76.
145. Ibid., 72.
146. As per amendment introduced via an ordinance in 1978 (and available at https://data.globalcit.eu/), the following categories of persons were to either retain or lose their citizenship:

(1) All persons who, at any time before the sixteenth day of December, 1971, were citizens of Pakistan domiciled in the territories which before the said day constituted the Province of East Pakistan and who (i) were residing in those territories on that day and are residing therein since that day voluntarily or otherwise shall cease to be citizens of Pakistan; (ii) were residing in Pakistan on that day but after that day voluntarily migrated to those territories shall cease to be citizens of Pakistan; (iii) were residing in Pakistan on that day and are voluntarily residing therein since that day shall continue to be citizens of Pakistan; (iv) were residing in those territories on that day but voluntarily came to Pakistan after that day with the approval of the Federal Government shall continue to be citizens of Pakistan.

(2) Any person who, at any time before the sixteenth day of December, 1971, was a citizen of Pakistan domiciled in the territories which before the said day constituted the Province of East Pakistan and who, being under the protection of a Pakistan passport, was on that day, or is, residing in any country beyond those territories shall not be deemed to be a citizen of Pakistan unless, upon an application made by him to the Federal Government in this behalf, the Federal Government has granted him a certificate that at the date of the certificate he is a citizen of Pakistan.

147. Balibar, *Citizenship*, 74.
148. The case of women was different. In most cases they desperately wanted to escape their abductor's household and be reunited with their families. In some cases, however, the women bearing their abductor's children had little choice. They had to make peace with their situation, as they feared rejection from their families for losing their "honor." Still, the question of consent was a tough one in the case of many such women who did not want to be repatriated. Ritu Menon and Kamla Bhasin, "Recovery, Rupture, Resistance-Indian State and Abduction of Women during Partition," *Economic and Political Weekly*, 24 April 1993, WS2–WS11.
149. Khayyam Chohan has recorded the lives and experiences of some of these children—now in their early eighties—who had little or no memory of their parents and were reluctant to be sent to Pakistan. As some of the interviewees recounted, they escaped from the refugee camps or local police stations, where they were kept after "recovery" from their foster parents. For details, see Chohan's YouTube channel, Desi Infotainer: https://www.youtube.com/c/DesiInfotainer.

Chapter 2: Quilting Islam

1. Partha Chatterjee, *I Am the People: Reflections on Popular Sovereignty Today* (New York: Columbia University Press, 2020), 87.
2. Ibid., 85–86.
3. Ernesto Laclau, *On Populist Reason* (London: Verso, 2005), 69.
4. Ibid.
5. Ibid., 70.
6. Ibid.
7. Laclau's theoretical methods have recently become popular with scholars of South Asian studies. The best example is Jurgen Schaflechner's *Hinglaj Devi: Identity, Change, and Solidification at a Hindu Temple in Pakistan* (Karachi: Oxford University Press, 2020). Sumrin Kalia's upcoming manuscript provisionally titled "Imagining Madina: Narratives and Networks of Islamic Populism" also uses Laclau's theoretical insights. The title of my chapter draws inspiration from a section on "quilting Hindutva" in Shruti Kapila's book. Kapila, *Violent Fraternity*, 97–98.
8. G. W. Choudhury, *Constitutional Development in Pakistan* (Karachi: Royal Book Co., 2007); M. Rafique Afzal, *Political Parties in Pakistan*, 3 vols. (Islamabad: National Institute of Historical and Cultural Research, 1998); Kausar Parveen, *Politics of Pakistan: Role of the Opposition, 1947–58* (Karachi: Oxford University Press, 2014).
9. For details about the Constituent Assemblies, the description of party strength, and other aspects of their history and working, I have relied extensively on Choudhury's *Constitutional Development in Pakistan*.
10. M. Rafique Afzal, *Political Parties in Pakistan, 1947–1958: Vol. I* (Islamabad: National Institute of Historical and Cultural Research, 2002), 194–95.
11. For details, see Allen McGrath, *The Destruction of Pakistan's Democracy* (Karachi: Oxford University Press, 1996).
12. Choudhury, *Constitutional Development in Pakistan*, 158.
13. Prathama Banerjee, *Elementary Aspects of the Political: Histories from the Global South* (Durham, NC: Duke University Press, 2021), 6–7.
14. Some recent works analyzing the Objectives Resolution include Yaqoob Khan Bangash, "Sovereignty and the Constitution," *Journal of Law, Religion and State* 7, no. 2 (2018): 129–51; Neeti Nair, *Hurt Sentiments: Secularism and Belonging in South Asia* (Cambridge, MA: Harvard University Press, 2023), ch. 3.
15. M. Rafique Afzal, ed., *Speeches and Statements of Quaid-i-Millat Liaquat Ali Khan (1941–51)* (Lahore: Research Society of Pakistan, 1987), 241.
16. Ibid., 161.
17. Nelly Lahoud, *A Study in Intellectual Boundaries: Political Thought in Islam* (London: Routledge, 2005), 7.
18. Ali Usman Qasmi, *The Ahmadis and the Politics of Religious Exclusion in Pakistan* (London: Anthem Press, 2014), 28.
19. *Imroz*, 4 April 1948.
20. *Morning News*, 16 October 1947.
21. Emad El-Din Shahin, "Government," in *Islamic Political Thought: An Introduction*, ed. Gerhard Bowering (Princeton, NJ: Princeton University Press), 69–70.

22. Patricia Crone, *Medieval Islamic Political Thought* (Edinburgh: Edinburgh University Press, 2004), 286–87.

23. Ibid., 287.

24. Roshain Abbasi, "Did Premodern Muslims Distinguish the Religious and Secular? The Dīn-Dunyā Binary in Medieval Islamic Thought," *Journal of Islamic Studies* 31, no. 2 (2020): 185–225.

25. Crone, *Medieval Islamic Political Thought*, 396.

26. Hans-Georg Gadamer, *Truth and Method* (London: Continuum, 2004), 305.

27. Ibid., 317.

28. Ibid., 322.

29. Ibid., 382.

30. "Pakistan Constitution," box 1, 2–3, Zafar Ahmed Ansari Collection (hereafter Ansari Collection), Freedom Movement Archives, University of Karachi. This report was signed and submitted on 30 April 1950. The name of the author has not been mentioned, but it must have been a jointly written document submitted by the board.

31. "Pakistan Constitution," box 1, 30 April 1950, 6, Ansari Collection.

32. Ibid., 7.

33. Ibid., 8.

34. Ibid., 9.

35. Crone, *Medieval Islamic Political Thought*, 300.

36. See Michael Cook, *Commanding Right and Forbidding Wrong in Islamic Thought* (Cambridge: Cambridge University Press, 2001).

37. "Pakistan Constitution," box 1, 30 April 1950, 9, Ansari Collection.

38. Ibid., 3.

39. "Pakistan Constitution," box 1, undated, 1, Ansari Collection.

40. Ibid., 2.

41. Ibid., 3.

42. Ibid., 4.

43. Ibid., 5.

44. Ibid., 3. These concept notes have been put together in the folder titled "Minutes of Various Sub-Committees Regard Board Talimate Islamia."

45. Ibid., 6.

46. "Boards Views and Comments on the Interim Report of the Fundamental Rights Committee," box 3, 1, Ansari Collection.

47. Ibid., 6.

48. *Fundamental Principles of an Islamic State: Formulated at a gathering of Ulama of various Muslim Schools of Thought under the Presidentship of Allama Syed Suleiman Sahib Nadvi* (Karachi: Published by Maulana Ehtishamul Haq Thanvi, Jacob Lines, Sadar, ca. 1951).

49. "Amendments Proposed by the Board of Talimat-i-Islamia to the Report (dated 3.10.52) of the Basic Principles Committee," box 3, 1, Ansari Collection.

50. Ibid., 2.

51. Ibid., 24.

52. Ibid., 4.

53. Ibid., 5.

54. There is a brief note at the end of the draft that indicates the pamphlet was adopted from an article published by Zafar Ahmad Ansari in *Dawn*.

55. "Views and Amendments of Reputed Ulema of Various Schools of Thought on the Recommendations of the Basic Principles Committee," box 2, 5, Ansari Collection.

56. Ibid., 5.

57. Muhammad Qasim Zaman, *The Ulema in Contemporary Islam: Custodians of Change* (Princeton, NJ: Princeton University Press, 2002), 98.

58. Crone, *Medieval Islamic Political Thought*, 281.

59. Wael B. Hallaq, *The Impossibility of an Islamic State: Islam, Politics, and Modernity's Moral Predicament* (New York: Columbia University Press, 2012).

60. "Mussawwida Dastur-i-Pakistan," box 1, Ansari Collection.

61. "Mussawwida Dastur-i-Pakistan," box 1, art. 31, Ansari Collection.

62. Ibid., 3.

63. Ibid., 5.

64. Ibid., 6.

65. Ibid., 8.

66. Gadamer, *Truth and Method*, 305.

67. Choudhury, *Constitutional Development in Pakistan*, 81.

68. "Extracts from the Minutes of the Meeting of the B.P.C. held on the 17th November, 1952," box 3, Ansari Collection.

69. "Amendments to the Constitution," box 1, 5, Ansari Collection.

70. *Morning News*, 18 October 1953.

71. Muhammad Qasim Zaman, *Islam in Pakistan: A History* (Princeton, NJ: Princeton University Press, 2019), 58.

72. *Morning News*, 22 October 1953.

73. Faisal Devji, *Muslim Zion: Pakistan as a Political Idea* (London: Hurst and Co., 2013), 204.

74. Ibid., 207.

75. Quoted in Devji, *Muslim Zion*, 201.

76. Neeti Nair has also covered parts of these debates on nomenclature in her recently published work. Nair, *Hurt Sentiments*, 168–74.

77. *Constituent Assembly of Pakistan Debates*, 27 January 1956, vol. 1, no. 58 (Karachi: Government of Pakistan Press), 2147.

78. *Constituent Assembly of Pakistan Debates*, 28 January 1956, vol. 1, no. 59 (Karachi: Government of Pakistan Press), 2182.

79. Ibid., 2184.

80. *Constituent Assembly of Pakistan Debates*, 29 February 1956, vol. 1, no. 80 (Karachi: Government of Pakistan Press), 3698.

81. *Constituent Assembly of Pakistan Debates*, 21 February 1956, vol. 1, no. 76 (Karachi: Government of Pakistan Press), 3367.

82. Ibid., 3370; *Constituent Assembly of Pakistan Debates*, 26 January 1956, vol. 1, no. 57 (Karachi: Government of Pakistan Press), 2078.

83. *Constituent Assembly of Pakistan Debates*, 21 January 1956, vol. 1, no. 76 (Karachi: Government of Pakistan Press), 1906.

84. *Constituent Assembly of Pakistan Debates*, 21 February 1956, vol. 1, no. 76, 3374.
85. Ibid., 3375.
86. *Constituent Assembly of Pakistan Debates*, 27 January 1956, vol. 1, no. 58, 2116.
87. *Constituent Assembly of Pakistan Debates*, 21 February 1956, vol. 1, no. 76, 3358–59.
88. Ibid., 3384.
89. Ibid., 3400.
90. *Constituent Assembly of Pakistan Debates*, 26 January 1956, vol. 1, no. 57, 2074.
91. *Constituent Assembly of Pakistan Debates*, 21 February 1956, vol. 1, no. 76, 3385.
92. Ibid., 3385.
93. *Constituent Assembly of Pakistan Debates*, 31 January 1956, vol. 1, no. 60 (Karachi: Government of Pakistan Press), 2248.
94. *Constituent Assembly of Pakistan Debates*, 1 February 1956, vol. 1, no. 61 (Karachi: Government of Pakistan Press), 2258.
95. *Constituent Assembly of Pakistan Debates*, 29 February 1956, vol. 1, no. 80 (Karachi: Government of Pakistan Press), 3670.
96. Saul A. Kripke, *Naming and Necessity* (Cambridge, MA: Harvard University Press, 2001).
97. Laclau, *On Populist Reason*, 102.
98. Devji, *Muslim Zion*, 202.
99. Naveeda Khan's ethnographic study on contemporary Pakistan gives an account of aspirational striving toward an idealized Muslim belief and practice—both at the statist and the individual level—and the contradictions, failings, and potentials of such efforts. See Naveeda Khan, *Muslim Becoming: Aspiration and Skepticism in Pakistan* (Durham, NC: Duke University Press, 2012).
100. Ibid., 95.
101. Laclau, *On Populist Reason*, 97.
102. Ibid., 97.
103. Ibid., 98.
104. Ibid., 100–1.
105. Ibid., 105.
106. Ibid., 133.
107. Ibid., 155–56.
108. Partha Chatterjee, *I Am the People: Reflections on Popular Sovereignty Today* (New York: Columbia University Press, 2020), 83.
109. I infer this point from Laclau's brief reference to the Kemalist project in Turkey. Laclau, *On Populist Reason*, 208.
110. Ibid., 227.
111. The note was issued from the Prime Minister's Office, Karachi, but undersigned by the president of Pakistan Muslim League. Its date, estimated on the basis of other documents to be found in this file that are part of the Prime Ministerial Secretariat record at the National Archives of Pakistan, is around August 1952.
112. "Amendments to the Constitution," box 1, 15, Ansari Collection.
113. "Amendments Proposed by the Board of Talimat-i-Islamia to the Report (dated 3.10.52) of the Basic Principles Committee," box 3, 24–25, Ansari Collection.
114. Ibid., 25.

115. "Amendments to the Constitution," box 1, 16, Ansari Collection.
116. Ibid., 16.
117. *Constituent Assembly of Pakistan Debates (Constitution)*, 24 October 1953, vol. 15, no. 13 (Karachi: Government of Pakistan Press), 415.
118. *Constituent Assembly of Pakistan Debates*, 23 January 1956, vol. 1, no. 60 (Karachi: Government of Pakistan Press), 1950.
119. *Constituent Assembly of Pakistan Debates*, 31 January 1956, vol. 1, no. 60, 2252.
120. *Constituent Assembly of Pakistan Debates*, 29 February 1956, vol. 1, no. 80, 3670.
121. *Constituent Assembly of Pakistan Debates*, 1 February 1956, vol. 1, no. 61, 2265.
122. *Constituent Assembly of Pakistan Debates*, 21 February 1956, vol. 1, no. 76, 3460.
123. *Morning News*, 18 February 1956.
124. Serial no. 94, PM Secretariat, National Archives of Pakistan, Islamabad, 452.
125. Ibid., 457.
126. Ibid., 449.
127. Ibid., 450.
128. Ibid., 449.
129. Qasmi, *Ahmadis and the Politics of Religious Exclusion in Islam*, 174.
130. Chantal Mouffe, "Religion, Liberal Democracy, and Citizenship," in *Political Theologies: Public Religions in a Post-Secular World*, ed. Hent De Vries and Lawrence E. Sullivan (New York: Fordham University Press, 2006), 322.
131. Ibid., 320.
132. Ibid., 322.
133. *Constituent Assembly of Pakistan Debates*, 21 February 1956, vol. 1, no. 76, 3461.
134. Mohammad Basheer Ahmad, ed., *Selected Constitutions of the World*, 2 vols. (Karachi: Governor General's Press and Publications, 1951). The first volume solely comprised constitutional drafts of various "Eastern" countries. As the editor explained it in the preface to the volume, the volume's composition was an intentional departure from the "general tendency to draw inspiration from the West in political and constitutional matters."
135. *Constituent Assembly of Pakistan Debates*, 28 January 1956, vol. 1, no. 59, 2200.
136. Ibid., 2193.
137. Ibid., 2194.
138. Ibid., 2194.
139. *Constituent Assembly of Pakistan Debates*, 21 February 1956, vol. 1, no. 76, 3448.
140. Quoted in Saadia Toor, "A National Culture for Pakistan: The Political Economy of a Debate," *Inter-Asia Cultural Studies* 6, no. 3 (2005): 326.
141. Ibid., 328.
142. Serial no. 50, PM Secretariat, 61.
143. Abul Mansur Ahmad, *End of a Betrayal and Restoration of Lahore Resolution* (Dacca: Khoshroz Kitab Mahal, 1975), quoted in Rachel Fell McDermott, Leonard A. Gordon, Ainslie T. Embree, Frances W. Pritchett, and Dennis Dalton, eds., *Sources of Indian Traditions: Modern India, Pakistan, and Bangladesh* (New York: Columbia University Press, 2014), 862–64.
144. *Constituent Assembly of Pakistan Debates*, 16 January 1956 (Karachi: Government of Pakistan Press), 1826–27. Among other items, the united opposition parties had de-

manded the establishment of naval headquarters in East Pakistan and an ordnance factory to make the region militarily self-sufficient.

145. *Constituent Assembly of Pakistan Debates*, 26 January 1956, vol. 1, no. 57 (Karachi: Government of Pakistan Press), 2094.

146. *Constituent Assembly of Pakistan Debates*, Thursday, 2 February 1956, vol. 1, no. 62 (Karachi: Government of Pakistan Press), 2321.

147. Ibid., 2323.

148. *Constituent Assembly of Pakistan Debates*, 31 January 1956, vol. 1, no. 60, 2213.

149. Ibid., 2213.

150. Muhammad Aslam Malik, *The Making of the Pakistan Resolution* (Karachi: Oxford University Press, 2001), 202. Emphasis added.

151. Attique Zafar Sheikh, Ashraf Ali and Malik Mohammad Riaz, eds. *Pakistan Resolution and the Working Committee of the All India Muslim League 1940* (Islamabad: National Archives of Pakistan, ca. 1990), 184.

152. Muhammad Aslam Malik, *The Making of the Pakistan Resolution*, 209.

153. Ibid., 207.

154. Ibid., 208.

155. *Constituent Assembly of Pakistan Debates*, 31 January 1956, vol. 1, no. 60, 2214.

156. Ibid., 2227.

157. *Constituent Assembly of Pakistan Debates*, 28 February 1956, vol. 1, no. 79 (Karachi: Government of Pakistan Press), 3640.

158. Sadia Saeed, *Politics of Desecularization: Law and the Minority Question in Pakistan* (Cambridge: Cambridge University Press, 2016), 5.

159. Ibid., 24.

160. Amanullah Memon, ed., *The Altaf Gauhar Papers: Documents Towards the Making of the Constitution of 1962* (Lahore: Sang-e-Meel Publications, 2003), 27.

161. Ibid., 304.

162. "Religious Problems of Pakistan," 12/CF/64, NDC, 2.

163. Ibid., 9.

164. Ibid., 11.

165. Ibid., 10.

166. Ibid., 5.

167. "Schemes for Modernization of Mosques and Training of Imams," 54/CF/60, NDC, 29.

168. Ibid., 30.

169. Ibid., 31.

170. Ibid., 34. The authors of the note observed that the Ramakrishna Mission attributed Marathas success over the Mughals to the religious revival infused by Sant Tukaram's devotional songs rather than Shivaji's prowess in military.

171. Ibid., 32.

172. Ibid., 36.

173. File no. 699, "Bureau of National Reconstruction—Short Term Plan for East Pakistan," NAP, 3.

174. Ibid., 3.

175. Ibid., 6.

176. "1) Compilation of the standard books on history 2) Problem of students indiscipline 3) Incorporation of President's autobiography in the text books 4) Publication of text books," 19/CF/67-II, NDC, 44.

177. Ibid., 44.

178. "Controversy on Dr. Fazalur Rahman's Book 'Islam,'" 331/CF/68, NDC, 3.

179. Again, it will require another detailed study to analyze the political rise of the ulema during the 1960s and give reasons for it. A microlevel study of Ayub Khan's basic democracies system gives insights into the processes that led to the emergence of the ulema as a political force and their success in electoral politics.

180. Jamal Malik, *Colonization of Islam in Pakistan: Dissolution of Traditional Institutions in Pakistan* (New Delhi: Manohar Publishers and Distributors, 1996). Salman Sayyid calls for decolonizing Pakistan to achieve an ideal Islamic state: "Decolonize Pakistan to Attain Riyasat-e-Medina: Salman Sayyid," *Straturka*, August 3, 2022, https://www.straturka.com/decolonize-pakistan-to-attain-riyasat-e-medina-salman-sayyid/. It is beyond the scope of my work to engage with Sayyid's argument. However, in his shrill partisanship for the former Pakistani prime minister Imran Khan, Sayyid overlooks the impact of self-Orientalizing notions about Islam in Khan's religious thought and the continuity of coloniality and its forms of knowledge and power among even Islamic scholars and their epistemologies in the postcolonial context. The decolonial praxis, therefore, must move beyond the political elite to impact a much wider intellectual spectrum. In other words, there is no decolonizing of Pakistan without decolonizing of Islam.

181. During the dictatorial rule of General Zia-ul-Haq, the Women Action Forum organized political resistance against discriminatory laws imposed by the military junta against women. Aurat March is a social movement that targets stereotypes about sexual and reproductive rights and challenges deeply embedded notions of patriarchy and sexism, often through cheerful sloganeering.

182. *The National Assembly of Pakistan (Constitution-Making) Debates*, 16 March 1973, vol. 2, no. 22 (Karachi: Manager of Publications), 1425.

183. *Dawn*, 16 July 2005, "Text of Hasba Bill," https://www.dawn.com/news/148019/text-of-hasba-bill. Imran Khan regime's National Rehmatul-lil-Alameen Authority served a somewhat similar purpose, albeit at a much smaller scale. Ostensibly, he has set it up to impart moral education to the Pakistani youth and to inspire them with lessons from the life of Prophet Muhammad.

184. *Pakistan Observer*, 19 December 1950.

185. Slavoj Žižek, *The Sublime Object of Ideology* (London: Verso, 1989), 95.

186. Ibid., 96.

187. Ibid., 105.

188. Ibid., 104.

Chapter 3: Making the State National

1. Judith Butler and Gayatri Chakravorti Spivak, *Who Sings the Nation-State? Language, Politics, Belonging* (Calcutta: Seagull Book, 2011), 3–4.

2. Ibid., 30–31.

3. Clifford Geertz, *The Interpretation of Cultures: Selected Essays by Clifford Geertz* (New York: Basic Books, 1973), 219.

4. Ibid., 220.

5. Ibid., 221.

6. Homi K. Bhabha, "DissemiNation: Time, Narrative, and the Margins of the Modern Nation," in *Nation and Narration*, ed. Homi K. Bhabha (London: Routledge, 1990), 294.

7. Arundhati Virmani, *A National Flag for India: Rituals, Nationalism, and the Politics of Sentiment* (Ranikhet: Permanent Black, 2008), 224–25.

8. Ibid.

9. For more details about the discussion in the Assembly on the new flag, its symbolism and ideas about alternative flag designs proposed in the press, see Sadia Saeed, *Politics of Desecularization: Law and the Minority Question in Pakistan* (Cambridge: Cambridge University Press, 2016), 70–86.

10. *Constituent Assembly of Pakistan Debates*, 11 August 1947, vol. 1, no. 2 (Karachi: Government of Pakistan Press), 22.

11. Ibid., 27.

12. Ibid.

13. *Pakistan Times*, 13 August 1947.

14. *Morning News*, 4 August 1947.

15. *The Pakistani Flag* (Islamabad: Directorate of Films and Publications, Ministry of Information and Broadcasting, Government of Pakistan, 1988).

16. The English translation of Iqbal's couplet is from an anonymously curated blog post on Iqbal's poetry. The website has complete works of Iqbal available online and selections of his works translated into English: https://iqbalurdu.blogspot.com.

17. Serial no. 464, "State of Affairs regarding the Flying of the Flag in Early Days of Islam" (N), Ministry of Interior, NAP, 10.

18. Serial no. 464, "State of Affairs regarding the Flying of the Flag in Early Days of Islam" (C), Ministry of Interior, NAP, 2.

19. Ibid., 2.

20. Ibid., 3.

21. Ibid., 13.

22. Serial no. 461, "Colour of Pakistan Flag" (N), Ministry of Interior, NAP, 6.

23. Ibid., 2.

24. Ibid., 40.

25. Ibid., 8. Given the popularity of the flag, especially for its use on such festive occasions as Eid, various private companies offered finely printed flags on the best-quality fabrics to adorn "shops, offices, factories, cinemas, schools, mosques, houses, streets and market places." Nadeem Omar Tarar, *The Colonial and National Formations of the National College of Arts, Lahore, circa 1870s to 1960s* (London: Anthem Press, 2022), 291 (e-book).

26. Monthly *'Aina-i-Qismat* (Lahore), August 2020. I was informed by the director of the National Documentation Centre at Islamabad that the cabinet division regularly receives mail from astrologers pleading that the Government of Pakistan change the position of the moon. As long as the moon is waning, they argue, Pakistan will not be able to flourish.

27. "Position of the Crescent and Star on the Currency Notes and Coins. Position of the Crescent and Star When Used as Emblem," 371/CF/48, NDC.

28. Serial no. 470, "Decision That the Position of the Crescent and Star Should Remain Unchanged so Far as the Pakistan Flag Is Concerned" (N), Ministry of Interior, NAP, 7.

29. File no. 478, "Question raised by the Ministry of FA&CR that the Crescent and Star Appearing on Currency Notes, Postage Stamps, Stationer and Other Government's Publications Etc. Should Be Drawn Facing North-West Instead of North-East but the Cabinet Decided That No Change Be Made in It" (N), Ministry of Interior, NAP, 4.

30. "Pakistan Flag," CF/Prog/77, NDC, 2.

31. Ibid., 4.

32. *Pakistan Flag*, 14–15.

33. "Man Arrested in Pakistan for Hoisting India Flag," *The News*, January 27, 2016, https://www.thenews.com.pk/latest/94171-Man-arrested-in-Pakistan-for-hoisting-India-flag.

34. "Flags to Be Flown on United Kingdom High Commissions, in India, Pakistan and Ceylon, on Special Occasions," DO 35/3287, NA.

35. Ibid.

36. *Pakistan Observer*, 31 July 1949.

37. *Pakistan Observer*, 2 August 1949.

38. *Pakistan Observer*, 24 July 1949.

39. *Morning News*, 24 September 1956.

40. *Pakistan Observer*, 4 August 1949.

41. *Morning News*, 29 March 1958.

42. *Pakistan Observer*, 4 August 1949.

43. Quoted in Michael E. Geisler, "Introduction: What Are National Symbols—and What Do They Do to Us?," in *National Symbols, Fractured Identities: Contesting the National Narrative*, ed. Michael E. Geisler (Middlebury, VT: Middlebury College Press), xxii.

44. Ibid., xxviii.

45. Ibid., xxix.

46. Alexis Schwarzenbach, *Portraits of the Nation: Stamps, Coins and Banknotes in Belgium and Switzerland, 1880–1945* (Bern, Switzerland: Peter Lang, 1999).

47. Yair Wallach, "Creating a Country through Currency and Stamps: State Symbols and Nation-Building in British-ruled Palestine," *Nations and Nationalism* 17, no. 1 (2011): 129–47.

48. For an overview of the ideological content of various Pakistani symbols, emblems, banknotes, and other official paraphernalia, see Raja M. Ali Saleem, *State, Nationalism, and Islamization: Historical Analysis of Turkey and Pakistan* (London: Palgrave Macmillan, 2017), esp. chs. 3 and 4.

49. S. Aijaz Husain, *History of the State Bank of Pakistan (1948–1960)* (Karachi: State Bank of Pakistan, 1992), 18; Tanveer Afzal, *Bank Notes of Pakistan in the State Bank Museum Collection (1948–2012)* (Karachi: State Bank of Pakistan, 2013), v.

50. Afzal, *Bank Notes of Pakistan*, v.

51. "Selection of Animal and Floral Symbols of Pakistan," 28/CF/50, NDC. Even after Jinnah's picture was introduced on the currency note, there was some public criticism. In a letter to the editor, A. K. Mian, of Tippera, objected to this "un-Islamic idea"

and wrote that there were better way to honor the memory of the founder of the state than printing his portrait on currency notes. *Morning News*, 28 December 1957.

52. Afzal, *Bank Notes of Pakistan*, vii–viii.

53. S. M. Ikram, Joint Secretary to the Government of Pakistan, "Summary for the Cabinet," 24 November 1950, "Selection of a Suitable Design for Adoption as National Floral Symbol of Pakistan," 317/CF/65, NDC, 3.

54. Serial no. 503, "Selection of Designs of Animal and Floral Symbols of Pakistan" (C), Ministry of Interior, NAP, 80.

55. Serial no. 503, "Selection of Designs of Animal and Floral Symbols of Pakistan" (N), Ministry of Interior, NAP, 13.

56. Serial no. 503, "Selection of Designs of Animal and Floral Symbols of Pakistan" (C), Ministry of Interior, NAP, 76.

57. Serial no. 534, "Selection of a Suitable Design of 'Jasmine'—the National Floral Symbol of Pakistan" (N), Ministry of Interior, NAP, 1.

58. Ibid., 3.

59. Ibid., 9.

60. Ibid., 18.

61. "Selection of a Suitable Design for Adoption as National Floral Symbol of Pakistan," 317/CF/65, NDC.

62. *Constituent Assembly of Pakistan Debates*, 22 September 1953, vol. 15, no. 1 (Karachi: Government of Pakistan Press), 2.

63. The translation has been taken from al-quran.info (http://al-quran.info/#3:173), a Denmark-based web platform providing English translations and commentaries of Quranic verses.

64. This information has been taken from the Information Ministry of the Government of Pakistan, available at http://www.infopak.gov.pk/Eemblem.aspx. According to Nadeem Omar, the new emblem was designed by Mehraj Muhammad—a local artist based in Dera Ghazi Khan and an alumnus of the Mayo College of Arts. Unfortunately, his name has largely been forgotten, and he is not credited for "the singular honor of designing the national emblem of the state of Pakistan." Nadeem Omar Tarar, *The Colonial and National Formations of the National College of Arts, Lahore, circa 1870s to 1960s* (London: Anthem Press, 2022), 292–93 (e-book).

65. Nihal Ahmad, *A History of Radio Pakistan* (Karachi: Oxford University Press, 2005), ii. The motto of Radio Pakistan is based on a Quranic verse (2:183), which translates as "Speak fair to the people."

66. Quoted in Emma Tarlo, *Clothing Matters: Dress and Identity in India* (London: Hurst, 1996), 18.

67. Lisa Trivedi, *Clothing Gandhi's Nation: Homespun and Modern India* (Bloomington: Indiana University Press, 2007), xvii.

68. Ibid.

69. File no. 1092-B, Muhammad Ali Jinnah Papers, National Archives of Pakistan, Islamabad.

70. *Relics of the Quaid-i-Azam: A Catalogue* (Karachi: Department of Archaeology and Museums, Ministry of Culture and Tourism, Government of Pakistan, 1980), 11. Emphasis added.

71. *Imroz*, 26 April 1948.
72. *Morning News*, 26 April 1956.
73. "Formal Dress for Officers in Civil Employ," 240/CF/48, NDC.
74. Ibid.
75. "Standard Portrait of the Quaid-i-Azam," 342/CF/49, NDC, 20.
76. Ibid., 37.
77. Serial no. 502, "Amendments to the Pakistan Names and Emblems (Prevention of Unauthorised Use) Act, 1957" (C), Ministry of the Interior, NAP, 31.
78. "Standard Portrait of the Quaid-i-Azam," 342/CF/49, NDC, 93.
79. See, e.g., Farahnaz Ispahani, *Purifying the Land of Pure: A History of Pakistan's Religious Minorities* (New York: Oxford University Press, 2017), 97–98; Nadeem Farooq Paracha, "Dressing Jinnah," *Dawn*, 25 December 2016, https://www.dawn.com/news/1304036.
80. Khawaja Abdur Rahim, foreword to *Iqbal: The Poet of Tomorrow*, ed. Khawaja Abdur Rahim (Lahore: Iqbal Academy Pakistan, 2004), v.
81. Khurram Ali Shafique, *Iqbal: An Illustrated Biography* (Lahore: Iqbal Academy Pakistan, 2010), 11.
82. Afzal Haq Qarshi, ed., *Iqbaliyat-i-Tasir (Iqbal ke Fikar wa Fan par Muhammad Din Tasir ke Maqalat)* (Lahore: Iqbal Academy Pakistan, 2010), 20.
83. *Nawa-i-Waqt*, 19 November 1949.
84. "Fortnightly Summaries of the Ministry of Education and Industries," 18/CF/49, NDC.
85. Rahim, foreword to *Iqbal*, viii–ix.
86. Ali Usman Qasmi, "Where the Twain Did Meet: The Genealogy of Muhammad Iqbal's Intellectual and Poetic Genius," in *Revisioning Iqbal as a Poet and Muslim Political Thinker*, ed. Gita Dharampal Frick, Ali Usman Qasmi, and Katia Rostetter (Heidelberg, Germany: Draupadi Verlag, 2010), 17.
87. Khalid Nazir Sufi, *Iqbal Durun-i-Khana, hissa duam* (Lahore: Iqbal Academy, 2012), 211.
88. Ahmad Nabi Khan, *Iqbal Manzil Sialkot: The Birth Place of Allama Muhammad Iqbal* (Lahore: Department of Archaeology and Museums, Ministry of Culture, Tourism and Archaeology, Government of Pakistan, 1977), 19–20.
89. Khalid Nazir Sufi, *Iqbal Durun-i-Khana: Hayat-i-Iqbal ke Khanagi Pehlu* (Lahore: Iqbal Academy Pakistan, 2003), 230.
90. This matter was discussed in the meeting of board of governors of Bazm-i-Iqbal on 18 July 1953. For details, see *Bazm-i-Iqbal ki Rudadain: 1950 ta January 1993* (Lahore: Bazm-i-Iqbal, 1993), 87. Once it had been published, the central government's Ministry of Information requested 5,000 copies of the pamphlet. An additional number of 4,500 copies were ordered for a reprint.
91. *Proceedings of the First Meeting of the Advisory Board of Education for Pakistan Held at Karachi from 7th to 9th June, 1948* (Karachi: Education Division, Government of Pakistan), 11–12.
92. Professor Dr. Ghulam Husain Zulfiqar, *Tarikh-i-Bazm-i-Iqbal: 1950 ta 2000* (Lahore: Bazm-i-Iqbal, 2000), 17.
93. *Iqbal Academy: Decade of Progress, 1958–68* (Karachi: Iqbal Academy, ca. 1968), 27.

94. Ibid., 22–23.

95. Ibid., 23.

96. Dr. Shafiq Ajami, *Iqbal Shanas: Alami Tanazur mai* (Lahore: Pakistan Writers Cooperative Society, 2011), 129.

97. Professor Dr. Ghulam Husain Zulfiqar, *Tarikh-i-Bazam-i-Iqbal* (Lahore: Bazam-i-Iqbal, 2000), 47.

98. *Iqbal Academy: Decade of Progress, 1958–68*, 9–10.

99. *In Memoriam—III (Iqbal Day Speeches and Articles)* (Karachi: Iqbal Academy, 1969), 10.

100. Ajami, *Iqbal Shanas*, 22.

101. Jagan Nath Azad, "When Was Iqbal Born?," in *Allama Iqbal ki Tarikh-i-Wiladat*, ed. Dr. Waheed Qureshi and Zahid Munir Amir (Lahore: Bazm-i-Iqbal, 1994), 47–48.

102. Ibid., 48.

103. Said Akhtar Durrani, "Allama Iqbal ki Tarikh-i-Paidayish," in *Allama Iqbal ki Tarikh-i-Wiladat*, ed. Dr. Waheed Qureshi and Zahid Munir Amir (Lahore: Bazm-i-Iqbal, 1994), 84.

104. Marghub Siddiqi, "Allama Iqbal ki Tarikh-i-Wiladat," in *Allama Iqbal ki Tarikh-i-Wiladat*, ed. Dr. Waheed Qureshi and Zahid Munir Amir (Lahore: Bazm-i-Iqbal, 1994), 45.

105. Zahid Munir Amir, "Muqaddama," in *Allama Iqbal ki Tarikh-i-Wiladat*, ed. Dr. Waheed Qureshi and Zahid Munir Amir (Lahore: Bazm-i-Iqbal, 1994), 14.

106. Dr. Waheed Qureshi and Zahid Munir Amir, eds., *Allama Iqbal ki Tarikh-i-Wiladat* (Lahore: Bazm-i-Iqbal, 1994), 355.

107. Amir, "Muqaddama," in *Allama Iqbal ki Tarikh-i-Wiladat*, 11.

108. Durrani, "Allama Iqbal ki Tarikh-i-Paidayish," in *Allama Iqbal ki Tarikh-i-Wiladat*, 87–90.

109. Aqeel Abbas Jafri, ed., *Pakistan Chronicle* (Karachi: Fazali Sons, 2010), 146.

110. Zulfiqar, *Tarikh-i-Bazam-i-Iqbal*, 47.

111. Sufi, *Iqbal Durun-i-Khana, hissa duam* (Lahore: Iqbal Academy, 2012), 153.

112. Khalid Nazir Sufi, "Ek Ghalat-Fehmi dar Ghalat-Fehmi ka Izala," in *Allama Iqbal ki Tarikh-i-Wiladat*, ed. Dr. Waheed Qureshi and Zahid Munir Amir (Lahore: Bazm-i-Iqbal, 1994), 35.

113. Ibid., 37.

114. Shaikh Ijaz Ahmad, "Allama Iqbal ki Tarikh-i-Paidayish," in *Allama Iqbal ki Tarikh-i-Wiladat*, ed. Dr. Waheed Qureshi and Zahid Munir Amir (Lahore: Bazm-i-Iqbal, 1994), 250–51.

115. Dr. Waheed Qureshi, "Allama Iqbal ki Tarikh-i-Wiladat," in *Allama Iqbal ki Tarikh-i-Wiladat*, ed. Dr. Waheed Qureshi and Zahid Munir Amir (Lahore: Bazm-i-Iqbal, 1994), 118.

116. Qureshi and Amir, *Allama Iqbal ki Tarikh-i-Wiladat*, 368.

117. Faqir Syed Waheed-ud-Din, "Tarikh-i-Paidayish: Ek Bari Ghalat-Fehmi ka Izala," in *Allama Iqbal ki Tarikh-i-Wiladat*, ed. Dr. Waheed Qureshi and Zahid Munir Amir (Lahore: Bazm-i-Iqbal, 1994), 29.

118. Jafri, *Pakistan Chronicle*, 453.

119. Azad, "When Was Iqbal Born?," in *Allama Iqbal ki Tarikh-i-Wiladat*, 61.

120. Amir, "Muqaddama," in *Allama Iqbal ki Tarikh-i-Wiladat*, 10–11.
121. Khaled Ahmed, "Jinnah—The Secular Mussalman," *Indian Express*, 1998.
122. Per "i) Biography of the Quaid-i-Azam ii) Preparation of the History of Freedom Movement of the Muslims of the Indo-Pakistan Sub-Continent," 149/CF/51, NDC.
123. PM Office Files, NDC, 126.
124. Per "i) Biography of the Quaid-i-Azam ii) Preparation of the History of Freedom Movement of the Muslims of the Indo-Pakistan Sub-Continent," 149/CF/51, NDC.
125. Sharif al-Mujahid, ed., *In Quest of Jinnah: Diary, Notes and Correspondence of Hector Bolitho* (Karachi: Oxford University Press, 2009), 98.
126. Ibid., 100.
127. Ibid., 123–24.
128. Ibid., 126.
129. *Morning News*, 16 January 1956.
130. *Morning News*, 1 February 1956.
131. *Report of the Commission of Enquiry, Set up by the Government of Pakistan, to Ascertain which of the Properties Left by Quaid-e-Azam Should be Preserved as Relics of National Value* (Cabinet Division Islamabad), NDC, 3–4.
132. Ibid., 6–7.
133. Ibid., 9.
134. Ibid., 11.
135. Syed Hashim Raza, *Hamari Manzil (Our Destination): An Autobiography of Syed Hashim Raza* (Karachi: Mustafain & Murtazain Ltd., 1991), 143.
136. Ibid.
137. *Pakistan Observer*, 17 August 1954.
138. Ibid.
139. Jafri, *Pakistan Chronicle*, 144.
140. Raza, *Hamari Manzil*, 152.
141. Fikri, "The Quaid-i-Azam's Tomb," *Pakistan Times*, 16 October 1960.
142. Ibid.
143. "Work in Progress on Quaid's Mausoleum," *Pakistan Times*, 25 December 1960.
144. *Quaid-e-Azam Memorial Fund Board: Report for the Period Ending December 31, 1973*, 2.
145. Ibid., 3.
146. "Rangers, ISI Officers Involved in 'Karachi Incident' Removed: Pakistan Army," 10 November 2020, https://www.geo.tv/latest/317832-pakistan-rangers-isi-officers-acted-over-zealously-army-chiefs-karachi-incident-inquiry-finds.
147. Carl Schmitt, *Political Theology: Four Chapters on the Concept of Sovereignty* (Chicago: University of Chicago Press, 2005), 36.
148. Butler and Spivak, *Who Sings the Nation-State?*, 73.
149. For a good collection of such songs from the pre-1947 period, see *Muntakhib Nazmain: Tehrik-i-Pakistan kay dauran Jalson mai parhe janay walay Tarane aur Qaid-i-Azam ke huzur Nazrana-hai-Aqidat* (Islamabad: National Archives of Pakistan, ca. 1986).
150. Shafi Aqil, ed., *Majid Lahori ki Harf-o-Hikayat* (Karachi: Fazli Sons, 2000), 112.
151. Rukhsana Zafar, ed., *The National Anthem of Pakistan: A Documented History*

Based on the Pakistan Government Cabinet Record (Islamabad: National Documentation Wing, 2009), 9. I am relying on the officially published record compiled by Rukhsana Zafar, along with the original cabinet division file from which Zafar draws her material. It is clear that Zafar has deleted significant parts of the conversation and correspondence on the national anthem—especially one member's proposals or opposition to the idea of adopting a national anthem—as she wanted to avoid the controversies or disagreements about the anthem while putting together the documents as part of an official publication. In my notes from the original cabinet division file, however, it is difficult to find the relevant page numbers either because of the poor scan quality or simply because the archivists have not numbered the pages continuously.

152. "National Anthem for Pakistan," 60/CF/48-1.

153. Ibid. In an earlier meeting held at the Ministry of Interior on 9 February 1948, the question of Western and Eastern music for the anthem came up. J. Welsh, composer to the UK royal family, had sent a piano composition that was played before the members of the Interior Ministry. Bukhari pointed out that a Western tune harmonized and sung to the accompaniment of a Western orchestra would not be appealing to Pakistanis. Similarly, an Eastern tune, he said, would "be a 'Swing' to the Western ears." Ibid.

154. Zafar, *National Anthem of Pakistan*, 39.

155. File no. 1010, Fatima Jinnah Papers, National Archives of Pakistan, Islamabad, 6.

156. Zafar, *National Anthem of Pakistan*, 43.

157. Ibid., 11.

158. File no. 1010, Fatima Jinnah Papers, NAP, 1.

159. Zafar, *National Anthem of Pakistan*, 54.

160. *Imroz*, 6 April 1951.

161. *Imroz*, 14 August 1951.

162. "Hafeez Jalandhari: Story of Creation of Pakistan's National Anthem (Part 2)—Exclusive for LAL," YouTube video, posted by Khursheed Abdullah, 19:42, https://www.youtube.com/watch?v=xEzd8CXf2_Q.

163. Zafar, *National Anthem of Pakistan*, 10.

164. "National Anthem for Pakistan," 60/CF/48-1, NDC.

165. Abul Asar Hafiz Jallandhari, "Dibacha," in *Pakistani Qaumi Parham aur Tarana*, by Younas Kamal Lodhi (Islamabad: National Book Foundation, 2016), 13–15.

166. Zafar, *National Anthem of Pakistan*, 20.

167. Ibid., 31.

168. Ibid., 32.

169. Ahmed Nadeem Qasmi, *Meray Hum Safar* (Lahore: Asatir, 2002), 136.

170. Aqeel Abbas Jafri, *Pakistan ka Qaumi Tarana: Kia hai Haqiqat? Kia hai Fasana?* (Karachi: Virsa Publications, 2010), 47.

171. Ahmad, *History of Radio Pakistan*, ii.

172. Younas Kamal Lodhi, *Pakistani Qaumi Parham aur Tarana* (Islamabad: National Book Foundation, 2016), 76–78.

173. Zafar, *National Anthem of Pakistan*, 2.

174. *Pakistan Observer*, 24 August 1954.

175. *Pakistan Observer*, 26 August 1954.

176. *Pakistan Observer*, 6 September 1954.

177. *Morning News*, 22 August 1954.
178. *Morning News*, 20 August 1954.
179. *Morning News*, 16 August 1954.
180. *Morning News*, 28 August 1955.
181. *Morning News*, 4 October 1947.
182. Firoz Mahmud, "Cultural Life in Dhaka: Pakistan and Bangladesh Period," in *400 Years of Capital Dhaka and Beyond: Volume II, Economy and Culture*, ed. M. Mufakharul Islam and Firoz Mahmud (Dhaka: Asiatic Society of Bangladesh, 2011), 314.
183. *Morning News*, 17 March 1958.
184. *Morning News*, 21 March 1958.
185. This inference is based on my reading of Butler's argument. See Butler and Spivak, *Who Sings the Nation-State?*, 58–59.
186. *Nawa-i-Waqt*, 30 August 1954.
187. Ibid.
188. *Nawa-i-Waqt*, 30 August 1954.
189. Ibid.
190. Ibid.
191. *Nawa-i-Waqt*, 1 September 1954.
192. Jafri, *Pakistan ka Qaumi Tarana*, 64–66.
193. The lyrics have been translated by Ali Raj, a doctoral student at Columbia University, who is locating the contestations about the national anthem in the longer history of Urdu poetics and aesthetics.
194. Zafar, *National Anthem of Pakistan*, 73–78.
195. Jafri, *Pakistan ka Qaumi Tarana*, 12.
196. Ibid., 29.
197. Bhabha, "DissemiNation," 304.
198. For the innovative designs that Pakistanis added to their flag to celebrate Independence Day, see Ayesha Jalal, "Beyond the Symbolic to the Significant," in *Mazaar, Bazaar: Design & Visual Culture in Pakistan*, ed. Saima Zaidi (Karachi: Oxford University Press, 2010).
199. Iqrar ul Hassan Syed, "Mazar-i-Quaid on Rent for 'Dates'. . . . Watch Sar-e-Aam this Saturday at 7:05 pm on ARY News," tweet, 21 February 2014, 12:30 a.m., https://twitter.com/iqrarulhassan/status/436583669080137728. In that episode, Syed Iqrar ul Hassan, an investigative journalist, claims that young couples "rent" the basement of the *Mazar* for sexual activities. The basement is the actual resting place of Jinnah, much in line with the tradition adopted by the Mughals for funerary monuments. The outward structure is symbolic of a *qabar*, while the body is buried deep inside the ground.

Chapter 4: Over the Moon

1. Muhammad Qasim Zaman, *The Ulema in Contemporary Islam: Custodians of Change* (Princeton, NJ: Princeton University Press, 2007). The chapter builds on Francis Robinson's foundational work on the contestation of authority in modern Islam. See Francis Robinson, "Crisis of Authority: Crisis of Islam?," *Journal of the Royal Asiatic Society* 19, no. 3 (2009): 339–54. I supplement my reading of Zaman and Robinson with Mashal Saif's insightful analysis on the overarching impact of the postcolonial state on the shap-

ing of ulema's thought and practices, whereby ulema, "despite contesting the state[,] ... take it as a fulcrum around which they structure their arguments." See Saif, *The 'Ulama in Contemporary Pakistan: Contesting and Cultivating an Islamic Republic* (Cambridge: Cambridge University Press, 2021), 14.

2. Mushirul Hasan, "Traditional Rites and Contested Meanings: Sectarian Strife in Colonial Lucknow," *Economic and Political Weekly* 31, no. 9 (1996): 543–50.

3. David King has written extensively about the use of instruments for calculating time, observing movements of celestial bodies and ascertaining the direction of *kaʿba*. See "Astronomical Timekeeping (c ilm al-mîqât) in Medieval Islam," *Actes du XXIXe Congrès International des Orientalistes* (Paris: L'Asiathèque, 1975), 2:2, 86–90; "Astronomical Timekeeping in Fourteenth-Century Syria," *Proceedings of the First International Symposium for the History of Arabic Science*, 2 vols. (Aleppo: Institute for the History of Arabic Science, 1978), 1:391–415 (Arabic), and 2:75–84 (English). "Astronomical Timekeeping in Ottoman Turkey," *Proceedings of the International Symposium on the Observatories in Islam, 19–23 Sept., 1977* (Istanbul: Millî Egitim Basımevi, 1980), 245–69; "Kibla. ii. Astronomical Aspects" [sacred direction], in *The Encyclopaedia of Islam*, new ed. (Leiden: E. J. Brill, 1979), 5:83–88, fascs. 79–80.

4. Stephen P. Blake, *Time in Early Modern Islam: Calendar, Ceremony, and Chronology in the Safavid, Mughal and Ottoman Empires* (Cambridge: Cambridge University Press, 2013), 18.

5. Ahmad S. Dallal, *Islam, Science and the Challenge of History* (New Haven, CT: Yale University Press, 2010), 6.

6. Ibid., 8.

7. Ibid., 9.

8. Lorraine Daston and Elizabeth Lunbeck, introduction to *Histories of Scientific Observation*, ed. Lorraine Daston and Elizabeth Lunbeck (Chicago: University of Chicago Press, 2010), 3; David Aubin, Charlotte Bigg, and H. Otto Sibum, eds., *Observatories and Astronomy in Nineteenth Century Science and Culture* (Durham, NC: Duke University Press, 2010), 6–7.

9. Martin Heidegger, *The Question Concerning Technology and Other Essays* (New York: Garland Publishing, 1977), 13–14.

10. Ibid., 16.

11. Martin Jay, "Scopic Regimes of Modernity," in *Vision and Visuality: Discussions in Contemporary Culture #2*, ed. Hal Foster (New York: New Press, 1999), 9.

12. Daniel A. Stolz, "'Positioning the Watch Hand': 'Ulama' and the Practice of Mechanical Timekeeping in Cairo, 1737–1874," *International Journal of Middle East Studies* 47, no. 3 (2015): 489.

13. Ibid., 494.

14. Ibid., 494–95.

15. Ibid., 501.

16. Daniel A. Stolz, *The Lighthouse and the Observatory: Islam, Science, and Empire in Late Ottoman Egypt* (Cambridge: Cambridge University Press, 2018), 143.

17. Ebrahim Moosa, "Shaykh Aḥmad Shākir and the Adoption of a Scientifically-Based Lunar Calendar," *Islamic Law and Society* 5, no. 1 (1998): 57–89.

18. Ibid., 71n46.

19. Ibid., 81–82.
20. Vanessa Ogle, *The Global Transformation of Time, 1870–1950* (Cambridge, MA: Harvard University Press, 2015), 164.
21. Ibid., 170.
22. *Maulana Syed Amir Ali*, trans. Fatawa Alamgiri (Lahore: Maktaba Rahmania, n.d.), 2:12–15.
23. Ali Altaf Mian, "Troubling Technology: The Deobandī Debate on the Loudspeaker and Ritual Prayer," *Islamic Law and Society* 24, no. 4 (2017): 355–83.
24. Ogle, *Global Transformation of Time*, 156.
25. Ibid., 160.
26. Mufti Muhammad Kifayatullah Dehalwi, *Kifayat al-Mufti* (Karachi: Dar-ul-Isha'at, 2001), 4:229.
27. Maulana Ashraf Ali Thanawi, *Imdad-ul-Fatawa* (Saharanpur: Zakaria Book Depot, n.d.), 4:161–63.
28. *Inqilab*, 2 March 1930.
29. *Inqilab*, 26 January 1933.
30. *Inqilab*, 6 August 1948.
31. "Musalmanon ki khidmat mai dard-mandana guzarishain," *Inqilab*, 12 August 1948.
32. *Pakistan Times*, 27 July 1949.
33. Serial no. 517, "Formation of Ruat-i-Hilal Committee and Adoption of a Lunar Calendar" (N), Ministry of Interior, NAP, 1.
34. Untitled Note, 16 March 1954, box 2, 1, Ansari Collection.
35. Ibid., 2.
36. Ibid., 3.
37. Serial no. 517, "Formation of Ruat-i-Hilal Committee and Adoption of a Lunar Calendar (N), Ministry of Interior, NAP, 3.
38. "1) Sighting of the Eid Moon 2) Festivals Depending on the Appearance of the Moon," 85/CF/61, NDC.
39. Ibid., 35.
40. Alasdair MacIntyre, *Whose Justice? Which Rationality?* (Notre Dame, IN: University of Notre Dame Press, 1988), 9–11.
41. Ibid., 362.
42. Ibid., 384.
43. Mufti Muhammad Shafi, *Ru'at-i-Hilal* (ca. 1961; Karachi: Idara al-Ma'rif, n.d.), 7.
44. Ibid., 11.
45. Ibid., 13.
46. Ibid., 21.
47. Ibid., 22–23.
48. Ibid., 33.
49. Ibid., 34–35.
50. Ibid., 36.
51. Ibid., *Ru'at-i-Hilal*, 36–37.
52. Ibid., 60–61.

53. Zayde Antrim, *Routes and Realms: The Power of Place in the Early Islamic World* (New York: Oxford University Press, 2013), 1.

54. Ibid., 91–92.

55. Ibid., 101.

56. Sarah Albrecht, *Dar al-Islam Revisited: Territoriality in Contemporary Islamic Legal Discourse on Muslims in the West* (Leiden: Brill, 2018), 35.

57. Wael B. Hallaq, *The Impossible State: Islam, Politics, and Modernity's Moral Predicament* (New York: Columbia University Press, 2012), 62–63.

58. Quoted in Dr. Muhammad Mushtaq Ahmad, *Ru'at-i-Hilal: Fiqhi wa Qanuni Tajziya* (Lahore: Kitab Mahal, n.d.), 113. In his treatise written in 1961, however, Shafi advised that the region with a different *matali'* should be allowed to celebrate Eid separately. Shafi, *Ru'at-i-Hilal*, 38.

59. Shafi, *Ru'at-i-Hilal*, 39–40.

60. Ibid., 49–50.

61. As Ahmad has pointed out in his book, *Ru'at-i-Hilal*, the requirement of *shahadat* is set for *hilal-i-shawwal* only and not for any other month of the Islamic lunar calendar. Even *hilal-i-Ramzan* is to be decided on the basis of *iwayat*.

62. Shafi, *Ru'at-i-Hilal*, 45–46.

63. Ibid., 41.

64. Ahmad, *Ru'at-i-Hilal*, 96.

65. Maulana Ja'far Shah Phulwarwi, *Ru'at-i-Hilal* (Lahore: Idara Saqafat-i-Islamiyyah, 1967), 19.

66. Ibid., 29.

67. Ibid., 38.

68. Ibid., 41.

69. Syed Hashim Raza, *Hamari Manzil (Our Destination): An Autobiography of Syed Hashim Raza* (Karachi: Mustafain and Mustafain Ltd., 1991), 120.

70. The author used both *Ramzan* and *Ramazan* spellings in the text. Ibid., 119–21.

71. Serial no. 517, "Formation of Ruat-i-Hilal Committee and Adoption of a Lunar Calendar", Ministry of Interior, NAP, 13.

72. Ibid., 15.

73. Ibid., 16.

74. Ibid., 41.

75. Ibid.

76. Ibid., 12.

77. Serial no. 517, "Formation of Ruat-i-Hilal Committee and Adoption of a Lunar Calendar" (N), Ministry of Interior, NAP, 5.

78. Serial no. 517, "Formation of Ruat-i-Hilal Committee and Adoption of a Lunar Calendar" (C), Ministry of Interior, NAP, 7.

79. Ibid., 9.

80. Ibid., 19.

81. Ibid., 49.

82. Ibid., 49.

83. Ibid., 49 and 58.

84. Ibid., 60.

85. Ibid., 10.

86. Ibid., 76. The letter was written in a eulogizing tone for Ayub Khan's regime with a prayer that he gets to rule Pakistan for eleven years—which he eventually did (1958–1969)—so that "poor science" (*baichari science*) could achieve what it had not been able to do under foreign rule followed by eleven years of postindependence governments. Ibid., 77.

87. Ibid., 79–80.

88. Ibid., 83.

89. Serial no. 517, "Formation of Ruat-i-Hilal Committee and Adoption of a Lunar Calendar" (C), Ministry of Interior, NAP, 86–88.

90. Ibid., 92.

91. "1) Sighting of the Eid moon 2) Festivals Depending on the Appearance of the Moon," 85/CF/61, NDC, 16.

92. Ibid., 41.

93. Ibid., 42.

94. Ibid., 48.

95. Ibid., 49.

96. Ibid., 51–52.

97. "Ashura—10th of Muharram," 438/CF/62, NDC, 2–3.

98. "Ruat-i-Hilal Committee and the Moon Controversy," 97/CF/67, NDC, 2.

99. Ibid., 3.

100. Serial no. 542, "Decision of Dissolution of the Central Ruat-i-Hilal Committee" (N), Ministry of Interior, NAP, 5.

101. Serial no. 542, "Decision of Dissolution of the Central Ruat-i-Hilal Committee" (C), Ministry of Interior, NAP, 4. The government had tried to address this issue by discussing the possibility of adding more ulema as members of the committee, but the idea was dropped as "it would amount to an abject surrender to the Mulla." Ibid., 4.

102. Serial no. 542, "Decision of Dissolution of the Central Ruat-i-Hilal Committee" (N), Ministry of Interior, NAP, 5.

103. Ibid., 7 and 9.

104. Ibid., 11–12.

105. Serial no. 542, "Decision of Dissolution of the Central Ruat-i-Hilal Committee" (C), Ministry of Interior, NAP, 13.

106. *National Assembly of Pakistan (Legislature) Debates* (Karachi: The Manager of Publications), 22 December 1973, 1003.

107. Ibid., 1005.

108. Ibid., 1006.

109. Ibid., 1007–8.

110. Ibid., 1008.

111. There were some disagreements on the membership of the committee as Begum Nasim Jahan insisted on representation for women members as well—a suggestion viciously opposed by Maulana Ghulam Ghaus Hazarwi. He said: "No matter what the issue is, this lady drags women into it. She does not pray even ten days in a month. She is deficient in reasoning (*naqis al-aqal*) and faith (*naqis al-din*). Should we follow

the respected scholars or these women? For no good reason (*khawam-kha*), she forces women [into everything]. She is forcing a woman into the Ru'at-i-Hilal Committee as well." *National Assembly of Pakistan (Legislature) Debates*, 23 January 1974 (Karachi: The Manager of Publications), 297. Begum Nasim Jahan stood her ground in a calm and dignified manner. In response to Hazarwi's verbal onslaught and claim that women could not become head of state, Jahan made a tongue-in-cheek remark about the two females heads of state—Indira Gandhi and Golda Meir—and reminded Hazarwi of their "achievements"—a snarky reference to India's military victory over Pakistan in 1971 and that of Israel over Arabs in 1967. Ibid., 298.

112. *National Assembly of Pakistan (Legislature) Debates*, 23 January 1974, 306.

113. Ahmad, *Ru'at-i-Hilal*, 138–40.

114. Abid Husain, "Moon-Gazing: Profile of Mufti Muneeb-ur-Rehman," *The Herald*, July 2016, https://herald.dawn.com/news/1153201.

115. He tweeted:

Step 1: Download app
Step 2: Select City and Month (Shawal)
Step 3 Go to Navigation part and click on Search option
Step 4 Write Moon
Step 5 Move your phone towards the direction of moon shown in App
You will find the moon right there Ch Fawad Hussain, 7:56 PM—4 Jun 2019

https://twitter.com/fawadchaudhry/status/1135923248858849281.

116. Mufti Munib-ur-Rahman, "Ru'at-i-Hilal par Abhas ka Tajziya," *Daily Jang*, 5 June 2019.

117. As Dr. Mushtaq Ahmad mentions, these jokes take an ugly ethnic turn as well. He cites an anecdote in which Pashtun students in a seminary were looking at the sky for the new moon when their Punjabi instructor quipped that those who consume *naswar* (a powdered tobacco) are able to see the moon early. The Pashtun students retorted that the moon could not be seen in Punjab because it would always become invisible in the cloud of hookah smoke. Ahmad, *Ru'at-i-Hilal*, ye.

118. Maulana Abdul Haq, ed., *Fatawa Haqqaniyya* (Akora Khattak: Jamia Dar-ul-Ulum Haqqania, 2010), 4:127.

119. Mufti Muhammad Farid, *Fatawa Faridiyya* (Swabi: Dar-ul-Ulum Siddiqiyya, 2009), 4:61. When the resolution to set up a central *ru'at-i-hilal* committee was being discussed in the national assembly, Maulana Abdul Haq shared an incident of when some military men visited him at his madrassah on the day of Eid and told him that, although they had offered Eid prayers, they were still keeping a fast because they did not want to celebrate official Eid (*sarkari Eid*). *National Assembly of Pakistan (Legislature) Debates*, 23 January 1974 (Karachi: Manager of Publications), 293.

120. Farid, *Fatawa Faridiyya* (Swabi: Dar-ul-Ulum Siddiqiyya, 2009), 4:136.

121. Ibid., 4:137.

122. Ahmad, *Ru'at-i-Hilal*, 30–33.

123. Mufti Muhammad Taqi Usmani, *Fatawa Usmani* (Karachi: Maktaba Ma'rif-ul-Quran, 2012), 2:170–71.

124. Vanessa Ogle, *The Global Transformation of Time*, 119.

125. Farid, *Fatawa Faridiyya*, 4:80–81.
126. Abul Hasnat Ali Muhammad Saidi, ed., *Fatawa Ulema-ye Ahl-i-Hadis* (Khanewal: Maktaba Saidiya, 1977), 6:183.
127. Ibid., 6:177.
128. Ibid., 6:199.
129. Usmani, *Fatawa Usmani*, 2:172.
130. Stolz, *The Lighthouse and the Observatory*, 11.
131. Vilashini Cooppan, "Time-Maps: A Field Guide to the Decolonial Imaginary," *Critical Times* 2, no. 3 (December 2019): 399.

Chapter 5: Scripting the National Time and Space

1. Paul Ricoeur, *Hermeneutics and the Human Sciences: Essays on Language, Action and Interpretation* (Cambridge: Cambridge University Press, 2016), 187.
2. Ibid., 187–88.
3. James E. Young, *The Texture of Memory: Holocaust Memorials and Meaning* (New Haven, CT: Yale University Press, 1993), 6.
4. Pierre Nora, "General Introduction: Between Memory and History," in *Realms of Memory*, vol. 1, *Conflicts and Divisions*, ed. Pierre Nora, trans. Arthur Goldhammer (New York: Columbia University Press, 1992), 8.
5. Ibid., 3.
6. Hyden White, *Metahistory: The Historical Imagination in Nineteenth-century Europe* (Baltimore: John Hopkins University Press, 1973).
7. Achille Mbembe, "The Power of the Archive and Its Limits," in *Refiguring the Archive*, ed. C. Hamilton, V. Harris, J. Taylor, M. Pickover, G. Reid, and R. Saleh (Dordrecht, Netherlands: Springer, 2002), 23.
8. Ibid.
9. Ibid., 23–24.
10. I have mainly relied on Rosie Bsheer's *Archive Wars: The Politics of History in Saudi Arabia* (Stanford, CA: Stanford University Press, 2020) to understand the importance and centrality of archive in crafting a national narrative for the nation. For studies on ideological indoctrination through history in case of Pakistan, see Ayesha Jalal, "Conjuring Pakistan: History as Official Imagining," *International Journal of Middle East Studies* 27 (1995): 73–89.
11. Krijn Thijs, "The Metaphor of the Master: 'Narrative Hierarchy' in National Historical Cultures of Europe," in *The Contested Nation: Ethnicity, Class, Religion and Gender in National Histories*, ed. Stefan Berger and Chris Lorenz (London: Palgrave Macmillan, 2008), 68.
12. The feeling of newness was not limited to nomenclature alone. Unlike India, which had inherited the bulk of major ports, capital cities, educational, training and vocational institutes, and administrative structures, the Pakistani state had to build most of its infrastructure from scratch. In the decade following 1947, there was a lot of activity in Pakistan where foundations for a "new building" were being laid down or a policymaking seminar being held for the "first time." In the newspapers of the late 1940s and early 1950s, one finds numerous such instances. For example, the building of Pakistan's State Bank was inaugurated by Jinnah in July 1948; Pakistan's first stock ex-

change was established on 18 September 1948; the first Pakistan educational conference was held on 27 November 1947; Pakistan's first Urdu conference was held on 26 March 1948 in Lahore; the first postage stamps were issued on 9 July 1948; the first batch of coins minted by the Government of Pakistan were issued on 1 April 1948, and the first currency notes worth five rupees were issued on 1 October 1948. One- and two-rupee notes were issued on 1 March 1949. These were by no means trivial to the project of establishing a distinct identity for Pakistan. In the case of such items as currency notes, the significance was in terms of not just design and aesthetic features but also in formally drawing a dividing line with India with the cessation of Indian currency as legal tender, symbolically signifying closure of a transaction. It showed the coming of age of the Pakistani state's sovereignty, as it had the basic infrastructure required for its functioning. All this information has been gathered from Zahid Husain Anjum, ed., *Encyclopaedia Waqait-i-Pakistan*, vol. 1 (Lahore: Nazir Sons, 2005); and Aqeel Abbas Jafri, ed. *Pakistan Chronicle* (Karachi: Fazali Sons, 2010).

13. *Pakistan Times*, 1 March 1954.

14. Ibid.

15. *Proceedings of the First Meeting of the Advisory Board of Education for Pakistan Held at Karachi from 7th to 9th June, 1948* (Karachi: Education Division, Government of Pakistan), 11.

16. *Guide to the Sources of Asian History: Pakistan* (Islamabad: National Archives of Pakistan, 1990), 2.

17. "Division of India Office Library and Building," 24/CF/48, NDC, 2.

18. Ibid., 3.

19. Ibid.

20. "Brief for Pakistan's Representatives in the Fact-Finding Committee Relating to the Assets of India Office," n.d., "Division of India Office Library and Building," 24/CF/48, NDC, 6. The file has not been numbered continuously, so I refer to the page numbers indicated in the brief.

21. Ibid., 6.

22. M. N. Safa, Member-Secretary, "Report of the Committee of Experts to Advise Government on the Disposal of the Assets of the Old India Office, London," 15 October 1955, "Division of India Office Library and Building," 24/CF/48, NDC, 4. The file has not been numbered, so I refer to the page numbers printed on the report of the committee of experts.

23. Ibid., 18.

24. Ibid.

25. Ibid., 11.

26. Ibid., 5–6.

27. Ibid., 6.

28. *Microfilm Holdings: From IOL&R and Other Sources Abroad (Series 1.1)* (Lahore: Government of Pakistan, Cabinet Division, National Documentation Centre, 1988), iii.

29. Atique Zafar Sheikh, ed., *Guide to the Sources of Asian History*, Series 8.1 (Islamabad: National Archives of Pakistan, 1990), 1:1.

30. *Proceedings of the Inaugural Meeting of the Fourth Session of the Historical Records and Archives Commission for Pakistan Held at Karachi on February 21, 1959*, 12.

31. File no. 1465, "Division of Lahore Museum" (C), Ministry of Education, NAP, 3.

32. M. H. Siddiqi, *A Handbook of Archives and Material on Pakistan Freedom Struggle* (Karachi: University of Karachi, 1988), xxiv. Siddiqi's introduction gives details about the technical tasks undertaken and expertise developed to preserve these documents in an efficient manner.

33. *Historical Records and Archives Commission for Pakistan: Proceedings of the Meetings of the Fifth Session Held at Dacca on 11th April, 1970* (Karachi, n.d.), 7.

34. Ibid., 19.

35. Achille Mbembe, "The Power of the Archive and Its Limits," 19.

36. Various contributions in Antoinette Burton's *Archive Stories: Facts, Fiction and the Writing of History* (Durham, NC: Duke University Press, 2005) address these themes, focusing on the link between narrative and archive in different parts of the world.

37. Muhammad Abdullah Qureshi, "Nisab-i-Tarikh aur Tarmim ki Zarurat," in *Tarikh aur Nisabi Kutub*, by Dr. Mubarak Ali (Lahore: Tarikh Publications, 2016), 172–76. This article was published on 17 August 1947.

38. *Nawa-i-Waqt*, 15 April 1949.

39. For a history of the Pakistan Historical Society and its contributions, see Dr. S. Moinul Haq, "Historical Studies in Pakistan with Special Reference to the Role of Pakistan History Society (A Brief Survey)" (paper presented at the National Conference on History and Culture, Islamabad, 3–5 July 1980). Since its inception in 1950, and within a span of thirty years, the society published about seventy monographs and held seventeen annual conferences. The society's monthly journal continues to be published to this day.

40. File no. 341, Fatima Jinnah Papers, NAP.

41. Ibid.

42. *Civil and Military Gazette*, 8 March 1952.

43. *Civil and Military Gazette*, 9 March 1952.

44. *Morning News*, 27 January 1954.

45. Dr. S. Moinul Haq, ed., *The Proceedings of the All Pakistan History Conference: First Session Held at Karachi, 1951* (Karachi: Pakistan Historical Society, ca. 1952), 7.

46. Dr. S. Moinul Haq, ed., *The Proceedings of the Pakistan History Conference (Sixth Session) Held at Karachi under the Auspices of the Pakistan Historical Society 1956* (Karachi: Pakistan Historical Society, 1959), 29.

47. Pakistan Historical Society, *A History of the Freedom Movement (Being the Story of Muslim Struggle for the Freedom of Hind-Pakistan) 1707–1947*, vol. 1, *1707–1831* (1957; Delhi: Renaissance Publishing House, 1984), vii.

48. Ibid., vii.

49. S. Moinul Haq, preface to *A History of the Freedom Movement*, vol. 4, *1936–1947, Parts I and II*, by Pakistan Historical Society (1970; Delhi: Renaissance Publishing House, 1984), v.

50. Pakistan History Board, *A Short History of Hind-Pakistan* (Karachi: Pakistan Historical Society, 1960), iv.

51. Ibid., 71.

52. Ibid., 108.

53. Muhammad Ali Jinnah, "Presidential Address by Muhammad Ali Jinnah to the

Muslim League Lahore, 1940," Columbia University, http://www.columbia.edu/itc/mealac/pritchett/00islamlinks/txt_jinnah_lahore_1940.html.

54. *Morning News*, 12 January 1956.

55. I. H. Qureshi, "Presidential Address," in *The Proceedings of the Pakistan History Conference (Eighth Session) Held at Peshawar under the Auspices of the Pakistan Historical Society*, ed. Dr. S. Moinul Haq (Karachi: Pakistan Historical Society, 1961), 23–24. In later writing, he cited the statement of a leader from Ghana: "We created Ghana," said a political leader of that country, "now the university should create Ghanaians." I. H. Qureshi, *Education in Pakistan: An Inquiry into Objectives and Achievements* (Karachi: Bureau of Composition, Compilation and Translation, University of Karachi, 1999), 124.

56. "The Role of the Ulema in Muslim Political Movement in Pak-Hind," 557/CF/67, NDC.

57. "Compilation of Books on (i) the need for a strong centre and (ii) the history of Muslims in East Pakistan," NDC, CF/35/65, NDC, 6.

58. Ibid., 6.

59. I. H. Qureshi, *Aspects of the History, Culture and Religions of Pakistan: A Series of Lectures by Dr. Ishtiaq Husain Qureshi* (Bangkok: Southeast Asia Treaty Organization, 1963), 15, emphasis added.

60. "Compilation of Books on (i) the Need for a Strong Centre and (ii) The history of Muslims in East Pakistan," NDC, CF/35/65, NDC, 10.

61. Serial no. 1253, unnamed file, Ministry of Education, NAP, 5.

62. Ibid., 6.

63. "Compilation of Books on (i) the Need for a Strong Centre and (ii) The history of Muslims in East Pakistan," NDC, CF/35/65, NDC, 7.

64. Ibid., 12.

65. Ibid.

66. Ibid., 14.

67. I. H. Qureshi, ed., *A Short History of Pakistan* (1967; Karachi: Karachi University Press, 1992), i.

68. Ibid., i.

69. Ibid., i–ii.

70. Yael Zerubavel, *Recovered Roots: Collective Memory and the Making of Israeli National Tradition* (Chicago: University of Chicago Press, 1995).

71. "Quaid-i-Azam's Birthday Celebrations," 223/CF/47, NDC, 3.

72. "Independence Day Celebration," 196/CF/48, NDC, 2. Few have publicly challenged the rationale of this decision. It is, however, interesting to note that the editor of the volumes of Jinnah papers published by the Government of Pakistan, Zawwar Husain Zaidi, used to mention 15 August as the independence date for Pakistan.

73. M. Rafique Afzal, ed., *Speeches and Statements of Quaid-i-Millat Liaquat Ali Khan (1941–51)* (Lahore: Research Society of Pakistan, 1987), 162.

74. *Pakistan Observer*, 21 April 1951.

75. "Observance of Id-e-Miladu-Nabi as a "State function," 284/CF/50, NDC, 5–6.

76. *Inqilab*, 14 August 1948.

77. Ibid.

78. "Proposal to Celebrate the Centenary of Independence Struggle of 1857," 511/CF/56, NDC, 16.
79. Ibid., 17.
80. Ibid., 18.
81. *Imroz*, 19 April 1951
82. *Proceedings of Lahore Municipal Corporation*, February 1952, item no. 787, Lahore Municipal Corporation Archives (henceforth LMCA).
83. *Proceedings of Lahore Municipal Corporation*, 19 February 1955–3 March 1955, LMCA.
84. *Proceedings of Lahore Municipal Corporation*, 20 April 1961–27 July 1961, item no. 164, LMCA.
85. *Proceedings of Lahore Municipal Corporation*, July–September 1968, item no. 136, LMCA.
86. *Proceedings of Lahore Municipal Corporation*, 19 February 1955–3 March 1955, LMCA.
87. *Proceedings of Lahore Municipal Corporation*, 9 February 1953, item no. 783, LMCA.
88. *Proceedings of Lahore Municipal Corporation*, April–June 1969, item no. 661, LMCA.
89. *Morning News*, 10 April 1957.
90. Abdul Alim Morris from Karachi had written a letter to the editor to congratulate the Commissioner of Karachi. *Morning News*, 18 October 1956.
91. *Pakistan Observer*, 18 May 1951.
92. *Pakistan Observer*, 19 May 1951.
93. "Proposal regarding Renaming of the Fuller Road as Nazrul Avenue," File No. 9N-7, Government of East Bengal, Home Department, Political Branch, Proceeding 570-B, December 1950, National Archives of Bangladesh, 1.
94. "Changing the Names of Streets and Towns etc.," 54/CF/62, NDC, 3.
95. Ibid., 3.
96. Serial no. 519, "Proposal to Change the Spellings of the Names of Certain Districts and Towns in East Pakistan" (C), 1.
97. Serial no. 519, "Proposal to Change the Spellings of the Names of Certain Districts and Towns in East Pakistan" (N), 4.
98. Ibid., 5.
99. Serial no. 519, "Proposal to Change the Spellings of the Names of Certain Districts and Towns in East Pakistan" (C), 10.
100. Ibid., 26.
101. *Morning News*, 1 April 1950.
102. "Renaming the Provinces of East Bengal and West Punjab," 293/CF/49, NDC.
103. Ibid.
104. Ibid.
105. *Pasban*, 17 October 1948. M. Alam Malic from Dacca similarly recommended renaming East Bengal and West Punjab into Pak-Bengal and Pak-Punjab, respectively. *Morning News*, 4 February 1950.
106. "Renaming the Provinces of East Bengal and West Punjab," 293/CF/49, NDC.
107. Ibid.

108. *Pakistan Observer*, 2 October 1950.
109. *Morning News*, 19 September 1950.
110. *Nawa-i-Waqt*, 27 October 1949.
111. *Morning News*, 11 July 1959.
112. *Morning News*, 24 July 1959.
113. *Morning News*, 23 August 1959.
114. *Morning News*, 27 January 1957.
115. Quoted in Jani Vuolteenaho and Lawrence D. Berg, "Towards Critical Toponymies," in *Critical Toponymies: The Contested Politics of Place Naming*, ed. Lawrence D. Berg and Jani Vuolteenaho (London: Routledge, 2009), 10.
116. Maoz Azaryahu, "Naming the Past: The Significance of Commemorative Street Names," in *Critical Toponymies: The Contested Politics of Place Naming*, ed. Lawrence D. Berg and Jani Vuolteenaho (London: Routledge, 2009), 63–64.
117. *Nawa-i-Waqt*, 23 November 1949. On this occasion, it was suggested the gate be renamed Bab-i-Nishtar in honor of Abdur Rab Nishtar, the governor of Punjab who performed this ceremony. The governor opposed this proposal.
118. Jafri, *Pakistan Chronicle*, 45.
119. *Pakistan Times*, 28 August 1947.
120. *Nawa-i-Waqt*, 23 January 1950.
121. Ibid.
122. See Paul McGarr, "'The Viceroys Are Disappearing from the Roundabouts in Delhi': British Symbols of Power in Post-Colonial India," *Modern Asian Studies* 49, no. 3 (2015): 787–831.
123. UK High Commission Karachi, 30 August 1960, to D. M. Cleary, Commonwealth Relations Office, "Cemeteries and Graves in Pakistan," R/4/296, India Office Records, British Library, 2.
124. "Nicholson's Column at Margalla," 321/CF/69, NDC.
125. "Future of Memorials Associated with British Rule in India and Pakistan," DO 142/255, NA, 56.
126. "Future Retention of Monuments Memorials and Tablets in India and Pakistan," DO 35/ 2137, NA, 212.
127. Ali Usman Qasmi, "Symbolic Redemption, Retributive Justice: The Significance of Anti-Colonial Iconoclasm as Radical Politics," *The Abusable Past* (blog), https://www.radicalhistoryreview.org/abusablepast/symbolic-redemption-retributive-justice-the-significance-of-anti-colonial-iconoclasm-as-radical-politics/.
128. *Nawa-i-Waqt*, 11 April 1949.
129. *Nawa-i-Waqt*, 28 August 1950.
130. *Nawa-i-Waqt*, 30 August 1950.
131. "Removal of Statues from Public Places," 40/CF/51, NDC, 2c.
132. "Removal of Statues from Public Places," 40/CF/51, NDC.
133. Ibid.
134. Ibid.
135. *Pakistan Times*, 22 July 1951.
136. *Civil and Military Gazette*, 27 July 1951.
137. Ibid.

138. "Future Retention of Monuments Memorials and Tablets in India and Pakistan," DO 35/ 2137, NA.

139. Ibid., 235.

140. "Foyle College, Londonderry, wish to secure Statue of Lord Lawrence from Lahore," DO 35/9043, NA.

141. UK High Commission Karachi to J. Gibson, Commonwealth Relations Office, 22 January 1959, DO 35/9043, NA, 15.

142. DO 35/9043, NA, 25.

143. DO 35/9043, NA.

144. K. M. Sheikh to Sir Olaf K. Caroe, 14 October 1959, "Statues: Removal of Statues of British Sovereigns and Officials in India and Pakistan—especially the Removal of Statue of Lord John Lawrence, Viceroy 1864–69 from Lahore to Foyle College, Londonderry," Mss. Eur F173/172, India Office Records and Private Papers, British Library (henceforth BL).

145. Caroe to Trotman, November [date unclear] 1959, Mss. Eur F173/172, India Office Records and Private Papers, BL.

146. E. W. Trotman, Secretary ICS (Retired) Association, to Mrs. Glenn, Secretary to the Board of Governors, Foyle College, 6 February 1962, Mss. Eur F173/172, India Office Records and Private Papers, BL.

147. "Removal of Statues from Public Places," 40/CF/51, NDC, 43.

148. *Imroz*, 24 April 1948.

149. "Removal of Statues from Public Places," 40/CF/51, NDC.

150. "Style and Titles of Her Majesty the Queen," 132/CF/52, NDC, 7.

151. "i) Accession to the Throne of Queen Elizabeth the Second ii) Memorial Service for the Late King iii) Resolution of Condolence on the Death of King George iv) Programme regarding Coronation Celebration of Her Majesty Queen Elizabeth the Second v) Memorial Service for Queen Mary," 36/CF/52, NDC, 2A-2B and 5-A-5B.

152. "Battle Honours Earned for the Battles Fought against Muslim and Our Own Countrymen under the Pressure of Foreign Rulers," 194/CF/60, NDC, 3.

153. Ibid., 10.

154. Michel Foucault, *Archaeology of Knowledge* (London: Routledge, 2002), 146.

155. Patricia Davison, "Museums and the Reshaping of Memory," in *Negotiating the Past: The Making of Memory in South Africa*, ed. Sarah Nuttall and Carli Coetzee (Cape Town: Oxford University Press, 1998), 145–46; Rosmarie Beier-de Haan, "Re-staging Histories and Identities," in *A Companion to Museum Studies*, ed. Sharon Macdonald (Oxford: Blackwell Publishing, 2006), 192–93.

156. Mrinalini Venkateswaran, "Museum Collecting and Constructions of Identity in Indian Punjab, 1947–1970" (PhD diss., University of Cambridge, 2020), 112.

157. *Proceedings of the First Meeting of the Advisory Board of Education for Pakistan Held at Karachi from 7th to 9th June, 1948* (Karachi: Education Division, Government of Pakistan), 10.

158. *Pakistan Times*, 20 June 1952.

159. B. A. Kureshi, "Lahore Museum (Then and Now)," *Lahore Museum Bulletin* 1, no. 2 (July–December 1988), 6.

160. Dr. Saifur Rahman Dar, "Development of Museums in Pakistan: Potentials,

Prospects and Problems," in *Museology and Museum Problems in Pakistan*, ed. Dr. Saifur Rahman Dart (Lahore: Lahore Museum, 1981), 15–16.

161. Serial no. 1456, "Request for the Establishment of a Museum at Swat," Ministry of Education, NAP.

162. Serial no. 1459, "Establishment of a Museum at Umarkot," Ministry of Education, NAP.

163. *Proceedings of the 6th Meeting of the Advisory Board of Education for Pakistan Held at Peshawar on 2nd to 4th March, 1954*, 37.

164. Serial no. 1328, "Establishment of a National Museum in East Pakistan" (N), Ministry of Education, NAP, 1.

165. Ibid., 5.

166. Ibid.

167. Firoz Mahmud, "Cultural Life in Dhaka: Pakistan and Bangladesh Period," in *400 Years of Capital Dhaka and Beyond*, vol. 2, *Economy and Culture*, ed. M. Mufakharul Islam and Firoz Mahmud (Dhaka: Asiatic Society of Bangladesh, 2011), 317; Andrew Amstutz, "A Pakistani Homeland for Buddhism: Displaying a National History for Pakistan beyond Islam, 1950–1969," *South Asia: Journal of South Asian Studies* 42, no.2 (2019), 237-255.

168. S. A. A. Naqvi (Superintendent of the National Museum of Pakistan), "Report on the National Museum of Pakistan for 1968–69," *Pakistan Archaeology* 6 (1969): 255–56.

169. *Nawa-i-Waqt*, 19 April 1950.

170. Tony Bennett, *Pasts Beyond Memory: Evolution, Museum, Colonialism* (London: Routledge, 2004), 5.

171. Serial no. 1446, "Proposed Construction of National Museum Building in the Burns Gardens" (C), Ministry of Education, NAP, 1.

172. Ibid., 2.

173. Ibid., 3.

174. Ibid., 4.

175. Ibid., 5.

176. Ibid., 6–7.

177. Ibid., 9.

178. Carol Duncan, "Art Museums and the Ritual of Citizenship," in *Exhibiting Cultures: The Poetics and Politics of Museum Display*, ed. Ivan Karp and Steven D. Lavine (Washington DC: Smithsonian Institution Press, 1991), 91–92.

179. Serial no. 1457, "Construction of a Building for the National Museum of Pakistan" (C), 11.

180. Ibid., 16.

181. Ibid.

182. Ibid., 18.

183. Michel de Certeau, *The Practice of Everyday Life* (Berkeley: University of California Press, 1988), 108.

184. Srirupa Roy, *Beyond Belief: India and the Politics of Postcolonial Nationalism* (Durham, NC: Duke University Press, 2007), 66.

185. Ibid., 15.

Postscript: A New Beginning

1. Aalene Mahum Aneeq, "To the Editor: Partition Refugee Relief and the 'Making of the Pakistani Muslim Citizen' in Punjab," in *The Routledge Handbook of Refugee Narratives*, ed. Evyn Lê Espiritu Gandhi and Vinh Nguyen (New York: Routledge, 2023), 240–51. Aneeq's essay focuses on refugee narratives in the post-Partition period as they wrote letters to the editors to demand assistance from the government in the rehabilitation process and put up an organized front to assert their rights as "Muslim citizens" of the newly established state.
2. *Imroz*, 12 June 1950.
3. *Pakistan Observer*, 5 August 1949.
4. *Nawa-i-Waqt* 18 November 1949.
5. *Nawa-i-Waqt* 18 November 1949.
6. *Nawa-i-Waqt*, 27 November 1949.
7. *Nawa-i-Waqt*, 2 December 1949.
8. For detailed discussion about themes relating to bureaucratic framing of a rational electoral arena, see David Gilmartin, *Civilisation and Modernity: Narrating the Creation of Pakistan* (New Delhi: Yoda Press, 2014).
9. *Nawa-i-Waqt*, 24 November 1949.
10. *Nawa-i-Waqt*, 24 November 1949.
11. *Nawa-i-Waqt*, 30 November 1949.
12. *Nawa-i-Waqt*, 24 November 1949.
13. *Nawa-i-Waqt*, 24 November 1949.
14. *Nawa-i-Waqt*, 2 December 1949.
15. *Nawa-i-Waqt*, 4 December 1949. Another reader, Tariq Faruqi, favored the practice, not out of pride for his identity, but aesthetic reasons. He said he rather liked the sound of Faruqi and it would be unfair to expect from him to remove it from his name. *Nawa-i-Waqt*, 4 December 1949.
16. *Nawa-i-Waqt*, 3 December 1949.
17. *Nawa-i-Waqt*, 15 December 1949.
18. The newspaper also published a poem by Tohid Nadwi Hoshiyarpuri titled *Tark-i-Nisab* (Abolition of Social Ranks) to support its notion of equality among citizens. *Nawa-i-Waqt*, 11 December 1949.
19. *Morning News*, 4 November 1956.
20. *Morning News*, 4 November 1956.
21. *Morning News*, 24 November 1956.
22. *Pakistan Observer*, 21 April 1957.
23. *Pakistan Times*, 4 February 1952.
24. *Morning News*, 26 April 1956.
25. *Pakistan Observer*, 14 October 1956.
26. *Pakistan Observer*, 18 October 1956.
27. *Pakistan Observer*, 24 October 1956.
28. *Pakistan Observer*, 24 October 1956.
29. Karl Marx, "On the Jewish Question" (1844), available at https://www.marxists.org/archive/marx/works/1844/jewish-question/.
30. Ibid.

31. Serial no. 487, "Use of Ceremonial Red Cloth" (C), Ministry of Interior, NAP, 2.
32. Ibid., 2.
33. Ibid., 3.
34. Ibid., 5.
35. Ibid., 10.
36. Ibid., 11.
37. Ibid., 12.
38. Ibid., 13.
39. Ibid., 18.
40. Ibid., 16.
41. On student-led protests, see Aslam Khwaja, *People's Movements in Pakistan* (Karachi: Kitab Publishers, ca. 2016). On workers' strikes, see Kamran Asdar Ali, "The Strength of the Street Meets the Strength of the State: The 1972 Labor Struggle in Karachi," *International Journal of Middle East Studies* 37, no. 1 (February 2005), 83–107; Layli Uddin, "'Enemy Agents at Work': A Microhistory of the 1954 Adamjee and Karnaphuli Riots in East Pakistan," *Modern Asian Studies* 55, no. 2 (March 2021): 629–64. On the farmers' movement, see Mubashar Rizvi, *The Ethics of Staying: Social Movements and Land Rights Politics in Pakistan* (Stanford, CA: Stanford University Press, 2019).

42. On surveillance, see Zehra Hashmi, "Making Reliable Persons: Managing Descent and Genealogical Computation in Pakistan," *Comparative Studies in Society and History* 63, no. 4 (October 2021): 948–78. On relief packages, see Ayesha Siddiqi, *In the Wake of Disaster: Islamists, the State and a Social Contract in Pakistan* (New Delhi: Cambridge University Press, 2019). On infrastructure and connectivity, see Naveeda Khan, "Flaws in the Flow: Roads and their Modernity in Pakistan," *Social Text* 24, no. 4 (2006): 87–113. On social programs, see Haris Gazdar, "Social Protection in Pakistan: In the Midst of a Paradigm Shift?" *Economic and Political Weekly* 46, no. 28 (2011), 59–66.

43. Partha Chatterjee, *Lineages of Political Society: Studies in Postcolonial Democracy* (New York: Columbia University Press, 2011), 198–200.

44. Ali Usman Qasmi, "Making Sense of Naya Pakistan," *Friday Times*, 21 September 2018.

45. Ravinder Kaur, *Brand New Nation: Capitalist Dreams and Nationalist Designs in Twenty-First-Century India* (Stanford, CA: Stanford University Press, 2020), 10.

46. Richard David Williams and Rafay Mahmood, "A Soundtrack for Reimagining Pakistan? Coke Studio, Memory and the Music Video," *BioScope: South Asian Screen Studies* 10, no. 2 (2019): 111–128.

47. Najia Mukhtar, "Using Love to Fathom Religious Difference—Contemporary Formats of Sufi Poetry in Pakistan," *Contemporary South Asia* 23, no. 1 (2015): 27.

48. Arif Hasan, *The Unplanned Revolution: Observations on the Process of Socio-economic Changes in Pakistan* (Karachi: Oxford University Press, 2009).

49. Hurmat Ali Shah, "Redefining Citizenship in Pakistan," *Himal South Asian*, 28 April 2020. https://www.himalmag.com/redefining-citizenship-in-pakistan-2020/. For an overview of the Aurat March and its charter of demands, see Alia Chughtai, "Pakistani Women Hold 'Aurat March' for Equality, Gender Justice," *Al-Jazeera*, 8 March 2019. https://www.aljazeera.com/news/2019/3/8/pakistani-women-hold-aurat-march-for-equality-gender-justice.

50. Andrew Schaap, "Enacting the Right to have Rights: Jacques Rancière's Critique of Hannah Arendt," *European Journal of Political Theory* 10, no. 1 (2011): 26.

51. Mohammad Waseem's voluminous recent work on political conflict in Pakistan serves as an excellent reference work for such a study. See Waseem, *Political Conflict in Pakistan* (London: Hurst, 2022).

52. Many Pakistani analysts see "the Imran Khan project" and this rise of his Pakistan Tehrik-i-Insaf (PTI) as yet another example of a military strategic asset gone rogue. According to them, the military relaunched Khan and infused life into his otherwise-dud politics post-2010 as it was looking for an effective third-party interjection to break the monopoly of established political parties—the Pakistan People's Party and the Muslim League (Nawaz Sharif group)—which had reached a mutual understanding following the signing of the Charter of Democracy in 2006 to not allow military interference and work together to strengthen democracy. Pro–Imran Khan analysts point out the rise of a new professional middle class, its aspirational values for meritocracy, and its disdain for corruption and dynastic politics, which they see as responsible for Pakistan's economic woes and the reason for Khan's meteoric rise in Pakistani politics. A "new Pakistan" was in the making, and Imran Khan became the charismatic leader who promised to bring it to fruition. It is not surprising, then, that analysts, observers, and ordinary citizens are highly partisan in their understanding of the current wave of protests. Khan's critics view the protestors as an entitled class, lacking political maturity, trying to force the military to restore to power their favorite leader and the only possible savior and a messiah figure. His supporters see the current moment as the emergence of a highly politicized middle class strongly invested in Pakistan's future, demanding rule of law and calling for elections to resolve the political crises. One needs to look beyond the simplistic dismissal of Khan's supporters as cult followers or the glorification of his politics as truly revolutionary to fully gauge the impact of ongoing verbal and physical assaults by the PTI against the military and its potential consequences in the years to come.

BIBLIOGRAPHY

Archives
National Archives of Pakistan, Islamabad
Fatima Jinnah Papers
Muhammad Ali Jinnah Papers
Prime Minister Secretariat Files
Ministry of Interior, Pakistan
Ministry of Education, Pakistan

Freedom Movement Archives, University of Karachi
Zafar Ahmed Ansari Collection

National Documentation Center, Islamabad

Lahore Municipal Corporation Archives

National Archives of Bangladesh, Dhaka

National Archives, Kew Gardens, London

Roberts Club Archive, Lahore

Libraries
British Library
Abdullah Malik Collection, Government College University Library, Lahore
Dayal Singh College Library, Lahore
Dhaka University Library, Dhaka
Hamdard University Library, Karachi
Lahore Museum Library
National Library, Islamabad
Punjab Assembly Library, Lahore
Punjab Public Library, Lahore
Punjab Secretariat Library, Lahore
Punjab University Library, Lahore
Research Society of Pakistan Library, Lahore

Newspapers and Journals
Civil and Military Gazette
Dawn
Imroz
Morning News
Nawa-i-Waqt
Pakistan Observer
Pakistan Times
Pasban

Court Case
Roochomal Daryanomal v. *The Province of West Pakistan* (1959), PLD.

Primary Sources
Afzal, M. Rafique, ed. *Speeches and Statements of Quaid-i-Millat Liaquat Ali Khan (1941–51)*. Lahore: Research Society of Pakistan, 1987.
Ahmad, Mohammad Basheer, ed. *Selected Constitutions of the World*. 2 vols. Karachi: Governor General's Press and Publications, 1951.
Al-Mujahid, Sharif, ed. *In Quest of Jinnah: Diary, Notes and Correspondence of Hector Bolitho*. Karachi: Oxford University Press, 2009.
Bazm-i-Iqbal ki Rudadain: 1950 ta January 1993. Lahore: Bazm-i-Iqbal, 1993.
Constituent Assembly of Pakistan Debates, 1947–56.
Fundamental Principles of an Islamic State: Formulated at a gathering of Ulama of Various Muslim Schools of Thought under the Presidentship of Allama Syed Suleiman Sahib Nadvi. Karachi: Published by (Maulana) Ehtishamul Haq Thanvi, Jacob Lines, Sadar, ca. 1951.
Guide to the Sources of Asian History: Pakistan. Islamabad: National Archives of Pakistan, 1990.
Haq, Dr. S. Moinul, ed. *The Proceedings of the All Pakistan History Conference: First Session Held at Karachi, 1951*. Karachi: Pakistan Historical Society, ca. 1952.
———. *The Proceedings of the Pakistan History Conference (Sixth Session) Held at Karachi under the Auspices of the Pakistan Historical Society 1956*. Karachi: Pakistan Historical Society, 1959.
Historical Records and Archives Commission for Pakistan: Proceedings of the Meetings of the Fifth Session Held at Dacca on 11th April, 1970. Karachi.
Iqbal Academy: Decade of Progress, 1958–68. Karachi: Iqbal Academy, ca. 1968.
Khan, Ahmad Nabi. *Iqbal Manzil Sialkot: The Birth Place of Allama Muhammad Iqbal*. Lahore: Department of Archaeology and Museums, Ministry of Culture, Tourism and Archaeology, Government of Pakistan, 1977.
Memon, Amanullah, ed. *The Altaf Gauhar Papers: Documents towards the Making of the Constitution of 1962*. Lahore: Sang-e-Meel Publications, 2003.
Microfilm Holdings: From IOL&R and Other Sources Abroad (Series 1.1). Lahore: Government of Pakistan, Cabinet Division, National Documentation Centre, 1988.
Muntakhib Nazmain: Tehrik-i-Pakistan kay dauran Jalson mai parhe janay walay Tarane aur Qaid-i-Azam ke huzur Nazrana-hai-Aqidat. Islamabad: National Archives of Pakistan, ca. 1986.

National Assembly Debates, 1972–1974. N.p.: various publishers. https://na.gov.pk/en/debates.php.
The Pakistani Flag. Islamabad: Directorate of Films and Publications, Ministry of Information and Broadcasting, Government of Pakistan, 1988.
Proceedings of the 1st Meeting of the Advisory Board of Education for Pakistan Held at Karachi from 7th to 9th June, 1948. Karachi: Education Division, Government of Pakistan.
Proceedings of the Inaugural Meeting of the Fourth Session of the Historical Records and Archives Commission for Pakistan Held at Karachi on February 21, 1959.
Proceedings of the 6th Meeting of the Advisory Board of Education for Pakistan Held at Peshawar on 2nd to 4th March, 1954. Karachi: Education Division, Government of Pakistan.
Quaid-e-Azam Memorial Fund Board: Report for the Period Ending December 31, 1973.
Relics of the Quaid-i-Azam: A catalogue. Karachi: Department of Archaeology and Museums, Ministry of Culture and Tourism, Government of Pakistan, 1980.
Report of the Commission of Enquiry, Set Up by the Government of Pakistan, to Ascertain Which of the Properties Left by Quaid-e-Azam Should be Preserved as Relics of National Value. Islamabad: National Documentation Center, Cabinet Division.
Sheikh, Atique Zafar, ed. *Guide to the Sources of Asian History*. Vol. 1, Series 8.1. Islamabad: National Archives of Pakistan, 1990.
Siddiqi, M. H. *A Handbook of Archives and Material on Pakistan Freedom Struggle*. Karachi: University of Karachi, 1988.
Zafar, Rukhsana, ed. *The National Anthem of Pakistan: A Documented History Based on the Pakistan Government Cabinet Record*. Islamabad: National Documentation Wing, 2009.
Zulfiqar, Professor Dr. Ghulam Husain. *Tarikh-i-Bazm-i-Iqbal: 1950 ta 2000*. Lahore: Bazm-i-Iqbal, 2000.

Secondary Sources
Abbasi, Roshain. "Did Premodern Muslims Distinguish the Religious and Secular? The Dīn-Dunyā Binary in Medieval Islamic Thought." *Journal of Islamic Studies* 31, no. 2 (2020): 185–225.
Adams, Laura. *The Spectacular State: Culture and National Identity in Uzbekistan*. Durham, NC: Duke University Press, 2010.
Afzal, M. Rafique. *Political Parties in Pakistan*. 3 vols. Islamabad: National Institute of Historical and Cultural Research, 1998.
Afzal, Tanveer. *Bank Notes of Pakistan in the State Bank Museum Collection (1948–2012)*. Karachi: State Bank of Pakistan, 2013.
Ahmad, Abul Mansur. *End of a Betrayal and Restoration of Lahore Resolution*. Dacca: Khoshroz Kitab Mahal, 1975. In Rachel Fell McDermott, Leonard A. Gordon, Ainslie T. Embree, Frances W. Pritchett, and Dennis Dalton, eds., *Sources of Indian Traditions: Modern India, Pakistan, and Bangladesh*. New York: Columbia University Press, 2014: 862-4.
Ahmad, Manan Asif. *The Loss of Hindustan: The Invention of India*. Cambridge, MA: Harvard University Press, 2020.
Ahmad, Dr. Muhammad Mushtaq. *Ru'at-i-Hilal: Fiqhi wa Qanuni Tajziya*. Lahore: Kitab Mahal, n.d.

Ahmad, Nihal. *A History of Radio Pakistan*. Karachi: Oxford University Press, 2005.
Ahmad, Rafiuddin. *The Bengal Muslims 1871–1906: A Quest for Identity*. New Delhi: Oxford University Press, 1981.
Ahmad, Shaikh Ijaz. "Allama Iqbal ki Tarikh-i-Paidayish." In *Allama Iqbal ki Tarikh-i-Wiladat*, edited by Dr. Waheed Qureshi and Zahid Munir Amir, 237–56. Lahore: Bazm-i-Iqbal, 1994.
Ahmed, Sufia. *Muslim Community in Bengal, 1884–1912*. Dhaka: University Press Ltd., 1996.
Ajami, Dr. Shafiq. *Iqbal Shanas: Alami Tanazur mai*. Lahore: Pakistan Writers Cooperative Society, 2011.
Akhtar, Aasim Sajjad. *The Politics of Common Sense: State, Society and Culture in Pakistan*. New Delhi: Cambridge University Press, 2018.
Albrecht, Sarah. *Dar al-Islam Revisited: Territoriality in Contemporary Islamic Legal Discourse on Muslims in the West*. Leiden: Brill, 2018.
Ali, Kamran Asdar. "The Strength of the Street Meets the Strength of the State: The 1972 Labor Struggle in Karachi." *International Journal of Middle East Studies* 37, no. 1 (February 2005): 83–107.
———. *Surkh Salam: Communist Politics and Class Activism in Pakistan, 1947–1972*. Karachi: Oxford University Press, 2012.
Ali, Nosheen. *Delusional States: Feeling Rule and Development in Pakistan's Northern Frontier*. New Delhi: Cambridge University Press, 2019.
Ali, Shaheen Sardar, and Javaid Rehman. *Indigenous Peoples and Ethnic Minorities of Pakistan: Constitutional and Legal Perspectives*. Surrey, UK: Curzon Press, 2001.
Alimia, Sanaa. *Refugee Cities: How Afghans Changed Urban Pakistan*. Philadelphia: University of Pennsylvania Press, 2022.
Amir, Zahid Munir. "Muqaddama." In *Allama Iqbal ki Tarikh-i-Wiladat*, edited by Dr. Waheed Qureshi and Zahid Munir Amir, 9–20. Lahore: Bazm-i-Iqbal, 1994.
Anderson, Benedict. *Imagined Communities: Reflections on the Origin and Spread of Nationalism*. London: Verso, 2006.
Aneeq, Mahum Aalene. "To the Editor: Partition Refugee Relief and the "Making of the Pakistani Muslim Citizen" in Punjab" in *The Routledge Handbook of Refugee Narratives*, edited by Evyn Lê Espiritu Gandhi and Vinh Nguyen, 240–51. New York: Routledge, 2023.
Anjum, Zahid Husain, ed. *Encyclopaedia Waqait-i-Pakistan*. Vol. 1. Lahore: Nazir Sons, 2005.
Ankit, Rakesh. "The Accession of Junagadh, 1947–48: Colonial Sovereignty, State Violence and Post-Independence India." *Indian Economic and Social History Review* 53, no. 3 (2016): 371–404.
Ansari, Sarah. "Subjects or Citizens? India, Pakistan and the 1948 British Nationality Act." *Journal of Imperial and Commonwealth History* 41, no. 2 (2013): 285–312.
Ansari, Sarah, and William Gould, *Boundaries of Belonging: Localities, Citizenship and Rights in India and Pakistan*. Cambridge: Cambridge University Press, 2019.
Antrim, Zayde. *Routes and Realms: The Power of Place in the Early Islamic World*. New York: Oxford University Press, 2013.
Anwar, Nausheen H. "Negotiating New Conjunctures of Citizenship: Experiences of

"'Illegality' in Burmese-Rohingya and Bangladeshi Migrant Enclaves in Karachi." *Citizenship Studies* 17, nos. 3–4 (2013): 414–28.
Appadurai, Arjun. "Full Attachment." *Public Culture* 10, no. 2 (1998): 443–49.
Aqil, Shafi, ed. *Majid Lahori ki Harf-o-Hikayat*. Karachi: Fazli Sons, 2000.
Arendt, Hannah. *The Origins of Totalitarianism*. New York: Harcourt, Brace & World, 1966.
Aubin, David, Charlotte Bigg, and H. Otto Sibum, eds. *Observatories and Astronomy in Nineteenth Century Science and Culture*. Durham, NC: Duke University Press, 2010.
Azad, Jagan Nath. "When was Iqbal Born?" In *Allama Iqbal ki Tarikh-i-Wiladat*, edited by Dr. Waheed Qureshi and Zahid Munir Amir, 47–63. Lahore: Bazm-i-Iqbal, 1994.
Azaryahu, Maoz. "Naming the Past: The Significance of Commemorative Street Names." In *Critical Toponymies: The Contested Politics of Place Naming*, edited by Lawrence D. Berg and Jani Vuolteenaho, 53–70. London: Routledge, 2016.
Balibar, Étienne. *Citizenship*. Malden, MA: Polity Press, 2015.
Banerjee, Prathama. *Elementary Aspects of the Political: Histories from the Global South*. Durham, NC: Duke University Press, 2021.
Bangash, Yaqoob Khan. "Sovereignty and the Constitution." *Journal of Law, Religion and State* 7, no. 2 (2018): 129–51.
Batalia, Urvashi. *The Other Side of Silence: Voices from the Partition of India*. Delhi: Viking Penguin India, 1998.
Benhabib, Seyla. *The Rights of Others: Aliens, Residents, and Citizens*. Cambridge: Cambridge University Press, 2004.
Bhabha, Homi K. "DissemiNation: Time, Narrative, and the Margins of the Modern Nation." In *Nation and Narration*, edited by Homi K. Bhabha, 291–322. London: Routledge, 1990.
Blake, Stephen P. *Time in Early Modern Islam: Calendar, Ceremony, and Chronology in the Safavid, Mughal and Ottoman Empires*. Cambridge: Cambridge University Press, 2013.
Bose, Neilesh. *Recasting the Region: Language, Culture, and Islam in Colonial Bengal*. New Delhi: Oxford University Press, 2014.
Bose, Purnima. *Organizing Empire: Individualism, Collective Agency and India*. Durham, NC: Duke University Press, 2003.
Brubaker, Rogers. *Citizenship and Nationhood in France and Germany*. Cambridge, MA: Harvard University Press, 1996.
Bsheer, Rosie. *Archive Wars: The Politics of History in Saudi Arabia*. Stanford, CA: Stanford University Press, 2020.
Burton, Antoinette. *Archive Stories: Facts, Fiction and The Writing of History*. Durham, NC: Duke University Press, 2005.
Butler, Judith, and Gayatri Chakravorti Spivak. *Who Sings the Nation-State? Language, Politics, Belonging*. Calcutta: Seagull Books, 2011.
Cagaptay, Soner. "Citizenship Policies in Interwar Turkey." *Nations and Nationalism* 9, no. 4 (2003): 601–19.
Certeau, Michel de. *The Practice of Everyday Life*. Berkeley: University of California Press, 1988.
Chatterjee, Partha. *I Am the People: Reflections on Popular Sovereignty Today*. New York: Columbia University Press, 2020.

---. *Lineages of Political Society. Studies in Postcolonial Democracy.* New York: Columbia University Press, 2011.
---. *The Nation and Its Fragments: Colonial and Postcolonial Histories.* Princeton, NJ: Princeton University Press, 1993.
---. *Nationalist Thought and the Colonial World: A Derivative Discourse.* London: Zed Books, 1986.
Chatterji, Joya. "South Asian Histories of Citizenship, 1946–1970." *Historical Journal* 55, no. 4 (December 2012).
Chattha, Ilyas. "Competitions for Resources: Partition's Evacuee Property and the Sustenance of Corruption in Pakistan." *Modern Asian Studies* 46, no. 5 (2012): 1182–1211.
---. "The Impact of the Redistribution of Partition's Evacuee Property on the Patterns of Land Ownership and Power in Pakistani Punjab in the 1950s." In *State and Nation Building in Pakistan*, edited by Roger D. Long, Gurharpal Singh, Yunas Samad, and Ian Talbot, 13–34. London: Routledge, 2016.
Chester, Lucy P. *Borders and Conflict in South Asia: The Radcliffe Boundary Commission and the Partition of Punjab.* Manchester, UK: Manchester University Press, 2010.
Choudhury, G. W. *Constitutional Development in Pakistan.* Karachi: Royal Book Co., 2007.
Cook, Michael. *Commanding Right and Forbidding Wrong in Islamic Thought.* Cambridge: Cambridge University Press, 2001.
Cooppan, Vilashini. "Time-Maps: A Field Guide to the Decolonial Imaginary." *Critical Times* 2, no. 3 (December 2019): 396–415.
Crone, Patricia. *Medieval Islamic Political Thought.* Edinburgh: Edinburgh University Press, 2004.
Dallal, Ahmad S. *Islam, Science and the Challenge of History.* New Haven, CT: Yale University Press, 2010.
Dar, Dr. Saifur Rahman. "Development of Museums in Pakistan: Potentials, Prospects and Problems. In *Museology and Museum Problems in Pakistan*, edited by Dr. Saifur Rahman Dar, 13–26. Lahore: Lahore Museum, 1981.
Daston, Lorraine, and Elizabeth Lunbeck. Introduction to *Histories of Scientific Observation.* Edited by Lorraine Daston and Elizabeth Lunbeck. Chicago: University of Chicago Press, 2010.
Davison, Patricia. "Museums and the Reshaping of Memory." In *Negotiating the Past: The Making of Memory in South Africa*, edited by Sarah Nuttall and Carli Coetzee, 143–60. Cape Town: Oxford University Press, 1998.
De, Rohit. *A People's Constitution: The Everyday Life of Law in the Indian Republic.* Princeton, NJ: Princeton University Press, 2018.
Dehalwi, Mufti Muhammad Kifayatullah. *Kifayat al-Mufti.* Vol. 4. Karachi: Dar-ul-Isha'at, 2001.
Delanty, Gerard. "Communitarianism and Citizenship." In *Handbook of Citizenship Studies*, edited by Engin F. Isin and Bryan S. Turner, 159–74. London: Sage Publications, 2003.
Derrida, Jacques. "Force of Law: The Mystical Foundations of Authority." In *Deconstruction and the Possibility of Justice*, edited by Drucilla Cornell, Michel Rosenfeld, and David Gray Carlson, 3–67. New York: Routledge, 1992.

Desogus, Paolo. "The Encyclopedia in Umberto Eco's Semiotics." *Semiotica*, no. 192 (2012): 501–21.
Devji, Faisal. "Illiberal Islam." In *Enchantments of Modernity: Empire, Nation, Globalization*, edited by Saurabh Dube, 234–63. New Delhi: Routledge, 2009.
———. "An Impossible Founding." *Global Intellectual History* 8, no. 1 (2021): 97–104.
———. "Muslim Nationalism: Founding Identity in Colonial India." PhD diss., University of Chicago, 1993.
———. *Muslim Zion: Pakistan as a Political Idea*. London: Hurst and Co., 2013.
Duncan, Carol. "Art Museums and the Ritual of Citizenship." In *Exhibiting Cultures: The Poetics and Politics of Museum Display*, edited by Ivan Karp and Steven D. Lavine, 88–103. Washington, DC: Smithsonian Institution Press, 1991.
Durrani, Said Akhtar. "Allama Iqbal ki Tarikh-i-Paidayish." In *Allama Iqbal ki Tarikh-i-Wiladat*, edited by Dr. Waheed Qureshi and Zahid Munir Amir, 83–91. Lahore: Bazm-i-Iqbal, 1994.
Eco, Umberto. *From the Tree to the Labyrinth: Historical Studies on the Sign and Interpretation*. Cambridge, MA: Harvard University Press, 2014.
———. *Semiotics and the Philosophy of Language*. Bloomington: Indiana University Press, 1986.
Farid, Mufti Muhammad. *Fatawa Faridiyya*. Vol. 4. Swabi: Dar-ul-Ulum Siddiqiyya, 2009.
Faruqi, Shams-ur-Rehman. *Sher-i-Shor Angez: Jild Chaharum*. New Delhi: Qaumi Council Bara-i-Farugh-i-Urdu Zaban, 2008.
Fatawa Alamgiri. Vol. 2. Translated by Maulana Syed Amir Ali. Lahore: Maktaba Rahmania, n.d.
Fischer-Tine, Harald. *Low and Licentious Europeans: Race, Class and White Subalternity in Colonial India*. New Delhi: Orient BlackSwan, 2009.
Foucault, Michel. *Archaeology of Knowledge*. London: Routledge, 2002.
Gadamer, Hans-Georg. *Truth and Method*. London: Continuum, 2004.
Gayer, Laurent. *Karachi: Ordered Disorder and the Struggle for the City*. New York: Oxford University Press, 2014.
Gazdar, Haris. "Social Protection in Pakistan: In the Midst of a Paradigm Shift?" *Economic and Political Weekly* 46, no. 28 (2011): 59–66.
Geertz, Clifford. *The Interpretation of Cultures: Selected Essays by Clifford Geertz*. New York: Basic Books, 1973.
Geisler, Michael E. "Introduction: What Are National Symbols—And What Do They Do to Us?" In *National Symbols, Fractured Identities: Contesting the National Narrative*, edited by Michael E. Geisler, xiii–xlii. Middlebury, VT: Middlebury College Press.
Gilmartin, David. *Civilisation and Modernity: Narrating the Creation of Pakistan*. New Delhi: Yoda Press, 2014.
———. "A Magnificent Gift: Muslim Nationalism and the Election Process in Colonial Punjab." *Comparative Studies in Society and History* 40, no. 3 (1998): 415–36.
Gorman, Daniel. *Imperial Citizenship: Empire and the Question of Belonging*. Manchester, UK: Manchester University Press, 2006.
Haan, Rosmarie Beier-de. "Re-staging Histories and Identities." In *A Companion to*

Museum Studies, edited by Sharon Macdonald, 186–97. Oxford: Blackwell Publishing, 2006.

Habermas, Jürgen. "The European Nation-State: On the Past and Future of Sovereignty and Citizenship." *Public Culture* 10, no. 2 (1998): 397–416.

"Hafeez Jalandhari: Story of Creation of Pakistan's National Anthem (Part 2)—Exclusive for LAL." YouTube video, 19:42, posted by Khursheed Abdullah, https://www.youtube.com/watch?v=xEzd8CXf2_Q.

Hallaq, Wael B. *The Impossible State: Islam, Politics, and Modernity's Moral Predicament*. New York: Columbia University Press, 2012.

Hansen, Thomas Blom. "Sovereigns beyond the State: On Legality and Authority in Urban India." In *Sovereign Bodies: Citizens, Migrants, and States in the Postcolonial World*, edited by Thomas Blom Hansen and Finn Stepputat, 169–91. Princeton, NJ: Princeton University Press, 2005.

Hansen, Thomas Blom, and Finn Stepputat. Introduction to *Sovereign Bodies: Citizens, Migrants, and States in the Postcolonial World*, edited by Thomas Blom Hansen and Finn Stepputat, 1–36. Princeton, NJ: Princeton University Press, 2005.

Haq, Maulana Abdul, ed. *Fatawa Haqqaniyya*. Vol. 4. Akora Khattak: Jamia Dar-ul-Ulum Haqqania, 2010.

Haq, Dr. S. Moinul. "Historical Studies in Pakistan with Special Reference to the Role of Pakistan History Society (A Brief Survey)." Paper presented at the National Conference on History and Culture, Islamabad, 3–5 July 1980.

———. Preface to *A History of the Freedom Movement*, vol. 4, *1936–1947, Parts I and II*. By Pakistan Historical Society. 1970; Delhi: Renaissance Publishing House, 1984.

Hasan, Arif. *The Unplanned Revolution: Observations on the Process of Socio-economic Changes in Pakistan*. Karachi: Oxford University Press, 2009.

Hasan, Mushirul. *A Moral Reckoning: Muslim Intellectuals in Nineteenth-Century Delhi*. New Delhi: Oxford University Press, 2007.

———. "Traditional Rites and Contested Meanings: Sectarian Strife in Colonial Lucknow." *Economic and Political Weekly* 31, no. 9 (1996): 543–50.

Hashmi, Zehra. "Comparative Studies in Society and History" 63, no. 4 (October 2021): 948–78.

Heidegger, Martin. *The Question Concerning Technology and Other Essays*. New York: Garland Publishing, 1977.

Hopkins, Benjamin D. "The Frontier Crimes Regulation and Frontier Governmentality." *Journal of Asian Studies* 74, no. 2 (May 2015): 369–89.

Hull, Matthew S. *Government of Paper: The Materiality of Bureaucracy in Pakistan*. Oakland: University of California Press, 2012.

Husain, Abid. "Moon-Gazing: Profile of Mufti Muneeb-ur-Rehman." *The Herald*, July 2016. https://herald.dawn.com/news/1153201.

Husain, S. Aijaz. *History of the State Bank of Pakistan (1948–1960)*. Karachi: State Bank of Pakistan, 1992.

In Memoriam—III (Iqbal Day Speeches and Articles). Karachi: Iqbal Academy, 1969.

Iob, Elisabetta. *Refugees and the Politics of the Everyday State in Pakistan: Resettlement in Punjab, 1947–1962*. London: Routledge, 2018.

Isin, Engin. *Being Political: Genealogies of Citizenship*. Minneapolis: University of Minnesota Press, 2002.
Isin Engin, ed. *Citizenship after Orientalism: Transforming Political Theory*. Basingstoke, UK: Palgrave Macmillan, 2015.
Ispahani, Farahnaz. *Purifying the Land of Pure: A History of Pakistan's Religious Minorities*. New York: Oxford University Press, 2017.
Jafri, Aqeel Abbas. *Pakistan Chronicle*. Karachi: Fazali Sons, 2010.
———. *Pakistan ka Qaumi Tarana: Kia hai Haqiqat? Kia hai Fasana?* Karachi: Virsa Publications, 2010.
Jalal, Ayesha. "Beyond the Symbolic to the Significant." In *Mazaar, Bazaar: Design & Visual Culture in Pakistan*, edited by Saima Zaidi, 182–87. Karachi: Oxford University Press, 2010.
———. "Conjuring Pakistan: History as Official Imagining." *International Journal of Middle East Studies* 27 (1995): 73–89.
———. *Self and Sovereignty: Individual and Community in South Asian Islam since 1950*. London: Routledge, 2000.
Jallandhari, Hafiz. "Dibacha." In *Pakistani Qaumi Parham aur Tarana*, by Younas Kamal Lodhi. Islamabad: National Book Foundation, 2016: 13-5.
Jamali, Hafeez. "A Harbor in the Tempest: Megaprojects, Identity, and the Politics of Place in Gwadar, Pakistan." PhD diss., University of Texas at Austin, 2014.
Jan, Ammar Ali. *Rule by Fear: Eight Theses on Authoritarianism in Pakistan*. Lahore: Folio Books, 2021.
Janoski, Thomas. *Citizenship and Civil Society: A Framework of Rights and Obligations in Liberal, Traditional, and Social Democratic Regimes*. Cambridge: Cambridge University Press, 1998.
Jauss, Hans Robert. *Literary Hermeneutics*. Minneapolis: University of Minnesota Press.
Jay, Martin. "Scopic Regimes of Modernity." In *Vision and Visuality: Discussions in Contemporary Culture #2*, edited by Hal Foster, 3–23. New York: New Press, 1999.
Jayal, Niraja Gopal. *Citizenship and Its Discontents: An Indian History*. Cambridge, MA: Harvard University Press, 2013.
———. "Faith-Based Citizenship: The Dangerous Path India is Choosing." *India Forum: A Journal-Magazine on Contemporary Issues*. https://www.theindiaforum.in/article/faith-criterion-citizenship.
Kapila, Shruti. *Violent Fraternity: Indian Political Thought in the Global Age*. Princeton, NJ: Princeton University Press, 2021.
Kaur, Ravinder. *Brand New Nation: Capitalist Dreams and Nationalist Designs in Twenty-First-Century India*. Stanford, CA: Stanford University Press, 2020.
Kaviraj, Sudipta. *The Imaginary Institution of India: Politics and Idea*. New York: Columbia University Press, 2010.
———. "A Strange Love of the Land: Identity, Poetry and Politics in the (Un)making of South Asia." *South Asia Multidisciplinary Academic Journal* 10 (2014): https://doi.org/10.4000/samaj.3756.
Khan, Ayesha. *The Women's Movement in Pakistan: Activism, Islam and Democracy*. London: Bloomsbury, 2019.

Khan, Faris A. "Translucent Citizenship: Khwaja Sira Activism and Alternatives to Dissent in Pakistan." In "Sedition, Sexuality, Gender, and Gender Identity in South Asia," special issue of *South Asia Multidisciplinary Academic Journal* 20 (2019).

Khan, Maryam Wasif. *Who Is a Muslim? Orientalism and Literary Populisms*. New York: Fordham University Press, 2021.

Khan, Naveeda. "Flaws in the Flow: Roads and Their Modernity in Pakistan." *Social Text* 24, no. 4 (2006): 87–113.

———. *Muslim Becoming: Aspiration and Skepticism in Pakistan*. Durham, NC: Duke University Press, 2012.

Khan, Pasha Muhammad. *The Broken Spell: Indian Story Telling and the Romance Genre in Persian and Urdu*. Detroit: Wayne State University Press, 2019.

Khosla, Madhav. *India's Founding Moment: The Constitution of a Most Surprising Democracy*. Cambridge, MA: Harvard University Press, 2020.

———. "The Possibility of Modern India." *Global Intellectual History* 8, no. 1 (2021): 105–13.

Khwaja, Aslam. *People's Movements in Pakistan*. Karachi: Kitab Publishers, ca. 2016.

Kia, Mana. *Persianate Selves: Memories of Place and Origin before Nationalism*. Stanford, CA: Stanford University Press, 2020.

King, David. "Astronomical Timekeeping ('ilm al-mîqât) in Medieval Islam." In *Actes du XXIXe Congrès International des Orientalistes*, 2:86–90. Paris: L'Asiathèque, 1975.

———. "Astronomical Timekeeping in Fourteenth-Century Syria." In *Proceedings of the First International Symposium for the History of Arabic Science*, 1:391–415 (Arabic) and 2:75–84 (English). 1976; Aleppo: Institute for the History of Arabic Science, 1978.

———. "Astronomical Timekeeping in Ottoman Turkey." In *Proceedings of the International Symposium on the Observatories in Islam, 19–23 Sept., 1977*, 245–269. Istanbul: Millî Egitim Basımevi, 1980.

———. "Kibla. ii. Astronomical Aspects" [sacred direction]. In *The Encyclopaedia of Islam*, new ed., vol. 5, fascs. 79–80, pp. 83–88. Leiden: E. J. Brill, 1979.

Kirmani, Nida. "Mobility and Urban Conflict: A Study of Lyari, Karachi." Crossroads Asia Working Paper Series, No. 28, University of Bonn, 2015.

Koselleck, Reinhart. *Futures Past: On the Semantics of Historical Time*. New York: Columbia University Press, 2004.

Kripke, Saul A. *Naming and Necessity*. Cambridge, MA: Harvard University Press, 2001.

Kureshi, B. A. "Lahore Museum (Then and Now)." *Lahore Museum Bulletin* 1, no. 2 (July–December 1988): 3–8.

Kymlicka, Will. *Multicultural Citizenship: A Liberal Theory of Minority Rights*. Oxford: Oxford University Press, 1996.

Kymlicka, Will, and Wayne Norman. "Return of the Citizen: A Survey of Recent Work on Citizenship Theory." In *Theorizing Citizenship*, edited by Ronald Beiner, 283–322. Albany: State University of New York Press, 1995.

Laclau, Ernesto. *On Populist Reason*. London: Verso, 2005.

Lahoud, Nelly. *A Study in Intellectual Boundaries: Political Thought in Islam*. London: Routledge, 2005.

Lakoff, George, and Mark Johnsen. *Metaphors We Live By*. Chicago: University of Chicago Press, 2003.

Lodhi, Younas Kamal. *Pakistani Qaumi Parham aur Tarana.* Islamabad: National Book Foundation, 2016.
Lutfi, Ameem. "Conquest without Rule: Baloch Portfolio Mercenaries in the Indian Ocean." PhD diss., Duke University, 2018.
MacIntyre, Alasdair. *Whose Justice? Which Rationality?.* Notre Dame, IN: University of Notre Dame Press, 1988.
Mahmud, Firoz. "Cultural Life in Dhaka: Pakistan and Bangladesh Period." In *400 Years of Capital Dhaka and Beyond: Volume II, Economy and Culture,* edited by M. Mufakharul Islam and Firoz Mahmud, 313–24. Dhaka: Asiatic Society of Bangladesh, 2011.
Mahmudabad, Ali Khan. *The Poetry of Belonging.* New Delhi: Oxford University Press, 2020.
Malik, Anushay. "Public Authority and Local Resistance: Abdur Rehman and the Industrial Workers of Lahore, 1969–1974." *Modern Asian Studies* 52, no. 3 (2018): 815–48.
Malik, Jamal. *Colonization of Islam in Pakistan: Dissolution of Traditional Institutions in Pakistan.* New Delhi: Manohar Publishers and Distributors, 1996.
Malik, Muhammad Aslam. *The Making of the Pakistan Resolution.* Karachi: Oxford University Press, 2001.
Mamdani, Mahmood. *Neither Settler nor Native: The Making and Unmaking of Permanent Minorities.* Cambridge, MA: Harvard University Press, 2020.
Maqsood, Ammara. *The New Pakistani Middle Class.* Cambridge, MA: Harvard University Press, 2017.
Marx, Karl. "On the Jewish Question." February 1844. https://www.marxists.org/archive/marx/works/1844/jewish-question/.
Masud, Tahir. "Manzil Pakistan." *Ankh Micholi,* August 1990, 93–99.
Mbembe, Achille. "The Power of the Archive and Its Limits." In *Refiguring the Archive,* edited by C. Hamilton, V. Harris, J. Taylor, M. Pickover, G. Reid, and R. Saleh, 19–26. Dordrecht, Netherlands: Springer, 2002.
McGarr, Paul. "'The Viceroys Are Disappearing from the Roundabouts in Delhi': British Symbols of Power in Post-Colonial India." *Modern Asian Studies* 49, no. 3 (2015): 787–831.
McGrath, Allen. *The Destruction of Pakistan's Democracy.* Karachi: Oxford University Press, 1996.
Menon, Ritu, and Kamla Bhasin. *Borders and Boundaries: Women in India's Partition.* Delhi: Kali for Women, 1998.
———. "Recovery, Rupture, Resistance-Indian State and Abduction of Women during Partition." *Economic and Political Weekly,* 24 April 1993, WS2–WS11.
Mian, Ali Altaf. "Troubling Technology: The Deobandī Debate on the Loudspeaker and Ritual Prayer." *Islamic Law and Society* 24, no. 4 (2017): 355–83.
Mohammad-Arif, Aminah. "Introduction—Imaginations and Constructions of South Asia: An Enchanting Abstraction?" *South Asia Multidisciplinary Academic Journal* 10 (2014).
Mongia, Radhika. *Indian Migration and Empire: A Colonial Genealogy of the Modern State.* Durham, NC: Duke University Press, 2018.
Moosa, Ebrahim. "Shaykh Aḥmad Shākir and the Adoption of a Scientifically-Based Lunar Calendar." *Islamic Law and Society* 5, no. 1 (1998): 57–89.

Morris, Pam, ed. *The Bakhtin Reader: Selected Writings of Bakhtin, Mededev and Voloshinov*. London: Arnold, 2003.
Mouffe, Chantal. "Religion, Liberal Democracy, and Citizenship." In *Political Theologies: Public Religions in a Post-Secular World*, edited by Hent De Vries and Lawrence E. Sullivan. New York: Fordham University Press, 2006.
Mukhtar, Najia. "Using Love to Fathom Religious Difference—Contemporary Formats of Sufi Poetry in Pakistan." *Contemporary South Asia* 23, no. 1 (2015): 26–44.
Nair, Neeti. *Hurt Sentiments: Secularism and Belonging in South Asia*. Cambridge, MA: Harvard University Press, 2023.
Naqvi, S. A. A. "Report on the National Museum of Pakistan for 1968–69." *Pakistan Archaeology* 6 (1969): 255–63.
Natarajan, Kalathmika. "The Privilege of the Indian Passport (1947–1967): Caste, Class, and the Afterlives of Indenture in Indian Diplomacy." *Modern Asian Studies* 57, no. 2 (2022): 321–50.
Nigam, Aditya. "A Text without Author: Locating Constituent Assembly as Event." *Economic and Political Weekly*, 22–28 May 2004.
Nora, Pierre. "General Introduction: Between Memory and History." In *Realms of Memory, vol. I: Conflicts and Divisions*, edited by Pierre Nora and translated by Arthur Goldhammer, 1–20. New York: Columbia University Press, 1992.
Ogle, Vanessa. *The Global Transformation of Time, 1870–1950*. Cambridge, MA: Harvard University Press, 2015.
Oommen, T. K. *Citizenship, Nationality and Ethnicity: Reconciling Competing Identities*. Cambridge, UK: Polity Press, 1997.
Pakistan Historical Society. *A History of the Freedom Movement (Being the Story of Muslim Struggle for the Freedom of Hind-Pakistan) 1707–1947*. Vol. 1, *1707–1831*. 1957; Delhi: Renaissance Publishing House, 1984.
Pakistan History Board. *A Short History of Hind-Pakistan*. Karachi: Pakistan Historical Society, 1960.
Pandey, Gyanendra. *Routine Violence: Nations, Fragments, Histories*. Stanford, CA: Stanford University Press, 2006.
Paracha, Nadeem Farooq. "Dressing Jinnah." *Dawn* 25 December 2016. https://www.dawn.com/news/1304036.
Parker, Lyn. *From Subjects to Citizens: Balinese Villagers in the Indonesian Nation-State*. Copenhagen: NIAS Press, 2003.
Parveen, Kausar. *Politics of Pakistan: Role of the Opposition, 1947–58*. Karachi: Oxford University Press, 2014.
Patel, Ian Sanjay. *We're Here Because You Were There: Immigration and the End of Empire*. London: Verso, 2021.
Perkins, Christopher Ryan "Partitioning History: The Creation of an *Islami Pablik* in Late Colonial India, c. 1880–1920." PhD diss., University of Pennsylvania, 2011.
Phulwarwi, Maulana Ja'far Shah. *Ru'at-i-Hilal*. Lahore: Idara Saqafat-i-Islamiyyah, 1967.
Preuss, Ulrich K. "Citizenship and the German Nation." *Citizenship Studies* 7, no. 1 (2003): 37–56.

Qarshi, Afzal Haq, ed. *Iqbaliyat-i-Tasir (Iqbal ke Fikar wa Fan par Muhammad Din Tasir ke Maqalat)*. Lahore: Iqbal Academy Pakistan, 2010.
Qasmi, Ahmed Nadeem. *Meray Hum Safar*. Lahore: Asatir, 2002.
Qasmi, Ali Usman. *The Ahmadis and the Politics of Religious Exclusion in Pakistan*. London: Anthem Press, 2014.
———. "Differentiating between Pakistan and Napak-istan: Maulana Abul Ala Maududi's Critique of the Muslim League and Muhammad Ali Jinnah." In *Muslims against the Muslim League: Critiques of the Idea of Pakistan*, edited by Ali Usman Qasmi and Megan Eaton Robb, 109–41. New Delhi: Cambridge University Press, 2017.
———. "Making Sense of Naya Pakistan." *Friday Times*, 21 September 2018.
———. "Portraying Jinnah—A Brief History." In *Finding Jinnah: Contemporary Art from Pakistan*, 25–42. Karachi: Furqaan Ahmed Collection, 2021.
———. "Symbolic Redemption, Retributive Justice: The Significance of Anti-Colonial Iconoclasm as Radical Politics." *The Abusable Past*. https://www.radicalhistoryreview.org/abusablepast/symbolic-redemption-retributive-justice-the-significance-of-anti-colonial-iconoclasm-as-radical-politics/.
———. "Where the Twain Did Meet: The Genealogy of Muhammad Iqbal's Intellectual and Poetic Genius." In *Revisioning Iqbal as a Poet and Muslim Political Thinker*, edited by Gita Dharampal Frick, Ali Usman Qasmi, and Katia Rostetter, 11–34. Heidelberg, Germany: Draupadi Verlag, 2010.
Qasmi, Ali Usman, and Megan Eaton Robb. Introduction to *Muslims against the Muslim League: Critiques of the Idea of Pakistan*, edited by Ali Usman Qasmi and Megan Eaton Robb, 1–34. New Delhi: Cambridge University Press, 2017.
Qureshi, I. H. "Presidential Address." In *The Proceedings of the Pakistan History Conference (Eighth Session) Held at Peshawar under the Auspices of the Pakistan Historical Society*, edited by Dr. S. Moinul Haq, 17–32. Karachi: Pakistan Historical Society, 1961.
Qureshi, I. H., ed. *A Short History of Pakistan*. 1967; Karachi: Karachi University Press, 1992.
———. *Aspects of the History, Culture and Religions of Pakistan: A Series of Lectures by Dr. Ishtiaq Husain Qureshi*. Bangkok: Southeast Asia Treaty Organization, 1963.
———. *Education in Pakistan: An Inquiry into Objectives and Achievements*. Karachi: Bureau of Composition, Compilation and Translation, University of Karachi, 1999.
Qureshi, Muhammad Abdullah. "Nisab-i-Tarikh aur Tarmim ki Zarurat." In *Tarikh aur Nisabi Kutub*, edited by Dr. Mubarak Ali, 172–76. Lahore: Tarikh Publications, 2016.
Qureshi, Dr. Waheed. "Allama Iqbal ki Tarikh-i-Wiladat." In *Allama Iqbal ki Tarikh-i-Wiladat*, edited by Dr. Waheed Qureshi and Zahid Munir Amir, 93–127. Lahore: Bazm-i-Iqbal, 1994.
Qureshi, Dr. Waheed, and Zahid Munir Amir, eds. *Allama Iqbal ki Tarikh-i-Wiladat*. Lahore: Bazm-i-Iqbal, 1994.
Raghavan, Pallavi. *Animosity at Bay: An Alternative History. Of the India-Pakistan Relationship, 1947–1952*. London: Hurst, 2020.
Rahim, Khawaja Abdur, ed. *Iqbal: The Poet of Tomorrow*. Lahore: Iqbal Academy Pakistan, 2004.

Rahman, Taimur. *The Class Structure of Pakistan*. Karachi: Oxford University Press, 2012.
Ramnath, Kalyani. *Boats in a Storm: Law, Migration, and Decolonization in South and Southeast Asia, 1942–1962*. Stanford, CA: Stanford University Press, 2023.
Rashid, Maria. *Dying to Serve: Militarism, Affect, and the Politics of Sacrifice in the Pakistan Army*. Stanford, CA: Stanford University Press, 2020.
Ray, Rajat Kanta. *The Felt Community: Commonality and Mentality before the Emergence of Indian Nationalism*. New Delhi: Oxford University Press, 2003.
Raza, Syed Hashim. *Hamari Manzil (Our Destination): An Autobiography of Syed Hashim Raza*. Karachi: Mustafain & Murtazain Ltd., 1991.
Ricoeur, Paul. *Hermeneutics and the Human Sciences: Essays on Language, Action and Interpretation*. Cambridge: Cambridge University Press, 2016.
———. *The Rule of Metaphor: The Creation of Meaning in Language*. London: Routledge, 2003.
Rizvi, Mubashar. *The Ethics of Staying: Social Movements and Land Rights Politics in Pakistan*. Stanford, CA: Stanford University Press, 2019.
Robinson, Francis. "Crisis of Authority: Crisis of Islam?" *Journal of the Royal Asiatic Society* 19, no. 3 (2009): 339–54.
Roy, Anupama. "The Citizenship (Amendment) Bill, 2016 and the Aporia of Citizenship." *Economic and Political Weekly*, 14 December 2019, 28–34.
Roy, Haimanti. "Paper Rights: The Emergence of Documentary Identities in Post-Colonial India, 1950–67." *South Asia: Journal of South Asian Studies* 39, no. 2 (2016): 329–49.
———. *Partitioned Lives: Migrants, Refugees, Citizens in India and Pakistan, 1947–1965*. New Delhi: Oxford University Press, 2013.
Roy, Srirupa. *Beyond Belief: India and the Politics of Postcolonial Nationalism*. Durham, NC: Duke University Press, 2007.
———. "Instituting Diversity: Official Nationalism in Post-Independence India." *South Asia: Journal of South Asian Studies* 22, no. 1 (1999): 79–99.
Saeed, Sadia. *Politics of Desecularization: Law and the Minority Question in Pakistan*. Cambridge: Cambridge University Press, 2016.
Saidi, Abul Hasnat Ali Muhammad, ed. *Fatawa Ulema-ye Ahl-i-Hadis*. Vol. 6. Khanewal: Maktaba Saidiya, 1977.
Saif, Mashal. *The 'Ulama in Contemporary Pakistan: Contesting and Cultivating an Islamic Republic*. Cambridge: Cambridge University Press, 2021.
Saleem, Raja M. Ali. *State, Nationalism, and Islamization: Historical Analysis of Turkey and Pakistan*. London: Palgrave Macmillan, 2017.
Sassen, Saskia. "Towards Post-National and Denationalized Citizenship." In *Handbook of Citizenship Studies*, edited by F. Engin and Bryan S. Turner, 277–91. London: Sage, 2002: 277–91.
Schaap, Andrew. "Enacting the Right to have Rights: Jacques Rancière's Critique of Hannah Arendt." *European Journal of Political Theory* 10, no. 1 (2011): 20–45.
Schaflechner, Jurgen. *Hinglaj Devi: Identity, Change, and Solidification at a Hindu Temple in Pakistan*. Karachi: Oxford University Press, 2020.
Schmitt, Carl. *Political Theology: Four Chapters on the Concept of Sovereignty*. Chicago: University of Chicago Press, 2005.

Schwarzenbach, Alexis. *Portraits of the Nation: Stamps, Coins and Banknotes in Belgium and Switzerland, 1880–1945.* Bern, Switzerland: Peter Lang, 1999.
Sen, Uditi. *Citizen Refugee: Forging the Indian Nation after Partition.* Cambridge: Cambridge University Press, 2018.
Sevea, Iqbal Singh. *The Political Philosophy of Muhammad Iqbal: Islam and Nationalism in Late Colonial India.* Cambridge: Cambridge University Press, 2012.
Shafi, Mufti Muhammad. *Ru'at-i-Hilal.* Ca. 1961; Karachi: Idara al-Ma'rif, n.d..
Shafique, Khurram Ali. *Iqbal: An Illustrated Biography.* Lahore: Iqbal Academy Pakistan, 2010.
Shah, Hurmat Ali. "Redefining Citizenship in Pakistan." *Himal South Asian*, 28 April 2020. https://www.himalmag.com/redefining-citizenship-in-pakistan-2020/.
Shahin, Emad El-Din. "Government." In *Islamic Political Thought: An Introduction*, edited by Gerhard Bowering, 68–85. Princeton, NJ: Princeton University Press.
Shani, Ornit. "Gandhi, Citizenship and the Resilience of Indian Nationhood." *Citizenship Studies* 15, nos. 6–7 (2010): 659–78.
Sharma, Nandita. *Home Rule: National Sovereignty and the Separation of Natives and Migrants.* Durham, NC: Duke University Press, 2020.
Sheikh, Attique Zafar, Ashraf Ali, and Malik Mohammad Riaz, eds. *Pakistan Resolution and the Working Committee of the All-India Muslim League 1940.* Islamabad: National Archives of Pakistan, ca. 1990.
Sherman, Taylor C. *Muslim Belonging in Secular India: Negotiating Citizenship in Postcolonial Hyderabad.* Cambridge: Cambridge University Press, 2015.
Siddiqi, Ayesha. *In the Wake of Disaster: Islamists, the State and a Social Contract in Pakistan.* New Delhi: Cambridge University Press, 2019.
Siddiqi, Dina M. "Secular Quests, National Others: Revisiting Bangladesh's Constituent Assembly Debates." *Asian Affairs* 49, no. 2 (2018): 238–58.
Siddiqi, Marghub. "Allama Iqbal ki Tarikh-i-Wiladat." In *Allama Iqbal ki Tarikh-i-Wiladat*, edited by Dr. Waheed Qureshi and Zahid Munir Amir, 43–48. Lahore: Bazm-i-Iqbal, 1994.
Singha, Radhika. "The Great War and a 'Proper' Passport for the Colony: Border-Crossing in British India, c. 1882–1922." *Indian Economic and Social History Review* 50, no. 3 (2013): 289–315.
Spivak, Gayatri. *Nationalism and the Imagination.* Calcutta: Seagull Books, 2015.
Stoller, Ann Laura. *Along the Archival Grain: Epistemic Anxieties and Colonial Common Sense.* Princeton, NJ: Princeton University Press, 2010.
Stolz, Daniel A. *The Lighthouse and the Observatory: Islam, Science, and Empire in Late Ottoman Egypt.* Cambridge: Cambridge University Press, 2018.
———. "'Positioning the Watch Hand': 'Ulama' and the Practice of Mechanical Timekeeping in Cairo, 1737–1874." *International Journal of Middle East Studies* 47, no. 3 (2015).
Sufi, Khalid Nazir. "Ek Ghalat-Fehmi dar Ghalat-Fehmi ka Izala." In *Allama Iqbal ki Tarikh-i-Wiladat*, edited by Dr. Waheed Qureshi and Zahid Munir Amir, 33–41. Lahore: Bazm-i-Iqbal, 1994.
———. *Iqbal Durun-i-Khana: Hayat-i-Iqbal ke Khanagi Pehlu.* Lahore: Iqbal Academy Pakistan, 2003.

———. *Iqbal Durun-i-Khana, hissa duam*. Lahore: Iqbal Academy, 2012.
Svensson, Ted. *Production of Postcolonial India and Pakistan: Meanings of Partition*. London: Routledge, 2016.
Tarar, Nadeem Omar. *The Colonial and National Formations of the National College of Arts, Lahore, circa 1870s to 1960s*. London: Anthem Press, 2022.
Tarlo, Emma. *Clothing Matters: Dress and Identity in India*. London: Hurst, 1996.
Thanawi, Maulana Ashraf Ali. *Imdad-ul-Fatawa*. Vol. 4. Saharanpur: Zakaria Book Depot, n.d.
Thijs, Krijn. "The Metaphor of the Master: 'Narrative Hierarchy' in National Historical Cultures of Europe." In *The Contested Nation: Ethnicity, Class, Religion and Gender in National Histories*, edited by Stefan Berger and Chris Lorenz, 60–74. London: Palgrave Macmillan, 2008.
Toor, Saadia. "A National Culture for Pakistan: The Political Economy of a Debate." *Inter-Asia Cultural Studies* 6, no. 3 (2005): 318–40.
———. *The State of Islam: Culture and Cold War Politics in Pakistan*. London: Pluto Press, 2011.
Trivedi, Lisa. *Clothing Gandhi's Nation: Homespun and Modern India*. Bloomington: Indiana University Press, 2007.
Turner, Bryan S. "Islam, Civil Society, and Citizenship: Reflections on the Sociology of Citizenship and Islamic Studies." In *Citizenship and the State in the Middle East: Approaches and Applications*, edited by Nils A. Butenschon, Uri Davis, and Manuel Hassassian, 28–48. Syracuse, NY: Syracuse University Press, 2000.
———. *Religion and Modern Society: Citizenship, Secularisation and the State*. Cambridge: Cambridge University Press, 2011.
———. "Religion and Politics: The Elementary Forms of Citizenship." In *Handbook of Citizenship Studies*, edited by Engin F. Isin and Bryan S. Turner. London: Sage Publications, 2002.
Uddin, Layli. "'Enemy Agents at Work': A Microhistory of the 1954 Adamjee and Karnaphuli Riots in East Pakistan." *Modern Asian Studies* 55, no. 2 (March 2021): 629–64.
Usmani, Mufti Muhammad Taqi. *Fatawa Usmani*. Vol. 2. Karachi: Maktaba Ma'rif-ul-Quran, 2012.
Vajpeyi, Ananya. *Righteous Republic: The Political Foundations of Modern India*. Cambridge, MA: Harvard University Press, 2012.
Venkateswaran, Mrinalini. "Museum Collecting and Constructions of Identity in Indian Punjab, 1947–1970." PhD diss., University of Cambridge, 2020.
Virdee, Pippa. *From the Ashes of 1947: Reimagining Punjab*. Delhi: Cambridge University Press, 2018.
Virmani, Arundhati. *A National Flag for India: Rituals, Nationalism, and the Politics of Sentiment*. Ranikhet: Permanent Black, 2008.
Vuolteenaho, Jani, and Lawrence D. Berg. "Towards Critical Toponymies." In *Critical Toponymies: The Contested Politics of Place Naming*, edited by Lawrence D. Berg and Jani Vuolteenaho, 1–18. London: Routledge, 2009.
Waheed-ud-Din, Faqir Syed. "Tarikh-i-Paidayish: Ek Bari Ghalat-Fehmi ka Azala." In *Allama Iqbal ki Tarikh-i-Wiladat*, edited by Dr. Waheed Qureshi and Zahid Munir Amir, 21–31. Lahore: Bazm-i-Iqbal, 1994.

Wallach, Yair. "Creating a Country through Currency and Stamps: State Symbols and Nation-Building in British-Ruled Palestine." *Nations and Nationalism* 17, no. 1 (2011): 129–47.
Waseem, Mohammad. *Political Conflict in Pakistan*. London: Hurst, 2022.
White, Hyden. *Metahistory: The Historical Imagination in Nineteenth-Century Europe*. Baltimore: John Hopkins University Press, 1973.
Williams, Richard David, and Rafay Mahmood. "A Soundtrack for Reimagining Pakistan? Coke Studio, Memory and the Music Video," *BioScope: South Asian Screen Studies* 10, no. 2 (2019): 111–28.
Young, James E. *The Texture of Memory: Holocaust Memorials and Meaning*. New Haven, CT: Yale University Press, 1993.
Zaidi, S. Akbar. *Making a Muslim: Reading Publics and Contesting Identities in Nineteenth-Century North India*. New Delhi: Cambridge University Press, 2021.
Zakaria, Anam. *Between the Great Divide: A Journey into Pakistan-Administered Kashmir*. Delhi: HarperCollins India, 2018.
Zaman, Muhammad Qasim. *Islam in Pakistan: A History*. Princeton, NJ: Princeton University Press, 2019.
———. *The Ulema in Contemporary Islam: Custodians of Change*. Princeton, NJ: Princeton University Press, 2002.
Zamindar, Vazira Fazila-Yacoobali *The Long Partition and the Making of Modern South Asia: Refugees, Boundaries, Histories*. New York: Columbia University Press, 2007.
Zerubavel, Yael. *Recovered Roots: Collective Memory and the Making of Israeli National Tradition*. Chicago: University of Chicago Press, 1995.
Žižek, Slavoj. *The Sublime Object of Ideology*. London: Verso, 1989.
Zulfiqar, Professor Dr. Ghulam Husain. *Tarikh-i-Bazam-i-Iqbal*. Lahore: Bazam-i-Iqbal, 2000.

INDEX

Aas, Amr bin, 314
Abbasi, M. W., 75
Abu Hanifa, Imam, 253
Afghani, Jamal-ud-Din, 117
Agha, Salma, 1–3
Ahl-i-Hadith, 279–80
Ahmad, Abul Mansur, 103, 139, 156, 171
Ahmad, M. B., 299
Ahmad, Mirza Ghulam, 145–6, 150
Ahmad, Muizuddin, 189
Ahmad, Mushtaq, 256
Ahmad, Nazir, 35
Ahmad, Salahuddin, 188
Ahmad, Sami, 191
Ahmad, Ziauddin, 315
Ahmadis, 10, 110, 129, 136, 144ff., 199, 270
Ahmed, Abasuddin, 224
Ahmed, Alimuddin, 320
Ahmed, Ashabuddin, 170
Ahmed, Dr. Muhammad Mushtaq, 277
Ahmed, G. A., 83
Ahmed, Hameeduddin, 70, 75–6, 79, 81, 102, 260, 348
Ahmed, Nazir, 224
Ahmed, Nur, 72
Ahmed, Sheikh Ejaz, 201–3
Ahmed, Sheikh Rafiq, 314
Ahsan, Raghib, 117, 135
Aina-i-Qismat, 180
Ajmal, Dr. Muhammad, 201
Akbar (Emperor), 4, 334
Akhtar, Malik M., 313
Akhund, Abdullah, 97
Al-e-Ahmad, Jalal, 195
Aleem, Shah Abdul, 197

Ali, Anwar, 249, 266
Ali, Chaudhry M., 224
Ali, Chaudhry Rehmat, 287
Ali, M. R., 85
Ali, Malik Barkat, 313
Ali, Maulana Ahmad, 263–4
Ali, Mohsin, 261–2
Ali, Syed Ameer, 136, 141
All Pakistan History Conference, 297 ff.
All Pakistan Women Association (APWA), 168
Allama Iqbal Open University, 201
Ambedkar, B. R., 24
Andrews, D., 184
Ansari, Zafar Ahmad, 118, Collection, 47, 116, 130
Ara, Begum Husne, 315
Arendt, Hannah, 16
Asad, Muhammad, 116–7, 178
Ashoka, 24
al-Ashari, Abul Hasan, 149
al-Ashraf, Naquib, 140
Ashraf, M. B., 298
Ashraf, M. S., 208
Aslam, S. M., 321
Aurangzeb (Emperor), 242, 300, 313
Aurat March, 168
Austin, John, 140
Ayub, S. M., 248
Ayyubi, Sultan Salahuddin, 313
Azad, Jagan Nath, 205, 229
Azad, Maulana Abul Kalam, 291
Azurda, Mufti Sadraddin, 310
Azzam, Abdul Wahab, 199

Badayuni, Abdul Hamid, 223, 258, 264, 330
Bai, Dadan, 80, 94–5
Bai, Shirin, 209–10
Bairagi, Banda, 321
Bakhit, Muhammad, 243
Bakhsha, Maula, 319
Banerjee, Prof. D. N., 318
Banori, Yusuf, 254, 277
Barelvi, Ahmad Raza Khan, 244
Barelvis, 164, 264
Bari, Mian Abdul, 139–40
Basic Principles Committee, 114, 120, 126–31, 134, 144–5
Battle of Karbala, 117, 235
Begum, Anwari, 2
Benjamin, Walter, 55
Bhashani, Maulana, 112
Bhutto, Zulfikar Ali, 143, 162, 171, 181–2, 197, 213, 270
Bhuyan, Rafiqur Rahman, 315
Bibi, Karima, 203
Bibi, Ta'ley, 203
Bilal, Hazrat, 314
Bilyameeni, Aziz Ahmad, 222
BJP (Bharatiya Janata Party), 6
Board of Ta'limat-i-Islamiyyah, 116–7, 119, 134–5, 145, 151, 168, 171
Bokhari, A. S., 289–90
Bolitho, Hector, 207 ff.
British Nationality Act of 1948, 57–8
Buchan, John, 13
Bukhari, Ataullah Shah, 313
Bukhari, Imam, 314
Bukhari, Z. A., 216–20, 228
Bureau of National Reconstruction, 165–6, 259, 316
Bureau of National Research and Reference, 304
Butler, Judith, 173
Butt, Qamaruddin, 79

Cabinet Mission Plan, 160
calendar (a national calendar for Pakistan), 307 ff.
Caroe, Sir Olaf, 328
de Certeau, Michel, 320, 339
Central Committee of the Quaid-i-Azam Memorial, 212
Central Ruat-i-Hilal Committee, 269
Chagla, Ahmed, 218–20, 225
Chakraverty, Raj Kumar, 72
Charagh Din, 2. *See also* Jagjit Singh
Chattopudhyaya, Sris Chandra, 146–7
Chaudhry, Fawad Husain, 273, 281
Chaudhry, Mufazzal Haider, 308
Cheema, Muhammad Hasan, 149
Chetumal, Sobhraj, 329
Chibhar, J. S., 53
Choudhry, G. W., 111–3
Choudhry, Khushi Mohammed, 213
Chughtai, Abdullah, 212
Chughtai, Abdur Rahman, 190
Chughtai, Muniruddin, 302
Chundrigar, I. I., 103
City of God vs City of Man, 11
Civil and Military Gazette, 47, 297, 326–7
Commission on National Education, 166
Committee on Fundamental Rights, 57
Committees on Minorities and Fundamental Rights in 1950, 114
Congress Party (India), 5, 19–21, 33, 112, 158, 160, 176, 191, 314,
Constantine, Justice, 99
Control of Entry Act, 88
Council of Islamic Ideology, 267
Council of Non-Muslim Leaders, 132
Criminal Investigation Department, 71–2
Crone, Patricia, 118–9, 122, 131–2
currency notes of Pakistan, 187 ff.
Curtis, Lionel, 13
Custodian of Refugees' Property, 51

Dal, Ganatantri, 112
Dalits, 19, 24, 343
Daraz, Umar, 182–3
Daryabadi, Abdul Majid, 117
Das, Basanta Kumar, 153–4
Daultana, Mumtaz, 140–1, 147, 154–5
Dawn, 47, 262, 304

Deobandis, 164, 206, 245, 249, 264–5
Department of Meteorology, 232, 249, 260, 262, 265, 266–7, 272
desecularization, 161
Dhar, Durga Prasad, 205
Din-i-Ilahi, 4
Din, Muhammad, 329
Dinshaw, Eduljee, 329
Directorate of Archives and Libraries, 289
Dutta, Bhupendra Kumar, 138
Dutta, Dhirendra Nath, 71, 176
Dutta, Kamini Kumar, 70

East and West Punjab Evacuee Property (Preservation Ordinance), 52
East India Company, 27, 289–90
Ebrahim, Sir Currimbhoy, 98–9
Ebrahim, Sir M. Currimbhoy, 98–9
Ecclesiastical Department, 260
Eco, Umberto, 30
Ede, James, 58
Eduljee, Nader Shaw, 329
Egeli, A. Vasfi, 212
Elahi, Yad, 83
evacuee property, 51

Farid, Mufti Muhammad, 276–9
Faruqi, Shamsur Rahman, 28, 31–2
al-Fasi, al-Arabi ibn Abd al-Salam, 237
Fatawa Alamgiri, 242
Fauq, Munshi M. Din, 205
Fazal Ullah, Maulana, 278–9
Fazaldin, 95
Federal Committee of Experts on Shariat, 122
Ferguson, W. S., 328
Firoz, S. H., 99–100
flag (national flag of Pakistan), 175 ff.
Freer, L. G. P., 327
French citizenship model, 15
Frontier Crimes Regulation, 9
Fundamental Principles of an Islamic State, 128

Gadamer, Hans-Georg, 44, 118, 120
Gandhi, Indira, 169, 201
Gandhi, M. K., 23–4, 38–9, 190–1, 194, 210, 217, 329
Gani, Ahmad A. R., 216
Gauhar, Altaf, 77
Gawadar, 7, 55, 100 ff., 353
Geertz, Clifford, 174–5
gemeinschaft, 11
George (King), 331
German citizenship model, 15
gesellschaft, 11
Ghalib, Mirza, 34, 310–1
Ghamidi, Javed Ahmad, 274
Ghaznawi, Rafiq, 218–9
Gilani, Manazir Ahsan, 117
Gita, 24, 137, 300
Gomez, Peter Paul, 137, 154
Gould, William, 26
Gujral, I. K., 205
Gurmani, Mushtaq Ahmad, 82–3, 140, 157–60, 189
Guru Granth Sahib, 2
Guru, Baba, 5, 107

Habermas, Jurgen, 16, 36
hadith, 121, 163, 236, 242, 251, 280
Hakim, Khalifa Abdul, 133, 135
Haleem, A. B. A., 298–9
Hali, Altaf Husain, 217, 310–1
Halim, Dr. A., 298–9
Hamidullah, Dr., 117–8
Hanifa, Imam Abu, 314
Haq, A. K. Fazlul, 112–3
Haq, Dr. Abdul, 134
Haq, Maulana Abdul (Akora Khattak), 276
Haq, Maulvi Abdul, 199, 223, 227, 314–5
Haq, S. Moinul, 297–9
Harijan, Lal Bai Velji, 79
Hasan, Imam, 314
Hasan, M. Alay, 320
Hasan, Maulvi Zafar, 333
Hasba Bill, 169
Hashim, Abul, 159

Hassan, S. Fida, 331
Hazarwi, Ghulam Ghaus, 268
Heidegger, Martin, 238
Herald, 272
Hindutva, 6, 17
Hingorani, G. K., 64–5
Historical Records and Archives Commission for Pakistan, 289, 295
Hitler, Adolf, 72, 148
Hobbes, Thomas, 40
Holderlin, Freidrich, 238
Huber, Dr. L., 200
Hunter, W. W., 311
Husain, Abid, 272
Husain, Akhtar, 320
Husain, Chaudhry M., 197
Husain, Colonel Imam, 291
Husain, Dr. Mahmud, 134, 298–9
Husain, Hafiz Kifayat, 313
Husain, Hakim M., 319
Husain, Imam, 235, 314
Husain, Mehmud, 113

idea of citizenship, 10 ff.
Iftikharuddin, Mian, 72, 112–3
Ikram, S. M., 188, 216, 296, 298–9, 302
Ikramullah, 325
Imroz, 47, 117, 125, 177, 192, 218, 329
India Office, 289–295
Influx from Pakistan (Control) Ordinance, 51
Inqilab, 202, 245–6
Iqbal, Dr. Javed, 201
Iqbal, Muhammad, 35, 38–9, 116–7, 178, 187, 190, 214–219, 226, 296; birth date and year of, 201 ff.; hagiography of, 196 ff.; state's interpretation of the role of, 199 f.
Islam, Qazi Nazrul, 199, 219, 222, 315
Islam, Riazul, 299
Islamic Reconstruction Department, 116–7
Islamization, 111, 161, 163, 167–8, 195, 274, 276, 353
Ismail, Muhammad, 279–80
Ispahani, M. A. H., 209

Jacob, John, 322
Jaffar, S. M., 299
Jafri, Syed Muhammad, 259
Jahan, Begum Nasim, 169
Jalal Hamid, 182
Jallandhari, Hafiz, 26, 216, 219–29, 341
Jang, Nawab Zain Yar, 212
Jasimuddin, 216, 219
Javid, N., 192
Jehangir (Emperor), 235
Jilani, Shaykh Abdul Qadir, 140
Jinnah, Fatima, 206–7, 209–10, 212, 217–8, 295–7
Jinnah, Muhammad Ali, 4, 39–41, 145, 152–3, 156, 159, 175–6, 180–3, 185, 187, 190, 229, 295, 321; August 11 speech by, 40, 152; hagiography of, 196 ff.; mausoleum of, 211 ff., 307–8; state narrative about, "205 ff.; "wardrobe" of, 190 ff.
Join Defense Council of India and Pakistan, 51

Kakwi, Arshad, 222
Kalidasa, 24
Karachi Agreement, 52
Kemalism, 161–2, 171, 232, 259, 267
Khaliq, M. A., 223
Khan, A. M. Mumtazuddin, 217
Khan, Abdul Samad, 321
Khan, Ataur Rahman, 139
Khan, Bacha, 275
Khan, Colonel Nur, 53
Khan, Dr. F. A., 209
Khan, F. A., 336–7
Khan, Faris A., 10
Khan, General Ayub, 101, 148, 150, 161–167, 171, 232–3, 259, 261, 267–8, 270, 274, 294, 301–2, 306, 319–20, 328
Khan, General Yahya, 166, 268
Khan, Imran, 143, 171
Khan, Liaqat Ali, 114–5, 171, 176, 179, 228, 307–8
Khan, Lutfullah, 219
Khan, Maulana Akhtar Ali, 220
Khan, Maulana Zafar Ali, 220

Khan, Mehmud Ahmad, 202, 204
Khan, Muhammad Aziz, 318
Khan, N. M., 329–30
Khan, Nawab Zulfiqar Ali, 205
Khan, Prof. Hamid Ahmad, 202
Khan, Sardar Shaukat Hayat, 82–3
Khan, Shaukat Ali, 184
Khan, Sir Zafarullah, 147, 181
Khan, Syed Ahmad, 34, 311
Khan, Wali, 275
Khan, Zafar Ali, 324
Kharas, J. G., 180
Khokhrapar, 78, 83–89, 105
khwaja sira, 10
Kifayat Ullah, Mufti, 243–4
Kingsway Camp (Delhi), 51
Kohli, Virat, 182
Koreshi, S. H., 148
Koselleck, Reinhart, 35
Kripke, Saul, 141, 171
Krishak Praja Party, 112
Kristeva, Julia, 230
Kumar, Ravinder, 53
Kundanmal, 77, 94

Laclau, Ernesto, 44, 110, 141–3, 150, 170
Lahori, Majid, 216, 223
Lahori, Maulana Ahmad Ali, 254
Lawrence, John, 323–4
Liaqat-Nehru Pact of 1950, 85–6
Locke, John, 40
Lodhi, Younas Kamal, 221
Luqman, Syed Raza, 261

MacIntyre, Alasdair, 234, 249
Mahamadi, R. A., 101
Mahmud, Dr. Abbas, 200
Mahmudabad, Ali Khan, 29
Majlis Ulema Shia, 263
Malik, Imam, 314
Malik, Majeed, 208–9
Malik, Muhammad Aslam, 158–9
Mallick, A. R., 302
Man, Paul De, 142
Mandal, Rasa Raj, 137

Manuel, Rex A., 218
Marshall, T. H., 10
Masud, Tahir, 4
Maududi, Maulana, 133, 144, 164, 268
Mehmud of Ghazna, 300, 304
Mehmudabad, Raja Sahib, 209
Mehra, J. K., 1–2, 5, 53. *See also* Salman, Ahmad
Meir, Golda, 169
Merchant, Yahya C., 212
metaphor, 28 ff.
Mihr, Ghulam Rasul, 202, 204
Mirza, Iskandar, 298
modernization of Islamic institutions, 163 ff.
Mohammad, Faiz, 189
Mohammedan Anglo-Oriental College, 136
Mohammedan Educational Conference, 136
Morning News, 208–9, 223–4
Morning News, 47, 208–9, 223–4, 301
Morris, Abdul Alim, 314
Mouffe, Chantal, 151, 170
Mountbatten, Lord, 183
Muhammad, Prophet, 52, 118–9, 122, 150, 162–3, 167, 175–6, 178, 185, 204, 236, 247, 251, 308, 317, 341, 343
Muhammad Ali formula, 114
Muhammad, Ghulam, 112, 115
Muir, Edward, 327
Mujib-ur-Rahman, Sheikh, 103, 112–3, 138, 139–40, 156–7, 160
Mujtahid, S. Jafar Husain, 117
Munib-ur-Rehman, Mufti, 272–6, 281
Munir-Kiyani report, 137, 144, 150
Muradabadi, Jigar, 219
Murshid, Maulana Ghulam, 1
Musharraf, Pervez, 171
Muslim League Legislators' Convention, 158
Muslim, Imam, 314
"Muslim Terminology", 134 ff.
Mussolini, 148
Mustafa, Zakia, 185

Nabi, Malik Ghulam, 314
Nadavi, Sulaiman, 117
Nadawi, Sayyid Suleman, 117, 135
Nadwi, Sayyid Suleman, 298
Nahar, Burun, 315
National Anthem Committee, 218
National Anthem of Pakistan, 214 ff.; text and official translation of, 221–2
National Archives of Pakistan, 47, 56
National Documentation Center, 47, 293
National Planning Board, 261
National Reconstruction Bureau, 165–6, 301
National Register of Citizens (NRC), 6
Naturalization Act of 1926, 60
Nawa-i-Waqt, 3, 47, 225, 296, 324, 335
Nazim-ud-Din, Khawaja, 113, 209, 297–8
Nazim, Dr. Muhammad, 298
Nazism, 16
Nehru Report of 1928, 21
Nehru, Jawaharlal, 19, 59, 183, 210, 323
Niazi, Maulana Kausar, 270–1
Niazi, Sajjad Sarwar, 218
Nicholson, John, 323, 328
Nigam, Aditya, 49
Nishtar, Sardar Abdul Rab, 113, 216, 154
Niyazi, Sayyid Nazir, 201, 204
Nizami, Hamid, 313
Nizami, Hasan, 311
Noon, Feroz Khan, 78

Objectives Resolution, 44, 114–6, 121, 171, 206
One Unit Scheme, 154, 156
Osmani, S. R., 184

Pakistan (Control of Entry) Bill, 71
Pakistan (Control of Entry) Ordinance, 51, 87
Pakistan Citizenship Act of 1951, 65, 67, 74, 87, 96, 98, 101
Pakistan Historical Society. *See* All Pakistan History Conference
Pakistan History Board, 299, 301

Pakistan Names and Emblems (Prevention of Unauthorized Use Act) of 1957, 194
Pakistan Observer, 47, 184–5, 222, 346
Pakistan Times, 1, 47, 70, 177, 192, 246, 325
Pakistan's citizenship policy in April 1956, 74
Panipat (Battles of), 4
Partition Council, 291, 292–4, 333
Pasban, 47
Pasha, Mehmed Ali, 239
passport (emergence of), 13ff.
Pehelwan, Gama, 313
Phulwarwi, Maulana Jafar Shah, 257
Pirzada, Abdus Sattar, 218
Poppalzai, Mufti, 275–6, 281
Powindah of Suleman Khel (tribe), 62–3

Qadir, Manzur, 150
Qadir, Sir Abdul, 199
Qasmi, Ahmed Nadeem, 220
al-Qasimi, Jamal al-Din, 243
Quaid-i-Azam Memorial Fund, 213
Quaid-i-Azam's Mazar (Protection and Maintenance) Ordinance of 1971, 214
Quasem, Abul, 93
Quran, 121, 123, 129–30, 135, 137, 153, 163, 167, 169, 189–90, 212, 217, 226, 251, 258, 261, 265, 310, 343
Qureshi, Abdul Ghafur, 177–8
Qureshi, Abdullah, 296
Qureshi, Dr. Ishtiaq Husain, 113, 134, 149, 207, 288–90, 294, 296, 298–9, 301–3, 305–7
Qureshi, Dr. Wahid, 202, 204

Radcliffe Award, 48
Rafiq, Sheikh Muhammad, 203
Rahman, Dr. Fazlur, 167, 267
Rahman, Fazlur, 297–8
Rahman, Ghazi Abdul, 178
Rahman, M. D. Altafur, 319
Rai, Lala Lajpat, 329
Ram, Sir Ganga, 329
Ram, Sita, 333

Ramrajya, 23
Rashdi, Pir Ali Mohammad, 139, 155
Rasheed, G., 178–9
Rashid, A., 224
Rashid, Abdur, 302
Rashid, Ayesha, 177
Raza, Syed Hashim, 211, 220, 258
refugees and citizenship, 49 ff.
Rehman, A. R. M. Fazlur, 90, 92–3, 96
Rehman, Javaid, 8
Rehman, Justice S. A., 196–7, 201
Renan, Ernest, 41
Ricoeur, Paul, 28, 284
Rida, Rashid, 241
Rightly Guided Caliphs, 119
Roochomal Daryanomal v. Province of West Pakistan (1959), 99
Roy, Kiran Sankar, 176
RSS, 138
Rumi, Jalal al-Din, 31, 314

Safdar, Captain, 214
Saha (East Bengali Hindu), 74–76
Salik, Abdul Majid, 223–4, 227
Salman, Ahmad, 1–3. *See also* Mehra, J. K.
Salmani, Islam, 211
Samad, Hafiz Abdus, 319
Samad, M. A., 67
Schmitt, Carl, 44, 214, 215, 226
Sen, Dr. Sukumar, 308
Sen, S. K., 137–8
Shafi, Mufti Muhammad, 117, 242, 249 ff., 271, 277, 280, 330–1
Shafi'i, Imam, 314
Shah, A. B., 62
Shah, King Zahir, 197
Shahab-ud-Din, Khawaja, 247
Shahab, Qudratullah, 101–2, 149, 150
Shahin, Emad El-Din, 118
Shakir, Ahmad, 239–40
Sharar, Abdul Halim, 35
Sharf-un-Nisa, 321
Shariat Appellate Bench of the Supreme Court, 129

Sharif, Maryam Nawaz, 214
Sharif, Mian Muhammad, 313
Sharif, S. M., 302
Shefta (poet), 310
Sheikh-ul-Islam, 132
Sheikh, Lt. Gen. K. M., 328
Shuja-ud-Din, Prof. Syed Abdullah Muhammad, 321
Shuja, Hakim Ahmad, 219
Sialkoti, Mir Ibrahim, 117
Siddiqi, Ayesha, 25
Siddiqi, M. H., 299
Singh, Hasa, 329
Sirat (Prophetic biography), 163, 188
Sirhindi, Sheikh Ahmad, 313
Smith, Dr. Whitney, 182
Smith, W. C., 135–6
Snelson, Edward, 61, 87
Sodi, Zaildar Thakar Singh, 2
Solaiman, Mohammed, 213
Staatsangehorigkeit, 14
Storey, Professor, 289
Subhani, Maulana Azad, 117
Sufi, Khalid Nazir, 198, 203
Suhrawrdy, Husain Shahid, 112–3, 140–1, 147–8, 157, 311, 313
Sukhdev, Seth, 71–2
Sunna (Prophetic practice), 121, 123, 128–30, 137, 153
Suroor, Aal-i-Ahmad, 201
Swami, Subramanyam, 6
Swaraj, 20

Tabassum, Sufi, 225, 227
Tagore, Rabindranath, 24, 215, 224
Talpur, Mir Ghulam Ali Khan 77, 80, 89
Taseer, M. D., 197
terminology. *See* "Muslim Terminology"
Thanawi, Maulana Ashraf Ali, 245, 314
Thanvi, Ehteshamul Haq, 223, 232
Thijs, Krijn, 287
Tilak, L. B. G., 329–30
Times, 303
Tirath, Swami Ram, 31

Union Jack, 183
Usman, Prof. Muhammad, 202, 204
Usmani, Allama Shabbir Ahmad, 117, 206, 280, 313
Usmani, Maulana Zafar Ahmad, 254, 264, 277, 280
Usmani, Mufti Taqi, 280

Vedas, 137
Victoria (Queen), 323, 325, 329
Vishandass, Herchand Rai, 329

Wafaq-ul-Madaris Multan, 264
Waheed-uz-Zaman, 302
Wahid-ud-Din, Faqir Sayyid, 204
Wahid, Sayyid Abdul, 202
Wali Ullah, Shah, 117

Walton Camp (Lahore), 51
Weber, Max, 11
Wheeler, R. E. M., 299
Windrush scandal, 60
Wittgenstein, Ludwig, 151
Women Action Forum, 168

Zafar, Bahadur Shah, 310, 311, 321
Zahiruddin, 103, 147, 157, 160
Zahooruddin, Atia, 184
Zakariya, Nawab, 321
Zakaullah, Maulvi, 35
Zamindar, 223
Zia-ul-Haq, General, 129, 150, 171, 195, 274, 276
Zionism, 16
Žižek, Slavoj, 44, 49, 170–1

ALSO PUBLISHED IN THE SOUTH ASIA IN MOTION SERIES

Boats in a Storm: Law, Migration, and Decolonization in South and Southeast Asia, 1942–1962
Kalyani Ramnath (2023)

Life Beyond Waste: Work and Infrastructure in Urban Pakistan
Waqas Butt (2023)

Colonizing Kashmir: State-building under Indian Occupation
Hafsa Kanjwal (2023)

Dust on the Throne: The Search for Buddhism in Modern India
Douglas Ober (2023)

Mother Cow, Mother India: A Multispecies Politics of Dairy in India
Yamini Narayanan (2023)

The Vulgarity of Caste: Dalits, Sexuality, and Humanity in Modern India
Shailaja Paik (2022)

Delhi Reborn: Partition and Nation Building in India's Capital
Rotem Geva (2022)

The Right to Be Counted: The Urban Poor and the Politics of Resettlement in Delhi
Sanjeev Routray (2022)

Protestant Textuality and the Tamil Modern: Political Oratory and the Social Imaginary in South Asia
Bernard Bate, Edited by E. Annamalai, Francis Cody, Malarvizhi Jayanth, and Constantine V. Nakassis (2021)

Special Treatment: Student Doctors at the All India Institute of Medical Sciences
Anna Ruddock (2021)

From Raj to Republic: Sovereignty, Violence, and Democracy in India
Sunil Purushotham (2021)

The Greater India Experiment: Hindutva Becoming and the Northeast
Arkotong Longkumer (2020)

Nobody's People: Hierarchy as Hope in a Society of Thieves
Anastasia Piliavsky (2020)

Brand New Nation: Capitalist Dreams and Nationalist Designs in Twenty-First-Century India
Ravinder Kaur (2020)

Partisan Aesthetics: Modern Art and India's Long Decolonization
Sanjukta Sunderason (2020)

Dying to Serve: the Pakistan Army
Maria Rashid (2020)

In the Name of the Nation: India and Its Northeast
Sanjib Baruah (2020)

Faithful Fighters: Identity and Power in the British Indian Army
Kate Imy (2019)

Paradoxes of the Popular: Crowd Politics in Bangladesh
Nusrat Sabina Chowdhury (2019)

The Ethics of Staying: Social Movements and Land Rights Politics in Pakistan
Mubbashir A. Rizvi (2019)

Mafia Raj: The Rule of Bosses in South Asia
Lucia Michelutti, Ashraf Hoque, Nicolas Martin, David Picherit, Paul Rollier, Arild Ruud and Clarinda Still (2018)

For a complete listing of titles in this series, visit the Stanford University Press website, www.sup.org.

The authorized representative in the EU for product safety and compliance is:
Mare Nostrum Group
B.V Doelen 72
4831 GR Breda
The Netherlands

www.ingramcontent.com/pod-product-compliance
Lightning Source LLC
Chambersburg PA
CBHW030601230426
43661CB00053B/1792